Verna Felton

BY FREDRICK TUCKER

Published in the USA by:

BEARMANOR MEDIA
P.O. BOX 71426
ALBANY, GEORGIA 31708
www.BearManorMedia.com

ISBN-10: 1-59393-524-2 (alk. paper)
ISBN-13: 978-1-59393-524-5 (alk. paper)

BOOK DESIGN AND LAYOUT BY VALERIE THOMPSON

TABLE OF CONTENTS

To my parents,
who taught me to appreciate
what they (and Verna Felton)
called "cute" shows

A NOTE FROM THE AUTHOR

Why write a biography of Verna Felton? I was consistently asked this question not only in casual conversations but also during interviews with individuals who actually knew the actress. One questioned whether there was an audience for such a book "in a world much changed" since Verna Felton's heyday. Another suggested that she did not deserve a book of her own but perhaps rather an inclusion in one that featured career profiles of sitcom second bananas. Yet another doubted that there was much of a story to tell at all. Such talk only provided more fuel for my research.

However, I did not know much about Miss Felton's background when I was asked to write her biography. I had fallen in love with her characterization of Hilda Crocker on television's *December Bride* when I was no more than six years old and from time to time, I caught some of her movies on television. I had tried to find out more about her, but like so many other supporting players, Miss Felton remained overlooked by contemporary film historians.

Delving into her background, I discovered that Verna Felton had led a most interesting life. As an amateur genealogist, I got swept up in her family history as well. While the average reader may consider some content as superfluous, I have chosen to include detailed information regarding my subject's relatives and intimates because their life stories might never be recorded otherwise.

Verna Felton's career spanned sixty-five years and encompassed nearly thirty years of stage appearances, countless radio credits, a top-ten television series, and twenty-four films—including six Disney classics.

Why not write a biography of Verna Felton?

FREDRICK TUCKER
JULY 20, 2009

CHAPTER 1

EAST MEETS WEST

The well-stocked shelves were lined with chamois skins, sponges, trusses, atomizers, brushes, combs, hair oils, perfumery, stationery, eyeglasses, and a full line of patented medicines. Prominently displayed was a newly installed soda fountain, shipped by train from the East, which attracted large crowds of interested observers. John B. Scott took great pride in his drug store on Main Street in Salinas City, California. The newspaper advertisements of his stock were footnoted with the assurance that he could be located at any time day or night since he lived in rooms above the store. Another onsite convenience for Scott's clientele in the summer of 1890 was the office of Horace Wilcox Felton, a physician-surgeon, who specialized in women's diseases.

From his office in Scott's store, Dr. Felton could walk south on Main to the San Luis Street house he rented from attorney Henry V. Morehouse. A Salinas City resident for two and one half years, Dr. Felton hoped to build his own home in the near future, but for now he and his wife were adjusting to a new family addition: daughter Verna Arline had been born on the third Sunday in July. The Felton house was suddenly filled with the piercing cries of a newborn girl, but for the doctor it was a time to rejoice because baby Verna was his only child. However, he wasn't without parenting experience; for the past four years he had been practicing his childrearing skills on his stepson Clayton, age seven.

Horace Felton, at thirty-seven, had been in the medical profession for seven years. The youngest of seven sons, he was not satisfied to follow the path of his father and brothers who were all farmers in the Midwest. But Horace came from sturdy Yankee stock, and like his forebears, he was unafraid to strike off into unknown territory and face far-flung challenges. The American branch of the Felton family stretched back to 1633 when Nathaniel Felton arrived in Salem, Massachusetts, as an eighteen-year-old sent over from England to scout the living conditions of the new colony. The following year, Nathaniel sailed back to the mother country to offer favorable reports, and in 1635, he returned to Salem along with his mother Eleanor and other family members. The following year, Eleanor was granted twenty acres on a rise of land, which would come to be called Felton Hill. Here, in 1644, Nathaniel's home—originally two rooms but

The Nathaniel Felton house as it looked in the 1880s. Today it remains as the oldest surviving home in Peabody, Massachusetts.

later enlarged numerous times—was built.

Because Nathaniel was a man of good faith and judgment he was frequently called to give his testimony about litigated estates. In 1692, when his neighbor John Proctor was tried for witchcraft, Nathaniel led a group to sign a testament vouching for the Christian character of the accused. However, it was all in vain. Proctor was executed on August 19 of that year. Nathaniel also vouched for the reputation of Rebecca Nurse, perhaps the most famous of the twenty individuals put to death during one of the darkest chapters of New England history. At the Rebecca Nurse Homestead in Danvers, Massachusetts, Nathaniel's name is listed on a stone monument, along with forty other neighbors who attested to the upstanding character of Nurse. Indeed, he and the others placed themselves under suspicion by defending their accused neighbors. Nathaniel's sprawling house and the one built by his son Nathaniel Felton Jr., still stand in 2009 on a maple-lined avenue—named Felton Street—in Peabody, just outside Salem.

Dr. Horace Felton's own grandfather Robert Felton had fought for liberty during the American Revolution and later moved his family to upstate New York where his youngest son Nelson—Horace's father—was born in 1812. Around 1836, Nelson took as his bride Emily Raymond, three years his junior. Over the next fifteen years their Oneida County farmhouse, situated in the heart of upstate New York, was filled with the lively sounds of seven growing sons. Of the six who lived to adulthood, the youngest was Horace Wilcox Felton, born on

(LEFT) **Nelson Felton, Verna's grandfather.** (RIGHT) **Emily Felton, Verna's grandmother.**

November 14, 1852. When Horace was just a lad, Nelson moved the family to Fond du Lac County, Wisconsin, where Nelson's brother Robert had relocated in the mid-1840's. Ten years previous to Robert's arrival, this territory, part of the Winnebago Indian nation, had been wilderness. Then came the mass migration of thousands of New Yorkers, Pennsylvanians, and New Englanders, including the Feltons.

Nelson Felton became a prosperous farmer in this new territory. According to the 1870 Federal Census records, his real estate was valued at $9000, and his personal estate was worth the exacting amount of $1645. The family farm, totaling 160 acres, was situated in the Rosendale community in Fond du Lac County's Springvale township. By this time, Nelson's older sons Merritt, Alanson, Albert, and Theodore were off on their own. At home still were newly married George and seventeen-year-old Horace, both laborers on the family farm. Nelson's ventures met with continued success, and he was considered one of the most prominent and wealthy farmers in Rosendale. In the spring of 1878, his handsome new residence was nearing completion when he suffered a fatal heart attack on the night of May 30. Soon after his burial in Rosendale Cemetery, Nelson's widow Emily moved in with son Albert. Meanwhile, Horace set off to seek a living other than farming.

Horace chose medicine as his course of study and relocated to Oshkosh where he trained for a while under Drs. Thomas P. Russell and George M. Steele. When Horace decided to enroll at Rush Medical College in Chicago in the fall of 1881,

Dr. Russell provided the necessary references. While a student at Rush, he participated in clinical instruction at the Central Free Dispensary as well as at the Cook County Hospital. His studies were completed in early 1883 when he received his degree of Doctor of Medicine.

By August of that year, Dr. Felton was residing in Grant County, New Mexico, where he was first granted the license to practice medicine. His stay in this state was rather short-lived; by the next April he was certified by the Board of Examiners at San Luis Obispo, California, to practice in that state. It is uncertain how long he stayed in this area, but by July 1885, he had made his way north to Sierra County. There, between the north and south forks of the Oregon Creek, in the remote little mining town of Forest City, Dr. Felton opened his practice.

Forest City, elevation 4600 feet, lay at the base of the southern slope of Bald Mountain in southern Sierra County. The town was given that appellation in 1854 by a consensus of area residents. Gold had been discovered in the forks of nearby Oregon Creek around 1851. According to James J. Sinnott's *History of Sierra County, Volume III*, "Forest City grew rapidly with the locating of many mines. In 1853 the population of the town was 'over four hundred,' which had swelled by 1854 to one thousand. By this latter year there were at the least fifteen mines of significance in operation at the town or in the vicinity." Prosperous times lasted until the mid-1860s, and then the mines played out. However, the early 1870s brought another boom to Forest City with the discovery of the Bald Mountain mine, one of the great drift placer mines of California. Good fortune lasted another ten years until a terrific fire flattened the town on March 16, 1883, destroying over eighty buildings. However, the hardy citizens of Forest were experienced in overcoming such hardships; the 1883 fire was the most recent of three such devastations. They rebuilt their town with remarkable speed.

At the time of Dr. Felton's arrival in Forest City, one resident, Mrs. Clara Van Alstine was enduring a serious financial hardship and a great emotional burden of her own. Abandoned by her husband Edward eighteen months earlier, Clara had found it necessary to give up the older of her two young sons to a childless couple in the nearby county seat of Downieville. Subsequently, she was forced to eke out a meager living for her younger son and herself by finding work wherever possible. In the summer of 1885, she was operating a private summer school in her home for the miners' children of Forest City.

A first-generation American, Clara was born in the Sierra County mining village of Port Wine on July 13, 1863. Her father, David Lawrence, born in Dublin, Ireland on December 4, 1835, arrived in America, perhaps as a teenager. His elder brother George, quite possibly an original forty-niner, had been become a United States citizen in 1854, having made his application for citizenship in neighboring Plumas County. Like his brother, David sought his fortune in the gold mines, settling with George in the Port Wine section of northern Sierra County, some ten miles northwest of Downieville, the county seat. George married soon thereafter, but David worked hard and saved his money for several years.

(LEFT) **David Lawrence, Verna's grandfather.** (RIGHT) **Agnes Lawrence, Verna's grandmother.**

Then, on January 25, 1860, at Port Wine he took as his bride twenty-two-year-old Agnes Gleason, a native of Thurlis, Ireland. Their infant daughter was christened as Clara Winder Lawrence on July 29, 1863, by the Reverend B. Morris, officiant of the Immaculate Conception Catholic Church in Downieville. (This structure still stands in 2009 on the same knoll, its white bell tower reaching far above the tall pines.) Clara's middle name was derived from the surname of David's fellow miner, an English immigrant named Edward Winder. The two men must have shared a close bond because each of their firstborn children was named for their father's friend. Winder's firstborn, David Lawrence Winder, preceded Clara by three months.

Interestingly, Clara Lawrence and Downieville were also of the same age. The town was incorporated the very same year she was born, although Major William Downie, a Scottish prospector, had settled the area soon after gold was found on this fork of the North Yuba River in 1849. Word of this discovery soon brought hundreds, and then thousands, of prospectors into the area. By the mid-1850s, Downieville was the fifth largest town in California. At the time of Clara's parents' marriage, the population of Downieville had reached an astounding 16,000. A photograph taken in 1865 shows a mix of rustic store buildings—some of brick or stone construction—and whitewashed cottages, houses, and churches. (Among the businesses was the office of the town's newspaper, *The Mountain Messenger*, which remains today as California's oldest continuously published weekly. Another unique fact about the *Messenger* is that Mark Twain was once a staff writer.) The photograph also reveals that the surrounding mountainsides appear completely denuded of any trees.

By the time of Dr. Felton's arrival in Sierra County twenty years later, the gold strikes had diminished considerably and Downieville's population dwindled, but the charm of the town, now lying in a forested canyon, remained. A writer in 1882 offered this description: "I write from the quaint little town of Downieville, which in its day was teeming with thousands of eager gold seekers, but now has settled back into a pretty mountain village. Its situation is the strangest of any I have ever seen. Nestling at the base of lofty mountains that seem to rise but a few rods away from it, which enclose it as in a basin; with a width not possibly more than a quarter of a mile and extending up and down the river of less than half a mile. Downieville presents a delightfully novel appearance to one born and bred in a country flat as a kitchen floor, so to speak."

Clara Lawrence.

David Lawrence was granted full citizenship in 1868, the year following the birth of his younger daughter Mary. His wife Agnes evidently either died following Mary's birth or when her daughters were very young. By the time little Mary died on January 27, 1870, David had moved his family thirty-five miles south of Port Wine to Grass Valley in Nevada County. With the end of the Gold Rush, some miners, like David Lawrence, were forced to find other employment, such as hard rock mining. The federal census, taken five months following Mary's death, reveals a widowed David working in a Grass Valley quartz mill, stamping ore mined near there. Since her father David was away at the mill all day, it was necessary for little Clara to lodge with other families. An early tintype image of her reveals a tiny somber girl with closely cropped hair, posing stiffly in her hoop skirt and pantaloons. Over the next fifteen years, David Lawrence moved wherever the work was, living for a while in Nevada County, California, and then in Storey County, Nevada. Soon he had accumulated enough means to enroll Clara in the convent school operated by the Daughters of Charity in nearby Virginia City, but she was unhappy there, and according to family tradition, ran away at age fifteen.

By 1880, Clara had moved back to Sierra County to live with her uncle George Lawrence, now the successful proprietor of the Union Hotel, home to twenty-five miners in Forest City. His ad in the *Mountain Messenger* boasted: "First class in every respect. Tables first class. Large, Airy Rooms. Neat Servants. Good Accommodations. Board and Lodging by the Week $6. Board by the week $5." Operating the Union Hotel was a family affair; George's wife and four children assumed the duties of running the "first class" establishment. His wife Mary received praise from an anonymous *Messenger* correspondent in 1878: "Mrs. Lawrence has her hotel fitted up in good style, and somehow the lady of the house is possessed with the faculty of inspiring her guests with the idea that they can do not better elsewhere, consequently her house is generally full." Clara earned her keep, too, by waiting on tables in the hotel dining room, alongside her first cousin Agnes Lawrence, named for Clara's late mother.

At times, things could be rowdy around the hotel and in Forest City. Since the remote area was without police protection, sometimes the citizens had to handle certain situations without the "long arm of the law." One such incident occurred in February 1883 when Agnes "Aggie" Lawrence paid off a hotel employee, a Chinaman who was called Big Dick. He watched her as she took $10 from her bureau drawer, then sneaked back in her room later, only to be caught there by her father. Dick told George Lawrence that he was there to ask Aggie about buying a chicken for Chinese New Year. Soon after that, $126 was found missing, and George immediately started for Chinatown to find Dick. He met the Chinaman on the bridge, but before George could say anything, Dick exclaimed, "I no took your money, Mr. Lawrence!" The *Messenger* further reported, "George collared him and led him up town. When it got noised abroad, the people got ropes and threatened to hang the thief, but more prudent counsels prevailed, and upon his countrymen returning the stolen sum, he was released. It was a narrow escape for the Big [*sic*] heathen." Perhaps some of the citizens were sobered enough by reminiscences of the most infamous incident in the history of nearby Downieville. In 1851, a crowd of white men had lynched a Spanish woman named Juanita after she stabbed to death one of their own.

One of the miners lodging at the Union Hotel in the summer of 1880 was twenty-three-year-old Edward Van Alstine, a native of New York. His older sister Lizzie lived five doors away with her husband James McGregor, secretary of the Bald Mountain Mine Company. It was perhaps James who secured a mining job for Ed Van Alstine (sometimes spelled Van Alstyne). Ed made the acquaintance of Clara Lawrence as she performed her duties as hotel waitress. Her days and nights were busy, filled with food preparation, clean-up, and waiting tables. Breakfasts were substantial in those days, usually consisting of oatmeal or corn meal mush, bacon or ham, eggs, toast or hot cakes, and coffee. The hotel also packed lunches in tin buckets for the miners. The evening meal included a choice of two meats, a soup, vegetables, fruit, pie or cake, and coffee.

Whether over a cup of coffee or as she cleared the supper dishes, an attraction developed between Ed and Clara. A whirlwind courtship ensued, and the couple eloped to Downieville, where they were married by Father Curley of the Immaculate Conception Church on Sunday, July 4, 1880. Clara was of the Catholic faith, and while there existed a Catholic church in Forest City, there was no resident priest there. On occasion Father Curley traveled from the Downieville parish to hold Mass in Forest City, as well as in nearby Alleghany.

On the day of the marriage ceremony, Clara Lawrence was nine days shy of her seventeenth birthday. When notice of the marriage ran in the *Mountain Messenger*, Clara asked that it also be printed in the Virginia City, Nevada, papers so that her father, residing near that place, would be informed of her change in marital status. The young couple quickly became the parents of two sons, David Howard Van Alstine, born on June 13, 1881, and George Clayton Van Alstine, born March 24, 1883.

Clayton's birth came just a week after a devastating fire destroyed most of the town. On March 16, the fire started on Main Street in the rear of a hotel called the Forest House. Soon the entire roof was ablaze, and the inhabitants barely escaped with their lives. The fire hoses, which had been allowed to dry rot, burst when the water valve was opened, so the citizens of Forest City stood by helplessly as the fire crossed the road and raced up Main Street, reaching the last business in town and destroying everything in its path. In less than two hours from the time the fire was discovered, eighty-two buildings—including George Lawrence's hotel—were reduced to a blackened ruin. The damage was estimated at over $200,000, but the insurance on the destroyed property amounted to only one fourth of that. The homes of James McGregor and several other prominent residents were lost in the inferno as well.

Gifts of money, groceries, provisions, bedding, and lumber soon poured in from surrounding towns and communities. By late spring, at least a dozen structures had been rebuilt. George Lawrence had been delayed in rebuilding his establishment due to a lingering illness brought on by the cold he caught while exposed to the elements on the night of the fire. On June 9, it was reported in the *Messenger* that he would erect a "large and commodious" hotel on the site of the Forest House, but in a related article in the same edition, it was announced that he had sold his interest in that parcel of land to Archie Henderson and James McNaughton. Less than a week later, George bought McDonald's Hotel—three stories tall with a steeply pitched roof to handle heavy snows—in Downieville, renamed it the Capitol Hotel, and relocated there before month's end. Evidently he had realized that his fragile health would not provide the fortitude required to reconstruct in Forest City. Clara Van Alstine was sad to see the departure of her uncle. In the absence of her father David, Uncle George had been like a father to her. She had even named her second born son after him.

More sadness enveloped Clara on January 21, 1884, when Ed, who had grown too fond of gambling and alcohol, deserted her and the boys for the big-city attractions of Sacramento. Twenty-year-old Clara was forced to depend on the help of nearby relatives and friends as she struggled to support her two tiny sons. Gone were the more carefree days when she could visit family and friends in Downieville, taking a thrilling nine-mile stage ride down the treacherously winding Mountain House Road. How long that first winter alone must have seemed, trapped in a snow-covered house with a two-year-old and an infant.

Later that year, Clara Van Alstine moved to Downieville and became acquainted with Elizabeth Millar Wiggins, the twenty-nine-year-old wife of the town's saloon-keeper. "Lizzie" and her middle-aged husband James had been married for nine years, but their union had produced no children. James Samuel Wiggins had been born in Chicago in 1839 and came west with his father in 1852. With the exception of the war years, he had been a resident of Downieville since 1853, holding various positions, including pony express rider and mule train operator. His wife Lizzie, born in Australia in 1855, was the eldest child of James C. Millar, a Canadian who had settled his family on a Sierra County farm soon after the Civil War ended. (It should be noted that this Millar family was in no way connected to the Lee Millar family mentioned in subsequent chapters.) Soon it was arranged for this childless couple to help Clara by taking in her older son, three-year-old Howard, and rearing him as their own.

Meanwhile, Clara found a job opportunity in Forest City so she moved back there with her toddler Clayton. On occasion, she was able to visit with Howard in Downieville, and the Wigginses sometimes brought the boy to Forest City to see his mother, so it seems that open communication was maintained between the two parties. Only conjectures can be entertained about the explanation offered to Howard concerning this great change in his life. However, the little boy—already showing a physical resemblance to his grandfather Lawrence—was soon answering to the name of Howard Wiggins.

The summer of 1885 brought Clara more grief when her uncle George Lawrence died on August 7, never having recovered from the prolonged illness dating back to the fire two years earlier. Shortly before George died, Clara's father David, who by now had relocated from Nevada to Idaho, came to Downieville to visit him. He remained for the funeral, conducted in the Masonic Hall, which drew one of the largest crowds of mourners ever seen in Downieville. David's eloquent "card of thanks," published in the *Messenger* a week later, does not resemble the language of a rugged miner, so perhaps he had acquired an education either before entering that field of endeavor or after becoming very successful in the same. David left town a week after the funeral for his home in Bullion City, a small mining town in southern Idaho.

As Clara was mourning her own recent loss, the nation was grieving for former President Ulysses S. Grant who died July 23. When Forest City citizens decided to hold a memorial service for Grant on August 8, they asked Dr. Horace Felton to speak on behalf of the organizing committee, despite the fact that he was very much a newcomer, having opened his practice scarcely two weeks before. The

Forest City, California, in the 1880s.

service was quite a somber affair beginning with the church bell tolling sixty-three times, once for every year of Grant's life. A brass band played a funeral dirge, after which the choir sang fitting anthems such as "Silently Bury the Dead" and "Rest" and an orator eulogized the former president. Photographs of the occasion show school girls outfitted in white dresses and flower-bedecked hats, young lads in knickers, and bearded town fathers in three-piece suits. These expressionless citizens stand before an elaborate covered platform, built just for the occasion and draped in black crepe, fresh evergreen boughs, and American flags. High in the center of the platform they affixed a black sign with the message: "The Great Hero U.S.G. Surrenders July 23rd, '85." Below the message appears a clock face showing the exact time of Grant's death, a perfect example of Victorian Americans' obsession with mortality.

As the summer wore on, Clara Van Alstine grew weary of waiting for her husband Ed to return to the family he deserted eighteen months earlier. The solitary task of rearing her small son, not to mention the separation anxiety she certainly experienced with her older son living miles away in another home, surely created lines of worry across Clara's young face. Finally realizing that her present predicament was hopeless, Clara began divorce proceedings in late September. The court ruled in her favor on November 2, granting her custody of the children. Clara put her tragic marriage behind her and promptly reassumed her maiden name. Only twenty-two years old and single again, she remained an attractive young woman with pale eyes and soft curls framing her fair-complected face.

Dr. Horace Wilcox Felton.

At thirty-three, the newly arrived Dr. Horace W. Felton cut a fine figure himself. His farm bred physique leaned toward the stocky side. His full head of slightly wavy hair was neatly trimmed and created a definite contrast with his luxuriantly wiry beard, which obscured the greater part of his full face. A Roman nose complimented his strong features, including eyes that revealed an intelligent yet adventuresome nature.

Two weeks following Clara's divorce settlement, a correspondent for the *Mountain Messenger* noted that Dr. Felton was well liked by the Forest City citizens, coyly adding that one unnamed resident evidently held him in higher regard than the rest. In December, the newspaper hinted at a budding romance between the doctor and Clara Lawrence when it reported that they had paid a short visit to Indian Hill, a small mining town about twelve miles west, where they visited the residence of Mr. and Mrs. Edwin Ketchum, the stepfather and mother of Clara's former husband, Ed Van Alstine.

Perhaps kindly Dr. Roderick Stocking Weston, the local druggist, assisted Dr. Felton's courtship of Clara. Dr. Weston had arrived in Forest City in 1854 and made his living as a miner until ten years later when he opened a drug store. Twice widowed by the time he became postmaster in 1860, Weston held this position until one year before his death in 1888. Highly respected by all in Forest City, he was also the town's telegraph operator for over twenty years and a regular correspondent for the *Mountain Messenger*. A Massachusetts native some thirty years Dr. Felton's senior, Weston "lived his life on the bright side," often inquiring of the young fellows in town, "Why don't you get married?"

Dr. Felton took his friend's advice to heart, and in the spring of 1886, he proposed to Clara. When she accepted, he quickly realized that the income from his small-town practice would not be sufficient for a wife and a stepson, so he opened an additional practice in Pike City, ten miles away, where he made visits once a week.

The wedding was held in the Forest City home of young widow Mary McNaughton on the evening of May 25, 1886. The house was filled with flowers sent from Nevada City and San Juan, California. At nine o'clock the bride and groom stood under a wedding bell made entirely of white roses, a gift from John West, owner of the local saloon. In the presence of twenty-five friends, the ceremony was performed by Dr. Weston, whose many hats also included that of justice of the peace. Clara wore a gown of cream-colored silk adorned with white lace and flowers. Her bridesmaids were her cousins, the Misses Kate and Maggie Honold, daughters of her father's sister Margaret.

After the ceremony, a wedding supper was served at the Hooper House, a local hotel. The social column of the *Messenger* reported: "There were not wanting different varieties of wine on the table, but, such were the abstemious habits of the company, that scarcely a cork was drawn, and the wine, for the most part, was left untouched. The toasts to the prosperity and happiness of the newly-married pair were drank [*sic*] in cold water, though none the less sincere. After the supper there was an adjournment to the sitting-room, where pleasant conversation, jokes and repartee were engaged in till a late hour, when each pair departed for their respective abodes, after exchanging friendly adieus, feeling in their own hearts conscious of kind wishes for the future welfare of the two just setting out in married life, and that no unfriendly breeze may wreck their bark ere it attains the desired haven."

Dr. Felton's desired haven was evidently not the remoteness of Forest City where the once fabulous yield of the Bald Mountain mine—along with the opportunities for lasting fortune—had begun to diminish by 1886. He told the *Messenger* in midsummer that he was moving his wife and stepson to Illinois for two years, but soon thereafter it was reported in the same newspaper that the Feltons had moved to Wisconsin. Whether the doctor's destination was his home state for a reunion with his mother and brothers, or whether it was Chicago (where he might receive further medical training at his *alma mater*) cannot be determined. However, things obviously did not go as planned, as the Feltons were back in Forest City by November of the same year. The locals welcomed him like the fabled prodigal, and the Knights of Pythias elected him as one of their officers only one week after his return.

Dr. Felton was indeed a trusted physician, as evidenced by the summons he received from the county coroner in early 1887 to go to Pike City where the resident doctor had committed suicide. (Dr. Felton's autopsy revealed morphine poisoning.) But at the same time, his personality must have been of the kind allowing for an occasional good-natured jab. For instance, in January of 1886, a Forest City correspondent for the *Mountain Messenger*, identified only as "A Tongue," penned this playful little nudge: "Dr. Felton and W. N. Hooper are now off the sick list. The attacks were not very severe, hence they managed to be(e)ar up under it." Another item hinted that the good doctor enjoyed gambling.

The Feltons moved into a new house in Forest City on October 10, 1887. However, with another harsh winter approaching, Dr. Felton once more felt the itch to relocate. Two years previously, he had passed through the town of Salinas City, California, some 250 miles southwest, stopping long enough to treat a female patient. Now he thought of the flatlands of the Salinas Valley again, wondering if this would be a more desirable place to practice than the rugged Sierra Nevada. By mid-November, he determined that it would be better to make the move before the winter snowstorms hit the mountains.

Meanwhile, Clara Felton had spent the past eighteen months of marriage without enjoying a permanent reunion with her older son, Howard, who continued to reside with James and Lizzie Wiggins in Downieville. By now, the boy had assumed the surname of his foster parents and was a first grade pupil in the local school. Even so, the Feltons and Wigginses were evidently on friendly terms with one another: social items in the *Mountain Messenger* reveal that they were frequent visitors in each other's homes. Therefore, it presumed that they were all in agreement that Howard should remain in Downieville. It is even possible that the Wiggins couple had legally adopted Howard by the time the Feltons were ready to leave Forest City. Whatever the case, Clara Felton must have felt sharp pangs of loss as she bid farewell to her firstborn and to the county of her birth. She would make return visits the following two summers, but after that, decades would pass before Clara Felton saw Sierra County again.

CHAPTER 2

DESTINY STEPPED IN

The Feltons' move to Salinas City was completed in late November 1887. The doctor rented a small cottage for his family on Lincoln Avenue, one door north of the Methodist Episcopal Church South, a plain, frontier-style building embellished with a Gothic belfry. Then Dr. Felton set up his office on the east side of Main Street. On December 1, his initial ad appeared in the *Salinas Weekly Index*: "H. W. Felton, M. D., Physician and Surgeon, Office-Main Street, opposite French restaurant, Salinas City, Cal. Special attention paid to the diseases of women." Indeed, he was a specialist. In 1890, the *Index* mentioned that he had performed surgery to remove a cancerous tumor from the breast of a female patient. Dr. Felton practiced obstetrics at this time as well.

With a population of about three thousand, Salinas City (officially renamed Salinas in 1919) wasn't a very large town, but as the seat of Monterey County, it was a busy place. It boasted eight thriving churches, thirteen lodges, and a unit of the Grand Army of the Republic, an organization made up of Union veterans of the Civil War. The Women's Christian Temperance Union convened weekly at the Baptist Church, and their auxiliary for younger women met once a month. In addition, according to the *Salinas Daily Index*, Salinas boasted nine hotels, fifteen general merchandise stores, four meat markets, four livery stables, six blacksmith shops, ten insurance agencies, one brewery, one soda water factory, and twenty saloons.

Compared to nearby Monterey where the majority of folks spoke Spanish, one writer declared that Salinas City was a town of "purely American character." Indeed its population was predominantly Protestant, and the residents of this valley town depended on the surrounding grain and dairy farmers. By 1885, Salinas boasted the state's largest flour mill south of San Francisco, producing five hundred barrels a day. The town was supplied with telegraph connections, a city gas works, a water company, an electric ARC light company, and three newspapers, making it one of the most modern for its size in the state. At least ten doctors and two dentists were practicing in Salinas City by the advent of the Feltons, including a woman doctor, May C. E. Gydison.

Main Street, Salinas, California, 1887. COURTESY OF THE MONTEREY COUNTY HISTORICAL SOCIETY, INC.

When Dr. Oliver Trimmer decided to relocate to Pacific Grove in July of 1888, Dr. Felton moved his business into Trimmer's vacated space in John B. Scott's drug store where the hottest selling item was California Fig Syrup, hailed as "Nature's own true laxative" and guaranteed to dispel headaches, colds, and fevers. Dr. Scott was one of the pioneer citizens of Salinas City, moving there in 1868 to work as a postal clerk. When he arrived, the little town was in its infancy. Four years earlier, the first merchants had set up shop after Salinas was chosen as a Southern Pacific Railroad terminus. In 1872, Salinas City was not only incorporated as a city, but it also became the county seat when it was decided that Monterey—the original county seat—was too distant from the other parts of the county. Around the time Dr. Felton moved into Scott's store, he also moved his family from Lincoln Avenue into a house owned by fellow colleague Dr. Thomas Clay Edwards. This house was situated on the west side of South Main Street, near West San Luis Street, three doors from the slough bridge. The Felton and Edwards families had become close friends, even spending the 1889 Fourth of July holiday together at the seashore in Monterey.

During the ten months following Dr. Felton's move to Dr. Scott's store, the *Sailnas Weekly Index* reported two unusual medical cases attended by Dr. Felton. The first involved a disturbed jail inmate who took his own life by overdosing on laudanum, and the second involved Mrs. J. B. Scott, wife of the druggist. Upon examination, Dr. Felton recommended her admission to the insane asylum at Stockton, a particularly difficult decision since he worked daily with Dr. Scott in the drug store.

Dr. Felton became a medical patient himself in early April of 1890 when he came down with a severe case of catarrhal pneumonia. With his colleagues and wife attending him daily, he made an adequate enough recovery by May 1 to move the family residence from South Main Street to a quieter location at 121 East San Luis Street, a house recently vacated by Henry V. Morehouse and his family. Morehouse, an attorney, had been living in this house for a number of years while renting it from his law partner, Samuel F. Geil. When Morehouse decided to relocate to San Jose, he purchased the house from Geil to retain as rental property. Thus, the Feltons became Morehouse's first tenants. The home, bought by Geil in 1883, was probably built in the early 1870s by Henry S. Ball. While no photograph exists of the house, it is likely that it was built in the Italianate style, quite the rage at the time. (When the author visited Salinas in 2006, few examples of this style remained in this neighborhood, but just around the corner from this site, at 415 Soledad Street, there stood a house from that period. The house the Feltons lived in at 121 East San Luis Street no longer exists. In its place in 2006 was a house of Spanish style, dating to the 1920s.) In 1890, the flat streets in this neighborhood were all made of dirt, as were the sidewalks, typically abutted by picket fences enclosing the yards of the residents. Over the housetops, one could easily glimpse the Santa Lucia Mountains to the south and the Gabilan Mountains to the east.

Dr. Felton's recovery from pneumonia was not quite complete by the time he moved his family to the East San Luis Street house. It was customary in the late nineteenth century for those convalescing from lengthy or chronic illnesses to vacate to more rustic surroundings to achieve a full recovery. On May 12, soon after Dr. Felton got his family settled in the new home, he and James Jeffery, proprietor of the leading hotel, spent a week's vacation on the ranch of Charles Joy, outside the city on the Arroyo Seco, a tributary of the Salinas River. Clara did not accompany him, as she was by that time seven months pregnant and, following the social mores of the time, remained out of public view.

Sunday, July 20, dawned clear. No rain had fallen in Salinas City since April. The dusty streets were quiet; the Southern Pacific trains ran only twice a day on the Sabbath. But in the Felton house there was much activity. Clara had gone into labor. The Feltons' firstborn would be their only child, a girl they named Verna Arline Felton. Although her birth was not recorded at the county courthouse, it is highly probable that Verna was delivered by her father since he specialized in women's healthcare. A standard announcement appeared in the Salinas Weekly Index on July 24: "BORN. FELTON—In Salinas, July 20, 1890, the wife of H. W. Felton, M.D., a daughter." This miniscule mention and a sepia-toned cabinet card of Verna at age three months, taken by local photographer John Edmund Bacon, are the only primary sources proving that Verna Felton was ever a resident of Salinas City.

In fact, Verna never got to know the city of her birth at all. On June 8 of the following year, her father opened a practice in San Jose, sixty miles north of Salinas City. The *Salinas Weekly Index* bade him this farewell: "He is a genial gentleman and skillful physician, and leaves a good practice here which he has built up during his three years' sojourn among us." For seven weeks, Clara and her children remained in Salinas until Dr. Felton made arrangements for them to join him in San Jose. In the interim, Clara bore the responsibility for caring not only for her two children, but for her father as well. David Lawrence, suffering from

Verna Arline Felton, age three months, fifteen days.

tuberculosis, had previously moved into the Felton home in Salinas. In early May, Clara accompanied him to the small town of Jolon, some seventy miles south of Salinas where he remained for two months in a care facility to take treatments to improve his health. By the time Clara and her family packed up their possessions to leave Salinas, David had returned to Salinas. On July 29, 1891, Clara gathered her children and her father and boarded the train bound for San Jose, where Dr. Felton had rented accommodations on the upper floor of a store building at 392 East Santa Clara Street.

Life in San Jose was an adjustment for the Felton family since the city was eight times the size of Salinas. The commercial activity of the city was centered at the intersection of First and Santa Clara Streets where large banks occupied all four corners. The downtown also featured distinctive churches, hotels, and elaborate commercial buildings. A 237-foot Electric Light Tower straddling the juncture of Market and Santa Clara Streets was a San Jose landmark recognized worldwide. The impressively large City Hall was less than five years old when the Feltons arrived. The Letitia Building (still standing in 2009 on South First Street) and Verna were of an age, both products of 1890. The Feltons also witnessed the 1895 completion of a new post office building at the corner of Market and San Fernando. Constructed of high quality sandstone in the Romanesque style, this public building, with its imposing clock tower, resembled a stately fortress. The San Jose Normal School, built in 1881 by the state to train elementary teachers, stood with a commanding presence at the center of Washington Square. This was all before the advent of the automobile; most streets in San Jose were still made of dirt. Many of the eighteen thousand citizens rode trolley cars.

In this bustling and beautiful place Dr. Felton, one of two dozen physicians in town, achieved a certain degree of success as an obstetrician but was required to supplement his income by serving as the medical examiner for an insurance company called the Covenant Mutual Benefit Association. His medical offices were housed downtown in Rooms 41 and 42 of the Knox Building. Located at the northwest corner of First and Santa Clara Streets, this substantial two-story brick structure was built for $30,000 in 1866 by Dr. William J. Knox, who opened San Jose's first bank there. (Described as being as strong as a fortress, it survived the great earthquakes of 1868 and 1906. Only a hardworking wrecking crew could demolish it in 1945 to make way for the downtown store of the J. C. Penney Company.) Like most medical professionals of his day, Dr. Felton kept "banker's hours," opening his office from 10 a.m. until noon and from 2 p.m. until 4 p.m. six days a week. However, to his credit, he was accommodating enough to open each evening from 7 p.m. to 8 p.m. and for an hour on Sunday afternoons. In late August 1891,

Dr. Felton during his practice in San Jose.

the *San Jose Mercury* reported that Dr. Felton had been appointed the physician-surgeon for the San Jose district of the Southern Pacific Railroad Company. The territory of the district covered the narrow gauge from Newark to Felton and the broad gauge from San Mateo to Gilroy and from San Jose to Almaden. It is possible that an old friend provided the connections for Dr. Felton to land this position. Henry V. Morehouse, the attorney from whom the doctor had rented his Salinas home, was now residing in San Jose and representing the Southern Pacific Railroad. Morehouse would later become a California state senator.

On the morning of March 2, 1892, David Lawrence, Clara's father, finally lost his long battle with tuberculosis. His death occurred in the East Santa Clara Street home, but contemporary newspapers do not reveal details of a funeral or burial. His official death record, provided by Dr. Felton, indicates that David was married at the time of his demise, however no widow was named among any documents. David Lawrence was fifty-six years old.

In June 1893, Dr. Felton moved his family to a more suitable residence at 159 Vine Street, a one-story dwelling located farther away from the commercial district than the previous rental. In April 1895, Dr. Felton moved his office one block away to the home of his fraternal order, the Knights of Pythias Building, at the northwest corner of South Second and East San Fernando Streets. He would not remain there for long.

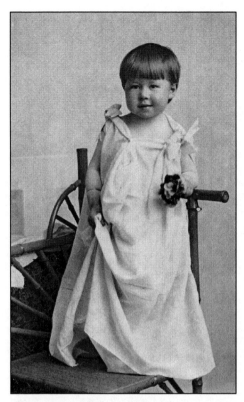

Verna Felton, May 20, 1893.

On July 30, 1895, he abruptly closed his practice, announcing his move to South San Francisco, where he would immediately assume duties as physician for the Western Meat Company, a concern whose majority stockholders included Chicago millionaire meat packers P. D. Armour and G. F. Swift. Situated on eighty acres fronting the San Francisco Bay, the company had begun operation in December 1892. The site included stockyards, abattoirs, and a large packing plant for the handling of beef, mutton, and pork. The company's average annual sales were close to $4 million. Almost three hundred men were employed there, and most were residents of South San Francisco, then a small town of less than seven hundred.

Considering the size of the town, the move must have seemed to Dr. Felton's family like a step backwards. In fact, one wonders if his wife and daughter ever resided in South San Francisco at all. A social item appearing in the *San Jose Mercury* on January 13, 1896, indicates that they indeed relocated when the doctor left San Jose, but they may not have actually resided in the same town with him: "Mrs. Dr. Felton and little daughter Verna have returned to San Francisco, after a visit of two weeks with Mrs. L. M. Pinard." The city, with much more to offer than South San Francisco, was only ten miles away. It is logical therefore to believe that Clara and Verna resided there, and the possibility seems even more plausible when one considers the fact that by this time, Clara had family living there.

Since at least 1889, William George Lawrence had been a resident of San Francisco. Born in Chicago in 1860, he was the only son of Mary Ann Lawrence, a sister of Clara's father David. According to family lore, Mary Ann had married a man named Jeremiah O'Connor, but upon either his untimely death or their divorce, she found herself in dire financial straits. Her unwed brother James, also living in Chicago, took her and her small children into his home to live—but with one stipulation: they must all assume the Lawrence surname. William grew to manhood in the Windy City, and learned the trades of plumber and then gas fitter. Around 1885, he married Isabella Ure Short. Four years later, accompanied

Verna and her mother Clara Lawrence Felton, San Jose, circa 1895.

by their firstborn and Mary Ann, the family moved to San Francisco, where William started his own business. Clara Felton must have met this eastern branch of the family by 1894, because in that year William's third daughter was named for her.

If Clara and Verna did live with the Lawrences during this time, it must have been at times a rather frustrating situation. Dr. Felton was miles away on his job; his wife and daughter knew no one else in the city. If they held any sway over the doctor, then perhaps they influenced his ultimate decision to return to San Jose, a scant ten months after leaving his practice there. Fortunately, Dr. Felton found that his old office in the Knights of Pythias Building was still vacant. He opened up for business the first week in June and apparently remained in practice there for the next several years. The Feltons were equally fortunate finding a dwelling—they moved right back into the house on Vine Street. Almost right away, Dr. Felton became active in several fraternal organizations, holding offices in both the Triumph Lodge of the Knights of Pythias and the San Jose Council (No. 591) of the National Union.

Meanwhile, Verna, a round-faced cherub with big brown eyes and curly dark hair, passed a happy childhood in San Jose. She accompanied her mother everywhere, including weekly mass and social outings, like picnics at Alum Rock Park, located seven miles outside the city. When she was old enough, Verna was given piano and art lessons, but she enjoyed physical pursuits as well, such as horseback riding. According to a bit of lore later perpetuated by Verna, her first appearance on a stage of any sort occurred when she was hardly more than six years old. Each fall, the Catholic Ladies' Aid Society of San Jose held a giant fundraising event, usually lasting for three days, at Turn Verein Hall. The ladies set up booths selling everything from lemonade to fancy homemade goods. Delectable lunches were served, and dances were held in the evenings. In addition, there was some form of daily entertainment given on the stage of the hall. This is most likely when Verna took her first bow—as an amateur performer, of course. She may have even been part of a group who danced or sang. Moreover, Verna's participation in the fundraiser may have been an impromptu appearance since her name does not appear in the detailed lists of festival performers published in the San Jose newspapers each autumn from 1896 through 1899. Almost forty years later, when Verna was interviewed over San Francisco radio station KPO, she could not exactly pinpoint the time when she became stagestruck. Of those early years in San Jose, she reminisced, "I don't remember that I had any ambitions at the time to be an actress, but I suppose there was some little spark hidden away. I recall memorizing lines that appealed to me and comedically [sic] dramatizing situations. Whenever some club entertainment was presented in or about San Jose, I did my little bit in the way of recitations."

In either the latter months of 1898 or early in January 1899, the Feltons moved once again, this time to a one-story dwelling located at 450 West San Salvador Street. This dwelling was located on the west side of Guadalupe Creek in what was then called the "suburban" Gardner district of San Jose, an area which later became part of the city's first annexation in 1911.

The Gardner district had been named for community leader William Gardner. In 1872, Gardner, a New Hampshire native, had moved to San Jose where he operated a grocery store at 77 South First Street. In 1887, he bought one of the ten-acre ranches that were being divided from a 320-acre tract bounded on the east by Guadalupe Creek, on the west by Bird Avenue, on the north by West San Carlos Street, and on the south by Willow Street. (In 2006, this location was immediately west of the juncture of Interstate 280 and State Highway 87.) Gardner built his own home at what would later be 659 Delmas Avenue, but in those early days, there were hardly any homes in the area, simply open fields and orchards. Since this section was very swampy, Gardner led efforts to have it drained. Then he actively sought buyers for the lots he divided from his ten acres. When owners of the other ranches followed suit, the area became so populated that it was necessary for a school district to be organized. Gardner led these efforts as well, and around 1892 a temporary school was opened in a butcher

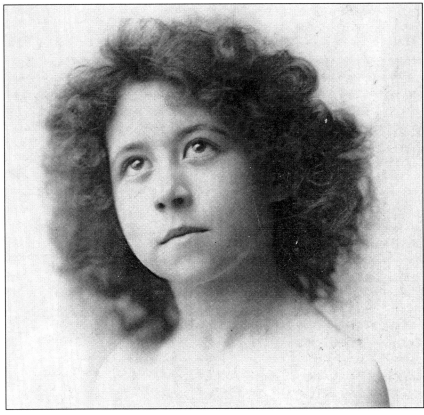

Pre-career portrait of Verna, circa 1898.

shop. In May 1893, voters decided to construct a two-room school building at 524 South Martin Avenue (now Illinois Avenue) to serve students in grades one through eight, but a struggle over appropriations soon followed. In 1894, when the new building was finally a realization, the community's residents wholeheartedly agreed to honor William Gardner by naming the school for him.

From her house on West San Salvador Street, Verna Felton could easily walk to Gardner Grammar School. Curiously, her name first appears on the school's honor roll for Grade One students published in the *San Jose Daily Mercury* on January 28, 1899. Since she was not mentioned on any of the earlier Gardner School honor rolls published the previous fall, one must wonder if her parents had enrolled Verna in the first grade following the Christmas holidays of 1898— although by this time she would have been eight and one half years old. If Verna had started first grade at age six, as most children did, she should have been in the *third* grade during the 1898-99 school year. Whether she had attended other schools in San Jose prior to moving to the Gardner district is not known. Nor is there any indication that a prolonged childhood illness or other mitigating circumstance may have kept Verna from starting school at age six.

To compound this mystery, Verna was twice recognized again as a first grade honor roll student in March and June of 1899, but she was not promoted to the next grade at the close of the school year. Since her advancement would not occur until the end of January 1900—a full year after her enrollment in the Gardner School—it lends credence to the belief that Verna had never attended any other school. The school system obviously required students to spend a full year in each grade, but it seems that promotion could occur at midyear if a student had enrolled at the same time the previous school year.

In the meantime, the spring of 1899 brought life-changing events for Verna Felton, beginning with her father's decision to return to Salinas. Evidently, the wanderlust had filled his heart again, or perhaps he had grown dissatisfied with things in San Jose. Maybe he was terminated from the employ of the Southern Pacific Railroad Company. Although a 1960 retrospective article in the *Salinas Californian* asserts that Dr. Felton had been offered a position in Salinas with the Southern Pacific, no contemporary documents at the time of his move support this. Whatever his motivation, Dr. Felton made a brief trip to Salinas City in late February to determine if the move would be advantageous.

Upon his return to San Jose, Dr. Felton informed his family and friends of his decision to relocate. On March 6, just before leaving San Jose, he attended a banquet in his honor at the Knights of Pythias Hall where the members of the San Jose Council of the National Union presented him with several testimonials which were "accepted in a feeling and fraternal manner."

During his absence, he arranged for Clara and Verna to board with family friends just down the street until he could send for them once the school year ended. It is surmised that Clara's son Clayton, now sixteen years old and perhaps finished with his schooling, was still residing with the Feltons at this time. From the time he was very young, Clayton had forsaken his father's surname for that of his stepfather, but whose idea this was is uncertain. Perhaps the doctor wanted his stepson to have his own name since he had been the only father the boy had actually known. Or perhaps it was Clara's request that Clayton use the name of Felton, preferring to eradicate the memory of her ill-fated marriage to Ed Van Alstine. As for Clara's elder son Howard, he was now eighteen and residing with his adoptive parents in Oakland where he was employed as a sales clerk in a bakery.

When Dr. Felton arrived in Salinas City to practice for the second time, he hung out his shingle in rented rooms over Sieghold's Jewelry Store on Main Street. He promptly advertised his services in the *Salinas Daily Index*, along with the city's seven other physicians, including his old friend, Dr. Thomas C. Edwards. During Dr. Felton's absence things had begun to boom in and around Salinas, despite a catastrophic drought the previous year. Consequently, the county's farmers were increasingly interested in the prospects of irrigation, and the newspapers that winter were full of reports about this new venture. Claus Spreckels, the "Sugar King," had been enticed by the Salinas Board of Trade to construct a major sugar refinery on the banks of the Salinas River. Spreckels promised it would be the world's largest sugar beet processing factory. Construction had begun in 1897 and was nearing completion when Dr. Felton came back to Salinas City in the late winter of 1899. On Main Street, brick buildings had replaced earlier wooden structures. Elaborate Queen Anne-style homes had risen along Central Avenue, among them the future birthplace of novelist John Steinbeck. Things were looking up for Salinas, destined to become an agricultural giant in the century ahead.

However, Dr. Felton's own future was not shining as brightly. At forty-six, he had lost his trim college physique and was experiencing the symptoms of "neuralgia of the heart," or a condition that modern physicians would diagnose as a mild heart attack. A younger colleague, Dr. Samuel B. Gordon, began treating Dr. Felton for this condition shortly after his arrival in Salinas. Dr. Felton spent lonely spring evenings in his rented rooms, anticipating Clara's steadying presence once she and Verna moved from San Jose. He and Clara had agreed it would be best not to uproot Verna until she completed her first year in school. For the time being, his only companion was a small dog he had brought with him from San Jose.

Clara and Verna, accompanied by a Mrs. Conrad, a family friend, arrived in Salinas on Sunday, April 30, for an overnight visit with Dr. Felton. When they returned to San Jose on the Monday morning train, it was without any suspicion of the events soon to transpire. On the afternoon of May 3, a representative of the Upjohn Pill Company made a call on Dr. Felton around half past three. When he knocked on the office door, Dr. Felton's dog began barking. Thinking the door was locked and without trying the knob, the salesman left. About thirty minutes later, he returned. This time when he received no answer to his knock, he let himself in. Stepping into the inner room he discovered the lifeless body of Dr. Felton seated at his desk where he had been writing a letter. The salesman immediately rushed downstairs and summoned Dr. Gordon from his office across the street. Yet, it was too late. Dr. Gordon found that he could do nothing but notify the undertaker.

Dr. Felton had died suddenly of an apparent heart attack. The stunning news was telegraphed to San Jose, where Clara was boarding in the home of bank teller Leon Pinard at 505 West San Salvador Street. She hastily replied, requesting that her husband's body be shipped to San Jose the next morning on the first available train. The funeral was held in the Pinard home on the afternoon of May 5 with burial immediately following in Oak Hill Cemetery, one and one half miles south of the city limits on Monterey Road. Pallbearers were city leaders, including the county assessor Lewis A. Spitzer, attorney Albert Hoehner, and nurseryman-florist Emilio H. Bourguignon.

Clara Felton sadly began to pick up the pieces of her life. She was faced with the sobering task of returning to Salinas City to sift through her husband's personal effects, sort out his business records, and determine a course of action to settle his estate. She soon learned that she had been dealt a double blow. Not only was she a widow at thirty-five, but she was also practically penniless. Verna explained this predicament in a *Radio Mirror* magazine article, published in January 1948, "Daddy had had an enormous practice, but there was no cash, and the books were an undecipherable mass of notations: 'Pete, the blacksmith, grippe. Old Mrs. Mason, arthritis.' No dates. No amounts. We put them away with Daddy's medical library." However, in private, Verna ruefully admitted once to a family friend that her father had actually spent more of his time gambling than doctoring.

Before leaving Salinas on May 11, Clara ran a notice in the *Salinas Daily Index* asking those who were indebted to the doctor to "settle with Warren C. Johnson," who, curiously, was listed on the 1900 census of Salinas City as an unmarried carpenter. Whether she was able to collect on these debts is not known, but fortunately, Clara discovered that the doctor had had the foresight to provide for the care and education of his daughter. As a member of the National Union, he had taken out a $3000 life insurance policy with Verna as the beneficiary. Clara, appointed as Verna's guardian, was required to report expenses accrued to Francis J. Hambly, the young law partner of Henry V. Morehouse. While this money would help, it could not be used for the support of Clara or Clayton. The Feltons were still in need.

In the meantime, Clara kept such burdens to herself. Her young daughter continued her first-grade studies at the Gardner School, appearing on the honor roll again at year's end. Six months later, Verna was promoted to Grade Two. On February 12, 1900, Lincoln's Birthday—a holiday once celebrated with great fanfare in many parts of the country—the school presented a lengthy program of songs and poems in the late president's memory. As her contribution, Verna recited a patriotic piece, the title of which is long forgotten, but it's likely that the plucky nine-year-old took the stage without any sign of doubt. One month earlier she had delivered a recitation at a surprise party for members of the San Jose Council of the National Union.

Still, the ever-increasing need of finding a livelihood troubled Clara. She and Verna were still fortunate enough to continue boarding in the home of Leon Pinard and his family on West San Salvador Street, but their meager income (perhaps provided by son Clayton—by then of working age) afforded them few necessities and no luxuries. In both the 1948 *Radio Mirror* article and subsequent interviews, Verna maintained that her widowed mother had never previously acquired any job skills because she "was a rich man's daughter who never had to work a day in her life." (Of course, this was not entirely true, because during her stay in Forest City, Clara had worked as both a waitress and schoolteacher.) Verna further explained to radio historian Martin Halperin in a 1964 tape-recorded interview, "There was nothing in the world [my mother] knew *how* to do. And everybody tried to get her a job, but there was nothing she could *do*, except keep house and everything."

Years later Verna would maintain that up until the death of her father, she lived the same sort of childhood that most children lived. "In all probability," she mused during a 1933 radio interview, "I should never have become an actress if Destiny had not stepped in." No observation could be keener. Had Horace Felton lived, Verna would have moved back to Salinas to continue her life as a physician's daughter. She might have married at a young age—as most girls did in those days—and begun a family when she was in her twenties. But this was not to be. The death of Horace Felton, compounded by his widow's limited work experience, directly resulted in Clara's decision to utilize Verna's natural talents as a means of putting food on the Felton table. However, Verna's autobiographical responses in the 1933 KPO radio interview, as well as the 1948 *Radio Mirror* article and the 1964 Martin Halperin interview, make it sound as if Verna's career began accidentally. A thorough search of all available turn-of-the-century sources reveals everything to the contrary.

Verna's name did not appear on either the March or June 1900 honor rolls listed in the San Jose newspapers. Neither did it appear on the end-of-the-year promotion list submitted to the newspapers by the Gardner School. Nowhere do Clara or Verna, or Clayton for that matter, appear on the United States Federal Census for San Jose, taken in June 1900. Nor do any of them appear to have been enumerated in any other location during this census year. They seem to have vanished. But what could have been their motivation to leave San Jose? Could it have been to move closer to Clara's elder son Howard, now nineteen years old and living in Oakland, where perhaps Clayton could also find work? Did Clara have another plan of action? Evidence exists that she, in fact, did.

When asked by Martin Halperin in 1964 if she had had prior training to becoming a professional actress, Verna responded by saying, "Yes, I had had elocution [lessons]. There was a woman by the name of Ray Newman, and she was a very fine elocutionist in the normal school there at San Jose. I took [lessons] from her, but that was all. Just the elocution. Then we went up to San Francisco and took songs and dances."

This latter revelation, although sparse in its details, not only informs one of the whereabouts of the Feltons by mid-1900, but is also very telling of Clara's plan. Obviously, she relocated to the Bay City (almost sixteen times more populated than San Jose) because there were more opportunities for Verna to be trained in voice, dance, and the other arts. It is likely that Clara was encouraged by the Pinards and their circle of musical friends to pursue this course of action. Interestingly, the Feltons do not appear on the 1900 census for San Francisco either. However, in a city of that size, it would have been rather easy for someone not to be counted, especially in the case of the Feltons, who may have been somewhat transient, perhaps spending time in both San Francisco and San Jose. More than likely, they took up residence again with Clara's first cousin William Lawrence, who was now living at 211 Chattanooga Street. By this time, William's family had grown to include five daughters and a son. The previous September, his wife Isabella had given birth to twin girls, Virginia Ure and Verna Arline, the latter, of course being named for her second cousin. In years to come, these two namesakes would be distinguished in family conversations as "Big Verna" and "Little Verna."

Meanwhile, Clara reasoned that once Verna had received enough training from San Francisco coaches (and luckily for Clara, the child was a quick study), then she could begin a career on the stage.

During the 1964 Halperin interview, Verna explained more about her training in San Francisco: "We did tap dances then. No ballet. No one did ballet then, except the [adult] ballerinas. A child in a [dance] class never got ballet [lessons] . . . you were not supposed to be very healthy if you did ballet for a while . . . it was something in the toes. I'll never forget it—My mother would say, 'No, [ballet] isn"t healthy.' And I'd say, 'Well, it's awfully *pretty*.' She'd say, 'Yes, but it isn't healthy, and I don't want you to do it." So I never got to do ballet, but we did songs and dances and tap dances. But we never used the little taps like they put on [shoes now]. We had a cornucopia of white sand, and we'd come out and just before we'd do our number, during the introduction, we'd take all the sand and put it all over a part of the [stage floor] and throw it offstage for someone to catch and then do our dance . . . that's what everybody did [in those days], and we enjoyed [this style of dance]."

After several months of study, Verna was given an opportunity to shine. At the invitation of old friends, she returned to San Jose for a special performance at the Victory Theatre on June 25. The California Ladies' Brass Band, under the direction of Professor Fred Brohaska, made its first public appearance that evening. While the addition of several soloists amplified the concert, the *San Jose Mercury* also noted that "Miss Verna Felton of San Francisco, a talented young lady who has been making a great hit with coon songs and dances, has been secured to give several fine numbers for the concert." The experience, while not Verna's professional debut, afforded her the chance to perform in an auditorium setting. Hoping the performance would be an impressive addition to Verna's resume, mother and daughter returned to San Francisco to seek employment. Two months later, their hopes were realized.

Verna's first professional engagement was a one-week appearance at Fischer's Concert House, located at 122 O'Farrell Street in San Francisco. Ernest A. Fischer, the proprietor, had opened this theatre on March 19, 1900. Advertisements from the *San Francisco Chronicle* at the time of its establishment hailed it as "the handsomest music hall in America." However, Fischer's stiff competition included the more established theatres of the city, such as the Columbia, the Alcazar, and the Grand. Fischer proudly announced that he had hired August Hinrichs as the orchestra conductor, and for the first few weeks, members of the Lombardi Opera Company would perform acts from *Faust* and *Il Trovatore*. Admission was ten cents, much cheaper than at the other houses of entertainment in San Francisco.

Promotional photo of Verna taken at the time of her debut at Fischer's Concert House, San Francisco, 1900.

Before the engagement commenced, Clara dressed Verna in a frilly organdy costume with matching hat and escorted her to the Fred Bushnell photography studio on Market Street. The promotional portraits taken that day included one pose showing Verna demonstrating the Skirt Dance, a popular dance for young girls of the day. Although the costume is quite girlish, ten-year-old Verna's facial features display a definite maturity. Gone are the chubby cheeks of childhood; her more angular features were beginning to take shape. In fact, when this same pose was reproduced in a 1957 issue of *TV Guide* alongside a contemporary portrait of Verna, the likeness was quite unmistakable.

By the time Verna opened at Fischer's Concert House on August 26, 1900, gone were the members of the Lombardi Opera Company, boasting exotic names such as Antonio Vargas, Signorina Barducci, and Jose Badarocco. In their stead were Hadley and Hart, Maud Still, Brooke Eltrym, and Eudora Forde. At the bottom of the bill was "Little Verna Felton." In that day, most child performers were given titles such as "Little" or "Baby," as a means to distinguish them from adult artists and perhaps to provide more draw at the box office. Child prodigies were all the rage so theater managers were eager to hire especially talented tykes. No reviews of Verna's one-week engagement survive, but it is safe to assume that her brief act included songs and dances. Her first performance was a Sunday matinee at 2:15 p.m. Admission was ten cents.

Over the years, as Verna became more famous, she grew to completely disregard the Fischer engagement as her first professional engagement. She never mentioned it in interviews, and this leads one to wonder whether she was embarrassed by this obviously humble beginning. Fischer's Concert House ranked among the lowest on the list of San Francisco theatres. Although it continued to operate until the advent of the 1906 earthquake, it never re-opened following that disaster—doomed to become one of the city's forgotten theatres. Perhaps as an adult, Verna regarded her professional debut as inauspicious and therefore chose to keep silent regarding the short run at Fischer's. Privately, though, Verna did recognize this engagement as the beginning of her career. In a scrapbook of photographic portraits taken during her stage days—now a part of the Arts Library Special Collection at the UCLA Film and Television Archive—one photograph shows a playful pose of Verna wearing the frilly organdy dress. Underneath it appears Verna's handwritten caption: "First Professional Engagement. Fishers. [*sic*] San Francisco, Calif. 1899." The only thing erroneous in her notation, besides the spelling of Fischer's, is the date. A possible explanation for this mistake could be that Verna was under the impression that she began her career the same year as her father's death. Since most of Verna's career clippings, kept by Clara in other scrapbooks, are undated, perhaps Verna—years later—assumed she began her career at age nine in 1899. To amplify confusion, she sometimes told interviewers that she was *eight* years old when she became a professional performer. However, at age eight, Verna was still a first grade pupil at the Gardner School.

Most often Verna maintained that she was nine when her career began. A prime example of this occurred in September of 1959 when she spoke to an audience of two hundred show business friends gathered to celebrate her sixtieth year in the profession. "It all started when I was nine, at the Victory Theater in San Jose," she told the audience. "I played, of all things, Little Lord Fauntleroy." Since Verna was so closely identified the part of Fauntleroy during the first four years of her career, perhaps she considered this play her professional debut. Or even—in retrospect—maybe she thought this famous role, one normally played by boys, would make the story of her stage debut more charming than sharing a vaudeville bill with a motley group of comics and hoofers at Fischer's Concert House. It's also possible that, years later, Clara unintentionally misinformed Verna of her age at her debut, thus explaining Verna's notation of "1899" under the scrapbook photo of her wearing the frilly dress. In any event, when 1959 rolled around, Verna announced her sixty years in the business.

To her credit, though, Verna Felton, unlike some of her contemporaries, never fudged on her date of birth. In 1959, at that testimonial luncheon in her honor, she unabashedly declared, "And don't everybody stand up at once now and ask me my age. I was born at Salinas in 1890. That makes me 69."

It is perhaps very likely that Verna Felton really considered the engagement at Fischer's Concert House as her show business start, even though she never mentioned it in any interviews. What she did recount many times was how she was discovered by the Jessie Shirley Company.

CHAPTER 3

LITTLE VERNA FELTON

The deadliest natural disaster the United States has ever experienced was the hurricane that destroyed Galveston Island, Texas, on September 8, 1900. Over six thousand lives were lost, and as many as ten thousand were left homeless. Modern technology now estimates that the winds were between 130 and 140 miles per hour. A wall of debris about two stories high, created by a fifteen-feet storm surge, mowed down everything in its path. Meteorologist Isaac Cline, who witnessed the storm, later wrote: "In reality, there was no island, just the ocean with houses standing out of the waves which rolled between them." On September 12, the *San Francisco Chronicle* reported the aftermath: "The city is filled with destitute, bereft, and homeless, while in the improvised morgues are the rigid forms of hundreds of victims. Whole families are side by side." Galveston mayor W. C. Jones appealed to the nation for aid: "Not a single church, school or charitable institution, of which Galveston had so many, is left intact. Not a building escaped damage, and half the whole number were entirely obliterated. There is immediate need of clothing, food, and household goods of all kinds." Many cities, including New York, St. Louis, and Denver immediately responded to the plea. San Joseans heard the call, too, and among them was Charles P. Hall, proprietor and manager of The Victory Theatre.

On Monday, September 17, Hall ran a notice in the *San Jose Daily Mercury* announcing that a grand matinee for the benefit of the Galveston sufferers would be given on Wednesday. The prescient Mr. Hall realized that the popular Jessie Shirley Company, a troupe of actors and musicians currently appearing at the Victory, would attract a large audience. As the introductory act on the bill, they would perform one act of *The Country Girl*. Among the Shirley players that season was San Jose native Meta Marsky, who would be a natural drawing card, but Hall also invited other local talent to perform, including the Ariola Ladies' Orchestra, male soprano Alfie Von Bendeleben, child violinist Estelle Franklin Gray, and character vocalists The Berlin Sisters. Listed third on the bill was "Little Verna Felton, the clever child artist, for some weeks past at Fischer's, San Francisco, who will give specialties and dancing." (In truth, Verna's engagement at Fischer's Concert House had ended September 1, after only one week.) Senator Henry V. Morehouse was asked to make an address prior to the introductory act. Coincidentally, this was the same attorney who had been the Feltons' landlord in Salinas City ten years earlier.

For the benefit performance, Hall charged admission prices of 25 and 50 cents, considerably higher than his usual matinee prices of 10 and 20 cents. A large audience was expected as the local schools were closed in order to provide an opportunity for the city's children to attend.

No review of her benefit performance exists, but Verna definitely made an impression on the Shirley company manager Harry Smith, for on Saturday, September 22, the *Mercury* reported: "As a special feature, Manager Smith has engaged little Verna Felton, the clever San Jose child actress, to do specialties for the balance of the engagement. She will be seen at the matinee, to-night and to-morrow night." These "specialties" consisted of novelty songs and dances to be performed between the acts of the engagement's remaining plays: *Maid of the Mill, At the White Lion,* and *The War of Wealth.* Of her Saturday night performance, the *Mercury* reviewer noted: "Little Verna Felton's specialty was well received and warmly encored."

Despite her one-week engagement at Fischer's, Verna usually regarded her performances at the Victory as her first professional theatre experience. More than likely it was not her first time to experience the grandeur of the auditorium, as she and her mother were frequent theatergoers. The Victory, built at a cost of $50,000 by San Francisco mayor James Duval Phelan, was located at 57 North First Street. It had been named to honor Admiral George Dewey's 1898 victory at the Battle of Manila Bay during the Spanish-American War. That date was mounted above and in the center of the two impressive Byzantine columns marking the street entrance.

The Victory had opened with great fanfare on February 2, 1899, with a performance of *The School for Scandal* featuring Louis James, Kathryn Kidder, and Frederick Warde. All of San Jose's elite turned out, as well as many important San Franciscans. The *Mercury* described its opulence: "The entrance is of Byzantine style and coloring, and is thirty feet high . . . The entire length of the vestibule and main hall floor is laid with encaustic tiles. The foyer vestibule has a dome ceiling with skylight and art glass over the ceiling. The theater is decorated throughout in cream, white, and gold . . . The auditorium is seventy-three by seventy-five feet in size, and is capable of seating 1500 people. The main floor is divided into a dress circle and an orchestra, separated by nine loges, which may be used singly or in suites of two or three . . . The ceiling of the auditorium is surmounted by a dome twenty-seven feet in diameter, handsomely frescoed. Electric lights placed in the dome and masked in the arches and around the rear of the balcony and gallery girders flood the entire auditorium with a blaze of light . . . The auditorium is divided into a first floor, a balcony and a

The Victory Theatre, San Jose, 1899.

gallery. The auditorium has no sharp angles. All of the ceiling angles are curved, and all of the wall angles are curved . . . there are eight proscenium boxes, four on each side. They are richly decorated and enshrouded with elegant tapestries. The stage is the largest in the State with the exception of the Grand Opera House in San Francisco, being 76 x 36 feet. The drop curtain was painted by John Stanton of San Francisco. It represents a rural garden scene and is beautiful in conception and design."

Theatergoers in 1899 marveled at the Victory's commodious size and plush accoutrements. Indeed, the stage area was so immense that during a performance of *Ben Hur*, four horses galloped on treadmills for the famous chariot race scene. Some of the theater greats who played the Victory in its heyday were Maude Adams, Billie Burke, Mrs. Leslie Carter, Ethel Barrymore, Otis Skinner, Anna Held, George M. Cohan, Julia Marlowe, Guy Bates Post, and Sarah Bernhardt.

The Victory Theatre interior, San Jose, 1899.

The best shows on the west coast were booked here, enabling the Victory to maintain its reputation for many years as San Jose's finest theater. As the decades passed, however, it became part of the Pantages Circuit, packing in vaudeville audiences on the weekends. With the advent of sound motion pictures, the Victory was one of the first theaters to show "talkies." The heirs of James Phelan sold the building to the San Jose Amusement Company in 1944. Five years later the theater's name was changed to The Crest when the owners decided to make a complete break with the past, dropping vaudeville in favor of first-run motion pictures. This continued until Sunday, June 6, 1965, when the building—still very sound—was gutted by fire.

By 1900, Charles P. Hall, the original lessee and manager of the Victory, had been in the theatrical business for thirty years. A debonair gentleman, sporting a fine handlebar moustache, Hall resided in the sumptuous Hotel Vendome on North First Street. At one time he had been the private secretary of the great P. T. Barnum. Before coming to San Jose, Hall was the manager of the Bush Street Theater in San Francisco where he conducted a phenomenal business. In the day when a single play hardly ran more than one week, Hall booked some productions that lasted seven weeks. The *Mercury* sang his praises as being "on terms of friendly and business relationship with every manager and theatrical concern of any note in the Union and is kept in touch with every successful movement in the theatrical world." During the Victory's first year of operation, Hall brought to town such luminaries as tragedienne Nance O'Neil, composer-conductor John Philip Sousa, and heavyweight fighter-turned-vaudevillian John L. Sullivan.

For the Victory's first anniversary Hall engaged the Jessie Shirley Company for a run of eight nights beginning January 28, 1900. Hailed as "the best repertoire company on the road to-day," the Shirley company performed a different play for each matinee and evening performance. They arrived in San Jose after a tour of Canada, Washington, Oregon, and other California cities. The winter engagement was so successful that Hall booked them for a return engagement to begin September 16, a time destined to coincide with Charles P. Hall's impromptu benefit for the surviving victims of the Galveston Flood.

On the afternoon of September 19, 1900, Harry Smith, the business manager of the Jessie Shirley Company, sat back and keenly observed the local talent performing for the benefit. He was searching for a young girl to join the stock company. He wanted a child performer to charm the audience between the acts, as scenery was being shifted behind the curtain. Smith watched Little Estelle Franklin Gray play her violin. He listened to Loyola Mensing's "coon songs." But it was Verna Felton's "specialties and dancing" that appealed to him. Smith was so impressed with her performance that he sought out her mother. Clara, despite having no other prospects of income, was less than enthused about Verna becoming the family breadwinner, especially since it required joining a traveling troupe of actors. While many Americans enjoyed being entertained by such performers, the profession in those days was still considered by some as less than respectable. Verna later admitted that her mother "knew nothing of theatrical people and was very timid" about accepting Smith's offer.

Charles P. Hall intervened, assuring Clara that he had known Smith for years and that she would be delighted with the engagement. Clara's attorney also ran a check on the company for her and reported that its members were, indeed, reputable. In fact, during the 1964 Halperin interview, Verna stressed, "This lawyer said, 'Now, these are *lovely people*. And they're all together, they're a family-circle sort of people.'" In fact, some in the company were married and settled—a fact that swayed Clara's decision. Smith's own wife was actress Jessie Shirley for whom the company was named.

Verna recalled Smith's sales pitch to Clara: "We'd like to have a child actress, someone that would, for the matinee, play Little Lord Fauntleroy and then at night, between the acts, do a song-and-dance." Still Clara was skeptical. "Mother had always been intensely interested in the theatre," Verna remembered in 1933, "not as a profession, *oh no*, merely as entertainment. She never missed a play that came to town and, of course, 'fond child' was taken to all of them." But now Clara was absolutely horrified at the thought of her child on the stage. On the other hand, she had to face the fact that she and Verna were alone now, with no income. (The employment situation of Verna's half-brother Clayton, by now aged seventeen, cannot be determined for this period of time.)

Harry Smith offered to pay Verna a weekly salary of $18, according to an interview she gave the *Hollywood Citizen-News* many years later. At the time, the national average weekly wage was $12.74. Realizing that Smith's offer would solve their monetary problems, Clara finally agreed to allow Verna to join the Jessie Shirley Company, but with one admonishment: "Don't put any paint on her face!" It was one thing for her child to be performing on a stage but another to have her face made up like a common streetwalker. The good people of the Jessie Shirley Company finally convinced Clara that without stage makeup, the bright stage lights would make Verna look pale and unhealthy. Clara was thus introduced to the first of many theatrical techniques she would encounter in the coming months, for it was arranged for her to accompany Verna everywhere the troupe went.

As far as it can be ascertained, Clayton Felton did not accompany them on their travels with the Shirley troupe, probably because he was already gainfully employed. In fact, he was listed in the 1902-03 city directory of San Jose as a printer, and his residence was given as West San Salvador Street, in the home of Leon Pinard where the Feltons were boarding at the time of Dr. Felton's death.

Clara's eldest son, Howard, now nineteen, had moved with his adoptive parents from Downieville to Oakland in 1895. The 1900 census shows him employed as a bakery clerk and living with his widowed adoptive father James Wiggins, a wharfinger. However, it remains a mystery whether Clara had had regular contact with Howard following her move to San Jose.

By this time, all of Clara's other close relations were no longer living. As for Verna's paternal relations, it is doubtful that she ever met them, considering the great distance between San Jose and the midwestern states of Wisconsin and Minnesota. (It is possible that the Feltons could have taken a summer vacation trip to the Midwest during Dr. Felton's lifetime, but there is no indication of such a journey.) Verna's grandmother Emily Felton, aged 84, had died on September 8, 1900, coincidentally on the same day the hurricane hit Galveston. Eleven days before her death, she had suffered a stroke at the home of her son Albert Felton in Lemond, Minnesota. Her remains were carried the following day to Rosendale, Wisconsin, where she was laid to rest beside her husband Nelson, whom she had survived by twenty-two years. And so, with very few family ties to be broken, Clara and Verna left San Jose as members of the Jessie Shirley Stock Company.

Walter K. Waters, in his doctoral dissertation *George L. Baker and the Baker Stock Company*, asserted that there were three types of stock companies producing plays in America, at the turn of the twentieth century. The smallest companies operated on a shoestring budget and used inexperienced actors in their casts. The second type, also operating under a low budget, presented plays of a greater variety. Young, inexperienced performers made up most of the casts, but they also included some trained actors. The Jessie Shirley Company would probably be classified as such a company. The third type was known as "high-class" stock, and according to Waters: "These companies concentrated upon the presentation of the latest New York successes as they became available for stock production and could boast full companies of actors with experience as well as full stage settings built to imitate as closely as possible the settings used in New York for the original productions of the plays."

Like most traveling stock companies, the Jessie Shirley Company performed a different play each night of their engagements, which typically began on a Sunday and continued for eight nights. Matinees were performed on Saturdays for the benefit of the schoolchildren who typically would not attend evening shows. At the Victory, admission prices for evening performances were ten, twenty, and thirty cents, depending on where the seat was. It is amusing to note that thirty years later Verna would recall that her early ambition was to be not a "high-class [actress], just a 10-20-30 cents one." Waters, describing the stock company of this period, affirmed that it "was, in many ways, a theatre of the people," noting that "it reflected the tastes and prejudices of the community, served an educational function and provided entertainment and a needed escape from everyday living."

A basic stock company required fourteen actors: the leading man and woman, the juvenile man and ingenue, the young comedian, the character comedian, the character man and woman, a second woman, a "heavy" and four utility actors. According to Waters, "a child actress might be added to this list to play either boys or girls as the scripts demanded." For the 1900-01 theatrical season, the Jessie Shirley Company employed twenty-one stock members, including the band members.

When Verna joined the Shirley company, the leading lady was Jessie Shirley herself, born the daughter of a Baptist minister in Payson, Illinois, in 1866. At eighteen, in Marion, Iowa, she married fellow Illinois native, twenty-five-year-old Harry Wilbur Smith, who had been engaged in the theatrical business nearly all of his life. After winning considerable approbation for a private theatrical performance, Shirley seriously contemplated becoming a professional actress. In 1894, she made her professional bow in Cedar Rapids, Iowa, with the Gibley troupe. One year later, she arrived in California as a member of the Sam T. Shaw Company while Smith was serving as its orchestra conductor. By 1896, Shirley was billed alongside Shaw, the leading man. This relationship lasted until the following year when she and Smith departed from Shaw to establish the Jessie Shirley Company.

When the Jessie Shirley Company performed at the Victory in the fall of 1900, their ensemble included Marie Baker, Effie Bond, Meta Marsky, George McQuarrie, H. W. Gilbert, William Abrams, Tom B. Loftus, Charles Lowe, Leslie Greer, W. V. Skinner, and C. F. Ralston. It also boasted a uniformed band orchestra, which played between the acts and featured W. J. Drew, popular for his xylophone solos.

The Victory's promotional ads in September 1900, boasted that Miss Shirley had recently returned from the East where "she secured elegant new costumes and a repertoire of high class Eastern productions." Included in the September repertoire were *The Sheaf of Arrows*, billed as a comedy-drama set in 1630 New

Amsterdam; *For Liberty and Love*, described as a Cuban melodrama involving such unlikely character names as Carlotta Casanova and Mario Novarro; *The War of Wealth*, a popular Wall Street melodrama written by Charles Dazey which had premiered in New York in 1896; and a dramatization of Ouida's 1880 novel, *Moths*—the Victorian equivalent of a modern Harlequin romance novel—which addressed racy topics like adultery, domestic violence, and divorce.

As a regional stock company, Jessie Shirley and her troupe toured both Northern and Southern California, Oregon, and Washington. "That's as far as we went; we'd turn around and come back," Verna explained in 1964. "We loved all those towns. And we'd do a new play every night, which was very wonderful for us for experience which *now* we use so well in television and radio." Life on the

Jessie Shirley, 1903. UNIVERSITY OF WASHINGTON LIBRARIES, SPECIAL COLLECTIONS, UW28323.

road meant that Verna could not attend regular schools so she had to be tutored. One of the female members of the Jessie Shirley company doubled as her teacher. "That's all [the education] I got, all through life," Verna told Martin Halperin in 1964. As for theatrical training, Verna relied upon the older and experienced members of the troupe for coaching and criticism. She also learned from the audience, which quickly showed its approval or disapproval for an actor's performance.

Prior to joining the Shirley company, Verna had been billed as "Little Verna Felton," but someone, perhaps Jessie Shirley or Harry Smith, strategized to change her stage name to the even more infantile "Baby Verna Felton" for the 1900-1901 theatrical season. Souvenir calling cards were printed using this moniker, even though some newspaper ads still identified her as Little Verna Felton. By 1901, the Shirley company also employed a false promotion technique with its claim that this child prodigy was a mere eight years old, when, in fact, Verna was nearing her eleventh birthday. Evidently, Verna was small for her age, or how else could this promotional ploy have worked? (This discrepancy harkens back to Verna's days as a student at the Gardner school in San Jose. The fact that her eighth birthday had passed before she entered the first grade remains unexplained.) Her true age would be masked for several years to come, very likely part of the plan to promote her as a child phenomenon and thereby increase ticket sales.

Undated newspaper clippings glued into makeshift scrapbooks—evidently assembled by Clara—chronicle Verna's rise to fame, beginning with *Little Lord Fauntleroy*, a production Verna long considered as her first professional appearance with the Shirley company. Actually, Verna's first role with them was not *Fauntleroy*. Not long after the troupe left San Jose on their way north, Harry Smith gave Verna one or two words to speak in *At the White Lion*, an English pastoral play recently produced in London by Herbert Beerbohm Tree, an actor-producer known for his lavish Shakespearean productions. Soon, however, Verna mastered the lines of *Fauntleroy*, and she began performing it regularly as the troupe headed for the northwest. The fall of 1900 was spent touring mainly in Oregon and Washington.

Using one scrapbook as documentation, Clara listed some of Verna's stage roles and their corresponding plays during the first four years of her career. Among the fifty roles, at least seventeen were boys' parts, including that of Cedric Errol in *Fauntleroy*. Verna's athleticism lent itself well to these roles. Fortunately, her naturally curly hair was easily concealed under boys' caps. For the *Fauntleroy* role, however, she wore it shoulder-length, as some small boys did at the turn of the twentieth century. Naturally, she was dressed in the lace collar, velvet coat, and knee breeches forever identified with the character.

The story of *Little Lord Fauntleroy* concerns Cedric Errol, a Brooklyn boy who suddenly finds himself the sole heir to a British earldom. Cedric, now Lord Fauntleroy, and his widowed mother leave America for England. There Cedric lives with his gouty old grandfather who refuses to allow the boy's mother to reside in his castle. Later a crisis shames the earl into asking her for forgiveness. However, when the earl intends to teach his grandson to become an aristocrat, the boy inadvertently teaches the old man that an aristocrat should practice compassion and social justice towards humans in his care. By the play's end, the earl is becoming the kind man Cedric always believed him to be.

Verna performed the *Fauntleroy* part nearly one hundred times while she was with the Shirley company. It became the signature role of her early career. When she played it for the first time in Portland, Oregon, on February 22, 1901, the drama critic for the *Oregonian* observed: "The talented child who took the [title] part invested it with just the boyish carelessness and dash one naturally looks for, and so free from the ordinary child player was her acting that she carried the audience by storm. Her scenes with the surly old earl were particularly good, while her acting of the more pathetic parts made handkerchiefs necessary to a very large number of the women in the audience." To promote the matinee performance of *Fauntleroy* the following day, the manager of Cordray's Theater ran a large photo of Verna (taken during the engagement at Fischer's Concert

Verna Felton in the signature role of her early career, Cedric Errol of *Little Lord Fauntleroy*, 1901.

House the previous summer) and enticed mothers to "have their children meet little Verna, who will wait on the stage to shake hands with and talk to all her little admirers."

When the Shirley company returned to Verna's hometown of San Jose in May, 1901, the *San Jose Mercury News* praised her performance: "The character of little Lord Fauntleroy is one particularly suited to her winsome sweetness and spirited intelligence, and she not only enjoys the distinction of being the youngest actress who has ever donned the velvets of Mrs. Burnett's little hero, but she has been pronounced by many competent critics the cleverest. Certain it is that she holds her audience in the palm of her little hand, bringing laughter and tears at will."

In 1964, Verna reminisced, "They'd have *Little Lord Fauntleroy* for matinees. And I tell you that *hundreds* of children, it seemed like, would come. I'll never forget Oregon City— I never have seen so many people in my life! So that night they had arranged for me to shake hands with everyone. So all these children came up, and I shook hands, and I shook hands, and I shook hands till *7 o'clock.* And the matinee would be out about a quarter to five. It was seven or after. And they had to take me home in a, well, in a hack, in those days. Took me home in a hack. And my hand was like it was broken. Couldn't move it. They had to send for a doctor and bind it all up . . . My mother said after this, *'No more hand-shaking! Say hello, how are you, but that's all.'* But I had a very great experience. The people were nice, all the people were nice—a good company."

Harry Smith continued to employ local talent in productions, just as he had initially used Verna for the latter half of the San Jose engagement in September, 1900. Later that fall, one little freckle-faced kid who attended a matinee in Jacksonville, Oregon, soon found himself hired to appear onstage in a brief scene with Verna. His name was Vance "Pinto" Colvig, the eight-year-old son of a local politician, whose skinny legs and uncombed hair were found to be the perfect image needed for a small part. His three lines were to be delivered while handing Verna a cat. Colvig later recalled, "I was so entranced working with Verna that I just stood there on stage, grinned at the audience, and held onto the cat. She pulled and the cat started yowling, but I didn't let go until she took off her shoe and hit me on the head." One can imagine the ensuing laughter from the audience, which probably made Colvig grin all the more. A born cutup, Colvig later became a circus clown, a vaudevillian, and a cartoonist before delighting Disney audiences with his original voice characterization for Mickey Mouse's friend, Goofy.

By January 7, 1901, the Shirley company had returned to northern California, appearing for the first time in the city of Oakland, at the Macdonough Theatre, where they scored successes with their usual repertoire of *Trilby, Moths, The Country Girl*, etc. Shortly afterward they once again made a tour of the northwest, including an engagement beginning on February 17 in Portland, Oregon at Cordray's Theatre. The *Morning Oregonian* reported:

The Country Girl, an old comedy in a new dress, was presented at Cordray's last night by the Shirley Company to a house that filled every seat and crowded the available standing room. It was the first appearance of the company in Portland, but it was cordially welcomed and the applause, which was almost continuous, showed it made a most favorable impression. The play is an entirely legitimate comedy with lines that are charming in their quaintness and a vein of quiet humor that is a refreshing change from the uproarious farces which are common now-a-days. The stately figures of the men, clad in silk stockings and knickerbockers, the odd, but charming costumes of the women and the atmosphere of powdered wigs and courtly bows was in fact so much of an innovation from Sunday night's performance that the house was considerably surprised at first, but soon caught the spirit of the piece and was not slow expressing appreciation.

Although Verna was misidentified as "Vera Tilton," she was credited with giving a "very clever speciality." Following the end of the run, the *Oregonian* published a less enthusiastic summary of the engagement: ". . . while it did not play to the business it merited, it made many friends who will welcome it in the event of another appearance here. The company could be strengthened in many places, but it makes no pretensions of being great, and there can be no question that it gives the audience its money's worth."

On Sunday, March 10, the Jessie Shirley Company opened for a week's engagement at the Third Avenue Theater, billed as Seattle's "only popular priced theater." It was the first time the company had played in that city since the fall of 1899. Of the four plays presented, *La Belle Marie*—in which Verna filled the small role of Patsy Walsh—received the most kudos. Although Broadway critics found it coarse and clumsy when it debuted in 1889, the drama was welcomed by stock company audiences. The heroine was a young, adventuresome runaway who rehabilitates a handsome flophouse denizen in the slums of New York City. The *Seattle Post-Intelligencer*, in its summary of the week's theatrical offerings, was liberal with its praise for both Jessie Shirley and Verna. Theatre-goers were unable to find standing room at the *Fauntleroy* matinee.

Monday night's production was *Nell Gwynne* (also known as *Sweet Nell of Old Drury*), a farce-melodrama by Paul Kester, based on the largely legendary life of the English actress who became the mistress of King Charles II. Kester's play had only endured for eighteen performances when it opened on Broadway the previous December, but, like many New York flops, *Nell Gwynne* was immensely popular among the touring companies. According to John Wilson's biography, *Nell Gwyn: Royal Mistress*, Victorian writers "suppressed or bowdlerized her bawdy sayings, choosing to ignore those facts of her life which collided with the legend of her goodness . . . canonized her as Saint Nell the Good, disinfected and triumphant,

Promotional photo of Verna, circa 1900.

a kind, generous, charitable, unseeking, loyal, friendly—and completely mythical—character." Indeed, the *Tacoma Daily Ledger*'s glowing review of Shirley's performance as Gwynne bore no mention of a wanton woman, but instead praised the play's "witty dialogue" and "picturesque period." In contrast, when the Ralph Cummings stock company produced the same play four nights later at the rival Tacoma Theatre, it only received lukewarm notices.

The same could not be said for Verna's "specialties" and matinee performance of *Little Lord Fauntleroy*. While admitting that Verna could not be "more at home" in this dramatic role, the Ledger favored her solos: "An attractive feature of the program was the singing and dancing of Baby Verna Felton. She has a fine voice and uses it with charming effect. She was recalled again and again, until the audience wearied itself with applause."

The Tacoma engagement was followed by a successful two-week return to the Third Avenue Theater in Seattle beginning on March 31. In addition to the aforementioned *Moths, Nell Gwynne, The War of Wealth*, and *La Belle Marie*, the Shirley company planned to stage *Trilby, The Sheaf of Arrows, The Country Girl*, and *The Ugly Duckling*, the latter three never having been previously performed in Seattle. Broadway producer David Belasco had employed his protégé Mrs. Leslie Carter in the leading role of Kate Graydon in *The Ugly Duckling*, Carter's 1890 Broadway bow. Described as a "social drama," the misleading title had nothing to do with Hans Christian Andersen's classic tale. *Trilby*, Paul Potter's dramatized version of the George DuMaurier novel, had been the most memorable success of the 1894-95 Broadway season. It proved to be a hit for the Shirley company as well. The *Seattle Post-Intelligencer*'s reviewer gushed, "No presentation of *Trilby* in Seattle has been better played or staged." The plot revolves around Trilby O'Farrell, a bohemian girl whose life is consumed by an evil mesmerist, Maestro Svengali, the man who hypnotically forces her to pursue a singing career, thus making himself quite wealthy. The character of the hypnotist became so widely known that now the name Svengali describes anyone with irresistible hypnotic powers.

Verna received good notices for two matinee performances. *Little Lord Fauntleroy* was performed on April 13, while the previous Saturday was reserved for a double bill of *Nell Gwynne* and a one-act "dramatic gem," *Editha's Burglar*, with Verna in the lead as Editha. Based on a short story by *Fauntleroy* author Frances Hodgson Burnett, *Editha's Burglar* had debuted on Broadway in 1887 starring the great Shakespearean actor E. H. Sothern and child actress Elsie Leslie, the Shirley Temple of her day. Editha is a nine-year-old girl who surprises an intruder in her home. Fearing that the burglar will harm her sleeping father, Editha keeps the burglar engaged in conversation until he has finished his task. In the end it's revealed that the burglar is her actually her biological father, who had long ago parted from Editha's mother after breaking her heart. Verna's characterization of Editha charmed audiences, rivaling her portrayal of Cedric Errol in *Fauntleroy*.

On Tuesday, April 9, W. M. Russell, the manager of the Third Avenue Theater, invited all members of the touring companies currently performing or sojourning in Seattle to attend a special matinee performance of the Shirley company's *The Country Girl*. The innovative event was termed as a "professional matinee," which at the time was something of a fad in the East. Among those in the audience was Madame Helena Modjeska, reputed to be the leading female interpreter of Shakespeare on the American stage in the 1880s and 1890s. Her three-night engagement at the Seattle Theater was promoted as part of her farewell tour of the United States. While it is not believed that Verna was among the cast of *The Country Girl* matinee, she certainly must have performed some of her specialties, as she typically did between the acts. After the matinee ended, Verna was introduced to Madame Modjeska, who congratulated her performance and predicted for her a bright future. Their meeting was described one month later in a *San Jose Daily Mercury* publicity piece whose author noted that, although Verna received many other tributes and was showered with multiple gifts during the two-week Seattle run, she remained modest and sensible, beloved by all. In the meantime, the Shirley company returned to Tacoma on April 14 for a week's run, every bit as successful as the March engagement.

Verna had been with the Shirley troupe for nine months when they returned to San Jose for a week's engagement at the Victory Theatre beginning on Saturday, May 11. Verna's ever-growing trademark role of Cedric Errol in *Little Lord Fauntleroy* fostered great anticipation for the Sunday evening performance. The *Mercury*'s drama critic predicted that with Little Verna Felton in the title role, it would be the strongest attraction of the engagement. The review the next morning was glowing: "The fact that the Shirley Company had lost none of its popularity in San Jose was demonstrated last night by an enthusiastic audience which packed the Victory Theater and from the frequent bursts of applause it is safe to infer that everyone was well pleased . . . Miss Shirley gracefully abdicated the post of star to Little Verna Felton, a San Jose girl, who filled even her admirers with wonder at her clever rendition of the title role. She combines all the simplicity of childhood with the charming *naivete* of an accomplished actress." *Fauntleroy* was so popular with San Jose citizens that it was repeated for the following Saturday's matinee. Verna had arrived; she was the only actor, besides Jessie Shirley, who was billed in the Victory's daily newspaper ads.

The company played to packed houses all week long despite serious competition from one of the greatest public events in the history of San Jose, a three-day festival called the Carnival of Roses, held in honor of President William McKinley. For six months Mayor C. J. Martin and his committees had planned the extravaganza, which included band concerts, automobile races, speeches, fancy dress balls, pyrotechnic displays, and three parades, including an illuminated bicycle-motor vehicle parade on the second evening of the carnival.

The parade route included elaborately decorated First Street, right past the Victory Theater. Evergreen garlands, accented with American flags, were suspended across the street at intervals of fifty yards. The great electric tower at the intersection of Market and Santa Clara Streets was a mass of ninety-seven waving flags. St. James Park bustled with activity as ladies from all over the county worked to decorate specially built arches with freshly cut flowers of every description. Store windows held extravagant displays, and private homes were festooned with bunting, colorful flowers, and portraits of McKinley. The city agreed to finance the lighting of several hundred Japanese lanterns for the three nights. Hundreds of out-of-town visitors, including five hundred automobile owners participating in the nighttime parade, crowded into San Jose to enjoy the festivities. The governor of Ohio, McKinley's home state, wired that he and a delegation from the Buckeye State would attend the carnival. Last-minute preparations for all of these festivities were underway when Verna Felton and the Jessie Shirley Company arrived in San Jose.

President and Mrs. McKinley were due to arrive on Monday afternoon, May 13, for a carriage tour of the city. The following day had been set aside for the presidential parade, but when the president's wife, a sickly epileptic, fell ill in Del Monte on Sunday, it was necessary to change these plans. After Mrs. McKinley was taken to San Francisco to recover from her attack, her husband decided to cancel plans to lead Tuesday's parade in San Jose. However, he did leave her for a few hours on Monday to appear at the Carnival of Roses. As many as ten thousand people witnessed his ride through the city, crowding the streets with wild enthusiasm and patriotic devotion. Some three thousand San Jose schoolchildren, all dressed in white and waving small flags, lined the canopied fairyland of First Street. Perhaps somewhere nearby stood Verna Felton, no longer a student of the San Jose public schools, but now a professional actress. Maybe she saw William McKinley, in frock coat and top hat, pass in a handsome landau drawn by four spanking black steeds. Perhaps she was one of the children to whom he smiled down. Or perhaps she was waiting for him to arrive at the reviewing stand at St. James Park where he would be presented with a colossal bouquet of flowers arranged on a wooden-framed pyramid that measured twenty-five feet high and sixty feet in circumference. Naturally this was not a typical bouquet, not one the president could take with him, but it was built as a symbol of the loyalty and patriotism of the women of the Santa Clara Valley. Two thousand women had contributed flowers from their own gardens, bringing them in wagons and buggies for two days previous. San Jose deserved every right to call herself the Garden City for everywhere one looked were roses, tulips, poppies, amaryllis, lilies, and carnations. McKinley's subsequent ten-minute speech boasted of the grandeur of California's natural resources and the warm hospitality of its people. After ending his speech with a promise to uphold the United States Constitution, the president left the cheering crowd to return to the bedside of his ailing wife.

On the following day, throngs of people in their finest clothes lined the parade route. If Verna was there, and she certainly must have been, she witnessed the horse-drawn floats, every inch covered in flowers and greenery and festooned with ribbons and streamers. All of the San Jose public schools sponsored floats, with each representing a theme, such as Washington Grammar's "The Old Oaken Bucket" and Grant Grammar's "Fairy-Land." The float of Verna's *alma mater*, The Gardner School, while not as elaborate as the others, depicted the "Horn of Plenty." Its four black horses were covered in white blankets of fringed mesh, and, truthfully, appeared more attractive than the float itself.

Meanwhile, during the remainder of the week, the Shirley company thrilled audiences with performances of *Trilby, The Country Girl, The Ugly Duckling, East Lynne, Cumberland 61*, and a repeat of *Nell Gwynne* (which featured Verna in the role of Zet) on the final evening. On the afternoon prior to the last performance, company ingenue Meta Marsky, the San Jose native, married fellow actor Tom Loftus, who served as the troupe's character comedian, at her parents' home. This union drew the Shirley family circle even closer, and it would not be the last time a marriage was born among company members. On May 20, the newlyweds and their theater family left San Jose for a two-week engagement at Oakland's Macdonough Theater, where they performed *Cumberland 61* and the comedy *Caprice* for one week each. The engagement ended with a Saturday matinee of *Little Lord Fauntleroy*.

Since Verna was the only child in the stock company she had to make her own amusement when her lessons were completed and her lines were learned. She studied the performances of the other actors, perfecting not only her lines, but memorizing theirs as well. She was said to be a perfect mimic, giving imitations of such characters as Trilby O'Farrell and Svengali from *Trilby*. Her quaint observations about stage life afforded endless amusement to the other members of the company. She became their darling. They affectionately called her "Babe," possibly derived from her stage name, Baby Verna Felton. It was indeed as Clara's attorney had insisted: this company was like a family.

Many years later Verna was hard-pressed to recall anything really drastic that happened when she was a part of the company, other than an experience in Oceanside, California. "When it was raining, or anything like that, I was always the one that the drummer had to carry to get to the theater, so I had to go on his back. The theater [at Oceanside] was way on the top of a hill, and the hotel was below. So the drummer said to me, 'Com'on, Babe, we'll go.' And I said to the man, 'How do we get up there?' The man said, '*Just follow the light.*' I said, 'Is there no path?' He said, '*Just follow the light.*' So we followed the light. We fell into *holes*, we fell into everything. And believe me, we had a *full* audience that night, and it was *raining*, you know like California does [get] rain, when it rains. It was really something."

When the company returned to San Jose for an eight-night engagement beginning September 1, 1901, there was a new actress among their ranks. Eighteen-year-old Virginia Brissac played Henriette to Miss Shirley's Louise in *The Two Orphans*, a melodrama set during the French Revolution. The play had been one of the greatest theatrical successes in America since 1874, and its popularity with West Coast audiences had not waned.

Years later Virginia Brissac went on to become one of Hollywood's busiest character actresses, appearing in almost 150 movies, including *Dark Victory, Destry Rides Again, The Little Foxes, Monsieur Verdoux, The Snake Pit,* and *Rebel Without a Cause.* Forty years after their Shirley Company days, Brissac and Verna crossed paths in a crowded elevator in the Broadway-Hollywood Department Store on North Vine Street. Recognizing Verna after all those years, Brissac cried out, "Baby Felton!" Their fellow passengers looked around and then smiled because the person Brissac addressed was not a baby at all, but instead was a stout, middle-aged, lady with plenty of gray hair. Verna said at the time, "I never was so embarrassed in my life," especially later in the hat department when she noticed two women who had been in the elevator looking at her and chuckling.

Verna in one of her many "trouser roles," circa 1901.

Verna almost made a career out of playing little boys' parts during these early years, and *The Sultan's Daughter,* which was performed on September 3, 1901, was a prime example. Verna was cast as James, the "up-to-date" son of Josiah Hopkins, a "victim of circumstances" in this comedy, which starred the diminutive Miss Shirley as Tuluna, a sultan's daughter who magically comes to life from an oil painting purchased by Josiah.

On September 6, while the Shirley company was still in San Jose, President William McKinley was shot by assassin Leon Czolgosz in Buffalo, New York. The president was greeting well-wishers at the Temple of Music, a part of the Pan-American Exposition, when the attack occurred. Like the day he appeared in San Jose almost four months earlier, McKinley did not have much time to spend at the exposition, but he wanted to make an appearance and shake as many hands as possible. Concealed in Czolgosz's bandaged hand was the deadly revolver. The president was shot in the stomach before security guards realized what was happening. Upon hearing the tragic news, many San Joseans recalled the previous May when McKinley had graced the Garden City as the guest of honor for the Rose Carnival. No doubt they remembered the admonishments published then in the *Mercury*: "Don't throw flowers at the President or Mrs. McKinley. Don't try to shake hands with the President. Don't drive in front of the President's carriage." Surgery was performed there on the grounds of the exposition, but the bullet was never retrieved and gangrene set in, killing the twenty-fifth president of the United States on September 14.

Meanwhile, the Jessie Shirley Company continued its 1901-02 tour of the coast states, stopping at many of the same cities and towns where they had performed the previous season. On March 9, they opened an unusually lengthy engagement at Portland's Cordray Theatre, where they played for four out of the six subsequent weeks. In addition to productions from the previous fall, the repertoire included old standbys such as *For Fair Virginia, Dad's Girl, A Farmer's Daughter, A Young Wife, The Octaroon,* and *Camille.* During this run, Verna received no recognition in the *Oregonian*, aside from a brief mention that she contributed a "charming specialty." Before the troupe departed for Olympia, Washington, Jessie Shirley garnered her usual share of attention in the press. However, all was not rosy. The *Oregonian's* columnist, in his weekly summation of dramatic offerings, criticized the company's lack of skillful supporting players.

In late spring, Harry Smith, the business manager for the Shirley company, accepted an enticing invitation from Harry C. Hayward, manager of The Auditorium in Spokane, Washington, for the troupe to appear there for one week. This offer was even more appealing because of an unprecedented stipulation that if the troupe proved to be a hit with local audiences, the engagement would be lengthened to as many as ten weeks. Hayward realized the necessity of popular-priced productions in the Northwest, but at the same time he wanted to insure that the stock companies were of the highest quality for the price. The Auditorium's popular prices were 15, 25, 35, and 50 cents, considerably higher than the Victory's. Matinees on Wednesdays were 10 and 25 cents. Hayward, in his capacity as manager of The Auditorium, was a member of the Pacific Amusement Company whose other members included William Russell of the Third Avenue Theater in Seattle, Dean Worley of the Lyceum in Tacoma, and J. F. Cordray of Portland's Cordray Theater. Hayward and the rest were set on making stock companies a vital part of their bookings for the coming seasons. Hayward's arrangement with the Jessie Shirley company resulted in the lengthiest stay little Verna would have in any city since being a San Jose resident in the years before her father's death. From September of 1900 until June of 1902, Verna had spent practically each week in a different city or town on the Pacific Coast or along the railroad lines of the interiors of California, Oregon, and Washington.

Harry Smith decided it best to open the Spokane engagement on June 9 with *Under Two Flags*, originally produced on Broadway by Charles Frohman and David Belasco the previous year. Miss Shirley, shown in character in a photograph in the Spokane *Spokesman-Review*, played the *vivandiere* Cigarette in this dramatization of Ouida's 1867 novel. The entire Shirley company was introduced to Spokane in this same newspaper article: George D. McQuarrie, Frank McQuarrie, H. D. Chambers, Tom B. Loftus, H. W. Gilbert, William R. Abram, Leslie C. Greer, W. A. Roberts, C. F. Ralston, George Stone, W. A. Redder, Ben Benton, Fred Henderson, Robert Shaw, William Skinner, Harry W. Smith, Miss Jessie Shirley, Miss Laura Adams, Miss Meta Marsky, Miss Helen Hamilton, Miss Clara Lawrence, and Little Verna Felton. Spokane audiences were pleased with *Under Two Flags*, which played for four nights, and the local drama critic was impressed by Shirley, McQuarrie, Abram, and Marsky. At the end of the week Hayward made a deal with the company to remain for the summer.

Little Lord Fauntleroy was chosen for the first Saturday matinee on June 21, and the *Spokesman-Review*'s drama critic was anticipatory: "This is one of the sweet plays that was so immensely popular some 10 years ago that several companies had to be sent on the road in order to meet the public demand, and as the Shirley company is said to give an excellent production, the matinee performance is likely to be as enjoyable as were those when the play was first produced." However, no review of the matinee appeared in the subsequent edition so it is uncertain what the reviewer thought of Verna's performance. But Verna did get a nod in his review of *For Fair Virginia*: "As Julian, the lad, Verna Felton was capital." While this particular critic was normally not very generous with compliments, he did admit that the Shirley company was giving the best performances at popular prices ever seen in Spokane. He further praised the company: "Taken altogether, the organization is a well balanced one and the plays it has produced heretofore have been well worth seeing. It is certainly far ahead of anything that has been offered in the way of a summer stock attraction, and if the productions keep up to the standard of those already offered, the theatergoer may count on an enjoyable evening any time he visits the Auditorium."

Curiously, Verna was mentioned in the *Spokesman-Review*'s notices only once, and her name never appeared in The Auditorium ads as they had back in San Jose. Whether this was because hers was a recognizable name among San Joseans or because the Shirley company was not promoting her as much is left to speculation. Another curiosity is that over the course of nine weeks *Little Lord Fauntleroy* was staged only once. Verna's usual routine of performing her "specialties" between the acts is not documented either, leading one to suspect that they were not part of the evenings. Perhaps manager Hayward thought Spokane audiences were above this type of amusement.

While the drama critic's daily reviews began in the most pleasant tone, there were little barbs throughout, particularly about the age of the plays being produced. He saved his most candid comments for the *Spokesman-Review* edition of August 10, the day before the Shirley company's final performance: "For a repertoire company producing good melodrama, comedy and society plays at popular prices the Shirley organization is above the average. It is not a great company and there are weak points in it, but for giving a good average performance without any serious blemishes, and as a company striving to please the average summer audience, it is far ahead of any similar organization that has ever played in the northwest. Miss Shirley is a hardworking, conscientious little actress, who puts the best she has into her efforts, with the result that her performances have been uniformly even and clean cut. Of course, she has not been as successful in some parts as in others, and there are perhaps some peculiarities about her work that might call for criticism. At times she is a little stagy and her elocution often takes on affectation. An unnatural laugh, too, is made use of more frequently than is necessary, and when worked to excess through a performance of two hours becomes objectionable, if not irritating. But these are minor defects that have not sensibly marred Miss Shirley's general work, which has been enjoyed by many thousands during her engagement here . . . George McQuarrie has an excellent stage presence and not a little dramatic force, and is likely to be heard from."

A native San Franciscan, the twenty-nine-year-old McQuarrie was indeed heard from. After leaving the Shirley company in 1909, McQuarrie made both his Broadway and film debut in 1916 under the stage name of George *Mac*Quarrie, and the following year he played George Washington to Alice Brady's title role in the silent picture *Betsy Ross*. With the advent of the talkies, he appeared in many, including *Abraham Lincoln, King Kong, Duck Soup*, and *The Mighty Barnum*. His younger brothers Frank, Murdock, and Albert MacQuarrie all acted in films as well.

It was George MacQuarrie's acclaimed portrayal of Svengali from *Trilby* that Verna mimicked so well. She observed carefully all of the actors, but especially McQuarrie and Jessie Shirley. In years to come Verna would play many of the same roles as Shirley. Since no film exists of either Shirley or Verna during their stage careers, one wonders to what extent Verna's performances were patterned after Shirley. If she heeded the *Spokesman-Review*'s criticisms of Jessie Shirley, Verna also learned what not to do.

One of the most remarkable consequences of Verna's stage career was that her mother took up acting as a profession as well. Here was Clara Lawrence Felton, who initially was quite opposed to her daughter's exposure to "life on the wicked stage" but now was, as Verna described her, "a woman absorbed by the theatre." She watched as Verna was given lessons in singing, dancing, stage movement, vocal projection. Clara observed all the behind-the-scenes operations of the stock company day in and day out. It was beginning to get in her blood, just as the profession was becoming more and more natural for Verna. After less than eight months accompanying the Shirley company on its tours, Clara got into the act. The play *East Lynne* may have been Clara's acting debut. A handbill from the May 6, 1901, production, listing her as "Miss Clara Lawrence" in the role of Susanne, was carefully mounted into one of the makeshift scrapbooks detailing Verna's early career. However, nowhere among these clippings is there mention of a gentle giant waiting in the wings, a man destined to change the lives of the Felton females forever.

CHAPTER 4

---•·•·•---

A MAN NAMED PEARL

If Destiny stepped in when Verna's father died, then Providence put Pearl Allen in her path to take Dr. Felton's place. As stage manager for the Jessie Shirley Company, twenty-nine-year-old Pearl met the Feltons when they joined the troupe in 1900. At six feet-one, his towering frame supported a considerably rotund body—upwards of 350 pounds—but his soft features revealed a gentleness that made being in his company a delight. As a former actor and musician, Pearl had not only gained experience in front of the footlights, but he had also acquired considerable knowledge about all the workings backstage. From the wings, he had watched little Verna grow as a performer, while becoming very fond of her and her mother Clara. Soon, Pearl Allen was to become the most influential man in the life of Verna Felton.

When discussing his career choice many years later, Pearl was quoted as saying, "Phooey on traditions." He had realized from an early age that he cared not to pursue a future in his father's blacksmith shop. Even his given name was nontraditional. Born Pearl Ruben Allen on September 11, 1871, in Chico, California, he was the eighth of twelve children. Pearl's father, Albert Allen, was born in 1833 in Ontario, Canada, but married the Ohio-born Anna Bethia Whitcomb in Mower County, Minnesota in 1856. Three years later, they made the five-month trek westward across the plains with Albert's parents in a covered wagon, finally reaching their destination of northern California.

By 1864, the Allens had settled in the northern Sacramento Valley town of Chico, founded four years earlier by General John Bidwell, a member of the first overland wagon train to cross the Sierras. By 1870, the predominantly male population of Chico numbered about five thousand. According to Tim Bousquet, researcher and former editor of *The Chico Examiner*, "With its wooden sidewalks, general and drug stores, multiple saloons, and fighting miners and ranch hands, Chico could have been lifted right off the set from a western movie . . . Saloons did a booming business and were often open all night, hosting card games and sporting roulette tables." Chico easily earned the reputation of a rowdy, drinking town where a brothel district, called the Tenderloin, was openly tolerated by city

Pearl Allen, circa 1902.

officials who needed a safe outlet for the thousands of single men coming through town, either by stagecoach or by rail. The Chinese made up one tenth of the town's population, inhabiting two "Chinatowns" on the east and west ends of Chico. Most Chinese residents worked in laundries or hotels, while others were employed as domestic servants by middle-class families.

The Allen Brothers' brass quartet, Chico, California, circa 1889. Left to right are Arden, Pearl, Leslie, and Ray.

At the time of Pearl Allen's birth, his father was employed as a teamster, but in subsequent years he supported himself as a blacksmith. By 1884, the Allens were living on Eighth Street in Chico and awaiting the birth of their twelfth child. While it is not known either how or when little "Pearly" (as he was identified on the 1880 Federal Census) was bitten by the acting bug, it must have happened when he was a very young and impressionable playgoer in Chico. As a young fellow, he formed a band with three of his brothers to perform at local functions. By 1890, Pearl felt the desire to abandon the simple life he had known from the time of his birth. He resolved to become an actor, and if that proved impractical, he was prepared to become connected with the stage in some other capacity. His early years in this field of endeavor are not recorded, but it is certain that before his twenty-fifth birthday, the musically talented Pearl had joined the stock company of Sam T. Shaw, a barnstormer who had quickly built a reputation for his troupe in many towns along the West Coast.

The son of a grocer, Sam T. Shaw, was born in Monroe County, Iowa, in 1861. Like the Allen family, the Shaws were musically inclined. When Sam Shaw formed his own stock company in the Midwest in the early 1890s, he hired Harry W. Smith as its orchestra conductor. Soon, Smith's wife, the former Jessie

Shirley, decided to get in on the act. She quickly became the troupe's leading lady, and not long afterward the company's success led them to northern California where they performed for the remainder of the decade. By May 1896, when the troupe was slated to play the Armory Hall in Woodland, California, the ad in the *Woodland Daily Democrat* screamed, "Shaw's Big Company in the repertoire of the Latest Comedies and Dramas, supporting the famous Character Actors, Sam T. Shaw and Miss Jessie Shirley." The Shaw company was, indeed, aptly named; they boasted twenty-three actors, thirteen band members, and seven orchestra members. Within ninety minutes of the troupe's arrival in Woodland on that spring day, they began drumming up business with a street-parade ballyhoo, a customary practice among traveling stock companies and circus troupes of the day. Shaw's parade consisted of his band members, dressed in clownish costumes to depict the bucolic *Farmer Stebbins*, the title character in their opening comedy that evening. The *Woodland Mail* reported that Shaw's band "gave a most novel and comical 'Farmer' street parade," furnishing excellent music. In addition to this, the band gave a second concert on the street outside the Armory Hall just prior to the evening performance. Two free daily concerts, just like these in Woodland, seem to have been Shaw's customary "drawing card" in each town where his troupe played. According to the *Woodland Mail* on the morning following their first performance of *Farmer Stebbins*, the troupe "took the house by storm and won all hearts . . . Sam T. Shaw as Silas Stebbins was a grand success. He is great as a 'Farmer.' Jessie Shirley is a charming little woman in manner, presence and song. Lew Rose is a corking, jolly good actor and so are all the rest."

In 1897, Jessie Shirley and Sam T. Shaw parted ways when she and her husband Harry Smith, by then Shaw's business manager, established their own stock company. Shaw hired the respected H. S. Duffield, who had previously been the business manager for the T. Daniel Frawley Company, to replace Smith. Meanwhile, Pearl Allen remained as a musician with the Shaw troupe which included leading man Sam T. Shaw, leading lady Marie Howe, "heavy" Al Hallett, the well-known "low comedian" M. J. Hooley, husband-and-wife team William and Birdie DeVaull, and a dozen more players. Al Walcott was the conductor of the company's operatic orchestra while J. J. Atkins led the fifteen-piece brass band.

On October 3, 1897, the Shaw company opened a week's engagement at Hall's Auditorium in San Jose, managed by Charles P. Hall, who would later become the manager of the Victory Theatre, where Verna Felton was discovered by the Jessie Shirley Company. One wonders if perhaps seven-year-old Verna saw the Shaw Company perform at the Auditorium that fall since Clara reportedly took her to see many touring productions during those days.

Touted by the *San Jose Daily Mercury* as "an evenly balanced company of stars," Sam T. Shaw's Big Company received further praise that week: "One of the best evidences of worth in a troupe is its ability to repeat. This is what Shaw's does. For instance, this season it has thrice played engagements in Fresno—a critical city—and each time to the largest possible business, and on each occasion with increasing demand for admissions." However, in a review later that week, the drama critic for the *Mercury* admitted: "It lacks of course the finish and symmetry and leadership of the great stock companies, but its members leave nothing wanting in endeavor and in earnestness. There is, judging from last night's cast in *The Westerner*, no weak timber in the organization, while there is a good deal of special and strong merit."

When Pearl Allen was interviewed by the Vancouver *Sunday Province* in 1933, he recalled performing with the Sam T. Shaw Company "in the Vancouver Opera House at the time when it was just a block from the tall timbers." Pearl elaborated, "Duke Ricketts was the manager then, and the building stood back from the wooden sidewalk with nothing to it that could be called a front."

As the Shaw Company traveled its way up and down the Pacific Coast, Pearl Allen, like a true apprentice, hungrily absorbed knowledge of every part of the business. Shaw saw Pearl's true potential and consequently promoted him from musician to business manager. By the time the Shaw Company returned to San Jose to open an engagement on Easter Sunday, 1899, at the newly established Victory Theatre, the successful troupe numbered thirty. The *San Jose Daily Mercury* boasted of its "up-to-date plays, elegantly equipped from a scenic standpoint, elaborately costumed and carrying their own silver cornet band and symphony orchestra." The successful troupe now numbered thirty.

Unfortunately, by the following year, Sam T. Shaw's Big Company had disbanded, due to the nervous breakdown of its proprietor. According to a press release, Shaw's rapidly failing eyesight brought on excessive worry, which led to the breakdown. Shaw moved back to his parents' home in Albia, Iowa, where his condition became increasingly worse. In August 1900, he was admitted to the Iowa State Hospital for the Insane, where he died the following year, three weeks before reaching his fortieth birthday. His early demise was much regretted, and after his death his name was always used with the highest regard. In October 1903, Charles E. Royal, a former member of Shaw's company, published the following tribute in *The Tacoma Daily News*:

> 'Twas just before the curtain rose
> Not so very long ago,
> And everyone was jesting
> As they do before the show;
> We were reading all the "Monograms"
> Which were written on the wall—
> There were names of all descriptions,
> Some familiar to us all.
> And as we read on down the line
> I heard someone declare

That only "Dubs" and amateurs
Would fix their "Monos" there.
I'm going to show you where they're wrong,
Perhaps you think the same.
But lots of real good fellows
Carelessly inscribe their names.
We came to one on the list
Written boldly on the wall.
'Twas the name of one you all know well,
Now gone beyond recall.
And there just as he'd placed it,
I could almost yell "Hurrah!"
Was the name of one we all loved well,
'Twas poor old "Sam T. Shaw."
Someone had drawn a square around
To preserve it from the rest
And wrote "He Was a Good Fellow,
A Prince Among the Best."
Those words read like a sermon,
For they filled all eyes with tears,
And they brought back many memories
Of happy bygone years,
And altho' some may be too "swelled"
Or it may be 'gainst the law,
I'm not too proud to have my name
With "POOR OLD SAM T. SHAW'S."

Upon the dissolution of Shaw's company, Pearl Allen called on his old friend and former Shaw leading lady Jessie Shirley for help. She and her husband promptly hired Pearl as their stage manager. As a member of the Shirley troupe, Pearl was therefore present on the fateful day of September 19, 1900, when Verna Felton sang and danced during that benefit performance at the Victory Theatre in San Jose. Though neither Pearl nor Verna knew it then, their lives would forever after be intertwined.

In 1902, after several years as a troupe musician with additional experience behind the scenes, Pearl, by now almost thirty-one years old, decided that he was knowledgeable enough to form his own popular-priced stock company. He was confident in his abilities to book engagements, but he was also assured that his artistic talents would successfully lend themselves to the aesthetic components of the position. As described by theatre historian Walter K. Waters, the duties of a stock company's stage director of this period were varied: "A stock director had to be capable of handling many details at once. He had to assign the roles, supervise the rehearsals, design the stage settings, choose properties and costumes, and attempt to enforce a universal interpretation of each play upon all those concerned with the production. The stock system simplified some of his work for him; for much of the casting followed the pattern set by the organization of the company and many of the sets were merely imitations of stage settings originally used for the plays in New York."

As director, Pearl would act as a disciplinarian during rehearsals, directing the players and their movements. The tight schedule of weekly engagements, coupled with a different bill each evening, allowed no time for improvisation or inspiration on the parts of the actors. Pearl knew that he would need to plan every detail of the performances before rehearsals began. He would also be required to ensure a smooth performance by overseeing the work of the stage carpenter, the scenic artist, the stage electrician, and the property man. At times he would be needed to act in the productions himself.

Pearl realized that as long as he remained with the Shirley company, his talents in these areas would remain unused. As the 1902 summer season wore on, Pearl began carefully planning the creation of his own company. He determined that the ideal time to break with the Shirley company would be at the end of their nine-week run in Spokane, Washington, in early August. Realizing that the debut of a new stock company would coincide perfectly with the upcoming fall theatrical season, Pearl arranged for the Allen Stock Company to open its initial engagement in mid-September. A key element in successfully orchestrating the entire endeavor would be Pearl's enticement of actors to join his fledgling company. Again, timing was crucial. The cooler months of fall brought turnover to each and every stock company. Just as teachers changed school assignments in the fall, likewise, actors sought better situations with rival stock companies. Pearl waited for the best time to approach his old cronies, currently employed in other companies, with offers to join his new troupe.

While ethics prevented him from enticing the adult members of the Jessie Shirley company to become part of the Allen Stock Company, Pearl did not hesitate to broach the subject with Clara Felton. In Verna, Pearl saw a great talent virtually untapped by the Shirley company. While it's true that the Smiths had recognized her ability first, they had allowed her career to stagnate somewhat during the 1901-02 season. During the Spokane engagement, Verna was hardly ever featured in advertisements or mentioned in the daily reviews. Only once during the nine-week run did the Shirley company produce *Little Lord Fauntleroy*, while *Editha's Burglar*, the other Shirley production which featured Verna heavily, had evidently been a neglected piece of their repertoire for months. Aside from the notable male role of Julian Esmond in *For Fair Virginia*, Verna was relegated to perform her "specialties" between the acts of other productions, such as *Under Two Flags, Trilby,* and *The Sultan's Daughter*. The Saturday matinees were no longer Verna's time to shine either, for on those days Miss Shirley assumed the spotlight as leading lady in productions of *Nell Gwynne, East Lynne,* and *The*

Deacon's Daughter. When Pearl Allen told Clara of his plans to begin his own company, proposing to utilize Verna in productions that would advance her career, she wisely chose to accept his offer.

When the Jessie Shirley Company ended its Spokane engagement on August 9, Pearl Allen, Clara Felton, and Verna Felton withdrew from its ranks and bid the troupe farewell as Jessie Shirley, et al., boarded a train bound for Sacramento. It is possible that the Feltons returned to San Jose, the city they still considered home, for a brief period of rest and reunion with old friends. But it is more likely that they followed Pearl to a new location, perhaps San Francisco, where Verna could begin rehearsing new plays he had chosen especially with her in mind.

During the early years of the twentieth century, a stock company manager could chose his plays from two sources: the standard repertoire of the nineteenth century or the newer plays controlled by the play rental agents in New York. He was forced to seek out plays primarily designed for balanced casts. For the most part, these plays, according to historian Walter Waters, "were of modern origin and had been produced on the New York stage. Many of them had been toured throughout the country, first in the expensive Syndicate-controlled theatres and then in the smaller second-class houses, which offered the so-called popular-priced attractions. Finally the plays were placed in the hands of play agents or play rental firms which granted production rights to low-budget producers and stock managers in return for which the firm was paid a fee or royalty which it divided according to contract between itself and the owner of the play. The newer and more successful the play, the higher was the royalty required."

Arthur Hobson Quinn, the author of *A History of American Drama: From the Beginning to the Civil War,* criticized the stock companies of this period, stating that they "contributed little to the creation of drama, for they contented themselves with the reproduction of Broadway successes." However, Quinn admitted that these companies "did present often the only opportunity for playgoers to see plays that were worthwhile." Walter K. Waters believed that this was the most valuable function of the stock companies, explaining that "it was not within the province of the stock producer to present new works or to experiment, for his was a commercial undertaking. He had to assess his audience's desires and satisfy them. If he wanted to present a play which might alienate a portion of the community, he had to prepare the public for it carefully. He had to balance the high costs of spectacular productions against the possible advertising value such presentations might have. He had to provide a varied program acceptable to all and give his performers an opportunity to appear to good advantage throughout the season. Programming a season of between thirty and forty plays was not an easy task, and the stock manager had to be sensitive to his audience, his cast, and his finances at all times."

For the initial season of the Allen Stock Company, Pearl ably assembled a varied repertoire of both old and new plays, none of which had been recently produced by the Shirley company or by the now defunct Sam T. Shaw Company. The earliest play he chose was Lester Wallack's drama *Rosedale*, originally presented in New York in the fall of 1863 for a run of 125 performances. Thereafter it was repeated season after season for nearly twenty-five years. By the time Pearl Allen chose *Rosedale*, it was enjoying somewhat of a revival across the country. Based on an English novel, *Rosedale* was the tale of the widowed Lady Florence May, who stands to lose her inheritance should she remarry without the consent of her late husband's uncle. Pearl decided that the part of Lady May's bratty son Arthur would be a perfect part for Verna.

Pearl found a similar character, although more amiable, in that of Bob Crockett, nine-year-old nephew of the title character in Frank Murdoch's *Davy Crockett*, which had been originally produced in Rochester, New York, in 1872. Well-known actor Frank Mayo had made a career of playing Davy in numerous productions, beginning in that year and lasting until his death in 1896, making *Davy Crockett* the best-known of the American frontier melodramas. Pearl was certain the comic part of squirrel-shooting Bob would be played by Verna with appropriate spunk.

Both *Rosedale* and *Davy Crockett* were published for the first time in 1940 in a volume of Barrett Clark's series *America's Lost Plays*. Editor Hubert Heffner cited both plays as having no literary value or literary pretension: "They were each written as stage pieces and conceived entirely in terms of their immediate theatric values. Thus they are excellent examples of that cleavage between literature and theatre that had arisen in the eighteenth century and continued down through the nineteenth to the renascence of the modern drama." Heffner demonstrated that these two plays followed the pattern established by refined melodrama, with the author relying upon suspense and pathos as a means to tell a thrilling and effective story. Heffner further explained the elements of melodramas: "The characterizations are very slightly and roughly sketched. They are usually mere examples of the types to be found in all melodrama: the hero, the heroine, the villain, and the comic. Again, as usual in melodrama, these authors employ a form of immediate surface realism in their compositions which undoubtedly served to give these works verisimilitude to their contemporary audiences. The use of music and the employment of elaborate pantomimic scenes are characteristic of this type of drama and of the technique of the period." (This last statement explains the necessity for the orchestra and/or band utilized by the stock companies of the period. Indeed, upon studying the scripts of *Rosedale* and *Davy Crockett,* references are found to background and lead-in music, particularly in the latter play which employed the tunes of "Auld Lang Syne" and "Home, Sweet Home.")

While most plays produced by stock companies made no pretense of being high comedy or great tragedy, Heffner asserted that they are historically significant because they reflect the theatrical interests and tastes of their age. He further credited these plays as being "a part of that development towards a distinctively, though not a self-consciously, American drama which marks the writings of our playwrights of today."

Pearl Allen's third selection for the 1902-03 season, *A Player's Night Off*, written by Thomas W. Robertson, was first produced in 1864. A romantic comedy set in the eighteenth century, it was sometimes called *David Garrick*, a work of fiction based on the famous English actor of the same name. For this production, Pearl ordered elaborate silk and satin costumes as well as exquisite wigs to resemble the powdered coiffures of the day. Next, Pearl chose Harry P. Mawson's 1891 drama *A Fair Rebel* as a vehicle featuring Verna as Joan Fitzhugh. However, the main characters in this Civil War play were a Union officer and his lover, a Southern girl.

However, the most expensive production Pearl opted to stage was the English melodrama *Master and Man*. Although it was a Broadway flop when first produced in 1890 with the great Richard Mansfield in the lead, *Master and Man* was popular among American stock companies at the turn of the twentieth century. Mansfield had played the "man"—the vile Humphrey Logan—who earns his living as an ironmaster's foreman. Pearl employed a large force of San Francisco stage carpenters to build the scenery and special effects needed for the iron foundry scenes. For this production Verna would again fill a male role, that of Johnnie Walton.

In addition to these "tried and true" selections, Pearl commissioned New York playwright Howard Wall to write two plays especially for Verna. The first was a comedy-drama, *The Power of Wealth*, featuring Verna as plucky little heroine Toddy Graham. The second commissioned work by Wall was *The Real Lord Lenox*, a comedy designed for children's Saturday matinees, which Pearl intended as a replacement for *Little Lord Fauntleroy*, Verna's signature play for the Jessie Shirley company. In *The Real Lord Lenox*, Verna was set to play the lead character, nicknamed "Morey the Mouse." Morey, an English boy descended from an earl, is returning from South Africa when he is separated from his mother during a shipwreck. The sailor who saves him brings the boy up in a rough manner. Through the efforts of kindly Dick Sparks, Morey's protector, they discover the boy's mother and consequently his right to his title.

Pearl also selected songs suited for Verna's "specialties" repertoire, including the 1901 Harry Heartz number, "The Good Little Sunday School Boy." One can easily picture Verna adding appropriate facial expressions to this amusing number:

> *A good little boy was a-walking down street, Just out from the Sunday School.*
> *When some wicked young fellows he happened to meet, Just out from a game of pool.*
> *They were Walter and Richard and Henry likewise,*
> *And the good boy was Bobbie, as you may surmise,*

And he frequently took some remarkable prize, Out of the
Sunday School!
Out of the Sunday School, Bobbie! Out of the Sunday School!
The good little boy, That we always enjoy, Out of the Sunday
School!

When Bobbie had spotted these very bad men, Just out from a
game of pool,
And he knew at a glance they were onto him then, Just out of
the Sunday School!
They guyed his good clothes and they mocked his good face,
Their manners were low, and their language was base,
And they frequently mentioned a very bad place, Far from the
Sunday School!
Far from the Sunday School, Bobbie! Far from the Sunday
School!
A very bad place, All abandoned by grace, Far from the Sunday
School!

Then Bobbie laid lesson and hymn book one side, Just brought
from the Sunday School,
While those naughty fellows he piously eyed, Just out from a
game of pool.
He first tackled Walter and made of him meat,
With Richard and Henry he wiped up the street,
And then he returned all so quiet and neat, Back to the
Sunday School!
Back to the Sunday School, Bobbie! Back to the Sunday School!
While the boys he did drop, Were pulled in by a cop, Back of the
Sunday School!

Meanwhile, Pearl Allen had not a minute to spare as he organized his new troupe. Mindful of his limited budget, he was faced with the daunting task of hiring an entire company of actors who could handle all of the productions to be staged in the coming year. Pearl realized that his leading man and lady needed to be ones with considerable experience, and thereby would be more costly to hire. While the supporting players' services would not be as expensive, Pearl knew that an inexperienced actor could almost sabotage a production. Consequently, he was very careful in his selections for the troupe.

Pearl chose as leading man the handsome Will Walling, currently ending his first year in the same capacity for the Dewey Stock Company in Oakland. Pearl negotiated with Walling to also perform the duties as the company's stage manager. One year younger than Pearl, Walling had won rave reviews for his portrayal of Davy Crockett while performing with the Dewey company. (In fact, he had been presented with a silver mounted rifle, purported to be an original one used by Crockett himself.) Walling's acclaim as Crockett had led Pearl to choose *Davy Crockett* as part of the Allen company repertoire, even though the production required a considerable outlay for costumes and scenery.

Hiring Walling was a risky venture for Pearl because the former was a relative newcomer to the theatrical world. Born in Iowa in 1872, Walling had spent many years of his youth in Woodland, California. While employed there as a butcher for Mossmayer's Meat Market, Walling's talent for whistling was discovered when he performed at a community fair in 1898. Soon he was appearing at the Woodland Opera House where his musical ability was showcased as a speciality between the acts of touring productions. By the fall of 1900, Walling had joined the Elleford Stock Company, based in northern California, and the following fall he became a member of the Dewey Company, at which time he met fellow actor, Effie Bond, who became his wife in 1902. As part of Pearl's deal with Walling, Effie, once praised as "a pocket edition of bright feminity," was hired as well to serve as leading lady for the Allen Stock Company. Born in 1879, Effie, like Verna Felton, had spent her girlhood in San Jose. Her career began in San Francisco when she was quite young, playing boys' roles in productions of the T. Daniel Frawley Company. Later Effie became known for her characterization of Neodamia in Frawley's prodution of *The Gladiator*, and after joining other theatrical companies, she was a well-known figure along the stage circuit. Pearl, as well as Verna, had known Effie from their days together in the Jessie Shirley Company.

With Verna and the Wallings as his anchors, Pearl hired the remainder of his company, including comedian Frank Bonner of the Dewey Stock Company; Joseph Damery and his wife Lillian Clayes of the Grover Stock Company; an old Coast favorite Harry Belmour; two well-known San Francisco actors Ralph Bell and Miss Loraine Lyons; plus Herbert Clark, Sager Dean, Fred Henderson, Robert Shaw, William Bond, D. C. Ferril, F. C. Miller, Wesley Tilton, and E. J. Scott. (Some of the latter individuals were possibly members of the band.) Clara Felton, performing under her maiden name of Lawrence, was also an initial member of the Allen Stock Company, as was Pearl's twenty-three-year-old brother, Arden Whitcomb Allen, whose musical talents were ideally suited for conducting the company's band. Arden was also somewhat of a composer, for he wrote a march titled "Toddy's Troubles" as part of the musical accompaniment for *The Power of Wealth*.

Pearl shrewdly selected Woodland, California, as the place for the Allen Stock Company to make its initial bow. Since Will Walling was so well-known there, his name was considered to be a drawing card among the populace. Pearl made arrangements with E. C. Webber, manager of the Woodland Opera House, for a week's engagement beginning September 15, 1902. Pearl's promotional strategies included advance announcements in the *Woodland Daily Democrat*, including blurbs about himself, as well as lengthy articles about Verna and Will Walling, published daily during the week prior to the troupe's arrival. In the September 10 edition, Pearl was described as knowing "the Pacific Coast from end to end, and it is doubtful if any manager in the country is better able to provide for the requirements of the Pacific Coast audiences than he."

Arden Allen, shown here in a photograph taken in Hanford, California, in 1902. Arden was born in Chico on October 24, 1879, and outlived all of his siblings.

Verna's advance notices were equally exaggerated. In a front-page feature appearing on September 11, and very likely penned by Pearl, the headline boasted that Verna held the distinction of being the youngest leading *woman* in America: "Some time ago the San Francisco papers were filled with pictures of a young woman who claimed to be the youngest leading woman in America, at the age of 17. The young lady was nothing of the sort. The youngest leading woman in the world is little Verna Felton, who will shortly appear in the opera house with the Allen Stock Company. Little Miss Felton, who will play the leading part in the new melodrama, *The Power of Money* [*sic*], is just past her ninth birthday. She will appear as a young lady in this play, and from all accounts her work surpasses that of many an older player. The little lady has a wonderful amount of emotional ability, which she displays with all the *savoir faire* and aplomb of a Maude Adams or Florence Roberts. People often predict a brilliant future for the child on the stage . . . She has arrived, as the French say, and is now a thoroughly finished artist. Off the stage Miss Felton is merely a pretty, sweet-tempered child, with all a little girl's desire for play and amusement. She is a simple, good little girl, who minds her mother and tries to be as good as all little girls are supposed to be. On the stage she is quite another person. There she is all actress, and her work is never ended. She does most of her work at rehearsals, and the way she absorbs what she is obliged to study is a wonder to all who know her."

While this boastful bit of promotion may be viewed by some simply as hype, it does contain certain truths. Verna Felton was indeed a quick study, and by other accounts she did seem to be well-adjusted despite her fame. There are no indications that she was at all like some child prodigies who manipulated adults by employing temperamental behavior. Of course, her reported age was grossly inaccurate. By this time, twelve-year-old Verna was approaching puberty. While this inconsistency may have been very evident to the more astute observers in the audience, the above article's accompanying photograph, taken at least two years earlier, coupled with Verna's small stature certainly led some people to marvel at the talent of such a "young" girl.

Further advance praises were published in the *Daily Democrat* on the following day:

> Little Verna Felton, the child wonder, learned her part in *The Power of Wealth*, for example during two rehearsals, and while the grown-up members of the company were worrying and studying through their lines this child was ready with every speech. In *The Real Lord Lennox*, a play somewhat on the order of *Little Lord Fauntleroy*, only it is all fun and comedy, little Miss Felton has another leading part. Indeed, the play was practically written for her by a well-known eastern playwright. The little woman's brilliant work in *Little Lord Fauntleroy* is of course, remembered by all the theatre-goers of this city. Her best work has been, perhaps, the child part in *For Fair Virginia*, in which she was seen last season while a member of the Jessie Shirley company. Here is a part requiring not only great comedy sense, but ability to bring tears to the eyes as well. The little lady easily carried off the honors in that play.

With these words, Pearl Allen was proving himself to be a talented marketer, not only promoting Verna, but the entire company. However, it was clear that Verna was his ticket to success. His initial ad in the Daily Democrat boasted, "Little Verna FELTON and the Allen Stock Company."

Most of the Allen Stock Company arrived in Woodland on Sunday evening, September 14, one day prior to their opening. As their initial play, Pearl chose *Rosedale*, "a dramatic exposition of simple home life," hailed in the *Daily Democrat*'s advance press as having "survived half a century of constant use and still in active demand by theatre-goers of good taste and judgment." Readers were assured that the play would be presented by capable players and that the content would be "clean," compared to the "so-called modern play, which is merely another name for degeneracy and indecency." Despite all the glowing previews, the Allen Stock Company got off to an inauspicious start in Woodland. First of all, some of the company were detained *en route* from San Francisco on Monday and did not

This portrait of Verna was used as a publicity photograph shortly after the formation of the Allen Stock Company, 1902. She autographed it for J. Willis Sayre, a Seattle drama critic. UNIVERSITY OF WASHINGTON LIBRARIES, SPECIAL COLLECTIONS, UW26805.

arrive in time to completely rehearse *Rosedale*, a consequence that resulted in embarrassingly frequent flubs. In addition, the *Daily Democrat*'s reviewer believed that the play's many scenery changes complicated matters and created lengthy delays. However, Verna, receiving the best notices, "completely captivated her audience . . . by her clever acting and specialties." The next evening's performance of *Davy Crockett*, featuring Will Walling in the title role, received more positive reviews, especially for Walling, but the reviewer felt it necessary to apologize for an unpleasant incident. "As a rule, gallery audiences at the opera house are orderly and well-behaved," he asserted. There was an exception Tuesday evening that was very annoying to the remainder of the audience and embarrassing to the company. While Mr. [Joseph] Damery was making an announcement he was interrupted by a rude yawn from the gallery. The manifestations of disapproval [exhibited by his fellow audience members] were so prompt and forcible that the offense is not likely to be repeated."

By the third evening's presentation, *The Power of Wealth*, the *Daily Democrat* was singing the praises of the Allen Stock Company: "It is a rare thing to have an opportunity to witness such a finished performance at popular prices. There are a number of repertoire companies that annually make a tour of California. Some of them have two or three stars while the rest of the company is made up of men and women who are taken along to hustle baggage, play in the orchestra, take tickets and do other odd jobs off and on the stage, and in order to economize, they are entrusted with thinking parts in the bill. As a result such companies cannot do satisfactory work because they are not well balanced. The individual work of those who know their business is marred by the bungling of [others]. Although the Allen Stock Company is a new aggregation, and the season is young, it is not open to any such objection. There is no claim of superabundance of talent, but it may be truthfully said that no part is assigned in any cast except to a person who is capable of presenting it at least acceptably. Indeed, the company includes so many capable people that in every play so far presented it has been necessary to leave some of them out. The cast is not large enough to include them all."

The writer was also complimentary of Verna's abilitiy: "It is said that *The Power of Wealth* was written with the sole view of giving little Verna Felton an opportunity of exercising her extraordinary talents. In some respects the plot is quite ambitious. In others the hideousness of vice is rather overdrawn and the villains rather overplay their game. Nevertheless, it is a story of full action and having a wide range of character. There is no question but that little Verna Felton easily carried off the honors of the situation and made a nearer approach to the stellar rank than any other member of the company. She is as much a favorite with the company as she is with the audience. There is rejoicing on the stage when she makes a hit and she does not seem to be a bit spoiled by the success she has achieved."

The following day, the *Daily Democrat's* drama critic panned the company's production of *A Fair Rebel*, citing certain cast members for not knowing their lines. However, the writer did find the costumes and scenery most appealing. His subsequent critique of *A Player's Night Off*, a romantic comedy, was almost identical to that of *A Fair Rebel*, but the writer made this allowance: "It is indeed a small wonder that the members occasionally forget their lines when it is taken into consideration that this is the first week out of an entirely new organization, and that they are compelled to play a new piece every evening. We venture to say that no other popular priced company on the road, with the same limited experience, could give the satisfaction that the Allen Stock Company has given during its present engagement in this city."

The Woodland run ended on September 20, to a standing-room-only crowd, when the troupe presented the English melodrama, *Master and Man*. A large crew of stage carpenters had spent two weeks that summer on the construction of the production's elaborate sets. Included were the blazing furnaces of the iron works which proved to be impressive and well worth the expense outlaid by Pearl. Kudos were showered on Frank Bonner for his portrayal of the villainous hunchback Humpy Logan, a role erroneously hyped in the *Democrat* as one of the earliest successes of Broadway actor Richard Mansfield, known on both sides of the Atlantic for his dual roles of Dr. Jekyll and Mr. Hyde. (In truth, the Mansfield production of *Master and Man* flopped after less than two weeks.) Will Walling ended a very frustrating week, performing each play's lead while also managing the technical aspects of each production. He was caused further anxiety by those performers who found it difficult to remember their lines after rushed rehearsals of the six productions.

However, Verna continued to receive the lion's share of praise from the Woodland critic, who said, "Little Verna left a warm spot in the hearts of all the theatre-goers of this city." Indeed, on closing night, after performing the much requested specialty song "The Good Little Sunday School Boy," Verna was encored three times, ending with her clever parody of the 1900 hit song "Just Because She Made Dem Goo-Goo Eyes," a number created by lyricist John Queen and composer Hughie Cannon.

While Cannon is most famous for his 1902 jazz standard, "Bill Bailey, Won't You Please Come Home?", he sometimes partnered with white minstrel Queen to compose "coon songs," like "Goo-Goo Eyes." The term "coon song" is often used to refer to a genre of songs written and performed by both blacks and whites containing derogatory racial images, stereotypes, language and caricatures of African-American people and culture. These songs, highly popular in the United States in the early 1900s, were part of the Tin Pan Alley and minstrel traditions.

While no record exists of Verna Felton's parody of "Goo-Goo Eyes," it's possible that a few words were altered for her performance since the original version is a tale of a trouper who falls for a young lady in the audience. Anyone who has seen her perform in films and television can imagine the gusto she would have poured into songs like "Goo-Goo Eyes" and "The Good Little Sunday School Boy."

On the morning after the Woodland closing, the Allen Stock Company took a train for Hanford, California, over two hundred miles to the south, where a new opera house had recently opened. Trombonist Fred Henderson, a member of the company's band, hailed from Hanford, and Pearl used this connection to draw attention to their engagement there, just as he had done with Will Walling's association with Woodland. The advance press in the *Hanford Daily Journal* was identical to the pieces published in the *Woodland Daily Democrat* before the Allen company began its engagement there. Moreover, the troupe performed exactly the same repertoire at the Hanford Opera House as they had in Woodland, with *A Fair Rebel* receiving the best notices. Despite nightly competition from the county fair, audiences were sizable by the time the engagement ended on September 27.

A Fair Rebel received the best notices the following week in the *Modesto News*, which singled out Verna in its review: "Her description of finding her father's grave in her search over the battlefield was pathetic and drew tears to many eyes."

On October 6, the company opened in Pearl Allen's hometown of Chico, where the only venue was the Armory Hall, built in 1885 at Main and Fifth Streets. Its lessee, the Chico Guard, a local military company, sublet the building to host traveling shows, dances, and other public meetings. Known as the Chico Opera House on the stock company circuit, the two-story building featured an auditorium and stage on the second level and a drill and dance floor on the street level.

Once again, the advance press notices in the *Chico Daily Record* were contrivances obviously executed and used by Pearl multiple times during the season. Little Verna Felton was the only troupe member billed in the ads, and her name was above the title. The band gave a concert at 4 o'clock each afternoon in front of Frank Waterland's candy store, where advance tickets were sold. Despite all of this preparation and Pearl's connection to Chico, the audiences were less than record-breaking. A political convention commanded the free time of many of the town's residents that week. The *Daily Record* was pleased with the Allen Stock Company's featured player: "Little Verna Felton throughout the week was a worthy favorite, for though a child, she manifested herself as fully equal to the many difficult parts entrusted to her. She was especially delightful in *The Little [sic] Lord Lenox*." Actor Frank Bonner was chided by the critic for not being certain of his lines, but Harry Belmour, deemed as "the only blemish" in the performance of *Master and Man*, received the harshest criticism: "He had but two positions—one with both hands in his trousers' pockets for a long session, and the other with his right elbow in his left hand, and his right hand on his chin, to wait for a cue." Following the final performance on October 11, Opera House manager Claude Steinegul hosted a banquet at Dooley's Restaurant in honor of the troupe. Pearl Allen was confident that when his fledgling company returned to Chico in the spring it would make a bigger impression on his hometown citizens.

The Allen Stock Company spent the remainder of the month farther south in the Sacramento Valley towns of Placerville, Colusa, and Williams. Prior to the Colusa Theatre engagement, which began October 20, the *Daily Colusa Sun* hailed the company's band as its most important adjunct: "Mr. Allen, the manager of the organization, is a musician himself and he has organized his band and orchestra with almost loving care. It is his pride and joy." The article continued for several paragraphs, clearly dictated by Pearl:

> "We are becoming more and more elevated in our musical talents each year, and each year we demand better and better music. We do not wish to criticize the orchestras in any other

houses in which [they] play. They are all very good, but is it not reasonable that a trained body of men who give all their time to their music will produce better results, especially when they are all picked performers and are trained to fit their work to that of the players on the stage? We have tried to secure as good a band and orchestra as is possible to secure anywhere. Our performers are all solo players in their different line and all artists. It is our aim to have those who go to our performances amused throughout the entire evening. There will be no long waits between the acts because during the intermission there will be rendered what is in reality a brief concert. Music of both classical and that of lighter nature will be played with the aim to reach all classes and every taste of the music-loving public."

Due to their train being delayed, the Allen Stock Company did not arrive in Colusa until half past seven on the evening of their opening. This caused some "imperfections in the stage setting and delay between acts," but the audience seemed to overlook this while they enjoyed the band's entertainment. Pearl selected *A Fair Rebel* as the week's opener. Written by Harry Mawson more than ten years previously, the title character, played by Effie Bond, was a Southern girl who fell in love with a northern army officer, played by Will Walling. However, the principal episode of the drama included a re-creation of a historical event, the celebrated escape of 109 Union soldiers from Richmond's Libby Prison in 1864. Walling, Bond, and Lillian Clayes as Aunt Margie, the lovesick old maid, received rave notices, but the reviewer was carried away by Verna's performance: "The surprise of the evening was little ten-year-old Verna Felton as Captain Johnnie. This little Miss is certainly a wonder and does work that more than equals that usually done by her elders. She is just as cute as she can be, and if there was a man, woman, or child in the house that did not fall completely in love with her, we would like to know who it was." By now, Pearl's publicity scheme inched Verna's age one year closer to the truth, but the fact remained that she was still more than two years older than the press proclaimed. Meanwhile the *Daily Colusa Sun* lauded the Allen Stock Company as the best repertory company appearing in Colusa since the time of Sam T. Shaw.

Downpours of rain on three consecutive nights that week did not keep away the Colusa audiences. After seeing *The Power of Wealth*, the *Daily Colusa Sun*'s reviewer wholeheartedly agreed with Pearl's advance promotion: "She is justly entitled to the honor of being called the youngest leading lady in the world. Her bursts of sarcasm to Leonard Scott, the rich villain, were so natural that it seemed as though the little Miss had real hatred in heart for the man who caused her and her brother's wife so many heartaches and hardships. Her lighter comedy lines were handled just as well as her pathetic parts." As a result of audiences' requests, the theatre manager made arrangements for the Allen Stock Company to remain in Colusa an extra night for an encore performance of *A Fair Rebel.*

After a repeat engagement in Placerville the first week of November, the company opened a successful week in Sonora, where a writer for the *Tuolumne Independent* praised the band: "The Company's orchestra under the direction of Prof. Arden Allen discoursed during the evening catchy and tuneful numbers, many of which were encored by the pleased and satisfied listeners. This orchestra is the best that has ever played in Sonora with a traveling Company. It is worth the price of admission to hear them." Following Sonora, the Allen Stock Company played one week each in Angels Camp and Carters, arriving in Oakdale for a week's run on December 1. By this time, the *Oakdale Leader* boasted that the company was comprised of twenty-five members, including the musicians, "all of whom are high-class artists, and besides are reported as being perfect ladies and gentlemen." Near the close of the engagement, the reviewer praised Verna as "a prodigy" and declared her "as graceful as a fairy."

The Oakdale venue was Barkis's Opera House, which, according to Glenn Burghardt, director of the Oakdale Musuem in 2005, may have actually been the upper floor of a general merchandise store or a vacant store building converted into a public hall. By calling the venue an "opera house," Burghardt believed it was an attempt to make the Oakdale more "big town" like San Francisco. "These 'opera houses' played an important part in early Oakdale," stated Burghardt, "as they were the central meeting places and brought the traveling culture shows to the people who were not able to travel to the big towns."

One marvels at how ingenious the stock companies of that day must have been, to ready their productions in places not specifically designed for scenery, special effects, musical accompaniment, etc. Some venues certainly required considerable physical adjustments and perhaps even some artistic allowances.

On December 10, The Allen Stock Company opened in Sacramento for six nights and one matinee. The state capital's population, at thirty thousand, was far greater than that of any city the troupe had previously played. Unlike the smaller towns, Sacramento boasted several theaters, therefore lengthy newspaper reviews for the nightly performances of each traveling troupe do not exist. However, one newspaper clipping mounted in a makeshift scrapbook maintained by Clara Felton, describes the run at Sacramento's Clunie Theater: "Its week here was rough on the company financially, because of the cold weather, the preparations for the holidays, and counter attractions. The company is a clever organization with good people in the lead, and a strong feature is its juvenile or child actress . . . Its purpose is to return in April."

The Allen Stock Company arrived in Fresno on Dec. 17 for a brief run at the Barton Opera House. In the previous ten years, Fresno had become the most sophisticated cultural center between Los Angeles and San Francisco, due primarily to the construction of the opera house in 1890 by Robert Barton Sr., a retired mining and vineyard magnate. An eloquent critique published in the *Fresno*

Evening Democrat, quite obviously not one of Pearl's creations, demonstrated that Fresno was indeed a city whose experiences with touring companies were varied and many. Furthermore, the drama critic could not be deceived regarding Verna's true age: "It is to be said of the new aspirants for public favor that artistically and musically the company is much superior to other stock companies on the road and it is moderately safe to prophesy that if Mr. Allen's players stick together and maintain the standard set by last night's performance they will soon be favorites in Fresno. Little Vernie [*sic*] Felton of course is well known here and evidently retains her popularity, but although the infant phenomenon feature of stage productions is sometimes a drawing card, it does not always satisfy, and if truth be told Little Vernie has reached the between times period where she is too big to be "Little Vernie," and to be petted and coddled by indulgent audiences because of her babyhood, and is too much "Little Vernie" to be Miss Verna Felton and taken seriously."

Pearl Allen's troupe was so well received at Bagby's Opera House in Monterey that it played there for two weeks beginning on January 4, 1903. In addition to the six plays the company had consistently performed since the previous September, Pearl decided to add the "old, but ever new, favorites" *Hazel Kirke* and *East Lynne*. The latter, one of several adaptations based on a popular 1860s British novel by Ellen Price Wood, would earn the distinction by mid-twentieth century as the second-most popular play in American professional stage history, with *Uncle Tom's Cabin* being the top favorite. The title *East Lynne* refers to the childhood home of Lady Isabel Vane, who, as an orphaned teen loses the estate. Later she marries the new owner Archibald Carlyle and returns to East Lynne, but their happiness ends when Isabel is deceived by Sir Francis Levinson into believing that Carlyle is planning to replace her with his former flame. Maddened with jealousy, Isabel runs off with Levinson, who turns out to be the play's villain. By the time the sadder but wiser Isabel returns to East Lynne, her little son Willie is dying. In some versions, Isabel soon follows her son to the grave.

As an old-fashioned melodrama, *East Lynne* packed the houses of stock companies across the country for more than half a century. Joseph Shipley, in his *Guide to Great Plays* explained: "East Lynne, together with its like a hundredfold, has little growth of character, and little portrayal of rounded individuals. Its strength lies in emotional situations, which were unusual enough to rouse interest while natural enough to win credence. A person theatre-wise may smile on such a play; but to dismiss it would evince small grasp of theatre history, or of social shift. Through the nineteenth century, especially in England and the United States, the processes of democracy and of public schooling produced a wide population of newly literate, and just literate, folk, with—for the first time for such a class—a bit of leisure, and a bit of money to spend in it. Just as they had begun to learn the rudiments of the three R's, so they must have rudimentary plays when they began to learn the theatre. Of the emotional dramas appealing to an untrained but eager theatrical taste, among the most touching and tender, as well as the most popular, is *East Lynne*."

Naturally the role of Little Willie, the dying child, was perfect for Verna. While she could be charming and humorous in the delivery of her "specialty" numbers, she also skillfully evoked emotion from audience members with parts like Little Willie. The Monterey drama critic wrote: "Miss Effie Bond vividly portrayed the sufferings and remorse of the misguided 'Lady Isabel,' laying a veritable spell upon the sympathies of the audience, while Little Verna Felton, the talented child actress made a most pathetic figure as 'Little Willie,' and played the part to perfection." Shipley, in the above book, offers some background information on Verna's role: "It was a maxim, until the first World War upset tradition, that on the English stage a man could not call himself an actor unless, as a child, he had played little Willie." To the stock company audiences of the West Coast, the part looked pretty impressive on Verna Felton's resume as well.

When the two-week run ended in Monterey, the Allen Stock Company boarded the train for Salinas for a week's engagement, arriving at noon on January 19. It marked the first time Verna had been back to her birthplace since her father's death almost four years earlier. However, none of the usual advance press preceded their arrival. In fact, they merited only a slim but erroneous mention in the evening paper: "The Salinas public always has a warm spot in its heart for the Allens, who at one time were residents of Salinas." Of course, Clara and Verna had been Salinas residents, but that was long before Pearl Allen came into the picture. The following day the *Salinas Daily Index* set the record straight by identifying a photo of Verna as the daughter of the late Dr. Felton, formerly of Salinas.

There were vacant seats in the Salinas Opera House for the first four nights, but by Friday and Saturday evenings, the house was packed. On Friday evening, Verna filled a request to repeat her rendition of "The Sheeny Coon," a music hall number written and composed in 1898 by British songwriter Harry Castling. However, her jig dancing and singing specialty was surpassed by the company's trombonist F. C. Henderson, who awed the Salinas audience with his solo of Stephen Adams's 1892 religious ballad "The Holy City." After the Saturday matinee performance of *The Power of Wealth*, Verna was declared "the lion of the hour." In the audience were hundreds of Salinas schoolchildren who would have known Verna in a different light had her family remained in their city instead of moving to San Jose some ten years earlier. The *Salinas Daily Index* noted: "The Allen Company has put on far superior plays to many of the companies who come with reluctance to a city the size of Salinas and demand the highest prices for their performances." Pearl's plan to provide quality entertainment at popular prices was winning fans in every city the troupe visited.

A week later, after a successful run in Gilroy, California, the columnist for the *Gilroy Advocate* was singing praise for Pearl's company: "As a company they came as strangers, [but] they leave as friends. By all odds, they are the strongest, most

Verna, San Jose, California, 1903.

evenly balanced Company that have [*sic*] ever visited our city. We do not except the old Shaw-Shirley combination, as the two principal stars of this good old company had not as good support as the Allens' . . . The Band concerts have enlivened the main street during the afternoon, while the selections by the orchestra, under the intelligent leadership of Arden W. Allen, have been a treat and have added greatly to the success of the evening performances." The writer was equally complimentary of Verna: "A brighter or more wonderful child actress could not be found than little Verna Felton. In *The Real Lord Lenox* she has a part that calls for quick active work, and a keen insight into human nature. She is child-like and natural in her manner, yet possesses the tact, ease and intuitive knowledge of the veteran performer. She has made a great hit with everyone. At ten years she is a phenomenon—what will her future be?"

Two weeks later while performing in Healdsburg, California, Verna was invited by Professor Dewitt C. Smith to dinner at the home of Mr. and Mrs. George Madeira following the Friday night performance. While Verna was delighted with the tempting meal prepared by Mrs. Madeira, this occasion prompted her first interview with a member of the press. Regarding her evening as a dinner guest, Verna remarked, 'It seems like home to me. I get so tired of stopping at hotels. Oh, no, I'm not very far away from home, for mother travels with me, and our home is in San Jose. I am a California girl and I have been on the stage just two years." Verna's comments reveal a natural desire to have a place to call home, leading one to wonder if she missed attending school and having friends her own age.

Still this lifestyle surely must have been exciting for a twelve-year-old girl. As soon as the Healdsburg engagement ended, the Allen Stock Company made their way to San Francisco where they boarded the Pomona, a steamer owned by the Pacific Coast Steamship Company. After a voyage of sixteen hours, they docked in Eureka, California on February 16 for a week's run at the Ingomar Theatre. Following a performance of *Master and Man*, The *Humboldt Standard* easily found words of praise for Verna: "The little lady—she is but ten years of age— reads her part with a naturalness that is as refreshing as it is unusual, and with an entire absence of the self consciousness and precociousness so apparent in the average child phenomenon, and which may frequently be noticed even in those of a larger growth." Noting her several encores following *The Real Lord Lenox*, the reviewer called Verna a "pocket edition of Barney Bernard," a popular comedian whose Yiddish songs Verna had added to her repertoire.

One month later, the Allen Stock Company opened in Verna's hometown of San Jose, appearing at the Victory Theater where Pearl had initially met the Feltons. The March 14 edition of *The San Jose Daily Mercury* printed almost verbatim a bit of pre-engagement praise originally used when Verna played San Jose with the Shirley company in May 1901:

It is an interesting fact that California has given to the American stage its cleverest and best known people. The latest addition to the ranks is little Verna Felton, the 10-year-old daughter of the late Dr. H. W. Felton, once a prominent physician of San Jose. For two years little Verna was a member of the Jessie Shirley Company and its strongest feature. Her sweet, magnetic personality, her winning grace and dainty style, have carried the public by storm, and many are the hearts that have worshipped at the shrine of her big brown eyes and witching smile.

There is nothing stagy or affected about little Verna. She gives to her work the serious thoughtfulness of the true student, forms her own conception of each character given her and brings forth a finished production of each and every part with a keen intelligence far beyond ten years. Her memory is something marvelous, and she not only masters her own lines with ease, but there is hardly a scene in the immense repertoire of the Allen Company that she cannot repeat. She is a perfect little mimic, while her quaint observations afford endless amusement to the other members of the company . . .

So many have been the tributes bestowed upon this small maid, so many the gifts showered upon her, that were she any but the sensible little girl she is her head would be completely turned by this sudden and overwhelming success. With it all she is just a dear little sprite of a girl with a sweet, sunshiny nature and a tender, childish heart, loving all around her and beloved by all. San Jose has reason to be proud of its daughter, this sweet bud of brightest promise.

Little Verna herself is delighted with the thought that she is to appear before her San Jose friends, for though she has traveled much in the past two years, and has seen many beautiful places, San Jose is beyond question her favorite city, and her home and her many friends will undoubtedly welcome her return.

Verna did not monopolize the limelight that week; Effie Bond, also a San Jose girl, was awarded a special feature article in the *Mercury* three days later. However, Verna made news in that edition as well. On the third night of the engagement at the Victory, members of the San Jose Council of the National Union, a fraternal beneficiary society of which Dr. Felton had been a part, attended the performance of *A Fair Rebel*. Between the second and third acts, a delegation of the National Union members surprised Verna backstage with the presentation of an Elgin pendant watch, its solid gold case engraved with her name. As Judge Michael H. Hyland bestowed this gift, he told Verna that the organization wanted to show their appreciation for the efforts of her father in building up their local union. Witnesses recalled that the child broke down completely.

Pearl chose the Victory as the perfect venue to try out two new productions, *Shall We Forgive Her?* and *The Dangers of New York*. The former, a melodrama set in England and Australia and written by Frank Harvey, had lasted one month on Broadway in 1897 before enjoying a two-season tour. Rehearsals for the latter had commenced as early as January, immediately after Pearl received the script. This was the third work he commissioned from New York actor-playwright Howard Wall as a showcase for Verna's talents.

Since Wall's scripts were privately commissioned, it is very probable that they were never published. Hence, copies are possibly nonexistent today. While the plot of *The Dangers of New York* remains sketchy in contemporary newspaper reviews, they reveal that this "melodramatic comedy" featured Verna as Nellie Moran, whose personality one may only surmise by examining a photograph of Verna dressed as the character. From head to toe, Nellie presents a curious picture, almost as if she is a little girl playing dress-up with her mother's clothes. She holds a frilly parasol over her plume-bedecked pancake hat, from under which two stiff braids extend. A checked bow is tied at the throat of her tight bodice while a floral overskirt serves as a balloon-like bustle. Kid gloves cover her hands and sensible high-top shoes peek from under her muslin skirt. Her facial expression is one of lofty condescension, summoning images of what a delightful character Nellie must have been. Interestingly, Effie Bond, the troupe's diminutive leading lady, was chosen to play the male role of Nellie's love interest, Chip Nolan. Upon the script's arrival, in January 1903, Pearl announced to the *Monterey New Era* that rehearsals would commence at once, with its initial presentation planned to follow in about two weeks. For reasons unknown, it was not staged until March.

Speculations concerning the plot of *The Dangers of New York* are only enabled by the knowledge that its creator, the Indiana-born Wall, drew upon the literary works of his fellow Hoosier, George Ade. While very little is known about Wall, George Ade was certainly no stranger to the average American at the turn of the twentieth century. Ade was not only one of the most popular authors of his time, but he was quite successful as a playwright as well. His career was ignited by the humorous columns he wrote for the *Chicago Morning News* during the 1890s. Possessing a keen ear for dialect and an ability for finding humor in the ordinary, Ade brought to life true American characters, usually a farmer or citizen of the lower middle class. Sometimes the objects of his satiric fables were women, especially those with "laughable social pretensions." (The image of Verna Felton as haughty but dowdy Nellie Moran, the creation of Ade-imitator Howard Wall, suggests an example of one such female.) "Ade's use of everyday vernacular blew

Verna as Nellie Moran in *The Dangers of New York.*

the dust off of the late Victorian Era and brought a well-needed breath of fresh air into American theatre," asserted Joanne Mendes, archivist at his alma mater, Purdue University. "He satirized all levels of society without a trace of malice, inviting America to join him is seeing itself, idiosyncrasies intact, and giving us the freedom to laugh at ourselves." Since no copies of *The Dangers of New York* are known to exist today, one can only surmise that its characters were cut from the same cloth as some of Ade's characters. Wall's play was soon to be a popular favorite among the audiences of the Allen Stock Company, but he would never escape obscurity during the remainder of his career, which lasted at least until the World War I era.

Near the end of March, Pearl Allen's troupe played to packed houses at the Farragut Theater in Vallejo, California, where Verna wowed the audiences with her Barney Bernard imitation and the coon song, "De Pride of Newspaper Row." As director of the company's orchestra, Arden Allen also won fans with "Hiawatha's Dance." Then Pearl and his little band of performers made a triumphant return to the Allen brothers' hometown of Chico on April 6. At week's end, *The Chico Daily Record* trumpeted: "Little Verna Felton and Effie Bond were practically the whole show at the closing performance of the Allen Company at Armory Hall Saturday evening, and it was a number one show at that. Effie Bond as 'Chip' and Little Verna as 'Nellie' were just all that the audience would have them. They had mastered the street slang and they passed it out as though they were the real lovers they were portraying. Little Verna is a marvelous child, a most faithful, accomplished little actress on the stage, and a loveable little girl off the stage. Her accomplishments and the influence of being constantly admired by audiences have failed, as is seldom the case, to make her forward off the stage. Mr. Allen certainly has a star."

Successful runs followed in the towns of Oroville and Ferndale that spring, documented by undated newspaper clippings glued into the expanding scrapbooks maintained by Clara. One news item, from an unidentified source, reveals more about Verna's early career than any other. It appears that the journalist conducted an interview with Pearl and Verna, although neither is quoted in the article. The anonymous writer, admittedly a fan of Verna's work, asked thoughtful questions about her experience before joining the Allen company. From this we learn that she made her first appearance onstage in San Jose around the age of six with the Catholic Ladies' Aid Society. Details about her days with the Jessie Shirley Company are revealed as well, including a mention that her first professional role, albeit a tiny one, was in the Shirley production of *At the White Lion*. Verna admitted to the journalist that her favorite role thus far was that of Julian Esmond in *For Fair Virginia*, an interesting revelation because this play was not a part of the Allen repertoire but instead was a Jessie Shirley production. Verna, confessing she liked the comic songs in her repertoire the best, listed her favorites as "Beautiful Fairy Tales," "Smiles," "The Sheeny Coon," "Epha Saffa Dill," and "The Good Little Sunday School Boy." But the most amazing item in this feature article was the story of how Verna saved the day and avoided financial loss for the Allen Stock Company.

The incident occurred during the week they played the town of Ferndale when the actress who was cast as Dolly Dutton in *Hazel Kirke* was taken ill. It was necessary to postpone the production, substituting it with another from the Allen repertoire. This continued for several nights as Pearl waited for the actress to recuperate. On the final morning of the engagement, the actress said she felt well enough to perform that evening. Arrangements were made at once, and a large number of seats were promptly sold in anticipation of the evening's performance of the popular play. *Hazel Kirke*, written and originally produced for Broadway by Steele Mackaye in 1880, had been a perennial favorite on the stock circuit for twenty years by this time. All was set when the actress suffered a relapse by noon that day. Verna offered to go on in her place.

At first, Pearl was hesitant to accept the child's offer because he knew she had not actually studied the part. After another actor ran lines with Verna, they were all surprised that she knew every word, and she was given the part. Interestingly, the fact that twelve-year-old Verna would be playing the character of someone five years older did not seem to be an issue. All that was left to do was to go over the blocking for Dolly's scenes. That evening, Verna played the part of Dolly, the heroine's best friend, in a "most excellent manner." Whether she also appeared in her regular role of Methuselah, a young boy, is not clear.

The anonymous writer who revealed Verna's rescue of *Hazel Kirke* ended his column in this way:

> Off the stage [Verna] is a little girl playing with her doll and toys, just as any other child of her age would, but on the stage she is an actress of exceptional ability. Ten thousand children might have the same opportunities and advantages but there would only be one who could make the success out of her work that Little Verna has. If her life is spared and her work continued on the stage she will yet become one of the famous actresses who have done so much to lift up and ennoble the stage.

Little did this writer, or anyone else, realize that Verna Felton's life would indeed be "spared." Her acting career would last another sixty years.

By late spring, the Allen Stock Company had lost most of its original players, including Will Walling and Effie Bond. In their places were Russell Reed, Hayden Stevenson, Ethel Roberts, Georgia Francis, Charles E. Royal, Reginald Barker, Frank Walsh, and Sydney Platt. The company spent the month of June making new friends in Oregon towns such as Grants Pass, Medford, Salem, and Astoria. In the latter city, at Fisher's Opera House, the troupe performed in a benefit for the sufferers of Oregon's deadliest flood, which killed 247 people in the town of Heppner. This must have brought back memories of the Galveston

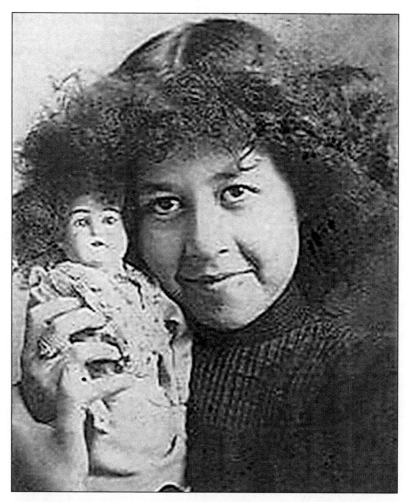

A print made in a photo booth showing Verna posing with her doll, circa 1902.

benefit in San Jose three years earlier. For the Heppner benefit, the company performed the first act of *A Black Heifer,* a rural comedy in which Verna was cast in the curious role of Scraps. She also sang two solos, "How D'ye Do" and "Go Way and Let Me Sleep."

In Salem, Oregon, the *Daily Journal's* drama critic noted that Verna's return to that city evoked memories of when she appeared there in *Little Lord Fauntleroy* with the Shirley company, lauding her for playing the "largest matinee that was ever assembled in the Grand Opera House." Nevertheless, the Allen production of *Hazel Kirke* drew only a fair audience among the Salem populace, despite its realistic storm scene, of which the reviewer noted: "When the window curtains began to wave, and the rain to rattle, more than one of Salem's fair women present involuntarily gathered her wraps about her shoulders." For her specialty numbers, Verna, described as a "charming little midget," was encored twice and then presented with a huge bouquet of pink roses. One spectator who found favor with others in the company felt compelled to express his delight poetically:

> *The man with the big violin*
> *You'll know by his rotundity;*
> *And Walsh has got a basso voice*
> *Unusual for profundity.*
> *The leading lady plays her part*
> *With vigor and intensity,*
> *And Little Verna makes you laugh,*
> *For that is her propensity.*

Of course, the rotund man was Pearl Allen, who played the bass violin in the company's orchestra. The "basso voice" belonged to Frank Walsh, who sang specialties between the acts.

By late June, the company had crossed the state line into western Washington where they would spend the remainder of the summer and most of the fall. On June 29, they opened for one week at the Olympia Theater. Two days later the *Morning Olympian* commented on their performance of *The Power of Wealth*: "The company was at a great disadvantage on account of the failure of the electric light service but were equal to the emergency, for as soon as kerosene lamps were placed about the house the show went on with very little delay." Verna's renditions of "Just Suppose" and "Smiles, Smiles, Simles" brought down the house that week. After an engagement in the city of Hoquiam, the troupe stopped in the small town of Elma to appear at the opera house for a week beginning on Monday, July 20, which was Verna's thirteenth birthday. The next day the local press related that following the performance of *The Power of Wealth*, the company gave Verna a surprise birthday party and presented her with a gold locket and chain. However, Pearl was continuing to mislead the public regarding Verna's true age; the newspaper reported that it was her eleventh birthday.

Other stops during the 1903 summer tour of Washington included Port Townsend, Chehalis, and Puyallup. Pearl freshened the company's repertoire with the additions of older plays like *Van the Virginian* (1874), *The Black Flag* (1882), and *Hearts of Oak* (1880), the last of which was written by James Herne and David Belasco, both known for creating plays which were more realistic than most nineteenth-century romances and melodramas. *Hearts of Oak* is the tale of a sailor Terry Dennison who falls in love with his adopted daughter Chrystal, who agrees to marry him despite her love for another man. Soon after Terry and Chrystal have a baby daughter, Terry realizes that Chrystal will never love him. After he goes away to sea, seven years pass with no word from him. Chrystal thinks him dead and marries her true love. One day Terry, old and sick, returns, finding the child, Little Chrystal, outside the house. After an awkward interaction, she comforts him by calling him father, and he dies contentedly in her arms. Although this plot may not be very different from melodrama, Herne and Belasco used none of the florid dialogue most melodramas employed in the nineteenth century. The story was made into two silent films productions, the first in 1914 and the second one, directed by John Ford, ten years later. In 1903, Verna, at age thirteen, played the part of Little Chrystal, a girl who was supposedly only seven years old.

Another role Verna continued to play into her teens was that of Editha, the lead in a one-act play, *Editha's Burglar*, which she had first played at age ten with the Jessie Shirley Company. Recalling Verna's successes with *Editha*, Pearl went one step further than the Shirley production. Knowing that one-act plays were not readily accepted on the touring circuit, Pearl chose the expanded version, a full-length drama simply called *The Burglar* and written in 1889 by Augustus Thomas, *Editha's* creator. According to Gerald Bordman, author of *American Theatre: A Chronicle of Comedy and Drama, 1869-1914*, "the old play served, with modification, as the middle section. The first act showed the burglar's earlier, happier married life, and the final act struggled to tie up all the loose strings of the original."

On October 18, after a week in Bellingham, the Allen Stock Company opened for the first time in Tacoma at the Lyceum Theater. The favorable notices it received from the surrounding towns greatly enabled this booking. Tacoma playgoers recalled Verna from her engagement there with Jessie Shirley two years earlier, but, as a reminder, her portrait was printed in the *Tacoma Daily News* as part of the advance press. Pearl Allen's portrait was also published in the *Daily News*, and curiously enough, so was a full-length pose of Clara Felton, dressed in plumed hat and resplendent cloak, captioned as "Miss Clara Lawrence, with Allen Stock Company." Interestingly, Clara's name does not appear on any of the existing playbills or in newspaper reviews, both prior to the Tacoma engagement and after it. The inclusion of her photograph in the drama section of that Sunday edition rouses speculations that by this time Clara and Pearl shared a certain affection for one another. After all, they had been in each other's company for three years, and due to the transience of their profession, little opportunity was afforded for either of them to establish lasting relationships with anyone, except the members of the troupe. It was only a natural consequence that they developed a fondness for each other. At thirty-two, Pearl was eight years Clara's junior—a situation seeming not to interfere with their budding romance. Furthermore, it is very obvious from existing documents, including photographs, that Pearl was very fond of Clara's daughter, not only because of Verna's ability to draw an audience, but also because of her winning personality offstage. Just as Verna described the Jessie Shirley Company as "a family-circle sort of people," the same could be said for the Allen Stock Company. It is doubtful that Clara ever imagined herself finding romance among the members of a stock company when she left San Jose that day in September 1900.

To awaken the memories of Tacoma theatre buffs, the Lyceum Theater's advertisements featured the name of Verna Felton four times the size of the subheading "With the Allen Stock Co." The opening bill, curiously renamed *Was She to Blame?*, was actually the company's old summer standby *Shall We Forgive Her?*, in which Verna was cast as comic relief in the supporting role of Nellie West, a young girl in love. This role proved that, at age thirteen, Verna was inching her way out of the child-phenomenon stage of her career towards that of *soubrette*, but ever so haltingly, for on the following evening she once again became little Editha in *The Burglar* and in the closing bill on October 25 she played the trouser role of Ned, an outcast boy, in *The Black Flag*.

On November 1, the Allen Stock Company moved up another rung on the stock-circuit ladder with an engagement at the Third Avenue Theatre in Seattle. A handbill announcing the week's run of *Shall We Forgive Her?* featured an artistic portrait of Verna around age nine, with bare shoulders and solemn eyes, cast heavenward. Below that in a large font: "Little Verna Felton." While the engagement was routine, it was destined to become the final time that Verna was exclusively billed with the word "little" preceding her name.

When the company returned to Tacoma for a four-night engagement on November 15, it was *Miss* Verna Felton who trod the boards at the Lyceum Theater. However, this new title did not signify that she was featured in a starring role or even that of an ingénue. Instead she was filling supporting roles such as Scraps, the waif in the rural comedy *A Black Heifer*, and Elsie in *Lost and Won* (also known as *The Fatal Wedding*), the latter role described in the *Tacoma Daily News* as "one of the strongest emotional child parts ever written."

While the troupe had been touring the western part of Washington that fall, Pearl had been making big plans for their future. After a year of traveling from town to town, he wanted the Allen Stock Company to make the transition from a touring company to a resident stock company. To accomplish this, he sought the help of fellow actor-manager Carl Berch, two years Pearl's senior.

The Michigan-born Berch had been a member of several stock companies before the turn of the century, including those managed by Frank Bacon, Carrie Clarke-Ward, and Landers Stevens. In the fall of 1901, Berch attempted to get his own company off and running, but after struggling one and one-half seasons, he retreated to the security of Stevens' company, based in Oakland. By October 1903, Berch got the familiar itch to move on. At the same time, Pearl Allen wanted to settle down and rest from the weekly road trips. The pair decided that their theatrical expertise would be a perfect mesh of management, stage direction, and production design.

When Berch and Allen learned of a potentially profitable venture in Vancouver, British Columbia, they chose that city as the location for the Allen company to establish residence. The Theatre Royal, at the corner of Pender and

Howe Streets, had recently closed there, and although it was a small venue (later promoted by Berch and Allen as "cozy"), the new partners knew that they could pack the house every night if they provided top-notch entertainment at popular prices (10, 20, 30 and 40 cents). The main competition in town was an establishment very familiar to Pearl from his days with Sam T. Shaw: the Vancouver Opera House, whose manager charged 25, 50, and 75 cents. Berch and Allen further emphasized their "popular" prices by christening their establishment as The People's Theatre. Berch was the sole lessee of the building, while he and Pearl shared the duties of managing the productions. Fred J. Dailey, formerly with the Norris & Rowe Circus, was hired as the business manager and treasurer.

The Allen Stock Company arrived in Vancouver on November 20 and on the following night, opened to a house "crowded to the doors." The selected production was *The Black Flag* with Carl Berch in one of the leading roles. To ensure that The People's Theatre lived up to its name, a keen strategy was exercised the following week. Berch invited all of the city's working boys to attend the performance of *Shall We Forgive Her?* on the night of Nov. 27, free of charge. Long before the scheduled time of performance, a "struggling crowd of youngsters surrounded the entrance in response to the invitation." The balcony was packed, while the lower part of the house, and even the aisles, were filled with delighted boys, who alternately hissed the villain and cheered the hero and heroine.

Following the success of this promotion, Berch devised other ways to draw the crowds. On December 11, he bought several hundred pounds of candy to be given away in small bags to every child in attendance at the Saturday matinee the following day. On the following Monday evening, nearly one thousand patrons deposited coupons in a lockbox for a chance drawing on a $50 bedroom suite. By midweek, over $4000 had been collected in ticket sales. The move to Vancouver seemed an instant success to both Carl Berch and Pearl Allen. Despite the holiday shopping season, box office records were being broken every day at the Pender Street theatre, and the Allen Stock Company raked in money both Christmas Day and New Year's Day. When the raffle of a diamond-studded lady's watch kept the house packed during early January 1904, the city's building inspector required that two side exits be added on either side of the building to ensure the prompt exit of patrons should a fire break out. A fire drill was later implemented, and the crowded house emptied in fifty-seven seconds.

Meanwhile, Pearl utilized some old standards to revitalize the company's repertoire, including *Ten Nights in a Barroom, Uncle Tom's Cabin,* and *The Count of Monte Cristo. Ten Nights in a Barroom,* a temperance melodrama based on the 1854 runaway best-seller by Timothy Shay Arthur, was described by a *Vancouver Daily Province* critic as "a new and considerably improved version of [an] old and somewhat threadbare drama." Pearl Allen brought the play up-to-date by adding a contemporary character, Carrie Nation, the zealous American prohibitionist known the world over for smashing saloon fixtures and stock with her hatchet.

Although Carrie and her brigade earned repeated curtain calls, Pearl realized that his calculation to brighten an otherwise gloomy production didn't actually succeed and so he closed *Ten Nights* on December 2, after only three nights. According to the *Daily Province* critic, "While nearly every member of the cast was well placed, the palm must be awarded to Miss Verna Felton, who as Mary Morgan, the drunkard's child, gave the best interpretation of that role ever seen here."

Uncle Tom's Cabin, with its impressive production values, proved far more successful, drawing capacity crowds for six nights beginning December 7. The *Daily Province* reviewer was candid in his criticisms, noting that the limitations of the small stage stinted the dramatic escape scene in which the slave Eliza crosses the Ohio River on a floating piece of ice and the "supposedly ferocious bloodhounds were rather sleepy-looking." However, he singled out one performance: "As the irrepressible Topsy, Miss Verna Felton was the life of the piece. This clever child-actress seemed quite in her element. Her interpretation of the familiar lines was decidedly original, and at the same time highly amusing." Perhaps Verna's experienced delivery of coon songs allowed for her originality in the blackface role of Topsy, an uncontrollable ragamuffin slave girl whom Harriet Beecher Stowe had based upon a minstrel-show character.

Besides Morey in *The Real Lord Lenox*, Topsy proved to be Verna's final outstanding role in the People's Theatre engagement, which totaled twenty weeks. In the remainder of the productions, her talent was utilized in much smaller roles, albeit ones repeatedly described by the *Daily Province* as "congenial." As she approached the age of fourteen, half of Verna's roles continued to be cheeky newsboys or street urchins. One reviewer, who probably never realized the accuracy of his prophecy, "It is hard to class little Verna Felton. She is only a girl in years, yet in talent she ranks with the best and the oldest of them . . . if Miss Verna keeps on, there will be a comedienne going from the People's some of these days who will be known in larger cities than Vancouver."

Besides Verna, the company boasted the addition of Irish tenor Allen Doone, whom Pearl had met in Seattle where Doone was managing the La Petite, the city's first movie house. Born Edward Doone Allen on September 3, 1878, in Amboy, Illinois, the twenty-five-year-old singer had built a considerable following in the Northwest as a racing cyclist during the last years of the previous century. Known as Eddie Allen, he and fellow racer Frank Cotter had toured Europe in 1900, competing in races in both Paris and Rome. Eddie was among the first to introduce motorcycles to Olympia, Washington, where he and Cotter built an early racing track. In 1902, when Eddie tired of racing, he moved from Spokane to Seattle to open La Petite. As a son of Irish immigrants, Eddie fancied ballads of that flavor, and spent his spare time composing his own works. While Eddie had no acting experience, Pearl recognized that his musical ability would lend itself well during intermissions. Since they shared the same surname but were in no way related, Pearl suggested that Eddie use "Allen Doone" as a stage name. Naturally, the name's ethnic ring would help audiences identify Doone as the fellow who sings the Irish airs. Pearl signed Doone for the Vancouver engagement, but he also hired his young wife Edna Keeley, who had been an actress since childhood. Just nineteen, auburn-haired Keeley was small and dainty, in marked contrast to Doone, whose height, dark complexion, lantern jaw, and good looks alone made him a drawing card. Consequently, Doone and Keeley were usually assigned juvenile leads, but on occasion found themselves entrusted with such respective character parts as a "picturesque Mexican villain" or a "Mother Hubbard."

Several onstage mishaps befell the Allen Stock Company during the Vancouver engagement. On December 28, actress Ethel Roberts seriously sprained her ankle during the murder scene of *After Dark*. Then on January 14, during the performance of *Larry Aroon*, Allen Doone, in the title part of the blacksmith, found himself in a challenging situation. One scene called for him to shoe a live horse, but midway through it, Doone discovered that the properties man had forgotten to leave a horseshoe onstage. There was no time to send for another, and there was no iron available to make another shoe. Doone was not going to be "so easily defeated," reported the *Vancouver Daily Province* the following morning: "Hastily heating one of his shoeing tools, he fashioned it into a very creditable shoe, and amid the plaudits of the large audience who had by this time discovered his embarrassment, he placed the shoe in position and finished out the scene in fine style." However, the most upsetting incident occurred during the week of December 11. During a performance of *Uncle Tom's Cabin*, actor William Bond sustained a serious cut below his knee, which became infected with blood poisoning. Six weeks later, after a lengthy hospitalization, which included several surgeries, Bond remained seriously ill at St. Paul's Hospital. The Allen Stock Company gave a benefit performance of *Forgiven* for the financially drained actor on January 26. Finally, on March 8, Bond was able to make the journey home to Colusa, California, where he hoped to recover completely. Standing at the steamer, waving their farewells, were most of the members of the company.

In the meantime, some players departed for greener pastures while others arrived in their stead. Both Ethel Roberts and Allen Doone had left Vancouver in February for a tour of the "coast cities," while Edna Keeley held on until March 25 before following them south. One new addition to the company received more press than any of the rest. On March 9, Miss Dorothy Davis, a San Franciscan actress who had performed with the Allen Stock Company during the previous summer tour of Washington, stepped off the Charmer, a steamer arriving from Victoria. Waiting her arrival was Arden Allen, younger brother of Pearl and musical director and orchestra conductor for the company. A summer romance had blossomed between Arden and Miss Davis, and after a faithful correspondence, she made the journey to Vancouver to accept Arden's proposal of marriage. Realizing the certainty of their respective families' disapproval, the young lovers had kept their plans secret. Dorothy, born as Phoebe Dorothy Jacobs in San Francisco on April 7, 1879, was the daughter of Jacob and Rachel Feig Jacobs, Prussian immigrants. According to Dorothy's granddaughter Daphne Allen, "My grandmother came from a Jewish family and was banished from the household for marrying a Gentile." However, Dorothy, who sang and played the piano, remained enamored with the thoughts of a stage career. Being married to Arden Allen would enable her to pursue this dream, even though it meant the end of her relationship with her San Francisco family. Arden's parents, though less demonstrative, did not approve of the union either. With marriage license in hand, the young couple left the dock and quietly hunted for the nearest clergyman.

When they arrived later at the People's Theatre for the afternoon rehearsal of *The Corner Grocery*, Arden

Dorothy Davis (*nee* Jacobs), stage and vaudeville actress, circa 1910.
UNIVERSITY OF WASHINGTON LIBRARIES, SPECIAL COLLECTIONS, UW26807.

shyly approached Pearl with the news of his marriage. At first, Pearl refused to believe him, but then he took one look at Dorothy and instantly began congratulating them both. Soon the entire company and the stagehands swarmed the couple with their best wishes. When someone demanded to know why the company had not been told of the nuptials in advance, Arden offered excuses, but they were not accepted. According to a tongue-in-cheek article appearing in the *Daily Province*: "A Kangaroo Court was held with Joe Whitehead [the company comedian] as presiding judge, and the musical director was found guilty and sentenced to play his own wedding march for the edification of the company. To the stirring strains all the members of the company executed a good old-fashioned Virginia reel, while little Verna Felton directed the figures from the stage mountain in the background."

Exactly one month later, on April 9, the Allen Stock Company ended its run at the People's Theatre with a performance of *A Mother's Devotion*, a melodrama written by company member James Rush Bronson. The twenty-week engagement ended without any explanation in the press, so one may surmise that some disagreement arose between Pearl and Carl Berch, since the latter continued to operate the People's Theatre for months afterward, though never securing another company like that of Pearl Allen. By mid-June, Berch was reduced to holding wrestling matches on his stage, an indication that The People's Theatre may have become a vaudeville house. Meanwhile, Berch took out ads in the *Daily Province* to entice pupils to join his drama school, which offered courses in expression, oratory, and fencing.

As consolation to the audiences who frequented the Allen Stock Company's performances at the People's Theatre, the *Daily Province* announced that Pearl Allen and company would return to Vancouver on May 2 to begin a season of stock at the City Hall. For whatever reason, this engagement never materialized. After leaving Vancouver, the troupe opened in Seattle on April 10 for two and one-half weeks at the Third Avenue Theater. Members of the sizeable company now included Rae Bronson, Dorothy Davis, Tom Loftus and his wife Meta Marsky, who had been part of the Jessie Shirley company in 1900, as well as twenty-three-year-old Russell Simpson, who later won film fame as Pa Joad in John Ford's *The Grapes of Wrath*. On April 28 in Olympia, they were joined by Allen Doone, fresh from a vaudeville stint at San Jose's Unique Theatre. Pearl seized upon Doone's racing-days popularity with Olympians to promote the Allen Stock Company's brief engagement of *Larry Aroon*. The realistic production featured live carrier pigeons, a brightly burning forge, and the requisite live horse for the blacksmith scene. Pearl timed it all perfectly. *The Morning Olympian* reported: "When the horse had been led away and Larry was left alone he softly drums on the anvil and sings that beautiful song 'A Handful of Earth from the Land of My Birth, From the Grove Where My Poor Mother Lies.' There was scarcely a dry eye in the house." Despite the generous coverage given Doone, Verna got a nod: "Little Verna Felton, grown a head taller since her last visit captured the audience with her cute acting and pretty songs. As the jockey in the horse-shoeing scene she did admirably."

It appears that the Allen Stock Company may have disbanded shortly after the Olympia engagement, owing most likely to financial difficulties. Allen Doone and his wife Edna Keeley sought their fortune in the East by joining the prestigious B. F. Keith Vaudeville Circuit. Likewise, Verna Felton resorted to vaudeville to keep food on the family table. Her whereabouts during the spring and summer of 1904 aren't easily tracked, but by June 14, she was back in Olympia, performing at the Edison Theater. Billed as a soubrette, she was described by one reviewer as "dainty, chic, and pretty." The dubious bill included comic F. H. Stansfield, whose specialty was mimicking barnyard fowl, and D's and D's Bronzed Moguls, "a thoroughly refined colored act."

Following a pattern that would be repeated more than once in the thirty years ahead, Pearl Allen and the Feltons, feeling the effects of lean times, returned to their native state of California. What exactly transpired in the following three months remains purely speculative, but it is likely that Pearl either sought financial assistance or employment from his family or he continued to manage Verna's career. It appears that the Feltons returned to San Jose for a while. By August 1, Verna was appearing there at the Unique Theatre, a converted storefront on East Santa Clara Street. Sid Grauman, not yet the impresario who would later build Hollywood's legendary Chinese Theatre, had opened the vaudeville house in 1903. The Unique was sadly inadequate when compared to the Victory, where Verna had made her bow in 1900. Although Grauman had hastily furnished it with eight hundred kitchen chairs and a single piano, it would prove to be a popular spot. A brief description of Verna's act, appearing in the *San Jose Mercury News*, sounds equally unimpressive: "There is a child—a little girl—at the Unique Theater this week that is quite clever. She appears with her father, or he may be a big brother, as a 'coon.' She sings, dances, and makes faces. The last accomplishment is the most amusing." One wonders if the father or big brother could have been Pearl Allen. Nevertheless, the writer complimented Verna's taste in clothes and her choice of selections, including the tried-and-true "How D'You Do?" Still it must have been a terrible disappointment to perform such drivel, especially in Verna's own hometown. Evidently her act was not successful enough to merit more than a few days' run. Three months later, Grauman would use the same stage to launch the career of singing waiter Roscoe "Fatty" Arbuckle, whose future

Verna as Duty Peck in *The King of the Opium Ring*, Third Avenue Theater, Seattle, 1904. UNIVERSITY OF WASHINGTON LIBRARIES, SPECIAL COLLECTIONS, UW28320.

success on the silent screen would be eclipsed by his trial—and subsequent acquittal—in the death of actress Virginia Rappe in 1921.

By early fall, Verna's career seemed to be back on track—if only briefly—when she joined the Frank Cooley Company, touring mainly in southern California. The two-week run began on September 26 at the Loring Theatre in Riverside. Wealthy Minneapolis businessman Charles Loring, who summered in Riverside, had built the 1,000-seat theatre in 1889. Frank Cooley, primarily known for his comedy roles, was the company's leading man. Cooley hired fourteen-year-old Verna as a soubrette to entertain between the acts, but he also cast her in supporting roles in eight of the ten productions. Earlier in the season, the troupe had played Reno, Nevada, where Cooley signed on a seven-year-old redhead named Olga Steck, who also sang and danced between the acts of the Riverside engagement. Steck would go on to become the first woman to establish a following on radio. This led to parts in a handful of Broadway musicals, including *Ziegfeld Follies of 1923* and *China Rose*. Steck's life ended in suicide when she plunged from the twelfth story of a San Francisco hotel in 1935.

Neither Verna nor Olga Steck received any press coverage in the *Riverside Daily Press*; that honor went to the company's leading lady, Gladys Kingsbury. A makeshift scrapbook maintained by Clara Felton reveals an assortment of clippings from this brief engagement, including playbills from *Tom Sawyer, A Daughter of Dixie,* and *The Silver Dagger*. Why Verna left the Cooley company on October 6 remains a mystery. Since the other clippings in this album are all from either Verna's days with Jessie Shirley or Pearl Allen, it is believed that her stint with the Frank Cooley Company was the only occasion during 1904 that she performed with any troupe other than the Allen Stock Company. For much of 1904 and early 1905, the whereabouts of the Feltons and Pearl remain a mystery, but it is quite reasonable to believe that Verna and Clara were in close contact with Pearl during late fall of 1904. The strong bond of friendship that had grown between Clara and Pearl would very soon ensure that neither financial difficulties nor physical distance would ever separate them again.

CHAPTER 5

━━━•◆•━━━

MISS VERNA FELTON AND THE ALLEN STOCK COMPANY

In the closing days of 1904, Tacoma, Washington was living up to its nickname, "The City of Destiny," so called because the area was chosen to be the site of the western terminus of the Northern Pacific Railroad in 1873. By the turn of the twentieth century, not one, but four, continental railroads terminated in Tacoma. Situated on a peninsula at the southern end of the Puget Sound, the city offered splendid views of Mount Rainier and Commencement Bay, attracting many visitors by rail. With a population approaching fifty thousand, the busiest spot in the city was at the center of downtown, near the intersection of Ninth and "C" Streets, where the theatre district was located. In a house on North "J" Street there lived a family whose fourth-born, a toddler named Harry Lillis Crosby and later called Bing, would one day share the movie screen with Verna Felton.

Tacoma was indeed a city of personal destiny for Verna. In this city, on December 15, 1904, her mother Clara Felton wed Pearl Ruben Allen. This union, which would not be broken for thirty-five years, provided Verna unwavering guidance and constant support as her stage career grew and developed. Pearl had always highly regarded her talent, and now, as her stepfather, he could guide her career with an even more personal touch. Pearl, Clara, and Verna made their first home in Tacoma at 621 South Tacoma Avenue, but later lived conveniently nearer the theater district at 911 South "C" Street. With Pearl's decision to re-establish his troupe as a resident stock company in Tacoma, the little family of three would finally be able to put down some roots.

The only available venue for Pearl Allen's company in early 1905 was the Edison Theater, a small nickelodeon, which had most recently housed a vaudeville show. The Edison was a part of the impressive Tudor-style Tacoma Theater complex, built in 1889 on the corner of Ninth and "C" Street. With brother Arden acting as proprietor and Pearl as business manager, the theater's name was changed to the Odeon, which reflected the building's original use. The *Tacoma Daily Ledger* explained: "Its name has been changed because the management wants everything new. The theater has a new company, a new idea of performance and

Verna in *My Lady Nell*, Odeon Theatre, Tacoma, 1905.

a new manager . . . A complete drama, that has not been cut down to a skeleton, will be presented with clever specialties between the acts, making a continuous performance of two and a half hours." The bills, which changed on Mondays, ran for six nights, just as they had during the Vancouver engagement. The opening bill on February 13 featured Verna in the title role of *My Lady Nell*, a melodrama set in an 1870s California mining camp. New members of the company included Clarke Wilson, Lee Morris, and Helen Davenport. Mrs. P. R. Allen, performing under the name of Clara Lawrence, completed the cast as Moll Casey. (Arden Allen's wife Phoebe was not performing as Dorothy Davis during this season because she was expecting their firstborn, Arden Joseph Allen, who would be delivered on March 12 in Tacoma.)

By now, Verna, at fourteen, had lost most of the round cheeks of childhood while the signature nose she inherited from her father had begun to appear more prominent. She posed for Tacoma photographer H. F. Coombs in her rustic *My Lady Nell* costume, but in another pose she looked every inch the soubrette, modeling a fluffy Floradora hat, off-the-shoulder dress flounced at the knee, black silk stockings and spool heels. Judging by all appearances, Little Verna Felton was no more. However, Pearl managed to squeeze out one last drop of the child phenomenon when he presented Verna in her signature piece *The Real Lord Lenox* one final week, beginning February 20. Renamed as *Morey the Mouse*, perhaps as a ploy to attract former Allen Stock Company patrons who might not recognize the plot hidden behind the new title, the play was performed daily at the 3 p.m. matinee and twice each evening at 7:30 and 9:00 p.m. Admission was ten cents for any seat in the house. One of Verna's specialties during this run was "Spooning in an Automobile," written by former troupe member Charles E. Royal.

After only four weeks at the Odeon, the Allen troupe packed up and moved to the nearby Orpheum Theatre at 923 South "C" Street. Pearl realized during the first week at the Odeon that its small stage and equally cramped auditorium were unsuited to their needs so when he was approached by rival theater manager W. H. Harbeck of the Orpheum, he signed on for an eight weeks' run. Business

Verna Felton the soubrette, Odeon Theatre, Tacoma, 1905.

was so fantastic, with scores of people regularly turned away, that Pearl and company remained at the Orpheum an additional six weeks, closing there on June 18. One novel tactic that enticed patrons each week was the positioning of a motion picture camera facing the exit, filming audience members as they left the matinee. The moving pictures were shown after performances the following week to the delight of chuckling audience members who pointed at the familiar faces on the screen.

After a brief rest, the Allen company began another run in Tacoma on July 3, this time at the Star Theater, formerly the Lyceum, at 312 South Ninth Street. This engagement proved to be one of the most profitable ones Pearl and Verna would ever know, lasting for an astounding sixty weeks. For their initial bill at the Star, actor William V. Mong was hired to star in the patriotic play *True to His Flag*. Born in Pennsylvania in 1875, Mong would go on to direct more than thirty silent films and appear in almost two hundred others, including *Cleopatra, Treasure Island*, and *The Last of the Mohicans*, until shortly before his death in 1940. In the coming decade, he would figure prominently in the lives of Verna and the Allens when they ventured into the film medium.

For the remainder of 1905, Verna would continue to win fans in Tacoma. Her audiences enjoyed her best when she played comedic roles, particularly those of tomboy or country bumpkin. One such heroine was Mulvina Sophie Hoskins in *Dad's Girl*, a comedy originally produced on Broadway in 1884. Mulvina is the adopted daughter of an old western roustabout who has earned a mint and retired to the East. Verna, as Mulvina, delighted audiences as she solves a series of thefts and murders. In *My Pardner*, a comedy sometimes known as *Tennessee's Pardner*, Verna also scored as Tennessee Kent, a girl from Smoky Mountain, Tennessee, who meets all sorts of Wild West characters during a search for her father in the hills of Nevada. (The play had nothing whatsoever to do with Bret Harte's 1869 short story of the same title, although both works involved mining camps and gamblers.) Souvenir portraits of Verna as Tennessee were given to theater patrons during the week of August 19.

On October 9, Pearl Allen unveiled a new production, The Heritage of the Red, written especially for Verna by the Allens' friend, poet and playwright Herbert Bashford, a resident of the Northwest who spent most of his time in Washington. Meg McIvor, the play's heroine, is the well-educated, imaginative, and romantic daughter of a respected frontiersman who has Native American ancestry. When she falls in love with a young Philadelphian landscape artist, Meg will not consent to marry him without his aristocratic mother's approval. The snobbish Mrs. Terraine, who has never met Meg, derides the idea of marriage with a girl who has "tainted blood." When Meg learns of this, she disappears, assumes the name of Frances Fairweather, and becomes a novelist. A year later Meg meets Mrs. Terraine at a seaside resort, and they become fast friends. When Mrs. Terraine learns of Meg's true identity, she admits that the "heritage of the red man" has not marred the beauty or accomplishments of Meg McIvor and readily consents to the marriage.

The Star Theater was crowded on the opening night of *The Heritage of the Red*, and the attendance increased at each subsequent performance. An article in the March 1906 issue of *Sunset Magazine* maintained that previous to the

Verna as Tennessee Kent in *Tennessee's Pardner,*
Star Theater, Tacoma, 1905.

creation of this play, successful dramas involving miscegenation contained
invariable denouements where proof was produced that the heroine did not have
"tainted blood." Therefore the writer saw Bashford's work as progressive and
quickly credited Verna for her ability to essay the role of Meg:

> Miss Felton was lionized for her pronounced victory in the
> first play written for her . . . Miss Felton is known as the child-
> star. She is only fifteen years of age. A child in years, thoughts
> and actions: her work is of a most remarkable nature. Time
> that can be spared from her duties at the theater, in which she
> is either engaged in portraying parts or in studying those for
> the coming week's bill, or in the casual routine duties of home
> life, is spent in the company of girls of her own age, all of them
> pupils at the public schools. Miss Felton is pretty, wears her
> well-tailored gowns tastily, and shows the utmost discretion in
> all of her actions. She is modest to a degree, and off the stage
> is an example to children of her age as to what a young woman
> of fifteen should be. Her homelife is ideal; all that an unselfish
> and respectful little miss should prove to be to her parents. She
> is gifted with a remarkable memory, studies assiduously, and
> performs her work admirably well.

The Tacoma Daily Ledger, however, did offer Verna some constructive criticism:

> Miss Felton's handling of the second act, where she leaves home and lover to make a name for herself and win Mrs. Terraine's consent, shows careful study and endeavor. It would, however, bear slight repression and a little less halting delivery which, by the way, does not always signify emotion.

Twice Verna found herself playing roles which Jessie Shirley made popular during their days together. On July 10, 1905, Verna opened with a week's performances as Louise, the blind sister in *The Two Orphans*, while Miss Desmond Kelly played the part of her sister Henriette. Originally produced on Broadway in 1874, Eugene Cormon and Adolphe d'Ennery's drama told the tale of two orphaned sisters living during the French Revolution who are separated after each is seized by unsavory characters. Louise is forced to beg for coins, even in the snowiest weather, on the porch of the church at the Place St. Sulpice. She and her sister, whose situation is equally miserable, are reunited in the end. The Broadway production was an outstanding success, and its star Kate Claxton bought the rights and toured in it, off and on, until her retirement. Shortly before Verna played Louise in the Tacoma engagement, the play had been revived on Broadway starring Grace George, Margaret Illington, and Clara Blandick, the last becoming world famous as Auntie Em in the 1939 film *The Wizard of Oz*.

Another role even more identified with Jessie Shirley was that of Cigarette in *Under Two Flags*, which opened on October 16. Verna, according to the *Tacoma Daily Ledger*, handled this difficult role "admirably," citing the play's success as dependent upon Cigarette, a *vivandiere*, or civilian provisioner to an army outpost, in this case one in Algiers. The hero, Bertie Cecil, played by leading man Russell Reed, falls in love with Cigarette, who saves his life on two occasions. In the concluding scene, she takes a bullet meant for him during a duel, dying in her lover's arms. Theda Bara would play this heroine in a silent film version in 1916, while Claudette Colbert essayed the part twenty years later with Ronald Colman as Bertie Cecil.

Throughout the Star Theater engagement, Verna continued to play boys' roles in productions such as *The Stowaway, Hills of Arkansaw, The Silver King, The Girl and the Sheperd*, and even *The Count of Monte Cristo*, in which she played Albert DeMorcef, who befriends the play's hero during his time in Rome. In a supporting role in the drama *In Indiana*, Verna brought down the house as Sammy Thatcher, a country boy who is forced to wear a barrel when his clothes are stolen during a skinny-dipping spree. In January 1906, Verna reprised her role of street urchin Ned in *The Black Flag*, a part she had first played in Vancouver two years previously. As an obvious promotional tactic to revitalize an older production, Pearl renamed the play *Brother Against Brother*. The *Daily Ledger*'s review of its initial performance provided Verna, now maturing toward womanhood, with a

A teenage Verna Felton, 1905.

rare negative comment: "If any criticism of her portrayal of Ned, the waif, is to be made it would be of little feminine touches which the dainty leading woman of the Allen company simply cannot help putting into her acting. When she is with Harry Glyndon, her friend, she occasionally betrays her sex by little caresses, which a boy would never think of giving a grown up man. In the fourth act, however, where, wounded by a revolver shot intended for her friend, she gives up her life for him, she does superbly."

In August 1905, Phoebe Allen, acting under the name of Dorothy Davis, rejoined the troupe after a rest following the birth of her son Arden Joseph Allen, Pearl's nephew. Pearl chose for her the role of Marguerite Gautier in a version of the classic drama *Camille*. Dorothy's portrayal of the doomed heroine was called "clever" by the *Daily Ledger*, winning her repeated curtain calls on opening night. Dorothy would perform as leading lady for the company until February 1906 when she was replaced by Marie Thompson.

Meanwhile Verna's mother, alternately billed in character roles as either Clara Lawrence or Clara Allen, earned positive nods here and there in the productions at the Star. She had once been noted as "weak" while performing *Trilby* in Vancouver in 1904, but since that time Clara had picked up many tricks of the trade. Following Pearl's coaching and the criticism of the more experienced players in the troupe, she began to come into her own as the company's character woman, and as such was expected to handle any assignment from an old street beggar to a grand dame. Clara, by now in her early forties, had developed the face and figure of a performer who could fill such roles. In the summer and fall of 1905, she sank her teeth into parts such as Prudence, the fair-weather friend of Marguerite in *Camille* and the domineering Mrs. Hay in *My Pardner*. The *Tacoma Daily Ledger* praised her as "natural and humorous" as Mrs. Terraine in *The Heritage of the Red*. As Bridget McNamara in *Caught in the Web*, Clara employed an effective Irish accent, owing that natural ability, of course, to the influence of her father who had been a native of Dublin. In years to follow, Clara would become a favorite with audiences who enjoyed her as an individual and an artist.

Pearl Allen made the news when an article appeared in the November 7 edition of the *Tacoma Daily Ledger*, publicizing his response to statements made by Arch Selwyn, a play broker for Selwyn & Company of New York and representative of the American Dramatists Club, who claimed that the Allen Stock Company was guilty of producing plays without paying the necessary royalties. Selwyn told the Seattle press that he made the trip to the Northwest to prosecute play pirates in the Seattle and Tacoma areas, specifically naming Pearl's company as one of those under investigation. "I have been expecting just such a thing for some time," Pearl told the *Ledger*. 'We have absolutely no fear of them, for the Sullivan & Considine company, which controls this house [The Star Theater], has always paid the royalties for the plays we use. In fact, the Selwyn company only recently sent us a list of their plays, but we have never used one, getting the greater of our plays from the Sanger & Jordan and Darcey & Wolfard companies. All they [Selwyn] will have to do is to investigate the matter and they will find that the Allen Stock company is not stealing any plays . . . John Considine, one of the proprietors of this house, is now in the East arranging for a new set of plays, but it will not necessitate his return to settle the matter. I think our name was mentioned as among the Seattle, Portland and Spokane houses to be prosecuted simply because we happen to be the only stock company now in this city.'"

Pearl's confidence in partners "Big Tim" Sullivan and John W. Considine was well founded. The pair had been successful and respectable proprietors of the Seattle vaudeville circuit for years. No news of any litigation appeared in subsequent editions of the *Ledger*, so it is assumed that Selwyn's investigation of the Allen Stock Company was absolutely groundless. Walter Waters explained the possibilities of such a situation in his doctoral dissertation, *George L. Baker and the Baker Stock Company*:

> An unscrupulous producer might obtain pirated scripts of the latest successes by dealing with firms which specialized in this illegal service. Such organizations sold only the scripts and not the rights to perform the plays. After altering the name of the play, the names of the characters and the locale, the producers presented the plays to the public. such practices not only defrauded playwrights and owners of their royalties, but hurt the honest stock producer who also needed new material badly in order to keep his audience's interest alive.

The following spring, another newsworthy event, far more unforgettable than Selwyn's unfounded accusations, occurred during the Allens' engagement at the Star. This tragedy would forever be associated with their eighteen months in Tacoma. On April 19, 1906, the *Tacoma Daily Ledger* screamed: "SAN FRANCISCO LAID IN RUINS: Conflagration Follows Earthquake and Flames, Sweeping on Unchecked, Envelop Whole Business District and Waterfront." Verna and the Allens anxiously read for details of the devastating fire and earthquake, still considered to be America's greatest urban catastrophe. The quake occurred on the previous morning at 5:12 a.m., with fires breaking out immediately and lasting, for what seemed like an interminable four days. By the next morning, the press estimated the loss of life at 1,000, but that number would soon grow to at least twice that amount. 28,000 buildings were destroyed, leaving half of the city's population homeless. Many sites familiar to Verna and the Allens were drastically affected, if not demolished. Fischer's Concert House, by this time known as Fischer's Theatre and located at 122 O'Farrell Street, where Verna performed for one week prior to being discovered by Jessie Shirley, was totally lost in the fire.

San Jose, the city Verna called home, experienced considerable damage as well. The block of South Second Street between Santa Clara and San Fernando Streets suffered tremendous destruction following the quake and the fire that rocked San Jose. Fortunately, water remained in the fire hydrants, so the blaze that swept northward and southward was soon brought under control. Falling victim to the quake were the Hall of Justice, St. Patrick's Roman Catholic Church, the new high school, and the annex of the Hotel Vendome, among many other landmarks. Ninety percent of the chimneys in the city toppled over. The stately Normal

School building, where Verna took elocution lessons as a young girl, was thought to have sustained the earthquake with just a few fallen bricks, but closer inspection revealed serious structural damage, this despite the addition of iron straps built into the brick work during construction in 1881. The edifice's stability had been hailed by the *San Jose Mercury* in 1892 as "second to no building in the State." However, it was never reoccupied following the quake, and it fell victim to the wrecking ball in 1908. The 3,000-pound brass bell once housed in this building's majestic tower can be found today on the grounds of San Jose State University, near the Tower Hall and Morris Dailey Auditorium. The Victory Theatre, where Verna and Clara met Pearl Allen during the benefit for the Galveston Flood victims and where Verna joined the Jessie Shirley company, survived with only damage to the building's front, which collapsed onto the ticket booth, located at the street entrance. A postcard of the scene revealed nearby potted palms left undisturbed. The Unique Theatre, which represented Verna's 1904 foray into vaudeville, was not so fortunate. The entire façade collapsed, and the structure was subsequently demolished.

Verna's brother Clayton was not among the San Joseans left dead or injured by the destruction, but he had other worries. At twenty-three, he had still not established himself in a lucrative career, and he tended to get into trouble. According to the May 14 edition of the *San Jose Mercury*, published less than a month after the quake, Clayton was sentenced to thirty days in jail for an undisclosed offense. Unfortunately, he would perpetuate this type of irresponsibility for most of his life. Perhaps his character flaws reflected the upheaval of his formative years. While yet an infant, he was abandoned by his natural father. At sixteen, he had lost the only father figure he had known. Consequently, Clara, while pursuing Verna's success, had been largely absent from San Jose for the past six years, leaving Clayton essentially on his own. Following his incarceration, Clayton would seek a fresh start in Oakland, where he would find work as a grocery clerk. To cut expenses he boarded with Clara's cousin William George Lawrence, an industrious electrician residing with his wife and seven children on Sixty-Third Street. Besides being grateful to her cousin for allowing Clayton to reside under his roof, Clara hoped that Lawrence would exert the proper influence on her wayward son. Fortunately, no one in the Lawrence household had sustained injuries in the recent disaster. Oakland, then California's second largest city, suffered considerable earthquake damage but escaped the devastating fires that crippled San Francisco.

Salinas, the birthplace of Verna Felton, was also badly shaken by the great earthquake, although there was no loss of life. Over 14 buildings were damaged, including her father's fraternal gathering place, the Knights of Pythias building. One structure, the Ford & Sanborn Dry Goods Store, was completely flattened.

Tacomans responded to the disaster spontaneously and liberally. By the evening of April 19, they had raised $15,000 and gathered 175 tons of provisions, including canned fish and beef, ham, bacon, crackers, condensed milk, flour, and potatoes, all of which was sent by steamer to San Francisco. Less than twenty-four hours after the catastrophe, H. M. Owens, the manager of the Star Theater in Tacoma, decided to host a benefit matinee with all proceeds going to the sufferers in San Francisco. The benefit, held on April 24, featured Verna and the Allen company in a playlet titled *The Littlest Girl*, as well as a musical program with acts provided by performers from other theaters.

Later that spring, Sullivan and Considine, who owned not only the Star but multiple theaters on the West Coast, offered Pearl a deal he found very appealing. The renovations of their theatre in Portland, Oregon, also named The Star, would be completed by third weekend of August. The partners wanted the Allen Stock Company to alternately perform, at eight-week intervals, in Tacoma and Portland. Pearl went one better, suggesting that he form another stock company, to be called Allen Stock Company #2, which could perform in Tacoma while the original company played in Portland and vice versa. For the second company, he chose a slate of new actors, headed by Bertha Knatvold, later to become one of Washington's leading suffragettes, and Ted Brackett.

On Sunday, August 19, 1906, the original Allen Stock Company ended its lengthy engagement at Tacoma's Star with matinee and evening performances of J. K. Tillotson's *Lynwood*, another Civil War drama whose main characters were on opposing sides, in this case a Kentucky belle and her lover, a Union officer. Souvenir photographs of the entire company were given to each patron on this final evening. One troupe member, Loring Kelly, a Tacoma native who had been with the company for fifteen months, elected to join the engagement in Portland. Engaged to be married in four months, Kelly decided to tie the knot while still in Tacoma, on the stage of the Star after the evening performance of August 16.

The original company, including Arthur Ashley, Charles King, Marie Thompson, Ethel Roberts, Forrest Seabury, Irving Kennedy, and Clara and Verna left for Portland where it opened on August 20 at the Star Theatre, located at Park and Washington Streets. According to Lester Schilling's doctoral dissertation *The History of the Theatre in Portland, Oregon 1846–1959*, the Star Theatre, which opened in early 1905, "never had a company that proved to be very popular until they booked the Allen Stock Company." It is clear from reading the August editions of the *Oregonian* that Pearl Allen had to prove his company's worth to the drama critics (and the public) in that city. Though the Star nor the Allen company received as much press coverage in this newspaper as the Baker Theater, the reviews were quite positive from the start, and the audiences flocked to the small theater, "newly painted and clean as a bandbox." Every seat was filled on opening night for the performance of the melodrama *Caught in the Web*. Prices were 10, 20, and 30 cents for evening performances while daily matinees cost 10 cents for any seat. Amazingly, the company performed matinees and evenings for twenty-one consecutive days until announcing that three afternoons a week would be reserved for rehearsals of the following week's production.

On August 28, the *Oregonian*'s A. H. Ballard, in his review of the second production, recognized the Allen product for what it was, but admitted that Portlanders were getting a bargain for the small admission price:

> Again melodrama, lurid, streaming, streaking, limpid, startling, terrific, thrilling, tearful, thundering, blazing! If I were a neophyte I would say, Shoot the luck, why cannot I sit down and give myself up to the absolute emotional debauch of this sort of limitless melodrama, and not think of trying to tell someone else about what happened afterward? But, oh, it is grandish! It is not only 'Arry and 'Arriet who attend. I see some of the best of them quietly going into the doors of the Star Theatre. The house cannot hold the people who try to get in each evening . . . the company might be improved upon in some details. But the performance is ample for the price. And the story as given hits the people's hearts and feelings with an unmistakably resounding thud. They all come out after the show wild-eyed, smiling, crying, glowing.

Pearl Allen knew what the people wanted, and once again he was playing to that same crowd, this time in Portland.

By this time, Verna's age was correctly reported as sixteen, but newspaper photographs of her wearing flower-bedecked gowns and a large pompadour make her appear several years older. While these feminine photographs appeared in the *Sunday Oregonian*'s theatre section, Verna was still winning rave reviews for her "trouser roles," especially Chucky in *The Stowaway* and Albert De Morcef in *The Count of Monte Cristo*. "She's a most promising young actress," the *Oregonian* asserted, "and, unless all signs fail, will develop into an important star sometime."

Verna Felton and the Allen Stock Company soon won a loyal following from Portland audiences. Lester Schilling, in his dissertation, explained how a resident company could achieve such success: "The very nature of the resident stock company allows it a closer relation to the community than the passing road companies are able to enjoy. The resident personnel become familiar figures on the streets as well as in the theatres of the community. Many bring families and establish homes, meeting their neighbors in the stores and shops of the town." Likewise, Walter Waters addressed the important relationship of a leading player, such as Verna, not only to the audiences but also to his or her company, stating that "fifty per cent of the actor's value to the company lay in his appeal to the public and in the local following he developed during his tenure with the company."

The Allen Stock Company faced some stiff competition while in Portland. George L. Baker had recently revived his own resident stock company after several unsuccessful seasons in the city. For the 1906-07 season, Baker had carefully assembled a troupe so strong that Eastern stock managers had offered to use Baker's company the following summer in their own stock houses. According to Waters, the Baker Stock Company was soon "regarded among actors as one of the four best stock organizations in the United States." When interviewed by Waters in 1962, Verna Felton, speaking of the Allen Stock Company, asserted, "We were every bit as good as the Baker Company; we were just younger and less experienced."

In his doctoral dissertation, Waters delineated the functions served by the Baker Stock Company during the first two decades of the twentieth century: "It was a source of civic pride because it was a locally organized and produced form of professional entertainment. It provided a needed social outlet for the community, a place to meet friends and enjoy a few moments of escape from the commonplace. Finally, it provided a source of plays otherwise not available to the community either because of the financial expense of such plays when offered by touring organizations or because of the lack of such organizations due to the relative isolation of a specific community." The same list could be used to describe the purposes the Allen Stock Company served during its fifty-five weeks in Portland.

For the thirty-seven weeks the Allen Stock Company played the Star, the bills were mainly melodramas, with Verna playing the lead in most. Some were strictly "old hat," particularly *Caprice, Moths, Two Orphans, Under Two Flags, The Sultan's Daughter*, all of which had been staged by the Jessie Shirley Company several years before. Verna assumed all of Shirley's roles in these productions, receiving high praise for emotional parts in *Caprice* and *Under Two Flags*, the latter for her "remarkable nerve and coolness" during the scene in which the heroine rides a horse up an incline. Later in the engagement, after months of melodramas, when Pearl moved Verna to more comic roles, the reviewer for the *Oregonian* was almost surprised to witness her capability in such roles, notably those in *Humbug, My Friend from India*, and *Deserted at the Altar*. Meanwhile, she garnered praise as Olga, the persecuted Jewess, in the melodrama *Lost in Siberia* and as Lady Babbie in James M. Barrie's *The Little Minister*. The latter play became a runaway success when it opened on Broadway in 1897 with Maude Adams as Lady Barbara, the daughter of a Scottish lord, who sympathizes with discontented weavers and their labor strike. When the Allen Stock Company's production of this play opened on January 7, 1907, the *Oregonian* asserted:

> No actress need hope to equal [Maude Adams's] role—that has
> long since been settled, but when a leading woman, particularly
> a very young one, succeeds in giving a performance of the part
> that disarms unkind criticism, her work is certainly worthy of
> unusual commendation. For that reason the work of Verna
> Felton at the Star this week is far and away above the

commonplace. Miss Felton plays the delightful heroine of Barrie's Scottish idyll with splendid effect, putting into it much of the charm that the critical associate with the part.

Despite this exceptional praise, the *Oregonian* held some reservations regarding Verna's ability, and understandably so. For the entire run at the Star, Verna was only sixteen years old. The *Oregonian* identified her as the "youngest leading woman in the West, if not in the United States." For this reason, the *Oregonian's* comments following the opening night of *Northern Lights* on April 15 are probably very appropriate:

> In the part of "the little Major" Verna Felton has an assignment that is well suited to her and she plays it well. If this clever young actress would confine her efforts to such parts she would achieve much better results than she has at times when she has essayed roles entirely too mature for a girl of her age.

The *Oregonian's* reviewer believed that Verna's best parts were her "country lass" or "trouser" roles. When the Allen Stock Company staged its final bill, *For Mother's Sake*, at the Star on April 29, the *Oregonian* hailed it as "one of the strongest bills the organization has offered since it opened its season at the Star last August." Verna received the sole credit:

> Verna Felton is good at anything in the show line. Last night at the Star where the Allen Stock Company presented "For Mother's Sake," a rural drama by Carrie Ashley Clarke, she undertook the difficult part of a boy. She not only attempted but filled the part and gave a performance or a character study of a real, human boy, of the kind full of daring and mischief, but also honest and upright. Any young woman can try to act as a boy, but those who can give a sensible interpretation of the trying part are as scarce as Negroes in Siberia. Miss Felton was everything that could be wished for. Last night she was an ideal boy. She took the part of Joe Pemberton, a bright little diamond, according to the programme. When a mere youth, Joe leaves his mother's and sets out to find the men who were responsible for his father's imprisonment, who is wrongly accused of murder. By chance he locates the right persons in a Western mining camp, and after many stirring episodes unites father and mother.

On May 6, the Allen Stock Company moved from the Star to the Lyric Theatre, a small but neat brick building at 133 Seventh Street near Alder Street,

Verna Felton, Portland, Oregon, 1907.

located there since being organized in 1903 by Lawrence "Larry" Keating and T. W. Murphy. (Keating, born in Illinois in 1872, was the father of actor Larry Keating, who played supporting roles on television's *The George Burns and Gracie Allen Show* and *Mr. Ed.*) Keating and Murphy were competing with several other successful Portland theatres, including the Baker, Marquam, and Heilig. When they disbanded their own stock company, Keating and Murphy asked the Allen Stock Company to move to the Lyric as a permanent fixture, hoping that their fans would follow them. Meanwhile, the owners of the Star did not miss a beat; Sullivan and Considine organized a new company, all of whom were new to Portland.

The Allens' first production at the 950-seat Lyric was the farce *Brown's in Town*, followed by the melodrama *Behind the Mask*. According to the *Oregonian*, Pearl's strategy was to "give plays of every character and avoid a monotonous procession of similar bills." He was successful in this endeavor, and the Allen Stock Company gained popularity during its stay at the Lyric. In general, Verna received warm reviews from the *Oregonian*, most notably in *The Girl from Albany*. The only negative comment in that paper was found in the May 28 review of the comedy *Polly Primrose*: "It is one of those girlish, unaffected parts which suit [Verna Felton] admirably and her work is excellent in every detail excepting that she occasionally forgets her Southern accent." For four weeks beginning June 16, Verna took a much-needed vacation, with Josephine Deffrey assuming the leading roles in her absence. Meanwhile, Clara Allen earned the title of "Portland's favorite character actress," garnering praise for her roles in *The Westerner, All the Comforts of Home* and *Whose Baby Are You?*, in which she played "as natural a 'Biddy' as one could expect to find, hanging over a back fence, and making reflections on the character of her next door neighbor."

On September 1, the *Oregonian* announced that the Allen Stock Company would be leaving Portland for San Jose, where Pearl had secured a theater of his own. It had been almost three years since the Allens and Verna had left California for the Northwest. It is quite possible that by the fall of 1907, the Allens and Verna were homesick for San Jose and their native state. Their steady runs in Tacoma and Portland had not afforded them a vacation of any length during this period. San Jose would provide the perfect location for a respite, considering that Clara and Verna still knew many people in that city with whom they could renew friendships. The Portland engagement ended on September 8 with a performance of *Jess of the Bar Z Ranch*, a melodrama of ranch life in New Mexico.

After arriving in San Jose, the Allens enjoyed a period of rest, or to employ theatrical vernacular, they "laid off." This respite also provided a time for planning and rehearsals for the upcoming fall season, as well as for necessary theatre renovations. Pearl had leased a small theater, formerly known as the Redmond, after its manager, Edward Redmond, abandoned it to move his stock company to the Jose Theatre. Pearl made improvements to this venue, renaming it the Auditorium Theater, and while he sincerely intended that the Allen Stock Company would become a permanent stock organization at the Auditorium, only a few days would pass before he would deeply regret this investment.

Opening night was October 20. A very mature photo of Verna appeared in that morning's *San Jose Mercury and Herald*. Her black décolleté evening gown, accented with matching elbow-length gloves and hair ornaments, made her appear much older than her seventeen years, certainly in stark contrast to how her San Jose friends remembered her as a young girl. Herbert Bashford, the Allens' friend who had written *The Heritage of the Red* with Verna in mind, was then a drama critic for the *Mercury and Herald*. In his review following the opening of the Allens' tried-and-true *Jess of the Bar Z Ranch*, Bashford was complimentary on the entire company, but especially of Verna: "Miss Felton, as Jess, played with the usual earnestness which characterizes her acting. There is nothing 'stagey' about her work. It seems to be the natural expression of one who lives the character portrayed, and she does nothing simply for effect." For the second week's bill, Pearl chose Eugene Walter's *The Undertow*, a political drama, which had opened and closed quickly that spring on Broadway. He snatched it up as soon as it became available to stock companies, perhaps because its plot was similar to the much more successful *The Man of the Hour*. Bashford was quick to notice the great expense outlaid on the realistic staging of the first act, which took place in the editorial rooms of a metropolitan newspaper. While *The Undertow* did not involve a great love interest like that of *The Man of the Hour*, Verna was on hand to play a reporter's sweetheart.

Then, on November 1, Pearl's daily advertisements in the *San Jose Daily Mercury* abruptly ended, a sure sign that things were not going well financially for the Allen Stock Company. While they had maintained their standard popular ticket prices of 10, 20, and 30 cents, the costs of managing a theater and its troupe far outweighed the box office. Its performances of *A Stranger in a Strange Land* were quickly cancelled, and by November 9, the entire company had retreated to Portland. Along the way, a washout in southern Oregon slowed their progress. Instead of arriving at the scheduled time of eleven o'clock on the night of the 11th, the train pulled into the Union Depot the next morning at four. With no taxis running, the unhappy troupe was forced to walk eleven blocks to their lodgings, the newly constructed Calumet Hotel on Park Street.

The Allen Stock Company re-opened at the Lyric, whose manager announced in the *Sunday Oregonian* that their return followed a splendidly successful engagement in San Jose. Such false promotional ploys were unnecessary. Portland audiences already loved Verna Felton and the Allen Stock Company, and they were eager to see more of their talent. Pearl lined up over twenty plays, a mix of old and new, that he had never before staged in Portland. Since the troupe was already familiar with their aborted San Jose comedy, Pearl staged *A Stranger in a Strange Land* for the initial week of their return. All of the returning players, including Verna, Forrest Seabury, Irving Kennedy, Charles Ayres, Clara Allen, and Marie Thompson, were greeted by a round of applause upon their entrances for the opening performance on November 18. While she did not have a major role in the featured play, Verna received kind words from the reviewer: "It must be said that Miss Felton is the whole thing when she is on the stage and deserves all honor."

Verna's popularity with Portlanders is further evidenced by a rather comical fashion spread featured in the *Sunday Oregonian* two weeks after her return to Portland. The article, written by an anonymous female reporter, but photographed by a man, traced the increasingly popular fad of shortened skirts for rainwear or shopping. Because Verna had been seen on the Portland streets wearing this new style, she was chosen to "illustrate the foolishness and the discomforts of the long skirt for street wear and shopping, as against the freedom and good sense of the short skirt." For decades the traditional street attire for women was dictated to include skirts that reached the ground and high-top shoes that left no skin or stockings exposed when a lady was required to lift her skirts to ascend steps, board streetcars, and traverse mud puddles. Verna was quoted in the *Oregonian* on December 1:

> "I haven't a single long skirt of my own," said the little actress with pride, "except of course my stage costumes, and if I'm going to demonstrate the agonies of the long skirt for The Oregonian, I'll have to burrow into mamma's wardrobe. My mother does not go in for the long-skirt foolishness either, but she towers above me some three or four inches at the waistline, and perhaps one of her skirts will do."

> Whereupon Miss Felton delved into the depths of the maternal clothes press and emerged with a green walking skirt.

> "Here you are," said she, as she slipped the garment over her head, seized a couple of bundles at random and popped open her mother's umbrella. "This is how we have to struggle when we go shopping in long skirts. Hat all askew, pompadour giving way under the strain, bundles bobbing about and gouging other people in the ribs, umbrella worse than useless, and skirts—well, look at the skirts. The best one can do is to grab a futile handful of the folds at the sides or front, and the rest must come trailing along in the mud. Ten to one somebody is going to step on that trailing length, too, and r-r-r-rip will go two or three yards of binding! Why, it distresses me to just to see some poor misguided woman suffering all these agonies, when she might be spared them all just by the simple means of whacking off the superfluous length with the family shears!"

> "Now just note the difference," said Miss Felton, slipping out of the long skirt and appearing in her own street costume. "I'll take up all these things I was struggling with before, umbrella, bundles and all, and show you how easy it all is when you wear the short skirt. Look! It's just as easy as eating bonbons!" and she demonstrated, with an untroubled handling of all the packages and a graceful tilting of the umbrella.

> "And there's something else, too," whispered the little actress to

the woman reporter, and waving the camera man into an adjoining room for a moment. "Do you know what one should wear under the short skirt? I am going to show you, and if you want a picture of it, I'll pose for you, just for the sake of comfort the tip may bring to a lot of other women who don't know about it yet!"

Off came the short skirt, and Miss Felton stood arrayed in the "bloomer skirt." The bloomers were of black cloth made extremely full, so as to serve all the purposes of a skirt, and were gathered in at the bottom by elastic bands. "They are warm and comfortable, and they cannot be blown by the four winds or tangle about one's limbs, as underskirts do," said she, "they're just dandy!"

While advocating short skirts earnestly, Miss Felton does not indorse the extremes to which some enthusiasts incline. "Ankle length," said she, "or the shoe top cut for the sloppy weather, will insure comfort and guarantee against bedraggling. There is no need to carry the short skirt to extremes."

Five photographs of Verna accompanied the article, including one of her wearing her favorite outdoor costume—a short skirt of cravenette cloth, high boots, a natty little street hat, and a warm astrakhan jacket. Also shown in the photograph was her beloved canine companion Teddy, the "official ratter of the Lyric theater," who accompanied Verna on all of her morning walks. Female theatergoers gobbled up features such as this, because actresses represented stylish fashion. What they didn't know was that each performer was expected to provide his or her own costume unless appearing in a period piece. Costuming could cause a serious problem for the actress because it was quite easy to fall far into debt in order to provide the necessary clothing for their roles. For instance, Louise Kent, the second woman at the Baker theater in 1907-08, was admired by the public as a well-dressed woman, but she left the company after one season as a bankrupt because she was unable to pay the bills she had accumulated at some of Portland's leading stores. Of course, Verna, as stepdaughter of the company's manager, probably never experienced this problem.

Verna was not the only member of the Allen Stock Company receiving press coverage. Clara Allen was proving herself as a talented character actress in each production, and her popularity with Portland audiences is demonstrated not only by her regularly featured portrait in the *Sunday Oregonian* theatre section, but also by the considerable mention she was given in the weekly reviews during late 1907 and early 1908. For her role as a mother-in-law "of the cayenne variety" in *All Due to Diana*, Clara received special notice: "And if any henpecked

Clara Allen.

husband or son-in-law ever suffered from woman, let him take in this bill and see how much more his sufferings would be increased if he were to have under the same roof a woman of the style portrayed by Mrs. Allen." She also won favor as Mammy Han, a blackface character in *Cumberland '61*, and as *Caught in the Web*'s Bridget McNamara, "one of the best Irish women seen in Portland for some time." During Christmas week, Clara played Verna's wicked stepmother in daily matinees of *Cinderella*, but her following role, the mother of a villain in *Man's Broken Promises*, afforded her the opportunity to fire a revolver, prop or authentic, for the very first time. A February 11 review of *The Lawyer and the Lady* reported, "Mrs. Allen scores a decided hit as Miss Melissa Whimple, the matronly gossip, and her well enacted disgust at the raptures of the 'city girl' [played by Verna] over a bulldog she has bought at an auction is excellently done."

In early February, Daniel Flood—an original partner with Larry Keating in the management of the Lyric—returned to that capacity, replacing T. W. Murphy. Flood immediately initiated some changes, especially in the types of plays produced by the Allen Stock Company. He wanted to give audiences the opportunity to see productions more elaborate than the string of rural comedies and melodramas staged since November. For this reason, the Lyric announced that on February 24 "the most ambitious effort of Verna Felton's career will be made this week when that talented young leading woman will make her first appearance in the great emotional drama, *Camille*." The Lyric management maintained that Verna, as a seventeen-year-old, would be the youngest woman in America to ever play the famous role of courtesan Marguerite Gautier, tubercular heroine of Alexandre Dumas's 1848 novel *La Dame aux camellias*. First adapted for the Paris stage in 1852, the play became known as *Camille* in the English-speaking world, where many versions of it were produced, starring such stage greats as Lillie Langtry, Sarah Bernhardt, Mrs. Patrick Campbell, and Madame Modjeska. The *Oregonian* asserted that these actresses and others "have made it a particular study and to this day the great names among the female contingent of those who serve the god Thespis essay this role when they would demonstrate their preeminence." However, none of the famous thespians listed above were anywhere near the tender age of seventeen when playing the role of Marguerite.

In his dissertation of Portland's Baker Stock Company, theater historian Walter Waters asserted that the leading woman of a stock company was usually an experienced player between the ages of twenty-five and thirty-five. Furthermore, he maintained that during the first decade of the twentieth century, "the roles of the leading actors usually required mature, adult individuals. It was only the exceptional young actress who could present herself convincingly in the role of a Leah, Sapho, or Zaza or in any one of the other typical dramatic roles in which the leading lady was to portray a 'woman with a past.'" Waters added that, "the very young or very old leading actors were to be found only in the smaller and cheaper companies." While it is true that the Allen Stock Company was not a well-known organization outside of its circuit and that their ticket prices were indeed inexpensive compared to their competition, nothing about the Allen productions could be called "cheap." On the other hand, it would be unfair not to consider Verna's privileged position as leading lady, afforded her in part because of her relationship to Pearl. Indeed it had been a quick transition from ingénue and second woman to that of leading lady. Yet Verna's seven years of stage experience must have brought her an awareness of the importance of such a classic role as Marguerite. The part was a distinct departure from the folksy characters whom critics had come to expect Verna to portray, but both Pearl and Daniel Flood believed that Verna had proved her right to aspire to powerful roles such as this.

The Lyric claimed the role of Marguerite was the "hardest test of an actress's ability," but one that Verna seems to have passed. The Oregonian's critic on the morning of February 25 appears to have been honest:

> Miss Felton is brave to attempt the part, but not foolhardy, as the result of her first performance at the Lyric last night demonstrated. The Lyric's leading woman gives a very creditable account of herself as the heroine of the greatest problem play that has yet been written. She has conceived the part well. She does not imitate and the spectator at once forms the opinion that the young actress is playing the part in accordance with her own ideas. There are a few false notes in her work, but not many, and in the main she sustains and gets all the significance out of the lines that the ordinary theatergoer could desire.

Rupert Drum, the company's leading man, won high praise for his part as Armand Duval, Marguerite's unhappy lover, while the supporting players were singled out for their accomplishments, including Forrest Seabury as Gaston, Charles Ayres as Baron de Varville, Marie Thompson as Nichette, Irving Kennedy as Gustav, Ella Houghton as Nanine, and Clara Allen as Prudence, a role she had played two years previously in Tacoma. (Probably the most famous Prudence is that portrayed by Laura Hope Crews in the 1936 MGM film version, starring Greta Garbo. Crews and Clara Allen were of similar physical appearance, so it is easy to imagine Clara giving life to this flighty, fair-weather friend of Marguerite.)

The actress who played Marguerite in the Allens' 1905 Tacoma production was Dorothy Davis, wife of Pearl's brother Arden. Coincidentally, while Verna was playing *Camille* in Portland, Dorothy was appearing in the same city as the leading lady over at the Star, in such productions as *Way Out West, Thanksgiving Day,* and *The Texas Ranger.* Meanwhile Arden was a member of a local orchestra.

Following *Camille,* Verna repeated her roles of Olga in Lost in Siberia, now renamed *By Right of Sword* as a ploy to attract patrons who might recognize the old title, and Chucky in *The Stowaway,* which would prove to be one of the last times she would play a trouser role. In *Our New Girl,* which opened March 9, she was "screamingly funny every moment" she was onstage as Katrina, a thick-headed German servant girl who, in spite of her good intentions, always did the wrong thing. While playing the lead in *Hazel Kirke,* Verna fell ill with the mumps on March 24, and was replaced by Marie Thompson for four nights until she, too, became ill. Since Clara had taken Marie's original role, Verna was forced to get up from her sick bed on March 29 to play the role of Hazel. She was even able to open the following night in a new production called *Captain Impudence,* set during the Mexican war.

The Lyric, and its productions, appears to have been treated like the proverbial stepchild by the Portland press, especially the *Oregonian*. In a special New Year's Day edition for 1908, featuring profiles and photographs of Portland's playhouses, the Lyric was noticeably ignored. Images of the other playhouses were prominently displayed and their corresponding histories were documented in this special issue. A similar slight was evident each week in the *Sunday Oregonian's* theatre section, where announcements of the Lyric's current production rarely made the first page. Only once did a photograph of Verna appear on this first page alongside other performers at the Heilig, the Marquam Grand, the Empire, the Baker, and the Star. Additional photos of Verna, Clara, Marie Thompson, Charles Ayres, and other members of the Allen Stock Company always appeared on the second page. Was this because their establishment, a house who still charged "popular prices" of 10, 20, and 30 cents, was not taken as seriously as the others who commanded higher ticket prices? The Heilig, Marquam, and Empire theaters were homes to touring companies, while the Baker and Star, like the Lyric, housed resident stock companies. The Heilig theatre was the most expensive in the city, demanding $2.00 to $0.75 for tickets and thereby catering to patrons of upper income.

According to the research of Walter Waters, author of the dissertation *George L. Baker and the Baker Stock Company*, the Heilig productions were often "sadly disappointing. On too many occasions, the stars were surrounded with poor supporting actors and the performances were, as a result, unbalanced." Such stars included Mrs. Leslie Carter, Nance O'Neil, and De Wolfe Hopper (later the husband of Hollywood gossip columnist, Hedda Hopper). Though the touring companies could appeal to their audiences by offering performances by well-known stars, they could not develop a loyal following such as the Baker, Star, and Lyric companies were able to do. According to Waters, "Few, if any, of the touring stars were known personally to the audiences and there was, actually, little rapport between the touring organizations and the local viewers." Still the managers of the resident stock companies had to employ different strategies to entice their regular patrons to return. Beginning with Verna Felton's debut performance in *Camille*, Daniel Flood of the Lyric began showing reels of silent films between the acts to keep audiences amused during the long waits for scenery changes. He continued the use of this plan for the remainder of the Allen Stock Company's engagement. Ironically, this novel medium of entertainment, and later their successors with sound, would bring an end to stock companies across America.

In late spring 1908, Pearl received an enticing offer from William Bowen Sherman, an entertainment entrepreneur in Calgary, Alberta, who had made arrangements to lease a venue he deemed appropriate for stock company performances. Sherman, an Ohioan born in 1868, had entered show business as a circus performer while still in his teens, later working for the Ringling Brothers and the team of Forpaugh and Barnum. By 1905, after fire claimed his

Ontario theatrical investments, Sherman had formed his own stock company in Calgary. When this endeavor failed, Sherman waited a year before re-entering the entertainment business, a move that proved advantageously strategic.

During the previous fall, he had opened a cavernous skating rink on the edge of the downtown area. When not used for skating, this arena could seat almost fifty-five hundred people for special concerts and events. Sherman was on the brink of building a veritable entertainment empire in Alberta, as well as becoming recognized as the greatest showman Calgary would ever know. In 1908, he set his sights on a building formally known as the Vaudette, on Fifth Avenue East. He planned to renovate this 800-seat auditorium as Sherman's Garden, so named because he intended to install a palm garden where theatre patrons could purchase ice cream, soft drinks, and candy while attending performances. Once his physical plans were achieved, Sherman began to consider lucrative choices for an opening engagement. His connections in the entertainment world had made him aware of the successes of the Allen Stock Company, almost eight hundred miles away in Portland. He was determined to engage this troupe for the opening of Sherman's Garden on June 4.

Meanwhile, Keating and Flood of the Lyric had grown dissatisfied with the small amount of money they were making under their arrangement with the Allen Stock Company, this according to an interview Verna gave Lester Schilling in 1959. When Sherman's offer arrived, Pearl Allen decided it would be best to leave Portland. Besides, he saw the new venture as a way to introduce his troupe to new audiences and make new business connections. The Allen Stock Company had not played in Canada since its Vancouver engagement at the short-lived People's Theatre in 1904. Pearl had long felt a fondness for America's northern neighbor, and this affection, as well as his keen instincts, led him to contract with Sherman to appear for the summer season at Sherman's Garden. Little did the Allens or Verna know that this new engagement would lead to their close connections with Canada and its citizens for the next twenty-five years.

CHAPTER 6

-•◦•-

THE ALLEN PLAYERS: EN ROUTE THROUGH CANADA

On May 31, 1908, the Allen Stock Company ended their long run in Portland. Verna, who had spent two of her formative teen years in that city, was sad to leave the many friends she had made there. The *Oregonian*, while known for being less than generous with its coverage of Allen Stock Company productions, redeemed itself with this farewell notice: "During the course of its long local career, giving seven night performances and four matinees, each week the members of the Allen Company have been called upon to play a round of parts that might well dismay the average actor. There has been a sufficient variety of plays presented to thoroughly test the versatility of the members of the company. These pieces have ranged from melodrama of the most strenuous sort to the most suppressed and quiet dramas. There have been farces, and spectacular offerings, romantic plays, wild west cowpuncher affairs, and problem plays. Everything in the category from *The Man from Mexico* to *Camille* have been on the tapis, and through all this wide variety the performances have been consistently worthy." Considering the *Oregonian's* previous treatment of the company and the Lyric itself, this was a fine time to sing their praises. Other companies would follow the Allen Stock Company at both the Star and the Lyric, but none seemed to be quite as popular as Verna Felton and the Allen Stock Company.

In Calgary, Sherman's Garden was not without its own competitors, but despite these counter attractions, the Allen Stock Company, according to the *Calgary Herald*, seemed to "hold its end" during the month of June, due perhaps to one unique change. It is not known whether it was Sherman's innovative tactic or Pearl's clever idea, but the Allen Stock Company presented a split bill during its summer season, with a melodrama produced on Monday, Tuesday, and Wednesday evenings and a comedy for the remaining three nights of the week. Across Alberta at this time, there seems to have been no Sunday performances whatsoever. In fact, the cities seemed to have shut down completely on the Sabbath. Summer productions included *A Country Girl, That Girl from Texas, Captain Impudence, Under the Magnolia*, and *The Westerner*.

After one month, the reviewer for the *Calgary Herald* was quick to notice that "Miss Felton is an emotional actress of exceptional merit, but displays her ability to a greater extent in the role of sweetheart rather than that of wife." This revealing observation reminds one that by this time, Verna, while capable of playing mature roles, was not yet eighteen years old. She had no personal experience with married life, or for that matter, with serious romance. Her adolescent years had been spent traveling from city to city with little opportunity to interact with anyone but her stage family. True, she had spent a lengthy time in Portland, but there is no indication that she had been courted by any of its young gentlemen. And newspapers items gave no hints of any backstage romances between her and the leading men of the company. Certainly, Pearl and Clara kept watchful eyes for such goings-on since backstage love affairs inherently possessed the potential for turning sour and consequently wrecking productions and ruining box office. Furthermore, the Allen Stock Company, an unusually intimate organization, prided itself on being a family-centered company. Correct behavior was strictly enforced. Verna recalled in 1959, "If you got drunk, you were through."

When *Under Two Flags* was produced during the third week of July, the *Calgary Daily Herald* called it the "most realistic piece of stage work ever seen in Calgary." The critic was wowed by the scenery and technical effects during the fourth act's famous gorge scene, complete with sandstorm. "It is about time that theater-goers here woke up to the fact," he sermonized, "that they have one of the best stock companies in Canada playing in Calgary today and showed their appreciation by their attendance. A company which never yet, in any instance can it be said, no matter how slim the patronage, has slumped in their work, going through it just the same as if they were playing to capacity houses." This bit of propaganda was effective enough to prompt Sherman to extend the bill for three extra nights. Effusive praise for the following bill, *Zaza*, was similarly productive. It, too, ran for an entire week.

Since Verna's *Camille* had met with success in Portland, Pearl decided to cast her as another "woman with a past," in the lead role of Zaza, the heroine of Pierre Berton and Charles Simon's French play about a music hall singer who becomes the mistress of a rich man. Zaza is a child of the gutter, of the street. She never knew her parents, and the aunt into whose care she was confided knew only one necessity, and that was drink. And so Zaza grew up without care, without love, without instruction. This bright, vivacious girl makes a hit on the boards of the Parisian concert halls, and when she is pursued by admirers, she accepts this life and becomes a courtesan, and without a twinge of remorse. After she falls in love with the wealthy Bernard Dufresne, she has hope of escaping this sordid lifestyle, but soon she discovers he is a married man with children. She renounces Dufresne, and his later efforts to win her back are met with indignant repulse. Zaza sadly returns to the halls and her old pattern of living.

Verna as Zaza, 1910.

When David Belasco produced *Zaza* on Broadway in 1899 with red-headed Mrs. Leslie Carter in the lead, some critics found it coarse and offensive, while others thought it moving and electrifying. Calgary audiences flocked to see Verna's interpretation of the role, and they were not disappointed. "Based upon exceptional opportunity for studying Miss Verna Felton, her interpretation of *Zaza* last night clearly proves she is a truly remarkable woman for her age," opined the *Herald* reviewer following the initial performance on July 27. "She is possessed to a large degree of that extraordinary dramatic and descriptive power which so many of our young actresses lack. Throughout the fourth and fifth act her audience is carried along with her until they see what she sees, laugh with her and weep with every turn of her pathos. She was surely born a natural actress, emotional, vivid, picturesque; she also tempers the sorrows of life with a good wit and consoling, quaint humor." Similar sentiments were repeated in the *Herald* the following day: "The roof should be battened down in more secure fashion, or the stormy applause, the terrific gales of hand-clapping may raise the rafters at any time, and let the noise escape to the clear heavens above. The performance could not be improved on. Verna Felton is great." William Sherman and Pearl Allen were impressed to read the writer's concluding comment regarding the audience, "The majority came out after the show wild-eyed, smiling, crying, glowing. What more can a showman give of satisfaction?"

After a long and strenuous week of *Zaza*, the Allen company settled down with the farce *All Due to Diana* before taking a brief vacation in Banff, a resort town in the Canadian Rockies. Two weeks later, *Camille* was the bill, running for a solid week, and raking in praise for Verna once again. The *Herald* critic compared the role of Marguerite Gautier to that of the unpredictable western prairie winds, but lauded Verna for being able to effectively represent such a character. "This clever company's version may have been often equaled, but it has been seldom excelled. The costumes throughout are splendid, and as good as those ever seen in any star cast."

During the early years of the twentieth century, many actresses became popular with audiences, particularly female patrons, because of the costumes they wore. They represented stylish fashion, as indicated by Verna's fashion spread in the *Sunday Oregonian* in the fall of 1907. Catherine Countiss, a leading lady with Portland's Baker Stock Company, explained the importance of costuming the actress in Portland's *Evening Telegram* in 1902: "She must be a classy dresser and must be able to undergo the coldest and most analytic feminine scrutiny without flinching, or her commercial value is depreciated. The cleverest actress will not be accepted in stock if she is sloppy or indifferent in her attire. Just as stock patrons idealize their favorites by endowing them with the attributes of the characters assumed, so do they love to see them decked out in silks, satins, and furbelows, reflecting the latest modes . . . As a matter of fact, beauty is not essential; brains are highly desirable, but clothes constitute an absolute necessity, if a leading stock woman expects to perpetuate her popularity." Verna, who, like many stage stars of her day would not be considered beautiful by modern standards, knew this all too well, and so did Pearl Allen. In the spring of 1908, Verna had introduced Portland audiences to a stunning Paris original, imported just for her. Designed in the popular Directoire or Empire style, revived that season by French couturier Paul Poiret, the white gown featured a lace bodice and sheath skirt with a matching lace inset panel. This style featured a rising waistline and narrowing skirt, much like the Empire gowns of the early 1800s, and required a longer corset, which constricted the hips instead of the waist. To counter this slimmer figure, milliners constructed hats that, by the end of the decade, would reach monster size. In fact they were the largest wide-brimmed hats since the age of Gainsborough. Similarly, Verna's Paris original was accented by a large white silk chapeau adorned with two drooping white ostrich feathers. Candid snapshots of Verna taken during this period and the early 1910s prove that she was quite the fashion plate, appearing often in the gargantuan hats of the day. Her fondness for hats would last her entire life.

The Allen Stock Company's sixteen-week engagement at Sherman's Garden ended on September 19 with the melodrama *A Great Temptation*. On the following day, the troupe arrived in Edmonton, where the *Edmonton Bulletin* drama critic, who met their train, cheerfully deemed them to be a "cosmopolitan crowd." However, this anonymous fellow was not so pleased the following night at the Edmonton Opera House when their initial performance of *Zaza* ran considerably past midnight, "Starting on time and the elimination of the tedious waits between acts would meet with the wishes of the public." Nevertheless, the audience remained attentive, warmly applauding Verna's scene in the fourth act where she, as Zaza, brokenheartedly drives away her lover once she realizes he is married.

Pearl had planned to stage *In the Bishop's Carriage* for the second half of the week, but when a cast member became ill, he substituted it with *Little Lord Fauntleroy*, featuring eight-year-old Baby Adele Meredith in the title role. Baby Adele received the lion's share of the notices, much reminiscent of Verna's kudos for her own portrayal of the title role some eight years earlier. However, Verna was given notice for her famous Directoire gown she had introduced in Portland.

For the next six weeks, the company alternated between the Edmonton Opera House and the Lyric Theatre in Calgary, where William B. Sherman had made arrangements to co-manage with Pearl for a three-week engagement. The Lyric, located on Eighth Avenue West, was owned by Sherman's friend, attorney James Lougheed. These two entrepreneurs would soon become business partners in several other entertainment ventures. While at the Lyric, the Allen Stock Company received its best reviews for a political drama called *The Undertow*, staged at an opportune time considering the approaching Dominion election, and for *In the Bishop's Carriage*, noted not only for its employment of that conveyance pulled onto the stage by live horses, but also for its novel use of the coming craze, an authentic horseless carriage. Based on a novel by Miriam

Michaelson, *In the Bishop's Carriage* told the story of a Philadelphia lawyer who reforms a girlish thief, Nance Olden. *The Morning Albertan* assessed Verna's role as Nance as "certainly not a pleasant part to play—too sordid for that—but full of opportunities for good acting."

Confident that his troupe could attract Edmonton audiences during the winter months of 1908-09, Pearl rented the Dominion Theatre at the corner of Third and Jasper Streets. Hastily built earlier in the year, the Dominion replaced the Kevin Theatre, which had stood on the same plot until its destruction by fire in 1907. The Allen Stock Company opened its Dominion engagement with a comedy of errors called *A Stranger in a Strange Land* on November 2. The Dominion was a smaller venue than the Edmonton Opera House, and following the opening night, the *Edmonton Daily Bulletin* critic felt it necessary to apologize for the situation, "A new hat has to be given time to fit, so the group of players at the Dominion must be given time to accommodate themselves to the contracted stage, the small theatre, and the general novelty occasioned by the change." By mid-December, the owner announced plans to remodel the Dominion into the "coziest theatre in the city." Verna was less tactful than either of the above in her appraisal of the conditions, calling it a "barn of a theatre" when the mercury dropped to 37 degrees below zero on January 3, 1909, freezing everything in the place, including the shoe blacking.

Edmonton winters were a difficult acclimation for most of the members of the Allen Stock Company, who were used to the warmer temperatures of Portland. In early November, the *Edmonton Daily Bulletin* had featured clothiers and furriers' advertisements detailing their lines of outerwear necessary for central Alberta winters, including men's raccoon, wombat, and dogskin coats and women's astrakhan coats with sable collars and cloth coats lined in grey squirrel or hamster. Less than a month later, a portrait of Verna wearing an astrakhan coat with upturned collar appeared in the same paper, perhaps to the delight of the local clothiers.

The miserable work environment, extreme winter weather, and the boredom of lifeless Sundays, made Verna very unhappy with Canada. The eighteen-year-old longed for Portland, anticipating the day when a return to the States would be possible. Although Verna seems to have been close to fellow players Ella Houghton, Marie Thompson, Charles Ayres, and Irving Kennedy, all with whom she tried to amuse herself in games of poker or cribbage during off-hours, her diary for early 1909 reveals the restlessness, and perhaps moodiness, of an adolescent. She reported a "big fight" with "old lady Henry," wife of the Castle Hotel's proprietor, on January 12, and another altercation with fellow actor Charles Ayres less than a week later. (He later gave her a bar of chocolate as a peace offering.) But she was overjoyed when the Dominion engagement ended on January 16 and the troupe moved to the larger venue of the Edmonton Opera House, built in 1906. Nearby was the Empire Theater, a "modern vaudeville house," which was part of the Sullivan and Considine circuit, and whose matinees Verna began to frequent. The bill there usually included singers, acrobats, comedians, and an orchestra. Patrons could also be entertained by the Kinetoscope, an early motion picture exhibition device designed to allow individuals to view films through a window in the cabinet housing the machine's components.

Curiously, the promotional advertisement for the January 18 opening at the Opera House listed as company manager, not Pearl Allen, but instead his wife Clara, leading one to surmise that financial reasons may have been behind this switch. In addition to this change, the troupe had been re-christened as The Allen Players, perhaps to coincide with the new engagement, giving everything a fresh start. The opening bill, as well, was given a new treatment. Pearl felt the title *Because She Loved Him So* was too melodramatic so it was changed to *The Green Eyed Monster* and was promoted as the "latest European success." Tickets sold for 50, 35, and 25 cents for evening performances. After a successful trial run of two nights, Pearl signed with the Opera House for an eight-week engagement, which proved to have its ups and downs. While *Sherlock Holmes* was a great hit and prompted several repeat performances, other productions like *The King of the Opium Ring* and *The Sultan's Daughter* did "rotten business," according to Verna. Meanwhile, things were not pleasant at the Castle Hotel, where the proprietress Mrs. James Henry was threatening to throw the Allen Players out following numerous disagreements.

However, Verna's spirits lifted after the evening of February 5, when she attended a much-anticipated dance, perhaps her very first such occasion. That evening she became instantly smitten with Jack MacNeil, a local druggist who was ten years her senior. Returning to the hotel after 3 a.m., Verna recorded the event in her diary: "The long looked for dance is over and we had a peachie, grand, glorious time. My debut. Dear old dance." The next three weeks proved to be happier than any she had spent in Alberta. She saw MacNeil practically every day, either at his father's drug store or at supper or during evening performances at the Opera House where he sat attentively in the audience's front row. After he walked her home on February 17, she wrote "Hurrah! At last." This may be an indication that she finally was experiencing the euphoria of young love, or perhaps her first kiss.

Other events made the end of Verna's sojourn in Edmonton more pleasant. On February 9, the situation at the Castle Hotel had become unbearable, and Verna began "packing like hell" in an effort to relocate to the Windsor Hotel along with the Allens and several of their players, including Kennedy, Ayres, Houghton, and Thompson.

The following evening was indeed eventful. The Symphonic Orchestra held a concert at the Opera House, with acts of *Paid in Full*, performed by the Allen Players, sandwiched between selections. Although ticket sales to the concert were not impressive, the ball, held at 10 p.m. in the Separate School Hall, was one of the social events of the winter season. A twelve-piece orchestra, featuring Pearl on the string bass, accompanied the dancers. MacNeil was there, making sure Verna had a pleasant time. She reported, "Ate so much cake, nearly died. Danced my head off."

The next afternoon, Verna began rehearsals for *Zira,* a drama set in South Africa and England during the Boer War. The Broadway production had been a triumph for leading lady Margaret Anglin in the fall of 1905. Verna, obviously a fan of the play's heroine, wrote, "I love her. Got a speech three pages long." She spent most of February 15 walking the streets of Edmonton, searching for a nurse's uniform for that evening's opening performance, which was hailed as "magnificent" by the *Edmonton Daily Bulletin*: "Miss Verna Felton played as she has never played before in this city. Those who want to see emotional acting of the highest type must see Miss Felton as Zira. At the close of the third act Miss Felton received three curtain calls."

When the Opera House manager booked the famous Canadian impersonator-comedian Jimmy Fax for the weekend of February 20, the Allen Players took advantage of the brief lay-off to travel to Daysland, Alberta to perform *The Sultan's Daughter* in the local theater. Upon their return on Monday, Verna used every opportunity to be with MacNeil, attending dances on Monday and Tuesday nights and a vaudeville show on Wednesday. After a late supper with MacNeil on Thursday, Verna enjoyed a long conversation with him once their walk ended at the Windsor Hotel. Despite Verna's light clothing and the frozen snow at their feet, she lingered with MacNeil on the sidewalk, hoping not to later rouse her parents' ire after climbing the stairs to their rooms. Once upstairs, when she saw that their light was out, Verna fully expected a "call down" the next morning due to the late hour of her return, but Pearl and Clara let the matter slide. Perhaps their lenience could be attributed to the fact that they intended to leave Edmonton in three days, with no plans to return. That evening, despite a head cold and sore throat, quite probably aggravated by the exposure the previous night, Verna impressed Opera House audiences with her performance in *Zaza*. The physical discomforts did nothing to cloud her memories of the prior evening with MacNeil, whom Verna called "the best chap ever." Their final afternoon together was spent on Sunday, February 28, taking a lovely sleigh ride around town. Although MacNeil promised to connect with Verna during the coming summer in Seattle, it appears that this never happened. On March 1, Verna found herself in a Stettler, Alberta hotel, wishing she were back in Edmonton, feeling many of the same sentiments she had two months earlier when she was longing for Portland.

The life of a traveling stock performer could be very difficult in many ways, considering the constant packing and unpacking, uncomfortable accommodations, unappetizing or unhealthy meals on the train, in boarding houses or hotels. For the most part, Verna had been fortunate with in all such circumstances during the last three years. Lengthy engagements in Tacoma, Portland, and to a lesser degree, Edmonton, had also provided opportunities for her to make friends,

Verna Felton at eighteen, Calgary, Alberta, March 1909.

which she seemed to do quite easily. But it also meant having to put those relationships on hold or even end them when it was time to move to the next city. Besides the situation involving Jack MacNeil, there must have been other bittersweet experiences related to Verna's transient lifestyle.

However, she made one friend who would remain faithful for almost sixty years. During the Calgary run in 1908, Verna had met twenty-year-old Ida Nellie Allan who was born in that city on July 13, 1888. Ida's father was Alexander Allan, a Scottish immigrant who opened a dry goods business in Calgary in

1884. Mr. Allan quickly became a prominent civic leader, serving as alderman, customs collector, and hospital board member. Although progressive, he never drove an automobile, instead buying a 1911 Maxwell for Ida who became one of Calgary's first women drivers, if not the first. Mr. Allan also inspired Ida to develop an appreciation for the arts. One night when she was about eight years old, her father attended a concert given by international opera star Madame Emma Albani. At intermission, Mr. Allan rushed home and woke Ida. "You'll never hear anything like her," he said as he got her dressed to go back with him for the second half. From then on, Ida became a regular attendee at plays and concerts. Perhaps that is how she met Verna.

Ida visited Verna in Edmonton for ten days in January 1909, and it was the first of many visits between the two women. When the troupe returned to Calgary that March, Verna spent most of her spare time in the Allans' home, playing bridge and dancing in the parlor on a rare Saturday night off. She borrowed Ida's mother's diamonds to wear in *Camille*, and her performance merited the huge bouquet of daffodils she received at the curtain call that evening.

After leaving Edmonton, Verna would not experience such an extended engagement for some time to come. Instead, the Allen Players trekked across Canada, passing the spring and summer with stops in cities in Alberta, Saskatchewan, Manitoba, and Ontario, and created a circuit they would repeat for the following six years. One of the first stops was Regina, Saskatchewan, during Easter week, where Verna's performances were received enthusiastically, despite cramped conditions on the small stage of the Regina Theatre. The bills did not vary from the repertoire established in Edmonton.

On June 22, the Allen Players opened in the city of Fort William, located in northern Ontario. Fort William, located on the Kaministiquia River at its entrance to Lake Superior, was a twin city to nearby Port Arthur. The three-week engagement was produced in the City Hall Auditorium, a venue that became uncomfortable during the summer heat wave until a number of electric fans were installed. The Fort William *Daily Times Journal* praised their production of *Zaza*: "Mrs. Leslie Carter, the creator of 'Zaza' was flattered by Miss Verna Felton in her interpretation of this many sided role. It would be a bold critic who would say that anything presented by Miss Felton was displeasing. In the Carter version 'Zaza' does a disrobing stunt in the first act. Miss Felton proved that that stunt is unnecessary to the success of the play and in fact that the cutting of the disrobing scene is a distinct improvement. The audience has more respect for the more modest 'Zaza" and is in better humor to sympathize with her when she steps across the 'dividing line.'" (Given the mores of one hundred years ago, it is difficult to believe that Mrs. Leslie Carter's "disrobing" scene would have actually involved nudity. Perhaps instead she was seen in her underclothes, a sight considered scandalous in most circles then.)

The reviewer also noted that the very hesitant audience cautiously held their enthusiasm until the end of the third act, explaining that *Zaza* had been often staged in Fort William by "counterfeit metropolitan productions." He credited Verna's performance alone for winning them over and evoking two hearty curtain calls at the end of the third act, a record for the Auditorium's current theatrical season. When the curtain fell just a few minutes before midnight, the audience was reluctant to admit that the play had ended, offering several more curtain calls and lingering in the aisles for a while afterwards.

On June 28, Clara Allen received the lion's share of praise for her part in the complicated farce *All Due to Diana*, in which she played a matriarch who ruled with a rod of iron. Impressive reviews like these increased the size of the house each night, so Pearl decided that they would extend their stay in Fort William for a while longer.

Pearl chose the military drama *Under Two Flags* for the evening performance of July 1 as a fitting end to the Canadians' national holiday, known then as Dominion Day, which commemorated the formation of the Dominion of Canada. The house was filled to capacity, and the same bill was repeated the following night. July 4 fell on a Sunday that year, so the Allen Players had the day off, spending part of the afternoon in Current River Park. The *Daily Times Journal* reported that the troupe, while being respectful to "the land of its adoption," could not allow the occasion to pass without displaying a bit of patriotism. Verna retrieved a miniature American flag from her trunk, while Charles Ayers produced a handkerchief displaying the stars and stripes, both of which were proudly displayed as the entire company stood on the park's highest peak and sang a number of patriotic songs. The Canadian spectators enthusiastically joined in three cheers for their southern neighbor.

When the Allen Players left Fort William on July 11 for a much needed vacation, the *Daily Times Journal* published a lengthy review of their engagement, citing Verna's best performance as *Zaza*. While recognizing her as a "premier" dramatic actress, the writer also allowed that she was better than the average comedienne and, given the opportunity, would be moderately successful in a musical. However, he did admit that Verna probably would not be a "world beater at the songbird game," but still better than some professional singers he had heard. Pearl was credited as a manager who knew the game, "both ends and through the middle from either direction," giving his audience what they wanted.

By this time, the Allen Players wanted a real vacation, away from life in a hotel or boarding house. They chose a site on Lake Superior called Silver Islet, located twenty-one miles off the shore of Port William, originally a silver mining community in the 1870s and now a summer destination for people from all walks of life. The Allen Players made the trip aboard a steamer named the "Niagara." While the small island's coastline was dotted with cottages, the Allen Players decided to rough it by camping five weeks under canvases, or tents. When they were not engaged in recreational activities, like playing ball or exploring the island's abandoned mining furnaces, they rehearsed a new slate of plays for the coming fall season.

On July 22, supporting player Ella Houghton left for a visit to her hometown of Portland, which she had not seen in over a year, leaving an emotional Verna and Marie Thompson terribly lonesome. Verna had grown fond of the younger Houghton since she joined the troupe during the Portland run. To relieve boredom and to earn a bit of extra money, Verna and Marie performed in a Port Arthur vaudeville house for two Mondays in August. By August 23, the company had returned to Fort William, where they were prepared to present several old standbys, including *Caprice* and *Tennessee's Partner*, and a few new plays, among them *Mrs. Dane's Defense* and *The Truth*. Most of September was spent performing these same plays in Manitoba.

As fall approached, the company headed further west, stopping in many of the same cities they had played on their way to Ontario. While most of the engagements for the remainder of 1909 lasted one week or less, the Allen Players maintained almost an identical repertoire in each town, including their successful productions of *Camille, Zira, In the Bishop's Carriage, Jim the Westerner, Zaza,* and *All Due to Diana.* Business was alternately good or "rotten," according to Verna, and the hotel accommodations were equally unpredictable. In Red Deer Verna found it deplorable that the staff rattled a cow bell up and down the halls to announce meals, while in Didsbury, she lamented that the "can was away out in the back yard." She disliked staying in Taber where the theatre was miles from the hotel, but she hated to leave Medicine Hat, which she labeled as "dandy." Verna would return to Medicine Hat numerous times, forming a steadfast friendship with one of its citizens in years to come.

Most of December was spent in Lethbridge, Alberta, where the Allen Players packed the house of the Lyceum during a two-week engagement, which began November 29. Verna and Clara both fell ill at the end of the first week. Verna barely made it through an evening performance of *Zira*, missing the matinee of *All Due to Diana* the following day, while Clara was forced to drop out of *Jim the Westerner.*

The following week, Verna was in fine form in the title role of *The Second Mrs. Tanqueray*, a production the Allen Players had added to their repertoire during an October engagement in Saskatoon. Verna played the tragic title character who commits suicide after realizing that a "woman with a past" has no future. First produced in London in 1893, *The Second Mrs. Tanqueray* scored a box-office hit despite the unsavory reputation of its title character, which had raised protests from conservatives. Fifteen years later, this play—as well as *Zaza*—still occasionally received negative reactions from the clergy and newspaper critics. However, the influence of European playwrights such as Ibsen, Sudermann, and Shaw was also being felt in the United States at this time. Theatre historian Walter Waters noted that during this period, "Intellectuals demanded that playwrights handle themes more realistically and comment on the shortcomings of the social order." But most stock producers catered specifically to families and not to these progressive intellectuals. Therefore, they had no desire to produce works dealing with indelicate themes, but some producers, including Pearl Allen, realized the popularity of such plays. As for the December 8 presentation of *The Second Mrs. Tanqueray*, the *Lethbridge Herald* conceded, " The story, while not particularly pleasing in its tragic end lost its unpleasantness in the keen interest that held the audience throughout." Two nights later another "fallen woman" packed the house when *Camille* was produced. Verna noted in her diary, "Like this bill best of all."

On December 17, 1909, the Allen Players arrived in British Columbia, where they would remain for five months. Their traditional Christmas Eve banquet was held at the Hume Hotel in Nelson, following a poorly attended performance of *Tennessee's Partner*. Since 1902, Pearl had hosted an elaborate banquet for his troupe, not only to celebrate the season, but to show his sincere affection for them as well. The Allen Players usually performed on Christmas Eve and Christmas Day so this happy meal together was their only holiday celebration. They also held a "Christmas Tree," a contemporary term used for the occasion when people exchanged Christmas gifts.

Inside the cover of her diary for 1910, Verna inscribed the same label Pearl used in newspaper ads: "The Allen Players, En Route Through Canada." An appropriate notation, as the troupe spent three fourths of that year in the Dominion. Almost all of January was taken up with an engagement in Revelstoke, British Columbia. On February 14, the troupe left Vancouver on the steamer "Joan" for Nanaimo, a city centrally located on Vancouver Island, thirty-four miles west of Vancouver. During their five-week engagement at the Nanaimo Opera House, they fell in love with the city, returning to it year after year.

The Allen Players made front-page news with each edition of the *Nanaimo Free Press*, which featured a review of the previous night's performance and a preview of the evening's production. The reviewer was most impressed with the performances of *Under Two Flags* and *Zaza*, the latter having become Verna's signature role. He lauded her development of the character from dance hall queen to chastened woman. "One can watch the budding of her true womanhood," he wrote on February 24. "In the terrible scenes with Bernard she was supreme. To English eyes and to English minds, Dupresne revealed himself a cad and a coward when he turned on Zaza, struck her, and threw her to the floor. Her love burns as deeply and flames as fiercely in her heart as ever, but she recognizes now the necessity for renunciation, for separation. In this climax of her emotional experience, Miss Felton was magnificent, and both tears and applause paid eloquent tribute to the realism of her acting." *Zaza* subsequently played twice more to packed houses, necessitating fifty additional chairs for the February 25 and March 10 performances. Many were turned away at the door, but those who witnessed the production agreed with the reviewer that it was far "above the highest standard of anything that has been seen here."

While the elaborate costumes and customized scenery for *Camille* drew praise on March 2, the *Free Press* critic felt that there was something lacking in the "spirit of the piece," explaining that the halting delivery in the early acts was perhaps indicative of insufficient rehearsal. However, he remained amazed at Verna's ability to pull off the famous death scene, considering her young age of nineteen. Her gowns for *Camille* were said to be some of the most beautiful dresses ever worn on the Opera House stage, especially one made of white satin with silver spangles she wore in the first act. And it did not go unnoticed that Verna had not worn the same gown twice during the entire run. The reviewer also found it impressive that Verna was adept at comedy roles, delighting in her ad-libs during *Our New Girl* and her solo of "I Wonder Who's Kissing Her Now" during *Hello, Bill.* When the Allen Players left town on March 27, the *Free Press* declared that the troupe had broken all theatrical records, staying longer than any other company. He complimented their exemplary conduct, recalling a different time when "members of the theatrical profession were regarded as hardly fit to associate in polite society, and on account of their profession alone were held to be undesirables."

Verna and her troupe similarly pleased the residents of Victoria when they played British Columbia's capital city the following month. Again her gowns stunned the playgoers, and many felt they were by far the best ever worn by a stock company star in Victoria. Verna received her best notices for the lead in *Mrs. Dane's Defense*, another "woman with a past," but one who, when exposed, sought to make a better world for herself. At the point of the play's climax, an audible sigh passed through the house, and when the curtain fell, many ladies in the audience were in tears, some actually sobbing. To entice repeat customers, Pearl publicized that actual photographs, and not half-tones, signed by Verna, would be given to everyone in attendance on May 5. When the lucky recipients clamored for an additional portrait of Verna in street clothes instead of the gratis "character" pose, Pearl complied by having dozens printed for the closing night of May 6.

After almost three years of being away from their native state, the Allens and Verna, weary but wealthier, began their journey to California on May 8, stopping along the way in Seattle, Tacoma, and finally Portland where they boarded the Shasta Limited, a luxury train operated by the Southern Pacific Railroad. They arrived in San Francisco on May 19 and two days later were relieved to be in San Jose at last. Verna still referred to this city as "home," for it was the one place in her twenty years where she had lived the longest. After a month's rest and reunion with old friends, Verna was contacted on June 23 by Ed Redmond, the actor-manager of the Redmond Stock Company, then appearing downtown at the Jose Theatre. Redmond, a talented comedian who nevertheless always seemed to struggle to maintain a stock company, had recently accepted the resignation of his leading lady Virginia Brissac, whom Verna had known almost ten years earlier when they played together as members of the Jessie Shirley Company. Brissac left

Redmond to join director Al Hallett in his newly formed company at Redmond's rival theatre, the Garden, in San Jose. When he heard that Verna was in town, Redmond immediately sought her as a replacement for Brissac, at least temporarily.

Verna was allowed to choose her opening bill, *Zaza*, and began rehearsals on June 28. Opening night was July 4, and while no review appeared in the *San Jose Daily Mercury*, the show appears to have done big business. Verna's leading man was the rugged Kernan Cripps, a Connecticut native who would go on to appear in over 200 films, usually as muscle-bound cops or bartenders. Redmond enticed Verna to appear for a second week at the Jose Theatre in a production of Ferenc Molnar's *The Devil*, a 1908 Broadway crowd-pleaser, which had made a star of George Arliss. For the San Jose audiences, Cripps gave a forceful interpretation of Satan in this peculiarly charming play, while Verna, showing "clever versatility," played a young married lady whom the Devil tempts her former sweetheart to woo. *The Devil* closed on July 17.

Afterwards the Allens and Verna, joined by brother Clayton, vacationed in nearby Capitola, a seaside town on the beautiful Bay of Monterey where an elegant 160-room hotel had been built in 1895. Capitola was perhaps the first resort on the Pacific Coast, with a history dating to the 1870s. The weeklong sojourn afforded the family leisurely days in the sun and surf, which especially delighted both Clara and Verna who were avid swimmers.

Clayton, now twenty-seven, was still a handsome bachelor. At five feet, eight and one half inches, he was taller than either of his siblings. While Howard favored their grandfather David Lawrence, Clayton shared Verna's dark hair and brown eyes. Even though a decade had passed since Clara and Verna left San Jose, Clayton had not endeavored to establish any roots. Nor was he acquiring any job skills. Clayton must have shared Dr. Felton's wanderlust. In 1907, he left his job as an Oakland grocery clerk and headed for Council Bluffs, Iowa, where he enlisted in the United States Army on July 26. He was immediately transported to Jefferson Barracks, a training station overlooking the Mississippi River near St. Louis, where he was made part of the Coast Artillery Corps. After a month, however, he was transferred to Company B of the Hospital Corps and shipped to the Presidio of San Francisco in preparation for a potential deployment to Cuba. Clayton never left the country, though. Instead, he became a deserter. When he met Verna and the Allens at Capitola, he was still on the run, hoping not to be discovered among the Bay City's 400,000 residents. Was his family aware of his AWOL status? No one can say for certain, but Clayton's erratic career pattern was undoubtedly a cause for concern. He was fast becoming the family ne'er-do-well.

On August 13, Verna and the Allens left San Francisco by boat for Seattle. The rough voyage made Verna quite seasick before arriving at their destination two days later. From Seattle, they traveled to Tacoma, where they reunited with all members of the troupe for a two-week engagement. Rehearsals began

Clayton Felton, Verna, and Pearl Allen vacationing at Capitola, California, 1910.

immediately for *Zaza*, which opened on August 28 at the Tacoma Theater, filling its standing room to the limit. "When Verna Felton left Tacoma four years ago with the Allen Stock Company, she was considered an unusually talented child," declared the *Tacoma Daily Ledger*. "Last night Verna Felton returned to Tacoma to demonstrate that she has developed into a capable emotional actress and she did so to the entire satisfaction of a house full of her old friends . . . she scored a triumph in the powerful climax at the close of the fourth act. Her acting of this scene was undoubtedly superior to that of any other actress seen in the role here in stock." Irving Kennedy, Clara Allen, and Ella Houghton all received praise for their roles in *Zaza*. After splendid business all week, Verna was "dead tired after that awful bill."

For the following week's bill, reviewers found the title role of *The Defiance of Doris* "much more suited to Miss Felton's youth than Zaza." Written expressly for Verna by former Tacoma citizen Herbert Bashford, *The Defiance of Doris* told the tale of a young woman who secretly marries the son of her father's bitter enemy. After an impressive two nights of *Doris*, Pearl was convinced to extend the Tacoma engagement a week longer than planned to present *The Second Mrs. Tanqueray*. The Allen Players had a break from *Doris* on Thursday, September 8, due to a one-night performance of *The Melting Pot,* which had been previously arranged by the management of the Tacoma Theater. The star of this touring production was Walker Whiteside, who had starred in the original Broadway production one year earlier. In the audience that evening was Verna Felton, closely studying the performance for methods she could use in her own future productions, but having no idea that some twenty years later she would be reunited with Whiteside in New York City stage circles.

For *Tanqueray*, which opened on September 13, Verna wore "several magnificent gowns purchased in New York" especially for the production. The *Tacoma Daily Ledger* observed of her characterization, "There is less careful blending of moods than theatergoers are accustomed to see in the part, but there is a strength and a convincing Aprilishness, with the showers and sunshine and thunder chasing one another in a way that suggests the inconsistent mental processes of a woman who has seen life only from the seamy side." Five days later, the troupe left Tacoma by car for Seattle where they took a boat to Victoria, British Columbia. From there, they rode the train to Nanaimo where they began their fall theatrical season in Canada.

At the Nanaimo Opera House, Verna drew the most crowds for her comedy role in *Miss Hobbs*, a satiric look at suffragettes. She chose *The Second Mrs. Tanqueray* as an appropriate vehicle to introduce the town to the latest fashion trend, the hobble skirt, which narrowed below the knees, restricting one's stride. Referred to by the *Nanaimo Free Press* as a "modern monstrosity," this impractical fashion was derided by newspapers on both continents for causing accidents as ladies alighted from streetcars and subways. Still actresses like Verna were compelled to wow audiences with the latest styles.

After seven weeks in British Columbia, the Allen Players returned to Alberta where they played two weeks at Lethbridge's Majestic Theatre, beginning November 7, 1910. The *Lethbridge Herald* saw fit to mention that this company was the only one in the West carrying its own baggage car. Furthermore, the abundance of scenery made it impossible for the railway employees at Lethbridge to check the baggage in their customary way. While this extra cargo created a great expense for Pearl Allen, he firmly believed that providing excellent production values, such as scenery, drew the crowds.

Meanwhile, Calgary's showman, William B. Sherman, invited the Allen Players back to his city after an absence of two years. They opened at the Lyric Theatre on November 28 with *The Defiance of Doris*. The following morning, the *Calgary Daily Herald* praised Verna as the best stock actress in the west, "Miss Felton expresses the dramatic moments of the play with such completeness of modulated voice and striking gesture that we do not expect much longer to have the pleasure of seeing her in stock companies. From our standpoint, she seems to have passed out of that class. Nothing finer has been witnessed in the west than her treatment of the third scene of the play last night." The writer added, somewhat less eloquently, that Pearl should be commended for having cast behind "the whole junk-pile of old-fashioned plays" and replacing them with the best modern dramas available. His wife Clara received her due amount of praise as well. For her role in *The Defiance of Doris*, the writer opined, "Mrs. Allen has the same unforced humor we always admired in her work. There never was any sense of effort in her lines. They were always spontaneous and therefore always hit the mark." Clara's performance in the following night's bill of *The Three of Us* pleased him even more: "It was worth the price of admission to see Mrs. Allen partaking of the luxuries of the breakfast table and wiping her mouth with the back of her hand . . . Her affects are so heartless, so unaffected and yet so true." One can imagine Verna watching her mother's subtle gestures and expressions, taking mental notes to be used in her future career as a character actress.

When the troupe returned to Regina in mid-December for two weeks, a large and appreciative audience welcomed them, but the *Regina Leader*'s reviewer did not think the opening bill, *The Defiance of Doris*, was "adapted to [Verna's] genius." While he felt her "uncommon histrionic powers" were well suited for a play like *Zaza*, he criticized Verna's "lavish exuberance" as Doris, because he thought it out of place in the "relatively familiar surroundings of American social life." At the same time, he marveled at the versatility displayed by Verna on her previous visit to Regina, citing it as "something like a landmark in the theatrical life of the city." This critic's favorite bill of the run was *The Heir to the Hoorah*, a 1905 comedy set in a mining camp and depicting the contempt of the polished East for the rough and ready West. In one scene, a group of uncouth miners pay a call on their pal who has become wealthy overnight as the heir to the Hoorah mine. Pearl Allen, featured as one of the miners, entered wearing white tie and tails, his costume unmistakably two sizes too small, accessorized with a tall pair of mining boots. As a broad smile crossed his round face, the audience became wild with laughter. The play was such a crowd pleaser that it was repeated twice during Christmas week.

Beginning with 1911 and continuing for the next four years, the movements of the Allen Players and Verna Felton are difficult to establish, due to the scarcity of online resources and the unavailability of Canadian resources for United States researchers. However, it is safe to assume that they continued to play exclusively in Canada, essentially following the same circuit they had established in 1909 and 1910, stretching from the Pacific Coast to the Great Lakes.

By mid-April, 1911, the Allen Players had crossed to Canada's western shore where they were enthusiastically welcomed by the playgoers at the Nanaimo Opera House. Pearl repeated his comic role in *The Heir to the Hoorah*, and when he entered in ill-fitting evening dress and demanded a drink, the audience "sat back and yelled." Verna attracted less attention for her performance in the drama *Magda* than for her choice of costumes for the role. She surprised Nanaimo by wearing a new creation, the harem skirt, essentially a long divided skirt. One amused reviewer remarked that it was difficult to tell whether to call the skirt "it" or "they."

From Nanaimo, the players headed to Victoria, where ticket sales were not as impressive, despite positive press. Again Verna's costumes for *Madga* received more coverage than the critique: "Last evening Miss Felton appeared in a coronation gown, a beautiful creation of royal red duchess satin, with a tunic about three-quarter length of royal blue chiffon, elaborately trimmed with a crystal fringe of red, white, and blue around the yoke and at the bottom in the form of a hobble. The entire costume is finished with silver cord, and there is also a large woven silver rose on the waist. The hose and slippers were chosen to match the predominating color in the gown, and Miss Felton had her hair tastefully decorated with an elaborate coiffure and surmounted with a single red rose."

Summer vacations for 1911 through 1914 were spent in Ladysmith, a picturesque little town on the east coast of Vancouver Island, fourteen miles south of Nanaimo. Founded at the turn of the twentieth century by industrialist James Dunsmuir, Ladysmith was first organized as a shipping port for coal from Dunsmuir's mines. Dunsmuir admired the peaceful locale so much that he had buildings moved there by both rail and oxen in order to build a recreation and dormitory complex for minors. By 1904, the bustling town was incorporated as Ladysmith. Upon the initial arrival of the Allen Players in 1911, Ladysmith boasted a population of 3300, including many Finns, Belgians, Chinese, and Croats.

On First Avenue stood the Opera House, a wooden two story building, unadorned except for colorful posters plastered to its exterior, advertising coming attractions to the movie theater housed on the upper level. Managed by a young man named James Haworth, the Opera House also hosted traveling shows. Three hundred people would have crowded it. Pearl approached Haworth about using the small venue for rehearsals of productions he had planned for the fall tour. When Haworth agreed, the Allen Players subsequently tried out their plays on matinee audiences who packed the house. According to Ladysmith resident Thelma Jones Paton, the admission charge for children was "the largest potato they could find in the sack, vegetable pit, or root-house." The potatoes were later donated to the new Ladysmith Hospital.

Clara and Verna, circa 1911.

The troupe had set up camp across the bay about a mile north of Shell Beach on a stretch of land that became known as "Allen's Green." They liked its sheltered cove so well that they made it a permanent camp upon their return the following summer. A number of cabins were built, with all the available comforts, and a Chinese cook was hired. Pearl invested in a very large motorboat, christened the "Zaza," after Verna's most famous role. Each summer the locals easily spotted the vessel as it ran back and forth between the camp and town. For the next several years, the troupe looked forward to returning to "Allen's Green" when the busy spring schedule ended in June.

Verna recalled this very special place in the 1964 interview with Martin Halperin, "We had a summer place outside of Ladysmith. And it's a beautiful spot up there, just beautiful. And we had a lovely home up there. We had it for about twelve years. Then they were surveying one time and we find out it was Indian reserve. And we had to give it up. Ah, it broke my mother's heart." When Verna visited Ladysmith in 1958, she returned to "Allen's Green," finding it an unoccupied shambles, "It was just all down-and-out and everything. Nobody keeps it [up]." Although the land had been designated as Chemainus Indian reserve as far back as 1877, the particular spot of Allen's Green was obviously unmarked. Though more than forty years had passed since the Allens lost their summer home, the regret was still strongly evident in Verna's voice, "Why couldn't they let us keep it and pay rent to the government or something?"

The Allens and Verna are included in the 1911 Census of Canada as residents of Victoria, British Columbia. While rife with errors, the document merits some attention, considering this was the first time Verna Felton ever appeared on a census record. Her birth came too late in the year to be recorded on the 1890 United States census, but even if she had been enumerated then, that particular census was later lost to fire. In 1900, when she and her mother were probably in San Francisco, they escaped the census taker. And in 1910, they were residents of Canada and, of course, were not included in the U.S. census that year. The 1911 Canadian census lists the threesome as roomers at the Dominion Hotel on Yates Street in the city of Victoria. Curiously, Pearl and Clara are listed as natives of Ontario, but Verna is identified as a United States citizen. Pearl's occupation is given as contractor, while Verna is listed as an actress. Their dates of birth are all incorrect, with Pearl being listed as three years older than Clara, who was recorded as forty-five years old. Meanwhile, Verna's age is shown as twenty-three, missing the mark by two years at least.

Unfortunately, little is known about the remainder of their theatrical engagements for 1911, except for the final five weeks of the year. The Allen Players' return to Lethbridge, Alberta, on November 27 was preceded by several curious items in the local press. It seems that the entertainment columnist, identified only as "Fidelio," for the *Lethbridge Daily Herald* had launched a campaign to increase citizens' appreciation for the performing arts. He found it deplorable that the attendance at three recent concerts had been as "slim as the eye of a needle." He urged readers to patronize the Majestic Theatre, where these concerts had taken place and where the Allen Players had been engaged for two weeks. Fidelio also felt it his duty to issue a slightly condescending reminder to the public, "Many managers of small, third-rate companies from the other side of the line have found to their sorrow that the people of the Canadian Northwest demand a higher standard of plays than the audiences in the United States." Nevertheless, he readily allowed that Pearl Allen was the exception to this statement. Indeed, the columnist informed Lethbridge readers that Pearl had strived to raise his standards in the selection of plays for his Canadian patrons. Despite the somewhat affected tone of this writer, the Allen Players' repertoire had, in fact, changed almost completely from the previous year, replacing those bills with "modern standard dramas." A few new members joined the troupe in the fall of 1911, among them Ethel Corley, a Pacific Coast actress and Harry Cornell, who had played leads in his own stock company in Butte, Montana, for the previous two years. In addition to these new talents, Pearl hired the Royal Hungarian String Quartette to perform selections between the acts.

For the opening bill, Pearl chose a dramatization of Leo Tolstoy's novel *Resurrection*, which had premiered in New York in 1903. "The principal roles," according to theatre historian Gerald Bordman, "were that of a count who recognizes how his thoughtless lovemaking has led a servant girl into prostitution, and the girl, whose life and spirit the count determines to save after she is exiled to penal servitude in Siberia." Verna played the servant girl Katusha, whose most dramatic scene occurs in the fourth act when she vehemently attacks the count during his visit at the prison. While Verna's performance evoked pity from Fidelio, he unhappily reported that many audience members giggled during Verna's distressful tirade. Were these Lethbridge patrons really too ignorant to realize the pathos of this emotion-charged scene? Or was Verna's performance so melodramatic that they found it ridiculous? Since none of Verna's stage performances, or those of her contemporaries, exist on film, it is impossible to either compare her ability to others or to determine if her acting style at this point in her career bordered on the melodramatic. However, the fact remains that by the age of seventeen, Verna had begun to break the bounds of both the "trouser roles" and the comic bumpkin persona to pursue works which won her acclaim as a tragedienne. And, for the most part, her critics were in awe of her artfulness at such a young age. As for the Lethbridge playgoers, perhaps they were simply uncouth, later proven by Fidelio's complaint that some had brought their dogs to the performance of *A Stranger in a Strange Land* on December 3.

While Fidelio thought the production of *The Spoilers*, a 1907 melodrama set during the Alaska Gold Rush, did not suit the Allen Players, he gave a favorable review for *The Lion and the Mouse*, a 1905 Broadway drama, which was a "thinly veiled, fictionalized account of Ida Tarbell's battle against John D. Rockefeller." He was also complimentary of *The Undertow*, *The Christian*, and *The Second in Command*. Verna was given another opportunity to play a wanton woman in *Sapho*, the story of a notorious courtesan who is unable to return the love of a smitten lover. The original Broadway production had rocked New York in 1900, especially after featuring a scene where the lover seizes the courtesan and carries her up a winding stair to her bedroom. That production was shut down by the police, and the star was arrested. No such thing happened in Lethbridge. Fidelio rationalized, "People now-a-days obviously like something well spiced." A week later, Verna appeared as Elspeth Tyrell in *The Road to Yesterday*, a comedy-fantasy, which had played successfully for seven months on Broadway in 1907. Elspeth, a modern English lass, dreams she has been transported back to the seventeenth

Verna as Elspeth Tyrell in *The Road to Yesterday*, Regina, Saskatchewan, 1912.

century, where everyone is the counterpart of a person Elspeth knows in the present. She has become Lady Elizabeth, fleeing a libidinous guardian, who is eventually slain by an outcast named Jack. Once Elspeth awakens, she realizes that the Jack of the present is the man of her dreams. After a two-weeks dose of "standard modern dramas," perhaps Pearl Allen realized it was best to leave Lethbridge laughing. The run closed with a bang on December 9, 1911, when Verna, in *Our New Girl*, played her one comic role of the engagement.

The Allen Players returned to Moose Jaw, Saskatchewan, for the first week of the new year. After a performance of *The Lion and the Mouse*, a reviewer for the *Morning News* predicted that Verna, "far too clever for traveling companies," would win her rightful place in New York "when the predestined time comes." From Moose Jaw, the troupe traveled east to nearby Regina where Verna wowed the audiences in *Resurrection, The Lion and the Mouse*, and *Sapho*. Between the acts, the impressive Royal Hungarian String Quartette continued to please, performing two numbers on January 9, "The Pearl Allen March" and "The Verna Felton Waltz," composed by orchestra leader Josef Schranko.

T. Herbert Chesnut, a reporter for the *Regina Leader*, got a rare glimpse behind-the-scenes when he called on the Allens and Verna at their cozy suite of rooms at the Kings Hotel. Expecting to find a room devoid of tasteful knickknacks and personal items, Chesnut was pleasantly surprised with the scene before him as a jovial Pearl ushered him into the apartment. Books and magazines were spread on a table. Attractive prints and family photographs were displayed here and there. Near a window in a rocking chair sat Clara, reading a book. Verna was rearranging things on a table while Marie Thompson was busy making tea using a spirit lamp at a side table. Pearl explained that the ladies liked to make their hotel rooms cosy and comfortable wherever they happened to be.

Before accompanying Pearl downstairs for an interview, Chesnut spoke with Verna for a bit. She related that the favorite of her current roles was Katusha in *Resurrection* because it called for a "complete reversal of one's nature." But Verna revealed that the roles she aspired to play were those written by French dramatist Victorien Sardou whose works *La Tosca, Fedora,* and *Gismonda* especially appealed to her. When she returned to Regina two months later for a brief run, *Regina Leader* columnist Adele Gibson compared Verna's appearance and mannerisms to the well-known English actress Constance Collier, "Her deep, full voice now subdued, now loud and strong, combined with her intonations of speech, and very wonderful facial expression, is a triumph of natural art in each personality she portrays."

By June 1912, one of Verna's dreams came true when Pearl staged Sardou's comedy *Les Divorcons* at the Victoria Theatre during their three-month run there. While this play was not one of Sardou's dramas Verna had hoped for, perhaps this was Pearl's wise choice. Cyprienne de Prunelles is a flighty wife who insists that her husband grant a divorce so that she can marry a cousin. The loving husband is naturally dismayed but he calmly sets a plan in motion. He agrees to the divorce, quietly hinting that he will be able to marry a more beautiful and intelligent woman. The ruse works, and Cyprienne remains Mme. de Prunelles. The role gave Verna "much opportunity for her diversified talent, at first pleading, then bewitching, then angry, and again imperious." The *Victoria Daily Colonist* found not a dull moment in this offering, "due to the vivacity of Miss Felton."

Verna Felton, Regina, Saskatchewan, 1912.

The 1912 repertoire also included a 1908 Broadway flop called *The House of a Thousand Candles*, which had become a sensational hit on the road and in stock. The Allen Players had first staged this mystery in Cranbrook, British Columbia, in the fall of 1910, but it did not seem to become a regular part of their repertoire until two years later. The plot involves a rich uncle who pretends to die and leaves his fortune to his nephew on the condition that he reside in the spooky mansion for a year. Eerie noises, secret passages, and the requisite suspicious butler provide complications. Verna played a dual role, appearing almost unrecognizable in one scene as a flirtatious youngster. Again her costumes were the subject of much discussion in the *Colonist*, particularly an Alice blue messaline veiled in black chiffon, accented by a matching straw hat trimmed in black ostrich plumes. Upon the Allen Players' closing on September 7, the *Colonist* touted it as the first stock company able to play a continuous season of three months in Victoria. Their immediate destination was northward to Prince Rupert for a brief engagement. Since they had been in Victoria since June 17, it is doubtful that they had much time that summer to relax at Allen's Green.

Verna looking a little dubious about her headdress, Regina, 1912.

By November 4, the company had reached Lethbridge where they opened at the Morris Theater for the first of two fall engagements. The highlight of the first run was Charles Hoyt's *A Contented Woman*, a comedy written for the New York stage in 1897, but not discovered by Pearl Allen until he received the script in the mail from an anonymous person, suggesting he present the play to Canadian audiences. The story involved a woman running against her husband in a mayoral race. Since the suffragist movement was gaining momentum by 1912, perhaps the sender wanted women to see how ridiculous it would be for a woman to run for public office. Pearl immediately accepted the play, but Clara voiced her opposition upon discovering that her role of suffragette leader Mrs. Jemima Crew required her to dress in men's clothing. Whether old-school Clara was an opponent to women's rights or she considered the costume a mockery to the suffragettes is unclear. But her genial husband persuaded her to don trousers, tie, and vest for a trial run of the play. The audience reaction was so overwhelming that it played in standing room conditions for a week.

One new member of the troupe undoubtedly found particular amusement with Clara's performance. This thirty-one-year-old novice, slight of build and with deep-set owlish eyes, was learning the ropes as he absorbed every performance of the Allen Players. The young fellow came in handy when carrying trunks and assembling scenery, but now and then he was entrusted with a bit part, as a waiter or porter. Like his mother, who also began her career without theatrical experience, this quiet, unassuming young man would learn all the proper stage manners by observing and copying the professional members of the Allen Players. The particulars of how and where he joined the company are not known, but that day must have been a joyous reunion for Clara Allen and her eldest son Howard Wiggins.

It is doubtful that Clara had had much contact with Howard after she moved to San Jose in 1891. And it is even more uncertain whether Howard, as a youngster, remembered that Clara was his actual birth mother; he was barely three years old when she gave him to the Wigginses to rear. The Wigginses and the Feltons maintained relatively frequent contact until 1889, the occasion of Clara's last visit to Downieville. Six years after that, Howard and his adoptive parents had moved to Oakland with plans to eventually relocate to Chicago, where James Wiggins had been born. This was delayed for several years, most likely due to the declining health of his wife Lizzie, so they remained in Oakland until after her death from uterine cancer on January 19, 1900. Within a few years, James remarried and moved his new wife and Howard to Chicago. Here, in 1910, Howard was living in the Vestibule Hotel on Van Buren Street while earning his living as a hotel clerk. On the census record for that year, he listed his mother's birthplace as Australia, which is exactly where Lizzie Wiggins was born. Perhaps not long after this, James told Howard the story of his adoption. Or maybe he knew all along that Clara was his real mother. It's possible that Clara sought out Howard and explained her dire situation in 1884 when Ed

Van Alstine ran off and left his little family. Perhaps she convinced him to move to Canada where he would have a steady job and family support. Whatever the case, he was reunited with Clara by the fall of 1912. And brother Clayton was not far behind.

1913 remains almost a complete mystery, but it is suspected that the Allen Players followed the path, by now very familiar, from Alberta to Saskatchewan to Manitoba, then backtracking to all the way to British Columbia. During the second week of May they received rave reviews for *Madame X* at the Nanaimo Opera House. Adapted from the French play *La Femme X*, this tear-jerker had run on Broadway for 125 performances in early 1910. It afforded Verna, not yet twenty-three years old, the chance to play a woman who "descends from the highest to the lowest dregs of society," one who was disowned by her husband when he learned of her adultery, one who has not seen her son for over twenty years. When she is brought to trial for her lover's murder, she is reunited with her son in the most unusual of circumstances; he is the prosecuting attorney. The *Free Press* called her performance " vivid, intense, and masterful."

The summer of 1913 was spent in rest and recreation at Allen's Green once again. After an evening performance at the Ladysmith Opera House, Pearl asked Helen Haworth, the sister of the proprietor, if she knew of a townsperson who would prepare a late supper for the players. She recommended that they contact Mary Ann Thomas, who readily agreed to cook a meal. Assisting Mrs. Thomas was her thirty-three-year-old spinster daughter Margaret, who was barely a year old when the family immigrated to Canada from South Wales in 1888. A friendship grew between the Allens and the Thomas family, and soon Margaret was hired to travel with the troupe as Verna's maid.

In the meantime, Verna's wandering brother Clayton Felton had become a part of the Allen Players. Wanted for military desertion, Clayton had eluded army officials for over three years until his apprehension in March, 1911. He was consequently forced to serve ninety days at the Presidio of San Francisco. How Clayton spent the intervening two years is merely speculative, but perhaps after this misadventure Clara insisted he join the rest of the family in Canada. Along the stock circuit, a budding romance grew between Clayton and Margaret Thomas, despite his dubious "track record."

By June 1914, the Allen Players found themselves back in Victoria after a full season on the circuit. The Royal Victoria Theatre, usually closed in summers, kept its doors wide open for the troupe, who opened with William C. de Mille's *The Woman*, a melodrama which had starred Mary Nash on Broadway for seven months beginning in the fall of 1911. Verna played the part created by Nash— that of Wanda Kelly, a telephone operator who thwarts the efforts of two corrupt congressmen to push through a bill legalizing railway overcapitalization. Before closing on July 4, the company presented *A Contented Woman*, which allowed Verna the opportunity of wearing "some charming frocks and a bewildering array

Verna Felton, 1914. GLENBOW ARCHIVES NA-2642-76.

of hats," a tactic her suffragette character uses to attract attention when delivering her campaign speeches. The production was considerably jazzed up with music, provided by a chorus of suffragettes and politicians, not to mention Verna's lively rendering of ragtime favorites.

While the Allen Players relaxed at Allen's Green later in the summer, distressing news arrived from Europe. On August 4, Britain, France, and Russia declared war on Germany and the Austro-Hungarian Empire. What would become the First World War had begun. For Canadians, the news came at the worst time due to serious economic situations at home, caused by plunging wheat yields following a severe summer drought.

The Allen Players' vacation at Allen's Green was cut short that August when drifting smoke from forest fires made camping almost unbearable. Sightings of a bear and several cougars, driven south by the fires, alarmed the company's women until Pearl and company packed up and headed back to Victoria, where he had already engaged a facility to house the Allen Players as a permanent stock organization. He chose the Princess Theatre on Yates Street, formerly a dingy, unattractive building. All summer workmen had been renovating the place, installing a raised house floor and 730 new opera chairs. Pearl chose for the August 17 opener Frances Hodgson Burnett's *The Dawn of a Tomorrow*, praised as "a little Sunday School lesson in the power of prayer" when it opened on the New York stage in 1909. Verna played a redheaded ragamuffin called Glad who befriends a wealthy Englishman set on suicide. Her cheerful outlook, despite her own dire situation, inspires the man to reclaim his life. To return her kindness, he eventually helps exonerate Glad's beau from criminal charges. "She enters into the cyclonic intensity of the child-woman's ever changing moods with deep understanding," crowed the Victoria Colonist of Verna's performance, "and presents a clear picture to the imagination."

For the remainder of the engagement, the Allen Players presented a mix of old and new, including the tried-and-true *Resurrection, Zaza, All Due to Diana, Madame X*, and the perpetually popular *Under Two Flags*. Ever since Verna had taken its leading role in 1905, the part of Cigarette had been one of her favorites. Now, almost a decade later, she was still getting requests to play the vivandiere. She recalled the role with fondness when interviewed by *TV Guide* in 1957. A nearly fatal mishap occurred during the tense scene where Verna was required to race a horse up an incline, which had been designed to resemble a hill in the desert. At the pinnacle, located offstage and not visible to the audience, the horse was supposed to descend a ramp, but missed his footing and fell fifty feet with Verna, who nonchalantly recalled, "I just kept his head up and we sort of wedged ourselves in between the side of the ramp and the brick wall backstage. Neither one of us got a scratch."

Pearl also pulled *The Stowaway* out of mothballs for a week's run in September. When he informed the players of his choice, it caused an absolute row. The troupe viewed the melodrama, first produced in 1888, as dated and artificial.

They predicted a dire failure, but Pearl Allen smiled and waited. He knew his audience. On opening night, "what might easily have proved a tiresome display of obsolete theatrical clap-trap," according to the *Colonist*, "was turned into a living, pulsating thing which sent shocks of joy into all who came into contact with it. The villains were both hissed and applauded, and glared in response with twinkling eyes." Verna, now twenty-four, "had the house topsy-turvy" with her monkeyshines as the London newsboy Chucky, just as she had done since she was thirteen. The occasion would mark the last time Verna appeared in a "trouser role."

Some of the company's new productions that fall were those recently made available to the stock companies. These included *A Butterfly on the Wheel*, lauded for its "absence of overacting," the comedy *Stop Thief*, a muckraking drama called *Fine Feathers*, the runaway Broadway success *Within the Law*, and a charming English comedy called *Green Stockings*, in which Verna played the elder sister whose spinsterhood stands in the way of her younger sister's marrying. To expedite the wedding, she creates an imaginary boyfriend for herself, only to kill him off in battle soon thereafter. Complications arise when a colonel by the same name appears at her door. According to the play, green stockings were traditionally worn by old maids at their sisters' weddings.

The highlight of the season, however, came in November, when Verna played the lead in *Peg O' My Heart*, a comedy by J. Hartley Manners, which had closed on Broadway in May after an astounding 604 performances. The *Victoria Colonist* raved, "Had Manager Allen searched through the entire file of comedies, old and new, he could scarcely have found one more suited to Miss Felton than *Peg O' My Heart*. In the first place, Peg is Irish, and Miss Felton inherits enough of the Celtic temperament to give her a completely natural mastery of the volatile characteristics of this race and of the fascinating brogue as well." Peg is the poor relation of a snooty but down-on-their-luck English family, who must teach her some manners or else lose an inheritance. Needless to say, the part of the unconventional Peg, creating an uproar in this very proper household, was indeed perfect for Verna, whose unlimited energy kept the play moving at a brisk speed.

Clara Allen also shared a bit of the limelight during the Princess Theatre engagement. Pearl cast her in the title role of *The Rejuvenation of Aunt Mary* in late August 1914. The comedy had achieved a modest success on Broadway back in 1907, starring May Robson as a crotchety spinster who must save her nephew from a blackmailing adventuress. Visiting him in the wicked city, she is surprised to find the place very appealing. In no time, she dons fashionable clothes, frequent cafes, smokes and plays poker with the best of them. One critic felt that Clara carried off the part with a "simple unaffected method." Her second chance to shine came the following February when she was cast again in a title role, *Mrs. Wiggs of the Cabbage Patch*, a goodhearted woman who tries to be a friend to everyone. According to the *Colonist*, Clara did not seem to be acting, "There is no straining after effect in her work. The beautiful lines of the part seem to come right from the heart."

Meanwhile, the romance which had grown between Clayton Felton and Margaret Thomas, Verna's maid, culminated in their marriage at "Breadalbane," the manse of the Presbyterian church in Victoria, on September 17, 1914. Both would continue as members of the troupe following their nuptials.

Plays like *Mrs. Wiggs of the Cabbage Patch* and *The Third Degree* entertained the Princess audiences throughout the winter of 1915, including soldiers stationed nearby who frequently attended performances. Clara told the *Colonist*, "So many of them we know by name or by sight from different towns in the Interior that it seems they are all good friends, and we certainly appreciate the splendid support they have given us this winter." Despite positive praise from the press, however, by March, the company was just not making a profit, even though they maintained their popular price range from fifteen to fifty cents per seat. Mentions of the troupe in the *Colonist* disappeared after a March 7 preview of *My Lady Nell* so it is believed this play was their swan song in Victoria. It quite possibly could have been their final performance in Canada that year, for the Great War was taking its toll.

CHAPTER 7

————•◦•————

CALIFORNIA

In the early years of the twentieth century, the mainspring of Canadian prosperity had been the rapid development of the Prairie Provinces, a land best suited to the production of wheat. Industrial Europe was willing to pay a profitable price for all that the Canadian prairie could supply, so Canada became one of the world's chief exporters of the grain. The drought of 1914 and the dearth of produced wheat put a serious strain on the nation's economy. In addition, more than fifty thousand people lost their jobs in 1914 and 1915 as the railway sector floundered under massive amounts of debt. Furthermore, construction activities shrank substantially from a lack of capital. Six hundred thousand men, equaling 20 percent of the pre-war labor force, entered military service. In these early years of the war, Canada's economic situation was indeed bleak.

The Allen Players were not exempt from financial difficulties. The war's effect upon luxury spending, including, of course, theatre tickets, was almost immediate. Recalling the war's effect upon Canada, Verna stated in 1964, "The First World War broke everybody that there was to break." Pearl found it necessary for the Allen Players to disband. The Allens and Verna returned to the States in 1915 with little hope of reorganizing the company there. After all, they had not performed in America for eight years, except for a brief engagement in Tacoma in 1910. While Verna's brother Howard accompanied them to America, Clayton Felton stayed behind in Duncan, British Columbia, where his wife Margaret was expected to deliver a baby in early summer, 1915.

There are indications that Verna became a freelance artist at this point, finding stage work wherever available in her native country. Attempts to find complete documentation of these engagements, however, resulted in a fruitless search through the proverbial haystack. Therefore, what follows is a sketchy account, unfortunately, of some of Verna's most successful endeavors and, conversely, some of her most disappointing ventures in the field of entertainment.

Considering the times, Verna was fortunate to find sporadic work during this period with various American stock companies, including those performing in the Shubert theatres in St. Paul and Minneapolis. She also played the Grand Opera House in Brooklyn and the Lyric Theater in Bridgeport, Connecticut, as well as the Castle Square Theater, an ornate venue located in out-of-the-way South Boston. Opened in 1894, the Castle Square, by the time of Verna's stint there, was managed by John Craig whose John Craig Players had been the theater's resident stock company since 1908. This stock company had become something of a pacesetter among stock companies prior to the United States' entry into World War One. Craig was famous for experimenting more daringly, and successfully, with new plays, new season planning concepts, and new staging techniques than his two predecessors. For three seasons, beginning in 1912, one member of the troupe was young Alfred Lunt, destined to become, with wife Lynn Fontanne, half of the pre-eminent Broadway acting couple in American history. Others in the company during this period were future Hollywood film performers Mabel Colcord, Henry Hull, and Donald Meek. The Castle Square company was considered one of the four most respected companies in the country. After appearing with this company, an actor could be assured of obtaining a position with almost any company having an opening. Most probably Verna thought that her tenure with the Castle Square would provide her with more permanent employment, but that was not to be.

Early in 1916, Verna was engaged to play in a production of *The Big Idea*, an unusual comedy written by A. E. Thomas and Clayton Hamilton, which made its Broadway bow in the fall of 1914, playing only three weeks before being yanked after mixed reviews. "Critics were torn between slamming the play's dullness and lauding its originality," wrote author Gerald Bordman in *American Theatre: 1914-1930*. The "big idea" was actually a plan devised by the two leading characters to write a play, using real events as their plot, making this a play within a play, but one in which the two plots converge and intermingle in the last act. When it failed on Broadway, plans were made for it to be produced the following spring in Chicago, where it was thought the public would be more receptive to "cleverness and fantasy." By early 1916, *The Big Idea* was appearing in many theaters across the country, the rights having been bought by Broadway producers George M. Cohan and Sam Harris. According to an article in the *Sacramento Bee*, Verna appeared in a production of *The Big Idea* in George M. Cohan's theater in New York City around this time. However, this claim remains to be substantiated after a thorough search of *The New York Times* failed to reveal that this play was produced in any of the city's boroughs at that time. It is possible that the *Bee* was misinformed, and perhaps instead Verna was performing in *The Big Idea* elsewhere within the state of New York.

According to the Bee, after this New York production folded, Verna signed to replace the former leading lady of the resident stock company at Sacramento's Grand Theater in a production of the drama *So Much for So Much*, an engagement doomed from the start. The play was scheduled to open on January 30, 1916, but snowstorms in the East delayed the arrival of the script. Instead, *The Big Idea* was staged, but this last-minute choice proved to be unwise. The Sacramento audiences, like those in the East, were not appreciative of the play's novelty. "*The Big Idea* is illogical and unconvincing, even preposterous," wrote the *Sacramento Bee* critic. "It has to limp along as best it can." Though he described Verna as "young and vivacious" and well suited for her role, he dismissed the play as a failure.

The following week, *So Much for So Much* received slightly warmer notices, but Sacramento audiences were definitely not interested. The curiosity seekers were instead packing the house at the nearby Orpheum where vaudeville performer Evelyn Nesbit was appearing. Nesbit, a former Broadway chorus girl, had gained notoriety following the "crime of the century," the 1906 murder of her former lover, architect Stanford White, by her jealous husband, Harry Thaw. To support herself following her divorce from the imprisoned Thaw, Nesbit took advantage of the notoriety by working the vaudeville circuit. Once a beautiful artist's model and the supposed inspiration for Charles Dana Gibson's classic creation "The Gibson Girl," Nesbit looked rather long-in-the-tooth, judging by 1916 newspaper photographs. Evidently her appearance on the Sacramento stage was equally unimpressive. The *Sacramento Bee*'s drama critic reported that she was frail and thin, adding that a woman seated behind him whispered to her companion that murder needed more provocation than Nesbit's skinny legs.

For Verna's third week at the Grand, the manager chose *All-of-a-Sudden Peggy*, a 1907 bit of fluff about an American girl whose mother conspires to marry her to an English lord. Instead Peggy falls for his younger brother and matches her mother up with the lord, thus becoming her own mother's sister-in-law. Clara Allen was engaged to play Peggy's mother, and was praised for fitting the part "with little fault to be found." The *Bee*'s critic found leading man Albert Morrison "pepless," citing him for "running on low gear while Miss Felton was on high." Verna was credited with doing her part "to save the show from developing into a doleful farce."

The reviewer was more favorable toward the next production, *The Spoils of War*, a drama purported to have been written the previous fall by a wounded French soldier during his hospital convalescence. During his recovery, Leon Mathoit had become a self-professed neutralist. His work endeavored to expose the mistreatment shown by captors toward those of a defeated nation, especially women and children. At the time, President Woodrow Wilson was still stressing his policy of strict neutrality, and this issue was foremost in the minds of watchful Americans. Audience members at the Grand applauded lines devoted to the subject of neutrality, but they also clapped loudly for lines regarding preparedness. "It is apparent from the lines that the play has been revamped and almost entirely re-written from the original . . . to fit America," observed the *Bee*'s critic. "Some of the lines sound as if they were cut from speeches delivered in Congress by representatives seeking the limelight." However, the reviewer was complimentary of the scenic and lighting effects, especially during the air raid on the town of

Linden, "There is plenty of noise, action, powder smoke, and the like to make the play lively." Verna was described as a "cyclone of passion and suffering" in the scene where she shoots an invading army general upon learning that his men ravaged her daughter. This praise indicates that finally, on the fourth attempt, the Grand may have had a hit on its hands, but without warning they closed their doors after the evening performance of February 24, citing financial difficulties. Once again, Verna was without work.

Verna and the Allens then retreated to San Francisco where Pearl sought employment with Patrick Edward O'Hair, the husband of his elder sister, Cora. O'Hair had founded a plumbing supply company prior to the 1906 earthquake. Pearl was hired as bookkeeper for P. E. O'Hair's wrecking department, presumably keeping track of records related to second-hand fixtures salvaged from demolition sites in the city. At this time, the Allens and Verna made their home at 1332 Scott Street.

With two exceptions, there is no evidence that Verna Felton was engaged in acting for a period of two years following her ill-fated Sacramento engagement in the winter of 1916. On July 9 of that year, she joined the New Orpheum Players, a repertory company who regularly performed as on the bill of the Oakland Orpheum, a vaudeville house at Twelfth and Clay Streets. The players, numbering twenty, included many former performers from Oakland's recently defunct Ye Liberty Theatre. Verna, as leading lady, opened with suave leading man J. Anthony Smythe in a three-act comedy *A Pair of Sixes*, which had enjoyed a successful run on Broadway in 1914. The action took place at the Eureka Digestive Pill Company, where its two partners frequently argue so much that their lawyer suggests a game of poker to decide who will leave the business for a year. The loser must also serve as butler for the winner, a situation which creates many complications as the loser tries to get the winner to call off the deal.

A behind-the-scenes drama was more newsworthy than the actual production. On the evening of July 11, an attempt was made to endanger the health of leading man Smythe. During the curtain call, he was presented with two huge bouquets of carnations sent by an anonymous party. A mystified Smythe bent down to examine them and detected an unusually pungent odor rising from the flowers. He deeply inhaled the strong scent in an attempt to identify it and in minutes became deathly sick. Smythe was removed promptly to his hotel, where a doctor examined the carnations only to surmise that a combination of obnoxious, though not necessarily fatal, poisons might have been used to spray the bouquets. The identity of the sender was never discovered, nor was the incident repeated. The next day Smythe was enough recovered, although appearing somewhat languid, to perform in the matinee of *A Pair of Sixes*.

Virtually an unknown to Oakland audiences, Verna received the briefest mentions in the weekly drama column of the *Oakland Tribune*, and even then was misidentified at times as "Ferna Felton," "Verna Fulton," and "Lorna

Felton." It appears she played with the New Orpheum Players for eight weeks or so before the dissolution of this company in early fall.

In early 1917, William V. Mong, who had briefly been a member of the Allen Stock Company in Tacoma twelve years earlier, approached her regarding a role in a new medium of entertainment. Mong, by now a veteran performer of over forty silent films and director of half as many, was casting for a new motion picture for the Crest Picture Company, set to film in southern California near Los Angeles. The screenplay, written by former attorney Lyman I. Henry, was based on the Old Testament book of Samuel, focusing on the friendship of David and Jonathan. Called *The Chosen Prince*, it told the story of David, the sheperd boy proclaimed by Samuel to become a great Israelite leader. Sent by King Saul to battle Goliath, David wins the admiration of Saul's son Jonathan, who becomes David's lifelong friend. Soon David is a favorite of Saul's court, exacerbating Saul's jealousy. Saul's unsuccessful attempts to kill David, who has married Saul's daughter Michal, fail, lead him to eventually drive David into a ten-year exile in the land of the Philistines. When Jonathan is slain in a battle with the Philistines, Saul kills himself in grief, and David is summoned by the Israelites to become their king.

Verna was cast as Michal, wife of David, who protects him from her angry father Saul. Edward Alexander and Charles Perley were chosen to play David and Jonathan, respectively. The part of Saul went to Noah Beery, who was destined to soon become a respected film actor, noted for his portrayals of cruel villains. Verna's mother Clara was hired to play David's mother, Nazbat, while Harry Holden was given the part of David's father, Jesse. Director William V. Mong filled the role of Samuel. Filming took place outside the small town of Monrovia, California, about twenty-five miles from Los Angeles, where the nearby foothills of the San Gabriel Mountains provided a realistic setting for the production.

Production of *The Chosen Prince* began in March and was completed in early summer. According to records maintained by the American Film Institute, the film's exact release date remains unknown. It is believed that it was never generally released to motion picture theaters. In fact, it may have been produced strictly for use by religious groups. Evidence exists that the film was available to the public by the fall after its completion. On November 20, 1917, the *Indianapolis Star* reported that the eight-reeler would be shown to members of the Grand Lodge of the Independent Order of the Odd Fellows, a fraternal organization dedicated to "elevating the character of man." It was still being screened three years later when the United Projector and Film Company distributed the film to educational institutions. For the next six or so years, at least until the advent of sound films, *The Chosen Prince* was shown around the country in places like church basements, Odd Fellows lodges, and Y. W. C. A.'s. Though the Internet Movie Database website lists an alternate title (*The Friendship of Jonathan and David*) for this film, no newspaper items located during the silent film era identify it by anything but *The Chosen Prince*.

The Motion Picture, Broadcasting, and Recorded Sound Division of The Library of Congress reported in 2006 that their organization deaccessioned their only copy of *The Chosen Prince* from their collection in 1988, following an unsuccessful attempt to preserve its extreme decomposition. No copies have been found to exist in other archives, but there is a possibility that the film could be in the hands of a private collector. The only known photographic evidence of Verna Felton's brief silent film experience is a collection of snapshots, probably taken by Pearl Allen, discovered in a crumbling album in Verna's attic in 2004. Most of the photographs offer behind-the-scenes views of Verna in her princess robes and pendulous gold jewelry and beads. She also wears the characteristic heavy makeup of silent film actors. Handsome Edward Alexander, as sheperd David, sports a curly blonde wig and sheepskin tunic. Clara Allen poses beside a camel with fellow actors Alexander and Holden while the mother of William V. Mong, a visitor on the set, stands nearby. In another candid shot, Mong, smoking a pipe, appears every inch the director in his military-style leather leggings and jodhpurs. Other scenes reveal the Israelite army in battle formation and the realistic sets created to resemble Biblical flat-roof dwellings. Verna never mentioned *The Chosen Prince* in any subsequent interviews, so one can only surmise from these photographs what the experience must have been like. She did write to her old San Jose friend Mrs. Clara Gairaud of her delight at being selected for the role.

Once filming ended, Verna and the Allens returned to San Francisco where they waited out the war, hoping for promising stage work. Verna's brother Howard joined them at 26 Steiner Street. As a former member of the Allen Players, he had also been displaced by the effects of World War One, but found new employment as a result. Howard became an oiler with the Bethlehem Steel Corporation in their San Francisco shipyard, where battleships were built and repaired. On September 12, 1918, Howard registered for the draft just two months before the end of the war, but, owing to that late date, he was probably never called into service.

Meanwhile, on the same day, his brother Clayton Felton had registered for the draft in Duckabush, Washington. Clayton had originally signed up with the Canadian Overseas Expeditionary Force in January of 1916, but it is doubtful that he ever fulfilled that obligation. Family tradition has it that around this time he abandoned his wife Margaret and baby son Ernest Richard Felton, who had been born in Duncan, British Columbia on July 6, 1915. Clayton's desertion sadly mirrored that of his own father Ed Van Alstine some thirty years before. He would never see his family again, and his son Ernest would grow up fatherless in a household where Welsh-born Margaret ruled with an iron hand. While he listed Margaret as his next of kin on the 1918 draft registration, Clayton claimed he was unmarried two years later when the 1920 census was taken. At that time, he was residing in Lilliwaup, Washington, where he made a living as a restaurant cook. Curiously, Clayton's birth date on the draft registration is listed as 1876,

Verna in costume as Michal in *The Chosen Prince*, 1917.

implying that he was seven years older than his true age of thirty-five and leading one to wonder if he wanted to appear older to escape military service.

In late April 1918, Verna teamed with former Allen Player Ethel Corley to appear for a single week's engagement at the Oakland Orpheum, a vaudeville house, in a sketch written by Corley called *The Answer* and described as an "intense dramatic bit with heart appeal."

Verna and Edward Alexander.

Clara Allen, Edward Alexander, and Harry Holden.

Director William V. Mong.

Location filming for The Chosen Prince.

Director Mong's mother, CENTER, visits the movie set. Looking on are Verna holding Kazan (EXTREME LEFT), Edward Alexander (CENTER), and Mong in costume as Samuel (EXTREME RIGHT).

In June, Verna received word of the death of Jessie Shirley, the actress who helped Verna break into show business in 1900. The fifty-one-year-old succumbed to cancer on May 29 at her home in Spokane, Washington, the city where Verna and the Allens had parted company with Shirley in 1902. Three years following this split, the Jessie Shirley Company had become a permanent stock organization at Spokane's Auditorium Theater, playing that house continuously for over four years. In early 1909, Shirley distinguished herself when she took on the country's most famous evangelist Billy Sunday in a spirited newspaper battle after he viciously attacked the stage, the theatrical profession, and its supporters during a Spokane campaign. As a daughter of a Baptist minister and a student of the Bible, Shirley stingingly defended her choice of profession in a lengthy, eloquent rebuttal, which appeared in newspapers across the country.

Not long after this, Shirley's company disbanded, but she spent the following eight years on the vaudeville circuit, mainly playing the west coast. Stricken with breast cancer in 1914, she continued to perform regularly following radical surgery. In the summer of 1917, she filmed a silent motion picture comedy, *The Man Hater*, for the Triangle Film Corporation in their Yonkers, New York studio. By October, her health had begun to deteriorate so she returned to Spokane to undergo an operation, which revealed the spread of cancer. She spent her final eight weeks confined to bed. By her side when death came was her husband Harry Smith, who first recognized Verna Felton's talent back in San Jose at the benefit for the Galveston Flood survivors. Verna would stay in touch with him until his death in 1950.

The static period from 1916 to 1918 must have seemed to Verna as the nadir of her career. For over ten years, she had been the leading lady in a successful stock company, earning recognition not only on the West Coast but across much of Canada. Now she was reduced to appearing in vaudeville, a medium which did not allow its performers to establish rapport with local audiences in the same manner as stock performers were able. In addition, the vaudeville theatres depended upon constant novelty in their programming because they chiefly appealed to the working classes who could barely read and write. Vaudeville audiences were not interested in stock plays, which usually contained long, intricate plots with abundant dialogue. In the 1910s, vaudeville was on the rise, becoming a more serious competitor for stock companies than ever before.

However, Verna was proud of her background in legitimate theatre, evidenced by her vocal tone during the 1964 interview with Marty Halperin when asked if she learned her skills on the vaudeville stage. Without condescension, but with immediate affirmity, Verna replied that the Allen Players performances were "all drama," meaning that they performed legitimate plays, most of which had first been produced on Broadway. She further delineated for her interviewer the difference between the two fields of legitimate theater and vaudeville, "See, vaudeville was just in these particular houses. There was Sullivan and Considine, like the little chap [Tim Considine] who's with the Fred MacMurray show [*My Three Sons*]. Well, [John Considine] was his grandfather . . . And then there was the Pantages circuit . . . and they were the vaudevilles." (Interestingly, actor Tim Considine's maternal grandfather was Alexander Pantages, the famous vaudeville impresario, while Tim's father was motion picture producer John W. Considine, Jr., son of the vaudeville producer.) Verna hastened to clear up any confusion about the song-and-dance routines she'd performed between the acts during her early days with Jessie Shirley and Pearl Allen. Admitting that these numbers were like those performed by vaudeville acts, she explained their necessity for stock playhouses, "Instead of letting an audience just sit, you know, and read their program or something, they had songs and dances between the acts. So it kept us going right through [from the songs/dances to the next act of the play]."

Appreciation for her stock experience, particularly with the Allen Players, was very evident in Verna's voice that winter day in 1964, as she sighed, "But I had very great experiences. The people [the playgoers and the stock company members] were nice, all the people were nice . . . a good company." At this stage in her life, almost forty years after her days in stock, Verna was hard-pressed to identify any specific stock experiences that were unusual or amusing, "There was always something doing, something that was happening, but I'm trying to think, as I tried to think last night as I was going to sleep, something definite, but we [The Allen Players] were a very peaceful company."

The same could not be said, however, for the company Verna signed with following her run at the Oakland Orpheum in 1918. Walter B. Gilbert, who spent that summer in Oakland, was scouting for new and talented players to begin a season of stock in Portland, Oregon, at the Baker Theatre. Gilbert had been an actor with the Baker company since 1913, and now, as its director, he had been given a certain responsibility by its managers to locate players of high caliber for the 1918-19 season. The Baker Stock Company had existed, in one form or another, in Portland since 1902, and its original owner-manager, George L. Baker, had produced and presented some of the most exciting stock productions to be seen on the West Coast. Its alumni included Fay Bainter, James Gleason, Thurston Hall, Edward Everett Horton, Florence Roberts, and William V. Mong. The new managers wanted to uphold the reputation of the Baker Stock Company as a first-class company producing the latest proven successes. As a result, they were able to choose selectively among actors "at liberty." And Verna certainly fit the bill. Not only was she adept at drama, comedy, and music, but she was also very available.

Verna signed on as "second woman," an actress who usually played the leading woman's confidante, rival, or the adventuress of the drama. While the particulars of her Baker contract are not known, Verna recalled in 1962 that a leading lady with the Baker company could expect to earn as much as $150 per week whereas most of the stock companies then were paying no more than $75 to $100 weekly to the leads. Second players could expect to earn about half the salary of a lead, still very good pay at the time. However, the job was quite demanding, considering that the leads and second people had to study a new and long role weekly.

Walter K. Waters, in his study of the Baker company, described a typical workweek: "The Baker company opened each new play with a Sunday matinee. On Sunday evening, roles for the next production were assigned . . . After the Sunday night performance, [the actor] went to his apartment and started the work of assimilating new lines for the new production . . . Most actors attempted to have their lines learned within two days after receiving their roles. On Monday morning at ten o'clock, the cast assembled in the theatre or rehearsal hall for the first read-through of the play and for the first blocking rehearsals . . . On Tuesday, the second half of the play would be blocked. On Wednesday, matinee day, the actors would gather in the morning for a complete run-through of the new play; and on Thursday, they usually had a day off. That is, they were not required to go to the theatre except for the evening performance . . . Friday was the day of the first dress rehearsal. The actors would appear in as much of their costumes as were finished . . . the performers were expected to know the production letter perfect. Saturday morning another full rehearsal would be held . . . On Sunday morning a final rehearsal was often held in preparation for the opening of the new play that afternoon." As Verna later put it, an actor in a company such as this, in any given week, was performing one play while trying to learn the next week's play as well as trying to forget the previous week's play.

In late August 1918, Verna packed her trunks for Portland, the city she had left in the spring of 1908 as a seventeen-year-old leading lady in a successful family-owned stock company. Now, ten years later, she was returning to "The City of Roses" as a second woman in one of the top four stock organizations in the country. Her stay there would be a stepping-stone to an entirely new adventure, one which would provide a reunion with someone from her past, someone whose devotion would forever alter the course of Verna Felton's life.

CHAPTER 8

———•◦•———

ENTER LEE MILLAR

On the afternoon of November 9, 1959, when Lester Lorenzo Schilling Jr. rang the bell at 4147 Bakman Avenue in North Hollywood, California, his mind was overflowing with new knowledge he had acquired in the last five days. Since his arrival from Portland, Oregon, Schilling had managed to interview seven veteran actors, all formerly connected with the Portland stage, including Mary Edgett Baker, Byron Foulger, Helen Kleeb, Edward Everett Horton, Myra Marsh, Rolfe Sedan, and the elderly Josephine Dillon, a former acting coach who had the distinction of being Clark Gable's first wife. From these individuals—most of whom had become busy character actors in film, television, and radio—Schilling sought information related to the history of Portland theatre for his doctoral thesis. Now on this autumn afternoon, he was prepared to conduct his final interview during his stay in Los Angeles, and his head was filled with questions for the grey-haired lady behind the door.

It had been forty years since Verna Felton's two-year stint with the Baker Stock Company in Portland, but her memory of that time was undimmed. Or at least for certain details it was. While Verna's tenure with the company was a successful one, both financially and professionally, the atmosphere backstage was often filled with tension, due in part to circumstances existing before she was hired. Since the fall of 1915, Milton Seaman and LeGrand "Lee" Pearl had been in charge of the Baker company and its theatre when the owner George L. Baker decided to enter politics. Seaman and Pearl, both of whom had been in Baker's employ since 1902, attempted to carry on his tradition of high royalty plays and fully mounted productions. However, when their first season left them virtually bankrupt, several investors came to the rescue in the fall of 1916. One was lawyer Clarence Vivian Everett, whose wife Alice Fleming had been the company's leading lady. At this point, George Baker insisted that his name not be associated with the new organization so it was named the Alcazar Players, borrowing the prestige of that famous San Francisco company. Although Seaman, Pearl, and Everett all wanted to invest in actors and productions as expensive and impressive as those

Baker had presented, they could not agree on other matters. For one, though Everett was the primary stockholder, his wife actually "ran the show," which worsened the situation between the partners. Everett, according to Verna Felton, "hated Seaman's guts."

In the spring of 1918, Everett pulled out, vacating the Baker Theatre and taking with him the majority of the Alcazar Players to a smaller theater, thus leaving Seaman and Pearl out in the cold. However, with the help of director Walter Gilbert, they assembled for the fall season an impressive new group of players, reorganized as the Baker Stock Company. J. Anthony Smythe, described as a "big athletic outdoors sort of chap," was hired by Gilbert as leading man. Both Gilbert and Verna had worked with Smythe in 1916— back in Oakland in *A Pair of Sixes* when Smythe had been delivered the toxic carnations. Curly redhead Betty Brice, a veteran of over thirty silent films in which she was billed as Rosetta Brice, was chosen as the new leading lady. Smythe and Brice had spent the summer of 1918 as leading players at the Ye Liberty Playhouse in Oakland.

A special article introducing these players and the rest of the company appeared in the September 1 edition of the *Sunday Oregonian*. Among those pictured was Verna Felton, sporting a huge brimmed hat and somber expression, her dark-circled eyes reminiscent of silent screen vamp Theda Bara. Demure and aristocratic Geraldine Dare, the ingénue, was also prominently featured in the layout. For the text of the article, drama critic Leone Cass Baer recreated a conversation between Seaman and herself in which he described each new member of the cast, including the character actors John G. Fee, George P. Webster, Lora Rogers, plus Anna McNaughton and her real-life husband Lee Millar. Seaman revealed that McNaughton had appeared on Broadway for three successive seasons with actor-writer Leo Ditrichstein, "who likes her comedy so well that he insists on writing a part for her into every play he presents." As for Lee, Seaman explained, "He doesn't pronounce Millar as if it were spelled Miller. It's like Mill-ahr, you know, stepping on the last syllable."

Changes within the company began almost immediately. Shortly before the September 8 opening and without explanation, J. Anthony Smythe was replaced by Albert McGovern, who had been a member of the Baker company three seasons earlier. While this adjustment had no negative effect, later changes led to dissension among the troupe. Verna summarized the situation for Lester Schillling, "Betty Brice left the company, but her replacement, Olive Templeton, couldn't come for two weeks. She was recovering from the flu. I played the leading role in *The Thirteenth Chair*. Wally Gilbert then put me in *Sis Hopkins*, which went over big. They [the theatre patrons] wouldn't accept the new leading woman, and by the end of the six weeks I was starred." While this is partly true, Verna inadvertently tangled the timing of certain events. A close inspection of the *Oregonian* sets straight her honest mistakes and fleshes out her brief summarization of the situation.

Betty Brice was with the company for five weeks, beginning with *De-Luxe Annie*, the story of a respectable wife who becomes a notorious criminal after a blow to the head renders her amnesic. Brice earned outstanding reviews, while Verna received a nod as a "delightful reformed adventuress." The following week the Baker Stock Company presented *The Thirteenth Chair*, a murder mystery which had been a Broadway hit two years earlier. The action occurs in a single evening in the Crosby mansion, where the affluent owners have planned a séance for after-dinner entertainment. Among the guests is social climber Helen O'Neill, the fiancée of the Crosbys' son, who is abashed to learn that the withered little medium hired for the occasion is her own mother, Rosalie La Grange, whose identity Helen would prefer to keep secret. The Crosbys hope that the séance will reveal the murderer of a friend of one of their dinner guests, Edward Wales. After everyone is locked in the room, Rosalie is tied to her chair and the lights are extinguished. Just as the medium is about to reveal the killer, Wales moans. He is found stabbed to death, but with no knife in sight. For a number of reasons, Helen is the prime suspect. To save her daughter, Rosalie uses all of her tricks to expose the real murderer. Suddenly the murder weapon, a knife which had been flung up into the ceiling, falls in front of one of the guests, revealing the killer.

The casting for *The Thirteenth Chair* seems to have given impetus to the unrest that continued throughout the company for two seasons. According to a 1962 interview conducted by Walter Kenneth Waters, another doctoral candidate whose dissertation focused strictly on the history of the Baker company, Verna stated that Betty Brice objected to playing the leading role of Rosalie because the character was much older than Brice's twenty-six years. Brice's distaste for the part was probably rooted in a desire to maintain her youthful screen image but was also accentuated by her awareness that contemporary playwrights now created leading roles requiring younger actors than those of the previous decade. When Brice refused to play Rosalie, Walter Gilbert, the director, asked Verna if she would accept the part of the crafty old medium, and she did. Although she was only two years older than Brice, Verna was undeniably adept at essaying this colorful character. What happened next backfired on Brice, who had assumed the secondary role of Rosalie's daughter Helen.

On the morning before the first performance, Brice and McGovern received anticipatory commendation from the *Morning Oregonian* for their "powerful" roles as the young lovers, but twenty-four hours later, the review's headline trumpeted, "ACTRESS IS WINNER: Verna Felton Scores Triumph in "The Thirteenth Chair." Leone Cass Baer, while allowing that she had not seen Margaret Wycherly as Rosalie in the Broadway production, opined, "The study of her given by Verna Felton is amazingly real and satisfying . . . There is a maternal brooding, a delicate satire and a splendidly sympathetic note in Miss Felton's portrayal of Rosalie La Grange." The youth-conscious Brice received a quick nod as being "colorful" and "girlish." While Baer also gave credit to John G. Fee for his subtle characterization as the police inspector and to Lee Millar for his "dramatic fervor" as one of the suspects, it was quite transparent that Verna Felton had won a fast fan in Leone Cass Baer.

The review for the next production, *Nothing but the Truth*, further supports this. While Betty Brice's lead role of Gwen "offered her few opportunities other than that of a pretty girl," Baer called Verna "the comedy hit of the evening" in a small supporting role as Mable, "attired in clothes that screamed across the footlights," wringing laughter from the Baker audience. For *Pals First*, Verna donned blackface for her comic part as Aunt Caroline, a Negro servant, a performance in "acute ebony" that Baer called "delightfully natural." The Baker audiences, though enthralled with Verna's supporting characterizations, demanded that she become the leading lady for the remainder of the season. Consequently, dissension developed within the company as various members of the organization took sides either with Verna or Betty Brice. Seaman was in a predicament, but nature soon took its course. *Pals First*, opening on October 6, turned out to be Betty Brice's final appearance with the Baker company. Four days later, Mayor George Baker ordered that all theatres, schools, fraternal lodges, and other places where large numbers congregated would be closed indefinitely to prevent the spread of what was then called "Spanish influenza," an epidemic sweeping the country that fall. Some time during the following weeks while the Baker remained dark, an angered Brice left the company, leaving the position of leading lady available. Rather than give in to audience demands or offer Verna a new contract as lead, Seaman sought an outsider to replace Brice.

Meanwhile, during the early morning hours of November 11, word of the armistice ran rapidly through Portland. The *Morning Oregonian* and the *Oregon Journal* pumped the streets full of newsboys hawking extra editions and yelling the ceasefire. The *Oregonian* described the scene best, "As magically as mushrooms, heads frilled and frowsy popped from the darkened windows when the newsboys passed, shouting their clan-cry of 'Uxtr-e-e-e!'" Industries tied their whistle cords, and churches pulled bell ropes "to the blister point." People dribbled into the dark downtown streets, which would soon become teeming with rejoicing citizens and remaining thickly crowded until after midnight. The biggest day in history had broken. An impromptu parade through the city ended in a tremendous traffic snarl with drivers honking horns, their vehicles festooned with flags and bunting. Children rode astride the car radiators, waving flags and blowing five-cent horns. "They were sugared with confetti," the *Oregonian* reported, "and the breeze twirled long streamers of gay paper behind them. Big gruff trucks, as incongruous as truckhorses on a race track, rolled ponderously by, with laughing, shrieking cargoes of merry lunatics. At the tail of every car and truck there jounced and jingled a clangorous string of cans and old metal. Someone rode by with an accordion wheezing away at the National anthem. Clear above the roar of the paraders and the surging sidelines the voice of a bugle lifted. Up the street, wholly oblivious of it all, marched a young mother and her little boy. The kiddie banged away at a toy drum and the mother was twanging raptly at a ukulele— and it didn't need the service pin she wore to tell a body that Dad was coming home." Although there is no record of Verna's reaction to the end of the war, it is certain she was in the thick of the celebration.

Meanwhile the influenza outbreak continued its unrelenting toll on American citizens. The Portland death rate was the lowest on the Pacific coast, with only 240 lives lost by November 2. On the same date, Seattle registered 389 deaths and San Francisco 1,279. Portland's mayor decided to lift the ban on theaters and other restricted places on November 16. The following day, the Baker Stock Company was ready to open its doors, even though it still lacked a permanent replacement for the departed Betty Brice. During the ban Milton Seaman had hired Olive Templeton for the job, but, unfortunately, her arrival from New York had been delayed by her lengthy recuperation from the same pandemic flu affecting Portland. So Seaman relied on Verna to temporarily fill the leading roles, the first of which was Bab in *Rich Man, Poor Man*, a Cinderella tale in which she could prove her versatility as not only a fine comic actress but also as a dramatic one.

For Thanksgiving week, Seaman arranged to stage an old favorite, but one that had never been available to stock companies before. Rose Melville, the actress who created the title role in the comedy *Sis Hopkins*, had continuously toured with the play since 1899, never permitting another actress to play the part. As soon as she released the play to stock producers, Seaman snapped it up, realizing it would be a perfect vehicle for Verna Felton. And Verna had been longing for the same opportunity for many years. Sis Hopkins, an Indiana hayseed, outmaneuvers the cad who plots to steal her family's farm and then, after marrying a yokel-turned-lawyer, enters local society with hilarious results. A large promotional photo of Verna in costume, wearing Sis's characteristic hairstyle of wired braids and gingham dress, appeared in the *Oregonian* on November 24, and that evening, the audience was packed even into the gallery. Portland playgoers had seen Melville perform the play numerous times, but this was the first time any other actress had played the part in their city. Leone Cass Baer crowed, "Just as that old truism holds good about there never was a lock made that some one couldn't undo, so it is that there never was a role created that someone else couldn't enact. Verna Felton plays Sis quite as well as Rose Melville ever played it. Possibly Miss Melville isn't going to lose any sleep over the assertion if it ever reaches her, but Miss Felton's Sis is just as quaint and weird and grotesque, with quite as many human splotches and delightful drolleries as is— or was—the famous original. Miss Felton goes Miss Melville several steps better, for Miss Melville couldn't dance, and the little Felton person shakes a wicked ankle and indicates more than a soul-deep knowledge of Terpsichore in her contribution to the programme at the girls' seminary." Supporting player Lee Millar again won commendation from Baer as a dress-suited villain, becoming somewhat typecast as such for the remainder of the season, while his wife Anna

McNaughton "bubbled over with fun and originality" as Parthenia Peckover, the head of the seminary Sis attends briefly. Verna's *Sis Hopkins* was such a phenomenal hit that literally hundreds of people were turned away at each performance. In the hearts of many, Verna Felton had become the new leading lady of the Baker Stock Company.

Into this atmosphere arrived thirty-five-year-old Massachusetts native Olive Templeton, whose acting experience boasted one Broadway production and four silent pictures. *Good Gracious Annabelle*, a bright comedy by Clare Kummer, was selected for Templeton's opening bill on December 1. When she made her first stage entrance that afternoon, there was an awkward and obvious silence. Curiously, the matinee audience did not offer its customary welcoming applause for the new leading lady. The *Oregonian*'s Leone Cass Baer diplomatically if lamely apologized for this slight, suggesting that the playgoers were so interested in the adventures of Annabelle that they simply forgot to clap. She knew all too well the real reason. The Baker audience, even though they saw fit to applaud Templeton by the end of the first act, wished Verna Felton were starring in the sprightly comedy. To compound matters, neither Templeton's popularity nor the box office receipts during her opening week were improved by the city health officer who pleaded with the public to prevent a resurgence of the flu epidemic by not packing the theaters.

However, the Baker audiences must have become more receptive to Templeton, if not gradually, for she remained with the company much longer than the six-week period of Verna's faulty recollection. In fact, Templeton held her position for six months, at first earning only cursory respect in Leone Cass Baer's columns. For instance, in *Blind Youth*, Templeton's second outing as leading lady, Baer deemed her performance as "satisfying," while Verna's supporting work was lauded as "exquisite." By late January, Templeton was receiving higher praise from Baer, but so was Verna Felton, making a competition between the two actresses seem likely. Verna was certainly the more versatile of the two, playing everything from an Indian squaw in *The Barrier* to a "vengeful, colorful Italian girl of the streets" in *Branded* to an alluring teenage vamp in *Upstairs and Down*. To compound matters, audience demand for farces that season had also provided Verna with many suitable comic roles, and Baer was unfailing in her generous coverage of Verna's every characterization. Olive Templeton's final appearance was in *Fair and Warmer* during the week of May 11, seven weeks before the season ended. Since she was married soon after that to John L. Flannery, a Chicago-based manufacturer of sewing machine needles, it is reasonably surmised that marriage was Templeton's real motivation for parting ways with the Baker Stock Company. She subsequently gave up acting, but resumed her career after her husband's death, eventually returning to Broadway and appearing on several New York-based television series such as *Mister Peepers*. Templeton died in New York in 1979 at the age of 95.

In 1959, Verna told researcher Lester Schilling that Mayor George Baker, whose wife was actually the legal owner of the Baker Theatre, was presented with a petition of ten thousand signatures requesting that Verna be returned to the position of leading woman. It is not clear if this impressive demand was to have occurred either during Betty Brice's tenure or after Olive Templeton's arrival, although the latter seems a more likely claim, one that remains unsubstantiated by searches through the *Oregonian*. This is not to imply that it didn't happen. Verna contended that this unprecedented tactic, initiated by fans, spread bad feelings among the company, emotions strong enough to linger into the following season of 1919-20. Nevertheless, Verna immediately replaced bride-to-be Templeton as the Baker Stock Company's leading lady.

Verna herself harbored ill feelings toward Milton Seaman and LeGrand Pearl, each of whom she emphatically referred to as "a son of a seacock" during respective interviews with doctoral candidates Schilling and Waters. Her dislike for Seaman could be traced to the days when the Allen Stock Company was a resident organization in Portland from 1906 until 1908. At that time, Seaman, as business manager for George Baker, had been left in charge of personnel when Baker went out of town. The leading man and lady of the Baker company, both unmarried, had become increasingly quarrelsome, so Seaman fired them, wielding accusations that they had broken the morality clause in their contracts by conducting an illicit relationship. Verna, then a seventeen-year-old performing at the Lyric, read about the brouhaha in the newspapers, but took the side of her fellow actors. Many years later she affirmed for Walter K. Waters that Seaman "trumped up against [the leading man and lady] charges which had no foundation at all." However, Verna chose not to divulge for Lester Schillling the reason for her equally low appraisal of LeGrand Pearl, treasurer of the Baker company. Perhaps she had never forgotten Pearl's reputation as a ticket scalper during his pre-Baker days, but more likely she still felt resentment towards Pearl, as well as Seaman, for the bitter way things ended between her and the two men in the spring of 1920.

Verna's working relationship with stage director Walter Bennett Gilbert, once described as a martinet by actor Larry Keating, seems to have been less stressful. Pennsylvania-born Gilbert, almost thirty-eight years old when he became the director of the Baker Stock Company in 1915, was also reported to have been "severe, sarcastic, and stern." Not too long before joining the Baker Company, just after the death of his wife Ida, Gilbert had washed his hands of his teenage stepson "Jack," an aspiring actor who would go on to become one of the screen's most popular matinee idols, John Gilbert. Trained as a comedian in his younger years, Walter Gilbert, according to Walter Waters, "expected his actors to know the rudiments of stage movement and protocol and was merciless when actors proved inept or inconsiderate in applying either." Certainly, in Verna Felton, he found no disappointment. By now she had been on the stage for nearly twenty years. One disagreement between the actress and her director, recounted by Verna for both Schilling and Waters, came during rehearsals for *Branded* in mid-December 1918. Verna was doubling that week, playing two different roles in separate acts, one as Dot Belmar, a celebrated brothel keeper, and the other as Roselinda, an Italian streetwalker. Although the play contained references to prostitution as well as drug addiction and white slavery, profanity was still very much taboo with Portland audiences at this time. Verna sensed this, and so she became reticent when she was handed the script and discovered that one of her lines was, "You're a goddam liar!"

Verna protested to Gilbert, "I can't give that line."

"Of course, you can, Verna," said Gilbert. "This is a new style of playwriting and acting. Anything goes. The audiences expect it."

"Not our audiences, Wally. Why, they'll freeze up on us and walk out. I just can't say it."

"Oh, yes, you can, and you will," Gilbert insisted.

Verna complied with Gilbert's ultimatum for the remaining rehearsals that week but held back on her delivery of the line until the day of the dress rehearsal, "Then I gave it all I had, and that was plenty."

"Stop!" shouted Gilbert who was watching out front. "All right, Verna, you win! It's too strong. Change it to suit yourself."

"And I did," smiled Verna. "I knew I'd win."

Verna was happily reunited with her family when the Allens and Howard, hopeful of employment, came to Portland in early 1919. Howard was hired for a few bit roles with the competing Alcazar Players, while Clara enjoyed a certain utilization as a character woman for the Baker Stock Company, beginning with *Daddy Long Legs* in late February and appearing sporadically until the season ended with *Merely Mary Ann* on July 5. To reduce lodging expenses, Verna and her family rented a suite of furnished rooms in the Wheeldon Annex, an apartment complex designed for transients. A four-room apartment at the Wheeldon featured an equipped kitchenette, bathroom, closets, and private entrance, all for about five dollars a day. Located on the east side of town, the Wheeldon was a convenient commute across the Willamette River to the Baker Theatre, situated in the heart of downtown.

On Sunday, May 17, 1919, Verna began her official stint as leading lady for the Baker Stock Company, opening in *The Straight Road*, a Clyde Fitch melodrama first produced in 1907. Seaman wanted to showcase Verna's dramatic strength in the part of Mary O'Hara, a Skid Row floozy, and he was not disappointed. Nor were the capacity crowds who attended the matinee and evening performances that day. The following week, *Oregonian* critic Leone Cass Baer recognized Verna's "acrobatic ability" as kittenish and petulant Zoie Hardy in the comedy *Baby Mine*, which included a scene requiring Verna's agility, jumping in and out of a bed repeatedly.

During Rose Festival week, beginning June 8, when Seaman knew Portland would be filled with visitors, he staged *Sis Hopkins* for the second time that season. When the previous fall's production starring Verna had gone over big,

Verna studying lines, circa 1919.

Seaman had wanted to extend it for a second week, but his reconsideration of Olive Templeton on a western bound train, studying her part for *Good Gracious Annabelle*, quickly put an end to the matter. Seaman could not justify asking Templeton to idly sit by for a week while her temporary fill-in packed the house with *Sis Hopkins*. Miss Baer sniffed, "Whatever Miss Templeton could do or could not do, one thing is certain. She would have made a mess of *Sis Hopkins*." Baer went even further by saying that most leading ladies would have turned up their noses at this role: "Leading women as a class and rule prefer only roles wherein they may be very beautiful, dress all over the place, be extremely desirable and supplied with brilliant dialogue. A Verna Felton happens to a manager only once in a lifetime. Miss Felton personally prefers the roles of character, and it is assuredly our profit that she does, for she puts her whole heart and acting into these parts. She is Sis Hopkins in every flicker of her eyes, every flirt of her pigeon toes and every move of her awkward body." In this one paragraph, Baer had summed up Verna's perfect niche, that of character actress. Though her days as Zaza, Sapho, and Marguerite Gautier were essentially behind her, she would continue to play "emotional" roles now and then, but like Baer and other critics before her, Verna recognized that her true talent, and passion, rested comfortably in comic character parts, roles that would be her future fortune with the advent of radio and television.

Baer's accurate estimation was further proven by her review of *The Unkissed Bride* on June 23. In this farce, Verna played the leading role of Kitty Blake, who agrees to participate in a mock marriage with her friend Fred Forrester whose uncle has promised him $50,000 on his wedding day. Even though Baer thought Verna charming in her dainty white satin wedding gown and long veil framed in orange blossoms, she much preferred that the part had been given to Geraldine Dare, the naturally beautiful brunette ingénue. Furthermore, Baer's most enthusiastic praise was offered not to Verna, but to the two character women (one of whom was Clara Allen), for whose roles she deemed Verna better suited. Meanwhile, audiences remained hopeful that Verna would return in the fall as the Baker Stock Company's leading lady.

Their wishes came true. On September 7, one week before Baker Company members returned from their two-month summer hiatus, the *Oregonian* ran a special article announcing Verna's return as the leading woman. Milton Seaman had received hundreds of requests that she be retained in this capacity, and Baer opined that Verna's success the previous season "established her beyond question as the most capable and popular leading woman who has appeared at the Baker in many years." New additions to the company included leading man David Herblin, recruited from New York, and fifteen-year-old Portland native Mayo Methot, who would become a strong Broadway presence before entering films and subsequently marrying an actor named Humphrey Bogart.

Returning supporting players included Lee Millar and his wife Anna McNaughton, both of whom merited promotional portraits in the September 7 edition of the *Oregonian*. During the previous season, Anna did not appear in as many productions as Lee, but when she did, Leone Cass Baer showered her with compliments. Anna's rotundity and skillful artistry made her well-equipped for comic character parts, and she often played women much older than her thirty-five years, among them decorous headmistresses and bold Irish landladies. In *The Great Divide*, Baer had found her "irresistible" as the ideal mother, dressed in stereotypical gray wig, black lace cap, and white fichu, and ironically playing the mother of Lee's character, whose wife was played by Verna. Interestingly, one month later, Anna and the equally versatile Lee played the parts of Verna's divorced parents in *The Divorce Question*, a bit of propaganda opposed to marital dissolution. The highest acclaim Anna received from Baer was her scene-stealing role of Lily the maid in *The Unkissed Bride*, prompting the critic to devote more press to her supporting part than to Verna's lead. Described as a female version of silent screen star Fatty Arbuckle, Anna played her role "with a nonchalance that was most refreshing. Nothing was too difficult for her, from getting stuck midway while trying to escape through [a] transom to fainting between the two men of apparent tender strength. Not least in her delightful attributes was the taste which led to the selection of pajamas of the most vivid, crashing and exciting hue and design." Meanwhile, Lee was awarded kudos for his performances in *De-Luxe Annie, Upstairs and Down,* and *Here Comes the Bride.*

The opening bill for the 1919-20 season was *Come Out of the Kitchen*, adapted from Alice Duer Miller's 1916 romance novel. Having played seven months on Broadway three seasons earlier, the original production had starred the accomplished Ruth Chatterton, whose ability Baer compared to the "strength and punch of a chocolate éclair." Ever the partial critic, Baer thought that Verna, in the same "sweetly-pretty" role, "made something out of it." Of the remaining thirty-two productions starring Verna Felton that season, her most acclaimed performances included *Hobson's Choice* (adored by Baer for Verna's "flat, toneless voice and the way she folded her arms and looked into space when everybody talked at her"), *The Naughty Wife* (whose jealousy Verna conveyed "through the medium of pantomime, a smoldering of the eyes, a nervous rat-a-tat-tat of her fingers, more expressive and Feltonesque than a volume of words"), *The Brat* (her performance deemed by Baer as far superior to that of Betty Brice the previous season, partly because of Verna's dancing ability), *The Willow Tree* (proving to be resourceful and versatile as a Japanese girl), and *The Five Million* (described by Baer as "one of the half-girl, half-woman roles she plays so realistically").

Leone Cass Baer, however, had a giant bone to pick with the management of the Baker Stock Company concerning the casting for *Pollyanna*, which opened on November 30. Based on the famous Eleanor H. Porter novel, the play version of the "glad girl" had enjoyed only a modest run on Broadway in 1916, when one reviewer described it as "peach melba drenched in syrup." Nevertheless, *Pollyanna* had become quite popular in stock presentations. Baer found fault with twenty-nine-year-old Verna playing the title role, and rightly so, for Pollyanna was a girl of twelve at the play's beginning and aged only five years by the end of the last act. Baer challenged a peculiar law of stock companies, wherein leading women seemed to always play the leading role no matter how youthful it may be. She thought that the part of Pollyanna would have been better suited to young Mayo Methot, who had been relegated to the male role of rough and ready Jimmy Bean. During the final act, when Pollyanna and Jimmy, both aged seventeen, talk of marriage, Baer thought the love scene totally "incongruous," especially noting Verna's sophisticated costume and hairstyle (a blonde wig) and Methot's undeniably feminine form not well hidden in trousers. Interestingly, as the season progressed, Baer became increasingly generous with her praise for Methot, often eclipsing mentions of Verna's contributions in subsequent productions, including *It Pays to Advertise*, *The Big Chance*, and *In Walked Mary*, the latter being a satire in which Verna essentially played the "straight woman" to the comic parts enacted by Methot and Claire Sinclair, the new character woman of the troupe.

In mid-February 1920, while *Daddy Long Legs* ran at the Baker, a touring company was spending the week at the Heilig, where they staged *The Bird of Paradise*, an idyll of Hawaii in which an American scientist falls in love with a native girl. The fiancée he forsakes was played by thirty-three-year-old Spring Byington, who would team with Verna Felton some thirty years later in both the radio and television versions of the situation comedy *December Bride*. Curiously, two other actors who would appear in guest parts on the television show were performing in Portland during Verna's tenure there; Edward Everett Horton was leading man for the Alcazar Players from 1917 until 1919, and Rolfe Edward Sedan appeared in summer stock at the same playhouse in 1919.

During her 1959 interview with Lester Schilling, Verna related an incident which could have shortened the 1919-20 season or even ended the life of the Baker Stock Company itself. The following, taken from Schilling's dissertation, illustrates the precarious position stock managers were being placed in by the growing shortage of theatres, available for stage shows:

> Claire Sinclair had been asking Verna Felton if she were interested in going to Salt Lake City to play with the Wilkes Stock Company there. Miss Felton indicated that she was not interested, but Miss Sinclair would frequently bring up the

subject. One day she said, "Mr. Wilkes is in town and wants to take you to dinner." When Miss Felton indicated that she was too busy to meet him, Miss Sinclair assured her that Mr. Wilkes would call for her by taxi and bring her to the theatre right after dinner.

Mr. Wilkes called for Miss Felton by taxi the next evening. As the taxi drove along, it was soon apparent that it was not heading for one of the downtown restaurants, where Miss Felton had supposed they would eat. The taxicab was soon heading out of town on what was known as the Stony Plain Road. Miss Felton explained that she could not go out of town for dinner, as she had to be at the theatre within an hour. "We're going to Mrs. Henderson's," Mr. Wilkes replied. Miss Felton did not know where Mrs. Henderson lived, but, as the taxicab sped along, it was becoming more apparent that she might be late to the theatre and that her host, Mr. Wilkes, did not care.

"Please take me back to town," the actress said, but the taxicab continued. "Let me out of this car, or turn around," she demanded, but Mr. Wilkes just sat there saying nothing. Seeing that the manager was determined in his purpose, Miss Felton turned her attention to the driver. She sat on the jump seat behind the driver and talked to him, she recalls, "like a Dutch uncle." She explained how she needed to be at the theatre and all the trouble she would cause the driver if he prevented her from getting there. Finally, she said, "Clarence Harrison happens to be a friend of mine." Clarence Harrison was the owner of the taxicab company and this statement accomplished its objective, for the driver stopped the taxicab. "If I let you out here, will you give me your word you'll forget about this?" said the driver. "I won't unless you turn around and take me back to town." She got to the theatre at 8:15 and the performance was soon underway.

It seems that Thomas Wilkes wanted to move his stock company to Portland, but could not obtain a theatre to play in. The Baker Stock Company's lease could be cancelled if they were closed for one day. Mr. Wilkes had arranged with the owners of the theatre building to pick up the lease if it should ever lapse. He had figured he could kill that evening's performance by preventing the leading lady from arriving at the theatre that night."

This botched subversion probably created friction between Verna and Claire Sinclair, character woman in the Baker Company, since it was she who plotted with Wilkes to lure Verna away from the theatre. The strain between the two actresses only intensified as dissension among the players mounted. Anna McNaughton, by now experiencing marital difficulties with Lee Millar, bowed out of the company just after Christmas 1919. Geraldine Dare, at odds with several company members, left the company in January, and soon after that, leading man David Herblin broke his contract, citing a backstage "restlessness" that had kept the company upset for some weeks previous. Milton Seaman was under such stress that he suffered a nervous breakdown that spring, leaving LeGrand Pearl in charge of managing the company for the remainder of the season. Unrest still existed between Verna and Seaman, as she explained to Lester Schilling, "There was dissension all through the company." This was not unusual, for a stock company's members were forced to work long hours under tense and confining circumstances, but the unpleasant atmosphere was something apparently very foreign for Verna Felton. She had Pearl Allen to thank for that. And so, when her forty-week contract was up in the spring of 1920, Verna kissed the Baker Stock Company goodbye. Although she would tell Lester Schilling that the unpleasant atmosphere was not her main reason for leaving, this statement leaves room for doubt.

Verna maintained that her primary reason for the departure was that she wanted to join her family in Tacoma, where Pearl had reactivated the Allen Players as a resident stock organization. But instead of following her initial plan of going there directly, upon completion of her Baker contract on April 24, Verna accepted a tempting offer to stay in Portland, if only briefly. Following her April 8 announcement of withdrawal from the Baker, she had been approached by Vivian Everett, the manager of the Alcazar Players, to star in his production of *Peg O' My Heart*. In 1919, Everett had secured the rights to stage the play, but soon after this, the play became involved in litigation over motion picture rights and was consequently withdrawn from stock when the legal action had been completed. LeGrand Pearl, who had acquired the same rights for the Baker in the spring of 1920, argued that he and not Everett held the rights to produce *Peg O' My Heart* in Portland. Both managers, with stubborn and deep-seated contention, staged the play the same week, beginning April 25. Verna's consent to appear with Everett makes one wonder if she were not thumbing her nose at LeGrand Pearl. On the other hand, Pearl Allen told the *Tacoma Sunday Ledger* that Verna had been made a "handsome" offer by Everett to play Peg.

Vivian Everett, perhaps motivated by retaliation, scored a coup by hiring the Baker company's leading lady. To her credit, Leone Cass Baer was impartial in her reviews of each production, while Verna, referring to the competing companies, recalled, "We both did big business." On closing night, following the performance, Verna received one of the greatest thrills of her professional life. As she stepped forward during her curtain call, every man in the first few rows of the house stood up and threw roses at her. Her Portland admirers had bought out the front of the house so that they could use this gesture to bid Verna farewell.

Meanwhile, over at the Baker Theatre, another player was performing his own Portland swan song. Lee Millar, after playing Alaric the "vapid English cousin" in his company's version of *Peg O' My Heart*, would return to his hotel room to finish packing his bags. The next morning he would leave on a train bound for Tacoma, Washington. Seated beside him would be Verna Felton.

It is uncertain whether a backstage romance had developed between Lee and Verna during their two years together at the Baker, but there are indications that this might have been the case. Not only were they together daily at the theatre, but they were also neighbors. Lee and his wife Anna resided in Apartment 501 at the Wheeldon Annex, while Verna and the Allens were nearby at Apartment 504. If the relationship between Verna and Lee changed from co-workers to lovers, then it quite possibly played a part in the dissension which plagued the company during the 1919-20 season. Conversely, it is conceivable that only a platonic relationship existed between the two actors prior to Lee's separation from his wife, the date of which is impossible to ascertain. Federal census records indicate that Lee and Anna were still together on January 6, 1920, although by this time they had moved across the river to a hotel on Salmon Street, within walking distance of the Baker. Was the move a conscious effort to distance themselves from Verna? Anna's final appearance in a Baker production took place the previous December 27, when she played Margot in *The Brat*. Her absence from subsequent productions leads one to wonder if perhaps she left the company in shame after Lee deserted her. It is also possible that Lee didn't abandon Anna until he left Tacoma; however, if this was the case, it seems unlikely that Anna would have been on hiatus for the four months previous to his departure.

Whatever the case, a newspaper article in the *Tacoma News Tribune* on May 1 leaves no doubt that Lee Millar had made a conscious decision regarding his future by the time he boarded that train for Tacoma. Headlined as "Matinee Idol Coming," the small but amusing piece promotes Lee as the new leading man for the Allen Players: "Girls, he's coming! Fluttering feminine hearts—young and near young—will flut another flutter. The romantic young things who just dote on powerful broad shoulders, soft wavy hair, gorgeous big brown eyes, soft melodious voice and that knightly bearing will find their idol in Tacoma May 9 . . . And he's single!"

Meanwhile Anna McNaughton had returned to San Francisco. By August she would be hired as a member of the Fulton Players in Oakland, appearing in very much the same type of roles as she had for the Baker Stock Company. More than a year would pass before Anna filed for an interlocutory decree of divorce with the Superior Court of California, on the grounds of Lee's "willful desertion."

Before going forward with an account of Lee's new venture in Tacoma, it is wise to examine his background and the story of how he arrived at this point in his life. Lee Carson Millar was born on February 20, 1888, in his parents' home

Lee Millar and Verna Felton, Portland, 1920.

at 1318 10th Street in Oakland, California. His first name was given in recognition of famed Confederate general Robert E. Lee, while his middle name honored his mother's family. Lee's forty-one-year-old father, John Edgar Millar, had been earning a living by performing San Francisco title searches since his early twenties. At the time of Lee's birth, John Edgar was partnered with Thomas B. Simpson in the San Francisco firm of Simpson & Millar at 522 California Street. Lee's mother, Kate, was John Edgar's second wife and stepmother of his ten-year-old son John Walter "Jack" Millar.

John Edgar Millar was born in New Orleans on January 9, 1847. His father, John Millar, born in New York around 1814, moved the family to California where, by 1860, he had become a successful Stockton saddler. Ten years later, the Millars were living on Kearny Street in San Francisco's First Ward, where the elder John continued to make saddles and harnesses and his Irish-born wife Maggie (*nee* Margaret Eccles) ran a large boarding house for single men. Meanwhile, twenty-three-year-old John Edgar had begun learning his trade as a searcher of records. In 1875, the Millars moved across the bay to the house at 1318 10th Street in Oakland. The following year, John Edgar married twenty-year-old Lizzie Anderson, a native of New Brunswick, Canada. In the fall of 1877, as they were anticipating the birth of their first child, Lizzie contracted typho-malarial fever late in her pregnancy. Jack was safely delivered on December 1, but Lizzie developed puerperal fever, leading to peritonitis, and died three days later.

A handsome young widower for almost ten years, John Edgar remarried in Stockton on April 28, 1887—this time to Kate "Katie" Carson, sixteen years his junior. Lee Carson Millar was their only child.

Both young Lee's paternal and maternal lineages boasted rugged California pioneers. Lee's mother, Katie Carson, was born on her parents' ranch near Stockton on January 4, 1863. At the time of her marriage, Katie's father, William McKendree Carson, was the supervisor for San Joaquin County, without a doubt a position of authority, but one which gave no hint to the colorful path which led him there. Born in 1829, Carson answered the call of the gold rush when he and two brothers sailed from their native Baltimore, Maryland to San Francisco on a six-month voyage via the Cape Horn in 1849. The Carsons were all carpenters so they readily found work in San Francisco, building a structure planned to be used as the city's first post office. However, the completed building was sold for another purpose. Later that year, Carson sought employment in Stockton where construction of the Stockton House, a large hotel, was underway. Earning between ten and twelve dollars plus board per day, Carson soon amassed enough wealth to purchase 215 acres of land on the lower Sacramento Road, about four miles north of Stockton.

In 1854, Carson married Mary Isabelle "Belle" Mitchell, the seventeen-year-old daughter of a neighboring farmer who led his family across the plains from their Indiana home in 1850. According to an interview given by Belle Mitchell Carson in the *Stockton Daily Independent* in 1927, her family camped on the Nevada side of the state line on the night of September 8, 1850, crossing the boundary the next morning in order that their advent into the Golden State would coincide with the day California was admitted to the union.

In 1856, William Carson purchased a ranch where the seven youngest of his eight children, including Kate, would be born. The rich peat soil and temperate climate made this area one of the finest agricultural regions in California. Carson took advantage of these natural resources, quickly becoming a progressive farmer and earning the distinction of operating the first thresher and reaper in the San Joaquin Valley, both machines which he had his father ship from Baltimore. Despite settling down in the valley he would call home for over fifty years, Carson still felt enough adventuresome spirit in 1870 to take his wife, their six children, and Old John, the family's Chinese cook, on a twenty-three-day voyage from San Francisco to New York. Midway they reached the Isthmus of Panama, where they disembarked for the train ride across the isthmus where they then boarded a second vessel. Their final destination was Baltimore where for two years they visited Carson's mother and siblings. Back in Stockton a decade later, Carson became county supervisor, a position he held for sixteen years. Besides his prosperous farming endeavors, he became known for his devotion to one public project, the construction of the San Jaoquin County Courthouse in 1895.

It is not known if the parents of Kate Carson and John Edgar Millar knew one another during the 1860s when both families were living in the Stockton area. Nor is it certain how these two individuals met. By the time Kate moved to her husband's 10th Street home in Oakland, it had been in the Millar family for twelve years. The head of the household was John Edgar's mother Maggie, widowed since 1882, who had performed as a surrogate mother to his son Jack since the boy's birth. Nearby was the Cole Grammar School, where ten-year-old Jack was enrolled and where Lee would one day attend. The Cole School was destined to become famous by another pupil's attendance; author Jack London studied there from 1887 until his completion of the eighth grade in 1891.

John Edgar Millar, forced into an early retirement due to an enlarged heart caused by arteriosclerosis, died of a related disease—chronic nephritis—at the age of fifty-four on November 21, 1901, leaving Katie a widow at age thirty-eight. She soon found the large house too expensive and difficult to maintain. Her mother-in-law had passed away nine years previously and her stepson, now a twenty-four-year-old real estate agent, had moved out on his own, occupying the house at 1314 10th Street with his wife Ida and her son Marlow Niles. Realizing that her own son would probably leave the nest one day, Kate began to consider a move to a smaller home. In 1904, she bought a lot two doors down at 1310 10th Street where she would immediately build an attractive two-family shingle style house with diamond-shaped casement windows. To supplement their income, Kate and Lee resided in the lower flat while the upper unit was leased to tenants.

Meanwhile, young Lee Millar, having finished his public education, pursued an interest in acting. To receive training, he enrolled with a local school, the formidably titled Jenne Morrow Long College of Voice and Dramatic Action. By age seventeen, Lee had joined The Bishop Players, a local stock company, sometimes referred to as Bishop's 30 Players. The company was organized in 1904 by artist-manager Harry W. Bishop, who, in the 1880s, had acted as a child under the name of Harry Morosco. As a venue for his players, Bishop built Ye Liberty Playhouse at 1440 Broadway in Oakland. It seated two thousand persons and featured the first revolving stage in America. For some time, Bishop rotated casts between his Ye Liberty Playhouse and the Majestic Theatre, owned by the Shubert Brothers, in San Francisco.

Lee Millar officially entered the theatrical profession in May 1905, when he joined the Ye Liberty cast of Tolstoy's *Ivan the Terrible* starring J. H. Gilmour. Lee's recollection of the production, recorded in a 1914 typewritten memoir of his career, was that he was given a small part when another member of the company had been taken ill. He continued to win minor parts until the evening of April 16, 1906, when he was offered a lengthier part in *Who Goes There?*, a farce set during the Spanish-American War. With comedian Walter Perkins as the lead, the production had played at Ye Liberty during the first week of April. On April 9, its cast had moved to the Majestic in San Francisco. It was here that Lee Millar was approached to fill in at the last minute, having to "jump into thirty-six sides in fifteen minutes notice." A "side," according to theatre historian Walter Waters, was a "piece of paper 8 ½ inches by 5 inches containing only the lines and cues for one particular character." Lee later reported of his impromptu performance, "[I] got away with it O.K." Less than thirty-six hours later, the great earthquake shook San Francisco, destroying the Majestic along with countless other buildings. Once valued at $83,000, the structure now was a total loss. Lee, safe at home in Oakland, quickly found himself unemployed. He also discovered that he had inadvertently saved a copy of the complete script for *Who Goes There?* Typically, the full script was kept exclusively by the director, but for some reason, Lee also had one, which turned out to be the only one not lost in the earthquake and the subsequent fire that destroyed much of the city. Afterwards Lee sent this copy to Walter Perkins, the star of the ill-fated production.

Later that spring, Lee was hired for a brief engagement in San Jose as the "juvenile man" in a company starring Frank Bacon, another of Bishop's players. A juvenile man, together with the ingénue, primarily served as the young love interest in a production. San Jose having been hit hard by the quake as well, Lee recalled that "things were in such a state down there that we only lasted about eight weeks." The company moved to San Francisco later in the summer, just as the city was getting back on its feet. On the practically the same spot where the Central Theatre had stood near Market and 8th Streets, a large tent had been built upon the ruins. Originally named the Park Theatre, this makeshift venue was soon renamed the Central, but Lee only played here a short time before he received a proposition from fellow actor Robert Downing.

Downing offered Lee a half-interest in two plays, one of which was the comedy *Running for Governor*, a major career departure for Downing who previously had been known for his roles in tragedies. Eighteen-year-old Lee accepted Downing's offer to invest in the tour; however, it remains a curiosity where such a young man would get the money. As part of the deal, Lee joined Downing's company for the 1906-07 season, beginning with a performance of *Running for Governor* in San Francisco on November 7. The company enjoyed a successful run in the west, but after the Chicago engagement, business in the Midwest and East was a disappointment.

A pleasant diversion from Lee's failing investment was the time he was able to spend with an attractive young lady in the company. Anna McNaughton, playing the daughter of Downing's lead character, had been a member of the Bishop Players back in Oakland, where she and Lee had been introduced. Born in Albany, New York, on October 15, 1883, Anna was the daughter William Henry McNaughton, a former New York attorney and now a manufacturer's agent in San Francisco. The thrice-married Mr. McNaughton had moved his family, which included Anna's older half-brothers William and Duncan, her stepmother Delphine and her stepsister Anna Ellis, to San Francisco in 1896. Anna attended the public schools of San Francisco, but soon after began appearing in small roles in plays in the Bay area. Eighteen-year-old Lee Millar was quite smitten with her. A 1911 *San Jose Mercury-News* photo of Anna, wearing a huge picture hat with towering egret feathers, reveals that she was quite a handsome woman.

Running for Governor had run out of luck by late spring of 1907. The tour ended in a one-night stand in Delaware. Lee reported a loss of $3,000, but philosophized optimistically, "Experience comes dear." Robert Downing returned to his hometown of Frederick, Maryland, to open a new theatre and dramatics school. That summer Lee and his sweetheart Anna McNaughton found five weeks' work in Albany, New York, coincidentally Anna's hometown. She and Lee were married there by a notary public on August 27. Lee was nineteen years old, but he listed his age on the marriage license as twenty-one, perhaps to make the gap between his age and Anna's seem closer than the four years it actually was.

During their first year of marriage, Lee and Anna successfully toured together in *The Kerry Gow*, a vehicle set in Ireland which had made its Broadway bow back in 1876. The tour began in the East and reached the West Coast before closing in Chicago. The young couple toured Nova Scotia with the Jim Huntley Company during the summer of 1908, not profitably, but Lee recalled, "We had a lovely time." A subsequent tour of the play *Quincy Adams Sawyer* ended in LaCrosse, Wisconsin, when the Millars left the company, following the Christmas Day performance. After a brief period of unsteady work at the Valencia Theatre in San Francisco, Lee and Anna joined Willard Mack's company in Salt Lake City, but the nine months spent there were disappointing because of Mack's alcoholic mismanagement. They ended their stay in Utah at Ogden's Orpheum Theater where they starred with William S. Donovan in *A Midnight Intruder.* The Millars were out of work for much of the remainder of the 1909-10 season, due in part to a lengthy illness which plagued Anna. The following season was not any more promising, but Lee was engaged for the first time as a stock company leading man in Seattle.

Lee and Anna were separated for the first time during the season of 1911-12. While Lee toured across Canada in a production of *The Barrier*, a melodrama set in Alaska, Anna, who now specialized in character roles, toured Nevada,

Lee Millar around the time of his first marriage.

California, Oregon, and Washington in *The Chorus Lady*, a sharp-tongued look at backstage life, hailed upon its Broadway bow in 1906 as "the most characteristic American play produced so far this season, and more vivid and real in many respects than any other." *The Barrier* tour closed in Pittsburgh on May 25, and Lee, in anticipation of using his last week's salary to buy his train ticket back to Oakland, sent all of his money home to Anna. When the run ended without a final payday, Anna wired the stranded Lee enough money to ride home in a smoking car. Unfortunately, this was a frequent occurrence among touring companies; managers often had insufficient funds to meet even the closing expenses.

The respective careers of Lee Millar and Anna McNaughton accelerated in the late summer of 1912, due to an opportune introduction to one of Broadway's most successful actors and playwrights. Lee and Anna had begun to perform regularly at the Alcazar Theater on O'Farrell Street in San Francisco, but when Leo Ditrichstein arrived from New York City to open his Broadway adaptation of *The Concert* at that theatre, Anna was engaged to join the cast, which also included Isabel Irving, Madge West, and Cora Witherspoon, the latter who had made her Broadway debut in the original production in 1910. The delightful Witherspoon would go on to appear in over thirty Broadway productions and fifty films, often as an acid-tongued presence. Only twenty years old when she first appeared in *The Concert*, Witherspoon enacted the part of a very elderly woman so perfectly that Ditrichstein brought her with him to the Coast for the San Francisco run.

Leo Ditrichstein possessed a keen ability to select strong supporting players such as Witherspoon. Now Anna was added to his company, and Lee would soon follow. The son of a count and the grandson of a famous Austrian novelist, Ditrichstein was born in Austria-Hungary in 1865. Educated in Vienna, he made his stage debut in Berlin in 1890. His reputation in Europe grew, and soon he was coaxed into appearing in the United States, where he mastered the English language in less than three years. As a member of John Drew's company, Ditrichstein's stage successes included *Trilby, Hedda Gabler*, and *Are You a Mason?* with actress May Robson. By the time of his arrival in San Francisco in June 1913, he had written or performed in over thirty Broadway productions. At the Alcazar that summer, he staged his own play *Such Is Life*, immediately hiring Lee Millar as one of the cast. Ditrichstein was so impressed with Lee that he asked him to go to New York in the fall to repeat his role on Broadway. David Belasco had agreed to produce, and the play was retitled *The Temperamental Journey.*

For most stock actors, this opportunity was a dream come true. Lee Millar was no different. For eight years he had learned the trade by experience, and his travels across the country with various companies had not only enhanced his acting skills but also allowed him a vision unequal to those stock actors who had never left the West. "New York producers looked upon inexperienced performers with aversion," asserted theatre historian Walter Waters. "Without experience, a young actor soon found that he could not find theatrical employment in the city that was the center of American theatrical effort." Fortunately, Lee Millar and wife Anna, who was also selected by Ditrichstein to appear in *The Temperamental Journey*, were in the right place at the right time. Ditrichstein opened new avenues for them, and Lee never failed to show his gratitude to the elder actor.

The Temperamental Journey, adapted by Ditrichstein from Andre Rivoire and Yves Mirande's *Pour vivre heureux*, opened at the Belasco Theatre on September 4, 1913. Ditrichstein played Jacques Dupont, a painter belittled by critics and unloved by his wife, played by Isabel Irving. When he fakes his suicide, the critics reconsider, and his wife begins selling fake Duponts to add to her bank account. He reveals that he is still alive and weds his faithful and loving model, played by Josephine Victor. After four weeks, the production moved to the Theatre Republic, where it played until Christmas. Plans were made for a tour to complete the season, but Ditrichstein fell ill. His doctor ordered him to rest at his Stamford, Connecticut estate for four weeks. Ditrichstein's wife Josephine graciously invited Lee and Anna to be their houseguests during her husband's recuperation, but eventually the tour was cancelled because the physician believed Ditrichstein needed to rest for the remainder of the season. Ditrichstein promised the Millars roles in a future production. Meanwhile, they filled their time performing in local stock, Lee in the Bronx and Anna in Hoboken, New Jersey.

During this interim, Lee ventured briefly into silent pictures after he received an offer to appear in *Across the Pacific*, filmed in Tampa, Florida during a six-week period in the spring of 1914. Produced by the World Film Corporation, the film was adapted from Charles E. Blaney's 1900 Broadway success by the same name. A convoluted melodrama, *Across the Pacific* told the story of Joe Lanier, a Montana miner who falls in love with his ward, Elsie Escott, played by Dorothy Dalton. She refuses his love at first, but then follows him to the Philippines, disguised as a fellow sailor on his ship. After their company is nearly wiped out by the enemy, she reveals her identity, and the couple is married. Unfortunately, Lee's role in the film is not specified in the scant production records available. The film was released on November 2 and proved to be fairly popular. When the Millars returned to New York, Lee filmed a second silent feature, this time for the Kalem Company, whose operations were based at 131 West 24th Street. Mainly using location shootings, the prolific company filmed over 200 productions in 1914. Since Lee did not record the title of the Kalem production in his career memoir, there is no way to know which of the two hundred features he filmed.

In late summer 1914, Lee and Anna began rehearsing for a new Belasco production, Ferenc Molnar's comedy *The Phantom Rival* starring Leo Ditrichstein and Laura Hope Crews, a prominent stage actress who would become familiar to modern film audiences for her character roles, notably that of Aunt Pittypat in *Gone with the Wind*. The play opened in Baltimore on September 28 before its Broadway bow on October 6. It was an instant success with the critics and the public, playing for 127 performances. Alexander Woollcott, drama critic for the *New York Times*, voiced his praise: "It ranks easily with the two or three best things it has been Mr. Belasco's wisdom and good fortune to produce. *The Phantom* Rival is one of the few really fine comedies of recent years."

When *The Phantom Rival* closed in January, Lee and Anna immediately followed Ditrichstein on a tour of *$2,000 a Night*, a comedy drama for which Ditrichstein collaborated with writers Frederic and Fanny Hatton. When that ended, they went home to Oakland where Lee joined the Orpheum Players, then

Leo Ditrichstein and Lee Millar in *The Great Lover*, 1915.

featuring James Gleason in a production called *Officer 666*, which opened August 1. The following week Lee starred in Sir James M. Barrie's Half an Hour, but Ditrichstein soon beckoned, and the Millars went East to rejoin his company again, this time in a tour of *$2,000 a Night*. Renamed as *The Great Lover*, this comedy opened as a George M. Cohan production on November 10, 1915, at the Longacre Theatre, starring Ditrichstein and featuring Cora Witherspoon and the Millars. Hailed by many as Ditrichstein's finest performance, the production played to packed houses for exactly seven months, cut short in its prime due to an eye illness plaguing its star.

As in previous summers, Lee and Anna made their way back to northern California where they would be reunited with their respective families and also find work again in Oakland, where they joined the New Orpheum Players, appearing first on July 2 in *The High Cost of Loving*. One week later, they were introduced to a young lady whose acting career had been hanging in limbo for about four months. Verna Felton joined the company as the leading lady for *A Pair of Sixes*, a comedy in which Lee also had a prominent role. (This was the same aforementioned production starring J. Anthony Smythe, the recipient of the toxic carnations during the opening night's curtain call.) Verna, Lee, and Anna appeared in most of the subsequent productions over the next six weeks until the Millars returned to Manhattan where they rejoined Ditrichstein's company in early September for a four-week run of *The Great Lover*, produced by Cohan and Harris at their newly acquired theatre, formerly known as the Candler. This engagement was followed by a national tour, which ran through May of 1917, including stops in Wisconsin, Ohio, Syracuse, New York, and Washington, D.C. The Millars were with it all the way.

By June 1917, Lee and Anna were again back in Oakland, where she had signed on as one of the Orpheum Players in a production of Cohan's *Get-Rich-Quick Wallingford*, starring Albert Morrison and Jane Urban. By August, Lee had become part of the Orpheum Players, now numbering twenty. Wally Gilbert had been brought in from the Baker Stock Company in Portland to direct the summer season at the Orpheum. Soon Gilbert would become quite instrumental in the lives of Lee, Anna, and Verna Felton, but for the intervening season of 1917-18, the whereabouts of Lee and Anna are just as mysterious as those of Verna. A thorough search of the *Oakland Tribune* for the summer of 1918 does not reveal the Millars returning to their old haunt, the Oakland Orpheum. Nor does Verna appear to have been a member of the Orpheum company that summer.

Nevertheless, by the fall of 1918, all three had been hired by Wally Gilbert to join the Baker Stock Company in Portland. This was a strategic move on the parts of all three actors since the Baker company was one of the four most highly respected companies in the United States, the others being the Castle Square in Boston, Elitch's Garden in Denver, and the Toledo Stock Company, all names which carried great weight on an actor's resume. An actor or actress who appeared with any one of these four companies could easily obtain a position with almost any company having an opening. In addition, the experience of belonging to one of the "Big Four" opened doors on the Great White Way.

Fast forward to the spring of 1920, when Verna began plans to rejoin the Allen Players, newly reactivated in Tacoma. Pearl Allen was ecstatic to hear of the availability of Verna's fellow actor Lee Millar, who had played mainly villains and character parts during his two years with the Baker Stock Company. The young but experienced actor came highly recommended by Verna, and Clara was equally impressed with his professionalism when she'd played in several Baker productions during the 1918-19 season. Pearl wanted Lee to direct the remainder of the 1919-20 season and assist with play selection. The Allen Players had been performing at Tacoma's Hippodrome Theatre since mid-February, following a month at the Liberty Theatre in Centralia, Washington, the site where Pearl had decided to revive the Allen Players. Since it had been nearly five years since Pearl managed his own stock company, he re-entered the profession cautiously at first, staging only Sunday matinee and evening performances each week for a month. While he was easily able to pay the royalties for some older plays like *A Stranger in a Strange Land*, *The Girl He Couldn't Buy*, and *The Governor's Daughter*, none of which were very popular with stock producers at the time, Pearl had to bide his time until the right situation came along to produce the newer plays, and in a newer and bigger location than Centralia. Pearl had always loved Tacoma, and his ambition was to make the Allen Players a permanent institution in that city, just as the Baker Stock Company had become such in Portland.

Pearl set his plan in motion, and after spending all of January in Centralia, he had acquired enough capital to move the company to Taoma's Hippodrome Theater on Pacific Avenue at Ninth Street. With only eight weeks left to fulfill her Baker contract, Verna was itching to leave Portland, and Pearl was anxious to have her back in the Allen fold, for her name as leading lady would be the drawing card he needed. In the meantime, he secured Marvel Phillips, who had been performing ingénue roles with the Baker, to fill the same type of roles for his productions. During the last week of April, Clara Allen was given a chance to shine as the lead in *The Rejuvenation of Aunt Mary*, reeling in adoring fans with her rendition of the old ballad "When You and I Were Young, Maggie," added to the play for a sentimental effect.

However, the additions of Verna Felton and Lee Millar to the Allen Players really cemented Pearl's reputation as a showman in Tacoma. Long before they arrived on the train from Portland on May 2, Pearl had been negotiating for the rights to produce many of the same plays the Baker Stock Company had staged during Verna's two years there. In fact, seven of the ten plays produced by Pearl between May 9 and July 17 were ones that Verna and Lee had performed in Portland, a wise move since their recent familiarity with those pieces would produce topnotch productions and financial successes for the Allen Players. Pearl insisted on charging "popular prices" of fifty-five cents for lower-floor seats and thirty-five cents for balcony seats, lower prices Pearl claimed than any other stock company on the Coast. He declared in the *Tacoma Daily Ledger*, "Every play in the Allen repertoire is of so high a standard that road companies would charge as high as $3 admission."

Pearl, confident of a coming resurgence of the public's interest in stock productions, told the *Tacoma Sunday Ledger* on April 25, "We are going to use Miss Felton in everything that is good and clean. We are not playing any of the suggestive or so called 'bedroom' farces. People want the best and most educational and that is what we are going to give them." Pearl also recognized Lee Millar's talent and expertise as the means to put the Allen Players at the forefront, enticing patrons away from vaudeville houses and moving picture theaters. Lee was hired not only as leading man, but also as director, and soon he won favor with the Tacoma critics for productions such as *The Brat and Which One Shall I Marry?* For the latter, the audience was amazed that he was able to finagle a way to make the set's kitchen sink produce running water. When a representative of the Shuberts, the renowned New York theatrical producers, passed through Tacoma on May 19, he attended a performance of this play. He commented the next day to the *Tacoma News Tribune*, "If I did not know it was a stock production I would have said that is was a little Belasco offering. Detail is not lacking in the minutest instance. The actors are directed to the acme of detail. The production is worthy of a first class organization."

Verna, meanwhile, was happy to be back in Tacoma, where she opened as leading lady in *The Brat* on May 9. During its rehearsals the previous week, she told the *News Tribune*, "It feels like home to be back in Tacoma, and in stock, too. I would rather be here in stock than in New York [on Broadway]. It was in Tacoma that I was first received recognition. As a child I won the warmhearted plaudits of Tacomans and now I am going to show my old admirers and the new ones I hope to win, just what I have done to merit their encouragement of years ago." Most of those who attended *The Brat* on the first few nights were, indeed, old admirers from when Verna played Tacoma fifteen years previously, but by Wednesday evening, new fans jammed the Hippodrome. They loved her brief dance near the end of the third act so much that they refused to allow her to leave the stage without a repeat of "her clever terpsichorean novelty." Meanwhile, the handsome Lee lived up to the promotional hype not only as matinee idol but also as gifted director, described by one reviewer as having "injected new life into the entire organization."

Other alumni from the Baker Stock Company soon followed Verna and Lee to Tacoma. Chubby little "Buster" Harrison, a three-year-old who had played the youngest orphan in the Baker production of *Daddy Long-Legs*, was engaged in late May to repeat his scene-stealing performance in the Allens' version of the comedy, one of the best-loved plays of the era. Buster's mother had been Verna's beautician back in Portland. As advance payment, clever Buster required a piece of candy before going onstage with the other child actors, and opened his mouth

Verna's brother Howard (Van Alstine) Wiggins, Tacoma, 1920.

wide for another treat the moment he exited the stage. An amusing incident involving Buster had happened in Portland during one of Verna's important scenes. He waited for a pause in her lines, and then he boldly blurted out the remainder of her speech, earning him the title of "Bolshevik Buster." The Wednesday matinee performance of *Daddy Long-Legs* that week broke all previous Hippodrome records. Buster would grow up to be known as composer Lou Harrison, often cited as one of American music's most original and influencial figures.

Oregon native and former Baker Stock Company member William Lee arrived from Portland to begin a month's run with the Allen Players on June 13. Thirty-year-old "Billy" Lee would assume some of the leading man roles to allow Lee Millar more time to direct. At this point, the remainder of the Allen Players included Clara Allen, Marvel Phillips, Allen Strickfaden, Carl Sihler, Lee Jaxon, Florence Spencer, and Verna's brother Howard Wiggins, who continued to fill small roles, like policemen and butlers. On October 26, with little sister Verna and fellow actor George Cleveland standing by as witnesses, Howard married a Tacoma resident named Elsie Schroeder. At least by this time, there was no doubt as to the groom's true parentage; he was identified on the marriage license, albeit with an alternate spelling, as Howard Van Alstyne, son of Edward Van Alstyne and Clara Lawrence.

Occasionally, Vera Jedlick, a twenty-year-old Tacoma girl, assumed other incidental roles in productions like *What's Your Husband Doing?* and *Sis Hopkins.* Her father Edward, a talented sign painter, had created scenery for the Allen Stock Company during their initial run in Tacoma back in 1905, when Jedlick was just a tot. Over sixty years later, Jedlick related an amusing anecdote about herself, one which she claimed to have occurred during the 1905-06 season when she was playing a small part in East Lynne. According to Jedlick's memoir, published in 1966 in *The Tacoma News Tribune and Sunday Ledger:* "In Act Four, Scene II, the divorced Lady Isabel [played by Verna], under the name of Madame Vine, has re-entered her former home disguised as a governess, to be near her own children. Her small son, William [played by Jedlick], on his deathbed, asks Madame Vine how long it will be before he dies. At dress rehearsal, Verna had impressed me with the necessity of speaking up so I could be heard 'way back in the last row. So on opening night, when Madame Vine asked, 'What makes you think you will die, William?', the enfeebled wee Willie, in a voice suddenly grown loud and lusty, proclaimed, 'I'M 'THERTAIN OF IT, MA'M VEEN!'"

Jedlick was visiting Verna on the set of television series *December Bride* when Verna told this same story to Hollywood gossip columnist Hedda Hopper. While Jedlick reported that Verna enjoyed sharing this particular tale with others, no record can be found of the Allen Stock Company producing *East Lynne* in Tacoma during the 1905-06 engagement or during their three-week run at the Tacoma Theater in 1910. Considering the passage of fifty years and Verna's countless stage productions, it's possible that Verna confused Jedlick with another child actress or another play with *East Lynne.*

However, Jedlick's memories of her second stint with the troupe in 1920 were undimmed forty-five years later when she recalled: "Rehearsals were always fun. Both Verna and Lee Millar were given to horseplay at times, and Verna's dog, a little Pomeranian spitfire named Kazan, often joined in the fracas. His was the only evidence of 'artistic temperament' I ever saw in the company. After his bath, he'd bark with fury and rush to bite the nearest ankle." Kazan had been a 1914 Christmas present to Verna when the Allen Players were performing in Victoria, BC. He was so tiny then that Verna carried him around in her muff. Verna had always loved animals, dogs especially, and Kazan became her fiercest protector, waiting patiently offstage during rehearsals, but keeping Verna in his sight at all times and refusing water or food until she exited the stage for her dressing room. During performances, he waited offstage quietly, and then after the curtain call, he yapped breathlessly until Verna led him to her dressing room. Sometimes

Verna with Kazan, Portland, circa 1920.

Kazan was featured among the cast, as he was in *Peg O' My Heart* in October of 1920, when the fluffy ball sat serenely on the lap of Marvel Phillips during two acts, that is, until Verna exited the scene, at which point he wiggled strenuously to reach her side. Jedlick recalled a lifelike Kazan imitator: "Lee broke up more than one rehearsal by sneaking up on hands and knees during a tense scene and barking sharply. Later he used this seemingly trifling talent in radio commercials for dog medicines!"

Jedlick was quick to add that performances were a different matter, "As with any group of seasoned troupers, performances usually went off smoothly. If somebody 'went up in their lines,' the others always managed to ad-lib until he picked up his cue. Only once in my experience with the Allens was there a real emergency. Fred Sullivan, the character man, suffered a slight paralytic stroke during an intermission, but played out the last act in a wheelchair. Verna ad-libbed a line or two about his having 'met with a slight accident,' which the audience accepted as all in the day's play."

As Verna had often recalled, Pearl Allen ran a tight ship. Jedlick remembered one of his house rules being that "members of the cast must not loiter in the lobby between performances. It would disillusion our public to see us as we really were, the actresses sans makeup and wearing conservative street clothes. Mr. Allen knew what he was doing: my friends envied me my love scenes with the handsome juvenile man, never suspecting that his endearments often smacked of garlic and 'likker.'" When the troupe left Tacoma, Pearl invited Jedlick to join the Allen Players, but her conservative father put his foot down, "No daughter of mine," he told Pearl, "will go traipsing around the country, living in cheap theatrical boarding houses and hotels." Easygoing Pearl took this comment not as a slur on his profession or company, realizing that Mr. Jedlick was simply a protective father.

Vera Jedlick submitted a photo of the Allen Players to accompany her newspaper memoir, and indeed, they were all wearing conservative attire, including hats. Eleven

Pearl Allen, Tacoma, 1920.

Verna Felton, Tacoma, 1920.

members, including Pearl, were pictured on the sidewalk outside the Hippodrome, with Lee, dapper in his snap-brim cap, and Verna, in a long plaid skirt and belted jacket with Kazan perched on her arm. As leading man and lady, they stand front and center, off the curb on the street level, perhaps even signifying that they were "an item" by this time.

On Sunday afternoon, July 11, 1920, the Hippodrome audience gasped when Verna, just a week shy of her thirtieth birthday yet masquerading as a twelve-year-old Pollyanna, tripped merrily onto the stage in a blonde curly wig and gingham dress. After nine weeks of seeing Verna as a mature leading lady in dramas and comedies, they were not ready for her turn as "the glad girl." However, by the end of the play, she managed to pull it off, as did Marvel Phillips as callow Jimmy Bean, whose true sex remained a mystery to many in the audience, according to the *Tacoma News Tribune*. *Pollyanna*, as the Allen Players' farewell performance for the summer, proved to be a huge financial success. The Wednesday matinee crowd, estimated at five hundred, by 12:30 p.m. had thronged the lobby and street outside the Hippodrome, vying for the chance at choice seats when the doors opened an hour later. Attendance records were broken for the remainder of the week. As a reward celebration for his company, Pearl took the Allen Players for a yachting cruise on the Puget Sound on Thursday afternoon, after which they landed at one of the island bathing beaches and enjoyed a picnic lunch and an afternoon of bathing.

The Hippodrome's manager was met with insistent demands that the Allen Players return in the fall for a winter season of stock plays. Without committing himself, perhaps as a publicity tease, Pearl promised to consider such an arrangement while the company was on vacation in the "Canadian wilds." Actually, Pearl and Clara were hosting some of the players, including Verna, Lee, Howard, Marvel, and Billy Lee and his wife actress Genevieve Robinson, at Allen's Green in Ladysmith for a well-deserved respite, perhaps for the one of the last times before it was forfeited as Indian reserve land.

On August 22, the *Tacoma Daily Ledger* announced the August 30 return of the Allen Players, with Verna and Lee as leading lady and man, but a week later Lee had been inexplicably replaced by Irving Dillon, a Stanford University graduate who gave up the study of medicine for the stage. Pearl chose not to reveal that his former leading man and director had suddenly accepted an offer from Broadway star Leo Ditrichstein to join the latter's road company in a tour of *The Purple Mask*, a ripsnorting romantic melodrama which had made a four-month Broadway appearance earlier in the year. Whenever Ditrichstein beckoned, Lee dropped everything and hastened to join him, a reaction understood by both Pearl and Verna. Career networking was just as important then as now, and an actor never knew when a touring show would lead to the Great White Way, a venue that Lee would have loved to perpetually haunt. Verna, no doubt, hated to see him go, but she probably felt assured that she'd see Lee Millar again. She had no way of knowing that two years would pass before this was possible. After the

The Allen Players on a cruise. From right to left, Marvel Phillips, Verna Felton, Lee Millar, Florence Spencer, Clara Allen (obscured), William Lee, Pearl Allen, and Howard Wiggins.

road tour of *The Purple Mask*, Ditrichstein took it back to the "subway circuit," a group of theatres, mostly located in Brooklyn and the Bronx, which regularly offered touring shows after their Broadway runs. Ditrichstein chose Leo Teller's Broadway Theatre in Brooklyn as the venue for *The Purple Mask* featuring Lee in a major supporting role. This association led to Lee's inclusion in the Broadway casts of two subsequent Ditrichstein comedies, *Toto* and *Face Value*, which debuted in March and December, 1921, respectively.

Meanwhile, others joined the Allen Players for the 1920-21 season back in Tacoma, including Walter Siegfried, a young Portlander who had directed Verna in the infamously competitive production of *Peg O' My Heart* just before she left Portland in May, 1920. Another new addition was George Cleveland, a thirty-five-year-old Canadian, who would go on to film over 150 motion pictures and win a new generation of fans for his portrayal of Gramps on the original Lassie television series in the 1950s. The entire company was given great ovations for their opening bill, *Come Out of the Kitchen*.

With Lee Millar away, Verna got her first chance to direct while supporting Dillon in *Nothing But the Truth* on September 6. Called a "howling success," the comedy centered on Dillon's character who bets $10,000 that he can tell no lie for twenty-four hours. Howard Wiggins and Florence Spencer won praise for their parts as a swindled bishop and a variety show chorus queen. Verna's first chance to shine that season came on September 27, when she played Ellen Neal in the 1915 melodrama hit *Common Clay*. Ellen, a housemaid, is seduced by the son of her wealthy employer. When she gives birth to their child and asks for his family's support, they call in an old family friend, Judge Filson, who recommends that the boy marry Ellen. When he refuses, a trial ensues, during which it is revealed that Ellen is the illegitimate daughter of the judge. Filson sends Ellen to Paris to study, and when she returns years later, as a rising prima donna, the father of her child proposes. Verna's performances were emotion-packed, and she explained her success to the *Tacoma Daily Ledger*, "I break down and cry every time I read the lines of Ellen Neal in the third act. I just can't help it. I try to put the emotion in the speech without resorting to tears, but they will come. It is the same thing with the other emotional roles I work in. Of course, I try to live the parts I play, but I feel the physical exhaustion at the end of my night's work when I break down the way I am doing in this week's play."

With the exception of two old chestnuts, *Way Down East* and *Madame X*, Pearl staged up-to-date productions for the remainder of the season, including *The Outcast* (deemed by Verna as ranking "with the best emotional dramas ever written"), *The Yellow Ticket* (in which Verna plays a persecuted Russian Jew), and *The Country Cousin* (in which George Rand replaced Irving Dillon as leading man). Two productions proved amusing for Prohibition audiences. In the English comedy *Green Stockings*, Clara Allen was afforded an unforgettable scene as a tipsy American. The *Tacoma Daily Ledger* described her subtlety: "Mrs. Allen does not depend on the usual series of unnatural staggerings to call attention to the fact that "Auntie" has hit the decanter for one too many. Her first drink is only the excuse for an indication. The second is accompanied by a nervous twitching of the muscles of her face, a curious eyeing of the hem of her skirt, and the third brings the little unsteadiness that authorities admit always accompanies a trio of "stiff ones." Clara received the noisiest ovation of all that evening. When *Fair and Warmer* was staged at midnight on New Year's Eve, the *Ledger* described the scene: "Fond memories of the merry, moist past were exhumed last night when Verna Felton wheeled out the 'Fizz Phaeton' with its clanking bottles of variegated hues and various concoctions, and the big crowd of midnight revelers howled and applauded until the scared scantlings in the old Hippodrome Theater shivered to their tiniest splinters."

A comedy called *Come Seven*, an oddity in that its entire cast performed in blackface, had run on Broadway for nine weeks in the summer of 1920. Since then it had been very popular with stock companies, and the Allen Players produced it on January 10, with riotous results. The comedy was based on a 1919 book by Octavus Roy Cohen, a young Jewish lawyer from South Carolina who often contributed Negro stories to *The Saturday Evening Post*. Lucille LaVerne, best known for her Disney voice characterization as the ugly hag who tempts Snow White with a poisoned apple, played the lead role of Elezir Nesbit in the Broadway production. When Elezir spots her diamond ring on the finger of the beautiful, high-living Vistar Goins, she suspects that her own "no-'count" husband Urias has pawned it. In fact, his friend Florian Slappey is the culprit,

Clara and Verna, Tacoma, circa 1920.

and when the two men try unsuccessfully to redeem the pawn ticket, they are paid $300 by the pawnbroker, who cannot produce the ring. Then they purchase a new "genawine" diamond ring for Elezir, who outwits everyone, for she now has two authentic rings. She had substituted a paste imitation when Vistar handed it to her to examine.

Verna and the other actresses, including Florence Spencer who played Elezir for the Allen Players production, spent days in downtown Tacoma searching for outfits garish enough for their characters. The *Tacoma Daily Ledger* also reported that "not a white countenance appeared throughout the play, and complexions varied from a light tan to a midnight gloom." Verna, as Vistar, sported a "light chocolate" complexion, and George Rand, as Urias, who enjoyed playing the role more so than he had with his former company one month previously, said, "The Allen Players are certainly marvels in Negro comedy."

Meanwhile, a long-lost relative in the person of Clayton Felton appeared on the scene about this time. Clayton, who had abandoned his wife and son some during the First World War, had been eking out an existence as a restaurant cook in rural Lilliwaup, Washington, about seventy miles northwest of Tacoma. By January 17, 1921, if not before, he had joined the Allen Players as a utility actor, a player who acted when and where he was needed. Often utility actors, explained theatre historian Walter Waters, were less talented or experienced members of the family of a principal performer. While Clayton's brother had also begun as a utility actor, Howard had made enough favorable impressions with audiences to advance to occasional character roles. Clayton was not as successful, although he appeared in several productions that season, including *Good Gracious Annabelle, Lombardi Ltd.*, and *What's Your Husband Doing?*

On February 7, Clayton, Howard, Vera Jedlick, and the entire company filled the huge cast of *Mrs. Wiggs of the Cabbage Patch*, the tale of a meddlesome mother with good intentions, originally produced on Broadway in 1904. Pearl defended the play's age by drawing attention to the record-breaking crowds that week. Meanwhile, Verna, filling the lead role, suffered what the *Tacoma News Tribune* called a "nervous breakdown" during this bill, but forced herself through each performance. The following week, an exhausted Verna lasted through only two performances of the very taxing *The Eternal Magdalene*, a modern morality play in which a biblical character comes to life in order to teach a lesson on the true meaning of religion. Verna left Tacoma for the remainder of the week to recuperate. By February 28, she was able to return to the stage in *Jim's Girl*, selected to commemorate the Allen Players' first anniversary at the Hippodrome.

It seems that Tacoma's patronization of the Allen Players declined sharply about this time. Thinking bad business was merely a temporary winter lull, Pearl kept operating at a loss for about two months. A last-ditch effort to keep Pearl's troupe in Tacoma was initiated by the local Moose Lodge, who canvassed the commercial houses of the city in an attempt to arouse recognition of the Allen Players as a civic asset. A mystified Pearl appealed to the *Tacoma New Tribune* on April 9: "There is no reason why communities the size of Tacoma, Portland, and Seattle should not jump in and support stock companies. This is especially true when the stock companies in all three cities are playing the best and the cleanest plays that have ever been written . . . It costs thousands of dollars a month to produce plays and maintain a stock company, and it is disheartening when a community the size of Tacoma does not respond . . ." Pearl decided to cut his losses and end the Tacoma engagement on April 24. He set his sights again on Canada, announcing that the Allen Players would conduct a summer tour for several months. Most of the company decided to go along, including Marvel Phillips, Allen Strickfaden, Florence Spencer, and newcomer Kathryn Card, who had been with the troupe for only three weeks. Card, a twenty-eight-year-old Montana girl, would be reunited many years later with Verna when she made guest appearances on television's *December Bride*. However, she would win small screen immortality for her occasional appearances as Mrs. McGillicuddy, the mother of Lucy Ricardo on *I Love Lucy*.

One stop on the tour was Regina, a city the Allen Players had not visited for eight years. On June 15, they opened for three nights at the Sherman Theatre, managed by their old friend W. B. Sherman, with *The Lady of the Scarlet Poppy*, a comedy-drama about "a woman who did not care," which afforded Verna the opportunity to wear lavish gowns, among them one covered in silver sequins and bedecked with a mammoth version of the signifying flower. The troupe proved so popular that Sherman asked them to remain for longer. Since they had previously booked engagements elsewhere, the Allen Players were only able to stay for two weeks, but they returned on September 5 for a three-month stay. The autumn's opening bill was *Polly with a Past*, a comedy first made popular by Ina Claire in 1917. Polly, played by Verna, is a housemaid who volunteers to pose as a French seductress in order to help Rex Van Zile win the girl of his dreams by inciting her jealousy. The remainder of their repertoire was repeats of Tacoma productions, except for *The Rainbow, Maggie Pepper,* and *Smilin' Through*. They closed the Regina engagement on December 3 with *The Lady of the Scarlet Poppy*, a repeat of their opener in June. One unique feature of the Regina engagement had been their invitation to admit free of charge the recuperating soldiers in the city's hospitals each Wednesday afternoon. At the end of the final matinee of the engagement, the appreciative soldiers presented Verna with a sheaf of roses.

There was hardly any rest between the Regina engagement and the next, except for what little sleep the Allen Players could enjoy while traveling almost five hundred miles by rail to Edmonton, where they opened on December 5 at the Metropolitan Theatre. *Polly with a Past* was the opening bill, and Verna was hailed by the *Edmonton Journal* for her exceptional "character work." After a subsequent performance of *Smilin' Through*, she was compared to Maude Fulton, who had written and starred in *The Brat*. Fulton would find later success as a screenwriter, among whose credits included *The Maltese Falcon*. On January 2, 1922, Verna admirably performed as director and lead in *The Brat*, even though suffering the ill effects of a head cold. In fact, she directed every production for the first eight months of the Edmonton engagement.

Verna's old Calgary friend Ida Allan, whom she had met in 1908 when the two were teenagers, was now an Edmonton resident. While Verna had remained single in the intervening fourteen years, Ida had become the wife of Missouri

Verna, Regina, 1921. Thirty-five years later, she would pull this dress out of mothballs to wear on television's *December Bride*.

native Robert Pitt Graves in 1912. Ida had met Graves, an engineer, when he had come to Calgary to supervise the construction of the Grand Trunk Pacific Railway there. By 1922, Ida was also the mother of two sons, Allan, age six, and Bobby, age three.

During the Edmonton engagement, Verna was a frequent visitor in the Graves home, and one evening, while helping Ida with Bobby's bath, she discussed the problem she was having locating local children to appear as the orphans in an upcoming production of *Daddy Long Legs*. Allan was nearby, listening. Later when his mother tucked him into bed, he volunteered, "Say, mother, you might go and tell Auntie Verna that if she likes, Bobby and I will help her out!" And that is just what happened. The little Graves boys filled the parts of orphans during the week of January 23, without showing the least bit of stage fright or self-consciousness. The reviewer for the *Morning Bulletin* was ecstatic about the play: "Even *Cinderella* is no more charming than this . . . it's truly a fairy tale dressed up and served in modern raiment."

Verna really loved directing the children. In fact, she loved being around children all the time, perhaps because she spent so much of her girlhood around adults. She decided to hold a special Friday matinee of *Sis Hopkins* on February 10 for Edmonton's school children. Concurrently, a popular silent picture called *My Boy* was playing across town at the Allen Theater. Verna decided to give away ten dolls depicting its star, Jackie Coogan, in a drawing that afternoon. She had learned well from Pearl the tricks sometimes needed to pull in the crowds, especially at a time when the flickers were enticing audiences away from live theatre.

Verna was not only a favorite with the youngest customers of the Allen Players, but she also made fans out of the young adult set. On the evening of May 13, 1922, a final match of the spring rugby season was to begin at Diamond Park between a team of all-star players, chosen from several teams in the Edmonton Rugby League, and the undefeated Edmonton Welsh team. Minutes before the game, Verna walked onto the field, escorted by Mr. George Dewe, honorary president of the league, who introduced her. Then, amid much cheering from both players and the large crowd of spectators, Verna gave the kick that started the match. Ninety minutes later she was in costume and waiting her cue for the final performance of *The Skirt*, two-thirds of which she spent wearing custom made leather chaps as a lovesick girl pretending to be a boy so she could be close to the rancher who spurned her.

The spring repertoire included other current plays, including the comedies *Three Live Ghosts, The "Ruined" Lady,* and *Adam and Eva*, of which the reviewer warned, "The tired businessman who conjures up visions of the Allen Players assembled in the Garden of Eden, leaning up against the well-known apple tree, is liable to be disappointed for the members of the company wear real clothes." Another notable bill, a "virile drama" called *The Man Who Came Back* featured the lead characters as drug addicts in an "realistic" opium den, a scene prompting the same reviewer to predict that it would serve as a "forceful argument against the pernicious traffic." An amusing incident occurred during the run of *Mrs. Wiggs of the Cabbage Patch*, in which Allen Strickfaden was cast in the juvenile lead of Sunday-school pupil Billy. There was to be a party after one performance, and someone had procured a "mickey of Scotch" in spite of Prohibition. With the

Verna with George Dewe, Edmonton, May 13, 1922.

bottle cached in Strickfaden's coat pocket, a prop man unknowingly shoved the coat under a table on stage. Later, Verna—in character—picked it up and said, "Why, this is Billy's coat." As she shook it, out tumbled the bottle and slithered across the stage. That evening, *Mrs. Wiggs* proved a real show-stopper.

Verna also hauled out *Zaza* once more. By now the drama had become old hat, however a recent operatic version staged in New York had renewed interest in the old story. The *Morning Bulletin*'s critic was skeptical of the Allen Players' production; he didn't think such an "emotional" piece could be effectively staged by a company who switched its bills each week. After the initial performance, he was very pleased, conceding, "Miss Felton still has many trump cards up her sleeve."

On June 12, the Allen Players moved from the Metropolitan to a roomier theatre called the New Empire, which offered a much larger stage and house, better ventilation, and no "disturbing street noises." Their first offering was another piece with which Verna was very comfortable: *Madame X*. Two weeks later, an even older melodrama was dug out of mothballs, mainly to capitalize on a screen version currently raking it in at box offices across America and Canada. Directed by D. W. Griffith, *Orphans of the Storm*, a tale set during the French Revolution which starred Lillian and Dorothy Gish, Joseph Schildkraut, and Lucille LaVerne, was produced on a grand scale by United Artists.

The Allen Players' version of the play, called *The Two Orphans*, was also produced with great attention to detail. Two scenic artists worked day and night for a week on the sets, and the costumes were quite realistic. Verna, reprising one of her first leading roles, played the blind orphan, "groping her tragic path through Paris," while Marvel Phillips "cleverly" played her sister, who was cruelly separated from her. Coming to their rescue was Chevalier de Vaudrey, in the person of a new acquisition to the company. Ten days earlier, this dashing young man had immediately left San Francisco once his tour with Leo Ditrichstein's *Face Value* had ended. When Lee Millar arrived at the New Empire, there was a sweet reunion with Verna and her family. Within moments he had become fast friends with the troupe members he had just met. On June 27, the *Edmonton Journal* lauded his performance as de Vaudrey, "With his fine stage presence and inexhaustible supply of 'pep' (if such a word may be used in describing a romantic character such as he plays this week) Mr. Millar made an instant hit."

For the following eight weeks, Pearl Allen had chosen plays very familiar to Lee, including *The Country Cousin*, *A Pair of Sixes*, *Baby Mine*, *The Trail of the Lonesome Pine*, and *Fair and Warmer*, most of which he had played with Verna during their days with the Baker Stock Company. *Camille* was dusted off for the week of July 17. Lee justified this selection in *Edmonton Bulletin* by saying the play was enjoying a revival across the American continent as well as in England. Verna revealed that when she had seen the great Sarah Bernhardt play *Camille*, she had "received an education," thus improving her ability to essay the role of Marguerite. Edmontonians were also familiar with the Divine Sarah; she had played *Camille* at the Old Empire some eight years previously, a performance still clear in the minds of many who would attend Verna's offering of the classic tragedy. As closely as can be determined, Verna's efforts were successful, despite audience discomfort, provoked as much by the three-and-one-half hours' running time as by the extreme summer heat enveloping Edmonton that evening.

Two members of the company bowed out with the final performance of *Camille* on July 22. Kathryn Card and Fred Sullivan joined the ranks of the competition at the Metropolitan, having completed sixty-eight and eighty-eight weeks, respectively, with the Allen Players. In a play of events that mirrored Verna's Portland swan song of *Peg O' My Heart*, both the Allen Players and the Metropolitan Players staged the same drama the following week. The Edmonton newspapers did not make an issue of the matter, nor did they reveal which company had tried to outmaneuver the other. The chosen vehicle was *The Passing of the Third Floor Back*, which had enjoyed lengthy runs on Broadway in 1909 and 1913. Lee Millar and Fred Sullivan played the leading part in each production, a Christ-like stranger "whose short stay transforms a cheap London boarding-house from a place of petty jealousies, petty thieveries, and petty gossip into one of hope, decency, and charity." Friends of both companies turned out to royally to get their favorites off to a flying start. The *Edmonton Bulletin*'s drama critic diplomatically praised neither production more highly than the other.

Verna in her automobile outside the New Empire Theatre, Edmonton, July 1922.
GLENBOW ARCHIVES ND-3-1642.

Meanwhile, Verna and Lee were quickly winning devotees among Edmonton's younger generation, including an impressionable teenager named Lotta Dempsey who would grow up to become a rather famous journalist, ending her long career with the *Toronto Star*. In 1966, Dempsey described the emotional effect these two matinee idols left on her: "To see this fabulous pair in a department store buying socks or hankies was almost more than the soul could bear . . . this couple had the earmarks of real professionals. He was debonair, attentive, dashing; she, regal yet warm, with a sense of presence and a floating cape and swathed veil or whatever was the glamour attire of the time." On an impulse, Dempsey left a party invitation—written "in deathless rhyme"—for Verna and Lee at the box office. However, the girl told neither her parents nor the other invited guests because she secretly doubted the celebrated pair would attend. "But come they did, arriving in such a haze of glory and trailing heady fragrance in Verna's wake: dressed exactly as they should have been, like something out of a Noel Coward drawing-room piece. We were, of course, frozen into mummified silence. My mother and two neighbor ladies, who never had been closer to an actress than they had to the Taj Mahal, were numb . . . But Verna and Lee were warm and generous and kissed all and had a piece of cake. They left us in a state of complete euphoria, having played one of their best scenes for thirty ordinary kids."

Lee Millar took his leave of Edmonton after the August 26 performance of the farce *Fair and Warmer*, but not without an understanding from Verna that they would be reunited the following year. Since the previous December, he had made no attempt to contest his wife's filing for a divorce decree. In another four months, the matter would finally be settled, and he would be free to marry. Before leaving Edmonton, Lee enthusiastically shared with Verna his hopes for a future with her—and not just in a professional sense. After an emotional farewell, he boarded a train for Chicago to rejoin Leo Ditrichstein, who was preparing to rehearse a new play, *Under False Pretenses*, written by a young man named Ben Hecht, predestined to become a prolific Hollywood screenwriter. Lee would remain in Chicago for eight weeks until the Ditrichstein company moved to the Garrick Theatre in Detroit for an additional tryout.

Verna in costume for *East Is West*, New Empire Theatre, 1922.

Meanwhile, back in Edmonton, Verna kept in close contact with Lee throughout the fall of 1922. His divorce from Anna McNaughton became final on December 18, while he was in final rehearsals for *Under False Pretenses*, which by this time had been renamed *The Egotist*. A week later, on Christmas Day, the play made its Broadway bow at the 39th Street Theatre with Leo Ditrichstein in the lead as philanderer Felix Tarbell, a role not unlike those he had played in his last half-dozen plays. *The Egotist* opened to lukewarm reviews, likely because critics, as well as audiences,

Lee Millar, Chicago, circa 1922.

were weary with Ditrichstein's characterizations of "imperfect lovers," roles best described by George Jean Nathan in his 1923 book *The World in Falseface*: "Ditrichstein has in the last eight or ten years permitted himself to appear only in such plays as would vouchsafe him the opportunity to show himself as a distingue and wistful roué who irresistibly seduces all the ladies in the cast save the ingénue, whom he gives over with a magnificently impressive gesture of self-abnegation to the calf-faced juvenile. The Ditrichstein vehicles have come to be so many dramatizations of a Fatty Arbuckle party, somewhat romanticized by the injection of white gloves, an Inverness coat and a top hat . . ." Felix Tarbell, the protagonist of *The Egotist*, fails at his attempts to philander, but finds himself the cuckold when his wife leaves him for a stockbroker, played by Lee Millar. Playgoers were apparently tiring of Ditrichstein in such roles, and so *The Egotist* departed after only six weeks.

In the interim, the Allen Players temporarily vacated Edmonton's New Empire Theatre on January 22, 1923, to allow two large touring companies to occupy the roomy venue. Verna and company moved to the nearby Temple Theatre. On Friday morning, February 2, during the production of *The Girl in the Limousine*, Verna received word from Lee to come to New York as soon as possible. *The Egotist* would sigh its final breath the following evening, and Lee, now available to marry, wanted Verna to become his wife before he left New York in Lee Shubert's touring production of *The Purple Mask*, a melodrama in which Ditrichstein had starred on Broadway in 1920. Verna had to make a hasty decision. Should she leave the Allen Players and Edmonton, where she had successfully given over five hundred performances? Was she ready to take the plunge and become the life partner of a man whose company she had shared for only three months out of the past twenty-nine? Verna had contemplated this decision for some time, in fact, ever since Lee left Edmonton the previous summer. Now, on this cold Edmonton morning, she was pressed to make a quick, but life-changing, decision. For advice she turned to her mother and stepfather, who both quickly gave their blessings. Her mother knew how important it was for a woman to have a supportive husband, while Pearl understood that this career move could bring Verna even greater fame and fortune. At thirty-two years-old, Verna weighed her options until she reached a firm conclusion. Happily, she wired Lee that she would leave Edmonton on the Sunday morning train.

The Edmonton newspapers wasted no time in announcing Verna's decision to end the Edmonton engagement, however, they erroneously reported that Verna would be making her Broadway bow in *The Egotist* as Leo Ditrichstein's leading lady. Whether this was an honest assumption on their part or they were misled by Pearl, perhaps even by Verna, is not clear. Over the past fourteen months Verna had become the city's darling, not only known for her theatrical versatility, but also for her willingness to lend assistance to many worthy causes sponsored by Edmonton's social and athletic circles. Now the public would be cheering for their local girl, whom they thought was about to take the Great White Way by storm, an almost impossible feat for a stock performer who had never once played New York and one that Verna would not accomplish for another six years.

Shortly after she made her decision to join Lee, Verna told the *Edmonton Bulletin*, "I will be genuinely sorry to leave Edmonton, really, I will, and I say that from the bottom of my heart." After her many fans read this interview, they packed the Temple Theatre on Saturday evening, bearing farewell gifts. Afterwards, about fifty friends hosted a farewell party in her honor at the home of Mr. and Mrs. John Michaels. Besides Verna's fellow actors and her pal Ida Graves, a number of the Eskimo Hockey Club players attended.

Earlier that day at the New Empire, a vaudeville troupe of Canadian soldiers known as the The Dumbells had twice performed a revue called *Carry On*. At the conclusions of both the matinee and evening performances, the group's founder Captain Merton Plunkett ran onto the stage with Verna in tow. He spoke briefly of the profound regard Edmontonians shared for Verna, and then she stepped forward. In a voice trembling with emotion, Verna expressed her regret at leaving and her gratitude for the support given to her and the Allen Players during their stay in Edmonton. Captain Plunkett then called for three cheers for Verna Felton, which the audience and the Dumbells gave with gusto.

On Sunday morning, accompanied only by her Pomeranian, Verna boarded an eastbound train for New York. Stopping in Montreal on Wednesday, she spent the day with Leona McIntosh, a young girl who had recently been crowned "Miss Edmonton," one of nine participants in the first Miss Canada Pageant. The previous fall, a committee of Montreal citizens had organized a carnival to promote the city as a winter-sports capital, later adding the selection of a winter queen to its social functions. This was Canada's reaction to the latest craze; the first Miss America had been crowned in 1922. While McIntosh and the other contestants would be judged on appearance and personality, the main criteria was their athletic ability on the ice rink. On the days before the judges' decision on February 10, McIntosh was swept up into a round of social engagements, one of which was dinner with Verna Felton on Wednesday evening.

The *Edmonton Bulletin* reported that Verna wired the Allens of their repast, but curiously, the news item also mentioned that Verna would make her Broadway debut at the 39th Street Theatre on February 19. For the second time, the paper erroneously linked Verna with Ditrichstein's most recent Broadway engagement. This indicates that someone was intentionally misleading the Edmonton press and its readers. Little did Edmontonians know that *The Egotist* had closed on February 3. In fact, on Monday, February 5, while Verna was crossing the plains, the 39th Street Theatre became home to Lee Shubert's production of *Mary the 3rd*, which would run there until June.

On Friday morning, February 9, Lee met Verna's train in Manhattan. They went immediately to see Benjamin C. Warren, the sixty-three-year-old Methodist minister who performed the marriage ceremony. The bride wore a street-wear suit of brown velvet but not without an accent signifying her favorite color—a

Portrait of Verna she labeled, "Off to New York to marry Lee Millar, 1923."

corsage of violets. Standing as witnesses were Lee's fellow cast member from *The Egotist* Gustav Bowhan and his mother Sibylla. That afternoon Verna met Leo Ditrichstein and the rest of the large cast of *The Purple Mask*. For the remainder of their stay in New York, the honeymooners stopped at the Portland Square Hotel at 132 West 47th Street, between Broadway and Sixth Avenue. Prior to their marriage, Lee had been residing nearby at the Hotel Bristol on West 48th Street. Perhaps he decided to change hotels because the Portland Square was a little more posh, or possibly its name appealed to his sense of sentimentality. After all, Portland was the original setting of the newlyweds' romance.

When Lee Shubert's touring production of *The Purple Mask* left New York in late February, Verna accompanied Lee who had been given a major role. Adapted by Matheson Lang from Paul Armont and Jean Manoussi's *Le Chevalier au masque*, the play was, according to theatre historian Gerald Bordman, "a ripsnorting romantic melodrama of the old, old school." Set in Napoleon's First Consulate, a masked count, played by Ditrichstein, employs many ruses to free a duke from his lower-class captors. Standing in his way is Brisquet, a clever Parisian police official, played by Lee. Bordman described the acting as "in keeping with the swashbuckling writing." Despite a less-than-impressive start in the East and Midwest, the touring production found its fans on the other side of the Rockies. However, a carbon copy of a portion of a letter, found among Lee's papers, reveals his acting caliber. Written to Lee Shubert from Grand Rapids, Michigan, on March 20, the unidentified correspondent, presumably Shubert's publicity agent, asserts, "I wish you could see [Lee's] performance. One critic said he was a greater actor than Ditrichstein, and that many of the audience thought the same. I am telling you this as proof of the quality of performance being given." Lee subsequently received equally fine notices in Kansas City, Denver, and Ogden City, Utah. By May 21, the company was appearing at the Curran Theater in San Francisco.

When a Southern Pacific Railway tunnel cave-in near Coram, California, seemed to threaten the troupe's tour of Northwest cities, including Portland and Seattle, Ditrichstein refused to let the obstacle get the best of him. The actors disembarked the train at the last station before the collapsed tunnel and took an automobile detour over twenty-nine miles of hilly and inferior roads to reach the next available depot. Six truckloads of scenery followed, arriving in Portland on May 29, a day later than the actors. It took the fragile Ditrichstein two hours to recover from the weary detour and the last leg of the train trip, but he and his wife took in a movie with Lee and Verna that evening.

The Purple Mask scored a hit the following evening with Lee equally sharing the acting honors with Ditrichstein. While the *Edmonton Bulletin* led Verna's fans to believe that she was featured among the cast of *The Purple Mask*, a close examination of the *Portland Oregonian* refutes this. That paper's drama critic, the indefatigable Leone Cass Baer faithfully listed the cast of characters and their respective players in each of her reviews. Verna's name was absent from the six female roles on the roster. Lee's role of the clever Brisquet called for him to masquerade as other characters, one of which—an elderly prefect—was handled so expertly that the audience was aghast at the revelation of his true identity.

Curiously, the imperious Miss Baer was not as kind in her estimation of another performer also appearing in Portland that week. Latin sex symbol Rudolph Valentino, whose film career had been stymied by an injunction initiated by Paramount Pictures, had resorted to open a national dance tour in order to keep his name in the public eye. The tour, sponsored by a cosmetics company named Mineralava, featured Valentino's wife Natacha Rambova, a former ballerina, as his dancing partner. Both Valentinos wrought the ire of Baer when they refused to keep an interview with her, one which they had requested, sending word through an under-secretary that "publicity was the one thing Valentino needed nothing else but." The next day, Baer derided not only Valentino's temperament, but his choice of sponsor as well. Calling him a "model for effeminate lads," Baer contemptuously described Valentino's wrinkle remover, "It is a kind of clay, you mix it with water and plaster it onto the face and gradually the clay hardens and you have to crack it off with an ax or something." As for his act, Baer thought the best thing was Valentino's orchestra, "a group of awning-tent clad Argentinians who certainly can play."

Lee and Verna spent much of the week renewing acquaintances with many of their Portland friends. "I have been consulting various owners of theater buildings and if I can get the theater I want," Lee told the *Oregonian* on June 2, "I will return this summer for a season of stock next year. We would call it the Verna Felton Players, and Verna Felton would play the leads." Verna explained their options if such a venture proved impossible, "We will both stay cast next year, Mr. Millar with Ditrichstein, with whom he has been for 12 years save for the years he was out here in Baker stock. As for myself, I shall look around and await my opportunity in exactly the type of play for which I am fitted and in which I want to appear. If I do not find it, I may travel again with my husband." While Lee intended to remain with *The Purple Mask* tour for its remaining six weeks, ending in New York, Verna revealed her immediate plans to rejoin the Allen Players in Edmonton on June 4 for the duration of Lee's tour.

A week later in Seattle, Ditrichstein suffered what the press termed a "nervous breakdown," and here the tour ended, as did Lee's professional association with the great star. Although Ditrichstein would return, without Lee Millar, to Broadway the following December in *The Business Widow*, the outing was a miserable failure. By December 1924, Ditrichstein, reluctant to risk his health any longer, decided to retire from the stage, lamenting that the United States offered no place for "a man of leisure." Assured that life in Europe would restore his health, Ditrichstein set sail for Florence, Italy, on December 16, where he lived out the remainder of his life. He died of heart disease at age sixty-three in a Viennese sanitarium on June 28, 1928.

With the transcontinental tour of *The Purple Mask* cut short, Lee joined Verna in Edmonton, where the Allen Players were winding up their own season at the New Empire. On July 9, Pearl scored perhaps the highest coup of his career, thanks to Lee, whose friendship with Leo Ditrichstein enabled the purchase of the rights to stage *The Purple Mask*. Believed to be the first stock producer on the continent to stage the drama, Pearl hailed the production as the "theatrical event of the season." To initially draw his audiences, Pearl compared the five-act swash-buckler to Douglas Fairbanks's popular silent film *The Mark of Zorro*. Lee was on such good terms with Ditrichstein that he had arranged the star's permission to bring all of the road show's elaborate costumes with him from Seattle. Since he knew every detail of the play, Lee, as director, while utilizing Pearl's financial support, would ensure that the staging of *The Purple Mask* be as extensive as a road show. Lee reprised his old role of Brisquet, and Verna took the leading female role of Laurette. The part of Armand, the "Purple Mask," was given to Allen Strickfaden, stalwart lead of the Allen Players for over three years. *The Purple Mask* played to capacity houses that week, but Edmonton audiences tended to prefer less sophisticated fare. Lee's intention was to stage *Fair and Warmer* the following week, but audience demand dictated that *Rebecca of Sunnybrook Farm* be its substitute, especially after the Allen Players announced they would end their season on July 21. The Allen Players left town soon thereafter for a lengthy vacation on Vancouver Island.

Instead of returning to Edmonton in the fall as Pearl had tentatively planned, the Allen Players opened its next stock season in Vancouver, where they had played during the 1903-04 season, under the name of the Allen Stock Company. In those intervening twenty years as Pearl traversed the continent, he claimed to have found no better city in which to live. "We looked on Vancouver as the coming metropolis on this Pacific coast and an ideal spot in other ways in which to live," Pearl later told the *Vancouver Sun*. "And we decided to grow up with it." Although there were those in Vancouver who tried to dissuade Pearl from establishing his troupe there, he refused to listen to these pessimists and their predictions of starvation.

The Allen Players opened at the Empress on October 29, 1923, in the midst of an unprecedented foggy season, which would almost destroy their business. The first two bills, *Polly with a Past* and *Six-Cylinder Love*, comedies that Pearl politely regarded as "child's play," were followed by the more powerful *The Passing of the Third Floor Back*, for which Lee's performance was called "poetic" by the *Vancouver Sun*. The following week the Allen Players departed from the usual, staging a Jerome Kern musical comedy called *Very Good Eddie*. With Strickfaden in the part played by Ernest Truex on Broadway back in 1915, the production allowed Verna a chance to use her "rich mezzo voice" to good advantage. Much of the remainder of that season's bills were old standbys, such as *Zaza, The Country Cousin, Nothing but the Truth, Merely Mary Ann, Camille, The Thirteenth Chair*, and *The Lady of the Scarlet Poppy*. Despite lackluster box office, Pearl hung grimly on to hope. In the coming months, he would not be disappointed in his determination to remain in Vancouver.

Several regular patrons felt compelled to respond to the company's efforts. Vancouver resident Francis Brodie, pleased that the Allen Players were attracting a "much better class than those who formerly patronized the Empress," wrote to Verna on December 2: "To me, as a psychologist, your portrayal of Zaza was exceedingly fascinating. The untrained, undisciplined and violent emotions of the erstwhile street-girl together with a natural charm and consciousness of inferiority is a combination difficult to reproduce, but I must say emphatically that you did it well."

Verna (with Kazan) in *Polly with a Past*.

William M. Galbraith, a former amateur theatrical nearing his sixtieth birthday, sent Pearl an appreciative letter on February 23. Comparing the Allen Players to similarly situated companies he had either patronized or worked with, Galbraith asserted the Pearl's troupe was second to none: "I have only missed some three presentations since you opened in the fall, and I often wonder how it is possible to make such a showing when you change the program every week. Good acting is not so much to be wondered at when the [company] plays only one program for the whole season, but it is the more to be praised when it is changed as often as yours is. I will not specially mention any one player, as they are all more or less deserving of commendation for their good work."

On April 21, 1924, *Mrs. Wiggs of the Cabbage Patch* was chosen for Easter week because of its appeal to children. To augment the supporting cast which required several parts for youngsters, Verna chose her brother Clayton's eight-year-old son Ernest Felton, who resided in the area. In addition she employed Verna and Louise Quain, twin daughters of an unnamed friend, only identified in the *Vancouver Sun* as a former member of the Allen Players. Perhaps the girls' mother was Marie Thompson who had been a member of the troupe over fifteen years earlier.

By this time, the maternal role of Mrs. Wiggs was more fitting for Verna than ever before; she was expecting a baby to arrive in June. Although no mention of the coming event appeared in the press, surely Verna's figure by this time revealed her condition, unless Pearl had devised some ingenious costumes. Amazingly, she played in

Verna, 1924.

every production through May 24, no small feat considering this was a time when mores dictated that women in the final stages of pregnancy refrain from appearing in public. Furthermore, pregnant women of this time would not have been allowed to continue their chosen profession, unlike today's career women who most often work right up to their due dates. Evidently, Verna's pregnancy was an easy one, for there is no record of any missed performances. Florence Lorraine Lyle, a Vancouver resident just returned from a season with the Intimate Art Theatre in New York, was chosen to fill the leading female roles during Verna's maternity leave, beginning on May 26. However, she was replaced by English actress Millicent Hallatt three weeks later.

Pearl Allen's great-niece later revealed an amusing story from this period in Verna's life, although Verna left no mention of it among her papers. "Verna once said that when she was pregnant," recalled Daphne Allen, "that one night in bed, she and her husband were sleeping side by side, with her belly up against his back, and all of a sudden the baby kicked. Lee felt it and quipped, 'This is the only baby who's kicked his father in the ass *before* he was born!'"

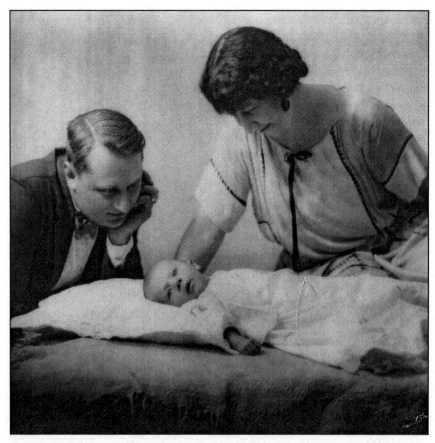

New parents Lee and Verna look admiringly at Lee Jr., Vancouver, 1924.

Friday the thirteenth of June turned out to be a very lucky day for Mr. and Mrs. Lee Millar. At 1:40 p.m., they became the parents of a nine-pound baby boy, whom they named Lee Carson Millar, Jr. Verna recorded in his baby book that they had originally considered naming him Lawrence Carson Millar, in honor of his grandmothers' maiden names, but instead they liked the ring of "Junior," rationalizing that "if he ever wants to change to Lawrence, his initials will be the same." On the afternoon of Junior's birth, most of the Allen Players were playing in a baseball game against the city firemen at a park known as the Powell Street Grounds. The news of his grandson's advent put a broad grin on the face of Grandpapa Pearl, who earned the distinction of playing errorless ball despite the fact that fifteen fielding chances came his way.

Congratulations poured in from so many well-wishers that it seemed all of Vancouver had either sent cards or phoned the new parents. Chief among them were telegrams from Lee's mother Kate Millar and his great friend Leo Ditrichstein. Faithful Empress patrons soon clamored to get a peek at the new baby, many suggesting that Verna introduce him onstage during the season

Four generations: Lee Millar Sr., his grandmother Belle Carson holding Lee Millar Jr., and Katie Carson Millar, Stockton, 1924.

opener in the fall. Meanwhile, during the week following Junior's birth, proud papa Lee, at age thirty-six, ironically played the sixty-year-old lead character in *Mr. John Graham of New York*, complete with grey wig, quavering voice, and slow step. On June 16, at the end of the second act, he was presented with a teddy bear tied with ribbons as a gift for his baby.

The season ended on June 28, but the Millars waited another three weeks before taking an automobile trip to San Francisco, with a stop along the way to visit Lee's mother and grandmother near Stockton. On the drive back to Vancouver in August, they bundled up Junior and put the top down. "He was in his basket," wrote Verna, "and we never heard a peep out of him."

The nurse Verna had hired right after Junior's birth quit shortly before the California trip, leaving the Millars in a bind. The late hours they kept necessitated the use of a nursemaid to look after Junior at their apartment during rehearsals

Lee Millar Jr., flanked by his father and paternal grandmother, visits the Millar family home in Oakland for the first time, 1924.

and performances. With the new season upon them, Verna decided to contact an old friend, "Connie" Conboy, to serve as a temporary nanny. She had known Connie for almost fifteen years—ever since the transcontinental tours of the 1910s—often buying gifts in Connie's jewelry shop whenever she was in Medicine Hat, Alberta. Now Verna wired Connie for help. Came the reply, "For no one but you." Born Mary Jane Mallett to English parents on October 19, 1859, in Park Hill, Ontario, the widowed Connie was now retired and eager to help the Millars. Her only child Leyton had died at age seven in 1894. Now Junior would become his surrogate, and soon Connie's position as nanny would become permanent.

In keeping with tradition, the Allen Players opened the Empress's fall season with a comedy, this time with Winchell Smith and Tom Cushing's *Thank You* on September 8. Vancouverites greeted each player with thunderous applause the instant they walked onstage. Clara, playing the village busybody Miss Blodgett, was compelled to pause on her opening line while audience members extended their congratulations to the new grandmother. Ovations for Verna and Lee were just as lengthy, if not more so. At the end of the second act, five female ushers made their way down the aisle, bearing tributes from admirers, including baby gifts, roses, and even bouquets picked from home gardens. Behind them followed Clara carrying a basket trimmed with pink ribbons. "People thought it a large basket of flowers," recalled Verna, "until I turned it to the audience and there [Junior] was sound asleep. It was my first appearance since his birth, and at the sight of him the packed house cheered and applauded for over five minutes. I took him out, and he looked around, blinked, and fastened his eyes on the footlights." From the house, Pearl Allen beamed with obvious delight at the thought of three generations of actors now in the family.

In Verna's dressing room after the performance, Junior's gifts, including white kid moccasins, a wool coat, and a silver cup, surrounded the sleeping baby. Regarding that evening's ovation, Verna confessed, "I was so excited. When he plays his first role, I'll die, I guess." Clara smiled at her daughter, "You'll feel like I did when you first went on the stage." A few months later, Verna would write to one of her friends in Portland, "Playing Junior's mother is the biggest and loveliest role I've ever had, and a starring adventure for me." Verna would echo this sentiment nine years later, when she opened her heart during a radio interview, "The biggest thrill I've ever known was not related to the stage, although I remember a certain ovation at the Baker Theatre in Portland which left me rather breathless with pleasure. At the time I couldn't think of anything that could possibly be more exciting, but the really great moment was the time my son was born." For the remainder of Verna's life this emotion would only intensify, as she generously and faithfully showered her love on Lee Carson Millar Jr., who would brighten many of the dark and lonely paths ahead.

CHAPTER 9

---◦◆◦---

HARD TIMES, COME AGAIN NO MORE

By the end of the 1924-25 stock season at the Empress Theatre, Pearl had given his detractors cause to reconsider their forecasts of doom and gloom, issued so freely when he announced opening a permanent stock engagement in 1923. In February 1925, he explained his company's lasting success to the *Vancouver Sun*: "The business today proves that I was justified in my faith in this city, but I also realize that part of our success is due to the fact that, while bidding for Vancouver patronage we also took a personal interest in the life of the city. In other words, we made ourselves boosters for Vancouver from the start. And Vancouver is boosting us today in return." Pearl failed to mention that the addition of Lee Millar to his company had provided it with much-needed new blood. Lee was not only a talented stage director, but he also made wise choices concerning play selection. With his influence, the Allen Players' repertoire was filled with more modern plays, some of which had debuted on Broadway as recently as one year before. While royalties for these plays were costly, their currentness proved profitable. Pearl and Lee supplemented these more expensive offerings with other contemporary works which had not yet found their way to New York, playing instead those parts of the country one Manhattan critic dubbed the "backwaters." Moreover, Verna's contribution should not be ignored as an important factor in the success of the Allen Players during this period. She continued to meet each new role, whether it be in a comedy, thriller, or romance, with remarkable skill and versatility.

In *Little Old New York*, which opened on September 22, 1924, Verna donned masculine attire once again, but this time she wasn't playing a male role exactly. She was playing Pat O'Day, an Irish girl who impersonates a boy in order to claim rights to a family fortune left only to male heirs. The other legal heir, Larry Delavan (played by Lee), becomes Pat's guardian when her father suddenly dies. At the end of the first act, Larry finds it necessary to spank the disrespectful Pat, much to the delight of those in the Vancouver audience who knew that Lee was Verna's real-life husband. In the end, Pat is so ashamed at the fraud perpetrated that she discloses that she is really a girl. This means Larry is the sole legitimate heir, but it doesn't really matter because he and "Patricia" find themselves falling in love.

Later that fall, real-life drama rivaled any of Pearl Allen's offerings. One evening during a performance, a twenty-four-year-old transient sneaked into Verna's dressing room and made off with over $2,000 worth of jewelry. Witnesses described him as five feet-three inches tall, about 140 pounds, fair hair and complexion. Local police were unable to trace his path for several weeks until a man fitting his description was arrested on vagrancy charges across the continent in Ottawa. Although he admitted his guilt, the jewelry was no longer in his possession and his pockets held only $260.

News of his apprehension reached Verna as she was rehearsing *Anna Christie*. Vancouver police detective George Sundstrum was sent east to bring the thief, identified as Henry Towers, back to the city via the Canadian Pacific Railway. Handcuffed together the two men reached Medicine Hat, Alberta, on November 18, where they waited several hours to change trains. Once aboard, and only three miles west of Medicine Hat, Sundstrum removed the handcuffs, preparing to retire for the night. He stepped a few feet away for a drink of water, and in one instant, Towers was gone.

Sundstrum ran to the next car where a porter informed that Towers had rushed through, knocking him sprawling and leaping over a passenger who was bending down in the aisle. At the rear of the car, the trap door on the back platform was open, and Towers took a headlong dive through it. Sundstrum jumped off the train but in the darkness could see nothing of his prisoner. He alerted the local police, and the entire night was spent searching Medicine Hat and vicinity, but to no avail.

Towers, in two days without anything to eat, made it over seventy miles on foot, arriving at the town of Robsart, Saskatchewan, not far from the United States border. In the interim, news of his sensational escape had been broadcast from a Regina radio station. When a restaurant patron in Robsart mentioned his resemblance to the description of the wanted man, Towers again fled but was soon apprehended. Handed over to Sundstrum, Towers was found to have cut his face severely on barbed wire in his leap from the train, narrowly escaping the loss of an eye. The two men finally reached Vancouver on November 24. On Wednesday, December 3, he was sentenced to serve three years in the New Westminster penitentiary. According to the *Vancouver Sun*, Towers "wilted perceptibly when judgment was passed upon him." The lost jewelry was never itemized in the Vancouver press, but it must have been stunning. Allowing for inflation, items that cost $2000 in 1924 would cost almost $25,000 in 2008.

Despite the loss, Verna knew it was necessary to turn her attention to the busy fall schedule. Several productions that season proved so popular that they were held over for more than one week, including the thriller *Red Light Annie*, featuring thieves, drug addicts, and prostitutes, and Eugene O'Neill's acclaimed *Anna Christie*, promoted by Pearl as "more powerful than the strongest sermon." But the most astounding success of the season was the runaway comedy hit *So This Is London*, which opened January 19, 1925. Pearl had staged two other George M. Cohan successes the previous fall, but they paled in comparison with this tale of two families, one American and the other British, who protest the marriage of their children. British solidity and conservatism are contrasted with American vivacity and slang until things work themselves out in the end with each family assuming characteristics of the other. Troupe newcomer Frank Vyvyan "scored a furor" as the English father, while George Taylor Jr. and Doris Brownlae excelled as the young couple. Verna filled a supporting role as the refined Lady Ducksworth who hosts a weekend visit for everyone at her country estate.

Pearl didn't intend to run *So This Is London* longer than two weeks, but, on February 2, when questioned about his plans, the *Sun* printed his response the following morning: "Well," drawled the genial Irishman, "I read in *The Sun* this morning that there are now a quarter of a million people in Vancouver. We've had about 20,000 of them so far, more or less, and there's no reason why the rest of 'em shouldn't see it too." He was joking, of course, but the play would run for another six weeks, breaking all of the city's theatrical records for attendance and length of run. Vancouver's telephone operators asserted that the Empress Theatre's line had become the busiest one in the city, prompting all seventy-eight switchboard girls (of that exchange) to attend the show en masse on February 9. Meanwhile, hundreds of disappointed patrons were turned away each week after the daily sellouts. One Saturday, conditions bordered on the riotous outside the Hastings Street venue when the mob was told there were no more seats. Surprisingly, many patrons came from as far away as Seattle to see what all the fuss was about. On March 9, a frantic man phoned twenty-five minutes before the curtain, saying his car was stuck in the mud forty miles away, but pleading that his seats not be sold, "I'll get there somehow!" The phenomenal eight-week bill, which ended March 14, was followed by the old reliable, *The Rejuvenation of Aunt Mary*, in which Verna and George Taylor Jr.'s jazz-style reprise of Clara's signature sentimental solo "When You and I Were Young, Maggie" shook the rafters.

The remainder of the spring line-up consisted of both old and new selections, among them *Spring Cleaning, Spooks, The Fool, Little Women* (in which Verna played Jo), and Verna's perennial favorite *Under Two Flags*. Verna's equestrian skills were tested in the latter when the police horse procured for the famous get-away scene proved uncooperative. "During rehearsal the animal turned around and looked Miss Felton in the eye," reported the *Sun*, "and then proceeded to do a whirling dervish in the center of the stage. All of which was Arabian enough, but not in the plot." As a replacement, Pearl was forced to utilize a bronco, a beast just as equally challenging. Verna, ever the animal lover, fed him sugar and baby-talked him for an hour until she won his confidence, then his friendship, and finally obedience. Once more the brave heroine Cigarette escaped the Arabs, who were described by the drama critic as "out-sheik[ing] anything Valentino ever attempted."

Verna, Vancouver, 1924.

Proud Papa: Lee Millar with his son, 1925.

On April 6, Verna's elder half-brother returned to the family fold and joined the cast of *The Love Test*, but this time he was acting under the name Howard Van Alstyne, an alternate spelling of his birth name. Howard had chosen not to follow the Allen Players into Canada when they left Tacoma in 1921. How he spent the intervening four years remains a mystery, but there are indications that he may have become widowed during this period. Why he now chose to acknowledge his birth name as his professional name is another puzzle. His adoptive father, James Samuel Wiggins, now eighty-six years old, was living out his final days at Saratoga, California, in a rest home established by a fraternal organization, The Independent Order of Odd Fellows. Death would take him on November 1, 1925.

Another member of the family got in on the act on May 11. Eleven-month-old Lee Millar Jr., now nicknamed "Spuddie," made his official stage debut as the youngest orphan in *Daddy Long Legs*. He only spoke one line, or to be more exact, two words ("Da-da"), but he was the hit of the bill, toddling onstage with the aid of a "hoop saddle on wheels," or what is today called a walker. "Vainly did Verna Felton and her bevy of 'orphan' kiddies endeavor to go on with their lines," reported the *Sun*, "for all eyes were on Lee C. Millar, junior, every ear was strained for some quaint baby coo, and gales of merriment greeted the precocious child's every odd movement and mannerism." The production also marked the farewell appearance of Lee Sr., and Verna, who planned to spend their summer vacation studying productions in New York and other eastern cities in order to line up new offerings for the 1925-26 season. In their stead would be Allen Stock Company alumni Allen Doone and Edna Keeley, both of whom had played juvenile roles during the 1903-04 season at the People's Theater in Vancouver. In the interim, Doone had become a household name in Australia and Tasmania, where he and wife Keeley staged Irish plays for more than a decade. Always one to maintain friendships and business contacts, Pearl prevailed upon Doone and Keeley to postpone a trip to London to fill in as "guest stars" during the final weeks of the 1924-25 season. Doone was happy for the chance to renew acquaintances with his Vancouver friends so this helped close the deal.

In the meantime, the Millars began the first leg of their 7,000-mile motor trip, stopping in Ladysmith, where they were able to spend some carefree summer days before heading to California. While there, "Spuddie," as he would be better known for the next decade, began walking on his own the day before his first birthday, an event celebrated at the home of friends, Mr. and Mrs. Edward Stock, in nearby Duncan, BC.

Despite their previous successes, the Allen Players did not return to the Empress in the fall of 1925. Instead, they opened on September 7 at the New Empire in Edmonton for eighteen weeks. By this time, the troupe numbered twelve and included most of the players from the prior season, including Clara (now billed as Mrs. P. R. Allen), Doris Brownlae, Millicent Hallatt, Howard Van Alstyne, father-son team George Taylor Sr. and Jr., and British man-and-wife,

Verna Felton the flapper, Vancouver, circa 1925.

Frank Vyvyan and Olive Eltone. Once described as a combination of Charles Laughton and Little Lord Fauntleroy, character actor Vyvyan was also a skilled artist. He presented Verna with a splendidly lifelike oil portrait of herself for Christmas that year.

New to the troupe was twenty-four-year-old Sherold Page, tall and debonair juvenile man. Born as Sherman Page Brown II in Seattle on September 8, 1901, Page's career had begun in 1920 when he left the University of Washington to become a member of an English troupe then performing in Victoria, British Columbia. His father, almost sixty-five when Page was born, humored this interest, but when Page wanted to use "Sherman Page" as a stage name, his mother suggested "Sherold Page," in honor of a family friend. Coincidentally, Page's father had graduated from Rush Medical College, the alma mater of Verna's father Dr. Felton. However, Dr. Brown really wanted to pursue a career with the railroad, so after a year he abandoned medicine and later became an executive for Northern Pacific in Seattle.

Like his father, Sherold Page followed his dream. By the time he joined the Allen Players, he had spent five seasons on the stock circuit, both in Canada and the States. Many times he had looked adversity in the face, going without food or lodging when paydays failed to arrive. Many years later he laughingly recalled playing a small town in Canada where the venue was nothing more than a meeting hall doubling as a barn, whose manager "opened these big doors and pushed the bales of hay out into the snow, as it was midwinter when we were there . . . a thousand below it seemed to me." Page's experience with the Allen Players was a sizable improvement and a welcome change.

Connie Conboy, Pearl, Howard Van Alstyne (inside car), unidentified man holding Spuddie, Clara, and Lee in Canada during the 1925-26 season.

For the eighteen-week engagement, Pearl and Lee chose an exclusive repertoire of comedies, the majority of which had been produced on Broadway within the past three years. The one exception was the melodrama *Common Clay*, selected by Pearl as the closing bill to showcase Verna's dramatic ability. The press remained fascinated with little Spuddie, but the lengthiest profile was published soon after the troupe's arrival in Edmonton the previous September when Spuddie was fourteen months old: "He has already acquired the art of turning a peculiarly characteristic somersault, crows like a rooster, imitates a butterfly, puffs like the once imperious but now forlorn Pomeranian 'Kazan,' demonstrates Daddy Lee's use of a pipe, and is willing to try anything from comedy to tragedy as the occasion demands."

The Allen Players closed their engagement on January 9, but ten weeks later they returned to the New Empire for a limited run, opening Easter Week with *My Son*, a drama which had unexpectedly run for over 275 performances on Broadway the previous season. Spuddie enjoyed another "walk-on" part in this tale of a Portuguese mother who set out to save her son from a life of crime. Other recent successes followed, including *The Family Upstairs, The Last Warning*, and *Why Men Leave Home*.

During the 1926 tour through Alberta, Spuddie had grown very attached to his nanny, Connie Conboy, whose first name he pronounced as "Coddie," an affection later alternately used with "Cod." (In future years, Spuddie and the rest

The Millars in Alberta, 1926.

Spuddie Millar, Regina, Saskatchewan, 1926.

of the family altered her nickname to "Codo," spelling it with only one "d," but pronouncing the first "o" as a short vowel.) Connie was accustomed to nicknames; her own family in Ontario had called her "Minnie." Her adopted family, the Millars and Allens, were fond of the practice as well. Verna was called "Babe" by her stepfather, perhaps because Pearl first knew her as "Baby Verna Felton." Lee Sr. used this same nickname for Verna, but sometimes he called her "Tootum." To confuse things even more, Spuddie was also alternately referred to as "Babe." For many years, Lee Sr. was known to his son as "Daddy Boy." In later years, to distinguish father and son, Verna would refer to Lee Sr. as "Big Millar" and Lee Jr. simply as "Millar." Clara's sons and son-in-law shortened her name to "Claire," while Pearl affectionately referred to his wife as "Pigeon." Spuddie called his grandparents "Nana" and "Bopa" (rhyming with "Poppa"). The use of nicknames was not reserved for members of this closely-knit family; Sherold Page was forever "Sherry," while later his wife Olive would become "Ol."

Bopa and Spuddie sledding in Canada, circa 1926.

By June 1926, the Allens and Millars reached western Canada where they vacationed for a short while before opening on June 28 for a month's run at the Orpheum in Vancouver. The repertoire included three farces and one thriller, *The Last Warning*, which featured the format of a "play within a play." This bill coincided with Clara's sixty-third birthday on July 13. Because of rehearsals and performances, there was little time during the day to celebrate, so the family indulged Clara's request for a midnight swim in the English Bay. "If the old folks can do it," Lee quietly said to Verna, "I guess we can." At one in the morning on her natal day, as Clara emerged from the briny water, she called out, "That's what I like about Vancouver. You sure can enjoy yourself if you've a mind to." Indeed, at sixty-three, Clara was quite youthful. Despite her rotund build, she was quite energetic and healthy. She was rarely sick, never missed rehearsals, and maintained a reputation for never muffing a line. She credited her good health to never "fretting over trifles or allowing herself to be upset when things go wrong." Daughter Verna would follow her example until the final years of her own life.

The movements of the Allen Players for the 1926-27 season are sketchy at best. It is believed that they spent these months touring smaller cities in the prairie provinces of Canada, perhaps ones never previously played. One of the few documented stops was Lethbridge, Alberta, where the Allen Stock Company had regularly stopped during its tour "*en route* through Canada" more than ten years earlier. As with many of the season's engagements, the troupe performed *So This Is London* at Lethbridge's Majestic Theatre for only two nights, November 1 and 2. Besides Verna and Clara, there appears to have been only three troupe members as holdovers from the previous two seasons: Frank Vyvyan, Olive Eltone, and Howard Van Alstyne. Without the talent of George Taylor Sr., who had enacted all of the older character roles before his departure, Lee was required not only to direct but also to fill Taylor's roles, such as Hiram Draper Sr., in *So This Is London*, a performance the *Lethbridge Herald* deemed as "exceedingly fine." Evidently, Lee was very believable as a man much older than his thirty-eight years, for his mother-in-law Clara played his wife in this production. Rarely had supporting players in the troupe been criticized for poor performances, but the unidentified actor playing the small part of an English servant received a rather harsh notice from the *Herald*'s reviewer: "Players who grossly exaggerate, and so make ridiculous, even a small part should be placed 'on the list' of Koko in the *Mikado*, to be led out for immediate execution." During the previous season, this part had been played by Howard Van Alstyne, but since Verna's brother had ten years of acting experience, it is likely that the criticism was directed at one of the newer members of the company.

This season had been like no other in the recent history of the Allen Players. Not since the company's earliest days had it been forced to travel so frequently to book engagements. The culprit seems to have been the increasing competition of both vaudeville and motion pictures. "The film companies were often able to obtain rights to recent plays even before the stock managers had had an opportunity to produce them," explained theatre historian Walter K. Waters. "The result was that more and more regularly the audiences began to attend the motion picture theatres, and attendance began to dwindle in the legitimate theatres." In 1926, Warner Brothers presented the first picture with synchronized sound effects and music—*Don Juan*—starring John Barrymore. This film would usher the advent of the "talkies" in just a few years, sounding the death knell for stock companies in Canada and the United States.

Pearl and Lee, with lives and livelihoods so steeped in the legitimate theatre, particularly found the changing times disheartening. Unfortunately, Pearl's attempts to find another Edmonton or Vancouver where the Allen Players could operate a permanent stock engagement for successive months were fruitless. One of their longest engagements began on December 28, 1926, at the Walker Theatre in Winnipeg, Manitoba, a city the Allen Players had never played before. Advance press for *So This Is London* hailed Verna as "a new star to Winnipeg's firmament, but one exceedingly popular in the western states and Canada."

Though the Allen Players performed at the Walker for only five nights, they arrived in Winnipeg a week early, rented a downtown apartment "for baby's sake," and according to Verna's notation in Spuddie's baby book, "lazed off Christmas week."

The company was well received in Winnipeg. As Lady Amy Ducksworth, Verna demonstrated "a certain breeziness that [was] captivating," according to the *Manitoba Free Press*. Conversely, Pearl was impressed with the Walker Theatre, built in 1906 by Corliss Powers Walker. With its magnificent vaulted ceiling designed to resemble the famous Auditorium Theatre in Chicago, the Walker boasted two thousand seats, elegant patron lounges, a deep stage, a huge fly tower, and broad wings to accommodate elaborate stage sets. Behind the stage was a three-story block devoted to dressing rooms, property rooms, and the scenery dock. Walker had aligned himself with the powerful New York syndicate run by the Broadway firm Klaw and Erlanger. For more than a quarter century, he would bring to the Walker a dazzling array of quick-changing bookings of top entertainments, everything from Shakespearean plays to ballets and operas. While there was no chance that the Allen Players could become a permanent stock organization in such an impressive venue, Pearl hoped that they would be invited for return engagements.

Early in 1927, the Allen Players began their westward journey with Vancouver as the final destination. Along the way, they stopped off in many of the cities they had visited in the fall, including a two-night run of the Anita Loos comedy *The Whole Town's Talking* at Lethbridge's Majestic Theatre on February 18 and 19. By mid-spring, the troupe had reached Vancouver Island, the place the Allens considered paradise. Here they would stop for a few days before departing for a lengthy summer vacation in California. Meanwhile, Walter Gilbert, Lee and Verna's old friend from their Baker Stock Company days, was beginning his thirtieth week as director of the Monte Carter Players at the Empress in Vancouver. When he heard that the Millars were back in town, he persuaded them to delay their vacation trip to join the Monte Carter Players for the final three weeks of the season.

Verna and Lee opened on May 9 as the leading players in *The Goldfish*, the tale of a young New York shop girl who manages to worm her way up through society to wealth and position through a series of marriages, only to find herself miserably unhappy. The second week's offering, *Stella Dallas*, the story of a woman who sacrifices her own happiness for the sake of her daughter, received better praise from the *Vancouver Sun*: "Miss Verna Felton displayed talent that was nothing short of genius. At times she touched the heartstrings as caressingly as a musician. At others she gripped and held one spellbound by the intensity of her elemental passions. Again she sent laughter rippling over the house in a wave of pure enjoyment." Playing the daughter's role in the production was twenty-three-year-old Glenda Farrell, an Oklahoma native who had been a stage performer since childhood. In the next decade, Farrell would become one of the most prolific screen actresses in the Warner Brothers' stable, most often playing brassy, fast-talking blondes.

This brief run with the Monte Carter Players offered Verna a break from the Cohan comedies she had performed for the past four years and instead gave her one last chance to shine as an "emotional actress." For the third and final week of her engagement, Verna starred in one of her old favorites from the 1910s, *The Second Mrs. Tanqueray*. The *Sun*'s review of her performance echoed the sentiments expressed in the critique of *Stella Dallas*, both being rather reminiscent of the notices Verna had received for melodramas of the previous decade. However, the writer admitted that Verna presented a more modern Paula Tanqueray than he had seen performed on the London stage some twenty years earlier.

The Allens and Millars witnessed theatrical history during this third week in Vancouver. The esteemed Shakespearean actor John Drew, Jr., now seventy-three years old and in failing health, was in town with a touring production of Pinero's *Trelawny of the Wells*, featuring an imposing roster of stage greats: Peggy Wood, O.P. Heggie, Estelle Winwood, Henrietta Crosman, Effie Shannon, Frieda Inescort, J.M. Kerrigan, and eighty-two-year-old Mrs. Thomas Whiffen. Though feeble and requiring the aid of his fellow actors to enter and exit the stage, Drew gave a "superlative rendition of his part with all his old polish and poise," Pearl remembered later. However, this performance was destined to be Drew's swan song. Doctors were summoned when he was unable to make the next performance, and it was decided to rush him to San Francisco and have all of his teeth extracted. Drew would die in that city on July 9, with his death being attributed to rheumatic fever and septic poisoning.

By June 13, the Millars had reached Lee's family's ranch near Stockton, in time to celebrate not only Spuddie's third birthday, but also the ninetieth birthday of Lee's grandmother Isabelle Carson three days later. Lee's mother Kate was now residing on the ranch to help her spinster sister Hattie care for their aged mother, whose keen mind remained a storehouse of pioneer history. One month prior to her ninetieth milestone, the local newspaper interviewed "Belle" Carson as she reminisced about her earliest days in San Joaquin County. From her porch rocker, she marveled at the steady automobile traffic whizzing past her shady home, recalling how impassable that muddy road could become during the 1860s when she was a young mother. But now, while surrounded by her descendants for a rare family reunion, the apple of Belle's eye was Lee Carson Millar Jr., the youngest of her great-grandsons. Spuddie was accustomed to the attention; he was doted on by a legion of female fans, including his grandmothers Kate Millar and Clara Allen, his beloved "Codo" Conboy, but foremost his devoted mother Verna.

Meanwhile, Pearl and Clara spent part of their vacation visiting scenes of their childhoods and early adulthoods. In Chico, they were the guests of Pearl's eldest sister Dr. Nellie Almira Allen, the first practicing female osteopath in the state of California. The highlight of the summer for Clara, though, was an automobile trip through her native Sierra County, which she had not visited since 1889. She reported that the scenes she encountered were not unlike those of her youth. Clara thought Downieville, in particular, looked very much the same.

One old acquaintance she definitely did not renew was that of her former husband Edward Van Alstine, now approaching seventy and employed as a ranch hand in neighboring Placer County. When Ed became ill later that year, his local lodge brothers took steps to admit him to the Odd Fellows home at Saratoga, only to be thwarted when he died of heart disease in an Auburn hospital during the early morning hours of January 1, 1928. His friends had never heard him speak of any relatives so they buried Ed Van Alstine in an unmarked grave at the Odd Fellows Cemetery in Roseville. Almost forty-four years had passed since he abandoned Clara and their boys in Forest City.

While visiting Chico, Pearl told his hometown newspaper the *Enterprise* that he had booked a lengthy engagement with the Walker Theatre in Winnipeg, to begin September 6, but for some reason or another this never came to pass. The Allen Players did not return to Vancouver that fall either, for when the Empress reopened on October 24, a new company—the United Players—was in residence. Among their twenty members were Allen Players alumni Allen Strickfaden and Frank Vyvyan, as well as gaunt Eily Malyon, another British character player who would create over eighty Hollywood film roles, mostly uncredited and almost always in the sinister vein. But where were the Allens and Millars?

It is possible that financial situations kept them in California following their summer vacation. A curious item appeared in the *Oakland Tribune* on February 2, 1928. From midnight until 2 a.m., KLX, an Oakland radio station, regularly broadcasted a musical request program called "Who's Up and Why?" When late-night listeners wired in to answer the show's title question, the newspaper printed their responses the following day. Lee and Verna wired, "We are just a couple of troupers enjoying other troupers' trouping." Does this mean that they were now only spectators? If they were out of work, at least the Millar house on 10th Street in Oakland afforded them a temporary and rent-free dwelling.

On April 10, the *Vancouver Sun* announced the return of the Allen Players to the Empress. Pearl stressed to readers that none of his policies had changed during the three intervening years, including clean wholesome bills and popular admission prices. Verna and Lee would take leading roles while Clara, Howard, and Frank Vyvyan, recruited from the now defunct United Players assumed character parts. In addition, Pearl brought from California a young couple: San Francisco ingénue Marjorie Spencer and Rollin Parker from the Fulton Theatre in Oakland. On opening night, April 16, after the first act of *Green Stockings*, Clara tripped over a carpet offstage and dislocated a kneecap. Refusing to bow out—despite unbearable pain—she made it through the remainder of the performance. During her scene as the intoxicated old lady, the audience roared with laughter while she groaned inwardly at every movement. The following evening, she showed herself again as a real trouper by taking the stage in a wheelchair.

A month of "light and airy" comedy dramas followed the opening bill, including *The "Ruined" Lady*, *Family Pride*, and *So This Is London*. Then on May 28, *Mother's Millions* offered a change of pace. Loosely based on the life of infamous Wall Street financier, the miserly Hetty Green, the play had been a hit for May Robson a few years earlier on the touring circuit. Verna played aged Harriet "Hattie" Breen, the world's richest woman: "She has treated her children with savage meanness, but she has secretly helped them to success. Her refusal to lavish them with luxuries, forcing them to shift for themselves while, unbeknown to them, she guides their destinies into suitable channels . . . and her reward has been the reputation of miserliness and meanness." When Breen's childhood sweetheart tries to ruin her son, she brings the villain to the point of ruin instead. He taunts her, "With all your wealth, you have been unable to hold the love of your children." Goaded by this taunt, Breen hurls discretion to the wind, and stakes her entire fortune on a wager that her children love her. The part satisfied Verna's penchant for character roles, and she proved her ability to play a character much older than her years. To enhance the authenticity to her appearance, she wore wigs fashioned of combings from Clara's gray head.

French Leave, opening on June 11, featured Verna as the wife of a World War One British officer who attempts to visit him at a rest retreat not far from the trenches in France by disguising herself as a Parisian chanteuse. She is caught by a blustering brigadier-general (played on Broadway by Charles Coburn in 1920 and by Frank Vyvyan in the Allen Players version), mistaken for a spy, and brought up before a military tribunal. But when the general learns the truth, he is forgiving. During one performance, an incident occurred which Verna would later cite as the most amusing experience of her stage career. In one scene, her character's scarf was supposed to be on a table, while another character was to hold it aloft and say, "It's hers." Verna recalled, "The scarf was not there at all. I had no handkerchief and my slip was fastened to my dress. I went behind a screen and took off my shorts. I crumpled them up and asked a player who would be passing by to put them on the table and to whisper to the actor not to unfold them. He started to do just that when he realized what he was holding. I think only the people in the first few rows knew what had happened."

A week later the Allen Players presented the perennial favorite *Mrs. Wiggs of the Cabbage Patch*. This time, Spuddie created a stir of interest in the part of Tommy, the fugitive who finds shelter with Mrs. Wiggs, played by Verna. Only a few days before Spuddie had celebrated his fourth birthday at home in the Felix Apartments on Jervis Street. A local newspaper called him "a citizen of the future," drawing attention to the fact that in his four young years, Spuddie had traveled over 40,000 miles, a feat contrasted with the life experience of his great-grandmother, who, at ninety-two, had not strayed far from the Carson ranch for the past sixty years. Indeed, Spuddie was something of a local celebrity, with his photograph appearing often in the *Vancouver Sun*. Late in the summer of 1928, when Vancouver native and Olympic athlete Percy Williams, recent winner of the 100-meter and 200-meter races at Amsterdam, returned to Vancouver, little Spuddie was part of the welcoming ceremony. The mayor presented Williams with a new automobile, but Spuddie, looking dapper in his wide-striped jacket, knickers, and knee socks, was chosen to present Williams's mother with a bouquet of roses.

The Empress closed its doors for summer vacation on July 7 after a week of *Linger Longer Letty*, a musical which afforded Verna the chance to sing several numbers, including the title song.

Over the past few months, Pearl Allen had begun to seriously consider the final fate of the stock companies. Many companies had permanently disbanded during the 1927-28 season, due to increased competition from motion pictures. On August 4, 1928, *The Perfect Crime*, the first live action motion picture with sound-on-film recording, had been released. Knowing that more would inevitably follow, Pearl decided to try something different for the upcoming season at the Empress. Instead of staging a weekly Allen Players production, he contracted for the appearances of ten or more road shows, many of them English. He promised Empress patrons that Verna Felton and the Allen Players would present plays during the short intervals between his contracted engagements. The first of these was a "play of intrigue" called *The Green Scarab*, in which Lee played an Egyptologist, collector of priceless scarabs, opening on September 17. Two consecutive productions followed, first *The Truth*—a 1907 Clyde Fitch relic— and then *The Great Gamble*, written by Jerome K. Jerome, the author of previous Allen Players production *The Passing of the Third Floor Back*. Deemed an "ignominious collapse" when it opened in London in 1914, *The Great Gamble* proved to be just that when performed at the Empress. Pearl brought Allen Strickfaden back to join the cast, but even his loyal Vancouver fans could not save the wretched play. Verna, Lee, Clara, and Frank Vyvyan were all on hand when it closed on October 6. Although none of them realized it then, *The Great Gamble* would be the final production in the twenty-six-year history of the Allen Players—an inauspicious finale indeed.

Though Pearl and Lee had feared the end of the stock era, they had held out as long as possible. Both realized that when stock ceased to exist, the stage would be deprived of its best training facility and the public would lose its source for good, inexpensive live theatre. The stock theatre of the early twentieth century had provided the training for some of the most versatile performers in the industry, including Verna Felton.

On October 29, when a tour of Garland Anderson's *Appearances* opened at the Empress, Lee Millar sat up and took notice. After a solid month of wondering where his career was heading, he suddenly saw an open window. *Appearances* had been the first play of black authorship to be produced on Broadway. Anderson, once a self-educated San Francisco bellhop, managed to get his autobiographical drama on the stage, but only with financial help from Al Jolson and New York Governor Al Smith. It debuted at the Frolic Theatre in the fall of 1925, causing quite a stir with its cast of both white and black actors. Heretofore, if a production required both white and black roles, white actors performed the Negro roles wearing blackface. Set in San Francisco, Anderson's story told of a black bellhop accused by a white woman of rape. At his trial everything seems to prove him guilty until the woman is shown to really be a light-skinned, blackmailing Negress. Hailed by the *New York Times* as "finely conceived, crudely wrought protest against lynch law," the original Broadway production of *Appearances* only lasted three weeks. But interest in the story did not die there.

D. J. Tallman's touring production of *Appearances* enjoyed twenty weeks on the road in 1928, including long runs in both Los Angeles and San Francisco. The Empress engagement was its first in Canada. Lee Millar envisioned *Appearances* as his ticket back to New York. After negotiating with the producer, Lee was hired to direct the Chicago production of a slightly rewritten version of the play, slated as a hopeful Broadway revival later in the season. Lee left Vancouver in late November to ready the production for a December 23 opening at Chicago's Princess Theater. Verna and Spuddie followed him on December 6.

Meanwhile, Pearl embarked on a new adventure of his own. He accepted an offer to manage the Vancouver Theatre, located at 761 Granville Street. The 600-seat theatre had been the original Orpheum when constructed in 1906. The first engagement—opening under Pearl's watchful eye on December 24—was the D'Oyly Carte Opera Company, performing *The Mikado, Iolanthe,* and *The Pirates of Penzance* during its two-week stay. Frank Hopwood, critic for the *Vancouver Sun,* paid tribute to Pearl upon his move: "With a knowledge of human nature, a great and loving tolerance for the faults of the human race, Mr. Allen is never worried. He has learned to take the bad with the good in about as hard a school as can be found—a school where knocks are perhaps more frequently met with than halfpence." Vancouver theater patrons knew Pearl as "Dad" Allen because after each performance he waited in the lobby to say goodnight to them.

Pearl and Clara maintained their residence in the Empire Hotel at 162 East Hastings Street. On the ground level of the establishment was a beer parlor, formerly the hotel saloon in the days before Prohibition. Beer parlors were not equipped with a bar; patrons were required to sit at one of the tables. No singing or entertainment was allowed either. The Empire Hotel Beer Parlor was operated by Mrs. Rose Elizabeth Low, a jolly, rotund lady who became fast friends with the Allens and Millars. She was assisted by her husband William Edward Low, with whom she had come from England to Vancouver in 1905. The childless couple took right to Spuddie so they were among numerous Vancouverites who were sorry to see him leave for Chicago with his mother.

In addition to directing the Chicago production of *Appearances*, Lee filled the minor part of Fred Kellard, whose Southern drawl afforded him the chance to hearken his father's Louisiana background. Verna was given the pivotal role of Elsie Benton, the bellhop's accuser. Though the *Chicago Tribune* was lukewarm

Spuddie surrounded by his gifts from Santa Claus, Bradley Hotel, Chicago, Christmas 1928.

in its reception of *Appearances*, it lasted nine weeks, and preparations were made for its transfer to Broadway.

Meanwhile, the Millars experienced a flurry of excitement one evening upon their return to the Bradley Hotel where they were stopping. Less than three weeks after the infamous St. Valentine's Day Massacre, which ended the five-year gang war between Al Capone and Bugs Moran, Lee and Verna were naturally cautious about their comings and goings in the crime-ridden Windy City. Just before going out for the evening on Sunday, March 3, 1929, they placed their savings of $700 plus their jewelry inside an envelope, which they put inside a larger envelope. The money and valuables were then deposited in the hotel safe. Later that night, while 250 guests slept undisturbed, four gunmen held up the hotel clerk, bellboys, and a few sleepy patrons. When the robbers rifled the safe, they evidently thought the Millars' envelope contained nothing valuable. It was later found unopened and tossed on the floor. The robbers' oversight afforded Lee and Verna a huge sigh of relief; they would soon need the money for the move to New York City.

Produced by C. Mischel Picard, *Appearances* opened at the Hudson Theatre on 44th Street on Easter Monday, April 1, 1929. After almost twenty-nine years in the business, Verna A. Felton (as she was curiously and unprecedentedly billed), made her Broadway debut. It was a red-letter night for her husband as well; Lee was directing his first Broadway production. Black actor Doe Doe Green, who had won laurels as the bellhop's buddy Rufus Jones in the original 1925 production, was brought back to repeat his comic role. The *New York Sun*'s Carl Helm deemed Green's reprisal as "one of the finest performances of the season." Recognizing that the play was "obviously designed to emphasize the philosophy that Truth will prevail and that a man can be anything he sets his heart on," Helm noted that Garland Anderson would deliver free lectures each noonday in the theater on "Success and Why It Is Available to All." On April 22, the production was moved to the Mansfield Theatre, where its forced run ended on May 25. *Appearances* was not the only disappointment that season. In fact, many playgoers could not remember a worse theatre season than the one of 1928-29. Most producers laid the blame on the talkies, but others cited inexperienced or tasteless producers rushing to make a quick killing. By this time, some of Broadway's best talents had deserted live theatre, most of them permanently, for the lights of Hollywood. "Even some of the great figures who remained did so because they were deemed unphotogenic," explained historian Gerald Bordman.

During the run of *Appearances*, Verna and Lee hosted a reunion of former Allen Players who were then appearing in various New York productions, including Ella Houghton, Mr. and Mrs. George Taylor Sr. and son George Jr., Guy Usher, and Sherold Page. Houghton, whose lengthy employment with the Allen troupe began in 1907 in her native Portland, was playing in a Broadway revival of *Under the Gaslight*. She would move to Los Angeles around 1934 and marry Geoffrey Shurlock, assistant to Joseph Breen, longtime director of the Production Code Administration for the Motion Picture Association of America. Houghton's acting career fizzled out, and she spent her last days as a malnourished recluse suffering from bone cancer. Ella Florence Houghton died at age sixty-three in 1953, the year before Shurlock succeeded Breen as the movie industry's censor.

Verna and Rupert LaBelle in a scene from *Appearances*, 1929.

In contrast, Sherold Page's lot in life was much lighter. After leaving the Allen Players in Edmonton in 1926, he joined another stock company which ended its run the following year in Dallas, Texas. Fortunately, the management paid his way to New York, where Page made his base, appearing in New York productions and on the road. He was advised to change his stage name because "Sherold" Page sounded too much like a musical comedy performer. So it was as Bradley Page that he performed on Broadway with Olga Petrova in *What Do We Know?* for 23 performances at Wallack's Theatre in late 1927. One year following the Allen Players reunion, Page would be introduced to a fellow actor who provided the spark for Page's future in Hollywood: William Clark Gable.

Meanwhile Verna found herself hobnobbing with some of Broadway's brightest stars at various events that spring. She and Margaret Dumont, current foil of the Marx Brothers in the Broadway production of *Animal Crackers*, were guests of honor at the April 30 benefit of the Metropolitan Theatre League, a service organization whose purpose was to introduce unknown talent to an audience of music lovers. Later Verna was among the fifty Broadway actors and actresses to be invited to attend a special matinee of *The Freiburg Passion Play* at the Hippodrome Theatre. The stellar list included Edward G. Robinson, Alfred Lunt, Lynn Fontanne, Thomas Mitchell, Ethel Barrymore, Clifton Webb, Katherine Cornell, Miriam Hopkins, Eddie Cantor, Ona Munson, Lenore Ulric, Donald Meek, Leon Errol, and Nydia Westman.

It seems Lee was frequently on the road during the summer of 1929, doing whatever he could to find work, mainly directing. Verna and Spuddie stayed behind in their apartment at 410 Cathedral Parkway on the upper west side. Despite social engagements with those in the theatre business, Verna found it difficult to find any stage roles following *Appearances*. The 1929-30 season, already weakened by competition from films, was devastated by the stock market crash. Half of that year's new Broadway productions ran three weeks or less. In desperation, Verna turned to Frank Hopwood of the *Vancouver Sun* to provide her a letter of introduction to New York's Theatre Guild, a theatrical society founded for the production of high-quality, noncommercial plays. It was all to no avail. So Verna continued to focus her attentions on Lee Jr. In a letter written on October 20 to Lee, who was then appearing in *The Demon* at the Poli Theatre in Washington, D.C., she reveals some of her frustrations with unemployment as well as the dynamics of home life:

> Dearest One:
> This is the longest, damndest [sic] day ever. It's the bunk . . .
> It's beautiful here today, just like Spring. Babe got peeved at Codo so slept with me after all last night. Had a great time moving all his clothes . . . Will get out $10.00 and pay Mrs. Davis tomorrow the 9.00 light bill. Babe has quite a bit of cold and throat cough. This a.m. at 8:30 he playfully threw serpentines all over me. Then he brought my breakfast to bed. He was waiter and Cod was cook. Don't forget to write Babe about the candy he sent wrapped up in cotton.
> Heaps of love, dear one.
> Always,
> Tootum

Lee Jr. added his own thoughts, surrounded with x's and o's, below Verna's message. He was still adored in Vancouver, evidenced by a piece which appeared that December in the Sun. Pearl related that Verna had taken Spuddie to a New

York theatre where the Mickey Mouse Club was giving an entertainment for disadvantaged children. During the performance everyone stood up to sing "America," which has the same tune as "God Save the King." Verna noticed that her son was singing just as lustily as the rest but was looking around at her in a rather bewildered way. After the song was finished, she inquired what was the matter, and Spuddie replied, "Oh, nothing much, Mother, only the others didn't seem to know the right words. They were singing 'My Country It Is of Thee' or something like that." The *Sun* dubbed the little Millar a "real Briton."

During a 1933 radio interview, Verna would recall, "The one truly nice thing about our marriage is that each is willing to sacrifice for the other. If Mr. Millar has an opportunity that excludes me, I am glad to step aside and let him take it. And when I have had an offer in which he is not included, he does the same for me." Both Lee and Verna had to go where the money was, even if it meant being separated by great distances for long periods of time. This arrangement would be a financial necessity for the next four years, due in part to the serious competition of the talkies, but later because of the 1929 stock market crash and the ensuing economic depression. Such circumstances would prevent Lee and Verna from sharing the stage for much of this period.

In June 1930, while Lee was engaged in production work for Broadway producer George M. Cohan, Verna sent the ever-faithful Codo on a short vacation to Toronto, after which she would join Verna and Spuddie in Vancouver where they planned to spend the summer with the Allens at their house at 790 Howe Street. Verna described the dynamics of daily life in a letter to Lee soon after her arrival:

> Dearest one:
> Still cold and rainy. DAMN. Dad took Babe out in the garden the other night and saw some toad stools so Dad picked them up with his feet. Babe yelled, "Oh, Bopa, don't please, don't. Don't you know that brownies and fairies live in toad stools and mushrooms?" And he put them all safely back in the ground and in the back yard we have bluebells and he stands in front just watching for a fairy to come out. It's so sweet to watch him. Be sure you tell the Bowhans [Lee's friend and fellow actor Gustav Bowhan and his wife] you never saw such reverence as he has for them. I am going down to get Codo in a minute. It sure seems funny to drive again. My little stick is still in the car far under the seat. It was in the car when stolen. The only thing that was taken out of the car was the lap robe. Rubber on one side, you remember. They stole that . . . It is a week today since I left you and it seems a year. Gosh! If I don't get a letter tomorrow, I'll have a fit. I wonder how you are, what you are doing, etc. I wrote Katie yesterday to let her

know we arrived OK. Did you see where the C.N.R. [Canadian National Railway] a day after I left got in a flood at Sudbury and several people were killed? Guess the C.P.R. [Canadian Pacific Railway] is the safest way after all. Mama is fine but terribly deaf. Babe has a grand time. He is the only one she can hear and he can shout to his heart's content. I did a huge washing yesterday, all electric, just great. Nana called, "Don't touch the things in the tub, they are mine." Babe flew at her, "Why, Nana, my mama wouldn't touch anything that wasn't hers, would you, Mama?" Awfully sweet. Bye bye, darling. All bodies fine but miss you heaps.

Tootum

Pearl was free during most of the Millars' visit. He had not booked a single act at the Vancouver Theatre since the first week of May. However, this good-natured man remained optimistic. For the fall he had engaged several English companies and one American Shakespearean troupe. Meanwhile, over at his old competitor the Empress, the British Guild Players under the leadership of David Clyde were becoming moderately successful. Their company included former Allen trouper Frank Vyvyan—dapper and handsome—and thirty-four-year-old Australia native Marjorie Bennett, sister of popular American silent actress, Enid Bennett.

At the same time, Clara Allen was planning to get back in the act but in a new medium. On October 1, she would debut over Vancouver station CNRV in a serialized musical comedy program called *Room and Board*. The story was set in a theatrical boarding house managed by Mrs. Timothy Harrigan, played by Clara. Boarders included a pianist, a singing theatre usher, a violinist, a theatre musician, a radio announcer, and a boxer called "One Punch" Monahan. A preview, published in an industry magazine called *The Microphone*, hailed Clara as "the best known stage personality in Western Canada," promising that the program would hold listeners' attentions with stories involving humor, tragedy, and romance. Verna just missed hearing her mother's radio debut, for she left Vancouver with Codo and Spuddie on September 22.

Verna returned to Vancouver, again without Lee, the following year when Pearl arranged for her to direct his productions featuring the Civic Repertory Players. Although he wasn't actually resurrecting the Allen Players, this new incarnation closely resembled it. Clara often had parts in the Civic Repertory plays, used as filler when Pearl did not have bookings from traveling companies. *Vancouver Sun* columnist R. D. Bouchette could not be fooled; he suspected that the Civic Repertory productions were an Allen family affair. Bouchette's columns reveal a fondness for the entire clan. He especially admired the work of Clara Allen, whom he compared to that great scene-stealer in motion pictures, Marie Dressler. And his description of Pearl is charmingly accurate:

It's bad taste anywhere to arrive at the theatre after the show has started, but in Vancouver it's worse than that. You're missing a part of the evening's entertainment, that's all, if you don't appear in time to see Pappa Perle [sic] R. Allen, welcoming the customers in. Pappa Allen stands inside the door leading to the lobby on a bee line from the ticket-taker. As the mob filters through he beams upon it individually and collectively with a sort of "bless-you-my-children-welcome-back-to-the-fold" expression. Nature was generous to Pappa Allen. He can display more starched shirt front than the drama critics of the three newspapers combined. The average columnistic shirt would be just another handkerchief to him. Pappa Allen looks so friendly there in the entrance that I have often wondered whether he is planning on handing out five-dollar bills, or pouring a few drinks.

That spring Pearl arranged a co-starring role for Verna in the comedy *Stepping Sisters*, which had been one of the previous Broadway season's surprise hits. To fill the part of the chief character, Pearl booked May Boley, a fat dumpling of a comedienne and veteran of over twenty Broadway productions. Five years Verna's senior, Boley had been born in Lynchburg, Virginia, and educated in the Washington, D.C. schools. Her talent for dancing had attracted the interest of a New York producer who sent her to that city where she was later employed by the Shuberts in several reviews and musical comedies. Since the mid-1920s, she had made a name for herself on the West Coast as well, performing with Charlotte Greenwood and others in touring shows. *Stepping Sisters* was set to open earlier in the year, but just as the production went into final rehearsals, Boley was called to Hollywood to film a western picture starring Gary Cooper. Cast as a frontier woman in *Fighting Caravans*, Boley recalled, "It was the worst thing that ever happened to me, learning to shoot. Imagine me—always afraid of a firecracker—being cast as a hard-boiled frontier woman. Finally I learned to shoot all right—three weeks after all the Indian extras had been sent off the lot."

Stepping Sisters, which opened on May 4, 1931, at the Vancouver Theatre for a week's engagement, told the story of three retired burlesque dancers, who, having achieved riches and respectability, are reunited in an unlikely coincidence of *fate*. Cecelia Ramsey, played by Boley, is determined to climb up in Long Island society and be president of the local women's club. She is shocked when she is advised that as part of her burden in a local charity fete, she must house three stage performers, one of whom is Lady Regina Chetworth-Lynde, played by Verna, "noted Shakespearean Reader from London, South Africa, and Melbourne." Cecelia's world starts to crumble when the lady arrives, for they recognize each other. They agree to keep their secret as former "stepping sisters." That secret comes out when the second guest proves to be another of their cohorts, the outspoken Rosie O'Toole, who has only accepted an invitation to the *fete* in order to expose "Chummie," a local married man who has shown her many favors. When Chummie turns out to be Cecelia's husband, she orders him out of the house. Only when her uppity neighbors snub her does Cecelia recognize who her real friends are. Toasting old times and new, the "stepping sisters" hold steins of beer to their lips as the play ends.

The *Vancouver Sun* critic, R. D. Bouchette, didn't hold back his praise for the Vancouver production: "If I had been wearing corsets last night when May Boley, Verna Felton, and the Civic Repertory Players scampered through *Stepping Sisters*, this review would never have been written. After the show they would have called the morgue wagon for my remains, or at least shipped me to the hospital with several broken ribs. [Boley and Felton] make a perfect team. Miss Boley has a line of humor as broad and thumpingly effective as a battleship. Miss Felton is cast in a role which gives her remarkably versatility full play. Personally, I would hand Felton the No. 1 bouquet for the evening's work, but I won't quarrel with anyone who prefers Boley. Verna Felton is indeed one of the most capable stage drunks we have ever seen." The play closed on May 9, marking the final time Verna Felton would perform in a stage production, though she may never have guessed it. Despite her thirty years as a stage actress, greater fame and fortune awaited her.

While Verna whiled away that spring in Vancouver, Lee was directing *A Lady in Pawn* at the Majestic in Chicago. He quickly moved from that to Frank Harvey's London melodrama *Three Men and a Woman*, for which Lee staged and directed its American premiere at the Columbia Theater in San Francisco on June 23. Set in a lighthouse off the coast of New Zealand, the drama unfolds as the lighthouse keeper's bored wife makes advances toward his mate. Before the two lovers can escape to the mainland, a third man arrives on the scene—a young and handsome thief. When the erring woman falls for the newcomer, a fight ensues between him and the mate. The latter is killed in the fight, and the young man throws himself from the tower into the sea. When a police officer interrogates the keeper and his wife about the deaths, the wanton makes eyes at him; she is still intent on escape. Inside her pocket is $3,000 she stole from the thief before he jumped.

Guy Bates Post played the keeper and Florence Reed his wife, while Broadway star Walker Whiteside was the mate. When all three were given excellent notices by the San Francisco *Chronicle*, the production was moved to Chicago's Blackstone Theatre for a limited engagement. Lee wired money to Verna to bring Spuddie and join him there, but he didn't have enough to pay for Codo's train ticket. Determined not to be separated from Spuddie, the enduring nanny paid her own way to the Windy City. William Desmond replaced Post in the Chicago production, now renamed as *Surf*. By month's end, the troupe had moved to St. Paul for another tryout. Christmas was spent in Detroit, where a rewritten version left Lee with serious doubts.

1932 was probably the darkest year in Lee Millar's life, but he unfailingly recorded its events in a small date book, providing a detailed account of the events leading to a major turning point in his and Verna's lives. On January 2, Lee took Verna to a Ford dealership to look at cars. Twice later that week he looked at other automobile makes. Despite the fact that his production of *Surf* was scheduled to make its Broadway debut in less than one week, Lee was making plans for a cross-country road trip. Weary of eking out a living in a dying medium, he was going home to California in defeat. He was not alone in his plight. By now 13 million Americans were unemployed. Forty percent of banks existing in 1929 had failed; cities teetered on the edge of bankruptcy. The Great Depression was reaching its height.

By the time *Surf* opened in Detroit, Lee had little faith in its future. However, after a prospective investor attended the evening performance on January 4, plans for a Broadway bow materialized quickly. One week later, the play opened in New York at the Lyceum with the same cast, although the title had reverted to *Three Men and a Woman*. Some complaints were made about the persistent and annoying artificiality of the offstage sounds of surf and storm. "Notice good considering what we have," Lee realistically recorded in his date book. However, it was not good enough. The show folded after eight performances. It was the swan song for both Lee Millar and Walker Whiteside, the latter who had once been considered among the most promising of young actors, but who, in the opinion of theatre historian Gerald Bordman, had "frittered away his career starring in exotic hokum more acceptable to the road than to Broadway."

After waiting about a week for his paycheck, Lee promptly bought two suits, overcoats for Verna and himself, and a 1929 Studebaker Commander. The Millars left New York City on the morning of January 30, accompanied by "Codo" Conboy, whose seven years' devotion had made her a family member. The thirteen-day trip afforded the travelers a chance to see both historic sites and natural wonders. They stopped in Lexington, Virginia, to see the tomb of Robert E. Lee, for whose family Lee was named. Before reaching Phoenix, Arizona, they marveled at the desert beauty near the Coolidge Dam. Finally, on February 11, they reached Hollywood, California, the symbolization of Lee's concession. The movies had won out over his beloved stage. After settling into their new home at the Bradford Apartments, Lee immediately began to look for film work, signing with the David H. Thompson Agency on North Vine Street.

Each day he networked among those he had known during their stage days. Chief among them was actor Bradley Page, whom Lee still addressed as "Sherry." Page had made the move to Hollywood the previous year after an interesting turn of events. In the spring of 1930, he had appeared in *Love, Honor, and Betray*, a Broadway drama starring Alice Brady, Glenda Farrell, and Clark Gable. Gable and Page had been born the same year, and they became good friends. Page suggested that Gable give Hollywood a shot, but Gable admitted he had already tried that. Because he had a dark tooth, he had only been used as an extra player in a dozen or so silents during the previous decade. Page still insisted that Gable pursue film work, not knowing that his friend would take his advice. The next time Page saw Gable was a winter day in 1931 when Page wandered into a matinee of a western film called *The Painted Desert*. Looking down from the movie screen, Gable was "large as life and twice as natural," recalled Page. Soon Page was on a train for Los Angeles to break into the same business. Arthur Landau, who also represented Jean Harlow, readily agreed to be Page's agent, and the job offers freely rolled in. Ironically, his first film was *Sporting Blood*, an MGM production starring Gable. Since then, Page had made five other films, quickly becoming typecast as an oily, mustachioed villain. He promised to help Lee make some contacts which would hopefully lead to employment.

One month later, however, Lee was still pounding the pavement. With savings depleted, he wrote to his half-brother Jack in San Francisco, asking for the loan of one hundred dollars. He also urged Verna to try her luck at breaking into films—through the Thompson Agency—while he peddled a script to various directors, including David Butler, all to no avail. Finally, on March 28, he was hired to record what he described in his date book only as "Tarzan records." Bradley Page was then the narrator for a radio version of the Tarzan stories, produced by Edgar Rice Burroughs. His connections got Lee the job; however, it is not known if Lee was hired as an actor or an animal imitator, the latter being a skill which would soon keep him in the black. But for now, this recording job was the only nibble either Lee or Verna had gotten since their arrival in Hollywood.

Yet, the Millars did not sit idle, waiting for the telephone to ring. They socialized with "Sherry" Page and his wife, the former Olive Meehan. They took in the latest movies. And many leisurely days were spent at the beach, until a letter from Lee's mother Katie arrived from Stockton on May 12. The elder Mrs. Millar was suffering from cancer, but a more immediate health problem, congestive heart failure, was causing shortness of breath. With her elderly mother and aging sister dependent upon her these last six years, Katie now needed the help and comforting presence of a younger person at the Carson ranch. Lee left Hollywood on May 14, arriving in Stockton the next day. He noted in his journal that the atmosphere at the ranch was terrible: "Got to get Katie away from here." Before his mission was accomplished, Kate Carson Millar died on May 19, in the home where she was born. She was sixty-nine years old. For Lee Junior's benefit, Verna recorded those final moments in a scrapbook: "Daddy was with her. He arrived on Sunday and she left Thursday 1 p.m. calling for you, Spuddie. 'Baby, Baby' were her last words." A dejected Lee wrote in his journal that day, "Just another victim in the whirlpool." Verna arrived on Friday, much to his relief: "Thank God Tootum's here." After the funeral on Saturday, Lee sighed, "At last Katie is off the ranch."

With probate matters to settle in Stockton and increasingly dire financial conditions to consider, Lee could not seek comfort in the happy memories of his

The Millar home at 1310 Tenth Street, Oakland.

mother. Nor could he take his family back to Hollywood. He resolved to move into the empty Millar family home at 1310 10th Street in Oakland. At least the large shingle house would be a rent-free home while he planned his family's future.

Verna often reminisced about what happened after the move to Oakland was complete. Katie's death had provided the impetus for Lee to consider a relatively new field of entertainment: radio. Although he and Verna had once considered the medium as a passing fad, neither could now ignore its growing importance. By 1932, the National Broadcasting Company (NBC) had leased the licenses and facilities of two San Francisco Bay area radio stations, KPO and KGO. The program staffs of both stations and that of NBC were combined into one collective staff of over 250 persons. "This included complete orchestras, vocalists and other musicians, and a complete dramatic stock company," explained John F. Schneider, historian for the Bay Area Radio Museum. The entire operation was consolidated under the roof of the Hunter-Dulin Building at 111 Sutter Street in San Francisco, where the broadcasting studios were located. However, at this time, KPO and KGO maintained separate transmitter facilities in San Francisco and Oakland, respectively. If the Millars could no longer play stock roles on the stage, perhaps radio could become a substitute medium.

In 1964, Verna explained this twist of fate to interviewer Marty Halperin: "I said to Big Millar [Lee], I said, 'Well, now, go out and see what this radio [industry] is like.' And he said, '*Radio* [industry] is like?' He said, '*What* is *radio* going to do? Do you think people are going to *sit home* in their chairs and *listen* to anything over the air and *enjoy* it and *stay* there?' He said, 'No!' He said, 'Well, we don't want to get mixed up into anything like that.' And I said, 'We want to *eat*. We've *got* to eat. If you don't go, *I'm* going to go. Either *you* go and find out about radio, or *I'm* going to go and find out about it.'"

Verna's ultimatum moved Lee to sigh reluctantly, "All right, if you insist, I'll go." With a chuckle, she recalled what happened when Lee, by then forty-four, with a growing paunch and graying hair, returned from San Francisco. "He came back about six o'clock, and he opened the door, and he said, 'Well, meet your new juvenile man!' And I said, 'My new *what?*' He said, 'Believe it or not, I am now a *juvenile* man. I'm not a *leading* man. I am right in there with all the youngsters, making love to them. In radio, you can't be *seen*, just your *voice* [is used].'"

During the 1964 interview Verna claimed that Lee obtained a radio position for her as well on this same day, although this is not documented in Lee's date book. In fact, according to that source, Lee was performing on radio for one month before Verna was hired by NBC. Lee's initial visit to the NBC studio took place on May 27, the first day after his arrival from Stockton. He was happily surprised to find an old theater acquaintance, Tom Hutchinson, employed as the program director. Lee was promptly hired, and on June 4 he rehearsed for *Bible Stories*, a children's program broadcast over KPO the next day. Whether or not Lee supplied the voice of a younger character is not known, but if Verna's claim that he was hired as a juvenile man is accurate, then Lee must have possessed a youthful voice.

The same cannot be said for Verna. Ironically, she was first hired by NBC as the voice of "the old Indian squaw" in the weekly serial *Ramona*, produced by Michael Raffetto and adapted by Wilbur Hall from Helen Hunt Jackson's classic novel. Bernice Berwin as Ramona headed a cast that included Thomas Kelly, Helen Musselman, Cameron Prud'homme, Henry Shumer, J. Anthony Smythe, and Pearl King Tanner. Although Verna liked to say that she was hired without an audition, it was not because her reputation as an actress was widely known. In the San Francisco area, she was virtually an unknown. In fact, she herself candidly admitted in a 1944 interview that Lee's connections won her the part on *Ramona*.

The first episode was broadcast from the NBC studio at 10 p.m. on Monday, June 27. Since the broadcast was so late in the evening, Lee accompanied Verna to San Francisco. At this time, there existed neither the San Francisco-Oakland Bay Bridge nor the Golden Gate Bridge. Usually when the Millars wanted to go into the city, they walked or drove to the Southern Pacific's 16th Street Station where they caught a train bound for the Oakland shore. There they would board either the "Creek Route" ferry or the Key System's ferry, both designed for passengers. But for this important occasion of Verna's radio debut, they decided to take the Studebaker into the city, necessitating the use of the Golden Gate Ferry, which they boarded at the Oakland Pier. Five weeks passed before Verna was needed again for her role. On this occasion, the Millars celebrated by having a pre-broadcast dinner with Lee's cousin Edith Williams and her husband, who lived in San Francisco.

Verna reprised her role as the old squaw twice more, on August 29 and on September 12, the final of the twelve episodes. Although a considerable number of her stage roles were character parts, Verna's venture into radio forever after defined her as a character actress. Within a year, she would confess an indescribable fondness for the new medium. Conversely, Lee remained reticent about his career change. For a person of his theatrical training and experience, it must have been somewhat deflating to accept positions where only his voice was heard, not to mention those occasions when he merely provided animal sounds. A decade later Verna told an interviewer that Lee had been happier working in the legitimate theatre. Unfortunately, Lee would never return to the stage.

Despite several performances over both KPO and KGO during June, Lee did not work again for three months. In late August, he was forced to ask his mother's brother Owen David Carson, a retired Oakland merchant, for a loan of $140 to pay the family's bills. "Uncle Onie" was a beloved figure not only to Lee, but also to those in his employ who benefited from his generosity and kindness. His unique personality and solid support had made him the revered Carson patriarch in the years following his father's death. He often traveled the road between Oakland and Stockton in order to keep an eye on situations at the family ranch. His aged mother Belle, now past her ninety-fifth birthday, was in a state of rapid decline. Though family members attributed this to the sudden death of her daughter Katie that spring, in truth, the old lady was suffering from cancer. On September 4, Belle took to her bed. In mid-September Lee was called to the bedside of his beloved "Gram," remaining there for a week until she rallied somewhat. She lingered until October 4, ironically outliving her family physician by one day. Belle Mitchell Carson had also outlived her husband and five of her children. Daughter Hattie would soon follow her to the grave, but Onie inherited some of his mother's longevity, living until 1943.

The month would not end before Lee was dealt another blow. His former wife Anna McNaughton was found dead in her San Francisco apartment on October 22, the victim of a cerebral hemorrhage at age forty-nine. The day before, as usual, Anna had reported to her accountant's job at a local insurance company, a position she had held for the last seven years. She, too, had felt the effects of changing times and had abandoned her theatrical career a few years after returning home from Portland, where she and Lee had parted ways in 1920. In the intervening years, Lee had kept in touch with his former wife through his cousin Bessie Carson Gunton, even visiting Anna on September 12 while in the city. Out of respect for their thirteen years of marriage, he also attended her funeral.

The triple loss of Lee's mother, grandmother, and former wife, along with the termination of his stage career, made the majority of 1932 almost unbearable. He could not have endured it without the love and support of Verna. Things would improve in the coming months, though. And that could be credited to his wife for insisting that Lee "look into this thing called radio."

CHAPTER 10

————•◦•————

RADIO DAYS

While the period of the 1930s and 1940s has been appropriately called by some as "Radio's Golden Age," radio historian John F. Schneider has asserted that "the decade from 1927 to 1937 can easily be termed San Francisco radio's 'Golden Decade.'" During this ten-year span, San Francisco was a "major origination point for many nation-wide network broadcasts." And Verna Felton and Lee Millar were part of the action.

Although the technical aspects of performing in this new medium could be frustrating for novices, Verna, within a year, found herself totally enthralled with broadcasting. When she joined the cast of *Ramona*, she discovered the most difficult thing to learn was not to project her voice as she had in the theater.

"[Michael] Raffetto would say to me, 'Verna, you don't have to play to the last boy in the gallery. There is no gallery.' The muscles in my abdomen would be aching when I went home after a broadcast from trying not to project and yet put emotion in my voice," Verna told Zuma Palmer of the Hollywood *Citizen-News* in 1944.

Twenty years later, she described these days to Marty Halperin: "The most difficult part was not looking at anyone. You're looking at your script and not looking at anybody else, because if you look up and then look down, you'd lose your place. You had to put your finger on it, if you were going to look up. You put your finger on it and look up and talk and then down. So that was the hardest thing. And talking loud. Of course, we [stage actors] had been taught to project, so if [there were audience members] in the balcony or the gallery, they had to hear you. So [when] we'd project on radio—BOOM, we were off the air! They'd say, 'Verna, don't talk so loud!' I'd back up and back up and then they'd put me [farther away from the microphone than the other actors.] That was really hard to adjust to."

However, this was not Verna's first experience with a microphone. Ten years earlier in February, 1922, while performing in stock in Edmonton, she was invited to sing during a special short wave radio broadcast going out to snowbound furriers in the Yukon. At the time Verna was overjoyed to participate in the new medium, but her biggest thrill came three months later when fan mail finally arrived from her "captivated" listeners.

Recalling her delight with the responses, Verna told an interviewer in 1933, "I think if I hadn't been so absorbed in the theatre just then, I might have gone completely radio. During the past year, I've wondered sometimes what made me wait so long."

At first Verna and Lee found it difficult to get regular work on radio. After a three-month dry spell in the summer of 1932, Lee landed a starring role in a fifteen-minute drama called *Doctor Dick*, which aired two mornings weekly over KGO, beginning October 4 and running through the end of the year. Verna, who was also a member of that program's cast, later remembered the earliest days at NBC when actors had to produce their own sound effects. "We were working in *Dr. Dix* [*sic*], when the first sound effects box, which was shaped like a casket, was wheeled on to the stage. While we were on the air it blew out the microphone used by Lee, then the one for the cast and finally another hastily brought in for him. Before the show was over we were working on the children's microphone, and were we uncomfortable! I think the greatest advance in radio since I have been in it has been in the engineering and sound departments."

Verna quickly picked up other radio work at NBC, including some gigs on shows like *Mad Cargo, The Man Who Laughs*, as well as a recurring role in *Little Orphan Annie*. Based on the popular comic strip, *Little Orphan Annie* had first aired on Chicago's WGN in 1930. The following year when it moved to NBC, it was broadcast from both its original city and from KGO in San Francisco, using two separate casts, of course. Featuring Floy Margaret Hughes as Annie in the San Francisco cast, the show caught on quickly with younger children because it was a serialized "thriller" just for kids. Before 1932 ended, Verna also had become a member of the network's National Players, who performed adaptations of literary works, such as Henry Francis Hasket's recent biography of King Henry VIII with Michael Raffetto in the title role.

By 1933, some NBC radio programs produced in San Francisco gained nationwide popularity, including *Winning the West*, scripted by Sam Dickson, one of San Francisco's best-known radio writers. Verna would appear on this western drama, as well as another one, *Death Valley Days*. In the latter she was once given the part of Maggie, an old Indian squaw—shades of her *Ramona* role. Her performance prompted one reviewer to cite it as one of the best portrayed characters of the week, noting that her "monosyllabic 'Me Come' and 'Me Go' speeches were eloquently characteristic of the type of western Indian she portrayed."

Verna's affection for these two westerns as well as for other early programs, such as *Captain Henry's Maxwell House Show Boat, One Man's Family,* and *The Mud Caves*, is quite evident in the recorded interview conducted by Marty Halperin in 1964.

In fact, when Halperin asked Verna to name her favorite radio show of all time, she did not cite any of the more memorable shows broadcast from Hollywood much later in her long radio career. Instead she described a much forgotten San Francisco serial which aired over KPO three afternoons a week, beginning September 27, 1933, and running into the summer of the following year.

"We had a comedy that we did—it never got out here [to Hollywood]—called *The Mud Caves*. It was the cutest thing that ever lived. It was all about the cave days and the problems that they had that we have today, just exactly the same. [For example], there would be moss on the walls, and they'd say they'd have to find something to cure the moss. Well, they'd go out and get oyster shells and things like that, and work it out, you know. It was so cute! A woman from the Berkeley Institute wrote it, and, oh, why she didn't keep up with it [I don't know], because it was wonderful!"

"But then—this was funny—I tried to buy it from NBC for a long time because I thought it was a good property. They had stored [the scripts] down the peninsula, you know, down around Sunnyvale. They had a great big place there where they stored it, where those salt things are. So when I came here [to Hollywood], one of the NBC men was already here, and I said, "Don, some day while you're around [the storage facility], see where *The Mud Caves* is. And I said I want to buy it because if I could sell it for TV, it would be wonderful, everybody in their leopard skins, you know, and the bones in the hair and all like that . . . so he went down to find out and came back in a week and he said 'Do you know what?' I said, 'No.' And he said they had this one big room where they had all these manuscripts and music and everything, and the atmosphere from this salt and the water and all had destroyed every one of them, and there was nothing but powder in that place! All those manuscripts—now think what they lost in that! These were all the original old ones they had. And I don't know what became of [the writer]. Stroud was her name—I tried to find her, but I never could find her. I thought maybe *she* had copies of them somewhere. Imagine a thing like that, when they opened it up to find nothing but white powder!"

The storage facility Verna described was actually part of a large transmitting complex constructed by NBC on the salt flats of San Francisco Bay near Belmont. A spray pond, located outside the spacious concrete building, contained water to cool the giant transmitter's tubes. As Verna explained, the combination of the water and the salt had deteriorating effects on the mishandled documents, by now perhaps too voluminous to maintain at the Sutter Street location. Equally regrettable is Verna's missed opportunity of buying the property for television production. She envisioned a television adaptation of *The Mud Caves*—which had also featured actors Frank Provo, Everett Glass, and Earl Lee—as being not unlike a live-action version of *The Flintstones*.

In marked contrast to the obscurity of *The Mud Caves* was *One Man's Family*, the most famous radio program to originate in San Francisco. Under the guidance of its creator Carlton Morse, the most important figure in San Francisco radio at the time, *One Man's Family* remained a national favorite for twenty-seven years. Debuting on April 29, 1932, it told the story of the everyday life of the affluent Barbour family, residing in the Sea Cliff district of San Francisco. Actor J. Anthony Smythe, with whom Verna and Lee had appeared in the 1916 Oakland stage production of *A Pair of Sixes*, played stockbroker Henry Barbour, the head of the clan. Minetta Ellen played his wife Fanny, while the Barbours' children were played by Michael Raffetto, Bernice Berwin, Barton Yarborough, Kathleen Wilson, and Page Gilman.

Verna told Halperin, "We didn't come out from the East until [*One Man's Family*] had been on for about nine [*sic*] months. The only time I ever [appeared on that show] was when Minetta was ill. She was ill for four weeks, and I went in and did the part."

The *Oakland Tribune* reported the situation on November 4, 1934: "The old tradition of the theater, 'The show must go on,' holds good in Radio, too. On a recent Friday night the *One Man's Family* episode was one long agony for Minetta Ellen, who has the role of Mrs. Barbour, gentle-voiced, kindly mother in the Carlton E. Morse serial of American family life. Although she was suffering from a severe case of ptomaine poisoning, she went through with her part. She collapsed as Announcer William Andrews was striking the NBC chimes at the end of the drama. She was taken to the hospital and on the following night, when the serial went on the air for Eastern ears, Verna Felton doubled for her."

Interestingly, Verna revealed to Halperin the admiration Morse felt for her ability. "So [Carlton Morse] often said to me, 'Well, if you'd been out [in California] before [the show debuted], you and [Lee] would have been Dad and Ma Barbour." While this timing may have seemed unfortunate for the Millars, the missed opportunity of becoming part of the immortal cast of Morse's program also left them available to hone their crafts on many other NBC programs without becoming locked into one series.

Scripts for radio productions arrived by mail at the Millar residence each week, allowing the couple to study their lines before the rehearsal, usually held one day prior to the broadcast. Of these days prior to the organization of the American Federation of Radio Artists (AFRA), Verna admitted, "The pay was not too great. You see, they used to take a 10 percent discount. So we used to get $10 a broadcast—less 10 percent, which went to NBC. We got $9, and NBC got a dollar. But when we did *Death Valley Days* or *Winning the West*—those were *high-priced* shows—they paid $15! We got $13.50 for each of them!"

An NBC program more obscure than *The Mud Caves* was a topical comedy called *The Jittersmythe*, written in rhyme and delivered in sharply cadenced readings by Verna and J. Anthony "Tony" Smythe, who wrote the oddity. They each received nine dollars for each performance, but when Smythe insisted he should be paid an extra five for writing it, the program was replaced by a better bargain, one starring Barbara Jo Allen who performed alone for nine dollars.

By mid-1933, Verna's NBC mailbox almost always contained a note from a listener who had been an admirer during her stage days, perhaps someone living on the Coast or in Canada who had seen her play *Camille* or *Under Two Flags*. In just one year's time, Verna had become such a well-known NBC personality that she was asked for an interview on KPO's *Personal Closeups*, a program sponsored by the magazine *Broadcast Weekly*, the leading radio guide of the Pacific Coast. The interviewer, a columnist for that publication, was identified only as Gypsy. While no recording exists of the fifteen-minute interview on June 18, a typewritten script, complete with corrections and addendums in Verna's hand, survives among Verna's papers. Examination of the script makes it obvious that Gypsy and Verna had met prior to the broadcast, discussing the questions and responses while someone transcribed their run-through. If the actual broadcast progressed as it was scripted, Verna shared many details about the history of her acting career, as well as personal information regarding marriage and family life.

Near the end of the interview, when asked her opinion about child actors becoming too "sophisticated" and "unnatural," Verna was to give this response: "Well, Gypsy, I think I should point out—and I believe this firmly—that it all rests with the child and his training. What's in a child will come out. True, there are many stage children who are artificial, but I think this artificiality would manifest itself in any walk of life. I can't get away from instinct, breeding, and training. My mother never permitted me to conduct myself differently in theatrical surroundings than she would have permitted me to conduct myself had we lived in a small conservative community. I was made to address adults with respect, disciplined just as other precious darlings are disciplined. At the risk of sounding 'preachy,' I cannot help but feel that parents mold a child's character. Children get out of hand, of course, but doesn't that happen to children the world over?"

A similar biographical piece was published on October 29 that year by the NBC Press Department in their weekly publication *NBC Advance Program Service*, but containing two blatant errors. The article reported that Lee proposed to Verna in 1923, at the close of a dress rehearsal for *A Pair of Sixes*, a stage production also featuring J. Anthony Smythe, Henry Shumer, George Webster, and Bert Horton (all of whom by 1933 were appearing on many NBC programs with the Millars). While these gentlemen and the Millars did perform in that production, the correct year was 1916, while Lee was still married to Anna McNaughton. Furthermore, the article reported that Lee and Verna, on the evening he proposed, slipped away just before the curtain rose, found an Oakland clergyman, and were married. Could this misleading information have been the fabrication of a zealous publicity man? Could Verna or Lee have misinformed their interviewer?

By the time of this publication, Verna had become the first and only NBC woman announcer in the west for Harold P. Burdick's *Do You Believe in Ghosts?*

Lee Millar and Verna Felton at the time they began their radio careers in San Francisco.

However, she was mainly known for dramatic roles in *Death Valley Days*, *The Story Teller*, and *NBC Drama Hour*. The latter program featured the National Players in dramatizations written by Samuel Dickson. Besides Lee and Verna, this acting ensemble included Michael Raffetto, Pearl King Tanner, and George Rand. These were happy days for the Millars, for they were both employed, often appearing together, just as they had done on stage.

An NBC press release described their relationship: "Like most happy marriages, theirs is marked by a contented comradeship founded upon the long knowledge of each other's characters. Their temperaments balance as perfectly as their acting does when they play together; Verna, says Lee, always knows before he does, when he is about to go up in his lines, and always manages to supply a cue and she feels happier in a part, stage or microphone, if he is near to offer a suggestion on how it is to be played."

Occasionally Verna was utilized in lighter fare such as *Carefree Carnival*, a program featuring western music and comedy skits, broadcast from the Community Playhouse in San Francisco, where it was hosted by homespun Charlie Marshall and featured Meredith Willson's Orchestra. On July 3, 1933, Verna shared the *Carnival* stage with a talented man-and-wife team called Tim Ryan and Irene Noblette, the latter who would later adopt her husband's surname as her professional name, winning the adoration of television fans as "Granny" on *The Beverly Hillbillies*.

Another occasional *Carnival* performer was Verna's fellow National Player, Barbara Jo Allen, who by 1935 was already delighting audiences with her man-crazy character Vera Vague, long before the character's heyday on Bob Hope's radio program. Allen and Verna's paths would cross many times before they reached the recording studios at Walt Disney Productions twenty years later when they each voiced one of the fairy godmothers in *Sleeping Beauty*. Born in New York City in 1906, Allen met husband Barton Yarborough when both were stage actors. Prior to their 1931 divorce, the Yarboroughs lived with their small daughter Joan on Webster Street on Oakland's east side, less than two miles from the Millar home.

By 1932, when the Millars moved to 1310 Tenth Street, West Oakland was a thriving, ethnically diverse neighborhood of over 280, 000 residents. For fifty years it had been the home of European Americans, African Americans, Portuguese, Irish, Mexican, Japanese, and Chinese immigrants who had settled there. World War One, creating employment opportunities in the shipyards, had brought another influx of workers to West Oakland. The Millar home, a shingle-style structure built around 1904, was actually one of the newer ones on a street lined with Italianate Victorians.

Lee and Verna, as well as Clara and Pearl Allen, had easily made friends wherever they traveled or lived. Their Oakland neighbors were no exception. Diagonally across from them, at the southwest corner of Tenth and Poplar Streets, was the grand home of Mr. and Mrs. John Blazic, who had bought their fourteen-room house in 1929. The Blazics had immigrated from Croatia when it was still part of the Austro-Hungarian Empire. Mr. Blazic had been an Austrian naval officer, while his wife Mary had once been a cook for Austrian emperor Franz Joseph I. Their son Albert Joseph Blazic lived with his wife Zora and their children, Albert and Betty, at 1311 Tenth Street, across the street from the Millars.

The younger Albert Blazic (hereafter referred to as Al) was one year older than Spuddie, and they became fast friends. Al found the Millars to be a fun-loving family. In 2005, he recalled: "In the summertime, Mrs. Millar would cart four or five of us young kids into the Studebaker and off we would go to Neptune Beach in Alameda. We'd all go over there and swim, you know, have a good time. Everything was always a good time, even when Mr. Millar was there. The kids would come into the [Millar] house and he would play the piano or sing, you know. We had a most wonderful upbringing there. At times, it was comical, really. 'There Is a Tavern in the Town'—that's the type of music we were playing. Mr. Millar never read music; he just played by ear. Mrs. Millar could read notes. It was fabulous! They were so kind to me." Over the years, Al became very close to Verna, whom he regarded as a "second mother." He also felt a deep admiration for Lee Sr., whom he called "a most wonderful man."

While Spuddie and Al attended the same school, they also spent much of their free time at the spacious Millar home, which had six rooms downstairs, and an equal number in the upstairs unit, which was unoccupied for the first three years they lived there. Al was particularly fascinated with the artifacts on display upstairs, mainly items left over from the time of Spuddie's grandfather, John Edgar Millar, who had served as a captain in the National Guard of California. "There were guns all over the place, swords, rifles, everything you could think of . . . all these stuffed birds in glass cases." The large barn out back also became the boys' playground.

In the meantime, Spuddie didn't sit on the sidelines while his parents were making the daily trek to San Francisco. Around 1934, he was hired to play the neighborhood toughie on a kids' radio show called *Wheatenaville Sketches*, heard over KFRC and sometimes known as the Billy Bachelor series. Bachelor was the newspaper editor in mythical Wheatenaville, as well as the guardian of twins, Peter and Pan.

In 1935, Spuddie acted before the cameras for the first time in a traffic safety film called *Remember Jimmy*, a local production intended to demonstrate the dangers of reckless driving. Spuddie played the title character who, after losing a leg as the victim of a careless driver, sadly spends his days watching his buddies play football. Spuddie made personal appearances at all of the East Bay Dads Clubs when the film was shown later that fall. Meanwhile, he tested for the screen part of Anthony Adverse as a young boy in the Warner Brothers production, but lost out to Billy Mauch.

The Millar house was frequently visited by Lee's nearby relations, including half-brother Jack and his wife Grace, as well as Uncle Onie and his wife Ava. Sometimes Clara's first cousin Maggie Honold Miller, also an Oakland resident, called on Verna. (Maggie would die in Oakland in 1967 at age one hundred.) Pearl's younger brother Arden, who had conducted the orchestra during the earliest days of the Allen Stock Company, had been a Bay area resident for about twenty years. Now he was a music teacher in the Oakland public schools. Arden and his wife Dorothy, residents of Richmond Boulevard, often joined the Millars for dinner and cards.

Meanwhile, Spuddie, enjoying his first experience with public school, was enrolled at the Cole School, just a stone's throw away. Codo, now serving as housekeeper, was on hand to have a snack waiting when he got home. Al Blazic described Codo as an "awfully nice person," adding, "The Millars took care of her and she [did likewise for] them."

Lee's 1932 date book reveals that he was something of a "shade tree" mechanic, always replacing parts on the Studebaker. He was equally handy around the house, making small repairs, painting, building furniture, doing laundry, and washing dishes. He spent a considerable amount of time refurbishing the upstairs flat. His mother had designed the house as a two-family dwelling as a way to maintain a steady source of rental revenue.

In 1935, when Pearl, almost sixty-four, decided to retire from theatrics, the Millars invited the Allens to occupy the flat upstairs. The living quarters were

Spuddie and Codo, Oakland, Halloween 1933.

large enough to include Clayton, who would later join the family there. And, for a brief time, even Verna's older brother Howard would become ensconced under the Millar roof.

Pearl had relinquished his position as manager of the Vancouver Theatre in 1933, but in a last-ditch effort he put his remaining dribble of faith in the competition. He joined forces with David Clyde's British Guild Players at the Empress. Each evening, he took his place in vestibule of the Empress to greet his friends, who had come to address the friendly giant as "Pop." However, this association lasted only a year. When the British Guild Players folded in 1934,

Pearl and Clara Allen, circa 1934.

Pearl knew this was the final defeat. He resigned himself to the fact that the dark days of the Depression, compounded by the insurmountable competition from the movie houses, had sounded the death knell for the stock companies of Canada and the United States. As Pearl reflected on his beginnings in Vancouver thirty years earlier, he admitted that the path then had not been strewn with roses, but there was always something to fight for. Now there was nothing left.

Pearl and Clara packed up their things at the Martinique Hotel, where they had been residing, bid farewell to its proprietor, their close friend Rose E. Low, and retreated to Oakland. Both had shed the corpulence of their youth, cutting fine figures for folks their age; they anticipated health and happiness in sunny California.

Once again as he had during World War One, Pearl turned to his family for employment. By now his sister Cora and her husband Patrick O'Hair were deceased, but their son-in-law John "Fritz" Bowman had helped parlay their San Francisco plumbing business into a highly successful parent company, which would one day support branches in fourteen California cities as well as Denver, Albuquerque, and Santa Fe. Pearl became a salesman for Bowman Plumbing Supply, the retail arm of P. E. O'Hair & Company, located on Devisidero Street in San Francisco.

Pearl's stepsons Howard and Clayton were not that fortunate or industrious. In 2005, Al Blazic recalled their brief tenures in the Millar house: "Clayton had a problem. My father obtained a job for him. That was back in probably '37, '38. He got him a job at Hall-Scott Motor Company, which isn't in business anymore, but [at this time] Clayton was living with Clara and Pearl Allen at 1310 [Tenth Street]. [Clayton] would trip down to the Japanese grocery store a block away and then he'd buy saki. He went heavy on saki. Well, the job didn't last long [after Clayton reported to work in a drunken condition]. And it made it bad because it was hard for my father to even get him a job because he didn't have a skill of any sort, you know. When Howard came, which I couldn't tell you how much later, [my father] tried to get *him* a job. I believe he *did* get him a job, but it was harder yet."

Meanwhile, Lee and Verna began to turn their attention toward Hollywood. Beginning in the early thirties, the American public increasingly desired to hear shows featuring their favorite Hollywood movie stars. To fulfill public demand, NBC pressured AT&T to construct a new circuit to open a second Pacific Coast network, terminating in Los Angeles instead of San Francisco. Once this was accomplished in 1936, it became economical to produce national programs in Hollywood on a wide scale. Almost immediately, NBC broke ground for its new $2 million Hollywood studios on a 4.5 acre tract at Sunset and Vine Streets. When the new facility opened for business on October 17, 1938, it not only included consolidated executive offices for the West Coast, but also eight studios, including four auditoriums that seated 350 persons each. At the time, it was the largest facility ever constructed for radio.

Beginning in 1936 and continuing for the next five years, virtually all of San Francisco's network programming moved to Hollywood. One of the first to leave was *One Man's Family* in August of 1937, even before the new NBC studios had been completed.

Meanwhile, the Millars had not wasted much time contemplating their own situation. By 1935, prior to the radio networks' move, Lee was considering possible employment opportunities in Los Angeles. According to Al Blazic, Lee went "down south, established himself in a hotel [on the outskirts of] Hollywood, and stayed there to make contacts." During this trial period, which Al estimated to last about eighteen months, Verna remained behind in Oakland with her parents, Spuddie, and Codo.

Promotional portrait of Verna taken shortly after arriving in Los Angeles, 1936.

In one of Lee's first Hollywood auditions, he beat out over twenty-five competitors—all canines—for the part of a dog in an adaptation of "*The Voice of Bugle Ann*" on *Lux Radio Theatre*, broadcast on CBS radio in July, 1936. Prior to this, Lee had just amused his friends with this talent. Soon it was to become his bread and butter, but he was already certain that a permanent transition to Hollywood was financially worthwhile.

Lee rented a stuccoed house at 846 Ford Street in Burbank, a home big enough for the entire family. He then invested in a used car, a little Durant coupe, enabling him to scoot around from one radio gig to another. By early August, Verna had resigned from all of her San Francisco-based radio jobs and was appealing to those in the industry who could help promote her own dramatic abilities for Hollywood-based productions. So the entire Millar family, including Codo, made the big move to southern California.

In the Millars' absence, the Allens moved downstairs to the more convenient lower flat and rented the upper flat to a neighbor. It grieved Verna to move over 350 miles and leave her aged mother, whose health was steadily deteriorating. Verna's only consolation was the assurance that Pearl, eight years younger than Clara and still hale and hearty, would provide loving care in her absence. Plus trustworthy neighbor Al Blazic, now a teenager, was readily available to run errands and chop firewood. In much less robust condition than Pearl was Verna's brother Howard, who, unknown to all, himself included, was suffering from chronic myocarditis. His sudden death at age fifty-seven, occurring in the Millar home during the early morning hours of July 31, 1938, would greatly worsen Clara's feeble condition. To comfort Clara, Verna and Lee Jr. made the trek from Los Angeles in the Millars' 1935 Ford Fordor Deluxe touring sedan. At the end of their visit, Al Blazic recorded the Millars' departure with his home movie camera. This rare film offers a quick glimpse of their affection for Clara. Standing at the curb, Lee Jr. catches his grandmother off-guard and while holding her face in his hands plants kisses all over her. Then Verna, looking smart in a pantsuit and marcelled bob, gives Clara a kiss on the mouth and wipes away the lipstick mark she left. Pearl stands nearby, exhibiting his trademark kind smile. Goodbyes like these were bittersweet; the Millars and Allens would not often see each other during these busy days.

Among Verna's first radio assignments in Hollywood were three appearances on *The Jell-O Program Starring Jack Benny*, broadcast over NBC in early 1937. On January 24 and February 7, she affected an exaggerated Southern accent to play the mother of skirt-chasing bandleader Phil Harris, one member of Benny's stable of talented supporting players which at the time included Andy Devine, Sam Hearn, and Blanche Stewart. Harris had grown up in Nashville, Tennessee, so his Southern accent was purely natural, but Verna's and that of the actress playing Harris's simpering sister Lucy-Belle left a lot to be desired. Still, Verna's big laugh on the January 24 broadcast came after she was introduced to raspy-voiced Devine: "Lucy-Belle, get the gentleman a *cawgh drawp*." When Verna appeared again on March 28—this time as a pushy stage mother of a brash girl named Millicent—her clipped speech was much more suited for the part than the molasses mouth she had used for Mrs. Harris.

With their financial future more certain, the Millars decided to put down some roots. On August 30, 1937, they bought a home at 4147 Bakman Avenue in North Hollywood. The three-bedroom house, with an English Tudor facade

4147 Bakman Avenue, North Hollywood, at the time of the Millars' purchase, 1937.

and a contrasting Spanish-style interior, had been built around 1924, in the days when North Holllywood was still known as Lankershim, named for an agriculturist who had bought 59,000 acres in the southern San Fernando Valley in 1871. The unincorporated town of Lankershim was annexed into the city of Los Angeles in 1923, and four years later it was renamed North Hollywood to draw in residents based on the glamour and appeal of the nearby film industry.

When the Millars moved onto Bakman Avenue, many lots still remained undeveloped. Commuting to Hollywood and downtown Los Angeles was relatively easy then; Valley residents rode the "Red Cars" of the Pacific Electric Railway. However, the Millars retained their trusty Studebaker. Spuddie, who now preferred to be called Lee Jr., commuted just over a mile to North Hollywood Junior High School each day.

Verna barely had time to unpack things in her new house before freelance jobs started rolling in. On September 13, she rubbed elbows with Hollywood royalty during a performance of an NBC play called "*Accent on Youth*," starring John Barrymore and his fourth wife, twenty-two-year-old Elaine Barrie. The Barrymores had made six appearances that summer on NBC's *Streamlined Shakespeare*, productions which reduced the Bard's plays to 45 minutes while modernizing some of the original language. When these dramatizations proved popular, the Barrymores returned for two modern plays in the same time slot. One was "*Accent on Youth*," the story of an aging playwright and the much younger assistant who is in love with him. Interestingly, the drama reflected the Barrymores' private

Al Blazic, Verna, and Lee Jr. enjoy Bradley Page's pool, circa 1936.

lives, as there was a thirty-three-year difference in their ages. Besides Verna, the Barrymores were supported by veteran performers William Farnum and Herbert Mundin.

A relative youngster in the cast, Hans Conried, at twenty, had been hand-chosen by Barrymore for the part of "Dickie." The senior actor, very impressed with Conried's versatility in *Streamlined Shakespeare*, had quickly become Conried's mentor. The adoration was mutual: Conried would name his eldest daughter Trilby for a character in one of Barrymore's greatest successes.

According to Conried's biographer Suzanne Gargiulo, the young fellow found among his fellow radio performers "a sort of extended family and friends he had missed growing up." When Conried later recalled this exciting period in his life, he revealed his friendship with another member of the *"Accent on Youth"* cast: "I remember my first years of radio stock-playing as an experiment in collective living, full of just as much frenzy, and just as much fun. We all spent our social lives with the same gang with whom we worked on the air . . . Lots of days I had nothing to eat but one of those foot-high milk shakes—ten cents and you had to cut it with a knife and fork. Lots of nights, I—and a lot of other 'great actors with small funds'—found in people like Verna Felton and Lee Millar friendly sort of people . . . who always had room at their dinner table for one or two more. It was a great period."

Another frequent visitor in the Millar home was Bradley Page, with whom Lee had stayed in constant touch during the four years the Millars were in Oakland. Now Page and his wife Olive had reached a certain level of prestige, residing in a comfortable home at 8751 Wonderland Park Avenue in the Hollywood Hills, a neighborhood once populated by some of the silent screen's biggest stars, including Tom Mix, Clara Bow, and Wallace Reid.

Page had forsaken his radio career when increasing film roles came his way. During the period from 1932 to 1937, he had filmed over seventy motion pictures as a freelance artist. Although most of them were "B" movies, he had supported the likes of Humphrey Bogart, Joel McCrea, Carole Lombard, George Raft, and James Cagney in others, mainly in gangster or villain roles. Page shared Lee Millar's dissatisfaction with the current situation of plays being squeezed out by the booming film industry. In fact, near the end of his life, he told an interviewer, "If the theatre had stayed healthy I would have still been in it. There's something else about the theatre, a psychological thing that comes to you from an audience. Also it's the length of the scenes. You play something as you would in ordinary life, you don't do that in pictures [because of the stop-start nature of filming]." Despite his misgivings toward the film industry, Page became one of the twenty-one founding members of the Screen Actors Guild in 1933.

While Bradley Page and Lee Millar bemoaned the decline of the stock companies, Verna reveled in her new line of work. Even late in her life, after she had spent more than sixty years in show business with half that time being on the stage, Verna still referred to radio as "my first love." She particularly relished two luxuries of performing on radio: freedom from wearing makeup and memorizing lines, not to mention the warm camaraderie among her fellow players. Verna soon became so active that she found herself bumping into the same stock performers at auditions and rehearsals. Many would become her friends.

In the fall of 1937, Verna recorded two installments of *The Cinnamon Bear*, a children's program, colorfully written by Glanville and Elizabeth Heisch and designed by the Transcription Company of America for syndication to local radio markets as a Christmas promotion. Sponsors inserted commercials for toys and children's products into the twenty-six cliffhanger-installments, which aired between Thanksgiving and Christmas. Verna appeared in the first and final installments, employing her stage-trained, clipped speech as the mother of young twins Judy and Jimmy Barton, but in effect she sounded more like their grandmother. When Mrs. Barton leaves the twins to search their attic for a silver star to adorn the top of their Christmas tree, a teddy bear named Paddy O'Cinnamon comes to life to help them. Informing them that he witnessed the Crazy Quilt Dragon steal the star and escape through a tiny tunnel in the attic wall, the Cinnamon Bear offers to shrink the children and lead them on a trek through Maybeland to catch up with the dragon and obtain the star. Along the way, they meet up with a wild assortment of charming characters, akin to those in *Alice in Wonderland* and *The Wizard of Oz*.

Andy Devine (LEFT) and Bradley Page in the 1935 Universal release *Chinatown Squad.*

The cast list for the production reads like a Who's Who of Old Time Radio: Joseph Kearns, Howard McNear, Gale Gordon, Elvia Allman, Lou Merrill, Elliott Lewis, Frank Nelson, and Martha Wentworth, most of whom would gain greater fame with the advent of television. Although these individuals were just beginning their radio careers, their unique styles were already taking shape. Joseph Kearns, chiefly known as the beleaguered Mr. Wilson on television's *Dennis the Menace*, was positively obnoxious as the Crazy Quilt Dragon. Gale Gordon exuded pomposity as a stork named Weary Willie, in a voice almost unrecognizable to fans who remember him as Lucille Ball's television foil. Howard McNear, who in later years would become Verna's North Hollywood neighbor, played Samuel the Seal, but without the nervous, fade-away delivery he made famous thirty years later as Floyd the barber on *The Andy Griffith Show*. And the inimitable Elvia Allman, mainly recalled as Kate Bradley's nemesis on *Petticoat Junction*, put in a brief performance as a snooty pelican. *The Cinnamon Bear* was repeated for many years each Christmas and remains a classic of old time radio.

The Millars had lived in their North Hollywood home barely six months when one of the worst disasters in Southern California history struck. Over the course of five days, from February 27 to March 3, 1938, ten inches of rain fell in Los Angeles County when two oceanic storms swept into Southern California. The resulting flood killed 115 people and destroyed 5600 homes. Mud and debris buried people in their homes, while motorists drowned attempting to cross

Lee Sr. and Lee Jr. in the back yard of 4147 Bakman Avenue, circa 1938.

raging torrents. Three transcontinental railroads servicing Los Angeles stopped operations because of bridge washouts and flooded lines. The Pacific Electric Railway, connecting Los Angeles to foothill cities including North Hollywood, was completely crippled. Public utilities were swamped by calls reporting broken gas mains and felled power poles.

"We went through the big flood," Verna later recalled, "but the big flood never touched us." One evening during the disaster Lee and Verna attempted to reach their residence on Bakman Avenue, located in a very flat section, but on higher ground than some surrounding streets. They found the low-lying intersection of Klump Avenue and Aqua Vista Streets, two blocks from their house, impassable. Plucky Verna, an excellent swimmer, decided to test the water's depth. Lee kept the car's headlights shining across the water, but just as Verna prepared to explore, a man approached and advised her to wait. He told her of a neighborhood druggist with a boat who was rowing people across the widest stretch of water. "We left the car with the lights on, and [the druggist] took me across, and the water was [sloshing] around inside the boat," Verna remembered in 1964.

The druggist let Verna out within a block from her house and then went back for Lee. It was dark on every street for the power had been knocked off. Trustworthy Codo was home though, waiting for the Millars to return.

Verna reminisced, "And when I came home, I had a housekeeper and she was so cute. This entire house was a mass of candles. She had candles in every place you could think. It looked like *The House of a Thousand Candles* (a play title from Verna's days with the Allen Players). And when I turned the corner, you know, looking, and I saw this blaze of light, you know. I knew it was her, and I knew I was home. It was the *most beautiful* sight I ever saw! She said, well, we had lots of candles and might as well use them. But that was an awful, an awful flood!"

The spring brought Verna an offer to appear again on Jack Benny's program, this time in two installments of "The Adventures of Tom Sawyer," a skit featuring the program's regulars as characters. She played delightfully fussy Aunt Polly to Jack's mischievous Tom. In one scene she packs him off to the school picnic.

AUNT POLLY
Thomas, did you brush your hair like I told you to?

JACK
Yes ma'm, I did.

AUNT POLLY
Well, then put it on and get going.

On this same show she was reunited with sound effects artist Pinto Colvig, who reminded Verna of the time she had bopped him on the head back in 1900 when the two were performing onstage in Colvig's hometown. Verna's next appearance on the Benny program would not occur until the next season's opener on October 2, when she reprised her role of Phil Harris's mother, but just briefly.

Notwithstanding her appearances on the Benny show and other comedies, Verna actively sought work on dramas when first breaking into Hollywood's radio industry. She and Lee particularly coveted roles on the prestigious *Lux Radio Theatre*, deemed by radio historian John Dunning as "the most important dramatic show in radio," boasting the biggest stars and budgets, as well as the most acclaim. Broadcast by CBS before a studio audience at the Music Box Theatre on Hollywood Boulevard (and beginning in 1940 at the more commodious Vine Street Playhouse), *Lux Radio Theatre* was hosted by the revered film director Cecil B. DeMille. Most Lux dramas were based on recent motion pictures, and whenever possible the screen stars repeated their roles for the radio version.

According to Dunning's *The Encyclopedia of Old Time Radio*, "At least fifty people were required for each broadcast . . . there were often twenty or more speaking parts, and when technicians were added, the crew overflowed the stage. Each play was a five-day commitment . . ." A history of the show, *Lux Presents*

Hollywood, written by Connie Billips and Arthur Pierce, was published in 1995. In it, actor Dix Davis recalled, "It was the most rehearsed radio show in the business, not only because it was [an hour] long, but [the producers] spent a lot of money on the show and they insisted on more rehearsals." In fact, a typical rehearsal schedule for *Lux* consisted of two-and-one-half-hour sessions each day beginning on Thursday and continuing through Sunday. Prior to the 6 p.m. Monday night broadcast, performers were expected to arrive for final rehearsals at 2:30 p.m.

When Verna and Lee first began appearing on *Lux*, the standard pay was $50 per week, an amount in startlingly sharp contrast to the money earned by the film stars appearing in these same productions. The highest paid actors included Clark Gable, Janet Gaynor, Claudette Colbert, Irene Dunne, and Cary Grant, who per week earned one hundred times as much as the *Lux* supporting players. Others, like Fred MacMurray, Rosalind Russell, David Niven, James Stewart, Merle Oberon, and Errol Flynn, earned slightly less. Once the American Federation of Radio Artists (AFRA) won the battle for a 125-percent wage increase in July, 1938, Verna and Lee and the other regular *Lux* performers were taking home between $75 and $100 per week.

Since all AFRA artists were paid on the same scale, it prohibited a "pecking order" among the regular radio performers and consequently helped to provide a warm, friendly working atmosphere. Verna recalled in 1964, "In radio, everybody got the same amount of money, except the high-scale [actors], but there was a sweetness and a warmth." This camaraderie fostered a generosity; when actors were unable to accept a part, they alerted others in the radio industry of its availability.

Lee and Verna would steadily appear on *Lux* from 1936 to 1941, with Lee chalking up twenty-eight broadcasts during this period and Verna ten more than he. Verna's first appearance on Lux only amounted to a brief commercial during the December 21, 1936, broadcast. She would not appear again on the program until over a year later, this time in a character role, in an adaptation of the 1935 RKO film *Alice Adams*. On the January 3, 1938, broadcast, Verna, though only forty-seven years old, played the snobbish Mrs. Dresser, a part created onscreen by character actress Zeffie Tilbury, who coincidentally was the same age as Verna's mother Clara. In subsequent *Lux* productions, Verna would inherit other roles originated on film by Hollywood's most prominent character actresses, including Helen Westley, Fay Bainter, Lucile Watson, Esther Dale, Beulah Bondi, Florence Bates, Gladys Cooper, Maude Eburne, and Margaret Hamilton.

In "*Ruggles of Red Gap*," the final *Lux* offering of the 1938-39 season, Verna joined a fine company of performers. Charles Laughton was the proper English valet whose services are won in a card game by Red Gap, Washington resident Charlie Ruggles. Both actors repeated their screen roles, as did Zasu Pitts who played Laughton's love interest. As rough-and-ready Ma Pettingill, Verna was equally delightful as the brutally frank mother-in-law of Ruggles who befriends

Laughton. When Ma shames her social-climbing daughter ("Effie, yer gittin' fat agin!"), one wonders if Verna used the same accent twenty years before when playing hayseed Sis Hopkins onstage in Portland.

A succession of maternal *Lux* roles followed, providing opportunities for Verna to play snide and provincial ("*The Awful Truth*"), fussy and flighty ("*The Sisters*"), disapproving ("*Made for Each Other*"), pushy and snobbish ("*The Rains Came*"), and delightfully brusque (as Parthy Ann Hawks in "*Show Boat*").

"*The Awful Truth*" marked the second time Verna and Lee had appeared together at the *Lux* microphone. Lee performed two small roles in this romance: a staid butler and a lively dog named Mr. Smith, the object of a custody battle between the leading players, Cary Grant and Claudette Colbert.

Chief among Verna's early performances for *Lux* was "*Made for Each Other*," in which she had the prominent role of Mrs. Mason, sharp-tongued and grudging mother of a timid son (Fred MacMurray) who has married against her wishes. The conflict between Mrs. Mason and her daughter-in-law Jane (Carole Lombard) is acutely felt, and when Jane asks the old woman to watch the couple's baby, the audience titters at Verna's terse retort: "That's what I'm *doing*. He'd choke if it wasn't for me!" Later when the baby is near death with pneumonia, the two women are reconciled when Mrs. Mason offers tender comfort, "You can't be lonely, either of you, as long as you have each other. You know, when you're lonely, *really* lonely, when you've no one to share things with, not even a loss . . . that's when you're *really* lonely."

Lee proved to be equally versatile in his Lux roles, often playing doctors, servants, foreigners, and on ten occasions, dogs. In the fall of 1936, when Lux producers again needed a canine mimicker for "*The Story of Louis Pasteur*," a dramatization requiring the sound of a mad dog, they called on Lee.

Subsequent turns as various dogs on Lux won Lee the regular role of "Rags" the schnauzer on the NBC serial *Those We Love*, debuting in January of 1938 and starring Nan Grey, Donald Woods, and Alma Kruger. In a press release for this program, Lee claimed that dogs, like humans, have their own personalities. Consequently, he asserted that he studied each script to get the feel of Rags' personality before attempting the proper bark. (Verna claimed that she herself, as well as Lee Jr., had appeared on *Those We Love*, though not in regular roles. However, these appearances, like many of her radio credits, remain unverified or undiscovered.)

Lee could go to great lengths for authenticity's sake. For his role as a beagle in the 1939 *Lux* season-opener "*The Awful Truth*," Lee caught a train to Lake Arrowhead to study the baying of his subject, because he didn't have a beagle in his repertoire.

Lee was adept at mimicking other animal sounds. During his San Francisco radio career, the producers of *Death Valley Days* needed the bray of a jackass and the howl of a coyote. Neither being available, they were about to change the script when Lee came to the front with an exact reproduction of each.

While some *Lux Radio Theatre* productions featured both Verna and Lee in the same broadcast, this was not a coincidence limited to that program. During 1938 they both appeared on *Big Town*, a crime drama airing on CBS and starring Edward G. Robinson as newspaper editor-*cum*-crime solver Steve Wilson. While Lee often portrayed an austere judge, Verna played a newspaper staffer who offered readers household hints. The same year an NBC afternoon serial called *Candid Lady* featured Lee as Bert Ladd and Verna as Aunt Julia. In addition, both Millars appeared from time to time on *Dr. Christian*, a light drama on CBS, starring film actor Jean Hersholt in the title role.

During the 1939-40 season, Verna and Lee starred multiple times in an NBC Sunday afternoon show called *I Want a Divorce*, designed to "give people practical advice on how to stay married through the medium of drama." Each week they played different characters on the verge of marital dissolution, but sometimes they did not play each other's spouse. On March 24, 1940, Verna played the exasperated wife of an unsuccessful inventor, played by veteran film actor Raymond Hatton. One month later, Verna played a nurse offering counsel to man-and-wife doctors, Gale Gordon and Lurene Tuttle, the latter refusing to abandon personal ambition to save her marriage.

NBC issued a press release for *I Want a Divorce* on December 1, 1939, in which interviewer Kenny Doyle asked the Millars how they managed to stay married for sixteen years. "We just follow a simple ten commandments of marriage," replied Lee. Whether the following list was actually composed by Lee and Verna is speculative, however some items do sound as if the couple's real-life circumstances dictated a few of them:

I.   Thou shalt use Flit [a popular insecticide in 1939] on the neighborhood gossip and on in-laws who try to run thy home.

II. Thou shalt build a picket fence with brick posts if she wants a picket fence and he wilt have one of brick.

III. Thou shalt eat thy crackers only in thine half of the bed.

IV. Thou shalt not require thy mate to punch a time clock on leaving or returning home.

V.   Thou shalt not argue in front of Junior about his taking the car or going to the movies.

VI. Thou shalt not leave the house or retire for the night in anger, lest one of you shall meet with illness or accident and the other live to regret it.

VII. Thou shalt wash, put on clean clothes and make thyself as attractive as possible before sitting down to the table.

VIII. Thou shalt give thy mate the biggest piece of pie.

IX. Thou shalt not make fun of thy wife's hat if she puts up with thy checkered suit.

X. Thou shalt not count ten to cool thy anger—thou shalt keep counting.

For good measure, the Millars toss in a couple of extra ones:

Thou shalt eat if it chokes you if thy wife thinks enough of you to prepare a new dish. Thou shalt not be stingy with praise for the efforts of thy mate.

During this period, Lee and Verna did not limit themselves to radio work. Both sought film roles but found them difficult to obtain at a time when the film industry was blessed with a multitude of accomplished character actors. Lee found a few tiny roles in pictures like *Make Way for Tomorrow, The Man They Could Not Hang,* and *Tomorrow's Children,* but often his scenes fell victim to the cutting room floor.

Verna fared a little better. Late in the summer of 1939, she filmed her first sound picture, the Technicolor adventure *Northwest Passage,* produced on a grand scale by MGM and directed by King Vidor. The film was based on the first half of Kenneth Roberts' 1937 novel about the exploits of a colonial military unit recruited by the British during the French and Indian War. The film's title is somewhat misleading: actually, the second half of Roberts' work focuses on the search for a northwest passage to the Pacific.

Set in the upper Hudson River Valley in 1759, *Northwest Passage* depicts the brave efforts of Major Robert Rogers, played by Spencer Tracy, to lead his rangers on a mission to annihilate a tribe of warring Indians. Rogers convinces young artist Langdon Towne, played by Robert Young, to join his company as a mapmaker. Towne, recently expelled from Harvard for creating an insulting sketch of the college president, is on the run for subsequently insulting a wealthy and powerful rogue in his hometown of Portsmouth, New Hampshire.

Principally shot on location in McCall and Payette Lake, Idaho, as well as Glacier National Park, the film employed the use of over 300 Indians from the Nez Perce reservation. On August 16, the principal players, including Tracy, Young, and Walter Brennan, returned to Southern California, where filming began at the MGM studio a few days later.

Robert Barrat (RIGHT) surveys the latest artwork created by Robert Young (SEATED) as Rand Brooks, Kent Rogers, Don Castle, and Verna Felton (STANDING) look on in *Northwest Passage.*

Verna played the gentle and sympathetic mother of Langdon Towne in a scene near the film's opening, just after he has returned home in disgrace from Harvard. When his prosperous father, ship rigger Humphrey Towne, played by Robert Barrat, reprimands Langdon for his misconduct, his mother asks for permission to speak. "I'm sorry Langdon's lost his chance to be a clergyman. He's a boy who's always wanted to share his feelings, and clergymen show their feelings on all occasions . . . Artists should show their feelings, too. And if he's going to be a painter, he's *got* to *feel* about things!" The elder Towne readily agrees with his wife, determining that the family will have to make the best of their disappointment. Mother, sensing Father's agreeable mood, then asks if Langdon may wear his father's Sunday shirt to call on his sweetheart Elizabeth Browne, played by Ruth Hussey.

Although her scene was brief, mobcap-and-fichu-clad Verna, with her softest voice and most humble manner, managed to accurately portray the role of a woman who knew her place but was also devoted to the welfare of her son. It is one of only two scenes in the entire movie dominated by a female.

Interestingly, Hussey received star billing in a role whose scant time onscreen matched that of Verna's uncredited part of Mrs. Towne. This can only be explained by Verna's position as a virtual unknown in the Hollywood film industry at the time. Furthermore, it's likely that Verna was chosen for her part because a lesser-known actress like herself could not ask for as much compensation as one of Hollywood's more established character actresses. And by the time *Northwest Passage* had begun production, MGM was looking for ways to offset its exorbitant pre-production costs. Therefore, plans for an "all-star" production were scrapped; roles intended for Wallace Beery and Robert Taylor, among others, were given to those with less substantial film careers.

In early November, Verna would return to the MGM back lot for one of the final scenes shot for an Ann Sothern feature called *Joe and Ethel Turp Call on the President*. The comedy-drama was based on a Damon Runyon story published two years earlier in *The Saturday Evening Post*. Sothern and William Gargan played the title characters, Brooklyn residents who seek the president's pardon of their mail carrier Jim (played by Walter Brennan), arrested for destroying a registered letter. For many years Jim has been in love with the recipient of the letter, all the while protecting her from the knowledge that her son is a prison inmate at San Quentin. When the letter arrives, Jim knows it will destroy the frail Kitty (played by Marsha Hunt) so he disposes of it. By a fluke, Joe and Ethel Turp are admitted to the president's office and inform him of the background information leading to Jim's arrest. Moved by the tale, the president pardons Jim and restores him to his mail route.

In the opening scene, Verna has five lines as Mrs. Murphy, the first neighbor Ethel turns to upon learning the news about Jim's arrest. With her gray-streaked hair and plump figure, Verna looked quite matronly in her housedress and apron, a striking contrast from her first film role twenty-two years earlier when she appeared almost vampish as the wife of David in *The Chosen Prince*. Filmed over a six-week period, *Joe and Ethel Turp Call on the President* was released on December 1, 1939, while *Northwest Passage* opened in theaters almost three months later.

During part of the time Verna was engaged in these MGM productions, Clara and Pearl spent an extended summer vacation in the Millar home. Clara, by this time, much thinner and quite feeble, was mourning the loss of both of her sons. Clayton had dropped dead of a heart attack at the age of fifty-six on May 12 in San Francisco. For some time previously, he had been living in that city, working in unskilled positions. Clayton's final employment was as a pantryman, probably in a large hotel or hospital. At the time of his death, he was no longer using the name Felton but instead was known by his birth name, George Clayton Van Alstyne. Sadly, Clayton had never reunited with the wife and son he had abandoned in British Columbia almost twenty-five years earlier.

Compounding the Allens' woes was their imminent displacement from the Millar home in West Oakland. Dozens of blocks, containing over 150 nineteenth-century wood-framed houses, were targeted for demolition during 1940. They would be replaced by Peralta Villa, one of the first public housing projects in California. Although some structures in this part of the city were dilapidated, Al Blazic, recalling their demolition, maintained that many were still in very good condition. The owners were offered less than market value and, in some

Pearl and Clara Allen visiting Verna's home in 1939.

cases, were pressured to accept these offers. Al's grandmother Mary Blazic was given a total of $2900 for her grand home and the house next door, which she also owned. Al remembered unhappily, "They said, 'Woman, you better take it because if you don't, we're going to condemn it.'"

Perhaps the Millar house was spared the wrecking ball because it was practically modern, compared to most of the houses in the vicinity. It was bought and moved to another location on Tenth Street. Consequently, Pearl and Clara Allen were forced to move into an apartment on Larkin Street in San Francisco, which at least was closer to Pearl's place of employment.

In the fall of 1939, a radio part came along that would not only bring Verna an estimable amount of recognition, but one that would also provide her, although indirectly, with several screen roles. At the close of the 1938-39 season, Jack Benny found himself in a predicament. Kenny Baker, the popular tenor on Benny's weekly show, decided not to return for the following season. After an extended search for a replacement, Jack signed an unknown, twenty-two-year-old Owen Patrick "Eugene" McNulty, later dubbed Dennis Day. Born in the Bronx, Day was a recent graduate of Manhattan College when he auditioned for Jack Benny in New York.

Regarding his new position, Day told interviewer Chuck Schaden in a 1976 interview, "I was scared stiff. After all, I had no great experience as far as singing is concerned with orchestras or appearing on [radio]. Here's the top radio show in the whole country and everyone was listening, so I was just very nervous and very scared. And I think that's why they brought in Verna Felton, who played the part of my mother. It was a buffer between myself and Jack until I got more confidence in myself on the show."

Mary Livingstone, in her biography of her husband, recalled, "Jack had met Day's parents, Mr. and Mrs. McNulty, dear people with thick Irish brogues and very sweet old-fashioned ways. That meeting gave Jack an idea. Since they wanted to keep Dennis the naïve, boyish type previously identified with Baker, why not introduce the character of Dennis' mother? But instead of being like the real Mrs. McNulty, a sweet lady, the mother of six, who spoke with an Irish accent and played the concertina, she would be a heavyweight—very domineering—or, as Dennis subsequently nicknamed her, 'my mother, the bricklayer.' Brilliant character actress Verna Felton was signed for the part."

But Verna almost didn't get the part of bombastic Mrs. Day. In 1964, she recalled the details of the situation: "Dennis, you see, was very timid. And when [he] first came on, why, he couldn't read lines. So they said, 'Well, what'll we do? He can sing, but he can't read lines.' So then this [Bill] Morrow, who was [Benny's] big writer said, 'Bring in a stage mother. He'll have a stage mother with him, and every time he *goes* to talk, let *her* talk.' Jack said, 'Good idea.' So they called an audition for everybody [interested in the part], and I came in, and Jack came through the office. He stopped and looked at me and said, 'What are *you* doing here?' And I said, 'I don't know. [I got a] call for an audition for Dennis Day's mother.' He said, 'Oh, *no*, no, I don't want you to play that part. Come on in here. I don't want you to play that part. So we went in [the room where the auditions were taking place]. And he said [to the writers], 'What'd you send for Verna for?' 'Well,' they said, 'she's a *natural* for it.' He said, 'Well, I don't want her. She works with us *all the time*.' They said, 'But *this* is the woman!' And [Jack] said, 'No, I don't want her to do it!' So, Janet Beecher was here at the time, and she auditioned. So they called me up and said, 'Well, Jack's decided Janet Beecher gets the part. And we could *kill* him!' I said, 'So could I.'"

"So, I was at the *Lux* rehearsal . . . this was on Saturday . . . and [the Benny company] rehearsed on Saturday. And I was over at the *Lux* theatre [across the street from NBC] rehearsing ["*The Sisters*"]. And pretty soon, just before we closed, they called over and said, 'Verna, be at rehearsal tomorrow at Benny's at 10 o'clock . . . *you're* going to do the part.' So when I went in the next morning, I ran into Jack, and I said, 'Thanks, Jack. That's very nice of you.' He said, 'Now don't thank *me*, because I *don't* want you in this part! I *still* don't want you! But nobody will have Miss Beecher nor anyone else, but I *still* don't want you in that part!'"

Despite Jack Benny's emphatic disapproval, Verna first appeared as Dennis Day's mother on Sunday, October 8, 1939, in the inaugural show of the season. About two-thirds into the broadcast, listeners were introduced to this domineering woman and her meek son. Upon entering, Mrs. Day promptly hands Jack the $1.65 bill for their cab fare to the studio. In a deep, almost grandiloquent voice, Mrs. Day answers every question Jack directs to Dennis. As an aside, Jack, asks, "How can a basso profundo like that have a tenor for a son?"

The following day, *Radio Daily* reviewed the broadcast: "As 'Mrs. Day,' Verna Felton was the perfect choice. In previous seasons, she had played the mother of Don Wilson, Phil Harris and nearly every other member of the cast—each time with a new dimension of versatility . . ." The character was an immediate hit. The following week, jokes about Mrs. Day's low register continued, including a big laugh when Mary Livingstone imitates the pompous matron.

Verna appeared as Mrs. Day a total of ten times that season, barking orders at Dennis, trading insults with Jack and continually arguing with him over Dennis's singing selections. As Dennis gained confidence, his mother was not needed as frequently, so Verna only appeared as the old "dame" (as Jack called her) once each during the two subsequent seasons. Day recalled in Mary Livingstone's biography of Benny, "During my second year on the show, when Verna Felton only came on once or twice, her presence was so strongly established, the audience *thought* she was there. I'd say things like: 'Mr. Benny, mother says it's time you gave me a raise . . . She thinks that for singing and mowing your lawn, I should be earning more than thirty-five dollars a week . . .' At which point, Jack would say with a disgusted tone: '*Your* mother . . . *your* mother, what does *she* know? And, all across the country, people laughed as they visualized the dressing down my mother was going to give Jack." Even in absentia, Verna helped to ensure that Dennis Day maintained a long stay on the Benny program.

Still, Verna was never given air credit for her part, prompting listeners to write in to newspapers and trade magazines asking who voiced the part of Mrs. Day. The character's popularity made it the first regular, or semi-regular, role to bring Verna wider recognition than anything she had previously done in radio.

Norman Siegel wrote in *The Cleveland Press*: "If Jack thinks he's the boss of the show, an imposter must have been taking his part on the air the past two weeks, for ever since 'Mrs. Day' has been around, she's been running the broadcast with

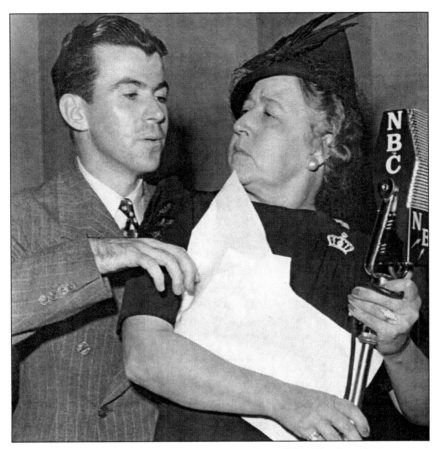

Dennis Day struggles with his mother (Verna) for a little attention during rehearsal for the Benny show, October 1939.

her booming orders. Although she's currently sharing the spotlight with Jack's new tenor, Verna isn't a newcomer on the program. She's appeared off and on during the past three years as the mother of Phil Harris, Don Wilson and nearly every other member of the cast, except that Equatorial Gable known as Rochester. And if Jack needs a 'mammy' for Rochester, Verna could also take the part, being an expert at colored dialect. A capable character actress, she looks the part of Dennis' domineering mother when she's at the mike. She scowls, waggles a forbidding finger, and looks menacingly over her glasses at Jack and Dennis."

Though anonymously, Verna even made Walter Winchell's column on October 25: "Jack Benny's Mrs. Day, a caricature on some of the more fiendish stage mamas, is a genuine comic innovation, and explains why he hangs onto his Crossley rating." The Crossley ratings were actually produced by the Cooperative Analysis of Broadcasting, Inc. and compiled by randomly calling residents of a city and asking them what radio stations or shows they had been recently listening to.

On November 23, Thanksgiving Day, almost 4000 children and their parents thronged Burbank's Union Air Terminal (now the Bob Hope Airport) in anticipation of the arrival of some very special visitors. Those children closest to the tarmac peered through the chain-link fence while others farther back sat on their fathers' shoulders to see over the crowd. A cheer went up when they saw the United Air Lines Mainliner land. When the door was pulled open, out stepped Mr. and Mrs. Santa Claus, clad in red velvet trimmed in white fur, smiling and waving at the crowd. All the way from their frozen home at the North Pole Mr. and Mrs. Claus had come to officially usher in the Christmas season in Los Angeles. Addressing the spectators from an elevated platform, Mrs. Claus expressed surprise at the scarcity of igloos and icebergs in Southern California. She graciously passed out "North Pole taffy" to the tots as her husband accepted dozens of "letters to Santa," all the while shaking hands with the crowd. The event was covered by the *Los Angeles Times*, featuring huge photographs on the front page of the local news section. Observant readers might have noticed a definite similarity between Mrs. Claus and Dennis Day's mother, apart from the former's snowy wig and warm smile.

Before the creation of Mrs. Day, Verna had usually filled sweet, grandmotherly roles. Now her colorful portrait of the domineering Mrs. Day, to a certain degree, led to typecasting Verna in a new vein: the battleaxe. But this was of no concern to her, as long as the job offers came rolling in. And they did.

Soon Verna was wanted for film roles of this ilk, beginning with *If I Had My Way*, a Universal production filmed in February 1940. Starring Bing Crosby and child actress Gloria Jean, the story involved a San Francisco steelworker Buzz Blackwell (Crosby) who escorts orphaned Patricia Johnson (Jean) to New York to live with relatives after her father is killed building the Golden Gate Bridge. Upon arrival, Buzz takes tomboy Patricia into an upscale ladies' department store to be properly outfitted.

When Buzz turns his back, Patricia's pet squirrel Crack scampers into the millinery department where an irritable customer Mrs. DeLacey (Verna) is trying on hats. As a saleslady places a creation covered in fruit and nuts on the dowager's head, Mrs. DeLacey looks in the mirror at the monstrosity, grousing, "It absolutely defeats me! Some man with a perverted sense of humor must be designing women's hats today. They all make you look ridiculous. This is the end! This one makes me look like a fruit salad! All I need with this is some whipped cream!" At that instant, Crack, who has climbed up Mrs. DeLacey's fur coat, appears on her shoulder, sniffing at the hat. She shrieks and throws off the hat, screaming that a wolf with fangs attacked her. When a floorwalker doubts her claim, the haughty woman leaves in an indignant huff.

Once *If I Had My Way* hit the screens, moviegoers would finally get to see Dennis Day's mother in action, for Verna used the same vocal inflections for DeLacey. Among other supporting players in the cast were Virginia Brissac, who had been Verna's fellow actor in the Jessie Shirley company, and Joe Whitehead, who had been part of the Allen Stock Company in 1905. On April 26, when this movie was released, Verna's name appeared near the bottom of the opening and closing credits. She was more pleased later that spring, when *If I Had My Way* played the Beacon Theater in Vancouver, and the management superimposed a special notice across Universal's standard newspaper ad, "Also featuring VERNA FELTON (Late Star of Vancouver's Own 'Allen Players')."

Three weeks after the release of *If I Had My Way*, news arrived of Clara's death at age 76 on May 18. Three weeks earlier, she had been admitted to St. Francis Hospital in San Francisco for osteomyelitis, a chronic bacterial bone infection. The previous year while visiting Verna, Clara had slipped on the bedroom floor, fracturing her right knee. Following the insertion of a Steinman pin to mend the knee, an infection had unknowingly developed. Consequently, cardiopulmonary problems compounded Clara's weakened condition.

The Millars made the sad trek to San Francisco for the funeral services on May 20. Then Clara's cremated remains were sent to Vancouver where family friend Violet Harvey took charge of their disposal. Clara, who had nurtured Verna's career since 1900, lived only long enough to witness the infancy of her daughter's Hollywood career.

In less than two years, Verna had lost her mother and both her brothers. While she was consumed by a busy career and the care for her husband and son, her stepfather was less anchored. Pearl sought solace in his friendship with the aforementioned Violet Harvey, who had been formerly employed as cashier at the Vancouver Theatre. Pearl encouraged the thirty-seven-year-old spinster to relocate to San Francisco, where she found work with the Wells Fargo Bank. Not long after, Pearl, now sixty-nine, proposed marriage. The ceremony, which took place in San Francisco on March 22, 1941, was officiated by a Methodist minister and witnessed by Pearl's brother Arden, just as he had for Pearl and Clara's marriage in 1904, the year Violet was born.

Meanwhile, the steady income from Lee and Verna's radio and film work afforded them several luxuries. They got rid of the Studebaker and the Durant coupe to purchase a black 1938 Packard 8 Touring Sedan, which Verna usually used, and a 1935 Ford Fordor Deluxe touring sedan, normally drive by Lee. Ferris Murdy, Lee Jr.'s best friend at North Hollywood High School, recalled those days: "Mrs. Millar was Lee's and my driver, wherever we wanted to go. I think it was a 1938 black Packard Sedan. She took us to dances with our girlfriends and to places like the Glendale Civic Auditorium and Pasadena Civic Auditorium. She [also] expanded my knowledge by taking us to shows at the Hollywood Bowl."

Murdy was also present when the Millars' swimming pool was completed in June 1940. The previous August, Lee and Verna had purchased the vacant lot next door to the south, spending the interim readying it for two improvements: the pool and a building at the rear of the lot, designed to house a rumpus room, a single-car garage, and a small workshop for Lee Sr. The rumpus room was

Pals Lee Millar and Albert Blazic Sr. enjoy an afternoon around the new pool.

finished in knotty-pine paneling, equipped with a stone fireplace, and decorated with Millar family heirlooms, including guns, knives, helmets, stuffed birds, an upright piano, and towering shelves of old books.

No one got more use out of the pool than Lee Jr., who shared his mother's love of swimming. Family tradition has it that the Millar pool was one of the first residential pools in the San Fernando Valley. Its completion merited a mention in the June 1940 *AFRA Bulletin*: "Verna Felton and hubby, Lee Millar, have always been swell pals to their young son, but the latest palsy-walsy demonstration was to provide a modern swimming pool and rumpus room in both of which Son, well along in high school, entertains his many friends."

In 1964 Verna recalled, "Of course, when school was out, you know, they would be here all summer long. You'd have *all* kids, just see heads bobbing. Big Millar [Lee Sr.] used to say, when we'd come in, 'Well, I wish there was one day I could come home and see the water there, but I can see *nothing but heads.* They'd bob, bob, bob."

The Millars' hospitality did not go unrecognized. On October 12, 1940, over thirty high-schoolers and their parents crowded into the rumpus room for a party in honor of Verna. As a token of their appreciation for the use of the swimming pool and for "her motherly interest and chaperonage during the summer months," they presented Verna with a dresser set, backed with black and rose tapestry and framed with gold filigree. Applause shook the rafters when teenager Jay Moss made the presentation. Afterwards, Verna showed home movies she had filmed of swimming parties she had hosted for the children that season.

Ferris Murdy, who frequently listened with Lee Jr. to Verna's performances on the Jack Benny program, shared a bit of the Millar family dynamics: "Verna was a great person, a devoted mother, and unforgettable. I spent many happy days with the family in her home and pool in 1939-1941 . . . She had many parties and swimming parties for Lee [Junior]. I think she was so close to him because he had rheumatic fever when he was younger. The fever left him with a limp. When I went there for dinner, she corrected Lee and me in etiquette and manners . . . We used to listen to her on the radio in a Jack Benny comedy show where she played Dennis the singer's mother . . . Mr. Millar was a fine gentleman and used to cut up and act silly in the swimming pool and did dog imitations, barking at us. Coddie, the housekeeper, was my pride and joy, and she used to fix Lee and me German hotcakes. I still fix them for my kids now, the same way she did. Take two eggs, two spoons of sugar, two spoons of flour and some milk. Make a real thin batter, make like a crepe, you know. Cook it in a frying pan, then put in on a plate and put fruit, jam, or sour cream on it and roll it up. They are so good . . . Mrs. Millar always said I was her 'second boy.' A lovely lady. You couldn't have asked for a nicer person."

The Millars' association with Walt Disney Productions began soon after Lee arrived in Hollywood in 1936. According to Dave Smith, archivist for The Walt Disney Company, a complete list of Lee's credits does not exist, but records show that he created animal sounds for many animated shorts, beginning with *The Worm Turns*, which was released on January 2, 1937. His other credits include *Don Donald, Magician Mickey, Moose Hunters, Mickey's Parrot, Farmyard Symphony*, and *Donald's Cousin Gus*. In 1939, Lee succeeded Pinto Colvig as the voice of Mickey Mouse's dog Pluto in the cartoon short Beach Picnic. He gave voice to the yellow pooch in at least nine subsequent shorts, ending with *A Gentleman's Gentleman* in 1941. In 2005, Smith verified that Lee's voice was used in *Pluto Junior*, released on February 28, 1942, but since The Internet Movie Database reports that Colvig provided the voice for Pluto in this short, perhaps Lee's voice was used for another character.

Verna joined the Disney family on October 12, 1939, when she tested for the part of Mrs. Hare, Thumper's mother, in *Bambi*. A week later she tested again, and although she was called back a third time on January 15, her voice was not used in the final production. Instead, the more youthful voice of Margaret Lee, nineteen years Verna's junior, was utilized. However, until the end of her life, Verna took credit for the role of Mrs. Hare. Anyone familiar with Verna's voice would deny this assertion after viewing the film. (The misconception is further perpetuated by the audio commentary for the 60th Anniversary Edition of *Dumbo*, released on DVD in 2001. When commentator John Canemaker summarizes Verna's Disney career during one of her scenes, he lists one of her credits as Thumper's mother.) Nevertheless, no one can argue Verna's participation in another Disney film, being produced at the same time as *Bambi*.

In 1939, Walt Disney bought the rights to a children's book called *Dumbo the Flying Elephant* by Helen Aberson and Harold Pearl. Originally planned as a short, *Dumbo* eventually became a full-length feature, albeit the shortest of Disney's animated pictures, with a running time of sixty-four minutes. It told the poignant story of a baby circus elephant whose outsized ears make him the ridicule of the other pachyderms. When a boy cruelly taunts him, Dumbo's mother spanks the youngster with her trunk, then fights the ringmaster and others as they take Dumbo away from her. When she is separated from Dumbo, he is shunned by the other elephants and falls into despair, only to be encouraged by a mouse who concocts a plan to make Dumbo successful, ultimately reuniting him with his mother.

Before the animation process began in August 1940, one preliminary task was the selection of voices for the animated characters. German-born Herman Bing, a veteran character actor known for his thick Teutonic accent, was chosen as the ringmaster. Folksy Cliff Edwards, who had gained immortality as Jiminy Cricket in Disney's *Pinocchio,* provided the voice of Jim Crow. Edward Brophy's raspy New York accent was deemed perfect as Timothy Q. Mouse, Dumbo's friend and adviser. Sterling Holloway's inimitable style won him the part as Mr. Stork, who delivers baby Dumbo to his mother. And Verna Felton, whose matronly voice had been judged inappropriate as Thumper's mother in *Bambi*, was bestowed a heftier part, the Matriarch Elephant of the circus troupe, undoubtedly an easy selection following her success as another opinionated and domineering female, Mrs. Day on the Jack Benny radio program.

All of these voices were important, because little Dumbo himself never speaks, doing all his work in straight pantomime. In previous productions, Disney had chosen not to use famous stars as voice actors but rather film or radio players whose names remained unknown to the general public. Parts played by these individuals were usually uncredited, either onscreen or on the air. When questioned, Disney typically refused to identify his voice actors for fear that audiences would associate his characters with a real person, thus spoiling the illusion. But after facing indignant protest and insistent curiosity from moviegoers and critics following the release of *Snow White and the Seven Dwarfs*, Disney relented, revealing to the press the identity of the five aforementioned actors in *Dumbo*. Individual photographs of the five, posing with sketches of their characters, were also released to newspapers and magazines. On October 19, the Sunday edition of *The New York Times* featured an impressive spread heralding Dumbo's arrival. Verna's photo, along with those of Edwards, Bing, and Brophy, was prominently displayed above a pose of the Matriarch Elephant. Despite all this attention none of these actors were included in the screen credits when *Dumbo* hit the theaters.

Whenever Verna was mentioned in one of the *Dumbo* press releases, she was always tagged as Dennis Day's mother, the most identifiable role of her career at this point. However, it would be years before the actresses who voiced the other three elephants were revealed to be radio veterans Sarah Selby, Noreen Gammill,

With sketches of her character behind her, Verna reacts as the Matriarch Elephant seeing Dumbo's large ears for the first time. © WALT DISNEY PRODUCTIONS.

and Dorothy Scott. Since Verna was not only the most famous of the foursome but a personal favorite of Walt Disney as well, she received special treatment. Being married to the man supplying the voice of Pluto didn't hurt either.

The Matriarch Elephant and her condescending cronies are of key importance to the plot of *Dumbo*. When Mr. Stork delivers the baby to Mrs. Jumbo, the other four elephants make a fuss over him. The Matriarch Elephant reaches down to tickle his trunk, causing a sneeze that unfurls the baby's enormous ears. He is then dubbed "Dumbo" by the cattiest of the elephants. Later after Mrs. Jumbo is imprisoned, the foursome blames Dumbo, calling him a freak. Resolvedly, the Matriarch Elephant intones, "His disgrace is our own shame." She instructs the others to ignore his existence. Later when Dumbo ruins their balancing act, which causes the collapse of the entire circus tent, he is added instead to the clown's act. The Matriarch Elephant, in a lofty and dramatic tone, leads the rest in a solemn vow, "He is no longer an *elephant*." But by the end of the movie, when Dumbo masters flying, these proud pachyderms get their comeuppance. In mid-flight Dumbo sprays them with bullet-like peanuts.

Vladimir "Bill" Tytla was the supervising animator for *Dumbo*, and in addition to those duties, he animated the five adult elephants, including the one voiced by Verna. Tytla subtly designed each elephant to move differently to show their individual personalities, basing his work not only on the vocals supplied by the actors, but by studying their corresponding facial expressions as well. The Matriarch Elephant is distinguished from the rest by having a higher headdress and a heavier figure. Her deep and imperious voice, as well as the heavy circles under her eyes, further substantiates her seniority.

Verna later expressed amazement at the resemblance between the Matriarch Elephant and herself: "If you'd been sitting there [watching *Dumbo*], you couldn't escape it. Because it was my face, you know, only with a great big trunk. It was *so* cute! We [Verna and her fellow actresses] would come down in the mornings and they'd have this work board for us. And each day you looked a little bit more like an elephant. First you started out like a person, you know, and pretty soon you looked like an elephant. Oh, it was fun!"

But sometimes the recording process could be arduous: "We worked all day long to get two [lines right]. One was 'Kootchie, kootchie, kootchie' and the other was 'Dumbo, Junior.'" (Actually the line was 'Jumbo, Junior,' spoken by Mrs. Jumbo, Dumbo's mother.) "And the one girl who said 'Dumbo, Junior,' she said it *every* way—'Dumbo, *Junior*'—'*Dumbo* Junior'—'*Oh*, Dumbo *Junior!*' *Every* way that you could think of saying [the line] till they found the one they wanted. That took us about two hours and a half. And I had the [line] with the trunk where I tickle him under the chin and say, 'Kootchie, kootchie, kootchie, kootchie.' We had to do that about two hours and a half until they got the 'kootchie, kootchie, kootchie' they wanted . . . That was a cute show."

The moviegoing public agreed. After *Dumbo*'s release on October 31, 1941, they ate it up like so much circus popcorn, clearly preferring it over Disney's *Fantasia*. *Dumbo* was colorful, charming, and simple. And it contained some of the most poignant scenes in any animated film, including the outstanding one where Dumbo visits his mother, imprisoned inside a circus train car. Her shackles prevent her from seeing her baby, but she extends her trunk down to cradle him and rock him during the song "Baby Mine."

This scene also impressed Verna, who shared her admiration for Disney's talents during the 1964 interview with Marty Halperin: "That little song she sang outside the jail . . . I said when you take *an ugly old trunk* of an elephant

The cast of *Point Sublime* featured (FRONT) Mel Blanc, Verna, Earle Ross, Jane Morgan, and Cliff Arquette. In the rear are announcer Carlton KaDell (LEFT) and producer Robert Redd, 1943.

and can do *that* and make people *cry*, it's really something." After *Dumbo*, Verna's association with Disney would continue for twenty-five years.

Late in 1940, Verna joined the cast of *Point Sublime*, a half-hour comedy-drama written by Robert L. Redd and sponsored by Union Oil Company. Debuting on Monday, December 16, and broadcast only to NBC listeners on the Pacific coast, the show took place in the fictional coastal town of Point Sublime. The main character Ben Willett, as decribed in the *Fresno Bee*, was an "eccentric, shrewd, but kindly old man who is the 'magnate' of Pointe Sublime, who knows everyone's business but has a knack of getting involved in difficult situations from which he succeeds in escaping only through luck." Ben, played by Cliff Arquette, owned the general store, the service station, the motor court, and almost everything else in the small village. Union Oil Company promotions called Ben a combination of Will Rogers and "your own Uncle Clem, back home." Veteran actress Jane Morgan played Ben's love interest, Evelyn "Evy" Hanover, former paleontologist's assistant now acting as housekeeper for Ben's rental cottages. (Although Morgan was twenty-five years older than Arquette, he ably used his vocal skills to match her more mature voice.) Other citizens were stuttering railway clerk August Moon (played by Mel Blanc), newspaper reporter Monk Rice (Fred MacKaye), and retired Texas millionaire Howie MacBrayer (Earle Ross), who rivaled Ben for Evy's affections. Verna lent her talents as the town gossip Hattie Hirsch, whose contention with Ben made her quite unpopular among the townsfolk.

On April 29, 1942, *Point Sublime* was broadcast from San Francisco as part of the dedicatory ceremonies for the newly completed NBC studio at the corner of Taylor and O'Farrell Streets. To tie the location into the plot of the evening's broadcast, writer Robert Redd had Ben and the other characters visit the Bay City, taking in the sights while Ben Willett pondered the necessity of wartime blackouts. *Point Sublime* continued to run on the NBC Pacific network until later that year when it switched to the Mutual-Don Lee network for two additional years.

Verna became best friends with actress Jane Morgan during the run of this show, and their close relationship thrived for over twenty-five years. Most of Jane's friends, including Verna, called her Janie, but her actual birth name was Jennie. She was born in England on December 6, 1880, to Welsh parents, Roderick Morgan and his wife, the former Emma Jane Evans. Before Jane reached her second birthday, she moved with her family to the United States, settling in Anaconda, Montana, where her father later became the blacksmith shop foreman with the Anaconda Copper Mining Company. Her childhood ambition was to be a concert violinist. At seventeen, she left home to study at the New England Conservatory of Music in Boston. She added vocal training to her curriculum and after graduation joined the Boston Opera Company, with which she doubled as violinist and singer for a short time. However, she returned to Anaconda in 1899 and began teaching violin and piano. Her musical services were in frequent demand for local concerts, weddings, and church services. Jane often found herself moving in the same social circles as another violin teacher in town. Leo Cullen Bryant, three years her senior and a native of Wisconsin, was also the orchestra conductor at Anaconda's Margaret Theatre. Romance blossomed quickly, and the young couple was married on February 17, 1901. For a short time, they flip-flopped between Butte and Anaconda, where both taught music, but in 1903 the Bryants opened a piano store in Nampa, Idaho. Business was not what they had hoped, and within two years they sold the store. The Bryants knew that their real calling was performing, so for the next decade they joined various theatrical companies in Salt Lake City, Denver, and Wichita. Their only child, a daughter named Aline, was born in Denver in 1905.

During World War One, job opportunities separated the family; Leo was violinist and musical director for the Shoreham Hotel in Washington, D.C., while Jane performed in plays in New Haven, Connecticut. Peacetime reunited them, and they relocated to the West Coast, where Jane was hired by the Thomas Wilkes Stock Company in Seattle for one season, performing in many of the same plays identified with Verna's stage career, including *Mrs. Wiggs of the Cabbage Patch*, *Peg O' My Heart*, *The Lady of the Scarlet Poppy*, and *Polly with a Past*. After the Wilkes company folded, the Bryants moved to Los Angeles where Jane became a regular performer in the Morosco Theatre Stock Company from 1923 until 1928. Like Verna, Jane sought radio work when the stock days ended.

She made her radio debut in 1930 in a program which featured silent film star Lew Cody. Prior to *Point Sublime*, Jane had appeared regularly on network serials *Brent House, Glorious One*, and *House Undivided*, in addition to guest spots on other shows like *I Want a Divorce, Dr. Christian,* and *Lux Radio Theatre.*

It is nearly impossible to mention Janie Morgan without also acknowledging Helen Rourke, as their lives were entwined for over fifty years. They met during World War One in New Haven, Connecticut, where Helen had been born on August 31, 1893. The granddaughter of Irish immigrants, Helen, a slender strawberry blonde, was the oldest child of Michael Rourke, a city fireman. To help her working-class family, Helen had become a saleswoman in a clock store by age sixteen. It is believed that she later became a sitter for Aline Bryant during Jane's nightly stage performances. Whatever the case, Helen moved with the Bryants to Seattle following the war and made her home on the West Coast with them for the remainder of their lives, except for a short period when she was a waitress in San Francisco. By 1940, Helen and the Bryants were residing at 1741 Cherokee Avenue in downtown Hollywood, where Helen had become a secretary for R.K.O. Radio Studio. When Verna and Jane became fast friends, naturally Helen was included in their social functions and consequently became Verna's dear friend as well.

By early spring of 1941, Verna was still primarily identified with the radio role of Mrs. Day, even though she had appeared on the Jack Benny program only once during the 1940-41 season. And that was in the season opener on October 6. However, promotional material for a new syndicated radio program, debuting on April 3, 1941, with Verna as a regular, featured photos of her with captions identifying her as "Dennis Day's mother."

This recorded comedy show was called *The Barrel of Fun*, starring screen comedian Charlie Ruggles. Sponsored by Acme Beer, the story was centered in Hollywood, where Ruggles operated The Barrel of Fun, a newly opened beer garden, financed by Mrs. Davenport, played by Verna. Others in the original cast included dialect genius Benny Rubin as Ruggles' foil and stooge, radio actress Margaret Brayton as LuLu Belle the hat check girl, and radio/film performers Leo Cleary, Edward Emerson, and Jack Mather. The half-hour show was formatted much like the Jack Benny program; musical interludes, furnished by the Lou Forbes Orchestra, the Singing Waiters, and the Barmaids Quartet, were interspersed throughout the comic plot of each show. The Acme Brewing Company, based in San Francisco, promoted *The Barrel of Fun* as "a beer program set in a high-class 'beer atmosphere' . . . Acme Beer flows throughout the entire show. The commercials don't sound like commercials because they are an integral part of the characters and the atmosphere of the program itself."

After the program met with success during the first thirteen weeks, it was revamped with everyone departing except Ruggles, Rubin, and Verna. Joining the cast were actors Hanley Stafford, Jerry Hausner, and the remarkably versatile Sara Berner. Art Gilmore became the announcer, while Dave Rose and his orchestra replaced Lou Forbes. Other music was provided by the Sportsmen Quartet and soloist Linda Ware.

Several extant recordings from *The Barrel of Fun*'s second thirteen-week run make Ruggles's talents seem wasted. Embarrassingly, he struggled to endure this tiresome venture's corny jokes, especially during his stand-up routine at the opening of each program. Most of the flimsy plots poked fun at Ruggles's character, who was prone to prevarication regarding his past prowess as college athlete, army private, etc. Meanwhile, Verna's character of Mrs. Davenport, or "Davvie," as she was called by Ruggles, leaned toward an imitation of Mrs. Day, often upbraiding the irresponsible Ruggles while injecting into the part as much fluttery charm as she could. The remainder of the cast, with the exception of Jerry Hausner as headwaiter Edgar, played a different part each week. Sara Berner was worth her weight in laughs, whether playing a hick Southerner, giddy sorority girl, or Brooklynese telephone operator.

On Tuesday, July 29, following a weekend pool party with *The Barrel of Fun* company, Verna and the show's other performers flew in a transport plane from Hollywood to March Field in Riverside County, where Bob Hope had held his first USO show on May 6. The *Barrel of Fun* broadcast was recorded in front of an audience of 5500 officers and enlisted men. While most of the stale skits on that broadcast revolved around Mrs. Davenport pressuring Ruggles to introduce her to a colonel, Sara Berner practically stole the show as Gladys Gush, a frenetically talkative girl from Glendale. Once the recording session was finished, the troupe continued to entertain the soldiers with more jokes, songs, and even dances, prompting Hedda Hopper to report in her newspaper column a few days later: "At March Field the other night when Charles Ruggles did his air show, Benny Rubin and Verna Felton, of my air show, put on an impromptu dance with a skidding fall at the finish that had the boys applauding for four minutes, and Benny Rubin saying under his breath to Verna, 'Stay down as long as they clap—I'm winded."

Hopper's newspaper column had been spawned by her popular and fast-paced fifteen-minute CBS radio program, which for three years, beginning in 1939, featured Verna in small parts, usually as a character in the commercials for Sunkist fruits, the show's sponsor. Twenty-five years later, when Verna had gained national fame on television, she and Hopper often joked about her humble beginnings on radio. However, during this period of her radio career, Verna was not above doing commercials for other shows like *Lux Radio Theatre, Fibber McGee and Molly,* and *Good News of 1939,* with the latter featuring her as "Mrs. Lee Millar" promoting Maxwell House Coffee.

In the meantime, Lee and Verna remained in demand for regular roles on *Lux Radio Theatre.* In fact, Verna appeared in half of the *Lux* broadcasts during the 1940-41 season. If she felt any frustration about her less than burgeoning film career, then Verna could have found consolation in knowing that on *Lux* she was supporting some of the biggest names in the film industry, among them William

The *Barrel of Fun* cast rehearsing at March Field. LEFT TO RIGHT are Charlie Ruggles, Benny Rubin, Sara Berner, Harry Lang, and Verna.

Powell, Paul Muni, Irene Dunne, Carole Lombard, Rosalind Russell, Ginger Rogers, Ronald Colman, and Shirley Temple.

Notable among Verna's roles that season were Loretta Young's doting aunt in *"Jezebel,"* Jack Carson's biddy-mother in *"His Girl Friday,"* and Alice Faye's devoted grandmother in *"Lillian Russell."* While most of Verna's roles for this season were maternal, a few allowed her comic ability to shine. As Don Ameche's meek mother in *"Vivacious Lady,"* she feigns faintheartedness each time his bombastic father (Lou Merrill) goes into a characteristic tirade. In one scene, she turns out to be a "vivacious lady" of her own when she daringly attempts to dance the La Conga (sounding quite like an incarnation of her future trademark character Hilda Crocker), but abruptly swoons when her husband enters, evoking much laughter from the studio audience. Verna has a few fun moments as Carole Lombard's wisecracking nanny in *"The Moon's Our Home,"* barks orders as a pompous couturiere in *"Model Wife,"* meddles into Shirley Temple's life in *"Captain January,"* and as a rough farmwoman trades insults with Wallace Beery in *"Stablemates."* Verna was a logical choice among the stable of *Lux* supporting players for the haughty Mrs. Van Hopper in *"Rebecca,"* the adaptation of Alfred Hitchcock's 1940 film. The incomparable Florence Bates, making her film debut, had deliciously portrayed this vulgar matron in the screen version, but

Verna frolics in the pool as husband Lee (LEFT) looks on. Standing nearby are Charlie Ruggles (WEARING SUNGLASSES) and Art Gilmore (EXTREME RIGHT).

unfortunately Verna's performance of the role, though abbreviated, lacked Bates's finesse.

Verna made lasting friendships with many of the regulars who performed on *Lux*, including fourteen-year-old Dix Davis, who, over the course of four seasons, played in eighteen *Lux* productions, half of which included Verna. In 2008, at age eighty-one, his admiration for Verna was quite effusive: "I enjoyed watching her so much. She was just a consummate artist, a really fine actress, and entertaining and funny—wonderful to watch. Of all the people I worked with—and I was very lucky—I played on a lot of network shows from about '39 to '49. And of all those people, and there were some really special people whom I got to know quite well, like Frank Nelson and Bea Benaderet and Elliott Lewis and Hans Conried, Wally Maher—these are some of my special, special people—Verna was Number One. We just developed a kind of close feeling for each other so whenever we ran into each other at a rehearsal, we sort of fell into each other's arms, you know, and we'd start playing Chinese checkers right away. I don't know how we got into that [game], but we got into the habit [of playing it]. I guess it was her set. I don't think I would have dared to bring a game like that to the studio. She *loved* playing Chinese checkers, and I, too, was a fanatic in those days about that kind of thing. And so we would sit down at the rehearsals and everyone would be sort of amused at the way we were going at Chinese checkers. That's how our friendship started."

It's entirely possible that Verna and Dix initially met at a rehearsal for a show other than *Lux*, but their first mutual *Lux* appearance thoroughly cemented the bond of camaraderie. During the first week of December 1940, they were engaged to provide supporting roles for "*My Favorite Wife*," starring Rosalind Russell. Dix played her son, and Verna appeared as her sweet and gentle mother-in-law. While Russell was loads of fun, neither Verna nor Dix were impressed with the young actor playing her husband. Dix recalled, "The actor who played my father acted like an absolute idiot. He came in and he was the typical Hollywood 'new' star. I had never heard of him. And he had *orange* hair. And he acted like an absolute idiot, like an arrogant young actor would. Verna and I thought he was a riot, so we made fun of him. Guess who he was? Laurence Olivier. He was doing some movie part, obviously was in the middle of filming it. He had his hair dyed blonde, orange blonde hair. We thought he was a nut!" It's likely that Verna, who frowned on displays of artistic temperament, could have instigated the playful mocking and snickering that she shared with Dix. It would not be the last time that they were partners in crime.

Lux rehearsals were often fun in other ways. Dix recalled, "Verna was such a cut-up. She was such fun. Somebody was sort of egging her on, I guess, and she got up and did a little dance, a sort of vaudevillian turn. And she said something like, 'I may be a little fat now, but look at those legs!' And she did have beautiful legs."

Later Dix saw a very human side to Verna. "There was a blind pianist named Alec Templeton who had a show [*Alec Templeton Time*] on NBC. A lot of us appeared on that. I was in the studio, and we were getting ready for the rehearsal and Verna walked in. Alec was sitting at the piano. And Verna walked in the door, and she came over toward us. Alec was talking to someone [else]. And Verna walked by [without speaking], you know, like you don't acknowledge a blind person because you don't expect them to notice you. And so she walked by. And Alec Templeton said, 'Oh, Verna, hello.' And you know why? She was wearing violet perfume! Apparently that was her signature perfume, so much so that when she walked into the studio, he knew she was there. Poor Verna could have fallen through the floor—she was so embarrassed because she had not greeted him."

"*My Bill*," the *Lux* presentation on March 3, 1941, provided an opportunity for Verna and Dix to share some especially tender scenes. In a supporting role, she played his terminally ill neighbor Mrs. Crosby, while Dix enjoyed one of the leading roles as ten-year-old Bill, the fiercely loyal son of a widow played by Kay Francis.

"Dickie Moore was originally cast in the part of Bill," recalled Dix, "and it turned out he couldn't read. Reading lines and making it sound like you're not reading is an art. And most kids can't do it. He was used to memorizing his lines, as stage people and movie people were. So when he started to read a line it sounded like he was reading, so they had to give up on him."

Dix's performance was exceptionally natural and touchingly sweet, especially in his scenes with Verna and Kay Francis. Just as Verna had succeeded in making turn-of-the-century audience members believe she was several years younger than her true age, so did Dix in this production. Conversely, Verna as Mrs. Crosby ably affected a tone much older than her fifty years. Interestingly, young Dix, though he counted Verna as a friend, regarded her as a grandmother figure, even though she had a son only two years older than he. Verna's love for children shone through in her affection for Dix, a love that would bind them closer when tragedy would strike later that year.

Although the rumblings of war grew louder in the summer of 1941, the Millars continued to entertain friends and family around their pool. Al Blazic, a recent high school graduate, spent an eight-week vacation at 4147 Bakman Avenue that summer. He recalled one party where Lee Sr. stood poolside in a full dress suit, imitating the principal of North Hollywood High School as he addressed the teenagers gathered there. When one prankster pushed him into the pool, Al and Ferris Murdy rushed to his aid to pull him out.

Al had visited the Millars each summer since their move from Oakland. He recalled in 2005: "When I first went down [to Los Angeles to visit the Millars], we would go to radio shows. That was really fantastic! You name 'em, I saw 'em! George Burns, Jack Benny, and all of them. There was one show in Hollywood— a stage show called *Your Witness*, a murder mystery. After it was over, you decided who did it. And it wasn't always the butler! Mr. Millar was involved in that show." Also during his time "down south," Al spent vacations with the Millars at Catalina Island and on the beach at Santa Monica.

Lee and Verna both doted on Lee Jr., and they always made his friends welcome in their home. Earlier that year they had shown their affection for him by purchasing a 1940 Buick 56 S Sport Coupe from the Howard Auto Company on South Figueroa Street. At a cost of $775, Lee Jr.'s vehicle was more modern than either of his parents' cars. Perhaps their attention was a little too generous. Seemingly, Lee Jr., as an only child, had come to expect the privileges afforded him by his loving parents. And at times he could take advantage of the situation by staying out too late or sleeping until noon while his father toiled in the yard. Al Blazic considered some of Lee Jr.'s behavior quite inconsiderate: "He was always on the damn telephone talking! How the hell could Mrs. Millar get her messages across or receive calls from people in the business? He'd be on the horn all the time!"

Verna filled several incidental roles in *Lux Radio Theatre* productions in the fall of 1941, including a fun bit as Mickey Rooney's uncouth landlady in "*Merton of the Movies*" and a brief turn as Edna May Oliver's crony in "*Lydia*." In this production, Oliver, considered by many as the film industry's premier character actress, repeated her film role as Merle Oberon's lovably crotchety grandmother. Show host Cecil B. DeMille noted in his welcome that it was an honor to have Oliver on the *Lux* stage. Rarely did Hollywood's famous supporting actresses fill the supporting roles in *Lux* productions, probably because their appearances were cost prohibitive. Instead, radio performers like Claire Verdera, Noreen Gammill, Margaret Brayton, Jane Morgan, Celeste Rush, Bea Benaderet, and Verna Felton regularly supported the film stars in the radio adaptations. (While film notables Zasu Pitts and May Robson could command $1500 and $1000, respectively, for *Lux* roles, Edna May Oliver was paid $1750 for "*Lydia*," second only to Oberon.)

Joining Verna in "*Lydia*" were Dix Davis and Barbara Jean Wong, both of whom had appeared with her six months earlier in "*My Bill*." Two years older than Dix, Wong at seventeen was adept at making her voice seem much younger. She quickly became an accomplice to Verna and Dix's studio shenanigans. The production of "*Lydia*" stands out in Dix's memory: "We [Verna, Dix, and Wong] would just keep each other *in stitches*, just giggling helplessly, making fun of Merle Oberon, in this case. We would be imitating her accent. And there was someone in this play called Bob [a role reprised by film actor George Reeves], and she would always say 'Buhb.' As kids, B. J. and I made a joke out of it, and Verna entered right in on the fun. We just had so much fun, imitating poor Merle Oberon and 'Buhb.' We even imitated the way the other actors said 'Lydia.' This just gives you some insight into the kind of person [Verna] was and the relationship we had. She was such fun to be with. I wish I hadn't been so young [then] because I would have loved to know her more as a friend after I grew up."

The *Lux* offering planned for Monday, December 8, 1941, was a frivolous comedy, "*The Doctor Takes a Wife*," starring Melvyn Douglas and Virginia Bruce. Verna had a double role as a doctor's wife and a department store customer. On the day before the broadcast, as the *Lux* performers were making their way to the usual Sunday morning rehearsal, the Japanese attacked the American naval base at Pearl Harbor, Hawaii. The studio immediately transformed into a beehive of activity, with the writers fretting over presenting such a trivial production at such a time.

On the following night, a few hours after President Roosevelt signed a declaration of war against Japan, *Lux Radio Theatre* began its broadcast with a stirring orchestral rendition of "The Star Spangled Banner," followed by DeMille's introduction: "Throughout America tonight this inspired music lifts every heart to new patriotism, as all of us join all of you in pledging full allegiance to our country. We've asked the Columbia Broadcasting System to interrupt our program tonight with any important news developments. We here in *The Lux Radio Theatre*, as well as you who are listening, want to keep in touch with any and all events bearing upon this national emergency. In the meantime, this theatre carries on as usual which, as you know, is one of the oldest and finest traditions of the theatre."

Lee reacted immediately to the attack on Pearl Harbor by becoming active in civilian defense and joining the Valley Police Auxiliary. Naturally, the news of war made Lee and Verna a little nervous because of the likelihood that Lee Jr., although then too young to be drafted, would one day be called into military service. Meanwhile, Lee Jr. was enjoying his final year at North Hollywood High, as well as gaining certain fame as an actor with the Little Theater of North Hollywood.

Two weeks after the declaration of war, Verna was back on the *Lux* stage for "*Remember the Night*," adapted from the 1940 Paramount film starring Fred MacMurray and Barbara Stanwyck, and being performed for the second time on *Lux*. The previous radio production, broadcast on March 25, 1940, featured MacMurray, Stanwyck, Beulah Bondi, Elizabeth Patterson, and Sterling Holloway, all recreating their excellent screen characterizations. The plot focused on Lee Leander (Stanwyck), an embittered shoplifter who learns the true meaning of love when she spends Christmas with the family of the assistant district attorney (MacMurray) who will prosecute her for her crime. Bondi portrayed the mother of the attorney, while Patterson played his spinster aunt, and Holloway their farm hand.

With Pearl Harbor still fresh in the minds of listeners, DeMille alluded to the new war in his introduction for the second presentation of "*Remember the Night*" on Monday, December 22, 1941: "*Remember the Night* is a the story of what makes the wheels go round in American life, ordinary American life, a way of life that won't be stopped by *anything*."

Unfortunately, the production lacked the charm of its initial presentation the year before. While MacMurray and Bondi returned for their original roles, the replacements for Stanwyck, Holloway, and Patterson failed to equal their predecessors. Jean Arthur, in the lead role, sounds too meek and countrified for the streetwise Lee Leander, and Felix Vallee in the role of Bondi's farmhand is embarrassingly inept.

Verna, as spinster Aunt Emma, was unable to duplicate the folksy charm of the delightful Patterson, whose rural Tennessee upbringing lent itself so well to the part. Patterson's Aunt Emma was more breathless and fluttery, full of just the right vocal inflections and other little touches so important in character parts. To Verna's credit, however, the role had been whittled down considerably for this second go-round, so she had less time to shine than Patterson. Despite Verna's attempts at a rural accent, the results were inevitable; the timbre of her voice is strikingly different from that of Patterson or Bondi. (For the previous production, Patterson had been paid $500, whereas Verna was paid $86 for an abbreviated version of the same role; even supporting film players could command as much as six to nine times more than the AFRA artists. Interestingly, this was not always the case. For instance, Clara Blandick, a veteran of over one hundred films, was paid scale for her performances on *Lux Radio Theatre*, including "*The Moon's Our Home*," which also featured Verna.)

However, others in the second production's cast exceeded those actors playing the counterpart roles in the previous broadcast. Bea Benaderet was very effective as the callous, hateful mother of Lee Leander, and Arthur Q. Bryan was superb as the blustery defense attorney. The production was also notable because it was the fourth and final occasion for Verna and Lee to appear together on the *Lux* stage. While Lee's distinguished voice could be heard briefly as a waiter, he also gave an excellent performance as a wailing dog inside the cold, ramshackle home of Lee Leander's mother.

Sadly, "*Remember the Night*" would be the final performance in Lee's illustrious career. Two days before this performance, Verna sent an ailing Lee to her physician Dr. Carl E. Lund, who diagnosed him with hypertension and told him to rest. So none of them was prepared for what followed a few days later. Around 11 o'clock on the morning of Christmas Eve, just after Verna and Lee had finished trimming their tree, Lee suffered a cerebral hemorrhage. Rushed to the Glendale Sanatorium and Hospital, he died soon after being admitted. Lee was only fifty-three, just one year younger than his father's age at death.

Friends and colleagues assembled for the funeral, which was held on the afternoon of December 27 at the Vernon F. Steen Chapel on Magnolia Boulevard in North Hollywood. Newlyweds Pearl and Violet Allen and Lee's half-brother Jack Millar were in attendance, as were the Blazics who made the trip down from Oakland.

Widowed at fifty-one, Verna had now lost four close relatives in less than four years. While Clara's death had been anticipated, as well as the demise of Verna's brothers given their own unfortunate situations, Lee's sudden passing was a fierce blow to Verna. Lee had been her rock. Their marriage had spanned eighteen happy years, half of them being rather lean ones, which had only drawn them closer. Alone, Verna would now have to provide all moral and physical support of Lee Jr., a seventeen-year-old high school senior, mourning the loss of the father he adored. Lee Millar's untimely death marked a sharp turning point in the life of Verna Felton, but she would rise to the challenge with courage and determination.

CHAPTER 11

WAR, WIDOWHOOD, AND RED

In November 1942, while vacationing in the California desert, newspaper columnist Hedda Hopper wrote a note of thanks to Verna for a recent gift: "What a sweet thing you were to buy me those hankies. I can't tell you how much I appreciate them. And I want you to know how much I love you. I may have met in my many years of living people as brave as you, but I don't remember who they were. The way you've carried on your work since your husband's death is an example everyone should follow. And while I haven't said much about it, believe me, I've thought about it a great deal. And I want you to know that you've made a real place in my heart."

Indeed, during the difficult months since Christmas 1941, Verna had faced life head on, and though she was hurting, not once did she shirk those career obligations already in place before Lee's death. In a *Radio Mirror* article published in January 1948, Verna recalled this difficult period, "I kept sane those first few months by working harder that I had ever worked in my life. Work continued to be the only way out."

Dix Davis, her young buddy from *Lux Radio Theatre* and other shows, recalled vividly her first appearance at an NBC rehearsal following her loss: "I'm not absolutely sure of the show, except that I can see the studio. It was Studio D, the largest studio in the building . . . It was a big show, and there were a lot of players. I remember Joe Kearns and Paula Winslowe and a lot of players were there. If I remember this correctly, I came and I was on time. And we were sitting around, and Verna hadn't come yet. And everybody was sort of hushed and speaking kind of quietly. And I don't know whether they told me then, or whether I learned later [that Verna had just lost her husband] . . . She came in late, and the whole cast was sort of *hushed*. They didn't want to talk to her. I mean, they didn't know what to say. She was [following] the classic [credo], 'the show must go on.' And she came in, and I greeted her and we sat right down and started playing Chinese checkers. And she didn't say anything to anybody else, and nobody said anything to her. And we just played Chinese checkers. And later somebody came up to me—I want to think [it was] Bea Benaderet, but it could have been somebody else—and said, 'That was the *best* thing you could have possibly done.' They weren't even sure she was coming in. She was very grief-stricken. Everybody in that group of radio players in those days adored Verna, and so they were very concerned."

Before Verna could probate Lee's will, which he had written eleven months before his death, she had to fulfill other obligations. Already scheduled for January, 1942, was the cutting of an additional thirteen transcriptions for her syndicated show, *The Barrel of Fun*, its new installments shortened to fifteen-minutes. In addition, Verna had signed to appear on *Lux Radio Theatre* for several upcoming broadcasts, the first being "*Smilin' Through*" on January 5, in which she appeared as the servant of Brian Aherne.

Four days later when Verna probated Lee's will, listing her as the only heir, she met an unexpected roadblock. Even though Lee Jr. had not been named as an heir, the law entitled him to receive a part of his father's estate. However, this could not take place until after Lee Jr. became of legal age. Consequently, legal matters regarding the estate could not proceed for another three and one half years. Nevertheless, Verna still had to pay taxes on the real estate and the automobiles, not to mention meeting their living expenses. Fortunately, she had no monthly mortgage payment. At the time of Lee's death, they owned 4147 Bakman Avenue, now valued at $7650, free and clear. However, her bank account with just over $3000 was monitored because, as joint tenancy, it was considered part of Lee's estate. It was quite obvious to Verna that she must endeavor to locate more radio work.

On January 12, Verna would give one of the most amazing performances of her career. She had been chosen for the villainous role of Madame Defarge in the *Lux* production of Charles Dickens's "*A Tale of Two Cities*," starring the gifted Ronald Colman, who reprised his role of Sydney Carton from the splendid 1935 MGM film production. Colman, in this radio adaptation, again seems born to play Carton. His mellifluous voice and that of his fellow Britisher, the production's leading lady Edna Best, make a stark contrast to Verna's gruff, embittered tones as Madame Defarge.

Hell-bent on revenge for the atrocities performed on her family by the aristocratic Evremonde brothers, Defarge harbors a secret hatred for every member of the offending family. In a climactic scene, during which one of the Evremondes is on trial, Defarge delivers a damning testimony that sends the man to the guillotine. In a voice that resonates with determination and scorn, Verna's stirring speech runs almost four minutes, escalating in volume and emotion until the final revelation.

Despite her excellent characterization, Verna's status as a secondary radio performer prevented her from sharing the customary post-performance on-air chat between Cecil B. DeMille and the film stars. However, she later confided to Al Blazic that once they were off the air, DeMille came to her bestowing praise, a commodity he rarely offered to *Lux* regulars.

For the rest of the season, Verna kept busy with *Lux* roles, although none were either meaty or memorable, with the possible exception of Mrs. Lydia Sandow in "*One Foot in Heaven*," broadcast on April 20. Mrs. Sandow is the wealthy parishioner of Methodist minister William Spence, played by Fredric March. He calls on her to ask for a sizable donation, but upon finding her not at home, he has a friendly visit with her gardener. When the self-righteous Mrs. Sandow learns of this, she forbids the clergyman to call on her servant because it puts her and him on the "same social plane." Spence refuses to comply with her mandate, and Mrs. Sandow huffs, "You are no longer my pastor. From this day on, I'm a Baptist!" (Instantly, the sound technician simulated a door slam, and the live audience responded with genuine laughter.) Months later, not to be outdone by other wealthy parishioners' gifts, a repentant Mrs. Sandow, in a childlike voice, asks to return to the fold, "I'll be good." (More laughter.)

In the meantime, three months had passed since America's entry in World War Two. Each week men from the radio industry, whether having performed in front of the mike or behind the scenes, were joining the armed forces. Their sacrifices did not go unnoticed by the women in their industry. Led by Verna, a group of volunteers, including actresses, secretaries, and wives of actors, organized the Radio Women's War Relief on March 26, 1942. Their mission was to communicate weekly via mail with those from the industry now serving as soldiers, sending them news of the careers they left behind. The women adopted the men as "godsons," remembering them each month with a package of soap, stationery, flints, lip ice, handkerchiefs, cigarettes, and trade papers. It is significant to note that the women's patriotic response to the war predated the days of rationing, which President Roosevelt would introduce a month later.

The original officers of the Radio Women's War Relief were Verna Felton, president; actress Mary Lansing, first vice-president; Helen McNear (wife of actor Howard McNear), second vice-president; Hazel Delphine, treasurer; Betty Buckler, secretary; Edna Payne (wife of actor Bruce Payne), recording secretary. The executive board consisted of actresses Lurene Tuttle, Jane Morgan, and Sara Berner, as well as Violet MacKaye, wife of radio actor Fred MacKaye, and Ruth Caton, wife of sound effects technician Floyd Caton. Other notable members include actresses Elvia Allman, Gloria Blondell, Mercedes McCambridge, Sharon Douglas, Pauline Drake, and Mary Astor.

Originally the Radio Women's War Relief met monthly in Verna's rumpus room, where they wrote letters and knitted gifts of sweaters, gloves, and socks for the servicemen. Knitting had been one of Verna's favorite pastimes since her youth, when an older actress advised her to try it as a way to pass time backstage. But Jane Morgan was the club's champion crocheter, donating multiple afghans for fundraising auctions. The group expended over $2300 in their first year alone. When the organization, renamed as the Radio Women's War Service, outgrew Verna's rumpus room, they made their headquarters at the Crossroads of the World (now known as Los Angeles's first shopping center), located on

Volunteers of the Radio Women's War Relief meet in Verna's rumpus room, 1942. Left to right are Alice Geronimi, Violet MacKaye, Verna, Helen McNear, Lurene Tuttle, and Sara Berner.

Sunset Boulevard in Hollywood. The RWWS met there on the third Friday night of each month. In one year the RWWS had grown to include 129 members who endeavored to furnish small comforts to 295 soldiers, sailors, and marines in places as far away as India, Iceland, New Guinea, Africa, Alaska, and the Fiji Islands.

Between radio rehearsals Verna spent many hours on the telephone, directing the organization's activities. She recalled those days, "We took care of all the boys overseas. Anything they wanted. One boy wanted golf balls, at one time, and we sent him a box of golf balls. [We tried to get them] anything they wanted or [find] somebody they wanted to get in touch with. Or if they'd be coming in, on a [furlough], and get up by New York, we'd say, 'So-and-so and So-and-so and So-and-so and So-and-so are there. Maybe you could get a job.' And they'd shoot in there, get a radio job or something, you know, before they'd go back."

In the meantime, Verna was anticipating Lee Jr.'s upcoming graduation from North Hollywood High School. With his college tuition a future concern, Verna realized that she needed to supplement her earnings from the evening shows like *Lux* and *The Pepsodent Show Starring Bob Hope*. When she heard of auditions for the lead in a syndicated daytime soap opera called *Aunt Mary*, Verna was one of the first to try out. The character of Mary Lane, according to radio historian John Dunning, was a "wise old lady philosopher who lived on 'Willow Creek Road'

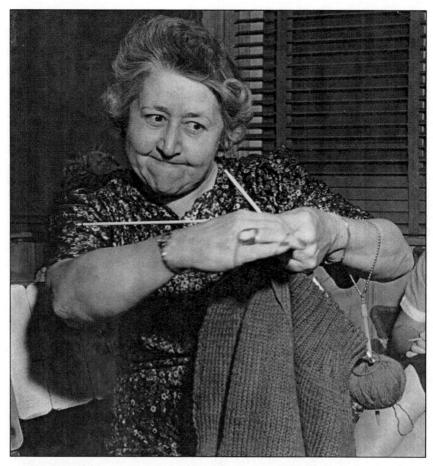

Verna knits herself into a frenzy in an effort to aid US servicemen.

and displayed great character in the *Ma Perkins* mold." The writers and director already had in mind just the type of voice they wanted for this generous, motherly character.

However, Verna's audition did not go well. During Marty Halperin's interview in 1964, Verna amusingly recreated the dialogue between her and the man conducting this audition.

In a melodramatic voice, she imitated the man as he interrupted her audition, "No! No, no, no, no! You bring me no *earth*! You give me no *earth*!"

Verna replied uncertainly, "You want *earth*?"

"Yes, I must feel *clods* in your voice! You have no clods in your voice." He suggested, "Why don't you go outside and sit down and *read* and *think* of *clods* and get the clods in your voice and *maybe* we can do it."

Trying not to laugh at the silly man's dramatics, Verna resignedly confessed, "No, I don't think I'll be able to get clods in my voice."

Verna arranging a project for the Radio Women's War Service.

As Verna exited into the waiting room, she saw fellow character actress Myra Marsh who was there to audition for the same part.

"What's going on in there?" Marsh asked.

"Go on in, Myra. They want someone who has *clods* in their voice," replied Verna.

"*Clods?*" exclaimed Marsh. "I'll give 'em *fertilizer!*"

When the auditions failed to provide a suitable actress for the part of Aunt Mary, someone suggested Jane Morgan, Verna's best friend in the radio industry. Morgan's audition was actually conducted via her home telephone, as Verna explained to Halperin: "He made her write down this whole [scene and then read it back to him over the telephone], which *I wouldn't have done*, and *nobody* [else] would have done, but Janie is so sweet, she *would* do it. And she did it, and *she* got the part!"

Meanwhile, as the Lux season wound down to its close, Verna landed a part on *Tommy Riggs and Betty Lou*, a summer replacement series for *The George Burns and Gracie Allen Show*. (Verna had appeared as one of Gracie's fellow clubwomen during that show's 1941-42 season.) Broadcast on Tuesday nights at nine, *Tommy Riggs and Betty Lou* was a situation comedy based on characters which actor Tommy Riggs had developed over the past decade.

According to radio historian John Dunning, "Riggs had a condition that doctors at the Cornell Medical Center, after X-raying his throat, described as bi-vocalism. This meant that Riggs could talk in his own voice—a deep baritone—or could assume the voice of a 7-year-old girl." Thus, Betty Lou was born. In earlier radio incarnations, she had simply been a little girl who appeared from nowhere, but in this sitcom, she was Riggs's niece.

Also heard in the show were Wally Maher as Betty Lou's nasal playmate Wilbur Hutch, Bea Benaderet as snooty neighbor Mrs. Wingate, Mel Blanc (using his Sylvester the Cat voice) as Uncle Petey, and Elvia Allman and Margaret Brayton as "the gabby gals on the telephone." Verna, employing an impressively authentic Irish accent, appeared as Riggs's talkative and outspoken housekeeper Mrs. MacIntyre.

The show debuted on CBS on July 7 and proved to be a popular favorite, doubtlessly due to its talented cast. It also afforded Verna the opportunity to keep in touch with one of her fellow *Lux* players, Bea Benaderet, who was practically Verna's neighbor, living about a half mile away on Moorpark Street in North Hollywood.

Another fun summer assignment was an occasional appearance on the *Rudy Vallee* program, broadcast on Thursday nights on NBC. The show's producer and writers had decided to forego their usual summer vacation, so for five weeks Groucho Marx was Rudy Vallee's guest star. On one of these shows, Verna played Marx's foil, a "military-minded screwball" Mrs. Ack-Ack Ackerman, for whom Vallee and his regular Joan Davis tried to arrange a date with Marx. In a most authoritative voice, Mrs. Ackerman makes Marx her "military objective" for the evening, with less than successful results. After their date, she asks Marx if he had ever been to a barn dance before. He replies, "Yeah, but this is the first time I ever danced with the barn itself!" Undaunted, Mrs. Ackerman fires a round of questions about Marx's military experience. When she asks if he has ever fired a machine gun, she punctuates her query with a questionable imitation of that weapon. Adlibbing, Marx comments, "Sounds more like a goat! Looks like the enemy's pretty safe." When Marx says he enjoys military "engagements," Ackerman suggests they make it a short one. "Okay," he replies, "Consider the engagement off."

On Monday, July 20, Verna's fifty-second birthday, she was part of the cast of the *Victory Theatre*, a summer series designed to raise money for the war effort. Each of several CBS series contributed one program during this summer run. In its first installment, the *Victory Theatre* presented "*The Philadelphia Story*,"

Mrs. MacIntyre (Verna), who eats everything in sight, wrestles a lollipop from Wilbur (Wally Maher) on *Tommy Riggs and Betty Lou*.

starring Cary Grant, Katharine Hepburn, and James Stewart. The studio audience enjoyed an amusing exchange between Stewart and Verna, playing the part of a soft-spoken librarian. Although not officially part of the *Lux Radio Theatre*, the broadcast followed the *Lux* format. Instead of commercials for Lux soap, there was a public service announcement for war bonds, in which Verna portrayed spokeswoman Mrs. Brown.

On this same evening, Lee Jr. had thoughtfully planned a special surprise for his mother, this being her first birthday without Lee Sr. Following the broadcast of "*The Philadelphia Story*," he took Verna out to dinner. During the interim, forty-five guests gathered at Bakman Avenue to await the Millars' arrival home. The surprise party that followed was among Verna's most memorable birthdays, and the guest list read like a Who's Who of Old Time Radio. Among those in attendance were members of the *Lux Radio Theatre* crew and players, including director Sandy Barnett and his wife Roberta; writer George Wells; announcer Melville Ruick and his wife, actress Lurene Tuttle; actor Ferdinand Munier and his wife, actress Charlotte Treadway; actor Bruce Payne and his wife Edna; actor Fred MacKaye and his wife Violet; actress Duane Thompson and her husband Bill Johnson; and actress Bea Benaderet and her husband, radio announcer Jim Bannon. From Verna's *Barrel of Fun* days came actress Sara Berner; actor Hanley Stafford and his wife Viola; and announcer Art Gilmore and his wife Grace. Representing the Radio Women's War Relief were four of Verna's best buddies: Jane Morgan; Helen Rourke; Helen McNear and her husband, actor Howard McNear; and Ruth Caton and her husband, sound technician Floyd Caton. Completing the guest list were the Millars' old friends, film actor Bradley Page and his wife Olive; radio producer Jim Fonda and wife Margaret; radio announcer Wendell Niles; Verna's doctor, Carl Lund and his wife; and Lee Jr.'s schoolmates Caddie Condon, Ferris Murdy, Duncan McKellar, and Jay Moss.

Two months later, Lee Jr. (hereunder referred to simply as Lee) enrolled as an eighteen-year-old freshman speech major at the University of Southern California. Although acting was definitely in his blood, Lee would become the first member of his family to study the dramatic arts in an academic setting. Teasingly, Verna would not let Lee forget that there was a time when he eschewed the acting profession. Once when he was a little boy, he had told Verna that he wished she were a store clerk instead of an actress.

Before Lee could become oriented to academia, his mother arranged for him to become a member of the cast of a *Lux* production of "*The Magnificent Dope*," starring Henry Fonda and Don Ameche. Although his part as a photographer consisted of only three lines, Lee earned $81.50, the same amount his mother earned for her brief part as Fonda's folksy mother.

Verna's other *Lux* roles that fall included an authoritative WAC sergeant in "*This Above All*," the meddlesome aunt of William Powell (who says she's like a mother-in-law to him) in "*Love Crazy*," the earthy Irish mother of Van Johnson in "*The War Against Mrs. Hadley*," and a gushing, giggling clubwoman seeking advice ("I always seem to have a great deal of trouble putting on those little rubber panties") from Bob Hope, a vaudevillian she mistakes for a pediatrician in "*My Favorite Blonde*."

One of Verna's most effective *Lux* characterizations that season was Judy Garland's crusty old granny in "*A Star Is Born*," which aired on December 28, 1942. Granny secretly finances the star-struck farmgirl's dream to make it big in Hollywood, but warns that she must never give up her dream no matter what trials come. Several years later, when Esther Blodgett has become a successful but unhappy movie star, it is the old lady who suddenly arrives to inspire her to continue her career. Interestingly, Verna's friend Jane Morgan plays an unsympathetic member of the family, Aunt Mattie, who sharply criticizes Esther's dreams.

Yet another *Lux* role brought Verna a bit of spontaneous recognition that fall. On November 9, she played a small supporting role of an old maid named Zeffie in "*Sullivan's Travels*," starring Veronica Lake and Ralph Bellamy. *Radio Life* reported that Verna "received an enthusiastic hand as she left the microphone. After the broadcast, Cecil B. DeMille came up to her and said: 'Verna, in the history of *Lux*, nothing like that has ever happened. May I congratulate you!'"

In addition to her Monday night appearances on Lux, Verna was a regular on five other series in the fall of 1942. First, she continued in her role of Hattie Hirsch on *Point Sublime*, also broadcast on Mondays but recently moved to the Don Lee-Mutual network. In the meantime, *Tommy Riggs and Betty Lou*, an audience favorite that summer, had been picked up for the fall season by its sponsor Lever Brothers, but moved from CBS to NBC. On Friday, October 9, Verna returned to that show in her role of housekeeper Mrs. MacIntyre, as did Bea Benaderet, Wally Maher, and Mel Blanc in their respective roles. Thirdly, Verna appeared regularly on *Today at the Duncans*, a fifteen-minute situation comedy heard thrice weekly on CBS. Frank Nelson and his wife-actress Mary Lansing played John and Mary Duncan, while Verna's buddy Dix Davis played their ten-year-old son Dinky. According to John Dunning, stories revolved around "planning meals with an eye on the ration book, driving to and from town on limited gas and rubber, and lending a hand to the war effort."

On October 25, Verna joined the cast of a delightful situation comedy *The Great Gildersleeve*—her fourth regular series that season—then in its second season on NBC. Although she had only made a single guest appearance on this show during its first season (as bossy neighbor Mrs. Beasley), writer John Whedon created a recurring role for her the following year.

Hal Peary starred as blustery Throckmorton P. Gildersleeve, a character he had originated on *Fibber McGee and Molly*. The ensemble cast of *The Great Gildersleeve* also included the fine talents of Lurene Tuttle and Walter Tetley as Gildersleeve's sophisticated niece Marjorie and acerbic nephew Leroy, Shirley Mitchell as honey-throated Southern belle Leila Ransom, Earle Ross as the irritable Judge Horace Hooker, Richard LeGrand as sniveling druggist Mr. Peavey, and the superbly authentic Lillian Randolph as Birdie Lee Coggins, Gildersleeve's Negro cook and housekeeper.

When Gildersleeve was hired as the town water commissioner in the fall of 1942, he soon found that the department was actually operated by its secretary, an "old hatchet-face" named Miss Fitch, played with matter-of-fact, rapid fire delivery by Verna. Miss Fitch, whose father had been the first water commissioner, ran a tight ship. Her no-nonsense attitude did not mix well with Gildersleeve's loquacity, frequently punctuated by his trademark chuckle. ("You're a harrrrd woman, Miss Fitch!") After two months, just when their relationship was beginning to become somewhat cordial, Miss Fitch suddenly and without explanation disappeared from the show. It didn't seem to matter that Miss Fitch, a thirty-three-year veteran in the department, had been depicted as a very unlikely candidate to voluntarily leave her post. However, three weeks later, on January 17, Gildersleeve began interviewing prospects for her replacement. He hired Bessie Barstow—played by Pauline Drake—a ditzy young lady in utter contrast to her efficient predecessor.

It is interesting to note that Verna had been associated with an earlier incarnation of the Gildersleeve character when she played the wife of Homer Gildersleeve on the February 21, 1939, broadcast of *Fibber McGee and Molly*. Hal Peary gave voice to Homer, the toastmaster of the Wistful Vista Rotowanis Club. On the evening of their annual steak banquet, when Homer's wife mistakes Fibber McGee as the club's guest speaker, McGee is eager to take the podium, as long as it means he'll be invited to dine with them. Interestingly, Peary would play a succession of Gildersleeves until the writers finally decided upon the given name of Throckmorton, actually named for Peary's street address back in Chicago. When "Gildy" became such a popular character, one of radio's earliest spin-offs was born, and Hal Peary was given his own show, *The Great Gildersleeve*, which began in August 1941.

The Rudy Vallee Show, Verna's fifth regular series for the 1942 fall line-up, would eventually provide her with one of her most famous radio roles ever. Rudy's show, sponsored by Sealtest, was broadcast on NBC on Thursday nights. No stranger to Vallee, Verna had appeared on his show as early as August 14, 1941. She played Cassandra, the irascible maid to series regular John Barrymore, the former screen idol who was by then in seriously declining health. When Barrymore died the next spring near the end of that season, the producers decided to revamp Vallee's variety show for the upcoming 1942-43 season.

In the show's new format, the suave Vallee became the proprietor of a village store, often visited by guest stars like Hedda Hopper, Basil Rathbone, George Jessel, Bert Lahr, and Lucille Ball. Comedienne Joan Davis, Vallee's guest star for eight weeks in late 1941, had been hired as a permanent member of the cast in January 1942. As the show's chief buffoon, she returned to support Vallee the following fall, along with three new zanies. Shirley Mitchell was signed to play Shirley Anne, the "village belle," who competed with Davis for Vallee's affections, while burlesque comedian Gil Lamb came aboard as goofy Homer Clinker, who carried a torch for Davis. But Verna's character would become the most outrageous and enduring addition.

Mrs. Two-Ton Greenbacker was a wealthy old widow who frequented the store. As her name indicated, she was rather overweight. Naturally, fat jokes abounded, fueled by Davis. While Davis, Lamb, and Mitchell received air credit for their roles, the actress playing Mrs. Greenbacker remained anonymous. Frequent radio listeners might have recognized that voice as Dennis Day's mother or Mrs. MacIntyre from *Tommy Riggs and Betty Lou*, but eventually the true identity of Mrs. Greenbacker's portrayer slipped into the press.

On November 12, 1942, the *Wisconsin State Journal* unflatteringly listed "Two Ton Verna Felton" as a member of the Vallee show. Verna took it all in stride. She

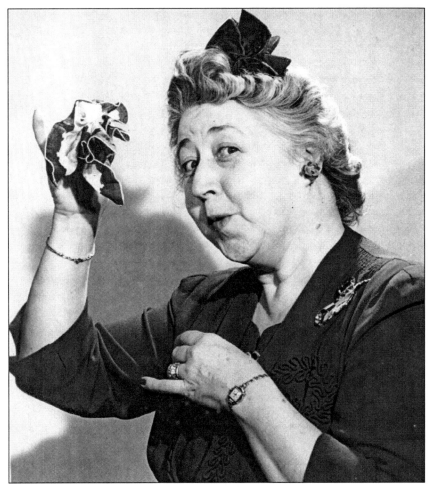

YooHoo! The original press snipe for this 1943 photo of Verna reads: "Working on the theory that love never comes too late, Blossom Blimp is very much the romantic on NBC's Rudy Vallee program."

would be the first to admit that she had let her figure go, and despite the frequent fat jokes, Verna enjoyed parts like Two Ton Greenbacker. In fact, she capitalized on it. Not only her voice but also her bulk helped Verna to easily lasso the parts of domineering old battleaxes or jolly dumplings like Mrs. Greenbacker.

Mrs. Greenbacker's stock holdings in wheat, copper, and railroads were inherited from her late husband. And despite her age, the old girl was still on the prowl. A self-professed romantic, she flirted with every male guest star on the show, hoping to make each one her future spouse. Mrs. Greenbacker was also somewhat of a misguided poet. Each week she recited a rather kittenish poem, afterward punctuated by a chipper "Woo! Woo!"

Early in 1943, Mrs. Greenbacker suddenly disappeared, and in her place was another wealthy matron, every bit as husky but endowed with a more lyrical name: Blossom Blimp. Her voice was exactly identical to that of the departed Mrs. Greenbacker. However, Blossom Blimp was bubblier, in fact at times quite shrill. Blossom's days as a coquette were far behind her, but "Blimpy," as the other regulars called her, was totally unaware of the fact. She frequently wore her graying hair tied up in girlish ribbons and fairly skipped into the store each week.

As a patron of the arts, Blossom Blimp was eager to spread culture among her fellow man. Instead of reciting poetry, however, she preferred works put to music. Each week she sang a little ditty, which she managed to work into the plot of the show. Originally, Verna chose from the repertoire of silly songs she had sung forty years earlier when she was a member of the Jessie Shirley Company and later the Allen Stock Company.

By the early spring of 1943, when Gil Lamb departed the Vallee show to pursue work in films and nightclubs, Blossom Blimp was rewarded with a beefier part. Consequently, the show's writers brought the character more up-to-date, substituting parodies of contemporary tunes for Verna's vaudevillian numbers.

Frequent guests on the Vallee show included some of Hollywood's best-known character players, including Joe E. Brown, George Tobias, Edward Everett Horton, and Arthur Treacher. The appearance of one such player stood out in Verna's memory twenty years later. Sixty-four-year-old Donald Meek, who made a screen career of playing milquetoasts, was cast against type as Shirley Mitchell's wacky uncle who proved to be somewhat of a wolf on the May 13, 1943, broadcast.

Verna recalled for Marty Halperin a mishap during Meek's appearance: "We had a cute little actor in the show once, Donald Meek. And we were working with him, and his dentures were a little bit loose, you know. Joanie was [at her microphone] across from him, and I was [beside him on the other microphone]. And all of a sudden he said something to Joanie, and he *spit*! And as he did, his dentures came right out of his mouth! Just like they were going into the [air]. He grabbed them and as he put them back in his mouth, [they went] 'click, click, click, click, click, click, click!' [When] Joanie saw them, *she just died*! She just turned and put her head down, [laughing]. Well, Rudy, is *such* a gentleman, you know, and always tries to [save embarrassment] for people. So he got up and started to talk, you know. Joanie couldn't talk! She said if you had ever seen those white things coming across the microphone at her. She said she *nearly* died. So the orchestra went on; Rudy turned around and started the orchestra. And they played a little bit until she got herself calmed, and then we were all right."

In 2005, Shirley Mitchell, whom Verna knew from *The Great Gildersleeve*, recalled the fun they shared on the *Rudy Vallee* show. "I adored Verna. We always had dinner in between shows [one broadcast early for the East Coast and a later show performed for the West Coast]. She kept us laughing constantly. She was a dear and wonderful actress."

Jack Haley (LEFT) and Blossom Blimp (Verna) feel left out as Shirley Mitchell and Joan Davis kiss Rudy Vallee goodbye on his final broadcast before joining the Coast Guard, 1943.

Mitchell left the *Rudy Vallee Program* at the end of the season, and so did the series star. Since the previous August, Vallee had been bandmaster for the 11th Naval District Coast Guard Band, generously contributing his radio salary to the Coast Guard welfare fund. When he was promoted from chief petty officer to lieutenant, Vallee decided to leave his radio show on July 1, 1943, due to the extra duties involved with the forty-piece band. Sealtest, the show's sponsor, chose Joan Davis to run Vallee's radio show for the duration, but still felt the show needed a male lead. Jack Haley was hired for that position, and the show was renamed *Sealtest Village Store*, set to open in August.

Verna continued to appear in small roles on *Lux Radio Theatre* throughout the 1942-43 season, mostly as a no-nonsense authority figure, such as an executive secretary in *"She Knew All the Answers,"* an orphanage matron in *"Are Husbands Necessary?,"* and a crusty but soft-hearted child welfare worker in *"The Lady Is Willing."*

In the meantime, Verna returned to the *Jack Benny Program* for its opening broadcast on October 4, 1942, making her annual appearance as Mrs. Day. Even though she continued to receive no air credit for the part, Verna had become so identified with Mrs. Day that she was never used for other roles on the Benny show. This changed in the spring of 1943, when Benny, ill with a severe case of pneumonia, chose Orson Welles to fill in for four weeks. Verna appeared as Welles's no-nonsense private secretary Miss Harrington, spraying the microphone with antiseptic before his arrival and taking dictation left and right after he assumes command of the broadcast.

Meanwhile, by May 1943, Lee had completed his first year in the Junior College program at USC. Caught up in the patriotic zeal sweeping the nation, he immediately enrolled in the university's newly established Navy College Training Program (Navy V-12 Unit). The program allowed students to complete degrees at civilian universities and earn commissions in the Navy and Marine Corps.

With Lee away from home most of the time, Verna kept busy in her spare time with the Radio Women's War Service. She also befriended her new next-door neighbors, the Stelters, who moved into the house at 4151 Bakman Avenue in 1943. Alex Stelter was born in Arizona in 1915; he had moved to Los Angeles five years earlier to pursue an acting career. Al's wife Margaret, whom he nicknamed "Trudy," was expecting their second child. Their daughter, a curly-haired blonde named Dolores, but called Dolly, was born July 11, 1942, about a year before becoming Verna's neighbor.

Verna, ever fond of children, longed to become a grandmother. In Dolly she found the perfect surrogate grandchild to shower with attention. The little girl freely returned Verna's affections, and when she began to talk, dubbed Verna as "DeeDee." From then on, all children who knew Verna well were invited to call her DeeDee. Dolly's little brother Steven Lee Stelter, named in honor of Verna's son, was born on September 27, 1943. These children and their parents became like Verna's own family.

In 2008, Dolores Stelter Neese recalled: "My parents moved to Bakman [Avenue] when I was one year old. My father was a struggling actor at the time, and he went by the name Clarke Stevens. He also was a stuntman, and it was his big dream to get into the movies. Well, DeeDee took a shine to this young family and tried to help my dad as much as she could. We were all very close. There was an elderly woman named Connie who lived with DeeDee. My brother was her favorite, and I was DeeDee's favorite. DeeDee liked us so much that—there was a fence that separated our properties—and she made a gate in that fence so that we could just come in and go as we pleased. I remember I still have pictures of my third birthday party, which DeeDee hosted. We were just always over there. My brother and I learned how to swim in her pool . . . She was a *wonderful* woman! She *loved* children! She just loved children! In the summer there would be seven or eight kids there every day, swimming in the pool. If she wasn't out there, her son was, or somebody was. We just had a wonderful time!"

"There was a period of time after I was born and while we were still living on Bakman, when my dad went into the USO. He had already been in the army in the mid-1930s. I guess because maybe he had already been in the army, he didn't have to go into fighting [during World War Two]. He [joined] the USO and went up to Alaska and had a sword-fighting show with his stuntman-partner. And I think Verna actually helped us [financially] at that point because my mother was not working then . . . And because she loved me so much, she wanted me to be a little model. So she got me my one and only modeling job. That was my

"DeeDee" and Dolly posing at the rear of the Stelter home, 1943.

short-lived modeling career! She was a genuine person with an *enormous* heart! She just did things for people and was so genuine . . . Those were just incredible years. They were magic."

Jack Benny's gang poses for a final picture before summer hiatus, May 31, 1942. LEFT TO RIGHT: (SITTING) **Verna Felton, Dix Davis, Jack Benny, Mary Livingstone, Sam Hearn, Blanche Stewart.** (STANDING) **Murray Bolen, sponsor's representative; Andy Devine, Ed Beloin, writer; Eddie "Rochester" Anderson, Bill Morrow, writer; Dennis Day, Phil Harris, and Harry Baldwin.**

The 1943-44 radio season proved to be one of Verna's busiest. She made eleven appearances that season on *Lux Radio Theatre.* Her outstanding roles included a fluttery society woman charmed by gambler Cary Grant in "*Mr. Lucky,*" Shirley Temple's meddling governess in "*Kathleen,*" and Betty Grable's wisecracking agent in "*Springtime in the Rockies.*"

On December 12, Verna made her only appearance on the Jack Benny program for the season, giving her best performance ever as Dennis Day's mother. The broadcast is noteworthy because Verna delivered a line that produced one of the longest laughs in the history of the show. The script called for Mrs. Day to enter the studio complaining to the ticket taker about Dennis's measly salary ($35 per show). Of Benny's frugality, she grouses, "Why, he's so cheap he sharpens his pencil in front of the fireplace so the wood won't go to waste!" Mrs. Day takes her seat on the front row of the studio audience, vowing to Dennis that she'll demand a pay raise for him from Benny at the close of the show.

After Dennis sings his number, Benny compliments him, saying he sounds better and better each week. From the background comes a cry hurled with all the fierceness of an angry baseball fan. "Then why don't you give 'im a raise!"

bellows Mrs. Day. Benny instantly recognizes her voice, but pretends to ignore her heckling by responding, "I'm sorry, madam, no autographs today." He tries to continue with the show when Dennis approaches.

DENNIS
"Oh, Mr. Benny?"

BENNY
"What, Dennis?"

DENNIS
"Guess who's sitting in the front row?"

BENNY
"I know, I know. I heard her."

DENNIS
"She wants to talk to you after the show."

BENNY
"I know she does. Now go sit down."

DENNIS
"It's about my salary."

BENNY
"Dennis, go over and *sit* down!"

MRS. DAY
"Stop *pushing* him!"

BENNY
"I'm not pushing him! And anyway, Mrs. Day,
you're not supposed to talk while the program's going on.

MRS. DAY
"My boy just sang, didn't he?"

BENNY
"Yes."

MRS. DAY
"Well, as far as I'm concerned, the *program's* over!"

BENNY

"Of all the nerve. And now, ladies and gentlemen—"

MRS. DAY

"Ahhhhhhhhhhhhhhhhh, shut up!"

Verna's delivery of the above line was filled with such punch and volume that the live audience rocked the studio with its laughter, which lasted an amazing twenty-three seconds. Of course, Benny's visible response to the line prolonged the laughter. According to Verna, he didn't see it coming.

She recalled in the Halperin interview: "You'll sort of hold back at rehearsal, you know. You won't really give it your all . . . I had this one line, and when I said 'Shut up!' to him I never saw a man *jump* so! And then he held his head down, and he started to laugh. And afterwards, he said no wonder [the writers] wanted you [for the part of Mrs. Day] . . . you scared the life out of me!"

After this broadcast, "Ahhh, shut up!" became Mrs. Day's trademark line. The writers would employ it multiple times in future shows, including two times when Verna was playing a character other than Mrs. Day. Actually, the first time Mrs. Day told anyone to shut up, the recipient was not Benny but his pet bear Carmichael, in the broadcast of October 29, 1939. However, on that occasion Verna delivered the command with less vigor. The audience response that evening was tepid compared to the broadcast of December 12, 1943.

In the latter show, Mrs. Day's tirade continues, as she appeals to the audience:

MRS. DAY

"Ladies and gentlemen, you should *know* what
this Waukegan weasel is paying my boy!"

BENNY

"Mrs. Day, there's a program going on!"

MRS. DAY

"He pays Dennis $35 a week, and because his song only takes two
minutes, he tells my boy he's making $17.50 a minute which that—"

BENNY

"Mrs. Day, you're not allowed to stand up on the seats!
And besides, this audience came here to see a show—"

MRS. DAY

"$17.50 a minute, which that chiseler says amounts to $186,000 a week!"

BENNY
"Now, Mrs. Day—"

MRS. DAY
"$186,000 a week! And my boy is dope enough to believe it!"

This hollering match continues until Benny demands that Mrs. Day come up on the stage to finish the discussion. When she trips on the steps, she claims Benny pushed her, and the argument is still heard over the closing credits. Despite this outstanding performance, Verna was once again given no air credit.

The same situation existed on another show that season when Verna occasionally appeared as Mrs. Hudson, the motherly housekeeper of Sherlock Holmes on the Mutual network series *The Adventures of Sherlock Holmes*, starring Basil Rathbone and Nigel Bruce, repeating their film roles of Holmes and Dr. Watson. John Dunning, radio historian, described the actors as "ribald cutups," while the show's director Glenhall Taylor called them "delightfully humorous and frightfully unpredictable."

In 1964, Verna herself recalled a slip of profanity during a broadcast of that show which featured Joseph Kearns as the evil Dr. Moriarity: "Oh, goodness sakes, the one Basil Rathbone said was just dreadful in *Sherlock Holmes*. The [crew was] in the booth, behind the glass. And we were outside—Joe Kearns, myself, and Rathbone. And Rathbone made a very funny remark, a horrible remark. And he brought it right out, and my goodness, 'he shot himself,' as he put it. We *died*! We couldn't answer. We looked up in the booth to get a signal what to do, and there wasn't anybody in the booth. Everybody had gone right down on the floor. Because they were in hysterics...so I worked with him just recently on the Social Security Hour and he said, 'Do you remember the last time we worked together?' I said, 'I'll *never* forget it.' But you get a word, you know, that is a habit, and [you feel like] you've got to [use] it."

During the same season, Verna had a recurring role on the *George Burns and Gracie Allen Show* as Mrs. Fannie Bundy, gossipy cleaning woman to the stars. Hired by Gracie on the February 1 broadcast, Mrs. Bundy charged ninety cents an hour but also finagled bus fare once a month—to her visit her daughter in Chicago. Each week when she visited the Burns home, blustery Mrs. Bundy provided some inside information on the evening's guest star, whether it was Adolphe Menjou, Cecil B. DeMille or Brian Aherne. Relaying the latest news to Gracie, the less than industrious Mrs. Bundy ("I can't talk while I work") often performed as a catalyst to the show's plot, like the February 29 broadcast when she told Gracie that Dorothy Lamour studied numerology. Gracie then campaigned to get George, whose personal number was seven, a costarring role with Lamour, who was searching for a leading man with the same number.

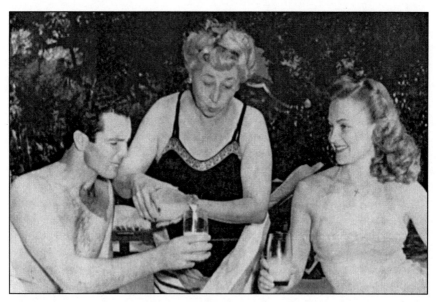

Blossom Blimp (Verna) serving Sealtest milk to Dave Street and Sharon Douglas.

Also that season, Joan Davis and Jack Haley were quite ably running the *Sealtest Village Store* minus the calm presence of former host Rudy Vallee, who was still serving with the U.S. Coast Guard. The format of the show for the 1943-44 season remained the same—comedy sketches interspersed with songs by fresh-faced soloist Dave Street and the Eddie Paul Orchestra. The show's staff of writers, which included Davis's husband Si Wills, employed a brand of humor which leveled insults at each character, but chiefly at the Davis character, who was depicted as "a homely, loud-mouthed wench who couldn't even be pin-up girl in a lonely Eskimo's igloo." In vivid contrast to the annoying coarseness of Davis's character was Haley's love interest, the suavely condescending Penelope "Penny" Cartwright, played by newcomer Sharon Douglas. While Davis and Haley swapped smart-aleck remarks, Verna was on hand again that season as Blossom Blimp, proving to be just as man-crazy as Davis by fawning over celebrity guests like Gene Kelly. And her song parodies had become an anticipated highlight of the broadcast.

The atmosphere of the *Sealtest Village Store* broadcasts was vividly described in the July, 1944 issue of radio magazine *Tune In*: "Right now, the Davis-Haley broadcast is a 3-ring circus, complete with acrobats. The two comics chase each other around the mike, do stumble-bum minuets during musical interludes, pound performers on the back until they almost lose their lines from laughing. The script takes quite a beating, both literally and figuratively. Joan and Jack use it to swat each other over the head. They kiss it ecstatically when a joke brings hearty laughter, tear pages out of it and throw them away when a gag fails to deliver. Favorite stunt for both guest stars and regulars, when they have a particularly harrowing insult to pay Joan, is to hold up their copy where the audience can see it and shake their heads to prove it was the writer's idea, not theirs."

The *Tune-In* writer failed to give Verna equal credit in these antics. On the broadcast of September 9, 1943, when Blossom was introduced to the visiting Frank Sinatra, Verna scored a 20-second laugh, the broadcast's longest. After casually greeting the pompadoured crooner, Blossom does a double-take, then gasps, "Frank Sinatra!!!" Then Blossom keels over in a dead faint, moaning "Oh, Frankie!! Ohhhhhh!" No doubt Verna, still a stage acrobat at fifty-three, exaggerated her fall to amplify the ensuing laughter. She knew her craft; the studio audience responded wildly. Young girls, obviously there to see Sinatra, squealed with laughter. Even Davis and Sinatra broke up, unable to continue with their lines. When Sinatra offered to help Blossom to her feet, Davis quipped, "No, don't strain yourself, Frankie. I'll call New York and get the same crew that raised the Normandy."

Embarrassed by her girlish reaction to meeting Sinatra, Blossom apologizes, "Oh, woo, goodness! Goodness! I'm afraid I made a spectacle of myself!" Then she breaks into one of her impromptu songs, so boisterous and off-key that it's followed by enthusiastic applause and whistles:

> *Fraaannnk-kie,*
> *You really send me when you sing!*
> *I love that 'dour!*
> *When you're crooning in the Store,*
> *You're the one that I adore!*
> *Yes, Frankie, Frankie, it's you!*
> *Woo! Woo!*

When debonair Rudy Vallee returned as a guest on October 28, bubbly Blimpy gushes about his contribution to the war effort and makes plans to see him at an upcoming military reception. She works in a reference to Al Dexter's current song hit when she admonishes Vallee, "Save every dance for me, and don't any of the other girls dare to cut in because . . . I'm a pistol packin' mama, and I'm shooting from the hips! Woo! Woo!"

On the January 13 broadcast, Blossom was pining for Humphrey Bogart, which led to her solo (to the tune of "Frankie and Johnny"):

> *If Blimpy and Humphrey were sweethearts,*
> *We'd rob every bank we could see,*
> *Though we'd end up in the jug,*
> *I'd still love that mug*
> *'Cause I know he's the man for me!*
> *Woo! Woo!*

Joan Davis assists Blossom Blimp on the diving board.

Verna's delivery of such ditties made Blossom a very popular radio character, while providing for Verna an escape from the long line of domineering roles. In creating Blossom the writers had employed one of comedy's oldest devices: incongruity. While the studio audience, who had the advantage of actually seeing the performers, could easily recognize the discrepancy between Verna's physical appearance and Blossom's girlish demeanor, the listeners at home had to use their imaginations. However, Verna's voice accurately conveyed Blossom's absurdity. A decade later, Verna would employ a little bit of Blossom in her greatest television characterization, Hilda Crocker on *December Bride*.

For Verna, the highlight of *Sealtest Village Store* came in the early spring of 1944 when the entire cast was invited to broadcast four weekly shows from military bases near New York City, beginning on March 23. While it was a great thrill to be back in Manhattan for the first time in a dozen years, Verna was also honored to entertain the servicemen. Of course, her absence from Hollywood meant that she could not perform on her other regular shows. And that meant she would not be paid for those shows. While Joan Davis was earning $100,000 annually for her radio work, Verna's supporting-player salary was nowhere close to that. She required the income from several radio series to earn a living. The National Dairy Products Corporation, the sponsor for *Sealtest Village Store*, had a solution for her loss of income.

In 1964, Verna was still amazed at their offer: "I had *five* [other] contracts then. They got me out of every one of them and paid me the salary of these five to take me to New York . . . I had this part of [Blimpy] and she was an awfully cute part and they didn't want to cut her out. They wanted her to go. And I had Lux Radio Theatre, and I had Burns and Allen, and I had Jack Benny and I had Judy Canova . . . there's a fifth one in there somewhere. I had these contracts, and they let me out. But I said, 'Well, I can't afford to lose all that money, and they said, 'We will pay you.' And they paid my salary . . . It was wonderful!"

Another *Village Store* regular who found the offer dazzling was twenty-three-year old Sharon Douglas. Born as Rhodanelle Rader in Oklahoma on October 16, 1920, Douglas had spent her teen years in Las Cruces, New Mexico. When her older brother moved to Hollywood to find work as a photographer, Douglas soon followed, hoping to become a film actress. With her brother supplementing her typist's income, Douglas took acting lessons and began auditioning for radio and film roles. She made her film debut in the spring of 1940 with a bit part in an Eddie Cantor picture, *Forty Little Mothers*, but that December Douglas won the leading role in WestCoast-based soap opera *Second Wife*, which also featured Jane Morgan, whom Douglas found "helpful and dear." When Douglas joined the cast of *Sealtest Village Store*, she found in Verna an equally accommodating co-worker. She later recalled, "Verna was always funny, sharp, and the hit of the show! She was like a mother to me. She was [also] a confidante and a good friend."

In a 2005 email correspondence with the author, Douglas wrote of her favorite experience on *Sealtest Village Store*:

> "I still remember with great fondness when in, I believe the Spring of '44, [Verna] and I traveled together along with the entire cast and crew of the Joan Davis-Jack Haley Sealtest show on the marvelous trains we had then, the Super Chief to Chicago and then changed to the elegant 20th Century Limited on to New York for month's stay broadcasting the show each week from a nearby military base . . . It was a heady and thrilling time for me as I was so young and never had been to New York. Verna and I were so close and had adjoining rooms at the famous old Madison Hotel off 58th Street. I would see many famous people in that lobby and in the elevator. Kitty Carlisle for one. The first night we arrived in New York with snow on the ground, we trudged through the slush across 42nd Street to one of the theatres to see a stage show of *The Merry Widow* which was a great production, even

Si Wills, Joan Davis, Sharon Douglas, and Verna at a party given for the cast of the *Sealtest Village Store*, Hampshire House, New York City, 1944.

though it was the only ticket we could get at the last minute. Later, through the courtesy of Jack Haley, we got tickets to the production of the famous *Oklahoma* with the original cast! Then we saw the wonderful Margaret Sullavan in *The Voice of the Turtle*. We saw others which also were fine and exciting, especially being with Verna who was an old vaudevillian, and so funny and light on her feet. Sealtest went all out entertaining us, taking us to '21' for dinner and Sardi's and many exciting affairs. They treated us like visiting royalty . . . We were so privileged to experience that luxurious train trip across the country and back because Joan Davis was afraid to fly!"

During his 1964 interview, when Marty Halperin asked Verna to recall any on-air mishaps, she instantly recalled a standout from the initial New York broadcast of *Sealtest Village Store*: "I know we were in New York at Mitchell Field and we hadn't taken the secretary along with us. So she was as mad as could be. And she said, 'Well, I just hope you get in a mess!' So Jack Haley, a nice fellow, was standing by me [at the microphone], and Sharon Douglas was with us. So we started the show and it was fine. And all of a sudden Joanie [who was at the other microphone] said something, and Jack and I looked at each other. We said our lines and looked at each other's scripts to see what had happened. Joanie went on talking, [but] *nothing* that we were talking about at all. So I got over and looked at her part and said, 'You're on the wrong page.' So we turned it around as quick as we could and gave it to her. Well, she went all to pieces! So then we were going along *beautifully* until we came to the end of it. So when we came to the end of it, she [returned to] the first pages that were in the first part [where she made the initial blunder]. How we got out of it, I'll never know!"

This incident was explained in detail in Jack Gaver's syndicated column "Night Life World," appearing in papers on Saturday, March 25, 1944. On the previous Thursday night, the *Sealtest Village Store* was broadcast from Mitchell Field, an air force base on Long Island, with actor George Raft as the guest star. Fifteen hundred men jammed into the post's attractive theater, decorated with murals of planes in flight. About five minutes from the end of the broadcast, Joan Davis began pawing frantically at first one page of her script and then another. Others gathered around the microphone began pointing urgently at their scripts to guide her to the next line. She covered with a laugh and told Haley to take the next speech. After a few seconds it looked like she had begun to find her way among her own pages. Then panic set in again.

Gaver explained the situation: "Final rehearsals were held in the afternoon and, as the case in any radio show, dialogue changes were penciled in right up to the last moment. Then corrected, final scripts were mimeographed for the night's performances. Miss Davis just happened to get a script that had two of the pages out of place. When she turned to page 20 she found herself confronted with page 22 while the others were on page 21. That caused the first trouble. The star fully expected to be in the clear when they got down to the bottom of page 22, but when she turned her sheet she was staring at page 21, not page 23."

Gaver also revealed some of the evening's visual antics, which at once delighted the servicemen but probably puzzled the radio listeners. The entire cast knelt and gestured profound salaams to each other as the program was announced. Davis made spectacle of licking her thumb and forefinger to turn script pages. She also kissed her script when a joke proved to be a hit. Gaver quipped, "If she had known what was to come later she probably would have made confetti of it."

The following Thursday night the show was broadcast from the United States Merchant Marine Academy at Kings Point, Long Island, where, according to the script, Davis was to be reunited with an old beau. On April 6, the cast, crew, and guest Roland Young performed from a stage at Hunter College in the Bronx, where the United States Navy had leased facilities to train 95,000 women as

Sharon Douglas and Verna Felton being royally entertained by Sealtest executives, New York City, 1944.

WAVES. The final broadcast of the *Village Store* sojourn, a week later, featured guest Edward Everett Horton trying to help Davis with her income tax return. Man-hungry Blossom Blimp, in the midst of redecorating her home, sang:

> *"I'm using every little scrap*
> *To build a pretty house!*
> *And then I'll get myself a great big cat*
> *And catch myself a spouse!*
> *Woo! Woo!"*

The *Sealtest Village Store* cast and crew had returned to Hollywood by April 20 when Alan Hale guested on the show. That week Verna resumed her other regular radio appearances as well. Twenty years later, when interviewed by Halperin, Verna listed the Jack Benny and Judy Canova shows as two of her six contracts for the 1943-44 season, but she was mistaken. Verna only appeared on Benny's show once during that season, and she would not become a regular on Canova's show until 1945. Instead it was *Point Sublime* and *The Adventures of Sherlock Holmes* for which she was under contract. The fifth contract, which Verna had difficulty calling to mind for Marty Halperin, was none other than the pun-filled *Edgar Bergen-Charlie McCarthy Show.*

Charlie Ruggles, Verna, Charlie McCarthy, and Edgar Bergen, January 2, 1944.

Comic ventriloquist Edgar Bergen had first appeared with his dummy, the wisecracking Charlie McCarthy, on Rudy Vallee's *Royal Gelatin Hour* in 1936. Since then, the pair had been a sensation, hosting *The Chase and Sanborn Hour* on Sunday nights on NBC. Verna made weekly appearances as different characters, all in the Mrs. Day vein and as such, perfect foils for Charlie. On January 2, she was reunited with *Barrel of Fun* co-star Charlie Ruggles when she played a bearded lady. She played Susan Hayward's mother in a caveman skit on February 6, and two weeks later she appeared as a bossy barber, receiving a double dose of insults from Charlie and guest W. C. Fields. On the March 12 broadcast, Verna was teamed with Ruggles again when she played a gruff lady hitchhiker.

Verna's most amusing character on the Bergen-McCarthy show appeared on March 6, the evening Cecil B. DeMille of *Lux Radio Theatre* guested. DeMille and Bergen had great fun during the broadcast, slyly alluding to DeMille's sponsor on his CBS show. When Verna, as a pushy civic leader, introduced herself to the gentlemen, she, too, got in a subliminal plug for Lux Soap, "I am Mrs. Dorothea Gilpatch of the Lobpope Busy Bee Club for the Collection of Kitchen Waste Fats and Theatrical Improvement!" *The Lux Radio Theatre* announcers regularly requested their listeners to save used cooking fat as a wartime effort to recycle, thus aiding the production of explosives, sulfur drugs, vaccines, synthetic rubber, and not least of all, soap.

When Mrs. Gilpatch, a pushy civic leader, announces that she sits on her club's board of directors, Charlie quips, "Well, that should give it some weight." Then when she is introduced to DeMille, who says he "directs people in the movies," Mrs. Gilpatch condescendingly inquires, "Oh, you're an usher?"

Since Verna was more often than not given no air credit, her name remained unknown to most listeners even though she had been a radio performer for more than a decade. Zuma Palmer, a columnist for the *Hollywood Citizen-News*, set out to rectify this situation. Palmer, who later stressed that she always tried to "give the little fellow a break," featured Verna in a two-part column on July 15 and 16, 1944, which not only listed some of her recent radio credits, but also divulged more about Verna than any other publicity since the live interview on KPO's *Personal Closeups* in 1933.

When Palmer asked Verna to compare her stage career to working in radio, she responded: 'There is one thing I have never got used to in radio, and that is the giving of advice to the director by members of a cast. I can't do it to this day. I may call attention to an error in the script or some small thing but in the theater we were taught the director was always right."

Verna also told Palmer that she hoped to live to see the day when casts would not sit on the stage during the entire radio broadcasts but instead make entrances and exits as in the theater. Perhaps Verna was indirectly referring to the antics of Joan Davis and Jack Haley when she told Palmer, "Ad libs and other mechanics of broadcasting when done on the stage distract the attention of the audience from what is being said by the players."

Palmer further reported: "One thing [Verna] finds difficult to do when sitting on the stage is having to laugh at jokes which are not funny. 'The ham in me likes audiences,' she said, 'but I believe many shows are better without them.'"

Later that year, Peggy Carter conducted a similar interview with Verna, which was published in *Radio Life* on December 17. Verna's only criticism of the radio industry was more guarded than her comments to Zuma Palmer: "I wish radio would adapt a little stage technique to its presentation. I think it would be a tremendous help." However, Verna quickly admitted, "I grew up on the stage, but it looks like I just grew up with radio. It's tops . . . Radio offers a pleasant existence for anyone. I like it because it gives me a chance to live a normal life. You know, when you travel all of the time, it gets pretty tiresome. You never get to know your neighbors, have a home, or even time to vote."

Indeed, this time in Verna's life was golden. The actual work involved in radio was not difficult, compared to her past career on the stage or the impending medium of television. Likewise, life on Bakman Avenue was very peaceful. Verna enjoyed entertaining friends beside the pool, in the rumpus room or on the badminton court. She was fond of bridge and other card games. When she had quiet time, she liked to read best sellers, noting that the current book-of-the-month selections were like the stories her mother once forbid her to read. Besides gardening, which was one of her loves, Verna really did not have many responsibilities at home. She had never been much of a cook. In the past Verna hadn't the time or the need to learn her way around a kitchen; she had grown up living in hotels and boarding houses. And since the second year of her marriage, Verna had relied on Connie "Codo" Conboy for all her domestic needs, including the care of Lee.

By mid-1944, Verna had hired a housekeeper to take over all of Connie's chores. And it was high time. Connie, stooped and frail, was approaching her eighty-fifth birthday. Calling her "the orchid of the family," Verna laughingly admitted in the *Radio Life* piece that the household actually revolved around Connie's wishes, which in turn revolved around Lee's wishes. "I don't think I count for much," Verna winked. Each time Lee came home from college, Connie sent the housekeeper out of the kitchen so that she could prepare his favorite dishes.

During the summer of 1944, some of Verna's contract shows went on hiatus for several weeks, which allowed her a more relaxing time at home. Her stepfather Pearl Allen came from San Francisco for an extended visit during this time. Approaching seventy-three, Pearl was still in good physical condition and had managed to keep his weight down during his retirement. They spent days by the pool, taking their meals outside, playing cards, and enjoying the antics of Verna's dogs, Skipper and Mike. Skipper, the senior of the pair, was a white Australian sheepdog who had been a member of the family since the Millars lived in Burbank, if not before. Mike, a rusty cocker spaniel, was the first of several Millar cockers to have the run of 4147 Bakman Avenue.

The house was quieter that summer without the comings and goings of twenty-year-old Lee. When physical problems plagued him that spring, he had withdrawn from V-12 program at USC without completing the second semester. The rheumatic fever he suffered as a child had caused increased muscular atrophy in his left leg, as well as arthritis in the femur joint. These conditions existed before Lee's enrollment in the Naval Reserve, and medical officers agreed that Lee never should have been accepted into the V-12 program. Before a medical discharge could be granted, Lee was required to spend eighteen weeks at the U. S. Naval Hospital in Long Beach for observation and medical survey.

Verna's only regular assignment that summer was her continuing role of Blossom Blimp on *Sealtest Village Store*. When Joan Davis and Jack Haley took an eight-week vacation, comic actor Edward Everett Horton stepped in as proprietor of the store. Writers concocted a ridiculous romance between Horton and Penny Cartwright, played by decades-younger Sharon Douglas. Billie Burke, duplicating her fluttery screen persona, was also on hand for six weeks and seemed much more of a match for Horton. In her own scatterbrained way, she merrily doled out Davis's brand of insulting humor, as in this exchange:

Billie Burke (singing)
Roll out the barrel, we'll have a barrel of fun,
Roll out the barrel—

Blossom Blimp (entering)
Hello, Miss Burke!

Billie Burke (laughing)
Oh, dear, instead of rolling it out, the barrel walked in by itself!
Oh, dear, Mrs. Blimp, it is you!

Blossom Blimp
Yes, it certainly is I.

Billie Burke
Well, come right in. What can I do for you?
I'm taking care of the store.

Blossom Blimp
Well, I came in to exchange this two-way stretch I bought here.
There's something wrong with the elastic!

Billie Burke
Really? What's wrong?

Blossom Blimp
Well, I sent it to the laundry, and now my two-way stretch
is four-way droop!

Billie Burke
Well, I can't understand it, Mrs. Blimp. You have a lovely figure!

Blossom Blimp (gushing)
Ooooh, thank you! You know, the other day a talent scout
with Paramount Pictures saw me. That's the studio that made
Road to Morocco and *Road to Zanzibar*. And they want me to appear in their
next *Road* picture with Bob Hope and Bing Crosby.

Billie Burke
Oh, do they want you play the part of Dorothy Lamour?

Blossom Blimp
No! They want me to play a steam roller on the road!

EDWARD EVERETT HORTON (ENTERING)
Oh, Billie! Billie!
(Seeing Blossom) Oh, Mrs. Blimp, you're here!

BLOSSOM BLIMP
Hello, Mr. Horton!

BILLIE BURKE
Eddie, have you heard? Paramount Studio
wants Mrs. Blimp for their next picture.

EDWARD EVERETT HORTON
Well, I'm not surprised at all. Blimpy would be wonderful in pictures.
She has such a winning smile!

BLOSSOM BLIMP
Oooooh, do you really think I have a winning smile?

EDWARD EVERETT HORTON
Yes, and it's such an unusual combination:
a winning smile on a losing face.

As America entered the final year of the war, Verna remained very busy with her own radio career. She filled typical roles in nine *Lux* productions during the 1944-45 season, including Lucille Ball's aunt in *"Lucky Partners,"* a role played by Spring Byington in the screen version. When *Lux* presented new treatments of three previous productions, namely *"Bedtime Story," "The Devil and Miss Jones,"* and *"A Tale of Two Cities,"* Verna repeated her original roles. Her finest *Lux* vocal characterization that season was Agatha Butterfield in *"Sunday Dinner for a Soldier,"* broadcast on February 19. Based on the 1944 Twentieth Century-Fox film, the show featured Anne Baxter and Charles Winninger as the heads of a rural Florida family who invite a soldier to dinner. In one of her meatiest *Lux* roles, Verna played their willful but goodhearted neighbor, the operator of a chicken farm often at odds with "that horrible old man," played with delightful crotchetiness by Winninger. Verna handled her part skillfully without slipping into caricature.

In addition to her regular role of Blossom Blimp on *Sealtest Village Store,* Verna made guest appearances during the 1944-45 season on *The Alan Young Show, Let's Listen to Spencer,* and *Cavalcade of America.* However, she was not needed as Mrs. Day on the Jack Benny show that season. Singer Dennis Day had joined the Navy in the spring of 1944, so Benny's writers had temporarily written him and his overbearing mother out of the program. Nevertheless, they did not allow Verna's trademark line to go to waste. Verna appeared twice that December as a different character, a Christmas shopper who bellowed to Benny, "Aw, Shudddup!"

All the while, Verna continued to supervise the efforts of the Radio Women's War Service, but, like many other Hollywood celebrities, she also volunteered her services by performing without pay on programs produced by the Armed Forces Radio Service (AFRS). Created by the United States War Department almost six months after the attack on Pearl Harbor, the AFRS provided entertainment for U.S. troops spread across the world. Shows were recorded on 16-inch wax discs in Hollywood and then broadcast over cooperating stations outside the United States. Some recordings were sent overseas in a "Buddy Kit," including a turntable.

Verna was heard most frequently on an AFRS musical variety program called G.I. Journal, designed to give information on activities of service personnel stationed throughout the world. Many of the *G.I. Journal* shows were recorded at the famous Hollywood Canteen, featuring the talents of guest hosts Linda Darnell, Jimmy Durante, Bob Hope, and Jack Benny. Mel Blanc was a regular, but occasionally he was joined by top supporting radio performers such as Bea Benaderet, Elvia Allman, Sara Berner, Jerry Colonna, and Arthur Q. Bryan. Verna appeared on this program at least ten times during the 1944-45 season, playing comic characters similar to those she had perfected on network shows.

Verna's March 9 appearance on *G.I. Journal* was perhaps her best. Groucho Marx was the host with guest stars Lucille Ball and Johnny Weissmuller. Just as she had demonstrated on the *Rudy Vallee Show* in 1942, Verna made an excellent foil for Marx. As millionaire Sessie Smugglemeier, she enters the offices of the *G.I. Journal* to place an ad for her missing cocker spaniel. When she tells Marx that in addition to her millions she has forty acres, he responds, "Yes, and I see you brought them with you. Let me put my arms around your subdivisions." His insults notwithstanding, Marx charms her, until Weissmuller enters. Then she swoons, "Johnny Weissmuller, come here, you big strong brute, and overpower poor, weak me!" Marx quips to Sessie, "I'm betting on poor, weak you."

On Valentine's Day, 1945, Verna was featured in a comedy skit on another AFRS program—*Mail Call*—starring Don Ameche and Marguerite Chapman as a young married couple. When their arrogant neighbor Mrs. Ritzmore, played by Verna, calls on them, the couple is forced to endure a melodramatic delivery of her prize-winning poem, "The Tale of the Flying Horse." Mrs. Ritzmore gushes, "Oh, it's nothing, really, but I do like to *scratch*." Ameche's character dislikes her immediately and sabotages the old girl's recitation, much to the chagrin of his social climbing wife.

For the duration of the war and even for three years after its end, Verna would appear on these and other AFRS programs, including the highly popular *Command Performance* and *Melody Roundup*, the latter in which she appeared as host Andy Devine's mother. One of her most amusing *Command Performance* appearances was hosted by Bob Hope on Christmas Day, 1944. In a prerecorded segment, Verna played a frustrated salesclerk trying to help the "feuding" Jack Benny and Fred Allen at the necktie counter. Frank Nelson also appeared as a prissy floorwalker.

In February, 1945, Verna reported to Republic Studios, known as the "B-movie factory," to film a small part in a prison drama called *Girls of the Big House.* Lynne Roberts plays a college professor's well-bred daughter who assumes the name of Jeanne Crail to date Earl Williams, a slick con-artist who frames her for robbery. Rather than have her father find out about her plight, Jeanne confesses to the crime. Believing she is covering for a known criminal, the district attorney sends Jeanne to a tough women's prison. When she finds it difficult to communicate with her father, Jeanne breaks out of jail to be at his induction ceremony as college president, all the while keeping her incarceration secret. She returns to prison to serve out her term, and after a series of cat fights and close calls, Jeanne is vindicated and freed. Verna appeared in two brief scenes as the college professor's testy housekeeper Agnes, who, despite her crusty exterior, likes to pamper Jeanne, especially by baking her favorite ginger cookies.

Later that spring, Verna joined the ensemble cast of *The Judy Canova Show,* airing over NBC. Thirty-one-year-old Canova, a native of Florida, had begun her career with her siblings in a New York nightclub. By 1941 she was starring in her own motion pictures, including *Sis Hopkins,* the same character Verna had played on stage twenty years earlier. On July 6, 1943, Canova's first radio show debuted on CBS and ran for one year, capitalizing on the country bumpkin persona Canova had made popular as a guest on the Rudy Vallee and Edgar Bergen shows. Canova's regulars included the gifted Mel Blanc as dry-witted Mexican handyman Pedro and Ruby Dandridge as Canova's devoted Negro cook Geranium. Although Geranium was a blatant racial stereotype, Dandridge's skillful performance rose above the standard. And garrulous Geranium's high-pitched cackle was simply infectious.

Canova resumed her radio show in January 1945, with a slightly altered format. At the bequest of her late uncle, Judy, along with Geranium and Pedro, moved from Rancho Canova to her uncle's fashionable Brentwood estate, presided over by his highbrow sister, Mrs. Uppington, or as Judy called her, "Aunt Uppie." If faithful NBC listeners thought Mrs. Uppington's voice or name sounded familiar, it was because Isabel Randolph, the actress playing her, had previously portrayed a snooty character by the same name for seven years on *Fibber McGee and Molly.* Rounding out the cast was Aunt Uppie's condescending butler Winchester, played by Joseph Kearns.

By late spring, Isabel Randolph was gone, and "Aunt Uppie" had transformed into "Aunt Aggie," played by Verna. Like her predecessor, Agatha Frost was Judy's wealthy aunt who resided in a Brentwood mansion. But Aunt Aggie was not uppity; instead she firmly supported Judy's attempts to break into society. She also worked hard to ensure that Judy catch the man of her dreams, Chauncey Van

Atwater, played by George Neise. Judy's competition in that department was debutante Brenda LaVerne, played by Sharon Douglas. Though a likable character, Aunt Aggie failed to stretch Verna's abilities; she was merely a "straight man," feeding the lines to laugh-getters Canova, Dandridge, and Blanc. Another negative was the show's time slot. Broadcast on Saturday nights at 10 p.m. Eastern time, the Canova show took up most of the cast's weekend because they didn't rehearse until the day of the broadcast. In December of that year, Canova told newspaper columnist Jack Haver, "I think I've got a good program if for no other reason than everybody on it enjoys doing it. We don't beat our brains out in the process, either."

Most radio stars, including Judy Canova, Jack Benny, George Burns and Gracie Allen, took the summers off, ending their seasons in June and returning refreshed in September. But supporting players like Verna could not afford such a luxury. By the time *The Judy Canova Show* completed its 1945 season, Verna had lined up summer assignments on shows like *Cavalcade of America* and the dramatic anthology *Romance*, which shared Canova's sponsors, Colgate Tooth Powder and Halo Shampoo.

Verna also appeared twice on *Wednesday With You*, a summer replacement series for Eddie Cantor's *Time to Smile* on NBC. She played Miss June Girthwaite, an obnoxious but comical guest at Cantor's lodge, the Cozy Cabana. While Cantor was on hiatus, his announcer and stooge Harry Von Zell was on hand to rebuff the advances of the impetuous Miss Girthwaite, whose shrill giggles and ample size suggested a blatant rip-off of Blossom Blimp. Even so, Verna's characterization was the only redeeming element of *Wednesday With You*; unlike Von Zell and regular Fred Martell, Verna knew how to get the most out of the miserable jokes.

Although the *Sealtest Village Store* did not go on hiatus that summer, Joan Davis was not a part of the zaniness. By this time, Davis had reached such star status that she decided to leave the *Sealtest Village Store* in the hands of Jack Haley and open her own radio show in the fall. She made her exit at the end of June, and comedienne Jean Carroll replaced Davis immediately. Just as quickly Davis began negotiations for Verna to follow her to CBS where they would begin a new series with a slightly altered format in September.

Concurrently with *Wednesday With You,* Verna was a regular on another summer replacement series, a CBS situation comedy based on Milt Gross's comic strip *That's My Pop*, starring film character actor Raymond Walburn as freeloading J. Gaylord Ginch who had held no regular job for over twenty years. He and his wife Gertrude and their son lived in the home of Ginch's unsympathetic and acerbic mother-in-law Mrs. Appleby, played by Verna. In one episode, as the distrusting Mrs. Appleby leaves on a week's vacation, she gives Ginch his allowance: one dollar. Often exasperated by Ginch's foolhardy schemes to avoid work and get rich quick, this old battleaxe found ample opportunity to use Mrs. Day's trademark line: "Awww, Shuddddupp!"

A landmark role in a revolutionary medium came Verna's way in midsummer when she was chosen to play the comic lead in a special telecast transmitted over W6XAO-TV, the country's first experimental television station. Founded by the late Don Lee, famed Cadillac distributor and pioneer broadcaster, the Los Angeles station was by this time operated by Lee's son Tommy. In 1939 Tommy Lee had built a new television studio and transmitter on the leveled mountaintop above the famous Hollywood sign. From this vantage point, one and one half times higher than the top floor of the Empire State Building, broadcasts could reach homes in the Hollywood Hills as well as those in the San Fernando Valley. The development of television had slowed during the war, but soon the infant medium would dramatically affect radio just as silent films and talkies had influenced stock companies.

In early August, Verna, as the title character, began rehearsals for the television comedy *Oh, Miss Tubbs!*, which was to be presented live, as were all Don Lee telecasts at the time, except for occasional newsreels and films. *Oh, Miss Tubbs!* was destined to become one of the forerunners of the television sitcom, although Verna perhaps never suspected that as she trekked up the winding road to "Mount Lee."

Oh, Miss Tubbs! was a radical change of pace for Verna, but in years to come, after scores of television appearances, she would almost forget that she ever did it. In 1964, when Marty Halperin asked Verna to name her first appearance on television, she cited *December Bride*. Then, as if being hit by a blinding flash of memory, she quickly retracted that: "*Oh!* Let's see how long ago—*years ago*—Peggy Webber—did you ever hear of Peggy Webber? Well, Peggy had written *Miss Tubbs*, this script—a *cute* script, *very* cute. Well, she had [hired] Earle Ross and a bunch of all of us [radio performers]. She wanted to put it on [the air] as the first [television sitcom]. So we did it up on the hill, you know, where Don Lee was, up on the hill."

After the telecast *Radio Life* profiled *Oh, Miss Tubbs!* in an article titled "Is Television Going to Be Like This?" The show's plot was summarized in eight captioned photographs depicting scenes from the play, which opened in Miss Tubbs's mathematics classroom at Andelusia Public School No. 2. In what appears to be an after-school tutorial, Miss Tubbs instructs solitary pupil Tennyson, played by thirty-year-old radio veteran Walter Tetley, looking appropriately nerdy in his horn-rimmed spectacles. Once her busy day is over, Miss Tubbs retreats to the home she shares with fellow spinster-teacher Cornelia "Corny" Udahl, played by Jane Morgan, and their housekeeper Guinevere "Guin" Slough, a younger and barefoot version of Ma Kettle, played by Selma Stern. Miss Tubbs wants nothing more than to relax, but Corny and Guin insist on hearing their favorite afternoon radio serial, which the girls refer to as a "strip," borrowing that term from serialized newspaper comics. Unable to discourage them, Miss Tubbs is forced to listen, and as she does, she determines that she could write much better scripts, especially with Corny's help. When Corny is doubtful of their abilities, the foolishly optimistic

Miss Tubbs instructs Tennyson (Walter Tetley) while the school janitor
(Arthur Q. Bryan) observes.

Miss Tubbs reminds her of their status in their college graduating class: "third
from the end." Finally she persuades Corny to join her as co-author. Then Miss
Tubbs naively solicits an investment from a local businessman, played by Eddie
Marr, whom she tells, "I've got a strip show which I want you to sponsor." He
misinterprets her, thinking she's talking about a burlesque show, and his interest
definitely quickens. Her confidence boosted, Miss Tubbs goes a step further and
seeks help from a realtor, played by Joe Granby, telling him that she and Corny
were "third from the end." Horrified that two mature educators are members of
a burlesque troupe, the realtor rushes to complain to their principal Basil
Chronkite, played by Earle Ross. Chronkite promises immediate dismissal, but
in a master coup, Miss Tubbs settles the situation, telling Corny that instead of
being dismissed they will merely be "called to an accounting" at a faculty meeting.
But Corny, instead of being overjoyed, breaks into tears because the meeting will
conflict with her favorite "strip show." It's all too much for Miss Tubbs, who
bellows, "Awww, Shuddddupp!"

Oh, Miss Tubbs! was the brainchild of nineteen-year-old college student
Peggy Webber, who wrote, directed, and produced it. Born in Laredo, Texas, on
September 15, 1925, Margaret "Peggy" Webber had begun writing radio plays at
age eleven. Her teen years were spent in Tucson, Arizona, where she was a leading
high school thespian. In fact, during her senior year, Webber played the lead in

"I've got a strip show for you to sponsor," Miss Tubbs tells an investor (Eddie Marr).

one of Verna Felton's former vehicles, *Peg O' My Heart*. She made her radio debut over KVOA in Tucson, and after her high school graduation in 1942, she enrolled in the University of Southern California. Immediately Webber was cast in the drama department's productions, and soon after sought roles outside the academic setting. Her first transcontinental broadcast was the serialized "*Of Human Bondage*" on NBC's daytime anthology series *Dreft Star Playhouse* in April 1944. A year later, she was known around town as a skillful radio dialectician.

Peggy Webber recalled her early years in Hollywood during a 2005 interview: "I was ambitious to break into television when I first came to Los Angeles. I felt that *that* was the future. And so I went to these experimental stations and would present my ideas, you know, of what I thought might make a show. And sometimes they would bite, and sometimes they wouldn't."

Oh, Miss Tubbs! was one of Webber's ideas that got past first base. Originally written as a prospective radio series, Webber had completed scripts for thirteen episodes when the property was chosen as a television adaptation, for which Webber also wrote the script. She directed all of the rehearsals at W6XAO-TV, but a previous contract to appear as Glenn Ford's co-star in *"Savage Encounter,"* an episode of the CBS anthology series *Columbia Presents Corwin*, prevented Webber from directing the telecast of *Oh, Miss Tubbs!* on Monday, August 6, at 8:30 p.m. (In 2005, Webber recalled that the telecast occurred on the same evening as the radio broadcast of *"Savage Encounter,"* but listings in the *Hollywood Citizen-News* confirm that the radio broadcast took place the following evening, August 7. Perhaps a rehearsal of *"Savage Encounter"* detained her from attending the telecast of *"Oh, Miss Tubbs!"*) Webber was terribly disappointed to miss the debut of her original work, but she had carefully coordinated all of the details with her cast and the camera director Jack Stewart during the final rehearsal.

Webber chose Verna as the lead character because she was already familiar with the actress's work. In a telephone conversation with the author, Webber recalled: "We had worked on comedy shows together, and I was always so impressed with her. She was so formidable and a very strong comedienne. She always knew how to *kick* the last speech, you know, to get a hand from the audience. It's a trick that a lot of stage people knew how to do, but not everyone in radio had that experience. She was *so* professional and *so* bombastic! I thought she was tremendous . . . I think it is very wonderful that you're writing about Verna because she was *it*. As far as I was concerned, there was no one who could do comedy as Verna Felton could. And she could make a show sing! When she would come on, boy, it would take off! And she just had a great command—powerful, powerful actress! Tell me today who there is who can do radio like *she* did it! It was something special. I have a theatre group, and we do regular radio programs that I write, but these are all prominent movie stars now because most of the radio people are gone. And there are *none* of them like Verna—I mean—she had that tremendous personality. The only person who came close was someone I used to direct on one of my television shows—Kathleen Freeman, who worked with me on her very first professional television show back in 1948 . . . She was similar to Verna. She could do similar roles."

For the rest of the *Miss Tubbs* cast, Webber instinctively chose actors with whom she knew Verna would interact well. Foremost was Jane Morgan whose style Webber described as being very different from that of Verna: "Jane Morgan was a lady, very refined. I would guess she was from New England or the South— I'm not sure. But she was very ladylike, very mellow. Her comedy was more of a straight man's line of comedy. Jokes would bounce *off* of her. And that's why I put Verna Felton and she as the two schoolteachers who lived together. I had other characters in the show that Verna had worked with in radio, in shows that I'd been on . . . And I cast them accordingly, because I knew that they worked well off of each other."

Webber found it amazing that Verna, at 55, took direction so well from a teenager: "She was complaining because she was going through the change of life right about that time. And she said, you know, 'I'm very tired, and I'm not feeling well.' She had to go see a doctor about her problems. So it was a difficult time, I remember, for her, but she was so generous to do this for me. I think she thought it was a good idea."

"It *was* an original idea. And I can't take full claim on that part because my girlfriend from college—I was going to USC at the same time—and my friend, who was an actress, older than I, had her master's degree and was going into school-teaching. And she would tell me the funny things that were happening [at school], and I got this idea. Because nobody at that time had done a comedy based on teachers. Teachers were kind of sacrosanct. Nobody wanted to make fun of them or tease them. And we were getting these headlines about teachers going on strike, and I thought, 'What an idea! This is so timely now to put this out while teachers are on strike and it's all stirred up in the headlines.' And so that's when I did it. I wrote it as a result of all that, plus what my friend Selma [Stern] would tell me what she was going through as a student teacher, you know, how different principals behaved."

As a way of thanking Stern for the inspiration, Webber cast her as Miss Tubbs's housekeeper Guinevere: "I wrote [the part] like a Marjorie Main character, and I wanted her to be a kind of hillbilly, but it was carried to an extreme [on the night of the telecast]." In Webber's absence that evening, someone thought it appropriate for Guin to appear barefooted. When Webber saw photographs taken that evening, she was pleased with every authentic detail except that.

Stern, the only surviving cast member of *Oh, Miss Tubbs!*, recalled in 2008: "I don't know what [Peggy] saw in me, but what I saw in her was this amazing child who already could draw people together, produce shows, write them, organize things—she could do everything! And on top of that she was such a darling—just an absolutely beautiful specimen of girlhood, then womanhood."

Stern had married that June and was in New York visiting her in-laws when Webber phoned her, asking her to return to California to be a part of *Oh, Miss Tubbs!* Webber picked up Stern at the train station, and rehearsals began almost immediately, with the longest session occurring on August 3. Stern's notes, dated August 6, reveal some of the dynamics of early television: "I've just come in from the television broadcast. Wow, what an experience! The studio is at the top of Mount Lee, 1700 feet above sea level. The road up is full of sharp, treacherous curves. The view up here is just gorgeous. Television acting seems to be more like pictures than like radio. The cameras and mikes are moveable and are located in the center. All around are the sets of the various scenes. The people who watched us [on the station's television] said that the screen is very small and the actors are very hard to see. All in all, the show came out quite well. Makeup for television is very simple—a very dark base, heavy eye and lip makeup. On the television screen everyone looks taller and thin . . . We got up there early to rehearse but we could have used a lot more time up there. Right now though they don't have the facilities for more rehearsal time because the studio is so hard to get to."

If she had been present for the live telecast, Peggy Webber might have helped Verna avoid an embarrassing incident that evening. Unlike filmed telecasts, which allow the cast and camera crew to stop at the end of each scene, live television required actors to move undetected from set to set while the cameras remained active. W6XAO-TV had several cameras in use for this telecast, and as each scene ended, its corresponding camera went to fadeout. Instantaneously, the camera for the following scene began telecasting. Because Verna was involved in practically every scene, she had to move quickly to reach the next set. One scene change was so abrupt that she did not have time to go behind the camera, the heavy lights, the cables, etc. Instead she had to pass in front of the camera, which she was told would fadeout before she made her move. For added insurance that she would not be caught moving to the next scene, Verna was instructed to duck as she passed the camera's eye. She did as she was told, but Verna detected some nervous movement and muffled hysteria from the cast and crew standing by. Then she noticed that the people in the sound booth, including her son Lee, were quite amused as well.

When the telecast ended, Lee asked Verna, "What did you think you were doing during that scene change?"

Still puzzled, Verna responded, "What do you mean?"

"You were getting ready to make your change, and all of a sudden you turn around, you go down, your fanny comes up in the air, you're squiggling along like a snake, and then you come up from the other side!"

Without Verna's knowledge, the cameraman responsible for the previous scene had failed to fade it to black, and so Verna's quick-change antics had been telecast as one of the industry's first bloopers. As she laughingly told Marty Halperin, "Me and my fanny were on the air!"

Although Verna considered *Oh, Miss Tubbs!* as a career milestone, she dismissed it, telling Halperin, "It was a cute thing, although nothing came of it. It was too new."

Actually, the telecast did spawn a radio audition, using the same performers. Webber recalled it vividly, "I recorded it later at NBC for a radio audition . . . I had made brochures up with the pictures of all the different actors, rented the studio orchestra at NBC, and just, you know, spent a lot of my own money. And Don Sharpe, who was an agent—I was working on the Harold Lloyd *Comedy Theater* at the time—and when I met Don Sharpe up in the sponsor's booth, I was writing on the script at the time. He said, 'What are you doing?' And I told him. And he said, 'That sounds like a great idea. What are you going to do with it?' I said, 'Well, I'm planning to make an audition at NBC.' He said, 'Who's going to direct it?' I said, 'Well, I don't really have anyone at this point.' And he said, 'I'll do it for you, I'll direct it for you.' And he was a very big agent, represented most of the big stars. He was with—I think it was—the Small Agency. At any rate, he was very prominent. And so I went on ahead on the premise that he was going to direct. And we talked on the phone two or three times, and he said, 'I'll

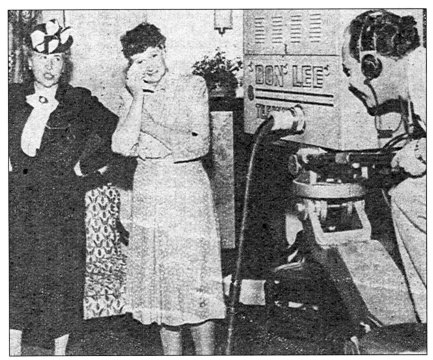

"Ah, Shuddup!" Miss Tubbs bellows at Corny (Jane Morgan) at the conclusion of *Oh, Miss Tubbs!*

be there.' And he [made a note of] the hour when the studio was going to be available and so on. And he didn't show up, of course. You know, when you're nineteen, people don't take you very seriously! And I had this great cast. And I had an ocarina band playing all the music, which I thought was correct for this kind of a show, in a little town, with a schoolteacher, and so on. So I had to direct it myself. And that was the first time that I had really tried to direct a group of stars in a radio show. So we did it, and I remember the night was very long. And I think I got home about 12 o'clock. And my dog—I had a big collie dog—my mother had gone to visit her aunt or something—my dog was bleeding all over the house. And I had to find a veterinarian who'd be open that night. So I got the dog to the vet, and they had to operate on her. And I remember they wanted me to be the assistant because they didn't have anybody else! And I had to assist in this surgery with this dog, and I *fainted*! Because I hadn't eaten all day, and I was exhausted. It was a very traumatic time!"

Webber would go on to perform in 8000 radio shows, 300 television programs, and 100 stage plays. Determined to revive radio drama, Webber founded the award-winning California Artists Radio Theatre (CART), acting as producer, director, and writer. As of this writing, CART was still going strong—Webber and Stern were among the cast of *The Wonderful Wizard of Oz*, broadcast on June 28, 2008.

In her youth, Stern toyed with the idea of a radio career, appearing occasionally in shows like *A Date with Judy*. However, her portrayal of the backwoods Guinevere in *Oh, Miss Tubbs!* inspired a prospective character for one of radio's biggest hits, but fate would not allow it. "There was some talk of me doing the part of a next-door neighbor of a maid played by a man," Stern said, recalling Marlin Hurt, a white actor who played a black domestic named Beulah. "Well, [the actor] died just as that was on the table, so that took care of that opportunity. I'm sorry he died anyway—'Did somebody bawl for Beulah?'"

Stern's association with Verna Felton did not end with *Oh, Miss Tubbs!* "I met her again. She was very, very nice to me. At one time there was a receiving line at some event with Bea Benaderet and, you know, a couple of other well known actresses. And when I came up, Verna said, 'Oh, girls, here comes competition!' And they all turned around and looked me over. And another time she said, "I don't know what you're doing, but you've got to quit doing that and get to work on this acting career full time." So that was very nice of her, you know, but I couldn't do it." Stern's family obligations required a more secure source of income than that of a struggling young actress. So she stuck to teaching, retiring after thirty-eight and one half years, twenty-five of those at Hollywood High School. In 1997, Stern revived her acting career, appearing in movies like *Bruce Almighty* and *Made of Honor* and television shows such as *Frasier* and *Nip/Tuck*.

Although Stern predicted that *Oh, Miss Tubbs!* would "go places," the telecast drew no notice from the *Los Angeles Times*. Much more important news filled the paper's morning edition of August 7, 1945. On the previous day, the United States had dropped the atomic bomb on the city of Hiroshima. Following the bombing of Nagasaki three days later, the world waited for Japan to surrender. On August 14, 1945, at 4 p.m. Pacific Time, President Harry Truman shared Japan's unconditional surrender with the nation via radio broadcast. The effect was immediate. All across the country, celebrations in cities awakened memories of the end of the First World War. In Seattle, the excitement swept over the city like a hurricane as people exploded from office buildings, manufacturing plants, and homes. Strangers embraced as reams of paper were thrown from the windows of offices above them. The scene was much the same in Portland, where Verna had celebrated the armistice in 1918. According to *The Oregonian*, "girls kissed sailors to signify the end of the war, and particularly exuberant sailors kissed girls at random." Portland's merchants were advised to remove items from display windows or pull down shades to prevent the merrymakers from being tempted to vandalize. San Francisco officials did not have that foresight. The wild celebration in the Bay City quickly turned into the nation's most violent display, with sailors, soldiers, and civilians creating a 30-foot-high bonfire from ripped-up war bond booths. Thirty liquor stores were looted, and every window along a busy three-block stretch of Market Street was smashed. Five people died as a result of the chaos, and thirty more were injured.

A rare glamour shot of Verna, 1945.

The *Hollywood Citizen-News* declared the celebration in downtown Los Angeles as the city's "mightiest." Parades of cars began forming shortly after 4 p.m. Commuters trying to get home from work were caught up in the jam that lasted until past well midnight. The *Citizen-News* described part of the scene: "A salty Marine with lots of overseas ribbons stood on the corner of First and Spring Sts., wearing a comic hat and blowing a New Year's horn. His girl friend was wearing the Marine Corps hat and the shore patrol said not a word . . . A conductor on a "B" streetcar, probably frustrated because he could not express his joy some way, grabbed the bell and clanged it continuously. A Negro bootblack on Main St. held an American flag and said in a monotone to each passerby: 'Ain't that nice! Ain't that nice!'" The intersection of Hollywood Boulevard and Vine Street was feverish with excitement. Some servicemen there were decked out in the loudest of civilian ties and straw hats, telling everyone that they were through with the service and the war. Film singer-comedienne Carmen Miranda danced on top of an automobile to the delight of the applauding onlookers. Meanwhile, the *Citizen-News* noted, "Worshippers, many with tears streaming down their faces, crept quietly into the city's many churches to give thanks to God for the victory that had come."

The nation was still rejoicing three weeks later when Joan Davis's new show debuted on CBS on September 3. After the broadcast that evening, Davis hosted her own celebration for the entire cast and crew at Slapsy Maxie Rosebloom's nightclub on Beverly Boulevard. The new show, sponsored by Swan Soap, was alternately called *The Joan Davis Show* or *Joanie's Tea Room*. It was set in the mythical town of Swanville where Davis operated a tea room. The show's format was essentially the same as that of the *Sealtest Village Store*; Davis played the same man-crazed female. Each show opened with announcer Harry Von Zell singing in a nasally mournful voice, "Poor Joan ain't got nobody. She's nobody's sweetheart now," before breaking into derisive laughter.

Verna, receiving second billing, played Rosella "Hippy" Hipperton III, who was practically a carbon copy of Blossom Blimp. Von Zell assumed a role similar to the one Jack Haley had played opposite Davis on the old show. Shirley Mitchell was recruited to play Joan's nemesis Barbara "Babs" Weatherby, a role not unlike her part of Shirley Anne three seasons earlier on the Sealtest show. However, the host of film stars who dropped in the Sealtest Village Store did not frequent Joanie's Tea Room. The absence of guest stars necessitated making the show's vocalist, popular tenor Andy Russell, part of the weekly plot. In addition, Davis's husband Si Wills, one of the show's writers, sometimes appeared in a comic role as Davis's whining brother-in-law Serenus.

Rosella Hipperton was an opera lover, the head of the local literary society, and the butt of Joan Davis's jokes. "Hippy" also flirted shamelessly with HarryVon Zell, chortling with delight for each bit of attention he returned. Upon entering the tea room, her standard chipper greeting was, "Hello, Miss Davis and Mr. Russell, *and Mr. Von Zell, **hellll-o**!*"

An amusing exchange occurred between "Hippy" and Joanie in the broadcast of December 10, 1945, when Joanie was temporarily working in a department store:

JOANIE
Now, do you want to buy a dress, Hippy?

HIPPY (CONDESCENDINGLY)
Buy a dress? From you, Miss Davis?

JOANIE
Sure. I'm helping Mr. Heppermyer out.

HIPPY (SMUGLY)
But you know absolutely nothing about style and fashion.
Your taste in clothes is *abominable!*

JOANIE
Oh, Mildred, you Pierce me!
But really, Hippy, I know just what you need—something "shick."

HIPPY (INDIGNANTLY)
Shick! Oooh, what ignorance!
It isn't "shick"—the word is *chic.* You need a French lesson!

JOANIE
The word is Schick—you need a shave!

The dynamics between all of the characters was never better typified than in the broadcast of January 21, 1946. While Hippy swooned over Von Zell, he much preferred Joanie, telling her in every show, "You know how I feel about you—I'm a man, and you're a woman!" Joanie, in turn, cared not for Von Zell's affections. Instead she carried a torch for Andy Russell, who only had eyes for the wealthy debutante Barbara Weatherby. Explaining their mutual dilemma to Hippy, Joanie schemed to get rid of Barbara. With her out of the way, Joanie could have Andy. Then Hippy could trap Von Zell. Joanie persuades Hippy to pen a phony letter to Andy from his "wife," asking him to come home to his three children in Peoria. Barbara takes the bait, and leaves a confused Andy, saying she'll never return. Von Zell and Andy discover Joanie' ruse, and they plot revenge. When Andy says he's going back to his real wife in Schnecktady, Joanie reacts just as they thought. Then the boys admit the truth. Hippy enters, and when she is upbraided by Barbara's father for participating in the ruse, she insists she's not ashamed of being an accomplice, in a throaty tremulo, "I'm *proud*! I did it to get

Verna playing Rosella Hipperton on *The Joan Davis Show*, 1946.

Harry Von Zell's love! To make him care for me, I'd move *heaven* and earth!" To which Joanie quips, "And she's the one that can do it, too!"

With additional air time and air credit, Verna had a better chance to shine as Rosella Hipperton. And Joan Davis's delivery was much less annoying than it had been on *Sealtest Village Store*. Harry Von Zell masterfully inserted plugs for Swan Soap into the middle and end of each broadcast, usually with Verna's help. As the season wore on, though, Von Zell began to poke fun at these insipid segues. While he often broke character, making smart aleck asides, Verna maintained her professionalism, never joining in. Just the same, their affection for each other remains evident in extant recordings of the show. However, perhaps the sponsor did not find Von Zell's adlibs so amusing. Before the season ended Swan Soap had hired its own announcer for the commercials.

During January 1946, while Davis filmed a Universal Pictures comedy called *She Wrote the Book*, she arranged for Verna to fill the minor part of an indignant matron. Verna's brief screen appearance could have been considered a cameo, had her face been familiar to moviegoers. Instead attentive radio listeners were perhaps delighted to recognize the voice of Davis's foil as none other than the lady they knew as Rosella Hipperton. And Davis saw to it that Verna was given a close-up despite the fact that the part hardly called for one.

Davis plays a plain-Jane college professor, Jane Featherstone, who agrees to help the dean's wife who confesses that she has written a scandalous tell-all under the pseudonym of Lulu Winters. The dean's wife persuades Jane to pose as Winters and to go to New York to accept $80,000 in royalty checks, which the authoress plans to donate to the financially strapped college. While in New York, Jane receives a head injury, resulting in amnesia. Later, when the book's publisher convinces Jane that she is actually Lulu Winters, she becomes the toast of New York, trading in her prim suits and horn-rims for furs and diamonds. A lecherous old shipping magnate Horace Van Cleve, played by Thurston Hall, romances Lulu, who finds it impossible to produce a second book. When she finally regains her memory, the professor rallies to convince Van Cleve to save the bankrupt college. When he refuses, she resorts to blackmail. She crashes his gala party on Long Island, where Van Cleve hopes to impress the governor with a new business deal. Maintaining her perpetration as Lulu Winters, Jane scandalizes Van Cleve's guests by cutting in on dance partners, practically roughhousing them. One she approaches is Mrs. Kilgour, the governor's wife, played by Verna. When Jane refers to the governor as "Cuddles," Mrs. Kilgour folds her arms and frowns disapproval. Fawningly, Jane coos, "Mrs. Kilgour, may I say you look lovely, utterly lovely. Beauty like yours is so rare, so exquisite, so to be envied." The flattery melts the icy dowager until Jane in the next breath turns to Van Cleve, "Why did you say she was a mangy old piece of burlap with a face like a barracuda?"

She Wrote the Book offered Verna a diversion from radio assignments, but she still preferred the latter medium. In fact, she was beginning to receive more calls for radio parts than she could fill. Verna's hectic schedule allowed her to appear on *Lux* only three times during the 1945-46 season, the final one being "*The Clock*" with Judy Garland on January 28. After that, Verna disappeared from all *Lux* productions for almost six years.

Just the same, Verna was kept busy with regular offers to appear on *Suspense*—radio's "outstanding theatre of thrills." *Suspense* was produced by William Spier, "the Hitchcock of the airlanes," whose attention to detail had such top film actors as Cary Grant, Charles Laughton, Fredric March, and Humphrey Bogart clamoring to be in its productions. John Dunning, author of *On the Air: The Encyclopedia of Old-Time Radio*, noted that Spier "required little rehearsal, just a few hours before air time. He wanted them tense at the microphone. They rewarded him with performances that were almost uniformly fine, matching the levels achieved by their underpaid supporting players, the professional radio people." When Verna joined the *Suspense* stable of supporting players—deemed a "veritable rep company" by Dunning—they included Joseph Kearns, Cathy Lewis, Wally Maher, Elliott Lewis, and Jerry Hausner. Sponsored by Roma Wines, the show aired on CBS on Thursdays at 8 p.m.

Although both print and online sources claim that Verna first appeared on *Suspense* as early as 1943, she did not make her debut on that show until October 18, 1945. These same sources even give her credit for Mary Astor's loyal maid in the episode titled "*In Fear and Trembling*," but it actually was Verna's friend Jane Morgan who played that part. Verna is incorrectly credited on at least seven other *Suspense* episodes as well. How could such a mistake be made? Spier, notoriously economical, prevented his supporting players from receiving air credit, so old-time radio fans have tried to piece together cast lists by identifying actors by their voices. Some of their efforts have resulted in blatant inaccuracies—mistaking Jane Morgan for Verna Felton especially seems illogical for the two ladies possessed distinctly different voices. Later, as Jane aged, her raspy voice deepened, making it even more distinctive.

During the 1945-46 season Verna appeared on *Suspense* six times, supporting stars like Henry Fonda and Alan Hale. Three of these performances are among the best of Verna's radio career. In one short season, *Suspense* had managed to showcase Verna's versatility more effectively than any *Lux* productions had in the past ten seasons. If she hadn't been in demand for comedy roles at the time, Verna might have become a regular on *Suspense*.

Verna's most emotional role on *Suspense* came at the end of the season on September 5, 1946. "*You'll Never See Me Again*" had a surprise ending, revealing the lead, Robert Young, as the villain. Verna played the spouse of a hit man (Joseph Kearns) whom Young hired to kill his young wife. When Verna's character is discovered as an accomplice to the plot, she breaks down in uncontrollable sobs. Although listeners must imagine Verna's facial and physical emoting, the vocal ability Verna demonstrates for this role dispels any doubt of her critical successes as a dramatic actress thirty-five years before.

In "*Pink Camellias*," the *Suspense* offering for December 27, 1945, Verna shines as the grumpy, invalid aunt of Marsha Hunt. Hunt plays Martha, a plain and timid girl who is beholden to her wealthy Aunt Abby. All day Martha keeps house, reads "sickening love stories" to the old woman, or shops for rich cakes and candies for gluttonous Aunt Abby. From her bed the fat old woman complains about everything. Jealous of Martha's youth, she makes snide remarks about Martha's lack of experience with men and then gloats about past lovers from her own youth. After Aunt Abby's nephew-by-marriage Neil arrives for a visit, Martha falls in love with him. Soon they plot to kill the old woman by putting arsenic in her cake. When they are successful, Neil turns on Martha and kills her.

On November 15 of that year, Verna appeared as a more colorful murder victim in "*Murder Off-Key*," which turned out to be the most delightful of all her *Suspense* roles. Zachary Scott played episode narrator Frederick Carlson, who's house-sitting the apartment of a friend away on vacation. He introduces Verna's character to the audience: "If I could just shut out that singing, I'd be all right. But it goes on pounding inside my head, and I keep hearing Violet screech those desperate, urgent scales. The first time I heard her I was sitting on the balcony outside the apartment, and everything was unnaturally still, the way it is late at night. And maybe that's why her singing sounded louder than it actually was. There was something abnormal about it, as though a control inside her had snapped and she couldn't stop that horrible noise that was coming from her throat. It went on, over and over again, rising and falling, and scraping the hot night to shreds." During this opening monologue, Verna, playing Violet Pondecker, is heard in the background, warbling scales in a comical, off-key manner that escalates until she sounds like a yelping dog. Then she segues into a brutal rendition of "Roses of Picardy," a popular tune during World War One. Carlson learns that Violet, a wealthy widow, thinks she has a trained voice, a notion perpetuated by her late husband. Violet is well past middle age but ignores that fact, piling her dyed hair up in curls and wearing lots of heavy perfume and makeup. In her youth she was a performer in the "thee-a-tah." Now she spends her days singing and doting on her yapping poodle Petty.

Violet is also fond of inviting young men to tea, and she wastes no time doing so for Frederick Carlson. "I have a special Chinese brand," she tempts breathlessly. "It smells like *dead flowers*!" Carlson finds Violet to be quite garrulous and affected, often quoting her dead husband. She coos, "My real name is Imogene, but he called me Violet—it's always *bean* my favorite color." Surveying her tragic efforts to hold on to youthfulness, Carlson begins to pity Violet, whose only comforts are Petty and her display cases full of expensive jewelry.

Several nights later, Violet is upset when Petty is missing. Blood and fur are found on the front bumper of Carlson's car, making him a suspect in the dog's disappearnce. He denies using the car on the night in question. Then the next night Violet is found strangled. Her apartment has been robbed of the jewelry and large amounts of cash she kept there. Carlson is fearful of an arrest until his friend Morley suddenly returns from vacation. Strangely, Morley refuses to vouch for Carlson by denying that he invited Carlson to stay there. Carlson now knows Morley wasn't out of town at all. He set Carlson up, making it look like Carlson killed Violet and her dog. Suddenly Violet's voice is heard, screeching "Roses of Picardy." Morley panics, thinking Carlson is trying to get him to admit he's the murderer. Just as he's about to shoot Carlson, the police break in and shoot Morley. Who was delivering the timely rendition of "Roses of Picardy?" A little girl next door had listened to Violet's off-key arias long enough to duplicate them exactly. (Of course, Verna's own voice was used as the little girl imitating Violet. Since Verna was a trained singer herself, it was quite the accomplishment that she could deliver such a realistic off-key performance.)

Two months after her brilliant portrayal of Violet Pondecker on *Suspense*, Verna left the *Lux Radio Theatre* stable of supporting players, not returning for another six years. About the same time, she turned over her role as Judy Canova's very proper Aunt Aggie to actress Ruth Perrot. Verna had other fish to fry. Plans to join a new radio program had been brewing for weeks. In December 1945, when Canova had broadcast three Saturday night shows from New York, Verna was not among the show's other regulars who made the trip East. Her newest contract would not permit her to be away from Hollywood for that long.

Everything was set for Verna to become a regular on this show when it debuted on December 4. Actually, the show was no stranger to NBC listeners; it was returning to the air after an absence of eighteen months. The show's popular star had been serving in the United States Army and was now back in Hollywood and ready to resume his career. His previous program, always highly rated, had skyrocketed him to fame. To insure his postwar return to the air, the show's sponsor, Raleigh Cigarettes, had been paying their star $1000 per week during his military service. His name was Red Skelton.

Skelton's postwar radio show followed essentially the same musical-variety format as his highly successful precursor, which had run for three seasons beginning in the fall of 1941. Each show was populated with Skelton's assortment of comedy characters, including Clem Kadiddlehopper, Dead-Eye, and Junior, "the mean widdle kid." Missing from the 1945 version were regulars Ozzie Nelson and Harriet Hilliard who had started their own show while Skelton was in service. Still very present was Skelton's ex-wife Edna Stillwell, who as his writer was responsible for his metamorphosis from small-time vaudevillian to radio and film star.

Verna, most likely aided by a ghostwriter, told the story of how she first met Skelton in the January 1948 issue of *Radio Mirror* magazine. The following excerpt is taken from her article titled "Love That Red-Head!": "Red and I were friends for a year before I even heard his radio show. We met backstage at NBC in 1940 . . . Sometimes Red and I would 'hit the hall' at the same moment, bob out of our adjoining studios during rehearsal for a quick breather. We were never introduced, just got to talking the way actors will . . . all right, I'll admit it, talking about ourselves. I was fascinated with Red's story, the Horatio Alger tale in which a gawky kid who began his theatrical career dancing in Walkathons in Vincennes, Indiana, climbed to the top in show business."

Verna and Skelton were interested to learn that their early lives somewhat mirrored each other. Like Verna, Skelton began his career at age ten, when his widowed mother needed financial assistance. However, instead of beginning with a legitimate stock company as Verna did, Skelton joined "Doc" Lewis's Patent Medicine Show, entertaining the crowd as the doctor's bumbling assistant. Subsequent stints in stock, burlesque, and vaudeville followed. Verna and Skelton each knew all too well the rigors of circuit life. Skelton met his first wife Edna in 1930 when she was an usherette at the Pantages Theater in Kansas City. Their paths twice crossed again the following year, and after dating only six weeks, they married. Young Edna had a talent for writing jokes, and soon she began writing for Skelton. For almost a decade they worked the circuits until Skelton hit it big with his first radio program. Verna found it easy to relate to Skelton in that way as well; she and her husband had earned their dues traveling across Canada together before entering radio. An added plus was Verna's discovery that Skelton's birthday was just two days before hers, although she was twenty-three years his senior.

"Red and I got to know one another very well, trading life stories, and we became fast friends," Verna wrote in the *Radio Mirror* article. "One day, while we gossiped in the hall, Red said, 'I'm going to have you on my show some day.' 'I can't wait,' I said, meaning it." But the wait was longer than either imagined it.

One of Skelton's most popular characters, dating back to his days on the stage in the 1930s, was Junior, the "mean widdle kid." Radio historian John Dunning best described Junior's shtick: " 'If I dood it, I gets a whipping,' he would muse. Then, after the briefest pause during which he allegedly reflected on the crime and its probable punishment, he'd say, 'I dood it,' and the vase would break, the window would shatter, the snowball would knock the postman's hat off. And Junior would have another sore bottom." Junior's "I dood it" became a national catchphrase in 1942; one of Skelton's films even bore that title.

It was obvious that such a successful character should be part of Skelton's return to radio in late 1945. Since Harriet Hilliard, who had played Junior's mother, was no longer available, Skelton had to come up with a new character to play off the mischievous tike. That's how "Na-maw" was born.

Verna explained the character's creation in *Radio Mirror*: "Red came back from the war with the Big Grandmother Idea. He had been looking, cooking, I think, for the right part for me. He said a lot of the boys wrote all the time to their grandmothers . . . there weren't any radio grandmothers. Edna thought he had something there, and set up auditions for the part. I was one of a dozen character women who tried out for the character. I came into the studio late, but very eagerly. I hadn't seen my 'little-boy' pal since before he put on his khaki pants. I looked about for Red. His voice sang out over the mike from the control room. 'That's my Grandma!' And that's all there was to that audition."

"Grandma," or "Na-maw" as Junior sometimes called her, was originally designed as a straight part to counterbalance Skelton's incorrigible brat. Employing

Verna and Red Skelton cutting the rug at a 1946 party.

a charmingly sweet voice, she gently admonished the little imp while Skelton got the laughs. For instance, on December 18 in the "Room for Rent: No Children Allowed" sketch, while they were inspecting a hotel, Grandma directs Junior's attention to a stained glass window. He protests, "Well, don't look at me—I didn't do it!" Grandma could be very indulging, but Junior could be just as unappreciative. When she turned her back, Junior, with a devilish grin, referred to her as a "trusting old soul" as he plotted new ways to wreak havoc on the household.

When Junior threatened to cut off a sleeping uncle's beard, Grandma gave her pat response followed by a throaty chuckle, "You wouldn't do that, Junior. You're kidding me! Ha! Ha! Ha!"

"You just keep laughing, kiddo," Junior winked with a smirk.

Gradually and subtly Grandma began to serve Junior a dose of his own medicine. In the January 22 sketch "Never Again," there was this exchange as Junior tried to fix a dripping faucet:

GRANDMA (CALLING)
Junior! Junior, are you banging on the pipe with an iron bar?

JUNIOR
No, Gwanma, I using me head.

GRANDMA
Well, *stop* it! Do you want to stir up all the rust?

A month later Grandma proves she can hand out the insults with sweetness when Junior questioned her about his birth in "The New Telephone" sketch:

JUNIOR
Was I a blessed event?

GRANDMA
No, you were a dirty trick.

JUNIOR
Was me mummy surprised when I was born?

GRANDMA
Yes, she was expecting a *child*.

When Junior thoroughly provoked Grandma, he feared she'd retrieve her hairbrush to "beat me within an inch of me underwear." Sometimes she did, too. Then Junior would stage one of his blubbering fits, full of false remorse. Grandma, assuming baby talk to comfort him, would pat him softly, "Bless his little heart." Then Junior, milking it, would echo, "Bwess me widdle heart!"

These sketches were always reserved as the final segment of the show, and they became the most popular.

As Verna further explained, the chemistry between Skelton and her clicked immediately: "From the beginning, we worked together as though we had been doing routines for years. We were in instant rapport—*simpatico*—whatever language you like, there's a word for it. On my side, at least, it was love. I really feel the deepest love for the boy. Nothing mystic, either—I have good solid reasons. If there is ever any disagreement about a line on the show, Red asks the cast's opinion. If we out-vote him, he backs down without an argument. 'You may be

Mutual Admiration: Red Skelton plants a kiss on Verna Felton's cheek while GeGe Pearson (LEFT) and Skelton's wife Georgia watch, 1946.

right, Na-maw,' he'll say, 'let's try it your way.' Not so big, you see, that he can be bigger, not so smart but that he is willing to learn."

Sixteen years later, when Marty Halperin interviewed Verna, a sincere love for Skelton was still evident in her voice. When listing her radio credits, she announced with pride, "I was with Red Skelton for five years. That was a nice adventure." She then explained to Halperin how the idea for Junior's grandmother developed, adding wistfully, "Five lovely years, just wonderful, had lots of fun."

Verna considered it a "dream job," and Skelton as a "dream boss." She explained in the *Radio Mirror* article: "It is traditional that the whole company barge over to the Brown Derby for supper after the broadcasts, and we linger over countless cups of coffee rehashing all of the slips and flukes of the show. He clings to us. We're a sort of hand-picked second family. I was grateful for all my years of barnstorming those first few weeks on the Skelton show, when I was just finding out about Red—how he will stop after the first line of a six-line speech if he feels like it (or cut out a joke completely if he sees someone in the audience he thinks the joke line might offend)—and he'll expect the other people in the routine to go merrily on, cue or no cue. I had worked like that for years, so it was no problem for me—but not every actor's nervous system can take it. Red expects more than routine efficiency from the people who work with him, and he should—for he certainly puts into his side of the bargain more than most people expect from a boss-employee relationship."

Verna makes a point with Red Skelton (RIGHT) while surrounded by Lee Millar Jr., David Forrester, and Georgia Skelton during a party at Rod O'Connor's home, May 1946.

Besides Verna, the cast of the 1945-46 Skelton show included announcer Rod O'Connor, singer Anita Ellis, David Forrester and his orchestra, actors Pat McGeehan and Wonderful Smith, and blonde actress GeGe Pearson. Born in Utah in 1911, Helen Rose Pearson, whose parents called her Ginger, began her career touring with her father's tent show in the Dakotas and Minnesota. Since then she had played in every entertainment medium except burlesque, even appearing in a fast flop on Broadway in 1933. Pearson's actor-husband Hal Gerard later gave her the nickname GeGe, which she began to use professionally. During an interview five months before Pearson joined the Skelton show, *Hollywood Citizen-News* columnist Zuma Palmer found Pearson to be more "animated" and having "more expression in her face than glamour pictures would indicate." An adept dialectician, Pearson played, among other parts, Clem Kadiddlehopper's twangy sweetheart Sarah Dew. She also gave an excellent imitation of Mae West in the Dead-Eye segments.

In his 1979 biography of Skelton, Arthur Marx noted that during the planning phase of Skelton's 1945 return to radio, NBC producers had to find "some competent bit part players who would not be thrown by Red's ad-libs and usually unreliable cue lines." Marx was evidently unaware of Verna's long list of estimable credits. She was no "bit" player, and she was more than competent. Others thought so, too.

On April 14, 1946, Verna was presented with *Radio Life's* Distinguished Achievement Award as the "outstanding feminine supporting player" for the 1945-46 radio season, undoubtedly due in part to her delightful turn as Junior's grandmother.

Not since she first played Dennis Day's mother had a part brought Verna as much recognition. Magazines and newspapers parenthetically identified her as "Gwanma" in order to help readers recognize her real name. As an even happier consequence, this landmark role influenced producers to give Verna air credit more frequently, particularly on shows for which she had previously performed without it.

One prime example of this was the *Edgar Bergen-Charlie McCarthy Show*, to which Verna returned in the spring of 1946. Bergen had persuaded an ailing W. C. Fields, by then a resident of the Las Encinas Sanitarium in Pasadena, to make another guest appearance on his March 24 broadcast. To make the situation more convenient for Fields, the Sunday rehearsal and broadcast were held onstage at the Pasadena Playhouse. When Verna saw Fields at the rehearsal she was saddened by his physical appearance. He was in the advanced stages of cirrhosis; his skin was a sickly yellow, and his abdomen was distended. Fields's failing eyesight prevented him from reading the script clearly, leaving everyone to wonder if he would make it through the broadcast. During the break Fields fortified himself with gin, vodka, and beer, served in his dressing room downstairs. When it was time for the broadcast, he staggered to the microphone. His delivery was slow but he managed to keep to the script, which essentially was a tragic satire of Fields's dilapidated state. Sadly, the performance foreshadowed the famous comedian's irreversible decline.

Borrowing straight from Fields's current plight, the sketch was set at the Creeking Springs Sanitarium, where Edgar Bergen and Charlie McCarthy go to visit Fields's character, a victim of the postwar housing shortage who's feigning illness in order to rent a room. Verna was chosen to play his foil, a battleaxe-nurse whom Fields says has the "soul of an ice cube."

VERNA (ENTERING)
(to Fields, gruffly) So you're sitting up, huh?
Well, it looks as if you're just about well.

FIELDS
(whispering to Bergen and McCarty) Isn't she a tough dame?

(weakly) Uh, frankly, Nurse, I don't think
I will—last—through—the—night.

VERNA
Good! Then I can rent this room out tomorrow!

BERGEN

That's no way to talk—he's a very sick man.

MCCARTHY

Why, he's within three fingers of death's door.
Why, look, he's shaking like a mint leaf!

FIELDS

(groaning) Water! Water!
(deliriously) What am I saying??

VERNA

Awwww, Shuddup! You're doing all right.

BERGEN

How could you tell?

VERNA

This morning he tried to blow the foam off the medicine.

BERGEN

Now, just a minute, Nurse, he's a sick man—

VERNA

You keep out of this, Curly!
Who do you think you are?

BERGEN

I'm Edgar Bergen!

VERNA

Yes, I know, and I'm Lana Turner!
Fields, why don't you pack up and go home?

MCCARTHY

He can't go home—he was thrown out of there, too.

VERNA

Ohhh, so that's it!

FIELDS (TO MCCARTHY)

Why don't you close your knothole,
you talking totem pole?

McCarthy
Why, you two-legged martini—

Bergen
Now, Charlie, remember we came here to extend the olive branch—

McCarthy
What's the use? He'll only trip over it.

Fields
One more crack, and I'll nail some runners on your stomach
and use you for a sled.

McCarthy
Oh, you "sleigh" me!

Fields
I've never been so insulted since the day I was born.

McCarthy
You weren't born—you were squeezed out of a bar rag!

Verna
(yelling) Here, get out of here, all of you!
Get out of here!

McCarthy (exiting)
Here we go again, here we go!

The Bergen show was second in the ratings that week, just behind *Fibber McGee and Molly*. It would be Fields's final radio performance. He died that same year, on Christmas Day.

In early summer *Radio Life* reporter Shirley Gordon visited Verna's home to prepare for a special profile to honor Verna as one of its award winners for the season just ended. The article, titled "Kilocycle Queen of Caricature," was published July 14. Gordon admitted being surprised to find Verna free for an afternoon interview, "We immediately discovered that she was due at a radio rehearsal that evening and slated to do two broadcasts the next day!"

"As a matter of fact," Verna laughed, "I'm on the air on CBS and NBC during the same half-hour tomorrow night. It'll be a tight fit."

Indeed, even though the regular season had ended for Red Skelton and Joan Davis, Verna had several episodes of *Suspense* lined up for the summer. She had also signed on to repeat her role of Irish housekeeper Mrs. MacIntyre for several

With the rumpus room in the background, Verna sits by her pool with dogs
Mike and Skipper, 1946.

weeks on *Tommy Riggs and Betty Lou*, which was then making a brief return as a
summer replacement series on CBS.

That afternoon Gordon and photographer Gene Lester followed Verna around
her house and yard, snapping shots of her tending her flower garden, playing
cards with Lee, posing with her pets, and playing the living room piano, a Millar
family heirloom. One pose showed Lee at his own piano in an upstairs room
which Verna had converted from attic space to be used as his "headquarters." It
afforded Lee some privacy away from the rest of the household, which at that
time was getting a little crowded.

The ever-present Codo, almost eighty-seven years old, and Verna's Swedish
housekeeper, a spry senior citizen herself, were not the only ones populating 4147
Bakman Avenue, which Verna jokingly referred to as the "Old Folks Home." Since
1945, Pearl Allen had been residing with Verna as well. Though his reasons for
relocating from San Francisco are not precisely known, it is quite possible that
Pearl, now seventy-four, might have received more daily attention in Verna's
home than from his young wife Violet, who continued to work a full-time job
with the Wells Fargo Bank. Whatever the case, their physical separation did not
end their marriage; all parties involved, including Verna, remained on good terms
with one another. She made Pearl as comfortable as possible in her home,
making sure to include "Bopa" in some of her own social activities.

Lee Millar Jr.

During the past year, Lee had tried his hand at composing music, radio announcing, and even starring in a short-lived radio program called *Son of Robin Hood.* One month after the *Radio Life* article was published, Lee joined a local repertory group known as The New Edition Players, organized by young actress Lisabeth Fielding. Fielding had devised a new concept; the repertory members would be descendants of professional actors. Besides Lee, charter members included established film actors Edith Barrett and Lloyd Corrigan as well as Bryan Kellaway, the son of actor Cecil Kellaway. Fielding's sponsors included Mary Pickford, Constance Collier, Sir C. Aubrey Smith, Selena Royle, Anne Seymour, and Vincent Price, who was then married to Barrett. Verna was a sponsor as well, but before the repertory company got off the ground, she encouraged Lee to pursue his stage career in the East. She felt if he were to be successful in film or radio, he needed the priceless experience of performing in stock. Lee eagerly set his sights on New York.

Meanwhile that summer, Verna took advantage of a less hectic work schedule. With gasoline and tire rationing a thing of the past, she was eager for a road trip. Verna especially craved a reunion with her Canadian friends, and her pal Mary Edith Stahl agreed to share the driving. Vancouver was chosen as their first stop; over a decade had passed since Verna had visited that city. She was anxious to reunite with hotel proprietress and friend Rose Low, who had lost her husband William to colon cancer earlier in the year. Later Verna would be especially glad she made the trip; Rose would die suddenly of a heart attack at age seventy-two on August 1 of the following year.

To cut travel expenses, Verna decided to use Lee's Buick convertible to pull a tiny house-trailer, a convenience allowing them to make stops along the 1300-mile journey—a pretty adventuresome plan for two unattached ladies. Verna and Mary Edith left Los Angeles on July 3, stopping off in San Francisco to pick up Violet Allen who would accompany them the rest of the way. These were the days before interstate highways so travel was no easy undertaking. To make matters worse, Lee's car kept breaking down. On one back road, it quit completely. The ladies were miles from a garage. Luckily, along came a young man who asked to assist them. Suspecting a faulty fuel pump as the source of trouble and thinking he had a used replacement at home, he soon returned and installed the pump. Gratefully, they were on their way again.

By July 7, they had reached Vancouver. The next day a reporter from the *Vancouver Sun* called on Verna at Rose Low's Marble Arch Hotel on Richards Street. She shared with him the sadness she felt earlier that day as she pulled her convertible up the corner of East Hastings Street and Gore Avenue. Instead of the imposing granite-fronted theatre she expected to find, there was a rather ordinary supermarket. The old Empress, Verna learned, had been torn down in 1940. Verna then regaled the journalist with stories of performances forty years past: "I have more memories of this town than I have grey hairs . . . I used to like the wonderful smell of new props backstage at the old Empress Theatre . . . I often wonder how far I really have gone since then. That was the 'legit' theatre. Not long ago I played a big role in a movie as—guess what?—an elephant!"

Verna was also quick to add that she had recently "sewn up two fat radio contracts" for the fall, returning to both the Joan Davis and Red Skelton shows. While no records of just how "fat" Verna's salary was for these programs, she was certainly far past the days of scale pay. A cancelled payroll check for her guest appearance on Rudy Vallee's show in November 1946, shows the after-taxes amount of $118.60. At that time, AFRA scale pay for actors in a 30-minute radio show was $37.51. However, actors like Verna, who were under contract to an agency, were generally paid higher than AFRA scales.

From Vancouver Verna's little caravan headed east for Edmonton, which happened to be Violet's hometown. There, Verna would reunite with her old Calgary friend Ida Graves, who had become a widow the same year as Verna. Ida had spent the interim visiting her three sons, but now she was settling into her

Neighbors gather to see Verna and her friends off on their Canadian vacation.

Edmonton home. Before reaching Edmonton, misfortune again met the little trio. Verna later blamed Canada's inferior roads, but whatever the cause, the car turned over in a ditch near Radium Hot Springs, some 500 miles south of Edmonton. Verna arrived at Ida's home "covered in bruises, but no broken bones."

The *Edmonton Bulletin-Journal* profiled Verna in an article on July 19, updating her old Edmonton fans on her recent endeavors while introducing her stage career to those too young enough to recall it. "Nostalgic memories of the golden age of the theatre in Edmonton were recalled with the return here on a visit of Verna Felton, one of the most popular actresses ever to tread the boards of city stages. As the leading woman of the Allen Players of happy days long since passed, she won a widespread following. And rightly so. With equal ease she could bring tears to the eyes of all while playing *Camille*. Then she would bring forth gales of laughter with the homely lines of *Sis Hopkins*. And just to top her versatility she would charm with a voice of the same general quality as that of Evelyn MacGregor of current radio popularity—in Karl Hoschana's delightful musical comedy *Madame Sherry*." While Verna confessed that she loved radio work better than any in her profession, she told the *Bulletin-Journal*, "The stage will never pass . . . the public wants drama." She assured readers that a future for stock companies definitely existed in the States, citing recent stage successes in New York and Hollywood and adding that Lee would leave Hollywood on July 24 to begin stage training in New York.

Meanwhile, newspapers back in the States ran a brief mention of a new radio series for which Verna was being considered. Dennis Day had been signed for a new half-hour radio program called *A Day in the Life of Dennis Day*, to debut on NBC on October 3. The July 28 press release noted that negotiations were underway to sign Sharon Douglas as the female lead, adding "expected to be included in the cast are Verna Felton and Joe Kearns." Verna and Kearns, as well as Bea Benaderet, John Brown, and Francis "Dink" Trout, had supported Day and Douglas in an audition for the series earlier in the year. Although Day played the same type of character as he regularly did on Jack Benny's program, this series was set in the mythical town of Weaverville where Day was a soda jerk, boarding in the home of Mr. and Mrs. Anderson, played by Trout and Verna in the audition. The domineering Mrs. Anderson greatly disapproved of Day's interest in their daughter Mildred, played by Douglas. Bea Benaderet was ultimately hired for the part of Mrs. Anderson, and she played it for most of the duration of the series.

At the same time changes were being made in the cast of characters for the *Joan Davis Show*. In August Shirley Mitchell announced that she was immediately giving up her radio career to make plans to marry Dr. Julian Frieden that November. Sharon Douglas, who had just become the bride of producer Edward Nassour on July 31, was chosen to fill the part of socialite Barbara Weatherby. Gone was Harry Von Zell; in his stead was Wally Brown as Joanie's boyfriend. Si Wills continued in his role of nincompoop Serenus, but writers decided that Rosella Hipperton's silliness had run its course. So they devised a new character for Verna to play—Joanie's irascible, dictatorial Cousin Cornelia. Although scant recordings exist from Joan's 1946-47 season, newspaper listings show that Joanie was continually trying to get rid of her bossy cousin. By season's end, she would get her wish. Verna would not return to the show in the fall of 1947, ending five years of being second banana to Joan Davis.

Verna found little time during the 1946-47 season to appear on other programs besides the *Joan Davis Show* and the *Red Skelton Show*. Two exceptions were delightful diversions. The first was a *Suspense* broadcast, "*The Man Who Thought He Was Edward G. Robinson*," broadcast on October 17. A shy, inhibited man named Homer J. Hubbard, played by actor Edward G. Robinson, is unhappily married to a nagging wife, played by Verna. He finds solace in going to the movies, particularly those starring tough-guy Robinson. Hubbard's wife callously ridicules his hobby, "I wish you were half the man that Edwin G. Robertson is!" Then Hubbard begins to fantasize that he is Edward G. Robinson, imitating the actor at home, at work, wherever he goes. His scornful wife laughs heartily, "Why don't you imitate Donald Duck or Shirley Temple? I think you'd find it easier." Later, after she humiliates him in front of their friends, Hubbard decides to kill her. When the real Edward G. Robinson comes to town, Hubbard seeks his advice on the proper method.

Verna's second guest appearance involved another tale of murder—"*Arsenic and Old Lace*," broadcast on November 25 as an episode of the *Screen Guild*

Theatre. Verna teamed up with pal Jane Morgan to play Abby and Martha Brewster, the Brooklyn spinsters who "help lonely old men find peace" by poisoning them. Both ladies turned in delightful performances, especially Jane whose vocal crackle was simply charming. Although Boris Karloff and Eddie Albert, playing the film roles of Raymond Massey and Cary Grant respectively, were credited as "starring" in this radio version, the evening clearly belonged to Verna and Jane. The versatile Joseph Kearns also shined as Dr. Einstein, played by Peter Lorre on film.

Midway through the radio season, Verna found herself filling in for one of her old friends on *The George Burns and Gracie Allen Show.* Since the spring of 1946, she had appeared on the show as a member of Gracie's club, The Beverly Hills Uplift Society, "a cultural group of intellectual ladies interested only in the artistic development of the cinema." Denounced by George as the bane of his existence, the women held their noisy gabfests in the Burnses' den. Verna played Frances Fowler while Bea Benaderet and Elvia Allman appeared as Blanche Morton and Clara Bagley, respectively. When Benaderet found it necessary to stop work during the last two months of her second pregnancy, Verna assumed the semi-regular role of Blanche Morton, Gracie's best friend.

Meanwhile, Red Skelton maintained his usual radio format and cast for the 1946-47 season. Junior and "Na-maw" continued to be the closing segment each week. Verna's popularity in the role is evidenced by her inclusion on Skelton's float in the 1946 "Santa Claus Lane Parade," annually sponsored by the Hollywood Chamber of Commerce. In a photo of the float, Skelton is attired a'la Fauntleroy—in his velvet knee britches and lace collar—while tethered around the neck with a fat rope, held on the other end by Verna, in colonial garb as Grandma. Well over a million spectators lined Hollywood Boulevard that night, craning their necks to catch glimpses of NBC radio stars whose floats were sandwiched between high school bands, mounted troops, cowboy units, civic groups, and clowns. Verna, Sharon Douglas, Paula Winslowe, and Eddie "Rochester" Anderson of the Jack Benny show were among the few supporting players featured in the parade; floats were mainly reserved for stars like Skelton, Benny, Dennis Day, Eddie Cantor, Roy Rogers, Judy Canova, and Fibber McGee and Molly. The *Hollywood Citizen-News* reported on November 23 that the record-setting parade "won a nip-and-tuck race with the rainmaker last night and was safely entered into the big book of super-scintillators today as the granddaddy of them all."

Verna confessed her affection for Skelton in the 1948 *Radio Mirror* article: "The best laughs are awfully close to drama, close to the hearts of the people. The laughs Red and I have had together, as well as the laughs we hope to get from you when we work together on the air, are that kind of laughter, for Red is the classic clown whose lips make jokes while his insides seethe with drama. Red is one funny man who really *could* play Hamlet. I am not joking. I think he is really great—a great actor, a great human being. I love him, the good, bad little boy—the complex, appealing adult."

Hal Peary (LEFT) and Verna clowning around at a party given for Red Skelton.

Skelton was equally demonstrative in his love and admiration for Verna. He presented her with two gifts, which she cherished always. One was a belt made of a gold chain with large gold medallions interspersed throughout is length. Verna's name was engraved on the largest of these, and on the reverse side was this message: "Award for Putting up with The Mean Widdle Kid, Love, Red Skelton and Edna." One of Skelton's hobbies was painting oil portraits of clowns. He gave one of his creations to Verna, which she proudly displayed in her home.

While Verna's friendship with Red continued to grow, she also socialized with his young wife Georgia. In 2006, Clyde Bowman, a great-nephew of Pearl Allen, recalled one of Verna's favorite stories about Red: "Verna and Red Skelton's wife—and there were several of the women that were associated with the show, either by being married to the people who were on the show or being in the show—they would get together and play bridge. Georgia and Verna were quite close, and they all played bridge together. One day Georgia was having bridge at her house. And Red came in from out in the yard—he'd been out gardening or something—he looked like hell. He was all sloppy and everything. And he was in the kitchen, looking at what she was going to serve for lunch. And she said,

Verna displaying the belt Red Skelton gave her.

'Now you get out of here. You can't come in here like that. I'm having the ladies over.' He said, 'Oh, okay.' So apparently what he did was he left. And then as soon as the ladies came and they all sat down to luncheon, the front door rang. And here was Red, all dressed up in a tuxedo. And he says, 'May I come in now?'"

A pensive Verna Felton in San Francisco on "I Am American Day," 1947.

Verna, unidentified man, Red Skelton, and Harold Russell, San Francisco, 1947.

In 1940, Congress had designated the third Sunday in May as "I Am An American Day," a time reserved to recognize newly naturalized citizens. Since then many cities held huge celebrations each year. In 1947, the *San Francisco Examiner* sponsored "one of the mightiest patriotic celebrations in the city's peacetime history," to be held at the War Memorial Opera House on May 18. Heading the list of the invited performers were Red Skelton and his entire radio troupe. *Examiner* photographs show Skelton with his arm around Verna's shoulder as they are introduced to the city supervisor upon their arrival in San Francisco the day before the celebration. Other performers on the program included Celeste Holm, Virginia Mayo, and 1947 Oscar-winner Harold Russell, who played the double amputee in *The Best Years of Our Lives*.

When the Skelton show opened in the fall, Lurene Tuttle joined the cast as Junior's indulgent mother who often took up for him when Na-maw was threatening to punish him. If his mother were not around when Na-maw went for the hairbrush, Junior would slyly threaten, "You lay a hand on me, and you is in trouble. I will tell on you! I know plenty, and I will tell." He would then dredge up some unflattering detail from Na-maw's past, which she would vehemently deny. Then he'd catch her off-guard and trick her into a confession. A prime example of this is found in the "A Little Boy and His Dog, Part 2" sketch on November 18:

JUNIOR
I will tell everybody that you used to be
Buxom Verna the lady wrassler, you was.

GRANDMA
(indignantly) I was no such thing!

JUNIOR
Oh, no?

GRANDMA
(insistent) No!

JUNIOR
(as an aside, yelling) Hey, Verna, do you think
you could beat Toe-Hold Harriet?

GRANDMA
(growling) Well, just put her in the ring with me,
and I'll strangle the moll!

NBC portrait of Verna, 1947.

Just as Joan Davis had arranged a part for Verna in *She Wrote the Book*, Skelton found a small role for Verna during the filming of *The Fuller Brush Man* at Columbia in December. Skelton played Red Jones, an accident-prone street cleaner in love with secretary Ann Elliot, played by Janet Blair. When he proposes marriage, she refuses his engagement ring and tells him that she will not marry him until he makes a success of himself. To help Red find a new job, Ann arranges to have him tested as a door-to-door Fuller Brush salesman.

Screenwriters Frank Tashlin and Devery Freeman seized upon the successful "Junior" segment of Skelton's radio program and included a variation of it in the film. In one house on Red Jones's trial route lives a mischievous redhead named Junior, played by seven-year-old Jimmy Hunt. As Red tries to enter the house via its Dutch door, Junior tricks him into spilling his samples case over the locked lower half of the door. Then when Red attempts to climb over it, Junior removes the salesman's shoe and tickles his foot with one of his own Fuller brushes. Red chases him inside where the devilish tyke drops the shoe into a fish tank.

When Red retrieves it, Junior lets out a yell for his grandmother, played by Verna. Eyeing the child with contempt, Red suggests that his grandmother buy a hairbrush "that's flat on one side."

She tries one, smacking her palm, "Oooh, my, that's a good one—has a lovely sting!" Just then, Junior takes aim at Red's eye with a slingshot.

Grandma is furious. "Junior! That calls for a spanking!"

Testing her, he responds, "You better not spank me, Grandma, or I will tell!"

"You'll tell what?"

He grins, "That you was a shimmy dancer in a side show!"

Grandma indignantly denies it, "Oooh, I was no such thing!"

Junior starts clapping and humming "The Streets of Cairo," the familiar tune usually accompanying cartoons of snake charmers or hootchy-kootchy dancers. Grandma, caught off-guard, enthusiastically shimmies, her hands in the air.

Suddenly realizing her grandson's ploy, she shrieks, "Junior!"

Red then offers Grandma the hairbrush, "Compliments of the company—I'm sorry we don't have one with a nail in it."

The Fuller Brush Man, released in May 1948, was a critical and commercial success, ranking among the year's top-twenty moneymakers. The 1947-48 radio season was equally successful for Skelton; the ratings consistently showed his program to be among the top ten.

Since she was no longer a regular on *The Joan Davis Show*, Verna was free to accept other regular parts that season. She was delighted to join the original cast members of *Point Sublime* when it returned to the airwaves on October 6 after an absence of three years. Its sponsor, the John Hancock Mutual Life Insurance Company, was somewhat uncertain about the show's return so it was initially broadcast only to Pacific Coast stations as well as a few Texas outlets. By year's end the show had proven itself, and the John Hancock company extended its sponsorship coast-to-coast over the ABC network, beginning February 2.

The season opener re-introduced listeners to the cast as Ben Willett, played by Cliff Arquette, came home from three years in Europe where he served the United Nations Relief and Rehabilitation Administration, providing help to areas liberated from Axis powers. Ben is welcomed at the train station by all of his old friends, including Evelyn Hanover (Jane Morgan), Howie MacBrayer (Earle Ross), and August Moon (Mel Blanc, employing his Porky Pig stutter). When Ben learns that loud-mouthed Hattie Hirsch (Verna) is seeking appointment as

Junior (Jimmy Hunt) outwits Red Jones (Red Skelton) while Grandma (Verna) looks on helplessly in *The Fuller Brush Man.*

the town's fire chief, he sabotages her efforts by riding a fire truck dressed as a woman and swaying the town council's decision.

Despite low comedy caricatures like Hattie Hirsch and August Moon, *Point Sublime* at times seemed more like a soap opera. Protagonist and chief do-gooder Ben Willett grappled with problems like helping scarlet fever victims, restoring hope and eyesight to a blinded war veteran, and reawakening affection in the heart of a bitter young mother. When he wasn't busy untangling someone else's life, Ben was sermonizing about current topics, like racial tolerance.

Of all the Point Sublime townsfolk, Hattie seemed to be on the receiving end of Ben's sermons most often. Her wealth and position enabled her to be a self-serving old meddler. Ben described her as the "kind of person you don't care for right at first and when you get to know her real good, you hate her." Each week Ben or one of his cronies would look out the store window and herald her arrival, "Oh, no, here comes that Hattie Hirsch!" Then she'd enter with a shrill "Hello, hello, hello, hello, hello!"

On the February 16 broadcast, when Hattie becomes head of the local Heart Association, she uses that position to further her campaign against Ben for county commissioner by plastering her photograph all over the fundraising booth. After Ben makes her see the error of her ways, a remorseful Hattie makes her typically loud and tearful exit. Just as typically, Verna's delivery received the episode's biggest laughs and applause. On the February 23 segment when Ben prevents Hattie from meddling in a love affair between two young people, she comes to her senses, extolling, "Oh, love, love, wonderful love!" Then a redeemed Hattie joins Evelyn Hanover in a duet, the curiously chosen "Pistol Packin' Mama." Verna and Jane's off-key antics, which have the studio audience going wild, are totally incongruous with the dramatic content of the show. *Oakland Tribune* reviewer John Crosby commented: "Rarely does a *Point Sublime* script run through its allotted half hour without a paroxysm of tears from somebody. Most of these little sermons wind up with everyone happily gathered around the Thanksgiving dinner . . . or grouped around a piano singing for dear life and damp with sentiment."

One wonders about the creative motive of the show's writer Robert L. Redd. Was *Point Sublime* intended to be a comedy or a drama? In episodes not featuring Hattie Hirsch, *Point Sublime* could be quite gripping, save for the annoying presence of August Moon. Jane Morgan regularly shines in her characterization of Ben's love interest, as does Cliff Arquette. Even Verna—her cartoonish entrances and exits notwithstanding—effectively emotes during her scenes. However, *Point Sublime* did not return to the air following its June 7 broadcast.

In late winter 1948, Verna returned to *The Judy Canova Show*, still stuck in its Saturday-night time slot on NBC. All of the old regulars were still on board: Ruby Dandridge, Mel Blanc, George Neise, and Joe Kearns. Although Verna initially filled in for Ruth Perrot in the part of Aunt Aggie, she soon created the role of Patsy Pierce, former silent film star. "Miz Pierce," as Judy called her, made her first appearance on March 27 when Judy solicited her friendship in order to advance her film career, a curious strategy since Miz Pierce had been out of the entertainment business for over fifteen years. The earthy Miz Pierce, who, according to her accent, must have been a Texas native, advised Judy about acting, publicity stunts, and romance. Occasionally the writers gave Verna a funny line, but, like Aunt Aggie, Miz Pierce merely served as Judy's sounding board. Still Verna did what she could with the part. She would continue to appear on the Canova show, which despite its tired material ran for another four seasons.

In addition to these recurring roles, Verna appeared four times on the *Burns and Allen* show during the 1947-48 season. Two of those appearances were as Gracie's Irish mother, visiting from San Francisco. The character was based on Gracie Allen's real mother, *nee* Margaret Darragh, a resident of the same city and the daughter of an Irish immigrant. On the show, Gracie's mother strongly disapproved of George. When Gracie asked her mother why she didn't like George, she responded in a thick Irish brogue, "I can't begin to tell ya—I'm only stayin' three weeks." During her stay, she harangued George constantly. When he tried to sooth her with a song about an aged mother, she bellowed, "Awwww, Shuddup!" (Verna continued to get a lot of mileage out of her patented line from the *Jack Benny Program*.)

Although her *Lux* days were behind her, Verna appeared on other dramatic shows that season, including *Suspense, Favorite Story, The Voyage of the Scarlet Queen,* and *The First Nighter Program*. In the latter she played the leading role in an episode titled "*Old Lady Shakespeare*," the story of 70-year-old former actress Laura Ravenswood, bitter that age has stolen her leading lady status. Though in frail health, Laura stages a comeback as the nurse in *Romeo and Juliet* in order to play matchmaker. She secretly wants her actor-son to fall in love with the actress assigned to play Juliet. When Laura's ploy works, the opening-night applause puts life back into the old actress. Verna gave one of her best performances in the part, being careful not to slip into caricature.

Meanwhile, her son Lee was actively pursuing his own career. Following Verna's advice, Lee sought to gain acting experience in Eastern stock companies. In the fall of 1946, he landed parts in several productions of The New York Imperial Players at Frank Dailey's Ivanhoe in Irvington, New Jersey. Verna and Pearl must have smiled when they learned Lee's first production was a three-night run of the old chestnut *East Lynne*, which the Allen Stock Company had performed numerous times almost a half-century earlier.

Several months later Lee, not wanting to trade on his father's fame, decided to perform as Steve Lawrence, borrowing his grandmother's maiden name. Subsequently he performed in several productions of New York's Equity-Library Theatre, founded by actor Sam Jaffe in 1943 as a showcase for young actors, directors, and technicians. In May 1947, Lee, now as Stephen Lawrence, appeared in a benefit production of *Hedda Gabler* at the Community Center Theatre on 89th Street. He spent that summer performing in stock at the Deal Summer Theatre in Deal, New Jersey.

While in New York that fall, he was signed to support Lucille Ball in a tour of the romantic comedy *Dream Girl*, which also featured Scott McKay, Hayden Rorke, and Andrew Duggan. Lee filled four small roles, including a district attorney and chauffeur, at $60 per week. The rigorous itinerary began on November 17 in Princeton, New Jersey, with weeklong stops in major cities and one-nighters in smaller towns. By the end of the tour, Lee had become a seasoned performer, experiencing similar situations faced by his family in the first three decades of the century—some venues were too small to accommodate the scenery, while others were huge auditoriums. The tour ended unexpectedly in Los Angeles on January 25, 1948, after Ball caught a flu virus that had plagued half the cast. Lee remained in California, and by midyear he had landed regular work on the juvenile adventure serial *Chandu the Magician*. He would stay with the series through April 1949, providing him with almost double the weekly salary of *Dream Girl*.

Verna on her boat.

During Lee's eighteen months in the East, when he was between engagements, he had required Verna's financial support. Luckily by now she was earning enough money to not only help him out but also support Codo and Pearl. With a reported 1947 income from radio assignments of $35,000 (approximately $334,000 in 2008 dollars), Verna could afford to enjoy a few luxuries. She enhanced her house in several phases, first by adding a service porch adjacent to the breakfast room. When it leaked, she built a room above it, thereby enlarging Lee's private space upstairs. The small living room windows were replaced with a picture window. Outside the dining room, a tiny patio was added facing the pool. And in the rear of the house, adjacent to the garage, a sturdy brick barbecue was built in a surrounding pergola. With all this building going on, Verna's friends began to jokingly call her "Mrs. Winchester," after the eccentric San Jose millionaire Sarah Winchester who, for thirty-eight years, continuously constructed her mansion to keep spirits at bay. In addition to these home improvements, Verna also made a sentimental purchase. Lee Sr. had always wanted to buy a boat but never got around to it. So now, Verna bought a small boat, docking it at San Pedro. She also purchased furs and jewelry, though not extravagantly. And in the summer of 1948, she planned a six-week Hawaiian vacation.

Verna booked passage on the S.S. Lurline, the crown jewel of Matson Navigation Company's white fleet, whose service route was Los Angeles-San Francisco-Honolulu. In 1932, the Lurline had been built especially for that route, but during the war she was assigned to the U. S. Navy for use as a transport vessel, carrying thousands of troops all over the world. After the war the Lurline was reconverted to luxury liner status—to the tune of twenty million dollars—and made her maiden voyage from San Francisco on April 15, 1948.

Hazel Delphine, Verna's Radio Women's War Service buddy and a frequent traveler to Hawaii, most likely sparked Verna's interest in the trip. Plans were made for Verna and Mary Edith Stahl to embark from the Los Angeles Harbor for the fabled islands on Monday, June 28, stopping first in San Francisco to pick up more passengers. When the Lurline docked in Honolulu five days later, the cruise ship arrived with a postwar record load of 753 passengers. Occupying a stateroom on the same voyage was Verna's old boss Walt Disney, traveling with his wife and daughters.

Verna and her fellow first-class passengers were pampered and indulged twenty-four hours a day. She passed the days lounging, playing deck games, or swimming in the outdoor pool. An inveterate game player, Verna was also pleased to find amusement in bingo, dominoes, and card games. At night there was dancing and a "midnight snack"—a staggering buffet of extravagantly garnished turkey, ham, and beef, not to mention a profusion of salads, side dishes, and desserts. And everywhere there was fresh fruit, on the breakfast table each morning and on the bedside table each night, and all times in between.

After five days of food, fun, and relaxation, Verna's tropical destination was in sight. She stood on deck to greet the soft, balmy air of the islands. As the Lurline prepared to dock, small craft arrived, bringing friends, family, and welcoming officials who climbed aboard to greet the travelers. "Outrigger canoes scattered a welcoming festoon of fresh-flower leis on the water," wrote the authors of *To Honolulu in Five Days: Cruising Aboard Matson's S.S. Lurline*. "Tugs came alongside, carrying hundreds of greeters, their arms full of leis for the arriving passengers. Young men dove for coins tossed over the ship's railing." Meanwhile, a press boat delivered reporters anxious to "get the scoop on traveling celebrities." Verna was among those interviewed; her beaming face, surrounded by a floral head wreath and copious leis of tuberose and plumeria, appeared in the newspaper the next day. Her five weeks in Hawaii were filled with nighttime luaus and sunny days on the beach. However, Verna's departure on August 7 was to be a sad homecoming. While she was experiencing her most extravagant vacation trip ever, back in North Hollywood the most important connection to her past—the last pillar—was toppling.

Pearl Allen, suffering from pneumonia, entered St. Joseph's Hospital in Burbank on July 19. Three days later he died of respiratory failure. An autopsy revealed that he had also been suffering from a bleeding peptic ulcer. Like Verna's mother Clara, Pearl was seventy-six years old at the time of his death. His widow Violet supervised the arrangements for cremation, but final disposal was postponed until Verna's return. Pearl's ashes were buried in the Allen family plot in his hometown of Chico on September 9.

Pearl Allen had been the most influential man in the life of Verna Felton. He more than ably filled the void left by Dr. Felton's death almost fifty years earlier. Pearl lovingly nurtured Verna as a child and wisely advised her as an adult. He had tirelessly promoted her stage career, and when that ended, Pearl supported Verna's move to radio. He then witnessed her rise in Hollywood and celebrated her successes. No one was prouder of Verna's accomplishments.

By this time, Verna's station in the entertainment world—where the busiest actors seldom received credit—was aptly summarized by an anonymous clipping found among her papers: "For the most part, however, supporting players remain the unknowns of radio. Men like Elliott Lewis, Jerry Hausner, Hans Conried, and women like Verna Felton, Agnes Moorehead, Bea Benaderet are vital parts of radio production. Without them, productions would level off to mediocrity and stars would lose their own lustre."

Things were about to change. In the coming decade, Verna's career choices would save her from anonymity and elevate her to immortality.

CHAPTER 12

DISNEY DAME

On a sunny Saturday, February 1, 1964, Verna Felton seated herself on a low sofa in her North Hollywood living room, while Marty Halperin sank into a nearby armchair upholstered in lavender velvet. Each held microphones connected to a large reel-to-reel tape recorder Halperin had brought to record his interview. A photographer was also present to document the event. Halperin's intent was to preserve Verna's memories of radio's heyday for future generations. As Verna shared amusing anecdotes about radio's golden age, Halperin politely and thoughtfully interjected comments and questions.

About halfway through the interview, Halperin posed, "I don't want to be too philosophical, but in looking backwards—in things you've done—is there anything you would have changed or . . . perhaps you had missed an opportunity—"

Without hesitation Verna cut in, "Yes, I would have never left Skelton." Then she repeated softly but with emphasis, "I never would have left Skelton." As a slight frown crossed Verna's face, she quietly admitted, "I was stupidly advised. And that's always been the regret of my life, that I left him."

What led Verna to make such a decision? Her association with Red Skelton had brought her more fame than the part of Mrs. Day on Jack Benny's show and at least as much recognition for her roles with Joan Davis, if not more. In addition to this, Verna's bank account had grown fatter since joining the Skelton show. So why would she give up this prize part and its rewards?

An inspection of Verna's fourth and final season with Skelton provides some answers. On September 3, 1948, Procter and Gamble, Skelton's sponsor for the new season, moved his show to Friday nights as a stronger lead-in for their series *The Life of Riley*. The switch had been brewing since April when Raleigh Cigarettes negotiated to loan Skelton to another sponsor due to his show's "heavy financial load." Skelton biographer Wes Gehring reported that Skelton's own weekly salary had skyrocketed from less than $1000 in 1942 to $7500 in 1946. While Verna's salary at the time is not certain, she would allude to its heftiness during the Halperin interview.

Namaw is not amused at Junior's antics, 1948.

Despite the efforts of the new sponsor, Skelton's ratings noticeably fell during the 1948-49 season. Few recordings of this season are available to old-time radio fans today, but those in existence pale in comparison to broadcasts of earlier seasons. Although "Junior" and his "Namaw" remained, their segment was quite obviously shortened. At the same time, a new regular character had been created for Verna—Mrs. Fussy, Skelton's grumpy neighbor who constantly battered Skelton with insults. Typical of Verna's breathless delivery as motor-mouth Fussy was her response to Skelton's simple "Good morning" greeting on one broadcast: "Welllll, aren't you the nosy one? Since when is it any of your business how I am? If you must know, I have indigestion, my feet are killin' me, and I'm seeing specks in front of my eyes, and one of those specks is *your head*!"

Midway through the season, another development heralded even greater changes for Skelton's troupe. In early 1949, William S. Paley, chairman of the board at CBS, scored a coup by enticing many of NBC's top radio artists to switch to his network for the coming season. According to Skelton historian Wesley Hyatt, Paley learned from an accountant "that performers could keep more of their money after capital gains taxes if they incorporated themselves as businesses and sold their shows to CBS," saving them 50 percent more than in previous years. Since NBC didn't offer such deals, Skelton, as well as Jack Benny, Edgar Bergen, and George Burns and Gracie Allen, signed to make the move to CBS for the upcoming season. Even though the potential existed for Skelton to retain more money than ever before, he, according to Verna, asked his supporting cast to take a salary cut for the 1949-50 season.

"I was big salary then. And I wouldn't cut," Verna confessed candidly to Marty Halperin. Dropping her voice, she added regretfully, "Which I should have! I never stopped to think [about the possible consequences], you know. I was happy [with Skelton, but] . . . 'Gee,' I said, 'since I don't have much longer to make the big money' . . . at my age, [I] won't go down.' They said, 'Well, that's for you to say.' So I did. And I've always regretted it. That was one of the biggest regrets I ever had—to leave him—because he was such a doll."

Verna's last appearance on the Skelton show was the broadcast of May 20, 1949. They would never work together again. When Halperin asked Verna if she had ever appeared on Skelton's subsequent television show, she responded, "No. No, he's never forgiven me for leaving him. It broke his heart." Since both artists remained active in radio following Verna's departure, naturally their paths crossed from time to time. There seems to be no evidence that, despite Verna's description of Skelton's reaction, the two were not on speaking terms on such occasions. In fact, one year after the split, Verna told *Radio-Television Life* that Red still greeted her as "Namaw" whenever they bumped into each other.

On July 24, 1949, the press announced Verna's withdrawal from the Skelton show. The following month, she was included for the first time in the *Academy Players Directory*—known within the film industry as the "casting bible"—a quarterly publication utilized by casting agents since 1937. In this edition Verna's agent was listed as Jack Weiner, who also represented Verna's friend Sara Berner, as well as other character actors such as Kathryn Card, Herb Vigran, and Frank Wilcox. Weiner would continue to act in this capacity until the end of Verna's career, but whether he was the one who "stupidly advised" her to reject Skelton's salary cut remains unverified, no matter how likely it seems. Since Verna's profile had never appeared in previous editions of the *Academy Players Directory*, her inclusion at this point indicates that she was no longer content to leave all of her eggs in radio's basket.

An additional bit of evidence reveals that Verna was considering other options before she even left Skelton. Among her papers were two reserved tickets—dated March 1, 1949—for an NBC radio audition identified as "MAMA KNOWS BEST

Nanaw attempts to teach Junior a lesson.

starring VERNA FELTON." A radio audition was similar to a television pilot; each was produced to entice prospective sponsors to buy it as a series. Unfortunately, Verna's shot at radio stardom failed. *Mama Knows Best* quickly faded away, leaving no mention in the local press even as to its premise. Coincidentally, Robert Young's popular radio program *Father Knows Best* debuted on August 25 of the same year, but there should be no confusion between these similar titles. *Father Knows Best* was a completely different show, produced after its audition was recorded on December 20, 1948, more than two months prior to *Mama's* audition.

Verna assuming a surprised expression, one she would often employ for promotional photographs, 1948.

While the Red Skelton and Judy Canova shows had dominated Verna's radio appearances during the 1948-49 season, she also found time to play comic parts on *Sealtest Variety Theater, Burns and Allen,* and *The Jack Benny Program,* as well as dramatic roles on *Screen Directors Playhouse, Suspense,* and *Hallmark Playhouse.* While these shows were on hiatus during the summer of 1949, Verna sought guest appearances on shows like *My Favorite Husband* and *Young Love.* Notable among Verna's other appearances that season was an episode of *The Adventures of Sam Spade,* in which she played a murder victim called the Queen Bee.

Meanwhile, Verna's decision to explore the possibilities of film roles paid off. No sooner than she had placed the listing in the *Academy Players Directory*, she won a small part in the pirate movie *Buccaneer's Girl* which began filming at Universal in July 1949, under the direction of Frederick de Cordova.

Yvonne DeCarlo played title character Deborah McCoy, a stowaway who falls for Robin Hood-like pirate Baptiste (Philip Friend), only to find he's really Captain Robert Kingston, a prominent member of New Orleans society. Fate reunites them at a party for which Deborah has been hired to sing. When Kingston's jealous fiancée Arlene Villon (Andrea King) learns that he and Deborah had previously known one another, she sabotages Deborah's solo. Throughout Deborah's selection, Arlene laughs loudly with another guest, a dowager dressed in black silk and ropes of pearls (Verna). When Deborah takes the rude women to task, they exit haughtily, only to be followed by the insulted entertainer. A catfight ensues. While Deborah and Arlene tussle on the floor, the intervening dowager is knocked on her backside. Despite the brevity of her role, Verna's veteran talents outshine the wooden efforts of DeCarlo and King. She was billed tenth in a cast of three dozen, even though her character was too minor to be given a name.

A far superior production was Nunnally Johnson's *The Gunfighter*, filmed at Twentieth Century-Fox two months later. Adapted from a story by William Bowers, *The Gunfighter* was one of the first westerns to focus on characters and dramatic development rather than shootouts. Set in the Southwest in the 1880s, its conflicted hero Jimmy Ringo, played by Gregory Peck, has built quite a reputation as a gunslinger. Weary of killing, Ringo would like nothing better than to settle down with his wife and son, but he finds himself a hunted man, challenged by cocky "squirts" wherever he goes. When Ringo's travels brings him to Cayenne, the town where his estranged wife lives, Marshal Mark Strett (Millard Mitchell), an old friend and former outlaw, asks Ringo to leave immediately. Refusing to go before Strett brings his family to visit him, Ringo holes up in the Palace Bar, setting the whole town abuzz. While most men avoid Ringo, two aim to cause trouble. One is a gangly smart aleck, bent on making a reputation for himself, and the other is a vengeful man who thinks Ringo killed his son. When Ringo discovers the latter poised with a rifle aimed at the door of the bar, he slips out the back way to go after him. Not wanting any more bloodshed, Ringo apprehends the man without a fight and locks him up in the empty jail. At this point a group of righteous townswomen, led by the venerable Mrs. August Pennyfeather (Verna), enter the marshal's office, intent on demanding Ringo's arrest. When they learn the marshal is out, they decide to wait for his return. Old Mrs. Pennyfeather seats herself and the other women surround her, as if she's the dowager queen and they are her royal court. She mistakes the hospitable Ringo for a deputy and begins to complain about the "notorious murderer" in town. Soon Marshal Strett arrives and politely introduces the ladies to the calm gunslinger standing in their midst. Then Verna, in one of the film's

Verna as Mrs. Pennyfeather in *The Gunfighter.*

rare comic moments, delivers a beautiful double take before registering chagrin and hastening her entourage out.

Although *The Gunfighter* was not a moneymaker upon its release in May 1950, its psychological edge is more appreciated by audiences today. It boasts fine performances by Peck, Mitchell, and Skip Homeier, as well as superb black-and-white photography by revered cinematographer Arthur Miller.

Mrs. Pennyfeather is greeted by Marshal Mark Strett (Millard Mitchell) while gunslinger Johnny Ringo (Gregory Peck) looks on.)

While live-action features such as *The Gunfighter* made Verna's face visible to a public who had only known her voice, she still preferred working in radio. However, she was delighted to find a happy medium at the Walt Disney studio, where she could enact her role without having to appear in front of a camera. Eight years had passed since she recorded the voice for the Matriarch Elephant in *Dumbo*, and since then, Disney had not created any voice parts befitting Verna's talent. During the war years, the studio had produced only instructional films and shorts, but now Disney was reviving a project he had been considering as a feature-length film since 1938: *Cinderella*.

As with *Dumbo*, Disney selected voice actors from the radio industry to give life to the characters in his new animated feature. Teenager Ilene Woods, a radio singer, was chosen out of 400 girls for the title role. The unsung Eleanor Audley, a Broadway veteran but relative newcomer in Hollywood, proved to be masterful as Cinderella's evil stepmother, while fellow radio performers Rhoda Williams and Lucille Bliss were appropriately effective as the ugly stepsisters.

Cinderella's fairy godmother leaves her with a gentle warning: "You must be home before the clock strikes midnight." © WALT DISNEY PRODUCTIONS.

Verna's mature voice made her a natural to play the kind but bumbling Fairy Godmother. During the recording process, she endeared herself to the young Ilene Woods, who told the *Chicago Sun-Times* in 2005, "I don't think the hard work was in my corner . . . I would go in and have such fun. Verna Felton, who played my fairy godmother, became one of my best friends for life." Verna recorded her part in just two sessions, once on May 19, 1948, and again on October 18, following her return from Hawaii. Her screen time would amount to only five minutes. Despite the role's brevity, it was one with which Verna would be identified for the rest of her life, possibly because of the Oscar-nominated song "Bibbidi-Bobbidi-Boo," a bouncy fan favorite whose repetitive lyrics never fail to attract children.

To guide the animation of *Cinderella*'s human characters, Disney insightfully employed live-action models. During this process, actors were carefully filmed to test continuity, staging, characterizations, and the interaction between the characters. According to American Film Institute records, film actress Claire DuBrey was used as the live-action model for the Fairy Godmother. However, Verna's fellow radio performer Sharon Douglas remembered in 2005, "As you know, [Verna] did the voice of the fairy godmother in the Disney 'Cinderella' film. And I well remember at the time her telling us that they photographed her for the animators so that they could use her gestures and mannerisms, even her 'look' to produce the character." Douglas's recollection is corroborated by Verna's 1950 interview with *Radio-Television Life* ("What's New With Verna") in which she described this same scenario. Since there is a definite facial resemblance between Verna and the film character, it's quite possible photographs of her face were helpful to animators, while DuBrey's movements were utilized for those of the fairy godmother. However, the fairy godmother's hefty arms and legs were obviously exaggerated by Disney animator Milt Kahl; neither Verna nor DuBrey were that corpulent.

It is interesting to note that Disney himself wanted the "fairy godmother to be a 'tall, regal' type . . . instead of a small, plump woman," according to Michael Barrier's *The Animated Man: A Life of Walt Disney*, published in 2007. Longtime Disney animator Frank Thomas said that Disney remained doubtful of an overweight fairy godmother until "the very end," when he saw animator Kahl's finished product. The character's resemblance to Verna Felton is unmistakable; animators clearly borrowed Verna's prematurely gray hair and expressive eyes.

Verna's voice characterization is right on the mark as well. As the fairy godmother, she is gentle, motherly, and comforting. But she displays enthusiasm and comic forgetfulness, too. She dominates the scene, transforming the pumpkin into the coach, the mice into horses, and the horse and dog into the coachman and groom, all the while singing that magical number "Bibbidi-Bobbidi-Boo." According to Jeff Kurtti, author of the book *Disney Dossiers*, "Legend has it that Walt Disney once told [animator] Marc Davis that the Fairy Godmother's transformation of Cinderella's rags into a shimmering ball gown was Walt's favorite piece of animation."

Walt Disney Productions released a special edition DVD of *Cinderella* in 2005, which included the documentary *From Rags to Riches: The Making of Cinderella*. Film historian John Culhane was among those interviewed: "And Verna Felton, the voice of the fairy godmother, had a voice that was so warm. She starts out at Disney as the voice of one of those unpleasant elephants in *Dumbo*, and you don't like her, but that was Verna Felton the character actress—the heart of Verna Felton is in the fairy godmother. She was a favorite of mine. I loved the quality of her voice."

By the time *Cinderella* opened in theaters on February 15, 1950, Walt Disney was in deep financial trouble. However, his newest film quickly became Disney's greatest box-office success since *Snow White and the Seven Dwarfs*, released twelve years earlier. According to Disney biographer Neal Gabler, "Cinderella had cost the studio $2.2 million. It would gross $7.9 million. And that didn't include what the film generated in sales of merchandise and music, especially since one of the film's songs, "Bibbidi-Bobbidi-Boo," became a popular hit and would receive an Academy Award nomination. The film, the failure of which would have sunk the Disney studio, would up rescuing it from financial disaster and spiritual despair."

Verna repeated her fairy godmother role in two subsequent productions. On June 30, 1950, Ilene Woods, Eleanor Audley, and Verna Felton reprised their film roles in a radio broadcast of "*Cinderella*" on *Screen Directors Playhouse*. Then on February 15, 1951, Verna and Audley supported Judy Garland in a non-Disney version of the tale on radio's *Hallmark Playhouse*. While the latter was not exactly a musical production, the dialogue was written in delightful rhyme.

Cinderella was not the only feature Walt Disney kept on the back burner during the war. Since 1938 he had been struggling to bring *Alice in Wonderland* to the screen. Described by Barrier as "a film Disney felt he *should* make but did not really want to," production began on *Alice* in the summer of 1949. Even Disney admitted, "we got in there and we just didn't feel a thing. But we were forcing ourselves to do it." And the finished product reveals just that. Its episodic format is strikingly different from previous Disney features. Leonard Maltin, author of *The Disney Films*, said it lacked "the essential thread that made Disney's best features hang together, and, moreover, it lacks *warmth*." Consequently, *Alice in Wonderland* is filled with tedious sequences, with one definite exception—the final episode involving the Queen of Hearts, vividly portrayed by Verna.

Following its established practice, Disney employed notable radio performers to voice the wild assortment of characters in *Alice*, including Ed Wynn as the Mad Hatter, Jerry Colonna as the March Hare, Bill Thompson as the White Rabbit, Dink Trout as the King of Hearts, and Joseph Kearns as the Doorknob. Film veterans Richard Haydn and Sterling Holloway played the Caterpillar and the Cheshire Cat, respectively, while ten-year-old London-born Kathryn Beaumont was chosen as the voice of Alice.

Just as with *Cinderella*, live-action films were employed to enable animators to work their magic, but this time many of the voice performers, including Beaumont, Wynn, and Colonna, played the same characters in the live action. However, instead of filming Verna as the "fat, pompous, bad-tempered old tyrant"—as denounced by Alice—the studio chose thirty-three-year-old actress Jody Gilbert, then best known as a 300-pound character on the CBS radio sitcom *Life With Luigi*. Gilbert's extreme rotundity more aptly matched the Queen of Hearts's image, as envisioned by Disney animators.

Early sketches of Disney's Queen of Hearts were clearly stylized versions of Sir John Tenniel's original illustrations, however Disney historian John Grant revealed that animators found it "financially impossible merely to turn them into 'moving drawings': Tenniel used too many lines, and animating them all would have taken forever." After animators showed Verna their sketches during her recording sessions in late 1949, she described the Queen to *Radio-Television Life*: "She's all made of hearts . . . her eyes are hearts and so are her nose and mouth and when she turns around, guess what she sits on? A big red heart!" This misleading "sweetheart" image clearly conflicts with the finished product; although the monarch's monstrous mouth transforms for a split-second into a red heart, there is nothing else symbolic of love in the character's image or behavior.

Disney veteran Frank Thomas was chosen as the directing animator for the character, but he encountered great difficulty in pleasing Walt Disney with his creation. Thomas shared his recollections of the Queen of Hearts with interviewer Christian Renaut for *Walt's People: Talking with the Disney Artists Who Knew Him*: "So I was supposed to take a funny character and do some stuff that I needed to be kind of strong. He looked at it and said, 'You've lost your comedy.' So I tried it funny. 'You've lost your menace,' and I asked, 'Now what is she doing in the picture? Give me some business and I'll give you a character,' and he said, 'No, you give me a character and I'll give you some business.'"

In the end, Thomas was successful; the Queen of Hearts is both a convincing threat and a delightful clown. Moreover, the lively action and Verna's brilliant vocal performance saves viewers from another in a long line of tiresome *Wonderland* sequences. As the Queen enters the royal garden she discovers that her playing-card guards have covered her white roses with red paint after realizing that they did not follow the queen's orders to plant only red roses. "Off with their heads!" she roars. She then challenges Alice to a game of croquet, using flamingos as mallets, hedgehogs as balls, and playing cards as hoops. When the game proves humiliating for the queen, she blasts Alice with her customary pronouncement, "Off with her head!" However, the diminutive king intercedes, suggesting that a trial would be in order. During the farcical proceedings, Alice insults the Queen and is forced to flee. As the queen and an army of cards chase Alice, the scene transforms into a nightmare sequence, ending with Alice awakening from the bizarre dream which transported her to Wonderland.

While Disney animation expert John Grant admits that the brutish Queen of Hearts is the "only real villain" in *Alice*, he opines that she is "only an ersatz one," lacking the subtlety of the average Disney villain, such as the seductive witches in *Snow White* and *Sleeping Beauty*. In fact, at times the Queen of Hearts, while roaring ferociously, is merely a grotesque buffoon. At one point the Cheshire Cat mischievously hooks the queen's skirt hem on the beak of the flamingo she uses as a croquet mallet. As she swings the bird, the cat's prank causes her to topple, exposing an ample backside, clad in heart-embroidered bloomers. Such ignominy was deemed unsuitable for a "real" Disney villain like *Cinderella*'s stepmother or *Sleeping Beauty*'s Maleficent.

However, most critics would agree with the Lewis Carroll Society's Brian Sibley who called Disney's depiction of the Queen of Hearts "the very embodiment of

Her majesty, the Queen of Hearts in *Alice in Wonderland*. © WALT DISNEY PRODUCTIONS.

the uncontrollable fury Carroll envisaged." Leonard Maltin wrote, "The climactic sequence with the Queen is quite funny, also benefiting from a particularly strong voice characterization by Verna Felton." Indeed, the Queen of Hearts is most likely Verna's most brilliant Disney characterization. Her Matriarch Elephant in *Dumbo* was appropriately snooty and her Fairy Godmother was charming, but the Queen of Hearts showcased Verna's ability to display both an impressive vocal range and a keen sense of timing. For many viewers, the Queen of Hearts sequence is the highlight of the whole movie.

Alice in Wonderland, released on July 28, 1951, was a box-office disappointment, with losses reported at one million dollars. The film's difficulties had escalated the production costs to more than three times that.

Disney historian Michael Barrier found the voices of Ed Wynn and Jerry Colonna to be inappropriate for their respective characters, but was pleased with the contributions of others, particularly Bill Thompson. Barrier noted in the 1978 summer edition of *Funnyworld*: "Thompson was more flexible than some of the other Disney regulars—Sterling Holloway and Verna Felton always sounded about the same, for instance." Barrier's estimation is correct; Verna's voice is always easily detected, whether playing a kindly grandmother, an Irish landlady, or a "boorish battleaxe," as one critic called the Queen of Hearts.

Could the real Verna Felton be as bombastic as some of her characters? There are definite indications that Verna had a temper, and she allowed it to show around her intimates. Even though she doted on her son, she could get quite angry with Lee. Family friend Lynn Morgan witnessed one of her tirades in the late 1940s: "Verna could be bombastic, yes. I know Lee ran over Verna's dog once, but he didn't run over it on purpose. It was an old dog named Skipper—a big old white dog they had . . . Lee was backing out of the driveway, and Skipper was getting old—and I mean *old*, about 14 or something. And evidently Skipper didn't get out of the way, and he killed it. Verna was very upset, very mad at Lee for running over the dog. I remember asking my mother, 'Lee didn't run over that dog on purpose, did he?' She said, 'Of course not, but you know how Verna is.'"

Verna filled Skipper's void by purchasing a mate for her cocker spaniel Mike. By 1950, Mike and Tracy became parents to a litter of pups, two of which Verna kept. Lee dubbed the female puppy Hildegarde, while Verna named the male after her favorite *Cinderella* character Gus-Gus, one of Cinderella's pet mice. The four cockers became Verna's constant companions throughout the 1950s, swimming in her pool, running in and out of their dog door, and sleeping in Verna's bedroom.

Besides Verna's canine friends, those of the human variety frequented 4147 Bakman Avenue during the late 1940s. Her busy social life remained a constant over the years, but around this time, an opportune innovation in the radio industry freed up Verna's Saturday evenings. Now radio shows could be recorded prior to broadcast and aired later during their regular time slots. In response to this growing trend, *The Judy Canova Show* ceased its Saturday-night live broadcasts beginning in the fall of 1948. No one was more delighted with the change than Verna; it allowed her an evening to socialize with her cronies from the Radio Women's War Service. The group's original monthly meetings, designed for knitting and letter-writing, had spawned other gatherings centered around food and recreation, mainly card games. A tight circle of twelve friends had formed in the interim. Prior to 1948 and for many years to come, Verna and her friends rotated their weekly card games among their individual homes. As canasta gained popularity in the late 1940s and 1950s, it became the ladies' game of choice.

Most of Verna's canasta cronies were within ten years of her age, and all of them were connected to the entertainment industry in one fashion or another. In a professional sense, Verna most closely identified with four who had performed with their spouses in stock: Jane Morgan, Gertie Virden, Charlotte Treadway, and Violet MacKaye.

While Jane Morgan's career history has been outlined in previous chapters, it is appropriate to note that by this time she had begun playing the character for which she is best known. *Our Miss Brooks*, debuting on the CBS radio network in the summer of 1948, starred film actress Eve Arden as spinster schoolteacher Connie Brooks. Jane played Connie's landlady Mrs. Margaret Davis, a daffy old soul whose culinary skills left lots to be desired. The ensemble radio cast also

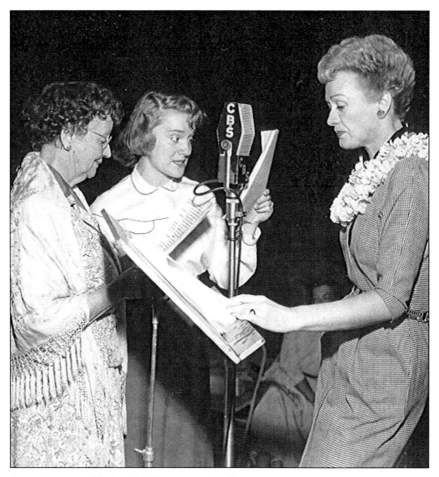

Jane Morgan, Gloria McMillan, and Eve Arden rehearse a scene from radio's *Our Miss Brooks.*

included Gale Gordon as Connie's blustery principal Osgood Conklin; Jeff Chandler (and later Robert Rockwell) as shy science teacher Mr. Boynton, Connie's love interest; Richard Crenna as squeaky-voiced student Walter Denton, and Gloria McMillan as Conklin's daughter Harriet. An immediate radio hit, *Our Miss Brooks* spawned a television incarnation in 1952, and for a while the two versions ran concurrently on both mediums, featuring the same cast. In 1956, the *Brooks* ensemble hit the big screen when Warner Brothers released a full-length feature film using the same title.

Around 1951, Jane and her husband Leo Bryant, who was now in the early stages of senility, moved to a spacious home at 4511 Camellia Avenue in North Hollywood, less than a mile from Verna's residence. The Bryants' home featured a separate wing for their longtime friend and cohabitant Helen Rourke, who was also one of the canasta cronies.

Another resident of Jane's household at the time was bespectacled widow Gertie Virden, an erstwhile stage actress. The daughter of a store clerk, Gertrude Dunlap was born on October 13, 1881, in Austin, Texas. Around 1903, she married actor-comedian Lewis "Lew" Virden, and together they formed their own stock company. For over a decade they toured the country, from New York to California, performing plays like *Number 44* and *The Wizard of Wall Street*. In the summer of 1906, when they were appearing as the vaudeville team of Virden and Dunlap at the Colorado Springs Opera House, they became acquainted with Leo Bryant and Jane Morgan, who were ensconced there as orchestra conductor and stock actress, respectively.

Proving herself the unconventional sort, Gertie shocked the city of Portland, Oregon, on March 3, 1911, by appearing on the streets in a pair of flaming red "harem" pants. Newspapers covering the story reported that men bystanders "took the innovation good naturedly." But when Gertie tried to board a streetcar, the women occupants turned up their noses and hurled such insults as "hussy," "cat," and "shameless minx." By the time three policemen came to her aid, Gertie was in tears, "Why will folks be so horrid! I think this new style is awfully cute, and not half so bad as the Directoire gown or the peek-a-boo. You wait and see if this new style won't be all the rage in a little while." Gertie attracted the same type of attention two weeks later when she tried wearing her pantaloons in downtown Oakland. Since Gertie's shocking display occurred in more than one city on the Virdens' tour, it seems it may have been more of a publicity stunt than fashion statement.

In 1916, when opportunities for stock companies diminished and even vaudeville proved fruitless, the Virdens settled in Los Angeles. Subsequently, Gertie appeared in at least one silent comedy film, *When Helen Was Elected*, but her acting career seems to have died soon after. As a means of income, Lew fell back on his carpentry skills while Gertie resorted to dressmaking. Childless and widowed since age forty-five, Gertie found new enjoyment in the weekly canasta gatherings, some of which were hosted at Jane Morgan's house.

Charlotte Evaline Treadway perhaps shared more in common with Verna than anyone among this group of friends. Like Verna and Lee Millar Sr., Charlotte and her husband-actor Ferdinand Francis Munier had enjoyed a healthy career in stock before graduating to radio and films. The only child of a dry goods merchant, Charlotte was born in New Orleans on May 18, 1893. Prior to her teen years, Charlotte's father moved the family to San Diego where she met fledgling actor Munier, whose father was also in the dry goods business. "Fred" Munier, whose stout build made him perfect for character parts, had once been a member of the Ed Redmond Stock Company in San Jose. In fact, he left the company in 1910, just one week prior to Verna's summer stint with Redmond. Although Munier joined Redmond's competition, it's likely that his path crossed Verna's while she was back in her hometown that season. Neither of them imagined that their families would become close thirty years later.

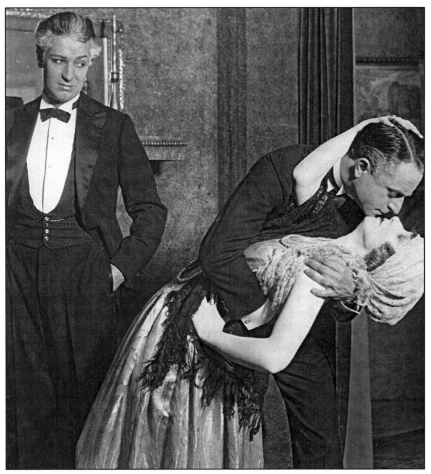

Harland Tucker makes love to Charlotte Treadway as Gayne Whitman forlornly watches in *The Gold Digger*, 1923.

Charlotte was nineteen when she married Munier and almost immediately began on-the-job training as his fellow performer in theaters across the country. It was a match made in heaven. In less than three years Charlotte was starring in *So Long Letty* for a twelve-week run at Oliver Morosco's theater in downtown Los Angeles. The Muniers subsequently became popular additions to several stock companies, including The Bishop Players (Oakland), The Thomas Wilkes Stock Company (Los Angeles), and The Henry Duffy Stock Company (Portland). Like the Millars, the Muniers sometimes found themselves separated by great distances, each finding work wherever they could. While Munier honed his craft as a stage director in San Francisco and Salt Lake City, Charlotte became the darling of the Morosco when she returned to perform there in 1922. Morosco productions that paired Charlotte with Harland Tucker or Gayne Whitman were consistently successful for the next several years.

By 1931, the Muniers were reunited when he began his film career, eventually appearing in over 100 talkies. Charlotte's films amounted to about one-fourth that, and while most were "B" movies, she did appear in several notable pictures, including *Dead End, The Women*, and *One Foot in Heaven*. The Muniers were also steadfast members of the *Lux Radio Theatre* stable, becoming friends with Verna and Lee Millar Sr. in the process. For many years, the Muniers made their residence at 956 N. Alfred Street in West Hollywood.

The Millars and Muniers worked frequently on *Lux* with handsome actor Frederic MacKaye who, along with his wife Violet, shared their theatre background. MacKaye's stage career dated at least as far back as December 1924, when he toured northern California as nineteen-year-old Fred MacKay in *Getting Gertie's Garter*. He married his wife, *nee* Violet May Neitz, when they were both members of Mac's Players in San Jose in 1927.

Violet, or Vi as she was called by close friends, was born on May 15, 1894, in Anacortes, Washington. By 1900, her mother had remarried and relocated the family to Los Angeles. Unlike Verna and Charlotte, Violet's acting career did not have its beginnings on the stage. Before she reached her twentieth birthday, Violet was a supporting player in silent pictures. Then she headed north, eventually settling in Vancouver, where she became a leading lady at the Empress Theatre, just a few years before the Allen Players would begin their tenure there. When she returned to California, she met Fred MacKaye.

After their marriage, the MacKayes moved to Los Angeles, where Violet's older brother Alvin James Neitz had become a film director and screenwriter. With his help, Fred and Violet launched their sound film careers. However, radio was more appealing to Fred so he made the switch. Meanwhile Violet turned her complete attention to Lynn, the daughter they adopted following her birth on December 7, 1938. In 1944, Fred became the director for *Lux Radio Theatre*, holding that position until 1950. The MacKaye family made their home at 1733 Sunset Plaza Drive in Hollywood, less than two miles from the Muniers. Violet usually picked up Charlotte on her way to the San Fernando Valley when the card game was held at Verna's or Jane's.

Vi MacKaye brought her sister-in-law "Myme" James into the card-playing fold as well. Myme (pronounced "My-mee") was born Marguerite Foss, the daughter of a San Jose blacksmith, on October 23, 1894. Around 1914, she married Violet's brother Alvin who later directed westerns for Republic and Universal using the name Alan James. Myme appeared in at least three silent pictures, two of which were directed by Alan. They lived at 6138 Afton Place in Los Angeles, about five miles from the MacKayes.

The remaining members of Verna's "card-playing crowd" were not performers in the industry, but they were connected. Helen McNear's husband Howard was a radio actor who broke into California stock companies before the stock market crash of 1929. A native Californian, Howard Terbell McNear was born on January 27, 1905, growing up in Berkeley and San Gabriel. By his twenty-fifth birthday, his parents were both dead, and Howard was supporting himself as a member of a San Diego stock company. He and Helen married in Fresno in 1935. Two years later Howard established himself as one of radio's top supporting players, amassing an excess of 1000 credits. His most famous radio role became "Doc" on *Gunsmoke*, but with the advent of television, Howard would win a legion of fans with his role of Floyd the barber on *The Andy Griffith Show*.

Helen McNear, *nee* Sadie Spatz, was born in New York on January 1, 1902. Her father William Lauerbach Spatz had immigrated to America in 1881 from Russia and subsequently married Freda Goldberg, also Russian born. Sadie, or Helen, was their oldest child. Mr. Spatz, a lifelong tailor, relocated the family several times, stopping to settle for brief periods in Kentucky, Denver, and Santa Fe. By 1920, the Spatz family had reached the seaside resort town of Venice, California, where the popular Helen was voted Miss Venice. Christopher "Kit" McNear recalled that in her youth, his mother Helen worked as a fashion model and for a while dated film comedian Stan Laurel. In 1923, Helen married the British-born Richard Jack Boston, whom perhaps she knew as one of her father's business connections since Boston was employed as a tailor's bookkeeper. Before their marriage ended in divorce about ten years later, Helen and Boston were sales clerks in a Los Angeles dry goods store.

Helen and her second husband Howard McNear lived at 3330 Troy Drive in the Hollywood Hills throughout the 1940s and most of the 1950s. Eventually, they moved to 4118 Bakman Avenue, just two houses down from Verna. Kit McNear recalled that by that time, the canasta girls also enjoyed playing a card game called panguingue.

Hazel Delphine, treasurer for the Radio Women's War Service, was the most likely candidate for that position since her profession was bookkeeping. Hazel grew up in San Francisco, where she was born to ironworker Bernard McGuirk and his wife Irene on October 3, 1903. According to several sources, Hazel never wed, but by 1929, she was using the surname Delphine. While her motivation for such a change is open to speculation, perhaps Hazel had tried to break into the entertainment industry using the new name. Or maybe Delphine simply sounded more appealing than McGuirk. Whatever the case, Hazel flip-flopped between the two names for several years. By 1932, she had moved to 1140 N. Gower Street near West Hollywood. For many years afterward Hazel was in the employ of the Harry Wurtzel Agency, located on Sunset Boulevard.

Two other office professionals helped to round out the "canasta circle." Mary Edith Stahl, employed with Benton and Bowles Advertising Agency, was born into a privileged existence in Chicago on July 27, 1901. Her father John M. Stahl, a highly successful newspaper editor, had been honored with two invitations to join presidential cabinets, first under Benjamin Harrison and twenty years later under Woodrow Wilson, but declined each offer. He married at forty to a woman half his age; Mary Edith was the eldest of their two children. In 1913, Stahl gave up his newspaper career to become president of the Farmers National Life

Insurance Company of America. He provided an excellent education for Mary Edith at the prestigious University of Chicago Laboratory School, in addition to travel opportunities all over the globe. Mary Edith resided in New York City before settling in California. Somewhere along the way, she met her longtime companion, Katherine "Katie" Robinson, who was born in Missouri on September 6, 1895. After her subsequent move to Los Angeles, Katie was hired as an editor for a leading movie magazine. Mary Edith and Katie made their home at 13435 Cheltenham Drive in Sherman Oaks.

The senior member of Verna's Saturday-night group was septuagenarian Mamie Bush, a round little lady with snow white hair. Mary Catherine Brown, nicknamed both "May" and "Mamie," was born in Ohio on January 14, 1874. At eighteen she married electrician Walter Dickey Bush who moved his young family from Cincinnati to Los Angeles in 1911. In both locations Mamie operated the family home as a boarding house to help support the couple's four sons, two of whom later became performers in silent pictures. The youngest son James—known to his friends as Jimmy—appeared in almost 100 films between 1930 and 1951. A handsome blonde, James Bush began his talkie career as a "younger leading man," supporting the likes of Marie Dressler, Ramon Novarro, Barbara Stanwyck, and W.C. Fields. In mid-career, he switched to character parts, playing sailors, policemen, and army sergeants. His credits included *You Can't Cheat an Honest Man, Gone with the Wind,* and *Since You Went Away.* Although they shared no scenes, James Bush and Verna were both in the 1939 film *Joe and Ethel Turp Call* on the President. Coincidentally, James's agent Harry Wurtzel was the boss of his mother's friend, Hazel Delphine. While James's parents eventually separated, he remained unmarried and lived with Mamie. By 1938, mother and son were residing at 3270 Laurel Canyon Boulevard, a spacious home they called "Bushaven," about two miles from Verna's house.

Besides the bond of show business, Verna found she had something else in common with half of the canasta crowd. Jane Morgan, Violet MacKaye, Myme James, Helen McNear, and Charlotte Treadway were each the mother of only one child. Violet MacKaye's daughter Lynn was privy to the gang's parties and games, especially following her parents' divorce in 1947. Since Lynn was totally Violet's responsibility, she accompanied her to the canasta parties, even sleeping in one of Verna's guest rooms on nights when the game ran too late. Later the gang taught Lynn how to play canasta and let her call numbers for bingo.

Lynn MacKaye Morgan's memories of the canasta cronies remained undimmed when she recalled in 2008: "They were all interesting women. It was very much fun, growing up around those women, I gotta tell you . . . Verna surely was an enjoyable person, but more than that. I will always remember her as a dear friend to my mother, especially during a miserable time in her life. Those ladies 'circled the wagons,' and there wasn't a holiday that she wasn't at Verna's or someone else's house, but usually it was at Verna's. Sometimes they let me prep a Thanksgiving dish or help with the salad for those great barbecues. There was a great seating

Ida Graves, Verna, and Violet MacKaye in Mexico, 1947.

area back of the main house, all set up perfectly for such social things. We always had a good time."

The canasta crowd also rallied around Charlotte Treadway when she was hit with a double whammy: the sudden death of her husband in 1945 and her own debilitating stroke soon afterward. Lynn Morgan credits the canasta gang with helping Charlotte overcome her adversity. They never left her out of their activities. They even took her along on vacations, no easy accomplishment for a time when accommodations for the handicapped were virtually nonexistent.

To help cheer Violet following her traumatic divorce from Fred MacKaye, Verna organized a "girls only" road trip to Tijuana and Ensenada in the summer of 1947. Ida Graves was enjoying a prolonged visit with Verna that summer, so she helped Verna load the little house trailer for the threesome's excursion. While Lynn stayed behind, she recalled another such trip, probably the following year, when Verna took Violet, Lynn, and Verna's neighbor Dolly Stelter to Mexico.

Dolores "Dolly" Stelter Neese recalled in 2008: "DeeDee had a little trailer, and she piled us all into her car one time and we went to Ensenada . . . Vi MacKaye liked to knit, and Vi knew that I liked to play with dolls. And she said, 'Well, I'm going to knit your doll a sweater.' You don't say that to a kid unless you really mean it, because every time I saw her after that, I said, 'Do you have that sweater?' And she finally had to whip it up quick so I'd shut up!"

Lynn Morgan's fondness for Verna's gang is quite evident: "They were all characters! What can I tell you! I remember Verna talking to the girls about John Kennedy screwing around. And you know, of course I was a Democrat—I didn't like to hear that! I thought it was a bunch of hearsay and crap. And actually she was right! You know, she was. So she must have gotten that from somewhere, and that was before he was president. He was senator and running for president at the time. I'd sit out there on the swing and listen to them talking. Verna was [conservative]. Helen McNear was the only Democrat in the bunch . . . oh, God, she was funny! I liked her; she was a character. Nothing was secret with her. Everything came out of her mouth! She swore, and she was funny. Howard McNear was just a charming and enjoyable person, just as dear as he was on *The Andy Griffith Show* . . . very, very enjoyable man, a gracious host and what killed me was he was always hanging out back at Verna's with the girls. If Helen was there, he was there! I enjoyed Howard a lot . . . Janie Morgan didn't entertain as much as Verna, but she was a gracious and good friend. She always got tickets for my friend Judy Johnson and me to sit in the audience and watch the *Our Miss Brooks* episodes being filmed . . . My uncle's wife Myme James was quite a bombastic woman, to say the least—she's the one who used to point at us and tell us to get out and be quiet—but she was a help and comfort to my mother and even came and lived with her for a while after I married . . . Mamie Bush's house was a fun place for a kid to play. Verna's son Lee was pals with Mamie's son Jimmy, and their pal Sterling Holloway used to hang out with them at the Bush home sometimes . . . and Ida Graves—she was a Canadian—she was more reserved—she got a kick out of them all."

Aside from the canasta crowd, Verna liked to entertain her neighbors, the Stelters. Dolores Neese recalled that her family dined with "DeeDee" several times in a formal setting, perhaps for a holiday or a birthday. Verna had grown very attached to Dolly and Steven Stelter. Around 1951, when they moved from Bakman Avenue, she was devastated. "We moved closer to the school I was attending," remembered Dolores, "because at that point my mother *and* father were working. My mother was a public health nurse. It was rare in those days for both parents to work, so we moved to a house only one block from the school. And DeeDee was brokenhearted that we moved."

But there were other children nearby whom Verna adopted as her own grandchildren. In 1948, Bernard and Thelma Witt Leff, a couple in their early thirties, and their toddler Debbie moved into 4157 Bakman Avenue, on the other side of the Stelters and two doors down from Verna. Mr. and Mrs. Leff were

Verna dries Sandy Leff after a dip in the Millar family pool as Lee looks on.

natives of Pittsburgh, Pennsylvania, but prior to moving to North Hollywood, they had lived in Cordova, Alaska, where Debbie was born on November 2, 1946.

Debbie recalled in 2007: "DeeDee immediately took a liking to my parents. And she relied on my father to help her with things around her house." Soon two little sisters joined Debbie: Betty, born on September 12, 1948, and Sandy, born on December 3, 1950. The Leff girls immediately became, in Debbie's words, "DeeDee's adopted grandchildren." Mr. and Mrs. Leff took Debbie to see Disney's *Cinderella* when it was released in 1950. When she recognized Verna's voice, she shouted out, "That's my DeeDee!"

One Christmas Verna knitted sweaters and matching hats for the Leff girls. Over the years knitting had become Verna's lifelong hobby. She told *Radio-Television Life* in an article published on September 1, 1950: "I started this hobby a long time ago to keep out of trouble. Once when I was a teen-ager appearing in a play, an older actress who was sitting next to me turned and asked, 'Child, haven't you anything to do?' When I told her all my work was at home, she left me with the advice, 'Always keep your hands busy wherever you are, then you'll never have to be a second party to anything that has been said.' I've remembered that all these years and now, when I don't want to listen or see something, I just keep my head lowered and purl like mad! I've never had a red face since!"

Among industry performers, Verna's knitting was legendary; she was said to never have been seen at rehearsals or broadcasts without it. When she was on *The Joan Davis Show*, Verna taught announcer Frank Bingman to knit, but he kept his hobby in the closet—until he learned fellow announcer Howard Culver shared the same interest. Later the two men donated their time at local military hospitals, teaching wounded veterans to knit.

Besides knitting, Verna enjoyed puttering around in her garden, tending her camellias. In summer she swam daily, sharing the pool with the neighborhood children but only after she had taught them how to swim. Although Verna's career schedule was hectic and her leisure time with the Stelter and Leff children was golden, there was still a void in Verna's life. Her son Lee, still somewhat dependent at 26, was essentially living his own life. However, Verna's sixtieth birthday was approaching; the proverbial clock was ticking. She issued a directive to Lee. According to Dolores Neese, "The way that I heard it from my mother was that DeeDee wanted grandchildren. And she put it to Lee, 'Find somebody—I want some grandchildren.'"

Lee chose as his bride Edith Iris Simmons, whom he had met in the summer of 1946 when they performed together as members of the New York Imperial Players in New Jersey. Actually, they did not get off to a good start. On the day they met, Edith was working a crossword puzzle. Lee leaned over and voluntarily gave her the answers to put in the empty blocks. Edith was irritated by his input, but a friendship grew as they moved on to other productions, including the Community Center Theatre's spring 1947 production of *Hedda Gabler*, with Edith in the title role. When Lee's 1948 tour of *Dream Girl* carried him back to the west coast, he and Edith continued to stay in touch.

In the meantime, Edith's acting career stalled, and she sought other ways to support herself. In the fall of 1949, she put her degree from the University of Maryland to use by teaching speech and fashion modeling at a school in Washington, D.C. By this time, Lee's career still was only inching along. He managed several radio appearances per month as well as an occasional telecast. By the time he considered marriage, Lee had filmed his first movie, a Universal-International western short called *Tales of the West*.

Edith Simmons, like Lee, was an only child. She was a year older, born in Richmond, Virginia, on May 12, 1923. Edith's closest relative was her recently widowed mother, nee Mabel Grace Walker, a fifth-generation Virginian and five years Verna's junior. When Lee proposed marriage to Edith, he suggested that she could pursue her acting career just as well in California as back East. This instantly appealed to Edith, whose lifelong dream was to be an actress. Once things were arranged for the two to be married, Verna happily converted her upstairs rooms into an apartment for the soon-to-be newlyweds. Lee mailed photographs of the new accommodations to Edith in Washington, since she would not have an opportunity to inspect them until her arrival for the ceremony. Meanwhile Lee and Verna arranged everything. They planned the wedding for Friday, August 25, 1950, at 4 p.m. in the Pueblo Oratorio, a chapel at the Chapman Park Hotel on Wilshire Boulevard. Following the ceremony, Verna would host a poolside reception at home. Since Edith knew no one else in Los Angeles, Lee even selected her bridesmaids from his set of friends. Edith would not meet her attendants until her wedding day.

A *Los Angeles Times* photographer snapped a shot of the bridal couple as they obtained a marriage license in the County Clerk's office on August 23. The following day, the photograph accompanied a small item titled "Nuptial To Turn Stage Romance Into Reality." Remembering their summer stock engagements, Edith told the *Times*, "Our words of love were all spoken on the stage in those days."

Two days later, the wedding party posed for photographs under Verna's backyard pergola, where she had arranged the buffet table. Edith—a natural model—looked stunning in her white satin. "Edith was magic," Dolores Stelter Neese remembered. Lynn MacKaye described her as "lovely, tasteful, and wonderful." Lynn, then eleven years old, was a junior bridesmaid, and Charlotte Treadway's son-in-law Steve Cardwell was one of the groomsmen. The rest of the wedding party was made up of Lee's friends. Verna, beaming, wore a lace formal and feathered hat, both in her signature shade of lavender. Now that her son was married, she hoped to soon hear a pitter-patter besides that of her four cocker spaniels.

Just as quickly as Verna gained a new family member, she lost another. The ever-faithful Codo passed away on September 1, exactly one week after Lee's wedding. Although she had been suffering from liver disease, senility, and osteoporosis, Codo had managed to attend the wedding and reception, even posing in a full-length gown with members of the wedding party. When she fell ill a few days later, Verna summoned her own physician Dr. Carl Lund, but there was very little he could do for the frail ninety-year-old. Mary Jane "Codo" Conboy had given almost one third of her life to the Millars; she had been a member of the family since Lee was three weeks old. With Codo's death, another important link to Verna's past was shattered.

The wedding party included, Codo, Verna, Steve Cardwell, Grace Simmons (SECOND, THIRD, FOURTH, AND FIFTH FROM LEFT), Lee and Edith, and Lynn MacKaye (EXTREME RIGHT).

Verna and Codo at Lee's wedding reception.

Meanwhile Verna sandwiched a few film roles into her schedule. Three months before Lee's wedding, she got her first taste of location shooting, in the desert no less. Verna traveled to Gallup, New Mexico, where an Irving Allen production, a western aptly named *New Mexico*, was already underway. Set in 1865, the picture pitted cavalry captain Lew Ayres and his unit against an angry Indian tribe betrayed by the captain's superior officer. Curvaceous Marilyn Maxwell was co-starred as Cherry, a platinum blonde singer passing through on her way to open a Las Vegas dance hall act, no matter how implausible that may seem for the period. Verna was assigned the part of Cherry's plume-bedecked aunt, Mrs. "Feathers" Fenway, who manages Cherry's engagements in "the theatre." When Ayres advises the women to return east, they stubbornly refuse and hire a stage to take them straight through Indian territory. Later, when their stage is attacked by Indians, the cavalry charges to the rescue. Cherry and Feathers retreat with the soldiers to an abandoned pueblo at the top of a mesa, but find themselves trapped there, surrounded by the angry natives. By the end of the picture, the Indians have killed almost everyone—including Ayres, Andy Devine, Jeff Corey, and Raymond Burr—in an attack on the pueblo. In an abrupt conclusion, Cherry climbs down the mesa with the Indian chief's young son, and into the desert they walk away. It is not clear whether "Feathers" lost her scalp during the attack; she is not shown during either the attack or the conclusion. Producer Allen hoped that the film would ignite interest in helping Native Americans, just as the recent releases *Home of the Brave, Gentleman's Agreement*, and *Pinky* had clamored for a square deal for their minorities. Critics weren't happy with the film's color process. The *New York Times* said the new Ansco print stock made the "cast, Indians included, look lobster-red." *New Mexico*, after making its world premiere in Alberquerque on May 5, 1951, was soon forgotten.

In December, 1950, Verna brightened a few scenes in the otherwise lackluster *Little Egypt*, promoted by Universal-International as "the story of the birth of the hootchy-kootchy, the dance that shook the world at the Columbian Exposition in Chicago in 1893." However, instead of a factual account of Fahred "Little Egypt" Mahzar, the exposition's original dancer, screenwriters concocted a love story between an opportunistic dancer and a swindler, promising the result to be the "hottest thing to hit Chicago since the fire."

Mark Stevens plays con man Wayne Cravat intent on swindling Cyrus Graydon (Minor Watson), a wealthy Chicago cigarette tycoon who has replicated a busy Cairo street as one of the Columbian Exposition exhibits. Cravat's unsolicited accomplice is Izora, a beautiful dancer who follows him to Chicago while posing as an Egyptian princess. Blackmailed by Izora (Rhonda Fleming), Cravat introduces her to Graydon and his social set, including the opinionated feminist Isabel Doane, played by Verna. Izora wins Mrs. Doane's approval when she suddenly lights up a cigarette in public. While the other ladies are stunned, Mrs. Doane is thrilled at this display of freedom and joins Izora in a smoke. Later, when public interest in the fair dwindles, Mrs. Doane—herself an astute

Cherry (Marilyn Maxwell) and Feathers (Verna) take cover during a fight with hostile Indians in *New Mexico.*

"businessman"—suggests that the emphasis should be on entertainment, not culture. She bolsters the fair's shareholders with the suggestion that Izora perform traditional Egyptian ceremonial dances at the Café Fez, part of Graydon's exhibit. Cravat balks at the idea, but Izora readily agrees. She secretly plans to dance the "hootchy-kootchy" in a revealing costume to embarrass Cravat and expose both their impersonations, hoping that it will bring Cravat, the man she now loves, back to his senses. While dancing, Izora deliberately provokes a brawl among some sailors and later telephones the police to report it. When Izora is arrested for inciting a riot, Mrs. Doane realizes that the negative publicity will boost reservations at the café, smugly telling Graydon, "Your fair's on the map now—larger than life! And who do you think put it there? A woman!" Cravat bails Izora out of trouble, but before he can get her out of town, Mrs. Doane arrives with her attorneys, seizing an opportunity from Izora's arrest to promote women's rights. She passionately claims that the city's women's clubs will support Izora's rights to dance; when the police sergeant threatens future arrests should Izora dance again, Mrs. Doane declares, "That's exactly what we want! And we'll keep it up night after night! Jail after jail! Court after court—until we come face-to-face with justice!" As a result, Graydon plans to insert photos of Izora in each of his cigarette packages to boost sales. When he plans a stage comeback for Izora as "Little Egypt," Graydon makes Mrs. Doane promise not to interfere. But in the midst of Izora's gyrations, the zealous matron whistles for the police, warning a dismayed Graydon, "Never underestimate the power of a woman!" Izora's hauled into court; Mrs. Doane's attorneys argue that it is a case of denial of women's

Mrs. Doane pitches her big idea to investors as her son Oliver (Charles Drake) and Cyrus Graydon (Minor Watson) listen.

rights. With the help of some perjurious character witnesses, the charges against Izora are dropped, and "*Little Egypt*" returns to a career on the stage.

After its initial preview at the Ritz Theatre in Los Angeles on July 23, 1951, *Variety* dismissed *Little Egypt* as "only so-so entertainment." While the reviewer praised the lavish sets and Technicolor atmosphere, the "major faults are the story, okay in theme but stretched out far beyond its own entertaining power." Indeed, the film today seems like a protracted episode of a 1950s sitcom. *Variety* criticized Frederick de Cordova's "static direction," while only nodding at Stevens and Fleming's "adequate" performances. "Best showings actually come from the supporting players. In the latter category are [Steven] Geray, Verna Felton, Kathryn Givney, and Fritz Feld."

Mrs. Doane (Verna) is delighted with the freethinking Izora (Rhonda Fleming) as her son Oliver Doane (Charles Drake) looks somewhat askance in *Little Egypt.*

Verna soon found that an occasional movie role was not enough to replace the income lost from her break with Red Skelton. Although she actively sought contracts for regular appearances on other radio shows, her efforts were largely unsuccessful. *The Judy Canova Show* remained Verna's only guaranteed weekly radio contract for the three seasons immediately following her 1949 departure from Skelton's show. Some may argue that exceptions to this are Verna's addition to the casts of two other summer shows in 1950, both of them quite short-lived. For several weeks Verna appeared as Mrs. Doolittle on the Jack Kirkwood comedy series *Much About Doolittle,* a summer replacement for Red Skelton's show.

Even more brief was Verna's tenure on another series that season; it was yanked off the air after only a few weeks. On July 2, William Powell debuted in an NBC comedy called *My Mother's Husband.* Less than two weeks later, Powell and NBC were named in a five-million-dollar lawsuit filed in federal court by the widow of Clarence Day, author of *Life with Father* and its sequels. Mrs. Day claimed that Powell's program infringed on the Day copyrights. Powell had played the leading role in the film version of Day's book in 1947, but the only similarity he saw was that both characters were "irascible fathers." To avoid controversy, Powell pulled the show's plug in August. Verna's part as the grandmother came to an equally quick end.

During the 1949-50 and 1950-51 seasons, Verna accepted one or two guest parts per month on radio shows like *Amos 'n' Andy, The Adventures of Ozzie and Harriet, Hallmark Playhouse,* and *Screen Directors Playhouse.* In comic roles she supported singer Gordon MacRae in The Railroad Hour installments of "*The Mikado,*" "*Irene,*" and "*Mademoiselle Modiste,*" attempting a French accent in the last. She appeared a half-dozen times on the detective drama *The Adventures of Philip Marlowe* in an assortment of similar roles such as a frowsy landlady, a pawn shop proprietor, and even a seventy-five-year-old kleptomaniac. Perhaps her most noteworthy turn on the *Marlowe* series was as criminal Bessie Dunsmuir in "*The Uneasy Head,*" broadcast on June 6, 1950. And on January 31 of the following year, Verna created the part of Burgess, the gruff housekeeper of Professor Joseph Warren, a recurring character on *The Halls of Ivy,* a comedy starring Ronald and Benita Colman.

During this period of time, Verna was called to appear as Mrs. Day on the Jack Benny program six times. However, Benny's writers were wise not to overutilize the character's standard line ("Awwwww, Shuddup!"), perhaps due to Verna's steady use of it on other shows. Since her skillful delivery of the famous line had been so successful with Benny audiences, the writers of other shows evidently saw no reason why their scripts should not benefit from its addition, particularly when Verna played battleaxes reminiscent of Mother Day. As a result, Benny's observant writers presented Verna with an occasional tirade, like the one she relished on the broadcast of May 28, 1950. When Mrs. Day barges into Jack's home to demand that Dennis be given two songs per show, Jack chastises her for invading his private home. With gusto she retorts: "What's private about it? You have a lemonade stand on the lawn, a jukebox in the living room, a pay phone in the hall, and a row of vending washing machines on the back porch!" Fourteen seconds of laughter and applause followed that line.

At the same time, Verna continued to prove herself as a dramatic actress. During the 1950-51 season, she completed seven radio productions for *Family Theater,* a dramatic anthology that, according to John Dunning, was "created by Father Patrick Peyton of the Holy Cross Fathers in an effort to promote family unity and prayer." The Mutual network donated the half-hour timeslot, but they stipulated that Peyton would pay the production costs. He also agreed that the weekly programs would feature a major film star in a top-notch production. The only commercial was "the continuous appeal for family prayer in America." One of the show's slogans became very familiar to listeners across the country: "The family that prays together stays together."

In a similar vein, Verna performed often in the syndicated radio series *Errand of Mercy,* sponsored by the Red Cross. The dramatic episodes, while appealing for donations, informed the public of the various services provided by the Red Cross. One critic stated that "Verna Felton gives another of her convincing performances" in a 1951 episode titled "*Orchids for Grandma,*" while employing a rather cryptic tease: "The play is concerned with a recurrence of that family miracle, the arrival of the first grandchild in a family. The Alton family, welcoming the new generation with mixed emotions, is awakened by a midnight crisis in the nursery to the realization that this child has been born into an uncertain world. In the actions of the Alton women after the crisis has been dealt with, there is a good example which many women will want to follow." No doubt Verna played the grandmother. Many familiar radio performers appeared alongside Verna in *Errand of Mercy*, including Lurene Tuttle, Jack Webb, Peter Leeds, Peggy Webber, Will Wright, Olan Soule, and Barbara Luddy.

Each spring for several consecutive years, Verna performed in *The Terrible Meek*, a traditional Good Friday production of Los Angeles radio station KFI since 1924. *The Terrible Meek* had debuted as a one-act play for three voices on Broadway in 1912. Its playwright, Anglo-American Charles Rann Kennedy, intended for it to be performed in total darkness, thus relying on the vocal strength of the performers. Consequently, radio producers had regarded it as quite conducive to their medium.

The play told the story of the Crucifixion, but with a twist. Written in modern-day speech and from an English standpoint, the characters were a Roman legionary who had a hand in the execution, a Centurion who had given the order for it, and the "Mother of the Son of Man." These three, while gathered at the foot of the cross, discuss events prior to, during, and after the crucifixion. The legionary speaks in a Cockney dialect, while the Centurion sounds more like a cultured captain in the British army. According to one contemporary critic, Mary uses the "ingrammatical [sic] dialect of an untutored British peasant-woman," prompting the same critic to remark, "The effect is somewhat as if Sophocles or Dante, let us say, were translated into slang."

Few reviews of the KFI productions exist, but *The Terrible Meek*'s thirty consecutive annual performances attest to its popularity. Some years the play was presented by more than one area station. In 1950, KNX, a competitor of KFI, launched their production of *The Terrible Meek* on Maundy Thursday as an episode of the *Skippy Hollywood Theater* featuring Lurene Tuttle, while the KFI version did not air until the following evening. The KFI production usually began at 10:30 p.m. and lasted forty minutes. It was also customary that complete silence would follow the conclusion of the play and remain unbroken until midnight.

As for Verna Felton's own religious affiliation, the influence of her Lawrence forebears was lasting; she remained a lifelong Catholic. Since moving to North Hollywood, she attended the St. Charles Borromeo Church on Moorpark Street, although not regularly.

On September 10, 1951, after a five-year absence, Verna returned to the *Lux Radio Theatre* stage for a production of "*Fancy Pants*," based on the 1950 movie starring Bob Hope and Lucille Ball. The stars repeated their film roles for the *Lux* broadcast, loosely based on *Ruggles of Red Gap*, a previous *Lux* production also featuring Verna. Hope "poses as an American actor who poses as a British valet and accepts employment with a family of uncouth ruffians," while Ball plays one of the ruffians. This version "left virtually nothing of the original intact, instead serving as an excuse for the high jinks of the two comics," observed *Lux* historians Connie Billips and Arthur Pierce. Indeed, Hope's performance resembles a stand-up comedy routine, while Ball delivers her lines as if she's bored to death. Verna, as Ball's uncouth mother, and Norma Varden, repeating her "to the manor born" film role, shine brighter than either Hope or Ball.

Verna followed up "*Fancy Pants*" with the Lux productions of "*The Lemon Drop Kid*" (assuming the Jane Darwell film role), "*My Blue Heaven,*" (as the "by-the-book" head of an adoption agency) and "*On Moonlight Bay*" (taking the Esther Dale role). On Christmas Eve, 1951, she repeated her role of the Queen of Hearts for the *Lux* version of "*Alice in Wonderland,*" a production accurately summed up by authors Billips and Pierce: "Shorn of their visual personalities for the broadcast version, the Mad Hatter, March Hare, Cheshire Cat, and others come across as grotesque and unpleasantly brash characters in an incredibly muddled story." Verna's characterization is sadly inferior to that of the Disney feature; what it lacks in feeling seems to be made up for in volume. Kathryn Beaumont, Ed Wynn, Jerry Colonna, Bill Thompson, Sterling Holloway, Joseph Kearns, and Doris Lloyd all repeated their screen roles for the dismal affair.

In the midst of steady radio assignments, Verna resumed her film career in September 1951, reporting to Twentieth Century-Fox for *Belles on Their Toes*. This much-heralded sequel to the 1950 hit *Cheaper by the Dozen* was based on the real-life story of the Gilbreth family. Clifton Webb played the father in the first film, but did not reprise his role since the sequel revolves around his character's widow and her struggle to keep the twelve children together. Myrna Loy returned as the mother, as did Jeanne Crain and Barbara Bates as two of the children. Verna was ninth-billed as meddlesome but wealthy Cousin Leora Simmons, who arrives in one of the opening scenes with an offer to raise two of the younger children in her own home. Bedecked in jeweled hat and floor-length fox stole, Cousin Leora can't remember the name of one of the older girls. Corrected by Anne (played by Crain), she shrugs, "How stupid of me! I always get you turned around." Anne rationalizes, "Well, there's so many of us." Demonstrating false sympathy, Leora breaks in with a downcast look, "Yes, isn't it heartbreaking? How are things?" Disgusted, Anne exits to find her mother, telling sister Ernestine (played by Bates), "Every time she comes here, she makes me feel like a charity case!" Mrs. Gilbreth (Loy) is no more receptive to Cousin Leora, calling her offer "outrageous." Leora tries to pressure her into a decision, but Mrs. Gilbreth puts her off until later that evening. When her cousin telephones for an answer, Mrs. Gilbreth, with all the children gathered round, refuses the insincere Cousin Leora, much to the delighted relief of the kids. Verna's scenes only amounted to a scant three minutes, but she made the best of them. Upon its New York opening on May 2, 1952, the *New York Times* called it "all-American apple pie," but noted the absence of the Gilbreth patriarch: "Seasoned with sugar and everything nice, *Belles on Their Toes*, is acutely needful of Mr. Webb's spicing."

Cousin Leora (Verna) causes unrest for Ann Gilbreth (Jeanne Crain), left, and her sister Ernestine (Barbara Bates) in *Belles on Their Toes.*

Three months after Verna filmed *Belles*, she mastered the part of another meddlesome old woman in the Twentieth Century-Fox production of *Don't Bother to Knock*, which began shooting in December. Based on the 1950 novel *Mischief* by Charlotte Armstrong, the drama tells the story of two strangers meeting in The McKinley, a New York City hotel. Nell Forbes, played by Marilyn Monroe in her first leading dramatic role, is an emotionally insecure girl still recovering from the loss of her lover in a plane crash. Her uncle operates one of the hotel's elevators, and when he learns that a visiting couple needs a babysitter for their young daughter Bunny, he volunteers Nell's services, even though she's never babysat. Meanwhile, pilot Jed Towers, played by Richard Widmark, arrives to reconcile with his former girlfriend, lounge singer Lyn Lesley, played by Anne Bancroft in her first film role. When Lyn refuses to resume their relationship, Jed returns to his hotel room.

Soon he looks out the window and notices a voluptuous blonde across the courtyard. She catches him looking at her and returns his gaze. When Jed determines her room number, he phones to invite himself over, not knowing that she is not a hotel guest and that Bunny is asleep in an adjoining room. Nell allows Jed into the suite, but she waffles between hesitancy and flirtation. Gradually, she warms up to him, and begins to think of him as her lost lover. Then Bunny abruptly reveals Nell's true position, angering Nell who views the girl as threatening a possible relationship with Jed. She shakes the child and orders her back to bed.

Despite his better judgment, Jed stays and later comforts the crying girl. When the child leans out the open window to look into the guest rooms across the courtyard, Nell places her hand on the girl's back as if she's going to push her. Jed grabs her in time and quiets the girl's screams.

Down below, snoopy Mrs. Emma Ballew (Verna), a permanent resident, witnesses this and becomes alarmed. Determined to learn what is going on, Mrs. Ballew charges upstairs with her longsuffering husband in tow. While Nell tries to answer the Ballews' barrage of questions through a cracked door, Jed slips into the adjoining room, exiting into the hall. The Ballews become more agitated when they see him hurry off. Mrs. Ballew quickly concludes that Bunny screamed because Jed had threatened Nell. She barrels into the suite to telephone the house detective, smirking to her husband, "Now aren't you glad you came up with me?" Mrs. Ballew gets no satisfaction from the hotel staff, who dismiss her complaint as one of her regular gripes. Eagerly she asks Nell, "Did he try to kiss you?" Mr. Ballew interrupts, "Emma, for once, be quiet. We're leaving!" As the couple exits, Mrs. Ballew glares at her husband, "If you ever dare to speak to me that way again . . ." He cuts her off, "Be quiet!"

This is the last we see of the Ballews, but things get tense inside the suite after the deranged Nell ties and gags Bunny in retaliation for Jed's departure. When Bunny's mother comes in to check on things, she and Nell get into a tussle, which is interrupted by Jed. Nell escapes but Jed tracks her to the lobby where she is threatening to kill herself with a razor blade. He talks her into giving him the blade, and the police are summoned to take Nell away to a hospital.

After *Don't Bother to Knock* opened in New York on July 18, 1952, Bosley Crowther of *The New York Times* questioned Twentieth Century-Fox's claim that Monroe was the hottest number to hit Hollywood in years: "There may be some grounds for that assumption, but if they also expect her to act, they're going to have to give her a lot of lessons under an able and patient coach." Crowther found the audience laughing during the "tense" scenes, while he agreed that Elisha Cook, Jr., as the nervous uncle with good intentions, was "a bit on the funny side, too, while the rest of the cast has trouble pretending to vast solemnity."

Admittedly, Verna's performance as Mrs. Ballew is fun to watch. Beneath her self-righteous posturing, the old girl possesses a healthy streak of voyeurism—she practically salivates when questioning Nell about Jed. Incidentally, that's not Verna's youthful high-pitched scream in the scene where Mrs. Ballew sees Bunny teetering on the window ledge, but clearly an uneven dubbing.

There are two more noteworthy asides about *Don't Bother to Knock*. First, Mrs. Ballew's dress is a dead ringer for one that Agnes Moorehead wore as slovenly Velma Cruther in *Hush . . . Hush, Sweet Charlotte* thirteen years later. In fact, it's quite possibly the same dress since both films were Twentieth Century-Fox productions. Secondly, Verna was one among a bevy of experienced radio actors in the supporting cast of *Don't Bother to Knock*, including Lurene Tuttle, Jim Backus, Olan Soule, Willis Bouchey, and Gloria Blondell.

Mrs. Ballew (Verna) questions Nell (Marilyn Monroe) about Jed (Richard Widmark) while her longsuffering husband (Don Beddoe) looks on in *Don't Bother to Knock.*

While Verna still strongly regarded radio as her favorite medium, she found herself inching toward the infant television. By 1950, many of radio's top performers were crossing over to the new medium, including Burns and Allen, Jack Benny, and Gertrude Berg. Red Skelton and Lucille Ball would make the move in 1951. Some of radio's leading situation comedies were converted as well, among them *The Life of Riley, Lum and Abner, Amos 'n' Andy, Beulah, Meet Corliss Archer,* and *A Date with Judy.* However, this was a time when most Americans didn't own television sets. To keep their radio listeners and to attract television viewers, some programs existed as both aural and visual versions. Still, the handwriting was on the wall—television was not some fad. By the mid-1950s, it was clearly evident that radio would never again be the preferred medium.

Even Jack Benny's sidekick Dennis Day made an early jump from radio to television. After five successful seasons, Day's radio show had ended in June 1951, although he continued to play Jack Benny's prize dunce on that program. The following year, Day was given an opportunity for a television show of his own, alternating with fellow singer Ezio Pinza's musical variety program under the umbrella title *The RCA Victor Show,* presented live on Friday nights over NBC.

Loveable Mrs. Day.

Day's biweekly show, which premiered on February 8, 1952, differed greatly from his radio series *A Day in the Life of Dennis Day*. Head writer Parke Levy, assisted by Norman Paul and Stanley Adams, borrowed straight from the Benny show, featuring some of the same gags, interspersed with Dennis's songs and imitations. Once again Day was a singer on the Jack Benny show, but although Benny was often mentioned, he was seen in only one guest spot. Even though Verna had not been a regular on Day's radio show, television producer Ernest Glucksman decided Mrs. Day was a necessary element for Day's television series so Verna came aboard. Kathy Phillips, who had been crowned the 1951 Miss San Francisco, was chosen to play Dennis's girlfriend Kathy Wilson, and Hanley Stafford rounded out the cast as Kathy's father.

The Dennis Day Show was telecast live on the West Coast but these were the days before videotape recording, so the producers created films of the transmitted television programs. These kinescopes, although lacking the clarity of live television, were the only way viewers in the East and Midwest could see a West Coast-produced show. The reverse was true also; New York-based productions were required to create kinescopes for the West Coast audiences.

After the series opener, the *San Mateo Times* critic Bob Foster wrote: "Dennis in just a single show has entrenched himself as one of the best among the new crop of distinctive personalities. He not only can sing but is actually a fine young actor, mimic, and comedian. Apparently NBC decided that Dennis would get the full treatment. The production was a bit thick, but still was some of the finest to come out of Hollywood. At the same time, the NBC people apparently were splashing around in the mire of formats trying to come up with one that would fit Dennis' talents. Why they did it all in one show is beyond us . . . Producer Joseph Santley called on Verna Felton to do the role of Dennis' domineering, bombastic mother, but perhaps some of the lines tossed up to her by the writers, Parke Levy and Stan Adams, were a bit too slapstick. At any rate, only Verna could do the kind of job required for the role."

At least one kinescope of *The Dennis Day Show* circulates among classic-television fans, and it demonstrates exactly what Foster described. Broadcast live on February 22, 1952, this second installment of the show surrounds Dennis's visit to a psychiatrist, all arranged by his overprotective mother. The show opens with Dennis, clad in apron and dust cap, cleaning his mother's house while singing to a photograph of Kathy. Hearing his mother approach and mindful of her disapproval of any relationship that would take him away from her, Dennis quickly swivels the frame to display Mrs. Day's portrait. "Oh, how sweet of you—singing to my picture!" she gushes. "Oh, I'm so glad you've stopped moping over that girl you met two weeks ago."

Later when Dennis learns that Kathy's father refuses to let "that poverty-stricken actor" see her, he moons for her and begins talking nonsense. Mrs. Day becomes concerned and hustles him off to the psychiatrist, "Come, dear, I'm afraid you've flipped your lid!" As the doctor tries to interview Dennis, Mrs. Day interferes, answering every question. At one point, she considers herself the patient and even pushes Dennis off the couch. Finally the doctor escorts her out and begins his analysis of Dennis.

As Dennis relates one of his recurring dreams to the doctor, the audience is transported to a medieval castle. Lord Wilson, Kathy's father, has her locked in a tower, protected from Dennis by the Black Knight (played by ex-heavyweight boxing champ Max Baer) and the Mad Baron (played by current heavyweight wrestling champ Baron Michele Leone). Between songs professing his love for Kathy, Dennis slugs Baer and flips Leone. Then, armed with his mother's feather duster, he fights off all of Lord Wilson's soldiers before becoming victorious, but not before doing a grand Sophie Tucker imitation. Thinking he is alone with

Mrs. Day upstages her own son, Dennis, 1952.

Kathy, Dennis reaches out for a kiss, "My mother doesn't know we're together!" Suddenly the helmet ventail of a suit of armor situated between the lovers snaps open, and Mrs. Day is revealed inside. "Dennis!" she roars as the camera zooms in on her glaring face. After the fadeout, Dennis awakens in the doctor's office with his mother standing over him. When the doctor learns Dennis has been working for Jack Benny for the past several years, he turns to Mrs. Day, "Well, that explains it—he's suffering from malnutrition!"

The *New York Herald Journal*'s John Crosby summed things up this way: "The new Dennis Day television show . . . may set back motherhood 2000 years which is all right with me. Mr. Day plays what I can only refer to as a mother-pecked young man and plays it with great conviction and sincerity. Mr. Day's mother, a little horror of maternity, is constantly lugging him off to an audition at NBC or to a psychiatrist or some such place where he runs docilely through his bag of tricks. Some idea of the degree of subservience to motherhood achieved by Mr. Day can be obtained from this small snippet of dialogue. Psychiatrist: 'Dennis, tell me how do you feel lately?' Dennis: 'Mother, how do I feel lately?' She even invades his dreams, a nice little Freudian note. The role of the overwhelmingly possessive mother has never been thought of as comedy material exactly and the fact that Mr. Day makes such use of it may conceivably indicate we are maturing slightly, at least in our attitudes toward motherhood, a topic which has been too sacred for too many years."

One episode that winter called for the gutsy Mrs. Day to upstage her son while he was singing. Attired in fishnet stockings and a skimpy dance costume bedecked with sequins and fringe, Verna unabashedly displayed her sixty-one-year-old figure as she cavorted across the stage. She was not above putting on a similar act when performing for an AFRA frolic the previous summer. While George Burns, George Raft, and Harry Ackerman delivered a harmonized version of the popular standard "M-O-T-H-E-R," Verna danced around in a cancan outfit, proving, as one columnist noted, "there's ginger in the old girl yet."

Radio performers like Verna soon found that preparations for television productions were more rigorous than radio performances ever were. After spending two hours observing a complicated rehearsal of Dennis Day's television show, Benny regular Phil Harris quipped, "The show should be titled 'A *Year* in the Life of Dennis Day.'" Later that season, when Mildred Ross interviewed Verna about the new medium for the July 4 edition of *TV-Radio Life*, Verna didn't mince words on the subject either. Although Ross tried to smooth things over by titling the piece "TV Is Duck Soup," Verna's true feelings for television work were transparent.

Verna first explained to Ross about her early stage career: "We'd do a different play every night for three weeks and another one for Saturday matinee. Our repertoire included twenty-one complete plays . . . and no scripts, just parts with cues. Talk about memorizing for television! Why, it's child's play compared to yesteryear. Like a juggler's, our memory patterns were always in motion. We forgot one play, learned one, and played in another, almost simultaneously."

Ross hailed Mrs. Day as Verna's most outstanding radio credit: "Her performance is always so convincing that one almost expects to meet in person a stern matriarch. Instead, Verna is a charming example of how to mellow gracefully; and we don't mean lavender and old lace. Lavender and spice would be more like it. Without reluctance, Verna freely expressed her opinions on one of television's weaknesses, the absence of theatrical 'know-how' among many TV directors. Because their experience is most closely akin to television's needs, stage directors have an edge over their radio and cinema brethren."

"In some cases," explained Verna, "the lack of coordination between the producer and the director is incredible. We rehearse with a producer all week and then the TV director takes over a day or so before air time and has us undo everything we've practiced all week. I believe camera angles should be worked out in advance by the producer and director, and not just before dress rehearsal."

"Pausing amidst her verbal barrage, Verna softened her anxiety by a quick smile as she almost apologetically said, 'I do not want to appear too critical, but do hope a helpful suggestion is taken for what it's worth. Furthermore, I sincerely believe that stock companies will supply much of television's talent—both actors and directors. After all, what else is good television but the stage put on camera?"

Despite the obvious permanence of television, Verna's allegiance clearly remained with radio. She saluted the radio thespians, who without the aid of settings, props, or gestures, used their voices to stir emotions. "The test for any good actor," she asserted, "is a script, a cold mike, and a convincing delivery. We devised a trick in the days of stock to hold the attention of our audience. In those days we'd gauge our audience reaction by dropping our voices lower and lower until we could hear someone rustle a program. Then we knew we were beginning to lose our audience and would boom our voices up again."

Why would Verna choose to be so candid in this interview? Perhaps it was just her nature, or perhaps by this time she already knew that she had nothing to lose—she would not be returning to Dennis Day's show when its second season began in September. In addition, Day would not be sharing the weekly slot with Ezio Pinza; he would be the sole star of *The RCA Victor Show*. In the meantime, the format had been changed completely; none of the supporting players remained. Instead of living at home with his mother, Day would reside in a "pricey Hollywood apartment he felt was necessary for his career ambition." Day explained the change to the press in the spring of 1953: "Verna Felton was wonderful as my mother, but the sponsors felt that the show made me too kiddish. I was too much like a 16-year-old boy, a sort of Henry Aldrich, and that confined me too much. The bachelor characterization has worked out much better." However, the sponsors were not entirely ready to free Day's character from any and all conflict with overbearing females. Big and blustery character actress Minerva Urecal was signed to play Day's cantankerous landlady as an effort to fill the vacant shoes of the departed Mrs. Day.

Despite Verna's derision of television production techniques, she evidently realized the new medium's potential. Less than a month after Dennis Day's first television season ended on June 6, syndicated newspaper columns reported that Verna was "begging NBC to buy the *Tugboat Annie* stories for her as a series." The character Tugboat Annie had been one of Marie Dressler's signature roles when she was the reigning queen of MGM in the early 1930s. Based on stories serialized in *The Saturday Evening Post*, Annie Brennan was a salty old tugboat captain who made her living piloting her vessel through the treacherous waters of the Pacific Northwest. Verna was unsuccessful in interesting NBC executives in the possibility, and with resignation, she told *TV Guide* in 1955, "If they do the show, they'll probably put some glamorous young actress in the part and call it 'Tugboat Anne.'" However, even as Verna gave that interview, plans were underway for the production of a syndicated series called *The Adventures of Tugboat Annie*. In an ironic twist, the title role would go instead to Minerva Urecal who had succeeded Verna on *The Dennis Day Show*. Filming would commence in Canada in 1957. One season's worth of episodes was first released in that country, where the show enjoyed considerable success. A year later *Tugboat Annie* was made available to stations in the United States, but it quickly flickered out.

Soon after the seventh first-season installment of *The Dennis Day Show*, real-life drama unfolded at Verna's home on Bakman Avenue. Shortly before 5 a.m. on Monday, May 5, 1952, while Verna was sleeping, her cocker spaniel Hildegarde began growling and then barking. Verna listened but heard nothing, so she told the dog to quiet down and go back to sleep. The persistent red-haired spaniel jumped on the bed and nudged her mistress's cheek until finally Verna rose to investigate the cause for the dog's alarm.

Looking through the crack in her bedroom door, the actress was horrified to discover smoke and flames on the other side. Her living room and dining room were ablaze. Painters had left a tarpaulin spread over a floor furnace vent, and it had ignited. Verna roused Lee and Edith, asleep in the upstairs apartment, and they all fled unharmed into the street. While the NBC publicity department later reported extensive damage to the house, the *Los Angeles Times* said the blaze was brought under control by firemen "in a matter of minutes" without any significant damage.

Later that day, Verna offered Hildegarde her choice of meats from the family freezer. She could not blame Mike and Tracy for not helping to warn her—they were asleep upstairs. But for Gus-Gus the actress had no kind look. He was asleep in the burning room—and slept right through it. "Poor Gus," Al Blazic laughingly recalled, "all he wanted to do was chase after balls."

Verna's little heroine would soon figure prominently in entertainment news. After Walt Disney decided to produce *Lady and the Tramp*, Hildegarde, or Hildy, was chosen as the live-action model for Lady. Verna called the picture a "family affair" because, in addition to Hildy's contribution, both she and Lee supplied voices for several of the roles. Whether the Millars were involved in the project before or after Hildy was recruited is not known. Of course, by this time Verna was quite familiar at Disney, having completed three productions there. Walt Disney had admired her talent ever since *Dumbo*. In fact, just after that film's release, he once introduced Verna as his "favorite elephant." Since *Cinderella*, he had begun calling her his "favorite fairy godmother." So it seems likely that Verna was hired first, and perhaps through conversations about the film's animal leads, she revealed that she had four cocker spaniels at home. The plucky Hildegarde, younger than Mike or Tracy and brighter than Gus-Gus, became the logical choice as Lady's live-action model.

By 1952, plans for *Lady and the Tramp* had been sitting on the shelf for over a decade when Disney finally decided to go ahead with the idea. Production files at the Walt Disney Archives indicate that Verna was hired early on in the film's production. She recorded the part of Aunt Sarah on four separate occasions, beginning March 30, 1953, and ending February 19, 1954. Lee voiced three parts—Lady's owner Jim Dear, the Dog Catcher, and the Man in the Pet Shop—which required seven visits to the Disney studio, beginning on July 2, 1953, and concluding the next May. Curiously, when Walt Disney Productions released a platinum edition DVD of the film in February 2006, its bonus documentary

Lady's Pedigree: The Making of 'Lady and the Tramp' revealed nothing about Hildegarde or Lee and very little about Verna. Such an omission leads one to wonder if the 2006 Disney staff knew the connection between the three. Film fans would likely consider it an interesting tidbit to know that the human counterpart of Aunt Sarah was not a dog-hater at all—in fact, she was the owner of Lady's live counterpart!

At the time of the film's release, the Disney public relations department promoted *Lady and the Tramp* as being based on an original story by Ward Greene. The 2006 documentary demonstrates that *Lady's* origination was not as simple as that. "It's hard to believe it actually took so long to get it up on the movie screen," admitted supervising Disney animator Eric Goldberg. "There's a lot of confusion about how *Lady and the Tramp* actually got to be made." According to the documentary, Disney story man Joe Grant owned a Springer spaniel named Lady in the late 1930s. When Grant's daughter was born, Lady was "shifted aside a bit." Disney suggested that Grant create a storyboard using that idea, in hopes that a full-length feature film could come from it. There was no Tramp in Grant's version, but there was a mean mother-in-law who came to visit, bringing a couple of Siamese cats. She would later develop into Aunt Sarah, the character played by Verna. In 1943, Walt was not pleased with the storyboard because he thought the piece was "too soft." The idea was shelved.

Several years later Disney read a *Cosmopolitan* magazine story by Ward Greene called "*Happy Dan the Cynical Dog.*" Disney realized that if a dog like Dan was paired with Grant's Lady, the necessary fireworks would result and make for a great film. Dan evolved into Tramp, as did a love story of "rich girl-poor boy."

So how did Lady evolve from a Springer spaniel into a cocker spaniel? The Disney animators and historians don't reveal that in *Lady's Pedigree: The Making of 'Lady and the Tramp.'* Nor do they explain the discovery of Tramp's live model. However, the animators spent hours perfecting their craft by observing the movements of various animals, as they searched for live action models for the leads.

The revered Frank Thomas was assigned to animate Tramp, as well as offer some input into Lady's animation. His widow Jeanette and son Ted are shown in the documentary, viewing Frank's 1954 home movies of dogs. "Frank was observing every dog in the neighborhood," recalled Jeanette. Perhaps Frank visited 4147 Bakman Avenue that summer, for there in 2005, in the dark dusty attic, Verna's family discovered a twelve-minute reel of 8-millimeter color film showing Hildegarde frolicking around the house and pool. The camera mainly focused on the dog—jumping, begging, barking, running, drinking, sitting, swimming, climbing the apartment stairs, going in and out the dog door, retrieving a rubber ball, and following Verna's gray cat Veronica. Verna is visible in several shots, as are the neighboring Leff girls who are attired in their customary swimsuits and bathing caps. Verna's other cocker spaniels are not slighted; the entire menagerie, except her parakeet, is part of the action. One take is shot from the same angle

Verna and her cocker spaniels on the day the 8mm film was made.

as many of the scenes in *Lady and the Tramp*—from the dog's perspective. The camera closes in on Hildy, showing only Verna's legs and feet, as they walk the length of the pool.

Other documentation retrieved from the attic proves Hildegarde's involvement in the picture. A yellowed clipping from the *Hollywood Citizen-News*, dated April 5, 1955, shows Verna and Hildegarde in the Disney studio surrounded by sketches of Lady. Regarding their roles, staff writer Ursula Baumann noted: "It took every bit of Verna's 57 years of acting experience to put over the part, too, because in real life she is the doting owner of four cocker spaniels. In fact, one of her pups, Hildegarde, modeled for Lady, the picture's cocker spaniel." Another item found in the same trunk makes Hildegarde's position more official. A glossy photograph shows Disney story men Ed Penner and Joe Rinaldi posing with, according to the attached press snipe, "Tramp and Hildegarde, who modeled for the hero and heroine—Tramp and Lady—of Walt Disney's first feature-length animated cartoon in Cinemascope, *Lady and the Tramp*." Many years later, Frank Thomas told interviewer Christian Renaut that Penner had spotted Tramp's live-action model while driving home one day. Unable to stop then to find the dog's owner, Penner returned to the area the following day only to discover from neighborhood children that the dog in question was a stray. Penner searched unsuccessfully until finally visiting the local dog pound. There he found the exact same dog, which he rescued from impending death.

This photo of Verna with Hildegarde accompanied the 1955 *Hollywood Citizen-News* article regarding their contributions to *Lady and the Tramp*. © WALT DISNEY PRODUCTIONS.

Set in New England at the turn of the twentieth century, *Lady and the Tramp* is really a love story, a charming tale boasting vivid characters and a delightful musical score. Lady's owners are a young married couple, identified only by the names Lady hears them call each other: Jim Dear and Darling. The faces of the couple, as well as the faces of all humans in the film, are rarely glimpsed because the camera angle is set low, from the dog's point of view. When a new baby boy is born into the household, Lady gradually becomes very protective of him. About six months later, Jim Dear and Darling go away on a trip, leaving the baby in the hands of fussy Aunt Sarah, who holds no high regard for dogs.

Upon arrival, Aunt Sarah chases Lady out of the baby's room but allows her devious cats Si and Am to have the run of the house. While the old lady is upstairs cooing at the baby, Si and Am create havoc in the parlor, shredding the curtains and upsetting the fish bowl. When they threaten to steal the baby's milk, Lady chases them all over the house, making a terrible racket. Aunt Sarah descends on the scene to find her precious felines pretending to have been attacked by "that wicked animal." As she scoops them up to carry them off to safety, Aunt Sarah positions them against her ample hips, and the audience is allowed to see her full figure as she climbs the stairs. Her turkey neck and hawk nose are comically contrasted with her oversized derriere. In the next scene, the old girl takes Lady to a pet shop to be fitted for a muzzle, but Lady bolts from the store, knocking Aunt Sarah to her feet. A quick pause of the DVD shows her sprawled across the floor, but also offers a clear view of Aunt Sarah's face. The sharp nose is a Disney original, but the jowls and upswept hairstyle are unmistakably those of Verna Felton.

Aunt Sarah significantly affects the plot later when she misjudges Lady once more. During a violent nighttime thunderstorm, an enormous rat creeps menacingly into the baby's room. Its unwelcome presence doesn't escape Lady, chained outside. After she sends Tramp into the house to fight it, she manages to break free to help him. The ensuing scuffle between Tramp and the rat wakes Aunt Sarah. Seeing the overturned crib, she jumps to the conclusion that Lady and Tramp were trying to attack the baby. She locks Lady in the cellar and calls the dog catcher for Tramp. In a dramatic chase-finish, Lady's neighboring dogs Trusty, an aged bloodhound, and Jock, a feisty Scottish terrier, prevent the pound wagon from reaching its destination. Tramp is freed, but Trusty, caught under the wagon's braking wheels, lies injured and appears dead. But weeks later as Lady, Tramp, and their newborn pups gather around the Christmas tree, a bandaged Trusty happily joins them.

According to various sources, Trusty was supposed to die in the movie, but Walt Disney did not want a repeat of the controversy surrounding the death of the mother deer in *Bambi* so the ending was changed. Verna related a similar story to Marty Halperin during their 1964 interview, but evidently she was a little confused on some details: "Oh, that was a cute show—*Lady and the Tramp*! And it was funny when they did it first, and they previewed it to the foreign press— and we were all sitting there. And old Tramp gets caught by the pound man, and he's going to be killed. And all of a sudden they put him in the dog pound, and they killed him. And the people yelled, 'No, no, no! No, no!' And [Disney executives] pulled it off the screen and said, 'Now what is the matter?' [Those people watching] said, 'No!—If he dies, we won't buy the film! If he dies, we won't buy the film—*nobody* will buy the film!' All of them [had] tears down their cheeks, and they said, 'We won't [buy] it!' And [Disney] had to take it and rewrite it . . . So he didn't die—he was saved and brought home to the family and all the little pups, you know, which was a prettier ending and a sweeter ending . . . That's a nice place to work: Disney—lovely place to work, *very* pleasant."

During this interview, Halperin was of the impression that the animation was drawn first and that the voice artists had to match their performances to the movements onscreen. When he asked Verna if she found that process difficult, she explained, "No, no, you see, you do it all yourself, you do it yourself, and then they put [your movements] into the animations. And then you may do something [with your facial expressions], you know, and [the animators] say, 'That's *it*! That's much *better*!' And then they scratch out a character, and it's interesting to watch how they do that."

By a strange coincidence Verna's explanations of the animation process were echoed in the segment "*Teaching a Dog to Talk*," featured in the bonus material on the 2006 *Lady and the Tramp* DVD. Bruce Reitherman, the son of Disney animator Wolfgang Reitherman, observed, "Disney was great at casting—in these subsidiary roles—talent and then animating great pictures to them . . . I can remember being with my dad for one reason or another and having [the animators] perk up in the room when they realized that an actor on the sound stage had just given them something—'Where's my felt pen? How can I get a quick sketch in to capture that little bit of sound that's going to be a personality?'"

Reitherman, who became a child voice actor for Disney, offered additional insight: "I can tell you from personal experience that it's not easy to act when you have nothing but a microphone to act to. The voices are always recorded first; the animation happens to the voice . . . The voice talent is a huge part of what makes these shows work, and in *Lady and the Tramp*, they had some terrific people to deal with."

Disney historian John Canemaker called *Lady and the Tramp* an "ensemble piece—it's like a little repertory company of voices." The gifted Bill Thompson, who had previously voiced parts in Disney's *Alice in Wonderland* and *Peter Pan*, and the authentic Bill Baucom, as Jock and Trusty respectively, ran away with every scene they were given. Co-composer Peggy Lee not only played Lady's owner Darling, but proved herself as a character actress with the parts of sassy stray Peg and the mischievous Si and Am. Stan Freberg contributed an inspired characterization of a fussy beaver, and Lee Millar delightfully injected a little bit of "Frank Nelson" into the pet shop owner, one of his three *Lady* roles. Veteran radio actress Barbara Luddy, forty-six years old at the time production began, supplied Lady's voice, while Larry Roberts, not yet twenty-seven, provided the voice of Tramp.

Lady and the Tramp, premiering in New York on June 22, 1955, was an enormous box office success—despite lukewarm reviews. Verna was especially proud of her family's contribution to this film. Today its nostalgic flavor, lifelike animation, and winning score hold up quite well; this combination ensures it as an enduring Disney classic.

During most of the eleven-month period that Verna intermittently recorded *Lady and the Tramp*, she visited the Disney studio at other times to record another forthcoming feature, one which Disney had envisioned as a masterpiece: *Sleeping*

Beauty. "He wanted to make this film as special and as different as he could. He wanted to make a film that he felt would be the pinnacle of achievement in animation," explained film historian Leonard Maltin in the documentary *Once Upon a Dream: The Making of Sleeping Beauty*, part of Disney's 2003 *Sleeping Beauty* Special Edition DVD release. While hoping to recreate the critical and financial successes of his two previous fairy tales *Snow White and the Seven Dwarfs* and *Cinderella*, Disney wanted Sleeping Beauty to have a more sophisticated look. "He didn't want it to look like *Snow White* done over with different characters," recalled animator Ollie Johnston.

More focused on the visual design than the story, Disney selected background artist Eyvind Earle to give the film a distinctive look. Since the story took place in the fourteenth century, Earle studied medieval art and architecture before creating a "stylized and modern" approach, a startling departure from the typically more realistic Disney product. In addition, Disney chose to shoot the film using a seventy-millimeter wide-screen process called Technirama, which, although fitting Earle's style perfectly, made the animation of characters extremely difficult. This format also meant that all of the backgrounds had to be more detailed, a factor which drove the film's escalating costs even higher. However, Disney told sequence director Eric Larson that he didn't care how long it took. *Sleeping Beauty* was to be a "moving illustration, the ultimate in animation." Unfortunately at that time, the Disney staff was already stretched thin; many had been pulled from feature films to work on Disney's three television series, numerous live-action films, as well as the Disneyland theme park. As a result, *Sleeping Beauty* took six years and six million dollars to complete.

Like all fairy tales, various versions of *Sleeping Beauty* had been passed down through the years. Disney's treatment was more like the Brothers Grimm story, but not without modifications suitable for a full-length motion picture. It followed the familiar tale up to a certain point. On Princess Aurora's christening day, the evil fairy Maleficent inflicts a horrible curse on the child: the princess is doomed to prick her hand on a spindle and die at age sixteen. The kingdom's three good fairies cannot completely undo this dreadful curse, but the youngest alters it so that instead of dying, Aurora will sleep until awakened by love's first kiss. The good fairies, whom Disney named Flora, Fauna, and Merryweather, vow to protect Aurora during the intervening years. Disguised as peasants, they take the baby princess deep into the forest where they plan to raise her as a foundling child. They even withhold her true identity from her, instead calling her Briar Rose. "The fairies really motivate a lot of what happens in that story," opined Ollie Johnston. "Without them, there wouldn't be any story. Everything they do is planned very carefully according to their personalities, and each of their personalities is different and strong, I think." The fairies carefully protect Aurora during her first sixteen years but are ultimately outwitted when Maleficent succeeds in enticing the girl to prick her finger on the cursed spindle. Then the real fight begins. Flora, Fauna, and Merryweather set out for Maleficent's crumbling castle to free the captive prince who can break Aurora's sleep. Though frightened by Maleficent and her hideous minions, the threesome is instrumental in aiding Prince Philip's escape and the ultimate destruction of Maleficent.

Verna was chosen for the part of Flora, the self-appointed leader of the three fairies. Her prior experience with Disney made her a logical choice. "Once the Disney team liked a voice," explained Disney historian Jeff Kurtti, "they tended to use them again and again." Verna's fellow radio veterans Barbara Jo Allen and Barbara Luddy were selected for the parts of Fauna and Merryweather, respectively. On June 24, 1953, the trio was called in to record lines for the first time, returning two weeks later for a second session. Then the production stalled while necessary revisions were made. Earle's artistic control of the picture became a serious issue because it dictated that the characters match the vertical stylization of the backgrounds. Most of the animated characters worked well as vertical designs, blending in smoothly with the static figures in Earle's backgrounds. However, Frank Thomas and Ollie Johnston, the animators assigned to creating the three good fairies, found this design impossible. A compromise was reached, and they were allowed to construct the trio more like traditional Disney characters. Johnston recalled that early on Walt Disney himself "toyed with the idea of their being all alike, but if they were there would have been nothing to animate—there was no play among them."

As with previous productions, the animators relied on live-action reference films to help perfect their craft. Many of Hollywood's best character actresses were called in to create these films, among them Spring Byington, Madge Blake, and Frances Bavier. Still photographs from the 2008 Platinum Edition DVD's documentary *Picture Perfect: The Making of Sleeping Beauty* reveal that the list also included Marjorie Bennett, Charity Grace, and Ida Moore. "All the actresses that came in—we saw lots of them—we made drawings of all of them," recalled Johnston.

Thomas and Johnston's earliest attempts, however, had the fairies looking more like gnomes or pixies. This may explain the high-pitched voices employed by Verna, Barbara Jo Allen, and Barbara Luddy in an early demo called "Riddle Diddle," included in the audio commentary on the 2003 DVD release, but ultimately dropped from the final film. The lyrics were set to an adaptation of the Silver Fairy theme from Tchaikovsky's *Sleeping Beauty* ballet. Some time earlier, Disney had realized that Earle's rich backgrounds called for something other than a traditional Disney song score. According to the 2003 documentary, the "instrumental popularity and celebrity of the ballet score, its indelible connection to the classic story and its storytelling sophistication led to [Disney's] decision to adapt the Tchaikovsky score for the animated feature." "Riddle Diddle" was written for a delightful scene in which the fairies resort to using magic after failing to make a birthday cake and dress for Aurora in the normal fashion. It's a fast-paced and tricky number, but the threesome pulls it off with apparent ease and charm. Of the three, Flora is definitely the musical leader, but the others are each given a moment to shine with a solo verse. The actresses' spoken exchanges sandwiched between the verses reveal that the personas of both Merryweather and Fauna would undergo dramatic changes between the time of this recording and the film's completion. In the "Riddle Diddle" number, Fauna is clearly the feisty one—much like the film's Merryweather—while Merryweather is meek and hesitant. In a startling contrast to the spunky Merryweather of the finished film, Barbara Luddy uses a soft, babylike voice. And as Fauna, Barbara Jo Allen employs a delightfully breathy vibrato, unlike the milder characterization used for the final film. Only Verna remains the same, although a trifle gentler than the screen Flora. In addition to their personality differences, the fairies' magic tasks in "Riddle Diddle" are completely switched around from the final film version. Instead of being in charge of the birthday cake, Fauna creates the gown, while Flora cleans the room and Merryweather handles the baking.

While "Riddle Diddle" didn't fit the rest of the film, neither did Thomas and Johnston's original animations designs for Flora, Fauna, and Merryweather. In their book *Disney Animation: The Illusion of Life*, they described the good fairies as "probably our most exasperating and elusive characters." Thomas and Johnston realized that they had to get a grip on the characters' individual personalities before they could proceed. "Until such characters have been 'found,' it is impossible to think of the story as anything but a collection of incidents," they explained. As they struggled with their assignment, Walt Disney seemed less than supportive. "Walt didn't have time or energy to come in to see the progressing work on *Sleeping Beauty*. He didn't have the creative juices on this one. They had to drag him in . . . I think that he had high hopes for it, but he never really got involved in it the way he thought he would," remembered Johnston.

From the start, Thomas and Johnston thought Flora should be bossy, but they later toned her down to "dominate without realizing she [was] doing it. She would be just a more aggressive personality and full of ideas." Next they had to find a way to play Merryweather off that character. It was decided that she would not always agree with Flora's decisions. "[Merryweather] is more impulsive and quick to act—more of a doer than the others but without an understanding of the big events around her . . . Fauna's character was the most difficult to find because we could not have another dominate personality." Finally, while vacationing in Colorado, Thomas met a lady who provided the inspiration for Fauna. He recalled, "She was supposed to read an inspirational poem at each meeting of her women's club, but when she arrived and could not find her prepared selection . . . she blithely pulled out something else, like a letter from her cousin in Indianapolis, and read it to the assembled ladies." Finally the triumvirate was complete.

Around this time, Thomas and Johnston made their drawings "cuter, more winsome, more appealing," although striving to keep within Earle's vertical style by giving them conical bodies when dressed as fairies. Leonard Maltin observed, "They retained the angularity of their costumes, somewhat . . . but the faces,

A disgruntled Merryweather poses as a dressmaker's dummy while Flora (center) struggles to create a gown for Aurora and Fauna attempts to make the princess a birthday cake—without magic—in this scene from *Sleeping Beauty*. © WALT DISNEY PRODUCTIONS.

though built on geometric shapes, still have a kind of cuddly, more Disney-esque feel to them."

While neither Fauna nor Merryweather resembled the actresses providing their voices, Flora certainly looked like Verna Felton, especially the expressions shown in her eyes and mouth. However, Flora's body, especially when garbed as a peasant, has the distinctive profile of character actress Madge Blake, who was counterbalanced by an ample bosom and backside. For the cottage scenes, the animators curiously dressed Flora in a 1950s skirt and black pumps, while hardly allowing Fauna and Merryweather to show their ankles. One can imagine Madge Blake wearing just such an outfit during the live-action reference films. While Johnston considered Fauna's personality reminiscent of the flighty persona forever associated with actress Billie Burke, her physical appearance rather resembles veteran actress Ida Moore, although minus Moore's button nose.

Jim Kurtti regarded the good fairies as the warmest and funniest characters in the film. "These sequences in the cottage illustrate the true performance skill of animators Frank Thomas and Ollie Johnston. The voices add enormously to the fairy characters." Ollie Johnston further emphasized the actresses' importance, "The voices are the things that really pin a character down because . . . the voice gives you the final way it should be handled and the timing on it."

Like Verna, Barbara Jo Allen and Barbara Luddy knew all about timing. By the time of *Sleeping Beauty*, they each had spent more than twenty-five years in the business. Verna had known both ladies since her early days in San Francisco radio; at one point all three were simultaneous residents of Oakland. Allen's Hollywood career was carefully documented in a 2003 *Films of the Golden Age* article ("Vera Vague: Of Mirth and Men"), but it omits details of her early life. Allen was born Marian Barbara Henshall in New York City on September 2, 1906. Although various references list her birth year as 1904, 1907, or 1908, U. S. Federal Census and Social Security records verify it as 1906. By age three, her affluent family had relocated to Long Beach, California. Her mother died when Allen was ten, and subsequently she traveled the world with her father Charles Thomas Henshall, a renowned horseman whose business interests often took him to Havana, Cuba, where he had invested in an upscale racetrack. In 1920, after her father's investment proved unwise, Allen returned to Los Angeles where she finished high school and attended the Southern Branch of the University of California, now known as UCLA. She also studied at the Sorbonne in Paris, recalling later, "I lived on the Left Bank for eighteen months and had the time of my life."

In mid-1927, when she returned to the States, she aimed for a fresh start and immediately joined a stock company, adopting the stage name Barbara Jo Allen. She soon crossed paths with a young actor named William Barton Yarborough, also recently returned from Europe where he had been performing on the London stage. In less than a year, they were married. Their only child, Barbara Joan, was born in Los Angeles in late 1928. Almost a year later, Allen made her Oakland debut with the Henry Duffy Players in the play *Boomerang*, directed by Ferdinand Munier. A succession of plays followed until both Yarborough and Allen broke into radio, becoming leading NBC players in San Francisco. In 1931, Allen made headlines when she obtained a Reno divorce and immediately married California lumber millionaire Charles Hooper Crosby—an impulsive and regrettable decision since the union barely lasted one month. During Allen's third marriage, to author Vernon Kansas Patterson, she moved to Los Angeles, where she entered films and resumed her radio career. Although her marriage to Patterson lasted longer than the previous two, it also ended in divorce. In 1943, Allen wed for the fourth and final time to radio executive Norman Morrell. They made their home in Woodland Hills on an eight-acre walnut ranch, populated by a menagerie rivaling that of Verna Felton: four dogs, a horse, and a ringtail monkey. Meanwhile, Allen's career blossomed; her films numbered more than fifty. However, in most of them Allen was credited as Vera Vague, a man-hungry ditz she had created for radio comedies as early as 1935. By 1948, Allen was weary of the Vera Vague persona and its effectual typecasting, so she abandoned her radio career to devote herself to raising orchids commercially. Five years later when *Sleeping Beauty* went into production, Allen was serving as the emcee of short-lived CBS-TV game show *Follow the Leader*.

Barbara Jane Luddy, the youngest of the fairy godmother trio, was born in Montana on May 25, 1907. Sources vary on the town of her birth, including among them Great Falls, Billings, and Helena. According to a 1908 Billings newspaper article, her parents married in that city, and it was here that her father, a former bowling alley manager, deserted the family the year Luddy was born. Her mother successfully remarried, this time to a physician, and the family resided for a while in the small town of Harlem. Later Luddy attended the Ursuline Convent school in Great Falls, where the nuns discovered that she possessed a remarkable singing range. She began a professional stage career as a child, but resorted to dramatic parts when her singing voice failed at age eleven. Subsequently, she played in stock, vaudeville, and even tent shows before being featured in string of silent films. In 1927, Luddy returned to the stage, subsequently touring Australia with Leo Carillo and the Duffy Players in 1929. The following year, she was back in Oakland performing with the same troupe, which now included Gale Gordon and Helen Kleeb. As the Depression deepened, Luddy turned to radio. In 1936, she began her long association with the *First Nighter* radio program, following the successful show to its new Chicago location the next year. In that city in 1942, she married radio announcer Ned Lefevre. They returned to Los Angeles several years later, and Luddy continued with Olan Soule on *First Nighter* until it ended in 1953. The *Oakland Tribune* once described the diminutive Luddy as "hardly reach[ing] the epaulets on a life-size statue of Napoleon." At four feet, ten and five-eighths inches, Luddy sometimes had to stand on a box to reach the microphone. Her radio pals called her "Biddy," but most never suspected that in her youth Luddy had valiantly battled polio. She was the perfect inspiration for Merryweather—and not just because of her size. The *Tribune* also described Luddy as having "blue eyes, dark hair, a happy disposition and a quick temper."

Leonard Maltin expressed his feelings about Verna, Allen, and Luddy in the 2008 documentary. "All of these women had such vast experience working . . . just with their voices, being able to express so much with an inflection, and it's not possible to measure how much they add to this movie."

Verna recorded the part of Flora during thirteen sessions, beginning in 1953 and ending in 1957, with the bulk of the voice work being completed in 1954 and 1955. Why did it take so long? For one thing, the majority of the film's lines belonged to the good fairies, so Verna, Allen, and Luddy were needed more often than some of the other actors. Mary Costa, who provided the singing and speaking voices for Aurora, offered another explanation during a 2005 interview with the author. "If the writers even changed a word, they would call us back to do the work. You couldn't drop a word in like you do today, because [the process] really was not a voiceover. Everything was done [according] to the voice . . . One time I was doing a signing with [animator] Marc Davis, and a lady came up and said, 'Miss Costa, how does it feel to be the voiceover for a classic Disney princess?' And Marc said, 'Forgive me, madam, but the voices were the ocean of sound upon which we animated.' [His comment] was so, you know, esoteric. I looked over and laughed at him, and he laughed, too, but he said, 'It's the truth.' He explained to her that words couldn't be dropped in—that they had to be animated again—if they decided to change any part or any sentence of a sequence. And they had to go back to the drawing boards and decide what they wanted. And then they told us [what to say] and they re-animated. It was really slow work, and of course, in between, Walt created Disneyland."

At twenty-two years old, Costa was a virtual unknown when she was chosen as the voice of Aurora. Many times since then Costa has told the story of her discovery by Disney, but it bears repeating here because Verna Felton was a sideline player in the sequence of events. Born in 1930 in Knoxville, Tennessee, Costa moved with her family to Los Angeles at age fourteen. Though musically untrained, Costa possessed a natural gift for singing—as well as for beauty—so she was encouraged to seek a Hollywood career. By 1952, she had acquired an agent named Ben Medford who one day escorted her to a studio audition for composer Victor Young. While there, Medford suggested that they meet Frank Tashlin, who had just finished directing Bob Hope in the Paramount feature *Son of Paleface*. Costa described Tashlin as "this big bear of a man, but so cordial, so nice and so funny . . . and I didn't care whether I got a part [in his next picture] or not because I thought he was so nice." Neither realized it then, but soon a courtship would develop, leading to their eventual marriage in the summer of 1953.

After an hour's visit, Tashlin walked Costa and Medford to their waiting car, and that's where they bumped into Verna, also visiting the studio. It seemed to Costa that Verna and Tashlin had worked together at some point, although she could not pinpoint the project. The connection may have been Disney; Tashlin was an animator there when Verna was recording *Dumbo*. Or perhaps he knew her from Red Skelton's *The Fuller Brush Man*, a screenplay which Tashlin had co-written with Devery Freeman. "[Tashlin] just absolutely loved Verna," recalled Costa, "and he would use her any time he could—in anything, you know, television, or whatever he was doing. And she was so funny and charming when I met her . . . When people really, genuinely amused [Tashlin], he would really laugh. I knew that he loved Verna because she really made him laugh out loud."

Two weeks later, Tashlin invited Costa to attend a dinner party where she might meet some influential people. After dinner, as people gathered around the piano, Costa was asked to sing. Seated next to her was Walter Schumann, musical director for Walt Disney. He was so impressed with Costa's rendition of "When I Fall in Love" that he invited her to audition for Walt Disney the following morning. Things went well, and the next day Disney himself phoned Costa to offer her the part of Princess Aurora.

Months later, in the Disney studio, Costa met Verna for the second time. "We had quite a reunion because she remembered me, and I remembered her . . . we were [together] in the recording studio about two or three times, the fairies and the prince and I. And [during rehearsal, Verna] would just cut up and have more fun with the prince, because she would take her pencil like it was a wand, and he was rather—he was a little bit shy—and one of the nicest people—Bill Shirley. And she jumped up on a chair to put this pencil over this prince's head and just broke us all up. And he started laughing, and everybody in the booth laughed. I shall *never* forget that, because, I mean, she was so agile. Just to know her was to adore her. And you know she was very, very animated when she spoke in true life. And the way [the animators depicted Flora] is exactly the way Verna was while recording this part." Costa was hard-pressed to recall any specifics about Barbara Jo Allen or Barbara Luddy, explaining, "They were entirely different personalities, but I was partial to Verna because she was always cutting up and keeping everybody in good humor. And so, all of my feelings toward her are just so happy. She just knew how to enjoy life, [but] the thing I admired about her was that when it came time to record, she just snapped into it. She had the highest professional standards . . . and as Walt Disney was a mentor to me, she was also."

Costa was also impressed with Eleanor Audley, who recorded the part of Maleficent: "She was just fantastic because when she stood in front of that microphone—I just wanted to go in one day—just listen to her record, and she wasn't that tall, but when she started to talk and speak that role, it was like she was *seven feet* tall! It was just amazing what she could do! And she was so nice— they were all just very, very sweet people. But they could go [quickly] into their characters. I found that Walt picked the people for this picture that were so highly professional that there was no time wasted, and they didn't mind coming back in when we had to re-do certain things."

One fact often ignored by reference books and internet sources is that Verna actually voiced two characters in *Sleeping Beauty*. While Verna, as Flora, held the record for the most speaking lines in the film, she also provided the voice for one of the most minor characters. In the opening scene of Aurora's christening, when the queen is distressed at Maleficent's presence, it's Verna's voice that softly utters the two brief lines given to the queen.

Sleeping Beauty was finally released on January 29, 1959. Despite a "massive promotional campaign," the film failed at the box office, grossing just $5.3 million and putting Disney in the red for fiscal 1960. Disney biographer Neal Gabler referred to the film as "the Sleeping Beauty debacle." Richard Schickel called it Disney's "nadir." Even Michael Barrier dubbed the "doomed" picture as a "hapless relic from what now seemed like a very distant period in the Disney studio's history." Leonard Maltin was more generous than most. While praising the film's realistic characters, "electrifying music," and "staggering" visual aspect, Maltin recognized its limited appeal. "*Sleeping Beauty* is a very good film, but more so for older audiences than for young children. The visual grandeur and the intricacy of the animation are lost on the tiny tots, who only want to see lots of color and movement." Luckily for today's older audiences, the 2003 and 2008

DVD documentaries and audio commentaries explain the painstaking efforts of the animators and voice artists to make this film, and in the process perhaps winning new fans for *Sleeping Beauty*. While it may not have been a moneymaker in 1959, its beautiful craftsmanship is not lost on faithful Disney aficionados. Borrowing John Lassetter's words, the film remains "a tour de force of directing, of storytelling, of animation."

In 1953, while Verna was shuttling back and forth to Disney's Burbank studio, she was also honing her craft as a television performer. While her first experience in the infant medium—1945's *Oh, Miss Tubbs!*—predated network television, Verna evidently did not appear on the small screen again until six years later. Her earliest documented network television appearance remains to be a segment of *The Colgate Comedy Hour*, airing on October 28, 1951. The host of this variety show was Eddie Cantor who appeared in a sketch "Maxi the Taxi," featuring Cesar Romero and Verna as taxi passengers. Her brief experience as a regular on *The Dennis Day Show* would shortly follow.

By the 1952-53 television season, many of the radio shows Verna frequented had made the transition to television, including *The George Burns and Gracie Allen Show, Amos 'n' Andy,* and *The Adventures of Ozzie and Harriet*. Verna soon appeared in guest spots on all three shows. As various characters, Verna lent her support on *Burns and Allen* three times during the season. On November 27, she appeared as Emily Beecher March, a children's guidance counselor engaged by Gracie to advise a ten-year-old boy against following his parents into show business. As she introduces herself to dizzy Gracie, she proudly announces, "I am affiliated with the Spencer Foundation." Gracie's gaze runs up and down Verna's tightly fitting business suit, "Well, you don't look affiliated." She confuses Mrs. March so thoroughly that the matron believes middle-aged Harry Von Zell, whom she observes floating a toy boat, is the child in need of career counseling. Thinking the situation is too peculiar, Mrs. March huffs out.

In the episode which aired the following February 19, Harry Von Zell complains about his income tax payment, telling Gracie that if he had a wife and three children he'd owe much less. Secretly Gracie decides to help Von Zell by placing an advertisement in the newspaper. Flashy divorcee "Babs" Rodney, played by Verna, arrives at the Burnses' house to answer the ad. Mistaking the cigar-smoking George as the matrimonial candidate, Mrs. Rodney girlishly flirts with him, "You can scatter your ashes on my rug any time!" When Gracie explains that it's Von Zell who desires a wife, Mrs. Rodney agrees to return later with her three "boys" to meet him. After Von Zell becomes aware of Gracie's scheme, he weakly protests to Mrs. Rodney whose brawny sons tower over her prospective husband. Gracie saves the day by announcing that Von Zell is already married to neighbor Blanche Morton. When he scoops a confused Blanche into his arms and rushes out, a disgruntled Mrs. Rodney grouses, "It wasn't worth putting my girdle on for this!" Verna's final appearance that season occurred on April 27 when she played an Irish cleaning lady befriended by Gracie.

On June 11, 1953, Verna made a brief appearance on *Amos 'n' Andy* as an authoritative nurse in the episode "Kingfish Has a Baby." When George "Kingfish" Stevens thinks his wife Sapphire is pregnant, he persuades Andy to accompany him to a night class for expectant fathers. Using a doll as a stand-in for a baby, the nurse attempts to instruct them in the proper care and feeding of an infant. The starchy nurse is not amused by their ignorance, especially after the men argue over who should hold the doll. When Andy yanks its leg off, it's the last straw. The nurse bellows, "This morning I had four cases of chicken pox. After that there were two cases of mumps, and a baby hit me in the head with a bottle. I missed my supper, and now you come in! I think I've given enough to the cause of medicine for the day—good night!"

Verna gave a more subtle and effective performance in "Whistler's Daughter," an episode of *The Adventures of Ozzie and Harriet*, which aired earlier that spring. As the most seasoned member of the cast, her natural performance shines in marked contrast with that of the other players. Playing the widowed Mrs. Whistler peddling homemade spot remover, she arrives at Ozzie Nelson's house, exhausted and suffering from aching bunions. Ozzie invites her inside to rest and, feeling sorry for her, buys five bottles of the cleaner. Mrs. Whistler promises to deliver the order later that afternoon, but at the last minute sends her attractive blonde daughter instead. When Ozzie ends up buying three magazine subscriptions from the daughter, his wife Harriet accuses him of having no "sales resistance."

Coincidentally, the same theme had been employed—to greater effect—by the writers of *I Love Lucy* three months before when Verna appeared in a small guest part. In "*Sales Resistance*," Lucy Ricardo falls prey to a fast-talking vacuum cleaner salesman. When her husband Ricky demands that she return it, Lucy is too fearful to approach the salesman for a refund. So, she decides to try to sell the machine to another unsuspecting housewife. When Lucy rings a doorbell on the next block, she's greeted by Mrs. Simpson, a snarling, disinterested older woman with unkempt hair, played by Verna. Employing the same hard sell used on her, Lucy throws a handful of dirt onto the woman's floor. Then she brandishes a ten-dollar bill, "Madam, that ten-dollar bill, that sawbuck, that one tenth of a C-note is all yours if my Handy Dandy Vacuum Cleaner fails to clean up all this dirt in two minutes flat!" With a hard look, the woman gruffly confirms Lucy's conditions and then accepts the offer. As Lucy scurries to plug in the vacuum cleaner, Mrs. Simpson wears a smug expression—she hasn't paid her electric bill so there is no power in the apartment. Discovering this, Lucy apologizes for the mess on the floor, "I don't know how you're going to clean it up!" Standing over Lucy, the displeased woman scowls, "*I* do!"

Although she's onscreen for less than ninety seconds, Verna expertly executes the part of slovenly Mrs. Simpson. The episode was filmed on August 29, 1952, but it was not Verna's first experience working with Lucille Ball in a comedy series. In 1949, she had appeared as a gossip on an episode of *My Favorite*

Mrs. Simpson "pockets" Lucy's sawbuck in "Sales Resistance."

Husband, the radio forerunner of *I Love Lucy*, which starred Ball, Richard Denning, Gale Gordon, and Bea Benaderet.

Ball evidently appreciated Verna's ability because she was chosen to play another character with a similarly no-nonsense flavor in the episode "*Lucy Hires a Maid*," filmed on March 27, 1953, and broadcast exactly one month later. After Lucy spends sleepless nights caring for the new baby, Ricky encourages her to hire a maid to help out but stresses that Lucy must be a firm employer. When Mrs. Porter, the prospective maid, arrives, it is she who conducts the interview. After inspecting the apartment as well as Lucy's appearance, she flatly outlines her own expectations and requirements. Mrs. Porter is ready to refuse the job when she learns that Lucy has neither a dishwasher nor clothes dryer, but Lucy entices her with the Ricardos' 21-inch-screen television. Things go downhill from there. For lunch Mrs. Porter serves Lucy an unappetizing peanut butter sandwich, but only after she has polished off half a roast beef ("that snively little leftover"), an entire head of lettuce, and the rest of the refrigerator's contents ("Well, *I've* got to eat, too, you know!"). Lucy is further frustrated when Mrs. Porter refuses to take care of the baby or his laundry, but she is too intimidated by the woman to fire her. Even Ricky, when confronting Mrs. Porter, cannot bring himself to serve her walking papers. The next day Lucy trashes the entire apartment to make the woman quit, only to learn that Ricky has already fired her via telephone. The episode has become a fan favorite over the years, mainly due to Verna's formidable expressions and body language.

Mrs. Porter expresses displeasure with Lucy's "leftovers" in the episode "Lucy Hires a Maid."

By more than one account, Desilu—the production company operated by Lucille Ball and Desi Arnaz—maintained a reputation for thriftiness, particularly in regard to supporting players who appeared on *I Love Lucy*. According to one such character actor, anonymously quoted in Bart Andrews's *The 'I Love Lucy' Book*, "They were awful cheapskates. We got paid the absolute minimums. If your part was small, they hired you for one day—the day of the actual filming—which gave you just one or two rehearsals." At the time, filmed television shows like *I Love Lucy* fell under the jurisdiction of the Screen Actors Guild, which specified that minimum payment for five days' work was two hundred and fifty dollars. Even so, there seem to have been some inequalities. Andrews pointed out that Verna earned two hundred and fifty dollars for her week's work on the "*Sales Resistance*" episode, while Sheldon Leonard, appearing as the slick salesman, went home with four hundred dollars.

Interestingly, Lee Millar appeared on *I Love Lucy* twice as many times as his mother. His initial episode ("*The Quiz Show*") was filmed on October 5, 1951, more than one year before "*Sales Resistance*" aired. In his first *Lucy* outing, Lee amusingly enacted the part of a bored radio station staffer whose job it was to wrangle applause from the quiz show audience. Although he was given no lines, Lee earned one hundred and fifty dollars for this performance. The most substantial of his four *I Love Lucy* appearances would follow three years later when he played the director of the Ricardos' ill-fated attempt at a live morning television show ("*Mr. and Mrs. TV Show*"). Like Verna, Lee was no stranger to working with perfectionist Lucille Ball, who made the move to television in 1951. While he had trouped across the country with her in a tour of *Dream Girl* in 1948, Verna had performed with Ball on various radio programs.

Prior to his initial work on *I Love Lucy*, Lee had populated radio programs like *Halls of Ivy, Hopalong Cassidy, Nero Wolfe, Dr. Christian*, and *Screen Directors Playhouse*. In 1949, he broke into television with a single appearance on *Armchair Detective*, a CBS game show in which studio contestants tried to solve mysteries acted out on stage. However, this was at a time when television was still considered by some as faddish, so radio assignments continued to dominate Lee's work schedule.

However, by 1952, Lee's television appearances far outweighed his radio gigs. His credits then included guest spots on such early television shows as *The Alan Young Show, Space Patrol, The George Burns and Gracie Allen Show, The Jack Benny Program, All-Star Revue, My Friend Irma, Life with Luigi*, and *The Dennis Day Show*. In general, these were small parts, as were many of his radio spots. But, in 1952, he landed a regular role on *Without Fear*, a KTTV drama series broadcast live in Los Angeles and San Diego and via kinescopes for San Francisco audiences. Jointly sponsored by the International Association of Machinists and the Machinists' Nonpartisan Political League, *Without Fear* meshed dramatic sequences with newsreel footage in a format to educate the public on such subjects as inflation, domestic communism, and international concerns. In addition to these early television appearances, Lee was soon able to list six feature films among his growing credits, including *Meet Danny Wilson, Hear No Evil*, and *Bonzo Goes to College*.

Unfortunately though, Lee's career would never enjoy the success of his mother's. True, he had been blessed with advantages that many other aspiring actors had not. He was born into a theatrical family, made his stage debut as a toddler, and was trained to dance, play piano, and ride horseback. By age twenty-five, he had acquired stage, radio, television, and film experience. Yet he seemed destined to fill only marginal roles, with most of them becoming character bits, particularly after his hair began to gray prematurely. Perhaps other physical attributes made him more suited for such roles. At six feet tall, his lanky frame seldom reached one hundred fifty pounds. And while Lee possessed conventional good looks, he was not matinee idol material.

Actress Peggy Webber, who worked with Lee in radio, recalled, "[Lee] didn't have what his mother had. He was good at what he did, but he wasn't like she was. She was a powerhouse! And he kind of melded into the background. But she knew how to take a part that was nothing and make something so fantastic out of it." Still, Lee enjoyed acting and continued to pursue it. His wife Edith also yearned for a career in entertainment, so Lee—and quite possibly Verna—used

Lee Millar, early 1950s.

their influence to win bit parts for her on many of the same shows with which Lee was associated, including *Without Fear, The Alan Young Show,* and *The Dennis Day Show.*

However, in the spring of 1953, Edith's acting pursuits were pushed aside. She and Lee were happily expecting their first baby to arrive that fall, but no one was more thrilled than Verna. The tiny apartment over Verna's kitchen was deemed inadequate for a growing family so the expectant grandmother converted her poolside rumpus room and its adjoining garage into a guesthouse, complete with nursery. On October 14, Edith gave birth to a six and one half pound baby girl at St. Joseph's Hospital in Burbank. In honor of Verna, her parents named her Lisa Felton Millar.

At sixty-three, Verna had become a grandmother. She telephoned her old friend Hedda Hopper with the news that she had finally caught up with her. (Hopper had become a grandmother a decade earlier.) Hopper printed part of Verna's announcement in her column a month later: "And wouldn't you know that the day of her birth I would be working. Fortunately the baby's father had the day off, and when I asked him who the baby looked like he replied, 'She's the spitting image of Martha Raye.'"

Just as Verna's home dynamics were changing, so was her career. Television's increasing stronghold would bring an end to her beloved radio days within two years of her granddaughter's birth. Verna's final radio series—*Meet Mr. McNutley* and *My Little Margie*—were produced concurrently on television as separate entities, although she did not appear in either of the video versions. The former, debuting on September 17, 1953, lasted one radio season and starred Ray Milland as English professor Raymond McNutley. Phyllis Avery appeared as McNutley's wife Peggy, while Verna assumed the role of Miss Josephine Bradley, dean of the all-girl Lynnhaven College. Verna summoned her best basso-profundo voice to embody the pompous and pedantic Dean Bradley, the thorn in McNutley's side. McNutley caused the dean an equal amount of exasperation, getting himself into situations potentially threatening to the college's fine reputation. McNutley notwithstanding, the stuffy Dean Bradley was relentless in her efforts to maintain a safe and proper atmosphere for students, even inspecting a new ice cream parlor near campus.

Sometimes the very proper Dean Bradley found herself humbled by McNutley. On May 27, 1954, in one of the show's final broadcasts, McNutley unknowingly buys a stolen mink coat for the faculty to give the dean. When the truth comes out and authorities confiscate the coat, Dean Bradley wags an accusing finger at McNutley. Shortly afterward, the roles are reversed when he learns that the staid Miss Bradley has won a mink coat in an advertising jingle contest. She confides in McNutley by singing her corny creation: "Grandma Rose's Buttermilk Mix for all your handy-dandy baking tricks! Get your culinary kicks with Grandma Rose's Buttermilk Mix!" McNutley shakes his head, "Dean Bradley, you're more to be pitied than censured." In the end they forgive each other: McNutley for buying stolen property and Bradley for entering a kitschy contest.

Meet Mr. McNutley's final radio installment aired on June 10, while the television version—although revamped for its second season—ended a year later. For the first season, Milland and Avery repeated their radio roles on the small screen, while Minerva Urecal assumed the role of formidable Dean Bradley. Urecal, in a coincidence worth noting, had beat out Verna for a television role again.

My Little Margie enjoyed a longer run on both radio and television than *Meet Mr. McNutley*. The television version of *Margie* debuted on CBS on June 16, 1952, as a thirteen-week summer replacement series for *I Love Lucy*. The comedy centered around 21-year-old Margie Albright and her gay-blade widower father Vern, each at odds over the other's romances. Gale Storm played Margie, and former silent film star Charles Farrell came out of semi-retirement to appear as the hapless Vern. Dubbed by one reviewer as "the unfunniest comedy show on the air," *Margie* was uniformly panned by critics but adored by viewers. When *Margie*'s summer run was up, fans flooded the network and the sponsor Phillip Morris with letters of protest. The show returned to the airwaves—this time on NBC—on October 4. After five episodes aired, the sponsor decided to move the show back to CBS, with plans for it to debut as a regular series on January 1, 1953, where it would remain until September before returning to NBC. Storm, Farrell, and the rest of the *Margie* cast, including Don Hayden, Clarence Kolb, Willie Best, and Gertrude W. Hoffmann, were summoned to immediately begin filming additional episodes.

In the meantime, Phillip Morris decided to cash in on Margie's popularity by creating a radio version for the considerably large number of Americans who were not yet equipped with television reception. (Even Palm Springs, California, the home of Charles Farrell, did not have access to television programs at this time. As the mayor of that city, Farrell responded to residents' requests and screened several *My Little Margie* episodes in the local movie theater.) So in a switch from the normal pattern, *Margie* debuted on radio six months after its television counterpart had been introduced. Storm and Farrell repeated their roles for the radio version, which premiered on December 7, 1952.

"I didn't know how they thought we could do a radio show when we were doing a TV show at the same time," recalled Storm in a 2005 interview with the author. "You know, when they came to Charlie and me and said, 'CBS wants to do a radio show,' we both said, '*When?*' Like what time do we have to do it in? They managed a Saturday or Sunday, I forget which. I was so busy and overworked, but I loved it. You couldn't have lived through it if you didn't love it . . . The interesting part about the radio show was the fact that we had a live audience. For the television show, we shot that like you would a motion picture. But the radio show was great; the performers were great. Verna Felton was just a dear. Everyone loved her."

My Little Margie aired as a transcribed CBS series on Sundays at 8:30 p.m. Producer-director Gordon T. Hughes was in charge of rehearsals, held just minutes before the transcription was recorded. Writer Frank Fox typically, but feebly, attempted to create each episode as a comedy of errors. As one commentator summed it up: "When Margie does something and Vern finds out, he decides to teach her a lesson. However, as Vern tries to teach Margie a lesson, she finds out and turns the tables by trying to teach him a lesson for trying to teach her a lesson."

Scatterbrained Margie and her father Vern lived in a high-rise Manhattan apartment. Their snoopy next-door neighbor was the much-married Mrs. Florence Odetts, played by Verna. Others dropping in were Margie's dimwitted beau Freddie Wilson (Gil Stratton), of whom Vern greatly disapproved, and Vern's grumpy boss Mr. Honeywell (Will Wright). Doris Singleton, and later Shirley Mitchell, appeared as Vern's love interest.

From the 1954 press snipe accompanying this photo: "A lot of *My Little Margie*'s complications on CBS radio stem from such incidents as this, where Margie (Gale Storm) is getting the latest unfounded rumor from her neighbor Mrs. Odetts (Verna Felton)."

Mrs. Odetts was prone to eavesdrop through the Albrights' keyhole before entering their apartment—without knocking—while never missing a beat as she jumped in on the current conversation. She was also quite free with her advice to Margie. And no matter the situation, Mrs. Odetts habitually related it to experiences with one of her six former husbands. When Margie contemplated marriage to Freddie, Mrs. Odetts mused about her own life, "Always a bride but never a bridesmaid!" When asked why she married so many times, the old girl replied, "Oh, I just did it for a lark! I gave all my husbands the bird!" Even though Mrs. Odetts was plainly a low comedy character, Verna gave it her best shot.

Fellow *Margie* cast member Gil Stratton recalled in 2005: "I loved working with Verna, you know, because she was terrific, and particularly with a live audience because she could mug with the best of them! Everybody loved her, and she was a terrific gal . . . *My Little Margie* probably had the worst scripts in the world; they were not very funny. And I remember Verna and I did everything but drop our pants on stage to get laughs and make it sound like it was funny even though there wasn't anything there to laugh at, really . . . The only [anecdote] I remember [about Verna] is that one time I came home, and I had some lipstick on my cheek. And my wife said, 'And *where* did *that* come from?' And I said, 'God, I don't know.' And she was kind of cold for a couple of days until I guess we did a *Margie* show . . . well, Verna was very effusive, and of course, she'd hug you and give you a kiss and everything like that. And I came home and said, 'I finally figured out where the lipstick came from.' She said, 'Where?' I said, 'From Verna Felton.' And she said, 'Oh my god, yeah, that was her color!' Verna was a special lady. She was just so great. Very professional. Whatever you [hope] to hear, that's what she was, you know, really just lovely."

On the television version of *My Little Margie*, eighty-one-year-old Gertrude Hoffmann played the role of Mrs. Odetts. It was to be one of the final roles of her career. Unlike Verna Felton, Hoffmann had become an actress rather late in life—at age 61, in fact—and only after her ornithologist husband accidentally hurtled down a rocky cliff while hunting specimens on San Miguel Island. The widowed Hoffmann was not content making the rounds of Santa Barbara dinner parties and teas so she informed her children of her plan to follow a lifelong dream of becoming an actress. A twenty-year career awaited her.

Hoffmann was born Eliza Gertrude Wesselhoeft in 1871 while her Americans parents were visiting Germany. She grew up in Cambridge, Massachusetts, where her father was a noted physician. In 1894, Hoffmann wed there, but after twenty-five years she relocated with her husband to Santa Barbara where he later became the head of the city's natural history museum. As an aspiring actress, Hoffmann made the move to Hollywood in 1932, spending the first nine months making the rounds at the studios, all to no avail. Since she had no agent, no studio would hire her. At the same time, no agent would take Hoffmann on because she had no acting experience. Finally she landed a part in a Warner Oland film at RKO. From then on Hoffmann earned a comfortable living with her portrayals of grande dames, although one of her most noted roles was a lifer in the prison film *Caged*. Her other films included Alfred Hitchcock's *Foreign Correspondent* and *Suspicion*.

Hoffmann was particular that her screen credits include her middle initial because she disliked being confused with another Gertrude Hoffmann, a Broadway dancer-choreographer who shocked audiences with her almost topless portrayal of Salome in 1908. Even today both women's credits and vital statistics are confused. Gertrude W. Hoffmann retired from acting in 1955 and died in Santa Barbara at age ninety-six on February 13, 1968. The dancer Gertrude Hoffmann (*nee* Kitty Hayes) was fifteen years younger and died in Los Angeles in 1966.

Unlike radio's Mrs. Odetts, Hoffmann's television character was only a semi-regular on *My Little Margie*, but when she did appear she outshined the rest of the cast. While not as gifted with timing or expression as Verna, Hoffmann's comedy approach was nonetheless effective. Nineteen years Verna's senior, Hoffmann looked even older than that, but as Margie's scheming accomplice, she proved herself a trouper. One episode called for Hoffmann to race down a studio street—while wearing a clown costume—and jump on a motor scooter. "I ran as fast as my legs would carry me," Hoffman beamed. While radio's Mrs. Odetts was outrageous for eavesdropping and flirtations, her more adventuresome television counterpart won laughs as she plotted to purchase race cars, speedboats, and flying lessons. Such modern pursuits were totally incongruous with Hoffmann's wrinkled face and outmoded attire, making her an effective comic character. But offscreen, the incongruity continued. Gale Storm recalled in her 1981 autobiography *I Ain't Down Yet*: "[Gertrude] was a trouper, though, and never failed. She had a problem, too. She didn't live in the real world . . . Between scenes she'd come up to me with a script and ask me what this meant or that meant—a slang phrase, for instance. I remember she asked me one time what a hot rod was. When I told her, she was so pleased. She had a sense of discovery about her, as if all of life were an adventure, and it came through on the screen." Hoffmann's rugged acting career didn't seem to dim her vitality; she drove her own car twenty miles to the studio daily.

In 2005, when asked to compare Verna's characterization of Mrs. Odetts to the character's television counterpart, Gale Storm diplomatically declined: "You don't really compare those people because they each had their own style . . . Verna Felton's was different from the one that Gertrude W.—she always wanted the W. in there—Gertrude W. Hoffmann played. And of course, people [didn't] get to know Verna Felton in a radio show the way they [did] in a TV show, but Verna Felton was so well known in the field of radio because she was such a fine actress. And she was a very valuable asset for our radio show. She was just a joy, just wonderful to work with and see her perform. And so I remember her vividly. You know, you never have time to get together socially because you're working too hard, [but] she was loved by everyone. And she had a wonderful, beautiful reputation for being a wonderful person as well as a very professional performer."

Both the radio and television incarnations of *My Little Margie* drew their final breaths in the summer of 1955. Entertainment columnist Robert Sokolsky announced on July 1: "On August 24, the National Broadcasting Company will take pity upon the nation's viewers and bring the *My Little Margie* television series to an end. This merciful decision will be roundly applauded although hopes are high that such capable performers as Gale Storm and Charles Farrell will be able to be back in the public's eye before too long." One month before the television *Margie* ended, CBS pulled the plug on the radio version, marking the end of Verna's career as a radio series regular.

My Little Margie in rehearsal: Clockwise from bottom: Gordon Hughes, director, unidentified man, Gil Stratton, Gale Storm, George Neise, Charles Farrell, Verna, and Will Wright, 1954.

Earlier Verna had ended her long associations with three other radio series. In the spring of 1953, Judy Canova decided to revamp her NBC radio comedy as a variety show for the following season. Consequently, Verna's characters, Patsy Pierce and Mrs. Dodge, were written out.

Meanwhile, Jack Benny discontinued his long-running radio program at the end of the 1954-55 season. Since 1950, Benny had been producing his radio and television shows concurrently but finally realized that the former medium had run its course. Verna, following her departure from Dennis Day's television series, had continued to appear sporadically as Mrs. Day during the final years of the Benny radio program. However, Benny's writers, realizing that the character had run her own course as well, resorted to using Mrs. Day merely as filler. On December 26, 1954, viewers heard Verna bellow her trademark line—"Eh, shuddup!"—for the last time, although her final appearance on the Benny radio program would not occur until the following February 13.

In that broadcast, Dennis Day throws a surprise party for Benny—a plot that borrowed heavily from a 1948 show. The resulting broadcast was a poor send-off for Mrs. Day and likewise Verna, who had injected so much life into the part. Benny and the show's producers slighted Verna in another way as well. For over eighteen years she had appeared on the Benny program, and not once was she given air credit, not even for this, her final contribution.

In 1958, Benny would rectify this omission during one of Verna's appearances on his television program. At the conclusion of the October 19 telecast, before bringing her out in front of the curtain, Benny announced, "Ladies and gentlemen, I would like to have you meet the lady who always and for years has played the part of Dennis Day's mother, who always hated me, you know—Miss Verna Felton!"

As for Verna's opinion of Benny, she told Marty Halperin, "That was a very fun show to do. He's a very nice man to work for, Jack is—he's a little nervous and very excitable, but he's fun."

Verna had been associated with only one other radio show longer than Benny's, and that was *Lux Radio Theatre*. With over one hundred *Lux* appearances to her credit, Verna appeared on the show for the last time on August 3, 1953, in a live broadcast of "*Romance to a Degree*,"an original play written by Kathleen Hite for *The Lux Summer Theatre*, a special summer replacement series for the regular *Lux Radio Theatre*. Directed by Norman Macdonnell, the summer series employed only one film star who was cast opposite a player usually limited to supporting roles on the air. In the case of series highlight "*Romance to a Degree*," Joseph Cotten was paired with Shirley Mitchell to portray strangers who meet on a train while en route to Los Angeles. Cotten played William Spring Smith, a small-town professor of literature with plans to earn a degree at UCLA, while Mitchell was Jenny, a star-struck girl with hopes of becoming Hollywood's newest discovery. Verna was handpicked to play Smith's aunt, former silent screen star Lily Spring who has deluded her Kansas relatives—including her nephew—into thinking that she's still living off her film fortune. When Smith phones his garrulous Aunt Lily to let her know he's in town, she puts him off, saying her house is filled with guests. The next day when she meets him for lunch at the Brown Derby, Smith is struck by her Hollywood tan ("We just turn brown to keep the Chamber of Commerce happy.") and her loquacity ("I wonder what kept her *out* of *talking* pictures!"). What Smith doesn't know is that his once affluent aunt is now so financially strapped that she operates her aging estate as a boarding house for show business has-beens, including a broken down Shakespearean actor (John Dehner) who poses as her butler. And she derives her suntan from standing on a Beverly Hills sidewalk, hawking maps of the movie stars' homes. Smith is later reunited with Jenny, discouraged because she's failed to break into the business. Later when Smith receives an unsolicited offer to become a screenwriter, he refuses it, wanting to have nothing to do with Hollywood fakeries. After learning the truth about Aunt Lily, he finds that Jenny is living the same kind of lie, telling her Oklahoma family that she has an agent and movie contracts. "You're not being true to your friends or yourself," Smith warns her. He attempts to encourage Jenny to go back home and be satisfied with small-town life, just as he intends to do. At first she refuses but then reconsiders, joining Smith on a bus for the Midwest.

"*Romance to a Degree*" was a fitting swan song for Verna's *Lux* career, providing her with the welcome opportunity to portray both warmth and humor. Ironically, her character's name "Lily Spring" combined the first names of a contemporary radio character and her corresponding player, a similarity surely not lost on Verna, who at the time was a regular on the same CBS comedy. The show was called *December Bride*, and it starred *Spring Byington* as *Lily* Ruskin.

CHAPTER 13

———•◦•———

DECEMBER BRIDESMAID

Whenever comedy writer Parke Levy explained the inspiration for his hit radio/television show *December Bride*, he boasted good-naturedly, "I'm the only guy who's made a fortune off his mother-in-law." However, Levy's mother-in-law did not fit the stereotypical—and much maligned—image of sitcom mothers-in-law. Neither did Lily Ruskin, the character Levy based on his wife's mother. Lily was cheerful, self-sufficient, helpful, open-minded, nurturing, and sweet. In short, she was almost perfect. Lily was also an attractive and charming widow, a fact not unnoticed by senior gentlemen wherever she went. But her son-in-law Matt Henshaw remained her biggest fan. In fact, Matt eagerly invited Lily to leave her Philadelphia home and move to Los Angeles to live with her daughter Ruth and him. As man of the house, Matt was very protective of Lily, patiently teaching her to drive and carefully guiding her investment decisions. Although Matt encouraged Lily to date and remarry, he cautiously screened her suitors, as if she were his daughter and not his mother-in-law. During *December Bride*'s first radio season, Lily came close to matrimony several times, hence the "bride" in the show's title. Levy would later relate that the title "epitomizes the winter of a woman's life." He claimed that its derivation was the sentimental ballad, "Will You Love Me in December as You Did in May?", written in 1905 by New York City's future mayor Jimmy Walker.

Since 1932, Levy had been writing for radio comedies while also doctoring scripts of Broadway shows. During these years he provided material for comedians Joe Penner, Ed Wynn, Al Jolson, Bert Lahr, and for a short while, Bud Abbott and Lou Costello. Beginning in 1941, Levy became one of the original writers for radio sitcom *Duffy's Tavern*, produced by his friend Ed Gardner, then the husband of actress Shirley Booth. Levy's longest association with any radio show, however, was *My Friend Irma*, for which he was writer-director for seven years, beginning in 1947.

Born in Philadelphia on April 19, 1908, Edward Parke Levy once claimed that he inherited his sense of humor from his shoemaker father, who told jokes to his customers while they waited. However, Levy's first published works were detective pulps, written while he was still a student at Temple University. "I was making so much money writing detective stories," he later recalled, "that after five and one-half years at Temple, I quit school." By that time Levy had become initiated into radio, writing jokes for comedian Jack Pearl.

As Levy's new career flourished, Hollywood film studios enlisted Levy's help on more than one occasion. Still, he preferred writing for radio and being based in New York. Eventually though, Levy decided to move his family—wife Beatrice, daughter Linda, and son Robert—to Los Angeles. Soon afterward he was inspired with an idea that later developed into *December Bride*.

In a 1955 *TV-Radio Life* interview, Levy explained the show's inception: "I actually got the idea for *December Bride* in 1946. My mother-in-law came out from Philadelphia for a visit. She had been a widow for several years, and she was suddenly being besieged by prospective suitors. I'll never forget one night when she was making a roast for dinner. One of her hopeful swains arrived with a twenty-two pound salmon he had caught and insisted on her preparing the fish instead. This wasn't so bad, but all during dinner he gave revolting discourses on the inner workings of all kinds of fish. Pretty soon not only the salmon on the table but the whole room was swimming in front of me. Watching my mother-in-law gave me an idea for a book about such mamas. I sent it to several publishers, all of whom liked it but most wanted a change made in one section." In the meantime, Levy's contract with *My Friend Irma* kept him tied up for the next five seasons so his manuscript just gathered dust.

Finally, in early 1952, he decided to convert part of his manuscript into a radio audition. Veteran film actress Spring Byington seemed a logical choice for the part of Lily Ruskin. She had spent the better part of twenty years playing sweet bubbly characters on screen, not to mention the fact that her liquid voice seemed to be made for radio. Levy was delighted to find that Spring—then suffering a dry spell in her career—was more than agreeable to star in the audition. Five years later, when interviewed by *Family Circle* magazine, she would refer to this "dark period" as "three years during which I did hit-or-miss stock and commercial films and personal appearances. Often I thought that I was really through." The actress was unprepared for the surprising change of luck that awaited her.

Meanwhile, other cast selections for the audition were finalized. Hal March, a thirty-two-year-old film and radio performer, was set to play Lily's son-in-law Matt, while radio actress Doris Singleton, also thirty-two, was signed as Lily's daughter Ruth. March would later gain recognition as the host of the infamous quiz show *The $64,000 Question* while Singleton would go down in history as Lucy Ricardo's nemesis Caroline Appleby on *I Love Lucy*. Rounding out the cast was the inimitable Hans Conried—then appearing weekly on radio's *My Friend Irma*—as the Henshaws' acerbic neighbor Pete Porter. Radio veterans Alan Reed, John Brown, Lou Krugman, and Barney Phillips handled the audition's non-recurring roles.

Levy hired Reuben Ship and Phil Sharp to write *December Bride*'s audition episode, which they titled "Lily's First Visit." Upon her arrival in Los Angeles, Lily introduces Matt and Ruth to Gus (Alan Reed), a fellow train passenger she met along the way. Practically before she's settled in the Henshaw home, Lily enters a whirlwind courtship with Gus, whose thrifty habits belie the fact that he is an investment tycoon. When he presents Lily with a stunning diamond ring, she concludes that he must have stolen it. She turns it over to the police, but in the meantime Gus reports it as missing. They bump into each other at the police station and accuse each other of thievery. When Gus learns that Lily doubted his integrity, he angrily calls off the engagement. But Lily's not a romance reject for long—the police lieutenant in charge of her complaint is so charmed that he asks her for a date.

The audition, produced and directed by Levy, was recorded on Thursday, May 15, 1952. Snatched up by CBS as a summer replacement series for *The Jack Benny Program*, the audition episode became the show's initial broadcast on Sunday, June 8. Thirteen subsequent episodes were produced that summer. While Levy acted as producer-director, he turned the writing over to Phil Sharp and Bill Freedman. Byington, March, Singleton, and Conried all continued to appear in their respective roles, while Bob Lemond served as the show's announcer.

Few recordings of *December Bride* are available today, but the summer run's second installment—variously titled as "Ice Box Stew," "Lily Cooking," or "Crunchies"—circulates among old-time radio fans. In this offering, Lily is courted by Oscar Primrose (played by Jim Backus of *Gilligan's Island* fame), a breakfast cereal tycoon. Boasting of Lily's talented culinary skills, Matt eagerly encourages Primrose's interest in Lily. Later, Matt incites Ruth's anger when he says he prefers Lily's cooking over hers. Lily steps in as peacemaker, deciding to change Matt's opinion by preparing an ungodly concoction for dinner ("You just empty the ice box, close your eyes, and stir."). Although she doesn't know it, Matt has invited Oscar home to sample Lily's cooking that same evening. When the millionaire arrives, Lily—thinking quickly—tells Oscar they have decided to go out for dinner. Instead, he offers to create his speciality: ice box stew.

The broadcast's most amusing scene, however, took place when Lily joined Oscar on a luncheon date. Even though she's a teetotaler, naïve and dithery Lily is convinced to imbibe. She chooses a drink called Horse's Neck, which rushes to her head, making her garrulous, giggly, and boisterous. When her beau reaches for her hand, she pleads, "Oscar, please don't take advantage of me—I don't know what I'm doing." A little later, though, she abandons all inhibitions, singing loudly, "I want to live! I want to live!" When she asks the waiter what he put in her drink, he confesses it was only ginger ale with a cherry. Spring Byington carries off the scene beautifully, playing one of the best radio "drunks" ever.

Less than one month into *December Bride*'s summer run, just as Verna Felton approached her sixty-second birthday, Levy offered her a guest appearance on the sixth installment of the series. He was no stranger to Verna's talents. Earlier that year, he had been the head writer for television's *The RCA Victor Show*, featuring Verna as Dennis Day's mother. For his new radio comedy, Levy concocted a colorful new character with Verna in mind. Though neither she nor Levy realized it then, the role was destined to vault Verna to the greatest fame she would ever know. The taping was set for Tuesday, July 8, 1952. At eight o'clock that evening, in CBS Radio's Studio C, Verna first brought the delightfully outrageous Hilda Crocker to life.

The episode, titled "Chicken Salad," aired five days later. When Matt realizes that Lily hasn't had a date in over a week, he's perplexed. He takes up the matter with Lily, who says that she's been spending all of her spare time with a new friend she met at the beach. "A cute little boy was playing in the sand," she explains. "He asked me to play with him and I did. While digging in the sand, we uncovered some old bottles, some clams, and Hilda." Although Lily describes Hilda as unattractive, unskillful in the kitchen, and untruthful regarding her age, she also finds her fascinating. In the meantime, Hilda, professing a disinterest in men, sweeps Lily away to bridge parties, charity bazaars, and art museums. When Matt finally meets the widowed Hilda, he understands her motivation behind this whirlwind of activity. "This dame has talked Lily out of fellows," he grouses. "It's all right for her to talk because she can't get a man anyway. If she stood on the docks at San Diego, the fleet would never come in." Intent on "rescuing" Lily from her new friend, Matt sets Lily up with Mr. Thompson, the lonely owner of a local hardware store, only to be disappointed when Lily refuses to date the man. After Hilda learns about Mr. Thompson, she suddenly asks Lily to make her famous chicken salad every day so she can to take it to the homeless mission. Several nights later Hilda shows up arm-in-arm with her movie-date—Mr. Thompson. "He proposed to me right between Mickey Mouse and Coming Attractions," she gushes. Lily wishes them luck, but Thompson says he won't need it. "I know my sugar dumpling here is a wonderful girl. She's sweet and she's smart and above all she's the greatest cook in the world. Nobody, but nobody, can make chicken salad like my Hilda."

Happy with this episode, Levy decided that the character of Hilda should become a permanent addition to the cast. This was arranged in time for Verna to appear in the last two installments of the show's summer run: "Lily Goes Into Politics" and "The Boulevardier."

December Bride was an instant hit. In fact, less than two months after its debut, columnist Ed Sullivan reported that movie producer Hal Wallis was planning a film version of the show. Wallis had recently produced *My Friend Irma* and *My Friend Irma Goes West*, both of which featured screenplay input from Parke Levy. Despite these prior connections between Wallis and Levy, a screen version of *December Bride* never materialized. The possibility of a "small screen" incarnation was a different story, and toward that end, Levy would work for the next two years.

Verna and Spring Byington during rehearsal for radio's *December Bride*, 1952.

By mid-August, industry insiders were already predicting that *December Bride* would be given a regular spot on the CBS fall schedule. The network made it official on September 5, when they announced that one month later the show would join the successful Sunday night comedy line-up, including *Our Miss Brooks, Jack Benny, Amos 'n' Andy,* and *Edgar Bergen and Charlie McCarthy.* Other CBS summer shows retained for the fall included *Gunsmoke, The Steve Allen Show, The Doris Day Show,* and *Horatio Hornblower.*

During the 1952-53 season, Hilda Crocker remained a regular fixture on *December Bride*, appearing in all but six of the thirty-nine first-run broadcasts. As Lily's best friend, she often dropped by the Henshaw house to get the latest news. Thrice married and widowed, man-hunting Hilda was free with advice whenever Lily encountered a problem with romantic or domestic life. She was chipper, wisecracking, and unflappable. Her sense of humor leaned toward self-deprecation. And she loved to eat. The following is an exchange from "Doc" (May 27, 1953):

HILDA
Oooh, that was a wonderful breakfast, Lily.
What time is it?

LILY
Twelve-thirty.

HILDA
Oooh, my goodness, I missed lunch! Oh, well, I guess
we must make some sacrifices when we're dieting.

Hilda was also quite a ham. As a former stage actress, she was given to impromptu solos, like "I'm Nobody's Sweetheart Now," which Verna sang with great gusto during the same broadcast. When Ruth asked if she had been a successful actress, Hilda replied, "Well, Helen Hayes wouldn't think so, but when I left Callahan's Cuddly Cuties, I left an awful big hole in the chorus—they had to hire three girls to fill up the gap! I wasn't *in* the chorus—I *was* the chorus!"

The addition of Hilda—a character in definite contrast to Lily—provided the series lead with a close friend, mirroring neighbor Pete Porter's relationship with Matt. While Matt adored Lily, Pete constantly made disparaging remarks about his own mother-in-law. But more often Pete's wife Gladys was the recipient of his acidulous barbs. Pete talked about her every week, but only on rare occasions did listeners actually hear a "loving" exchange between Pete and his strident wife. In fact, Gladys's voice was heard only five times during the run of the series. And on most of these occasions, she was only heard offstage, either yelling in Pete's direction while he visited the Henshaws or answering his yell for her. Typical of their vocal exchange was this scene from "The Actor" episode (March 11, 1953):

GLADYS
Peter! Peter! Peter Porter!

LILY
Pete, isn't that Gladys calling you?

PETE

It ain't the Voice of the Turtle. What a waste of talent!
She could make a fortune stampeding cattle.

GLADYS

Peter Porter, when I call you, why don't you answer?

PETE

Oh, did you call? Sorry, my lovely.
You've such a sweet, delicate voice I didn't hear you.

GLADYS

You come home at once!
I thought you were going to wash the dog.

PETE

I did, I did!

GLADYS

Peter Porter, throwing a bone into the bathtub and
telling him to get it is not considered washing the dog.

This particular episode was the first to feature radio veteran Alan Reed—later famous on television as Fred Flintstone—in the part of Pete. One week earlier, Hans Conried, who created the role, had bowed out of all his radio commitments to begin rehearsals for *Can-Can*, the Gwen Verdon musical which would mark his Broadway debut.

Versatile actress Hazel Shermet, fresh from two years' experience as Miss Duffy on radio's *Duffy's Tavern* and recently the bride of *Duffy* writer Larry Rhine, played the part of Gladys. In 2000, when she was interviewed by the Archive of American Television for their video oral history program TV Legends, Shermet recalled of *December Bride*: "Spring Byington was an absolute doll. She played a 'ding-y' character, but she was just a very sweet lady . . . that [show] was a lot of fun."

When Doris Singleton—who played Ruth Henshaw—was interviewed by the Archive five years later, she echoed Shermet's sentiments: "Oh, I loved doing that! It was fun because I had sort of a similar circumstance at home—my mother lived with [my husband and me]. And she was very young and very attractive—everybody liked her—but she didn't have a buddy like Verna Felton was to Spring."

During the 1952-53 season, *December Bride* aired at nine o'clock on Sunday nights until February 25 when it was moved to Wednesday nights at ten. On June 14, it was moved back to Sundays at nine, remaining in that slot until it went off the air on September 6. Despite being juggled on the CBS schedule, the comedy was so successful that CBS, half-owner of the show, wanted to transfer it to television, just as they had done with the *Our Miss Brooks* radio show. However, for some reason Hubbell Robinson, the executive vice president of programming in the New York office, did not want Spring Byington to star in the television adaptation. Parke Levy, who owned the other half, refused to accept anyone else for the part of Lily. During this impasse, the network's option to convert the property to television lapsed; the show now belonged to Levy. However, this all transpired without the knowledge of William S. Paley, the CBS chief executive.

In his 1976 autobiography, Desi Arnaz recalled that shortly after the CBS option expired, Levy came to his office at Desilu Productions to offer Arnaz fifty percent of the show in exchange for filming the pilot for *December Bride*. According to Arnaz, Levy wanted the show to be filmed in front of a live audience, just as its radio incarnation had been. In addition, he was greatly impressed with Desilu's three-camera technique used in filming *I Love Lucy*, *Our Miss Brooks*, and *Make Room for Daddy*. After Levy provided Arnaz with copies of the *December Bride* radio scripts, Arnaz deemed them to be easily adapted for television. He also agreed that Spring would be perfect for the television version, so he accepted Levy's offer.

Levy wanted Hal March and Doris Singleton to reprise their roles of Ruth and Matt Henshaw for the pilot, but it was not to be. Singleton, who had already filmed six episodes of *I Love Lucy*, recalled, "Lucy wanted Frances Rafferty to play Ruth—she was a very good friend of hers. So I did not get to do the show, and I was very unhappy about that." Ball and Rafferty, who made her film debut in 1942, had known each other since their MGM days. Dean Miller, a twenty-nine-year-old with seven films to his credit, was chosen to play Matt. For the comic part of next-door neighbor Pete Porter, Levy selected Henry Morgan, a film actor known better for drama, not comedy, in some sixty features. For *December Bride* though, Morgan was asked to change his professional name to Harry Morgan in order to avoid confusion with radio and television personality Henry Morgan. Arnaz chose *I Love Lucy* assistant director Jerry Thorpe to film the pilot, which was virtually a rewrite of the radio program's 1952 audition. Since the character of Hilda Crocker had not been created at the time of the audition, she was not included in the television pilot. But if the pilot sold, Levy wanted Verna to repeat her role of Hilda for the television series.

December Bride's pilot was filmed on Thursday, February 25, 1954, at the Motion Picture Center, a seven-acre lot rented by Desilu and located at 846 North Cahuenga Boulevard in Hollywood. Arnaz recalled, "Our studio audience reaction was great and we all felt we had a hit. Spring could not understand why the CBS people were not around. She told me Mr. Paley never failed to send her flowers at the beginning of each radio season and presents for Christmas with a note saying that her radio show was one of his favorites and how glad he was to have it on the network." Reluctant to tell Spring the reason for the absence of CBS representatives, Arnaz looked into the matter further and discovered that

The cast of television's *December Bride*: Spring Byington, Verna Felton (FRONT), Harry Morgan, Frances Rafferty, and Dean Miller, 1955.

Paley probably knew nothing of the expired option. When General Foods showed a definite interest in the pilot, Arnaz told their representatives to make sure that Paley was present when the pilot was screened in March. Paley immediately liked the film but was furious when he learned that CBS had dropped its option. He personally entered negotiations with Arnaz to buy part ownership in *December Bride*. Arnaz, known as the mastermind behind *I Love Lucy*, then demonstrated his own business savvy. He agreed to give CBS half of his ownership in the series on the condition that the network would give *December Bride* the time slot immediately following *I Love Lucy* on Monday nights. Things progressed quickly, and by April 1, Parke Levy flew to New York to complete his part of the deal with CBS. He would half-jokingly call this new venture his "bread on the waters" project.

Informed of her impending status as the lead in a television series, Spring Byington seriously considered the reality that she would soon be performing before a live audience each week. It had been almost twenty years since the screen actress had last appeared on Broadway—in the 1934 flop *Piper Paid*. Spring decided to test her mettle by accepting the title role in the fantasy-comedy *Mrs. McThing*, opening April 22 at the Alley Theatre in Houston, Texas. Despite this preparatory production, it turned out that she—and the rest of the *December Bride* cast— were unprepared for the rigors of performing for television.

Jerry Thorpe's directorial debut on the *December Bride* pilot proved to Arnaz that the twenty-seven-year-old son of film director Richard Thorpe was ready for his own show. Arnaz admired Thorpe's "fine technical" talents, but even more so his ability to earn the respect of a cast and crew who were all his elders. While

Thorpe was hired as *December Bride*'s director, Frederick de Cordova, then the director for *The George Burns and Gracie Allen Show*, was chosen as the show's producer. The rest of the *December Bride* production crew included members of Desilu's permanent staff, including production manager Argyle Nelson, art director Claudio Guzman, editorial supervisor Dann Cahn, set dresser Theodore Offenbecker, and composer Eliot Daniel. Under the baton of Wilbur Hatch, the show's bouncy theme music unmistakably shared the flavor of Daniel's already famous *I Love Lucy* theme.

When *December Bride* went into production the first week of August, all cast and crew assignments were set, except for one. Verna Felton's pre-existing contract with the *My Little Margie* radio show had become a roadblock preventing her from signing for the regular role of Hilda Crocker. *Margie*'s transcriptions were recorded each Saturday, the same day Desilu had scheduled its crew to film the weekly episodes of *December Bride*. Levy had created the part of Hilda with Verna in mind, so he was determined that she would be a part of the show sooner or later. Since Verna's contract with *Margie* allowed her to make guest appearances only, Levy decided to introduce Hilda in the third episode filmed. In the meantime, while contract negotiations continued, Verna would miss filming three episodes. Since the series pilot would serve as the first aired episode, there would be a total of four early episodes without Verna.

During this lull, Verna filmed a guest spot on *The Halls of Ivy*, another new CBS television comedy. For the show's second episode ("Professor Warren's Novel"), Verna reprised her role as Burgess, the gruff housekeeper of Professor Warren, played by Arthur Q. Bryan. Things go awry when Burgess secretly submits the professor's discarded manuscript ("The Heart of Passion") to a publisher and it becomes a best-seller—but only because its enticing cover art elicits a ban in Boston.

Verna's "guest spot" on *December Bride* was also filmed during this interim. By now she was no stranger on the Desilu lot. In addition to the two guest appearances on *I Love Lucy*, she had also appeared in Desilu's *Where's Raymond?* as the grouchy mother of Ray Bolger's girlfriend. During the second week of August, when Verna reported to Stage 4—where *December Bride* was filmed—she found that the television script for "Chicken Salad" was practically a carbon copy of the radio version, but with one notable addition. For comic effect, Hilda now had an insatiable appetite. When she meets the Henshaws for the first time, she exclaims, "Just call me Hilda, and I'm ready to eat anytime!" Then she stacks a great pile of hors d'oeuvres on her napkin ("for a rainy day"), and at dinner she can't converse without making repeated requests for butter, hollandaise sauce, and second helpings. When Matt offers her more melba toast, she refuses it, "Oh, no, I've got to draw the line somewhere!" As with the radio version of "Chicken Salad," Hilda plans all of Lily's social activities, much to Matt's disapproval. When he asks if Hilda shouldn't save some time from her busy schedule for dating, she gives him the most disinterested look and deadpans, "*Who* needs *men?*"

None of this was lost on the studio audience: they quickly caught Verna's subtle little gestures and inflections. By the time Hilda made her second entrance, it was obvious that Verna had won them over. She opened the door, and before she even uttered the first line, the audience chuckled expectantly. Verna's performance was clearly the highlight. Recognizing the episode's potential for hooking new viewers, Levy moved "Chicken Salad" up one week so it would become the second one aired.

On the evening of the "Chicken Salad" telecast, Lucille Ball was among the delighted viewers at home. Two days later, on October 13, she dictated a letter on Desilu letterhead, under which she instructed the secretary to type in red capitals: FAN LETTER TO VERNA FELTON. To this, Lucy added three handwritten exclamation marks. "Dear Verna," she wrote, "Just had to tell you how great you were on last Monday night's 'December Bride' show. Hope *we* have something worth your talents very soon. Love, Lucy." By underscoring "we," was Ball including Desi in hoping that they would have another guest spot for Verna on *I Love Lucy*? Or did she mean that they hoped for Verna to appear again on *December Bride*? The latter seems implausible since Verna had become a *December Bride* regular beginning with the sixth episode, which was filmed on September 4. Perhaps the very busy Miss Ball was unaware of Verna's new contract.

In any case, Verna brightened up the proceedings on *December Bride*'s first season—that is, when the script allowed her. Five weeks into her contract, Verna discovered that the popular part of Hilda had become almost a walk-on role. This may have been due to the fact that the scripts had been written weeks in advance of the certainty of Verna's contract, and therefore may not have originally included the character. In addition, the show's writers were relying on the old radio scripts, some of which did not feature Hilda. Consequently, once Verna was under weekly contract, it appears that they found it necessary to invent a quick exchange between Hilda and Lily for the already existing television scripts. To further complicate the first six weeks of filming, Levy employed a succession of five different combinations of writers. Whatever the case, Verna was not happy with the situation. This may explain Levy's cryptic note ("Verna *angry*"), written on his personal copy of the script for "My Soldier," the show's sixth episode and Verna's first appearance as a series regular. Of course, there could have been other reasons for her ire. Perhaps she found the technical aspects of filming to be confounding or possibly had some disagreement with director Jerry Thorpe, who was known to be difficult at times. It's unlikely that Verna was incompatible with the cast: by all accounts, the five of them got along famously.

By the time "The Gigolo" was filmed on October 23, Verna undoubtedly felt more secure with the situation. This is the first episode to feature the slapstick antics so closely identified with the character of Hilda Crocker. When Hilda becomes smitten with her mambo instructor Rinaldo Montez ("Ten dollars an hour—he's worth every wiggle!"), Lily sees the man for what he is: an opportunist.

Hilda takes aim at her mambo instructor (Fortunio Bonanova) in "The Gigolo" episode of *December Bride*, 1954.

Determined to expose Montez, Lily instructs a doubting Hilda to hide behind a folding screen while she flirts with an unaware Montez. When he speaks unkindly of Hilda and turns his affections towards Lily, Hilda erupts, "You double-crossing Don Juan! I'll break every bone in your body!" She chases him around the room, beating him with every available object.

Eventually, thirty-four episodes of *December Bride* would be produced for its initial television season. While one third revolved around Lily's romances, almost just as many involved her harebrained schemes to improve Matt's professional or private life. Like his radio counterpart, Matt was an architect for the firm of Gordon and Company. He and Ruth lived in a comfortable home, located at 728 Palm Drive (later delineated as North Palm Drive) in Westwood, California. Breadwinner Matt clearly saw himself as the head of the household, adamantly refusing to allow Ruth to work outside the home. He also controlled the family purse strings. ("It's a man's prerogative to say what his wife will have and when.") His chauvinistic attitude often led to domestic disputes, many of which Lily tried to resolve although not always successfully. In contrast, Matt was also devoted to his mother-in-law's well-being, both emotional and physical.

Hilda and Lily demonstrate their plan of attack for Pete and Matt in "Grunion Hunting," 1954.

Gradually the writers began to develop the best-buddy relationship between Lily and Hilda. With Lily as the instigator and Hilda her accomplice, they tackle pursuits atypical of average 1950s senior women. In "The Uranium Show" (January 31, 1955), the pair tromps through the desert, seeking the radioactive element in order to fatten their nest eggs. When one of Lily's more promising romances ends abruptly, the girls travel south of the border to forget the heartache, only to be mistakenly jailed for shoplifting in "Mexico" (March 14, 1955). They encounter shady characters in "Theatre Tickets" (April 4, 1955) when they bravely seek out a scalper who frequents a run-down pool hall. In "The Line-Up" (May 2, 1955), one of the season's best episodes, the feisty duo is arrested by mistake again, this time for "stealing" the Henshaw's furniture, which they had removed only for reupholstering. Occasionally their friendship was tested, as in "Gossip" (April 18, 1955), when Hilda takes offense at Lily's tactful attempt to break her comrade's habit of stretching the truth.

While Lily and Hilda evolved as the show's most lively and likeable characters, Pete Porter, bordering on misogyny, was the show's other source of comedy. His weekly zingers, aimed at Gladys and her mother, were at times screamingly funny. For the television version, Levy decided that Gladys and her mother should never be seen or heard, thus leaving it to the viewer to imagine their unappealing attributes, as described by Pete. Initially, Matt's neighbor gives him grief for liking his own mother-in-law, but by the telecast of "The Insurance Show" (February 7, 1955), Pete loses control and surprises everyone by kissing Lily, who has defended Pete to his boss. From then on, Pete is more respectful towards Lily, reserving his sarcasm for her pal Hilda.

However, critics did not find Pete or Hilda or any of the other characters very amusing. In general, they loathed *December Bride*. In his review of the "Chicken Salad" episode, John Crosby wagged a finger at the writers for their "imbecilic" script: "*December Bride*, a title that makes me slightly ill, is a series about a loveable mother-in-law who descends on her daughter and son-in-law and remains there, exuding lovableness, while they try to marry her off— a project for which she has very little enthusiasm. Her son-in-law—this is the switch—loves her. Her daughter loves her. She loves them both. Love runs rampant and, oh brother, is it tedious! I don't know how anyone figured a plot device like that could get off the ground . . . Miss Byington is a very experienced actress, but this thing doesn't give her much to do except smile and smile and smile. Incidentally, the very idea of putting a girl named Spring in something called *December Bride* seems highly improper to start with." Two months later, *TV Guide*, while admitting the show possessed a "certain amount of charm," opined that the scripts were "deliberately 'written down'" to viewers. Such negative reviews continued for the remainder of the season, prompting Levy to challenge one critic to "name another show anyplace, anytime, with a plot line similar to what the critic called 'unoriginal' in *Bride*." Levy was so certain of his claim that he offered $1000 if the critic was successful.

Unfortunately for Morgan, Rafferty, and Miller, another reviewer that first season was particularly unkind. After the premiere episode aired on October 4, critic Ellis Walker wrote: "Spring Byington does her usual first rate job of portraying a fluttery female in the new TV film series *December Bride*. But her supporting cast performed like fugitives from a daytime serial." Although his performance was typically a one-note song, Morgan effectively delivered Pete's insults with deadpan causticity. Frances Rafferty squeezed out a few believable moments as Ruth, but sometimes the character bordered on shrewishness. Despite his good looks, Dean Miller as Matt was often quite wooden. In fact, after four episodes, Levy had serious reservations about Miller's acting ability, noting in the margin of "The Chinese Dinner" script, "Dean Worries Me." In all fairness, Miller was a novice compared to either Morgan or Rafferty, who each had at least ten years' more acting experience.

Nevertheless, *December Bride* held onto *I Love Lucy's* viewers each week, despite some very mediocre offerings. Like other new television series—top-dog *I Love Lucy* included—*December Bride* would not hit is full stride until subsequent seasons. Despite the unflattering reviews, the show came in at number ten in the 1954-55 ratings. When General Foods promptly renewed it for a second season, Parke Levy celebrated by presenting Spring Byington with a brand new red roadster—"red for love," he said.

Both Spring Byington and Verna Felton found the production of a weekly television series to be more than challenging. In 1955 when responding by letter to movie fan Harry Wilkinson, Spring described her workweek: "TV is the most fascinating and the most frustrating thing I've ever done, also the most time-consuming. We shoot Saturday evenings with a live audience—like a stage show; do any retakes after the audience leaves. Also do trailers and commercials or what not then. Get home anywhere between eleven and one-thirty a.m. On Sunday learn my lines, Monday see the rough cut of the coming show, plan, design or buy wardrobe. Tuesday morning, shampoo, mail, wardrobe fittings, then start rehearsing at 12:30. Thereafter every day is rehearsing from 9:30 to 6 p.m. evenings, relearn the everlasting changes made in the script from day to day. Life is strictly on a catch-as-catch-can basis. Oh, for those leisurely days of pictures! TV is exciting, however, and I do love it!"

At first, Verna found the technical details of filming for television simply overwhelming, especially Desliu's three-camera method. She described the learning process to Marty Halperin in 1964: "Television was hard to adjust to. You see, we [had to adjust] to the three cameras—'Springie' Byington and myself, who had always been in show business, had always been in the theater. And we had to *remember* where our mark was—we'd have to *stand* on our mark, and [Dean Miller] would be over here, [Harry] Morgan would be here, and Frances Rafferty would be there. Well, we had to watch so that this shoulder didn't throw a shadow on his face in any way, or hers. And we were [positioned in] this way, [while] thinking of our lines and keeping on this mark that kept you in the mike, and [remembering other directions] so that she wouldn't get a shadow on her face, and I tell you, it was *something*!"

Verna also recalled times when the director gave the veteran actresses instructions contrary to their stage training. "Spring and I would sort of stop and frown and [Jerry Thorpe] would say, 'Well, Katzenjammer Kids, what have I told you to do now that you *can't* do, that you didn't do on the stage?' I'd say, 'He's talking down there, and he's telling the plot of the play, and we're up here making all sorts of noises and everybody will be looking at us and they won't hear the plot of the show down there, going on.' He said, 'The camera *isn't on you*.' He said, 'Just the audience is watching you. The camera is on this.' And, of course, naturally the dialog is louder [where the camera is aimed]. And we couldn't get that into our heads. It took us a good year to get through that. It was hard work, but we did it."

Even though Verna found the three-camera method difficult, she eventually preferred it to the one-camera technique familiar to her from motion pictures. "The only thing I found hard—and I *always* find hard in pictures—is after you *finish* a scene, and it's *over* and *oh*, you feel *so good* that it's over, then they call you and they have to take it from the other side! So you do it from the other side, and [sometimes] I can't recall how I said the line before. And you don't! You get to such a point, you know. They say it so many times, "Front! Side! Side!"

By the time the season ended, Verna was quite happy with her contribution to the show. As a bonus, *December Bride* was beginning to make Verna Felton— or at least Hilda Crocker—more of a household name. On June 4, 1955, a *TV Guide* profile emphasized her connection to Disney: "It's possible, thanks to a stint with Walt Disney, that Miss Felton is already the highest paid actress in TV. (Per spoken word, anyway). A five-word speech in a *Disneyland* auto commercial already has netted her $2500, counting royalties." (Despite her contract with *December Bride*, it appears that Verna was still relying on the supplementary income from such gigs. During the 1954-55 radio season, she continued to appear in her regular role on *My Little Margie* and occasionally contributed to Bob Hope's program as the comedian's mother.)

Bob Foster of the *San Mateo Times* sang Verna's praises in his entertainment column on February 28, 1955: "Several years ago, on a trip to filmland, we were talking with a couple of radio-television writers. Both of these men had long experience with most of the top radio shows. We asked them, who in their experience was the easiest person in radio to write for. We expected to hear some big name in reply but were surprised when they both said, 'Verna Felton, she's not only easy to write for, but she certainly can make a writer look awful darn good.'"

"Of all the roles I've played in radio, television and motion pictures, I think I most enjoy playing Lily's girl friend in *December Bride*," Verna told Foster. "Working with Spring Byington is just about as much fun as anybody my age could expect. She's marvelous and her very nature brings the best out in all those who work with her."

Indeed, there seems to have been a close camaraderie between the five principals. Verna was especially close to Harry Morgan, who, during a 1967 *TV Guide* interview, recalled of the *December Bride* set, "It was very pleasant. Five years went by like one." Frances Rafferty, who became great friends with Spring Byington, called the atmosphere "lovely." Spring's granddaughter San Baxley Michel, a frequent visitor on the set, recalled in 2008, "*December Bride* was pretty much devoid of high drama behind the scenes." Linda Kelemer, the daughter of series writer Lou Derman, attended many of the filmings and "was charmed by the ensemble cast, especially by Spring and Verna—the two most lovable characters, in my opinion. Lily and Hilda, with their outlandish pranks and hilarious gung-ho attitudes, were precursors of *The Golden Girls*. They actually made old age look fun!"

Dean Miller laughs on the set of *December Bride* as Harry Morgan pretends to eat part of Verna's fruity hat during the filming of "Alaska Show," 1958.

While one insider called Verna "the life of the company," Morgan also kept things hopping. Verna revealed to Halperin, "Television is awful [for practical jokes] because [unlike radio] they can stop at any time, you know. Harry Morgan, he is a great practical joker. He would make 'Springie' so *mad*! If some [prank] happened, she could just kill us! He always had a water pistol somewhere. I don't know how he'd ever do it, [but during rehearsal] he'd get this water pistol out and you could kill him! Or he'd get up in the flies, and shoot down, and it was always at the boy, it was always at Miller, Dean Miller."

Harry Morgan hams it up during rehearsals for "The Martian Show" episode of *December Bride*, 1959.

Morgan didn't limit his fun to unexpected water-pistol sprees. Parke Levy recalled, "Dean Miller . . . used to come to rehearsal always with a black luncheon box, in which he always had a hard-boiled egg and some bread . . . I'll never forget the day [Harry] sneaked into the dressing room and took out the hard-boiled egg and put a raw egg in. Dean always used to crack the egg on the edge of the luncheon box. Dean Miller chased Harry Morgan around the entire lot. He was livid, because naturally when he hit the egg it splattered all over him." In the spring of 1955, the frugal Miller used part of his savings to purchase a canary-colored Cadillac with red upholstery. Without losing any time, Morgan swiped Miller's lunchbox and painted it yellow on the outside and red on the inside.

Parke Levy, in his later years, took special pride in the fact that he gave Harry Morgan his first chance at comedy. Since his 1941 arrival in Hollywood, Morgan had been busy with dramatic roles in films such as *The Oxbow Incident, The Glenn Miller Story.* and *High Noon.* He was born Harry Bratsburg in Detroit on April 10, 1915. His toolmaker father moved the family to Muskegon, Michigan when Morgan was four years old. While in college Morgan took up public speaking and debating to enhance the legal career he planned but subsequently never achieved. While selling office equipment in Washington, DC, Morgan took up acting as a hobby. A summer stint at the Westchester Playhouse marked Morgan's professional debut—*At Mrs. Beams* with Frances Farmer and Mildred Natwick. Broadway scouts spotted Morgan; in 1937 he wound up in the role of Pepper White in *Golden Boy.* Seven Broadway productions later, Morgan found himself on a train for Hollywood, but not alone—he had married actress Eileen Detchon on September 1, 1940. By the time of *December Bride*, the couple had become the parents of four sons, including a set of twins.

Dean Miller, *nee* Dean Charles Stuhlmueller, was born in Hamilton, Ohio, on November 1, 1924. The eldest son of a physician, Miller was educated in private academies before studying medicine at Ohio State University. In January 1945, he enlisted in the army, serving as an infantry and field artillery sergeant for two years. When he returned to civilian life, Miller turned his attention to courses in radio broadcasting and advertising at Ohio State. After graduation he began his career as a radio announcer in Albany, New York, later becoming quite successful in a similar position at a Cincinnati station. His Hollywood "break" came while he was talking to three chance acquaintances on a California-bound train. He expounded his theories and opinions on motion pictures at length—unaware that his traveling companions were three of MGM's top executives—Dore Schary, E. J. Mannix, and Louis K. Sidney. Impressed by Miller's good looks and personality, they arranged for the young man's screen test shortly after their arrival in Hollywood. Miller was signed almost immediately after the tests were viewed. Consequently, he made five films in the next two years, beginning with *Skirts Ahoy* starring Esther Williams. An avid card player and horseman, Miller lived alone in a Beverly Hills apartment during his *December Bride* years.

Like Dean Miller, Frances Anne Rafferty was born into an affluent family. Her father was a business executive in Sioux City, Iowa, where she was born on June 26, 1922. When the Depression wiped out the family business, the Raffertys moved to Los Angeles. The following year when Rafferty was ten, a dance scholarship led her to study all phases of the art for the next seven years. Following her graduation from University High in Westwood, Rafferty attended UCLA, where she enrolled in pre-med courses. Again, like Dean Miller, her plans for a medical career were interrupted when she earned a cherished membership in the Hollywood Bowl Ballet Company. A promising career lay before her until she sustained a serious knee injury in the summer of 1941. Then her closest friend, actress Alexis Smith, suggested she enroll in a dramatics course directed

Dean Miller and Frances Rafferty on the set of the Henshaws' living room, 1955.

by Madame Maria Ouspenskaya. The revered actress-coach recommended Rafferty for a screen test with MGM, which resulted in a four-year contract, during which time she appeared in 34 productions, including *Dragon Seed, Mrs. Parkington, Girl Crazy,* and *Ziegfeld Follies.* Married briefly to Maj. John Horton in 1944, Rafferty wed a second time in 1948 to Thomas Raymond Baker, an aircraft executive. When *December Bride* went into production, the Bakers had a four-year-old son and a two-year-old daughter.

As the two senior members of the cast got to know each other, Spring and Verna realized that their theater background was not their only commonality. Each actress's father had been born in the same year and in the same state, and ironically both had died before their daughters reached the age of nine. Verna's father had been a medical doctor, as had Spring's mother. In their youth, both actresses had spent considerable time in Canada. As a consequence of their constant travel on the stock circuit, neither was a very accomplished cook. While Verna had always relied on live-in housekeepers, Spring paid a young lady to come three nights a week and prepare enough food to last several meals. Neither actress had owned a home until after settling in Hollywood, and both doted on their grandchildren. Even their given names were almost synonymous; "Verna" means "spring-like" in Latin.

Yet still, these ladies were very different individuals. A profile of Spring, printed in the *Syracuse Herald* on June 5, 1927, detailed her disinterest in the popular avocations of the day: "She does not swim, does not ride, cares naught for bridge, loathes sports, is not a pianiste [*sic*], and both sings and dances indifferently." Amazingly, this description was the complete antithesis of Verna's interests and abilities. (Spring would have probably abhorred the small talk circulating among Verna's canasta set.) While Verna's North Hollywood abode fairly bustled with friends and neighbors—not to mention a gang of kids splashing in the pool almost daily—Spring's two-story stucco house on North Beachwood Drive in the Hollywood hills was described by one writer as "lonely." Spring preferred it that way, but insisted, "I'm not really a recluse. My two daughters sometimes visit me with their husbands and children. But I work very hard on the *December Bride* show, and I'm determined to put my spare time to good use." Indeed, Spring devoted many spare hours to reading books on psychology, philosophy, space travel, and science fiction. However, each actress enjoyed life and kept young in her own way.

Verna was a packrat who saved almost every shred of paper related to her career and personal life, but Spring happily confessed that she didn't keep clippings, scrapbooks, or faded photographs. "It was a pleasure for me to burn every theatrical memento I ever owned," she laughingly told a reporter in 1950. "When a woman gets to be a character actress, it's her privilege to travel light. Why drag the past along with you?" Several years later, when discussing the same topic, Spring told another journalist that she preferred to "contain [her] experiences," instead of keeping a written record of them. By all accounts, it seems that the past was not important to Spring Byington. In fact, she never erected the simplest of monuments on either of her parents' graves, not even after attaining the financial status of one of Hollywood's busiest actresses. Those cemetery plots in Denver currently remain unmarked.

As an adult Verna never lied about her age, but Spring was given to shaving off as many as twelve years from hers, whether prompted by her publicity agent or propelled by her own whim. Particularly during the run of *December Bride*,

Spring Byington, whose film persona Hedda Hopper once described as "crisp, cuddly, peach-pretty and superlatively feminine."

when confronted by reporters, she consistently dodged the issue of age. One journalist jokingly referred to her birth date as "a better guarded secret than the Hydrogen Bomb." Another chalked it up to the actress's vanity, quoting Spring in a 1957 *TV Star Parade* article: "I simply won't give my age. It's a mistake to dodge your years. I don't mean to, but I think it's wrong to tick off each year as a milestone, as if each twelve months brings added wisdom. You can be dull— old—at six, sixteen, or sixty." Even Parke Levy didn't know her real age. In May 1958, he told Stanley Handman of the Canadian magazine *Weekend*, "I think Spring admits to 62, and Verna admits to 67." While Verna's age was reported accurately by Levy, Spring's was considerably off. For years after she died, speculations circulated concerning her true birth date.

According to her death certificate—as well as Social Security records and the 1900 Federal Census—Spring Dell Byington was born on October 17, 1886. Although her middle name was chosen to honor a family member, Spring disliked it so much that she refused to disclose it to journalists. To safeguard her true age during these interviews, she was careful not to mention any dates connected to the milestones of her life and career. However, for two particular newspaper articles, written over thirty years apart, she retold in chronological order the events of her early life. Using these details and various bits of corroborating evidence available today, a satisfactory account of Spring Byington's pre-Broadway days can be assembled.

Spring's father Edwin Lee Byington was born in 1852 in Ogdensburg, New York, but graduated from Victoria University in Cobourg, Ontario. In August 1884, following ten years of teaching on both high school and collegiate levels, Byington left Canada to accept the dual position of high school principal and superintendent of the public schools at Colorado Springs, a physical location he favored more than any on the continent, Spring later revealed. In the summer of 1885, he returned to Prince Albert, Ontario, to claim his longtime sweetheart Helene Maude Cleghorn as his bride. After a honeymoon trip across America, the newlyweds set up housekeeping in Colorado Springs at 321 North Weber Street, where Spring was born the following year. They remained there until 1889 when the professor accepted a similar position with the Boulder city schools. The situation there proved less than ideal, so after only one year the Byingtons moved to Fort Collins, where once again the professor served as school superintendent. The family had barely gotten settled in this new home when a second daughter, Helene Kimball Byington, was born. Unfortunately, the Byington household was in serious turmoil at the time: four-year-old Spring and her father were battling typhoid fever. Spring fully recovered, but the professor was left quite weakened by the disease. To regain his health, the family moved to Denver, but to no avail. Professor Byington died of chronic nephritis three days after Christmas 1891. He was thirty-nine years old.

Like the widowed Clara Felton, Mrs. Byington found herself without the necessary career skills to support her young family. Always interested in medicine, she ambitiously chose that field of study, packing off Spring and little Helene to live with various Canadian relatives while pursuing medical degrees in both Toronto and Boston. "Bad as the shifting was for our security, it was equally good for our mental flexibility," Spring told *TV Radio Mirror* in 1955. "We had to learn to adapt to new situations."

Completing her medical education in 1896, Mrs. Byington moved her daughters back to Denver to set up practice. Two years later, Dr. Mary Ford, one of Dr. Byington's classmates, moved from Chicago to join her medical practice. By 1900, the doctors and the Byington girls had settled in Highlands, an elite suburb of Denver. They resided in a large two-and-one-half story brick house, located at 3827 West 32nd Avenue. Spring attended the public schools in Highlands, graduating in 1904 from North Side High School, an imposing red brick structure trimmed in red sandstone. As a teenager, she expressed an interest in acting, and, encouraged by her mother, Spring enrolled in a local dramatics school. Most likely this was the Tabor Grand School of Acting, operated by Margaret Fealy, whose pupils also included Douglas Fairbanks.

Numerous career profiles of Spring Byington, published from the 1940s through the 1970s, state that the actress made her professional debut at age fourteen at Denver's Elitch Gardens Theatre. However, Spring would have turned fourteen in 1900, and records indicate that she did not actually appear on the Elitch stage until 1906. According to the interview in the *Syracuse Herald* from June 5, 1927, Dr. Byington had arranged for her daughter to meet Mary Elitch Long, who had first opened her summer stock theatre in 1891. Through Mrs. Long, Spring was soon filling "atmospheric roles," advancing to speaking parts at a salary of $15 per week. Spring recalled for the *Herald* that one of her fellow actors that summer was a Frederick Paulding. Elitch records reveal that Paulding was indeed a member of the company—once, during the 1906 summer season. Thus Spring's acting debut occurred just a few months before her twentieth birthday.

Following Spring's summer stint at Elitch Gardens, she promptly joined a small group of inexperienced young actors who decided to go on the road with a play. The director-producer was a former animal trainer, and the play was *Squire Thompkins' Daughter*, an obscure five-act drama written in 1901 by Arthur Buzzell. A catalog listing describes its "cunningly devised" plot as involving "forgery, mock-marriage, and mortgage foreclosure." Spring, as the company's leading lady, was assigned the title role of Milly Thompkins. On September 15, the production was scheduled to open the fall season of the Colorado Springs Opera House with a limited run of one matinee and one evening performance. When only eight playgoers showed up for the matinee, the theatre manager cancelled the evening show. Undaunted, the little band of actors took off for Kansas, where they lasted only two weeks.

Instead of returning home in defeat, plucky Spring stuck it out. She used part of her savings to make it as far as Kansas City, where she hoped to join another troupe. Allotting herself forty cents a day for food, she hid seventeen dollars under her hotel room's rug for train fare back home. However, before the week was up, she found a job with a road show. The months that followed were difficult, most especially for the lengthy separation from family and friends. In the spring of 1907, these feelings were compounded by the unexpected death of Dr. Byington, who suffered a blood clot following an attack of influenza. At the time, Spring was touring in British Columbia, more thirteen hundred miles away.

After her mother's estate was settled, Spring took her small inheritance and headed for New York. She landed a job in a vaudeville skit called *Cherrie* that toured the Orpheum circuit for 45 weeks. By September 1907, she had reached Baltimore's Maryland Theater. The *Baltimore Sun*'s review of *Cherrie* noted the "strikingly pretty young woman" named Spring Byington who "considerably heightened the charm of the piece." Around this time the budding actress was also actively seeking roles in New York, leaving promotional photographs with producers as she pounded the city's pavement. Among the files of famed theatrical producers Liebler and Company, currently housed at the New York Public Library, there is a cabinet card portrait of Spring, looking lovely in an elegant pompadour.

In 1908, Spring signed on with a New York-based acting troupe to perform an "English season" in Buenos Aires. While there and appearing in plays such as *Mrs. Wiggs of the Cabbage Patch* and *What Happened to Jones*, Spring met Roy Carey Chandler, a native of Akron, Ohio, and five months her junior. Standing six-feet, two-inches, Chandler towered over Spring, but his good looks, ambition, and well-connected family impressed her.

Before Chandler's first birthday, his photographer father decided to relocate the family to Buenos Aires. He spent his formative years in South America with family trips to Europe and New York. Developing an interest in theatrical production, Chandler began associating with Broadway producers and actors, as well as Tin Pan Alley writers cranking out America's popular tunes. He later became the vice-president of the All-Americas Theatrical Company, based both in Buenos Aires and New York.

A romance bloomed between Chandler and Spring in the fall of 1908, and they were married the following year. Residing the next five years in Buenos Aires, Spring became fluent in Spanish, while Chandler enticed theatregoers with live entertainment as well as screenings of American films.

Spring was often featured in Chandler's productions, but in 1914, she decided to pursue acting in the States, returning to the venue where she got her start— Denver's Elitch Gardens. However, Spring soon found it difficult to revive her career in America. During this period her plans were twice thwarted by maternity. Elder daughter Phyllis was born in the spring of 1916, and Lois followed seventeen months later. This must have been an extremely trying time in Spring's life. With her husband out of the country, she was solely responsible for the upbringing of their two daughters. Perhaps this physical distance separating the Chandlers contributed to the eventual dissolution of their marriage. Spring would not wed again.

In the interim, Spring's actions mirrored her mother's some twenty-five years before. She put her daughters in the care of family and friends while she sought positions in American stock companies, promoting herself as an ingénue-comedienne. From the fall of 1918 until well into 1920, Spring played the role of "the other woman" in a touring production of *The Bird of Paradise*, appearing in theatres all the way from Ohio to Oregon. Subsequently, she enjoyed a long run with the Stuart Walker Stock Company, based in Indianapolis and Cincinnati. In August 1923, the *Indianapolis Star* reported that Spring had not only co-written a play (*White Chips*) but that Broadway producer John Cort

Spring Byington, circa 1914.

would stage it in October. Perhaps the report was a little premature: instead Eva Le Gallienne and Basil Rathbone opened in *The Swan* at the Cort Theatre that October.

Undaunted, the actress continued to network until she met playwright Marc Connelly who in turn, recommended her to Winthrop Ames, the producer of Connelly's *Beggar on Horseback*, co-written with George S. Kaufman. The only

Spring Byington, circa 1930.

vacancy Ames had left was a small character part. She took it. "Any sacrifice for Broadway, not for Art," Spring later observed. *Beggar on Horseback* debuted on February 12, 1924 at the Broadhurst. Spring's adroit portrayal proved to be just the career boost she needed. For the rest of the decade and into the mid-1930s, she returned to the Broadway stage no less than nineteen times, sandwiching in summer stock engagements. Though probably they never met, Spring and Verna each appeared in Broadway productions in the spring of 1929. While Spring was enjoying a brief engagement in the comedy *Jonesy*, Verna was relishing her only shot at Broadway with the even briefer run of *Appearances*.

In 1933, Hollywood finally beckoned with Spring's first film feature role: Marmee March in the Katharine Hepburn version of *Little Women*. She later recalled the experience, "I approached it with pure terror. It was so different, suddenly they turned on the lights and camera and you had to act. You had to stand in the right place and look at the camera lens but not see it." Film fan-historian Gary Brumburgh estimated that Spring's first film role "was hardly what one could call a stretch, [but] it did ignite a heartwarming typecasting that kept her employed on the screen throughout the 1930s and 1940s." Indeed, she appeared in more than one hundred films during the twenty years following *Little Women*, including such classics as *Mutiny on the Bounty, Jezebel, Meet John Doe, Roxie Hart, Heaven Can Wait,* and *In the Good Old Summertime*. Although she usually played devoted mothers, grandmothers, or aunts, her role of malicious gossip Rebecca Perry in *Theodora Goes Wild* was a delicious departure. Her most famous film role, however, remains the only one that garnered her an Academy Award nomination: Penny Sycamore in Frank Capra's *You Can't Take It With You*. Despite Spring's voluminous film work prior to *December Bride*, her screen persona would forever after be identified with her charming characterization of Lily Ruskin.

Without a doubt, the same could be said for Verna Felton, whose performances as rambunctious Hilda Crocker brought her a certain new fame. Soon she, too, would discover firsthand the power of television exposure—not within the dazzle of Hollywood and its precincts, but within the very heartland of the nation.

As the end of *December Bride*'s first season approached, Verna was delighted to learn that she had won a major supporting role in Columbia Pictures' greatly anticipated film adaptation of the Broadway hit *Picnic*. One of 1953's critically acclaimed plays, *Picnic* had won a Pulitzer Prize for playwright William Inge and a Tony for director Joshua Logan. The studio paid Inge $350,000 for the film rights and began making careful choices to assure the film's critical and financial success. Columbia head Harry Cohn asked Logan to undertake his first solo directing assignment, while Academy-award-winning cinematographer James Wong Howe was chosen to shoot the Technicolor blockbuster in Cinemascope.

The story centers around Hal Carter, an ex-college football star turned drifter, who shakes up a small Kansas town during his twenty-four-hour visit, which coincides with the town's annual Labor Day picnic. Arriving by freight car, Hal wanders through town, seeking his old college friend, the wealthy Alan Benson. He stops at the house of sixtyish Helen Potts who looks after her invalid mother. When he offers to clean her yard, Mrs. Potts—perceiving his misfortune and charmed by his sincerity—invites him in for breakfast before he begins his chores. Meanwhile, next door, Flo Owens, a single mother with two daughters—beautiful Madge and bookish Millie—sits outside snapping beans while her girls quibble about boys. Joining them is Flo's boarder Rosemary Sydney, a spinster schoolteacher, who dismisses the prospect of marrying her occasional beau Howard Bevans and resigns herself to another approaching school year. Across the way, as Hal burns Mrs. Potts's trash, she offers to wash his shirt, which he

Verna Felton as Helen Potts in *Picnic*.

immediately strips off—inciting varying reactions from the four women next door. The sight of an athletic man arouses curiosity in both young Millie and Rosemary, although she declares scornfully, "He's as naked as an Indian!" Noticing Madge's attraction to Hal, Flo becomes wary of the brawny stranger—a reminder of the ne'er-do-well husband who abandoned her. She's further concerned to learn of Hal's connection to Alan Benson, who is currently dating Madge; Flo wants nothing to spoil her daughter's chances at marrying a millionaire's son. Nevertheless, she can't object to the invitation Alan extends to Hal to join him and the Owenses for the picnic.

During the festive afternoon, Hal joins Mrs. Potts and Millie in several contests, but Alan soon grows annoyed as he notices the mutual attraction between his old friend and his girlfriend. After Madge is crowned queen of the picnic, things quickly fall apart. As Madge and Hal begin a sensuous dance together, a jealous, drunken Rosemary lashes out and tears Hal's shirt when he attempts to pull away from her. Alan rebukes Hal, who rushes away with Madge in Alan's car. It is almost dawn before he takes her home and returns the car. He and Alan begin to fight, but Hal escapes, seeking refuge at Howard's bachelor flat. Later in the morning, Madge meets Hal in Mrs. Potts's yard where he declares that he loves her and wants her to come to Tulsa with him. As a freight train approaches, Hal dashes for the tracks, all the while beseeching Madge to join him. Uncertain, she runs off to her bedroom in tears. When Millie encourages her sister to follow her heart, Madge's doubts vanish. Determined, Madge catches the bus for Tulsa, leaving Mrs. Potts to comfort Flo.

Before Josh Logan was set as *Picnic*'s director, Columbia Pictures had already chosen one of its contract players for the part of Hal. At thirty-seven, Holden was generally considered "terribly miscast"—(to quote Darryl F. Zanuck)—for a character whom Inge had described as "an exceedingly handsome, husky youth." Holden chronicler Will Holtzman noted that by this time Holden had "the athletic physique of a man half his age, but his face had begun to crease, and the boyish features had begun to sag." Logan agreed that Holden was too old for the part, but "he was such a vital, virile, talented man and with such a youthful body, I felt that he would be strong in the part." Columbia starlet Kim Novak, while not Logan's first choice, was signed for the part of Madge after a disastrous screen test by Janice Rule, who originated the role. Film veteran Rosalind Russell practically leapt at the chance to play Rosemary, which had been played on stage by Eileen Heckart. Betty Field was set for the part of Flo, and seventeen-year-old Susan Strasberg, daughter of New York acting teacher Lee Strasberg, would play Millie. As Alan Benson, Madge's wealthy young suitor, Logan chose Cliff Robertson, fresh from a brief Broadway run with Helen Hayes in *The Wisteria Trees*. Logan gave the comic part of Bomber the newsboy to Nick Adams, whom he had previously directed in *Mister Roberts*.

Verna won the part of kindly Helen Potts, perhaps beating out at least one important contender because of her more familiar face. Stage actress Ruth McDevitt originated the role of Mrs. Potts on Broadway, but, with only one film credit to her name, remained a virtual unknown in Hollywood. To compound matters, McDevitt was appearing as the lead in the Broadway touring company of *The Solid Gold Cadillac* during the spring of 1955. So, it's possible that this prior commitment overruled any consideration that she should reprise her *Picnic* character. However, those familiar with McDevitt's work can easily imagine how effective she would have been in the screen role. Aptly described once by a theatre critic as "that splendidly fussy mother hen," McDevitt made the move to Hollywood a decade later and became a highly sought-after character actress.

Daniel Taradash, who wrote the screenplay for *Picnic*, insisted that the remaining cast could not be found in California, so Logan flew to New York to conduct screen tests with performers from the original Broadway cast. "Among them was Arthur O'Connell," recalled Logan, "who had been such a standout as Howard, the boyfriend of Rosemary, the spinster schoolteacher, that no one could replace him." Reta Shaw and Elizabeth Wilson, who had played Rosemary's cronies, also tested. "Josh had auditions—I remember them so well," reminisced Elizabeth Wilson in 2005. "We were put on film. Reta had to do it, and Arthur O'Connell. As you know, it was Arthur and Reta and myself that got into the movie, which broke Eileen's Heckart's heart." Heckart, described by Wilson as "brilliant" in the part of Rosemary, lost out because she was not yet known in the film industry. While Cohn saw Holden and Novak as surefire box office draws, he still wanted another big name for the picture. Since Rosalind Russell was in need of a career boost, she wasted no time in accepting the part. Meanwhile, newcomers Reta Shaw, Elizabeth Wilson, and Cliff Robertson were thrilled that *Picnic* would mark their film debuts.

Both Logan and Fred Kohlmar, the film's producer, insisted that *Picnic* be shot in Kansas, despite the expense this would incur. When the two men visited the city of Hutchinson and surrounding area in March, they decided the city's grain elevator skyline would be perfect for the film's background. Sites in the nearby towns of Nickerson, Halstead, and Sterling were also selected for location shooting. Hutchinson, with a population of 35,000, was the largest of these, so it was chosen as the film crew's headquarters. The studio rented about one hundred rooms downtown at the newly constructed Baker Hotel.

Before moving his cast and crew to Kansas, Logan asked Cohn for two weeks of rehearsals in Hollywood. Logan reminisced in his memoirs, "We had our first day of rehearsal on the sound stage. We read the script aloud and there were the usual nerves. Kim was almost impossible to hear, and Bill Holden did everything but leap on the table and stand on his hands in an effort to show that he wasn't nervous and also that he was young enough to play the part. Roz Russell and her fellow schoolteachers, Reta Shaw and Elizabeth Wilson, were on the button—using every second of the rehearsal day to take full advantage of the time to study their roles. Betty Field as Flo, the mother, and Verna Felton as old Mrs. Potts were the same. Susan Strasberg was duly respectful of all the older actresses, and Cliff Robertson just seemed to be grateful he was in the movies at last."

Almost two weeks later, on Saturday, May 14, Holden, Logan, and about fifty crew members arrived in Kansas by chartered plane. About 1,000 persons, mostly women, were at the Salina airport to greet them. Novak arrived in Hutchinson the following night, and the principals began filming on Monday morning. Back in Los Angeles, Verna, along with Russell, Field, Shaw, Wilson, Strasberg, plus Strasberg's mother and tutor, boarded the Santa Fe Chief for Hutchinson. Along the way, Colorado floodwaters necessitated re-routing their travel to Wichita, where the actresses disembarked. For the final fifty miles, they rode in automobiles driven by Columbia personnel, arriving at their destination late Saturday night, May 21. Arthur O'Connell, the final member of the cast to depart Hollywood, arrived in Hutchinson by air on Monday.

In Inge's version, the community picnic was an event that the characters only talked about; it was not an actual scene in the play. Filmmakers decided to include it to provide some extra color and spectacle. Halstead resident Mrs. Herman Hughes had called Josh Logan to suggest her town's Riverside Park as the perfect location for filming the picnic scenes. When he saw the site for himself, he agreed. No expense would be spared for this important part of the action. Columbia Pictures spent $5,000 on permanent improvements to the park, and they sought the most authentic props, including hand-cranked ice cream churns, an antique spring wagon-seat to be used as a swing, and six 50-gallon oil drums for trash cans. Locals were amused by the film company's extensive "imports" of Florida watermelons and ants from Connecticut, as well as a wind machine—to direct air currents in directions needed for filming. Adult extras for the picnic scenes were paid ten dollars a day, while children over six years were paid half that fee.

The first day of filming the picnic scenes was scheduled for May 23, but morning drizzles and heavy afternoon rain and hail prevented any progress. Fortunately, the main cast members weren't due on the set that day since Logan had only planned shots of some of the 300 locals who applied to be "extras." The following afternoon, Verna filmed her first scene—tossing rubber jar rings at a lollipop stick Holden gripped between his teeth, while Russell and Field attempted the same with O'Connell and Robertson. Between takes, Verna chatted with Mrs. Hughes, sitting in spectator seats near the cameras for her and her two small children. Verna, always attracted to little tots, wasted no time in getting acquainted. A photo of her with the Hugheses made the front page of the *Hutchinson News-Herald* on May 25. Irene Sommerfeld, another Halstead local, remembered, "Verna Felton would come and sit with us extras in a circle. It was just like she was a neighbor. We'd exchange recipes—she was a darling."

For the next several days, Verna at times found herself mobbed by television fans each time she appeared in public. In fact, *News-Herald* writer Paul Murphy, who profiled Verna's career on May 26, considered her more famous in Halstead than either Holden or Russell. "If you don't recognize her voice or her face, you obviously are just back from several years in the Andes. Even in the Andes, though, you'd probably hear of Verna Felton . . . At the set at Halstead, the policemen, who have to look twice to recognize some of the other stars, give a big smile and wave [to Verna]. And the public, sighting the familiar face from Channel 12, is all around." Verna didn't find their attention a nuisance at all. "It's really very gratifying," she told Murphy. The article—accompanied by a candid shot of Verna in one of her polka dot "Hilda" dresses—was the first to feature an interview with one of the *Picnic* cast members.

Hal (William Holden) enlists Mrs. Potts (Verna) as his partner for the ring toss game.

Of all the Kansans she met, Verna was most impressed with Irene Koeneke, a prominent physician whose late husband—also a physician—had authored a popular book some fifteen years earlier. When Dr. Koeneke learned that the actress who played Hilda was in town, she requested an introduction. But the doctor was no ordinary sitcom fan; she wished to share an interesting discovery with Verna. As part of her psychiatric practice at the Halstead Hospital, Dr. Koeneke found that *December Bride* episodes actually benefited older patients who had given up. "I want you to know what *December Bride* has done," Dr. Koeneke told Verna. "We use it at our women's classes—the women who are disgusted with life. We show them the [*December Bride*] films" to emphasize that not only are Lily Ruskin and Hilda Crocker older ladies who have fun, but the actresses playing their parts are themselves remaining active despite their advancing years. According to Verna, some of these patients were not as old as she, prompting Dr. Koeneke to point out, "See what they've done with their lives? They've made a little something with their lives, and you're sitting here down and depressed." With genuine appreciation in her voice, Dr. Koeneke confided, "Miss Felton, we've had more *success* through the psychology of that than anything we have [implemented]." As a token of her gratitude, she left Verna with a signed copy of her late husband's book, *The Horse and Buggy Doctor*. That evening Verna sat down and wrote a letter to Spring Byington, telling her it would be worth her time to take a trip to Kansas to see how well their television program was being received.

Verna during location shooting in Kansas for *Picnic*.

Meanwhile, the capricious spring weather continued to plague the production. On Wednesday, May 25, in the midst of preparing a nighttime scene, filming suddenly halted. As a public warning siren blared, people began to duck for cover. Elizabeth Wilson remembered that she and others were directed to go under a nearby bridge for safety. "While I was still trying to photograph," Logan recalled, "one by one the cast was beginning to disappear." Intent on finishing the scene, he strode after a few people, calling them to come back. He found Rosalind Russell lying flat in a ditch. "What the hell are you doing down there, Roz?" he asked. She urged, "You get down here, too. That's a tornado. It's right at us." Suddenly noticing a funny change in the air, followed by a "whooshing sound," he dove into the ditch on top of Russell. Within moments the wind roared across the landscape, stirring up dust and debris, cracking and snapping tree branches, snatching anything not fastened down. Seconds later, it was all over. Luckily, the tornado did not touch down in Halstead, but sixty-five miles away, the town of Udall lay obliterated. Seventy-seven people were killed, and only twenty of the town's two hundred homes were left standing. The *Picnic* cast and crew immediately joined the rescue effort, taking along many of their twenty-two trucks and their biggest lights to help recover bodies, clean streets, and assist injured folks into ambulances until early the next morning. On the following Sunday—the only day the film crew had off each week of the shoot—Logan, Kohlmar, Russell, Holden, and Nick Adams appeared at a Wichita baseball game to raise money for the tornado victims. To the delight of the roaring fans, Russell donned a baseball cap, pitched the first ball, and took some practice swings with a bat. (Kim Novak was not present since she had already agreed to appear onstage at Hutchinson's Midland movie theater prior to a screening of her current Columbia release, *Phffft*, starring Jack Lemmon and Judy Holliday.)

On a different stage in town, local amateurs known as the Hutchinson Prairie Players were learning their lines for a live production of *Picnic*, strategically planned to coincide with the film's production. On May 28, four days before their opening, these nine players spent a day studying their Hollywood counterparts filming the picnic scene.

Other extras at Halstead found the film actors equally amusing. Rosalind Russell gladly posed for fan photographs, and with her ever-present camera, turned the tables by taking pictures of the fans for her own scrapbook. Kim Novak, though, was a different story. "Whenever you'd start to take a picture of Kim, she'd hide," recalled Irene Sommerfeld. "She'd go behind a tree and peek out. She never did want her picture taken. It was kind of odd." But Sommerfeld found Nick Adams, like Verna, to be a crowd pleaser. "There was a rod going across that swinging bridge at the park, and Nick was always hanging by his knees on that thing! He loved to hang on that swinging bridge. He was just a young kid; he was full of fun."

William Holden, the other popular acrobat in the cast, left another lasting impression on Sommerfeld. At the time of the filming—being spring—the

Mrs. Potts (Verna) tries to win the balloon-blowing contest while Flo (Betty Field) looks on apprehensively.

cottonwood trees had begun releasing seeds in their downy casings. Unaccustomed to these floating bits of fluff, Holden worried that they were harmful. "He was just sure he got poisoned by them. He went up to the hospital and had a doctor check him out, see if he was okay. He just had a fit, and when that "cotton" would come around him, why, he'd fan and everything . . . Everybody kind of thought that was funny."

In the meantime, an opportunity arose for Verna to be "invited" into the homes of more Kansans—and to simultaneously promote *Picnic* and *December Bride*. Since the filming schedule for June 1 only called for nighttime scenes, Verna was free to appear in a televised cooking show on the local CBS affiliate, Hutchinson's KTVH. That morning she joined *Kansas Kitchen* hostess Charlotte Briscoe to "happily help with the kitchen chores." Station staffers were delighted to meet "Hilda" in person, agreeing that Verna Felton was as "unpredictable off screen as she was on," perhaps a polite indication that the actress didn't really know her way around a kitchen. Still, they declared Verna a "loveable personality in her own right."

More heavy rain on Friday, June 3, brought an abrupt end to nighttime filming at Riverside Park. Columbia officials decided to finish the three remaining sessions on a Hollywood soundstage, which would exactly duplicate the park site. Meanwhile, preparations had been made for location shooting in Nickerson, where filming began on Saturday night. The circa-1899 Dutch Colonial Revival home of eighty-three-year-old Mildred McFarland had been chosen to represent the Owens house, while the Elmer Beauchamp house next door would serve as Helen Potts's home. In April, not realizing the filmmakers were attracted by the weathered appearance of her house, Mrs. McFarland had it painted sparkling white for its film debut. To her dismay, one month later the production crew painted over the fresh white with dull yellow and gray for the aged neglected look befitting Flo's financial struggles. In the rear yards of both houses, weathered outbuildings and the adjacent tracks of the Missouri Pacific Railroad added a certain authenticity. Verna spent much of the second week and third weeks of June filming scenes outside the McFarland and Beauchamp houses.

Battling a hailstorm and intermittent rains, the crew began filming a nighttime scene in this neighborhood on June 4, attracting merely a handful of local spectators. On Monday when filming resumed, it seemed the whole town had turned out. The Nickerson Argosy reported: "The activity in Nickerson Monday night attracted an estimated crowd of over 2,000 persons. Visitors crowded onto lawns and yards of those living in the area. The reflection of the bright lights on the sky were visible for many miles. In fact, lighting on the McFarland home seemed as bright as daylight to film the night scenes." The 125-member troupe ate a midnight supper in the lunch room of the Reno Community High School, located across the street from the filming site. Expenses for the Nickerson shoot would run to $20,000 per day, with the city electrician reporting that "more electricity was used in the temporary substation in one night than the whole town of Nickerson uses in one month."

During all of this, a polite fourteen-year-old girl practically camped out at the filming site. Unlike most teenage onlookers, Eleanor Kirkpatrick wasn't motivated one bit by the star appeal of Holden, Novak, or even Russell. Instead, she zeroed in on the familiar actress who appeared on her television screen each week, closely following Verna's every move and utterance. "Eleanor was just infatuated with Verna Felton," recalled Eleanor's older sister Jean Shively in 2009. "She was like a grandmother figure, unlike all of the rest [of the cast], and she was just so kind to my sister who followed her around like a star-struck little teenager—which she was." According the editor of the *Argosy*, other spectators shared Eleanor's regard: "Everyone who is around Verna Felton says she is a very pleasant, retiring, natural sort of person."

On Tuesday, June 8, Eleanor—the youngest daughter of Nickerson's mayor—ran home to ask her mother, "Could I invite Verna Felton for dinner?" Thinking the actress would politely refuse, Mrs. Kirkpatrick gave her permission. Later that afternoon when Eleanor approached Verna with the invitation, the actress graciously accepted for the following evening. Her fellow actors were a little surprised by her quick acceptance, but Verna told them, "After looking at this girl, I just knew the invitation was all right and that I would enjoy myself." Unfortunately, Mrs. Kirkpatrick was due to undergo a medical procedure on Wednesday at a Kansas City hospital. Knowing that both her older daughters were good cooks, she left them in charge. On Wednesday evening, Eleanor and her father drove to Hutchinson to pick up Verna at the Baker Hotel. Waiting at the Kirkpatrick home, sisters Jean and Judy had prepared scalloped chicken and raspberry-marshmallow dessert from their mother's recipes. With them, little brother Mark and two of Eleanor's high school friends eagerly anticipated the guest of honor's arrival.

Nearly fifty-five years later, neither Eleanor nor Jean remember much about the conversation around the dinner table that evening, but Verna left Jean with the following impression: "She was just so ordinary and common, and not like you would maybe expect some famous person or personality to be. I would say she was just as common as, I'll say, my sister!" Eleanor, who appears in the film's final scenes as a high school student waving goodbye to honeymoon-bound Rosalind Russell, still warmly regards her brush with fame as "the highlight of my growing up: *Picnic* and having Verna Felton come to our house."

On June 16, with location shooting almost completed, Logan invited all of the locals to Hutchinson's Fox Theater, to see rushes of the film—and to hear words of appreciation of the cast. The large ad in the *News-Herald* featured photographs of Holden, Russell, and Novak, but Verna's name was listed next, above all of the remaining members of the cast, including Robertson, Field, O'Connell, Strasberg, and Adams. Her popularity with Kansans would be proved by the events of that evening. For the presentation, sandwiched between two screenings of Walt Disney's *Davy Crockett*, Logan presided on the Fox stage as emcee, while the cast sat at tables behind him. The house was full to overflowing with fans eager to hear what each actor had to say. When Holden was introduced, he didn't disappoint those who had witnessed his acrobatic talents during the shoots at the picnic and grain

Dinner guest Verna Felton, seated between Eleanor Kirkpatrick (LEFT) and Judy Kirkpatrick, reacts to Mark Kirkpatrick's "fish tale" as do Esther Naab, Linda Schlatter, and Jean Kirkpatrick.

elevators. Making a dramatic leap from his chair, Holden landed on a nearby table, which collapsed under him. Unruffled and thinking quickly, the actor quipped that his film character louses up things as well. Holden's stunt almost stole the show, but not quite.

"I knew Rosalind Russell, Bill Holden, and Kim Novak would get great hands," Logan later told writer Bennett Cerf, "but the real roar went up when Verna Felton, who played a relatively minor role, appeared on stage. And hers was the autograph all the kids fought for later. When I asked if Verna came from the Hutchinson area the answer was 'Shucks, no. Everybody knows Verna because she appears on a regular TV show called *December Bride!*'" Surveying the audience's zealous applause, Russell was heard to remark: "I've got to check into this TV thing." As a finale befitting the evening's feature film, the actors donned coonskin caps and sang "The Legend of Davy Crockett," which had reached number one on the Billboard charts earlier that spring.

On Sunday, June 19, the final day of location shooting, the sun came out after several gloomy days, just in time to film the swimming scene at Sterling Lake. That night and early the next morning, Logan and his cast took their leave of Kansas, either by air or rail. Once back in California, filming resumed at the studio and the Columbia Ranch, reaching completion on July 8.

Kansans were disappointed when *Picnic* did not make its world premiere there. Instead, the studio chose a limited California release in late 1955—in time for Oscar nominations, of which it garnered six, including best picture and best director. Following its general release in February 1956, *Picnic* became one of the top ten movies of the year, earning $6.3 million in box-office rentals. At the time it was critically acclaimed, but two decades later—in the wake of changing mores and cinematic trends—the film was often dismissed in retrospective reviews.

Even in 1956, *The New Yorker* had reservations: "William Inge's modest play, adapted to the vastness of Cinemascope under the direction of Joshua Logan, has become a sort of Middle Western Roman holiday. Mr. Logan's notion of an outing in the corn country includes a choir of at least a hundred voices, a camera so alert that it can pick up the significance of the reflection of a Japanese lantern in a pool and a soundtrack let loose in the most formidable music I've heard in my time at the movies. All this surging background stuff is applied to nothing more than the story of a kind of literate tramp who hops off a freight train in a Kansas town and sets every female heart to yearning." Yet, in contrast, by the end of the twentieth century, critics were praising the film's "resonant portrayal of small-town life during the Eisenhower era."

Still, it remains hard to deny that while Novak seems too passive and Russell tends to go "over the top," Holden was plainly miscast—and not just because of his age. Holden biographer Lawrence Quirk explained it almost perfectly: "Holden was to some extent limited to playing various extensions of his own personality, and the rootlessness, the dreamy escapism, and the unrealistic outlook of Hal Carter were fundamentally alien to Holden's temperament and mystique as a man." On the other hand, film scholar Steven Cohan, argues that Holden, despite his acting abilities, was "fundamental to the film's success," in part because his age was in direct contrast with his superb athleticism. Other critics today hail the film's well-drawn supporting characters and subplots and its authentic location settings. Arthur O'Connell's Oscar-nominated performance as Howard remains a standout.

To her credit, although there are a few instances where Verna Felton could have inserted a "Hilda Crocker" intonation, she never sinks into caricature as Mrs. Potts. The scene where Alan drives the women to the picnic is a case in point. Madge remains silent across the front seat, while Flo and Mrs. Potts occupy the back seat. Logan arranged this shot so that all four faces could be seen at once. While Flo pumps Alan for background information about Hal, Mrs. Potts silently observes the conversation. Verna's subtle reactions—registering satisfaction with Hal's football record, disappointment over his academic failure, reassurance of Hal's integrity, and hopeful approval of him from Flo—are skillful touches that enliven the scene.

From the time Mrs. Potts meets Hal, she's clearly taken with him. But what was her motivation? Daniel Taradash's final script omitted an important detail from Mrs. Potts's past—one that would have made the character's motivation clearer and more meaningful. Inge's play revealed that as a younger woman, Helen Potts ran off and got married, much to the displeasure of her clinging mother, who had the marriage annulled before the couple's wedding night could take place. Discussing Mrs. Potts's current situation, Flo tells Rosemary, "Sometimes I think she keeps the boy's name just to defy the old lady." This bit of exposition, were it known to *Picnic* film audiences, would make Verna's performance even more poignant in the scene following the picnic supper. In the glow of the sunset, Mrs. Potts and Flo are left alone while the others pair off and move to more secluded areas of the picnic grounds. As the two ladies gently sway in the wagon-seat swing, they listen to the soft voices drifting from the nearby community sing-along ("Nita, Juanita, ask thy soul if we should part!"). Reflecting on her rare outing and its temporary escape from the demanding cries of her invalid mother, Mrs. Potts sighs, "A day like this reminds me of when I was a girl . . . things I haven't thought about in a long, long time. Flo, you'll never know what it's meant to have you next door to me, watching your two girls grow up—it's made it easier."

In the play, Flo blames Mrs. Potts for the eventual romance between Madge and Hal ("The next time you take in tramps, Helen Potts, I'll thank you to keep them on your own side of the yard."), but the relationship between the two women is softened in Taradash's treatment. Verna is allowed another tender moment when Flo asks Mrs. Potts of Hal, "You liked him, didn't you, Helen?" The older lady replies, "Yes, I did. I got so used to things as they were, everything so *prim*, the geranium in the window, the smell of Mama's medicines, and *he* walked in. And it was *different*. He clomped through the place like he was still outdoors. There was a man in the house, and it seemed good." (In the final revised script, as in the play, Mrs. Potts continues, making her point even clearer: "And that reminded *me* . . . I'm a woman, and that seemed good, too." This line is not in the release print of the film; perhaps it was deemed too unsettling for 1950s film audiences to hear such a frank line from an actress approaching her sixty-fifth birthday.) For at least one modern *Picnic* fan, Verna's performance in this scene is a standout. In his online Amazon review, Michael C. Smith points out: "At the end of the film, [Verna Felton] glows in tender counterpoint to the dramatic ending. [Mrs. Potts] is the only person who understands Hal, even more than Madge. Her speech about having a man in the house is pure joy to watch. It is a small but important performance that frames the entire story with warmth and understanding." In the concluding pull-away shot, filmed from aboard the departing bus, Millie and Flo run alongside it. Likewise, Mrs. Potts hurries to the edge of her yard to watch the bus until it disappears, waving goodbye to the girl who reminds her of her youth.

Of all her films—including the immortal Disney features—Verna considered *Picnic* "the best picture I did." Not only was she was flattered to be included in such an expensive production—she was paid full salary from the time rehearsals began in Hollywood until filming concluded there some nine weeks later—but she was honored to be among such impressive company. Until the end of her life, she held a high regard for Josh Logan and marveled at the later successes of the novices among the *Picnic* cast, including Novak, Robertson, Strasberg, and Adams. "They're all stars now," she exclaimed when interviewed by Marty Halperin almost nine years after the film's completion.

Nevertheless, it is doubtful that Verna was intimate with any of the three leads. Kim Novak, who found the role of Madge difficult, remained by herself for most of the shoot, in preparation for her role. However, the young actress did send Verna a note of thanks on July 20: "Dear 'Mrs. Potts,' Thanks for being so wonderful to work with and know. Sincerely, Kim." As for the other two stars, Rosalind Russell tended to socialize with William Holden, who did not disappoint those hoping to catch some of his impromptu athletic stunts. He alarmed Logan when they shot a scene atop Hutchinson's grain elevator, 174 feet from the ground. Reaching the top, Holden strolled over to the minimal iron railing and leaned out to get a good view of the town. "Oh, my gawd! Don't do that," gasped Logan. "I've got to direct this picture and I can't talk with my heart in my mouth."

Another legendary escapade, varying from source to source, took place at the Baker Hotel in Hutchinson. According to his best buddy Ronald Reagan, Holden performed a daring handstand on the window ledge of his hotel room high above the street. Yet Logan's recollection was that Holden hung out the fourteenth-floor window by his elbow, while Russell reported in her autobiography that the actor dangled outside the tenth floor, holding on to the window ledge with both hands. And Cliff Robertson maintained that Holden stood on the same window ledge, poised as if to leap. In 2005, Elizabeth Wilson—by then the only cast survivor besides Novak and Robertson—confessed that at the time of filming she was oblivious to such goings-on: "I was so naïve, oh, Lord—and I wasn't that young either, I was what—32, 33, but I was so naïve! I heard stories later about William Holden's drinking and all the crazy things that happened." Logan described Holden as "simply a red-blooded American boy who wanted to have a good time, and believe me, he did."

With production completed, Verna did not want her newfound friends in the Sunflower State to think she had forgotten them. She found a discreet way to "wave to them" from 1400 miles away. When *December Bride* resumed production in late July, she requested a brief script addendum for "The Pizza Show," the first filmed episode of the second season. After Lily and Hilda are successful in helping a California restaurateur sell his business to join his ailing wife in Kansas, Lily reads his postcard to Hilda: "If you and Hilda need a job, come and see me. I have opened an Italian restaurant in Hutchinson."

Around the same time Verna returned to California, Disney's *Lady and the Tramp* premiered. While she was very proud of her contribution—and Lee's—to that film, she was even more impressed by another Disney milestone later that summer. On Sunday, July 17, Walt Disney opened his greatly anticipated Disneyland to invited guests and the media. The event was televised live on ABC and hosted by Art Linkletter, Bob Cummings, and Ronald Reagan. The eleven thousand ticketholders included celebrities Danny Thomas, Gale Storm, Frank Sinatra, Alan Young, Sammy Davis Jr., Jeanne Crain, Jerry Colonna, and Marjorie Main. Among the estimated seventy million watching the festivities from home was Verna's neighbor, nine-year-old James Simons. In 2008, Simons recalled that the event also received local television coverage: "[Verna Felton] was briefly on the air as one of the Disney stars who were invited to the opening day. That was a big deal in L. A. I'm pretty sure it was just invited guests that day, and she was on the list." However, that first day at Disneyland was not a "walk in the park." The summer heat registered over one hundred degrees, and to make matters worse, a plumbers' strike left many of the park's drinking fountains dry. The asphalt that had been poured just the night before was so soft that ladies' high-heeled shoes sank in. A gas leak in Fantasyland caused Adventureland, Frontierland, and Fantasyland to close for the afternoon. The park got such bad press that Disney invited some guests, especially members of the press, to return the following day to experience the true Disneyland. Verna's schedule didn't allow a repeat visit— she spent July 18 at Disney's Burbank studio, recording additional dialogue for *Sleeping Beauty*.

The remainder of Verna's summer was leisurely, compared to the hectic pace she had kept since the *December Bride* hiatus began in April. She swam almost daily in her pool, often joining the neighborhood kids, who probably got more use of it. "In that hot San Fernando Valley, those were the days when swimming pools were not terribly common," explained James Simons, whose family lived at 4167 Bakman Avenue. "DeeDee's pool was basically open to all the kids in the neighborhood. And the only rule was that really you had to ask permission first, not just show up. So, for many a year during my childhood, I spent most of my summer days there."

As a safety precaution, Verna would not allow any child who could not swim to get in the pool without her, so she taught the skill to many of the neighborhood children, including the Leff girls. She had established this procedure at least a decade before, when children of her friends visited, including Violet MacKaye's daughter Lynn and Duane Johnson's daughter Judy. Howard and Helen McNear's son Kit learned to swim there prior to 1955, when his family moved to 4118 Bakman. "I have a lot of fond memories of that time . . . We used to come and visit and drive down to her house and we lived in the Hollywood Hills, fifteen minutes away . . . Verna was a real gracious woman, very hospitable . . . I can vividly remember being on a little tuber in the pool, and she'd come around playing like a shark."

Verna extended swimming invitations to her fellow *December Bride* players and their families. According to Debbie Leff, most of them accepted. "Dean Miller would come over to go swimming. My sisters and I would help him rehearse and cue him on his lines, which seemed like a big deal to us." Frances Rafferty came with her husband and children, and occasionally Spring Byington brought along her daughter Phyllis Baxley and granddaughters San and Christine. Interestingly, Leff recalled that she never saw Harry Morgan at Verna's house, but juggling schedules for his four active sons may have been a little overwhelming.

The Leff family never regarded Verna as a celebrity, even when considering the famous people who visited her. To them, she was simply DeeDee, but still "a very, very big part of our lives," as Debbie Leff recalled in a 2007 interview.

VERNA AT HOME, 1955

Verna in her kitchen.

Playing a game around the pool with Lee, Edith, and Lisa.

Verna in her bedroom.

Verna and Edith in the living room. The 1925 oil portrait of Verna is seen on the wall.

Lois Blazic, holding Lisa Millar, is flanked by Sandy Leff (LEFT) and Betty Leff. In the rear are Frank Blazic and Debbie Leff, summer 1954.

Leff's abundant memories of her neighbor included those times when Verna would phone theLeff house during a rehearsal break on the *December Bride* set, just to find out what Mrs. Leff was serving for dinner. If she approved of the menu, she would call Lillian Nishijama, her housekeeper: "Lillian, I'm not having dinner at home—I'm going to the Leffs." She considered the Leff girls her own grandchildren, and she introduced them to everyone as such, especially when she took them to Disneyland for the first time. In the fall of 1956, she hosted Debbie's tenth birthday party in the largest room of guest house, where the children bobbed for apples and munched on popcorn. Another Halloween, DeeDee dressed Debbie up as a ragamuffin newspaper boy, dirtying her face for authenticity—perhaps just as some fellow performer had done for Verna when she was playing one of those boys' parts on stage more than fifty years before. As an Easter tradition, DeeDee gave the three girls two gifts: a candy egg with an eyehole to view the confectionary scene inside and a new bathing suit for the upcoming swim season. It was also customary for them to visit her on Sundays and share what they had learned in Sunday school class. And many times, DeeDee came to their house at nighttime to hear their bedtime prayers.

Verna with Lisa, 1954. From left to right are visible the guesthouse, garage, and pergola.

Kit McNear, who lived up the block, regarded DeeDee as "real" and "down-to-earth." Others, like James Simons, would agree that DeeDee seemed to be more of a hospitable neighbor than a television star. "She was very nice to all the kids, very wonderful about sharing. I think she took a lot of pleasure in having the kids over," he reminisced. "She always had three or four or five dogs. A whole little group of cocker spaniels, some of whose names I still remember to this day—Gus-Gus was my favorite, and Hildegarde—gosh, how things come back! [DeeDee] was just very sweet and generous. She didn't seem to take herself any too seriously." In fact, Simons vividly recalls Verna's lingering surprise over the response she received in Kansas that summer: "When she came back from filming *Picnic*, I remember her telling my mom that because of her exposure on *December Bride*, everybody in whatever little town they were in knew of her at that point. She was very impressed with the power of television as a media, that being a regular on a TV show kind of made you a celebrity." Celebrity or not, he added that Verna got along "quite well with most of the neighbors." A definite exception was one neighbor who tended to over imbibe. "[He] was over [at Verna's] at one point," recalled Simons, "and she read him the riot act and not to ever set foot on her property, and he never did."

Before Verna reported back to the *December Bride* set in late August, she found as much time as possible to play with her twenty-one-month-old granddaughter Lisa, whom Verna had described to a Kansas journalist as "the loveliest little girl in the world." The reunion with her family brought an extra reason to rejoice: Lee and Edith were expecting their second child that fall. With a growing family, the young couple had found it necessary to seek accommodations larger than Verna's guest house, but still, Verna didn't want her grandbaby too far away.

Grandmothers Grace Simmons and Verna Felton flank Edith holding newborn Kate and Lee holding Lisa.

She was more than pleased when Lee and Edith moved to 4172 Beck Avenue, only five blocks west of the Millar homestead.

Meanwhile, Lee's dwindling radio assignments had forced him to seek appearances in television commercials. Only occasionally did he land a role on a television series, such as *The Ray Bolger Show* or *My Favorite Husband*, but in recent months, he had become a semi-regular on *The Bob Cummings Show*, appearing four times as Sid Dorfman, Bob's air force buddy. Edith's duties as a young mother had temporarily stalled her acting career, and the situation would continue for at least another year. Exactly ten days past Lisa's second birthday, Kate Walker Millar, her baby sister, was born in St. Joseph's Hospital on October 24. Lee and Edith named their new daughter for Lee Sr.'s mother Kate Carson Millar and for Edith's mother Grace Walker Simmons. Again, Verna was beside herself with joy.

Verna's professional life was happy as well, and for good reason—the second season of *December Bride* turned out to be even more successful than the first. *Time* reported on March 12, 1956, that the show had "astounded the industry by elbowing its way into the top ten. Nielsen and Trendex place *Bride* No. 5; ARB has it tied for sixth (with *Disneyland* and *I've Got a Secret*). Videodex and Pulse report it 'consistently in the top ten.' No one is quite sure why." While CBS's Hubbell Robinson credited the ratings to *I Love Lucy*'s lead-in, Parke Levy argued that the show's success was the result of "basic sociological and psychological factors." "The show's message is that a woman can be attractive to men regardless of her age. It makes every dame over 45 think she's still desirable." Spring Byington, herself well-versed in psychology, viewed the message as being more important that Levy's summation. "Lily hasn't lost her appetite for life and is now free to do ridiculous things. She can play with life much more because she is mature of heart. She isn't stopped because other people are not doing it . . . If something appeals to the mature person, there is no really cogent reason for not doing it. Let us do it, let us not be bound by hidebound convention!"

Whatever the argument for its success, by now Parke Levy's creation was standing more on its own merits, due to fresh plotlines and fuller character development. By midseason, Levy had finally assembled a permanent team of writers, headed by Lou Derman, who had joined the show during the first season when the seventh episode's script ("Lily Is Bored") proved troublesome. Although Levy was listed as head writer for all scripts of the first and second seasons, it was Derman who actually cranked out a new collection of teleplays that diverted from those fifty-odd leftovers from the radio run. While almost one third of the first-season episodes of *December Bride* centered around the show's original premise—Lily's love life—only one fifth of second-season episodes were devoted to this theme. Second to Levy, Lou Derman was responsible for the success of *December Bride*.

Derman was born in New York City on September 27, 1914. Unlike Levy, he experienced no early aspirations to write. He studied at The City College of New York to become a Spanish teacher, but entered the U. S. Postal Service in 1937 when he found no teaching jobs available. Six years as a postal clerk yielded him fodder for articles in national magazines, and a literary agent—impressed with his comedy talent—suggested that he write for radio. The following year found him writing for Ed Wynn, then in succession, for a galaxy of headliners including Milton Berle, Eddie Cantor, and Jim Backus. From 1948 until 1953, he wrote radio's *Life with Luigi*. In the meantime, Derman maintained apartments on both coasts, traversing the country with his family—on the Super Chief—as the writing jobs dictated. In 1956, the income from *Luigi* and *Bride* allowed him to purchase his first permanent home—in West Hollywood. In his back yard, he constructed an office, where he sat at the typewriter as his Bride co-writers paced the room, throwing out ideas and snippets of dialogue.

"My father was a follower of Ralph Waldo Emerson," recalled Linda Derman Kelemer in 2006. "Indeed, his essays were kept in almost every room in our house—including the bathroom! Dad believed in goodness, integrity, truth: all values imbued in the character of Lily Ruskin." Like all writers, Derman derived motivation from personal interests and experiences, and, as he explained in 1958 to *Variety*, "then adapted [them] to our characters, and broadened, of course, for maximum spuffoonery [*sic*]." For instance, after he suffered through the "fish and poi and burnt pig" at a Hawaiian luau, he wrote "The Luau" (December 27, 1954). When Derman's wife wanted a poodle haircut, he held out for the curls. "She handed them to me one day, and that made a *Bride* story ("Ruth's Haircut," April 9, 1956)." Meanwhile, he assigned two of his hobbies—magic and photography—to the male characters on *Bride*. In "Handcuffs" (March 19, 1956), amateur magician Pete mistakenly locks Lily and Hilda together in a pair of "trick" handcuffs, while Matt joins a camera club in "The Beauty Pageant" (April 23, 1956). Such inspirations were molded into the same basic script pattern, as described by Derman in the *Variety* article: "There is an opening hook. The plot is advanced from scene to scene. There is a mounting crisis, a suspenseful curtain, further complications for the hero, leading to a big final obligatory scene. And if things get dull toward the middle, we throw in a subplot, at no extra charge to CBS."

Derman's scripts for the 1955-56 season effectively cement the friendship of Lily Ruskin and Hilda Crocker even more than those of the first season. In "The Shoplifter" (October 31, 1955), one of the finest *Bride* episodes ever, Hilda stands tall to defend Lily's reputation when she's mistakenly identified as a shoplifter. In "Handcuffs" (March 19, 1956), lovesick Hilda arranges dates with two different men on the same evening, so Lily agrees to be her stand-in on one of them—until the two friends become accidentally handcuffed together. Their devotion is tested in "The Texas Show, Part Two" (February 6, 1956), when Lily, fearing overweight Hilda won't make a good impression on her new Texas friends, schemes to put her on a diet and exercise plan. Hilda's discovery of Lily's ruse gave Verna an opportunity to evoke real pathos, quite a switch from her character's usual behavior. In a thoroughly delightful courtroom-dream sequence from "The Jaywalker" (April 16, 1956), Hilda refuses Lily's plea to tell the truth about what she witnessed on the day Lily was fined for jaywalking.

In a move that resembled a strategy used on *I Love Lucy* the previous season, Levy began utilizing—on a more limited basis—some of Hollywood's film stars to help increase ratings. Herbert Marshall, Dan Duryea, and Rudy Vallee played themselves in three respective episodes, "The Laudromat Show" (November 14, 1955), "High Sierras" (December 12, 1955), and "The Rudy Vallee Show" (January 23, 1956). (Lee Millar appeared as a photographer on the latter episode in what would be the first of his eleven bit parts during the run of the series.) Charles Coburn, who had previously co-starred with Spring Byington in several films, played a geriatric skirt-chaser in "Lily and the Wolf" (October 17, 1955).

Lou Derman approached two celebrities—not famous for their acting skills—to appear in guest shots. Spending many of his free hours at local wrestling bouts and boxing matches, he thought it would be fun to mix the *December Bride* characters with some famous athletes. Fifty-year-old Sandor Szabo, a native Hungarian and former world heavyweight champion wrestler, had been a huge draw in California matches during the previous two decades. Derman enlisted him to play Karl Manheim, a wrestler-singer married to Hilda's niece, in "The Wrestler"

News photographer Lee Millar appears unimpressed with the adoration Verna showers on Rudy Vallee, while her equally enthusiastic friends Cheerio Meredith (LEFT) and Almira Sessions stand by in awe.

(February 27, 1956). For the second-season opener "The Boxing Show" (October 3, 1955), Derman created a guest part for twenty-seven-year-old boxer Art Aragon, a New Mexico native who had grown up in Los Angeles. Known as "Golden Boy," Aragon was easily the most controversial boxing figure on the West Coast, often insulting reporters who attacked his arrogant displays both in and out of the ring. He was chummy with many of the Hollywood film set, including Derman, who often invited the "fast-talking and glib" boxer to parties in his home. Derman's idea worked—Aragon and Szabo's guest appearances proved popular enough that they were brought back again in following seasons.

Derman realized that a key element of comedy involves a situation that seems unlikely or incongruous. What then could be more incongruous than a sixty-five-year-old fat lady skipping rope with a muscled athlete less than half her age? Furthermore, Derman knew Verna was game for such a display. In "The Boxing Show," Lily and Hilda try to persuade Aragon to box in a charity fight to benefit underprivileged children. When he won't listen and continues to train, Hilda jumps into the rope with Aragon, delightfully lasting six turns of the rope. Banking on Verna's zestful attitude to make the scene work, Derman was not disappointed. In fact, it inspired him to write more physically challenging situations for the actress. In "Big Game Hunter" (November 28, 1955), she worms her way on elbows and knees through a dirty crawlspace to sweet-talk her exterminator boyfriend into posing as Lily's boyfriend. In "The Wrestler" she swings into the ring to distract Szabo's opponent, with hilarious results.

Hilda and Lily pose as teenage members of Desi Arnaz's fan club in
"Sunken Den," 1956.

However, Verna pulled off the most amazing stunt in "Sunken Den" (February 20, 1956). When trespassers Lily and Hilda find themselves locked inside guest star Desi Arnaz's house, they try to escape, setting off the security alarm. Their only access out is a window located over a sofa. Spring Byington gingerly climbs out first. From across the room Verna gets a running start, jumps on the sofa, and then dives headfirst out the open window—in hat, dress, and high heels! Since the original script simply called for Hilda to climb out the window, it's very likely that this stunt was Verna's own idea. Before rehearsals began, Parke Levy offered to hire a stunt double for Verna's flying leap. The idea insulted her. "You put a mattress outside that window," she growled, "and I'll go out head first." Later in the same episode, when she namboed with a young man, she ended her dancing spree with a huge pratfall.

To Verna there was nothing uncanny about a performer her age keeping up with the kids. She later explained to *TV Guide*: "Why gosh-a-mighty, I've been getting onstage and off by myself since I was eight. In my day we learned the physical rudiments of acting first. We didn't have chalk marks and doubles." Verna was injured on *December Bride* only once, and it was not her fault either. For "Lily and the Sailor" (April 30, 1956), she had to crawl across the floor during a barroom brawl. When a stunt man missed his chalk mark, he stepped on her fingers. "We aren't sure Verna Felton's delightful antics will ever net her a TV acting Emmy," said Leslie Lieber of the *Boston Herald*, "but we recommend her for the U. S. Olympic track team at Melbourne. The Russians have nothing like her."

Shortly before the season ended, Verna shared her views and opinions for journalist Vernon Scott in a May 3 UPI press release. Scott wondered aloud how a "frothy comedy series about a pair of middle-aged matrons" could push its way to number four in the ratings, topping all other competition, except Ed Sullivan's *Toast of the Town*, *The $64,000 Question*, and *I Love Lucy*. Verna, sipping a before-lunch cocktail, provided the answer: "We're successful because all the rest have forgotten about the middle-age audience. They depend too much on sex and glamour. After all, young folks are out having fun at night. Middle-age and older people stay at home watching TV, especially our show. We're a tonic for oldsters who worry about advancing years. The Halstead Hospital in Kansas uses our program as a psychiatric aid to old people who have given up. The nurses and doctors point to Lily Ruskin and Hilda to prove that older people can have fun. Spring isn't too far removed in real life from Lily, and I'm every bit as screwy as Hilda—she's eternally young. And I don't want to grow old either . . . I keep in shape—such as it is—by swimming almost every day in my pool and chasing my four cocker spaniels around. Although I live alone, I'm never lonely. The house is always full of my biddies—divorcees, widows, and other strays. I'm so busy I can't take time off to worry about getting old."

Several months before this interview, Verna began to plan how she would spend *December Bride*'s annual hiatus, which would begin on April 11. She had counted on re-teaming with director Josh Logan who had promised her a part in

Verna Felton liked this photo of "Hilda" so much that she had it duplicated to send to her multitude of fans in the 1950s.

his film *Bus Stop*, an adaptation of another William Inge play. Initially, location shoots in Phoenix and Sun Valley had been planned for summer, which would coincide perfectly with Verna's hiatus. When Logan found it necessary to move up filming to March, Verna had to bow out. However, two other *Picnic* alums— Betty Field and Arthur O'Connell—were given roles in this film.

Barbara Hale, Joel McCrea, and Verna enjoy a laugh during a break in filming *The Oklahoman*.

To make up for her missed opportunity, Verna accepted a small part—yet fifth-billed—in the low-budget Republic western *The Oklahoman*, which began filming in mid-May. Joel McCrea starred as John Brighton, a widowed physician living in the Oklahoma Territory in the 1870s, who finds himself at odds with wealthy rancher Cass Dobie (Brad Dexter). Dobie is intent on swindling a neighboring Native American out of his oil-rich land, but Brighton steps in to defend the Indian. The culminating gunfight between Brighton and Dobie leaves the good doctor standing. Barbara Hale, as young widow Anne Barnes, was on hand as McCrea's love interest, and Gloria Talbott delivered an impressive turn as the Indian's teenage daughter who's infatuated with Brighton. As Hale's wheelchair-bound mother, Verna, wearing a telltale wiglet and corseted frock, dispensed her opinionated views during three brief sequences. The film's predictable ending found McCrea proposing marriage to Hale while matchmaker Verna smirked confidently. Released almost a year after its completion, *The Oklahoman* failed as a moneymaker. More often than not, it was relegated to drive-in theatres, like the one in Cedar Rapids, Iowa, where the management proved that Verna Felton was still a drawing card in the heartland. While employing a studio-released newspaper advertisement, the Cedar Rapids Drive-In altered it to read: "JOEL McCREA in THE OKLAHOMAN with VERNA FELTON . . . TV'S 'HILDA' of 'DECEMBER BRIDE.'"

Costume test photo for *The Oklahoman*.

The summer of 1956 was pretty much like any other summer around the Millar household, except for one accomplishment which left Verna "bursting with pride," as described by a CBS press release. That August, Verna bounced onto the *December Bride* set to announce happily that she had just taught Lisa to swim. "She's the cutest thing, but she swims with only one hand—using the other hand outstretched to grab the nearest solid object. But she really scoots around the pool." As for Lisa's ten-month-old sister, Verna offered with a laugh, "I'm going to give Kate another couple of months to 'mature.' Then it's into the pool for her, too."

Near the end of the summer, Verna delighted in a rare guest appearance on a musical variety program. Since July 2, singer Vic Damone had been the host of his own CBS show, which served as a summer replacement series for *December Bride*. On September 24, Verna and Spring Byington joined Damone's guest star Celeste Holm in a half-hour of songs and fun. Verna, demonstrating a fine alto voice, took the lead in their duet of "Partners," mugging and dancing while the musically challenged Spring did her best to keep up. Reviewer Robert Sokolsky declared their rendition "one of the best light touches of the summer season . . . just the right amount of froth." Damone, too, was obviously happy with Verna's efforts—during the conclusion he enthusiastically introduced her as "Miss Verna Felton, wonderful star!" When he kissed her on the lips, Verna clutched her forehead, feigned a swoon, and staggered backwards, just short of a Hilda Crocker pratfall.

During the 1956-57 season, *December Bride* firmly held its enviable position as number five. Its plots—"as comfortable and commodious as an old shoe," said *Time*—usually featured Lily's latest "do-gooding" project. The show's original premise retreated farther and farther into the distance—only three of the season's thirty episodes centered on Lily's love life. Again, there was a smattering of celebrity guest stars, including Rory Calhoun and Marjorie Main—playing themselves—and repeaters Art Aragon and Sandor Szabo, but for the most part, storylines either focused on the Henshaws' efforts to sell their home or their later decision to remodel it instead. To reel in viewers, the shows featuring Calhoun and Main as prospective house buyers were strategically positioned at the season's start.

One month after the premiere, boxer Aragon returned to the *Bride* set to coach Pete's myopic brother-in-law, played by comic Arnold Stang, who had originated the role in a second-season episode. Stang, a personal friend of producer Parke Levy, received so much positive feedback for his interplay with Harry Morgan that by midseason Levy was considering the possibility of "working up a new TV series" for the two actors. By season's end, Levy had evidently concluded that Morgan should remain on *Bride,* but he still wanted Stang as a second banana in a new series, a plan that never materialized.

When the Henshaws' house failed to sell, Matt and Ruth decided to renovate it inside and out. The original design had been Early American, decorated with accent pieces like a grandfather clock, hooked rugs, and a cobbler's bench-coffee table. Matt's new design would be daringly modern, and it would require weeks of work. He decided it would be best if the family vacated during the renovation, so he planned a trip to the Midwest to call on several clients. Ruth, Lily, Pete, and Hilda all found reasons to tag along. For six weeks, the quintet was on the road, stopping in New Mexico, Oklahoma, Missouri, Illinois, and Indiana. When they returned to Los Angeles in "The Homecoming" (January 21, 1957), they were in awe of the sleek beauty of their new home, decorated in pale blues and soft grays.

Verna mugged her way through many of the third season episodes, but one outshines the rest. In "Ritzy Neighborhood" (November 12, 1956), Lily schemes to get a house buyer to renege on his deal with Matt. When his wife proves difficult to budge, Lily invites her club members, posing as undesirable neighbors, to meet the very staid Mrs. Crandall (Doris Packer). One pretends to be a kleptomaniac, another likes to give wild parties, and a third has a very intimidating dog. Hilda's disguise is the icing on the cake. Dressed in a black wig and outrageously long eyelashes, she waltzes in, swiveling her generous hips, to which a bright red sweater-dress clings. Her outrageous flirtations with Mr. Crandall send his irate wife straight out the door, and the deal is off.

In other episodes, Verna's flair for the physical is utilized almost as much as it had been in the previous season. In "Football Hero" (December 24, 1956), when she and Spring are disguised as football players, Verna gets knocked to the ground during the team's warm-up exercises but quickly rebounds. In a scene obviously created only to exploit Verna's gusto, she holds her own with a line of leggy chorines in "The Study Group" (February 4, 1957). When Hilda is frightened in "Duck Hunting" (February 25, 1957), Verna scores another pratfall—into a pool of water! As one *Variety* reviewer noted that season, "Miss Felton troupes broadly and indestructible, to nice effect."

How much of the real Verna Felton was evident in her characterization of Hilda Crocker? "She's a screwball in real life . . . Anyone who knows Mother can't help but note the similarity," her son Lee told celebrity-columnist Faye Emerson in a 1957 tongue-in-cheek interview. He cited several examples of Verna's real-life escapades, like the time she went to throw a pail of water off the back porch and threw herself along with it. "Then there was the night Mother was attempting to cover her shoulders in bed by tugging on a stubborn blanket that was caught somewhere," Lee continued. "Her hand slipped and—powie!—she socked herself in the jaw. Result: two broken fingers." Verna agreed with Lee's summation. "Who else," she asked, "but a screwball would lock herself out of the house at 5 a.m. and have to squeeze half of herself through the dog's little swinging door to open the inside door lock with the tips of her fingers?" Verna and Lee agreed that one of the goofiest things she ever did occurred when her boat lay at anchor. "The water was so calm and peaceful and the moon so lovely that Verna, somewhat hypnotized by the beauty of it all, decided to walk to the beach. She walked smack off the boat into six feet of water." Another incident was pure Hilda: "One

Spring Byington (LEFT) entertains at a Christmas party she gave the cast and crew of *December Bride* at Barraclough's in downtown Los Angeles, 1956. Verna is accompanied by her second cousin Virginia Lawrence Hier and Virginia's son-in-law Bob Hull, the TV/Radio Editor of the Los Angeles *Herald Examiner.*

day while floating majestically in an inner tube around her pool, the phone rang. In trying to disengage herself from the tube, it flipped over and held her submerged because her posterior was stuck tightly in the hole of the tube. 'What an embarrassing way to drown!' reflected Verna."

At sixty-six, Verna found it easier to perform physical stunts than to memorize lines. In her youth, she had been able to perform six different plays in one week, but now she found it difficult to learn new material each week. "Every actor," she said, "runs across lines that, for some reason, just won't stick in the mind. When I do that, I have a surefire method." Her method was pasting or writing or pinning cue words in odd places on the *Bride* set—places where she could look quite naturally while emoting for the all-seeing cameras. Prop men swore they had never seen her equal—she wrote cues across the breast of a dressed chicken in a market scene, scrawled them in chalk on a watermelon, pasted a word or two inside a humidor, or sometimes under the cradle of the telephone—wherever Verna's actions called for her to be at the time of the speech, and on whatever she was supposed to be holding at the time. Verna had learned this strategy from one who had perfected it. In the 1920s, her mother, haunted by a dreadfully bad memory, had worked out a scheme of pinning her script pages on the backs of furniture on stage.

Sometimes Verna enlisted the help of the *December Bride* prop men in supplying her script prompts. They wrote Verna's cue words onto a cake's frosting, a chocolate pie, sandwiches, bananas, even apples, all of these being perfect since Hilda always seemed to be eating. Once, Verna used nail polish to paint a cue on the bottom of a coffee cup. "I picked up the cup on camera, and darned if somebody hadn't filled it up! I had to gulp down a whole cup of hot coffee before I could see my words." Verna admitted that her system is a matter of convenience, "but I'd rather do it that way than cudgel myself constantly to memorize entire scripts, including the speeches of others which cue my lines."

However, Verna would find few places to hide her cues on the set of *Taming Sutton's Gal*, a backwoods melodrama which went into production in late April, about one month after *December Bride*'s 1957 hiatus began. The low-budget Republic feature, originally bestowed with the even more quizzical title *Back of Beyond*, featured a cast of only five and was filmed mainly on location in northern California in less than one month's time. John Lupton was cast as citified bank clerk Frank McClary who heads to the country for some pheasant hunting. He rents a room from feisty Aunty Sutton (Verna), whose seventeen-year-old niece Lou (Gloria Talbott) takes a liking to Frank. Unfortunately, so does the Suttons' nearest neighbor, sexpot Evelyn Phelps (May Wynn), the wife of dangerously jealous moonshiner Jugger Phelps (Jack Kelly). Things get really hairy when Jugger is wounded by a gunshot: he thinks Frank is responsible, but the culprit is his own wife who is anxious to escape her oppressive husband. A climactic showdown at the Sutton cabin results in Evelyn's death at the hands of Jugger, who is apprehended by Frank. Totally implausible is the film's conclusion, when Frank and Lou, who've known each other no more than three days, whisk themselves off to get married.

While the part of Aunty Sutton was more broadly written than Verna's last screen role of Mrs. Waynebrooke in *The Oklahoman*, Verna manages to capture the old girl's gruffness, even though brief "Hilda-esque" moments shine through. Mainly, Aunty is all bark and no bite. She passes her time rocking and listening to tawdry radio serials while smoking her own hand-rolled cigars, but she doesn't dare imbibe: "I don't hold with likker! Tobaccer's *good* fer your insides—but likker eats holes in ya." She also spouts words of wisdom for her niece's benefit: "Lou, I'm scared stiff you're a sissy. In fact, I wouldn't be surprised if ya growed up to be a woman . . . but a girl ain't a woman until she's in love—and then she's in trouble." Aunty tells Lou she's afraid she'll never catch a man because she's too feisty, but Lou gives as good as she gets, telling the old woman she learned it all from her. In the final scene, Aunty—with a ratty fur piece slung around her neck—accompanies the young lovers to town to get hitched. Just as they're about to kiss, Aunty leans forward from her seat in the rear of Frank's open jeep and sticks her lit cigar in his mouth. He throws it out, but this delights old Aunty: "I cotton to a man who ain't afraid to stand up his in-laws!"

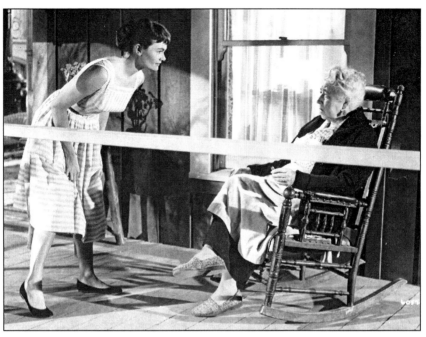

"Aunty, you're just plumb loony!" cries Lou (Gloria Talbott) after the old woman meddles in her love life in *Taming Sutton's Gal.*

"I'll bet he saw you looking moony-eyed and swimmy-headed," said Aunty Sutton, accusing Lou of being attracted to Frank McClary in *Taming Sutton's Gal.*

Verna's performance, though heavily caricatured, is really the only one of the five with any spark. In almost every scene she skillfully puffs on her "stogies," though in real life, according to family friend Al Blazic, she rarely even smoked cigarettes, except perhaps after a meal. Notable is the shootout scene when she goes for the sheriff in Frank's jeep, handling the vehicle with all the gusto of a rough-and-ready country woman.

Few of Verna's fans probably ever saw *Taming Sutton's Gal*, however. It was released on September 15, a scant four months after its completion, and most often shared a single weekend's double bill on drive-in screens with *The Wayward Girl*, another lackluster Republic feature which shared the same director and screenwriter.

For the fourth season of *December Bride*—premiering on October 7, 1957—the producers set out to prove that the series could survive without the powerful lead-in of *I Love Lucy*, which had ceased production the previous spring. Their chief strategy was to haul in a greater number of guest stars than ever before—including Rudy Vallee, Edward Everett Horton, Fred MacMurray, Ed Wynn, Sandor Szabo, Gilbert Roland, and Mickey Rooney—but with mixed results. Among these, "The Mickey Rooney Show" (April 14, 1958) ranked superior. Despite being the final episode filmed that season, Levy moved it up five weeks, burying lesser offerings at the end of the season, when warmer weather typically influenced viewers to tune in less often. This decision was not unique to the Rooney show; in fact, episode juggling was a consistent practice that season, most likely representing an effort to maintain ratings. The season's first episode to be filmed—"Ruth Goes Home to Mother"—was deemed so inferior after its completion in July that it was hidden among the holiday programs during Christmas week. Only those episodes filmed during the four weeks of November would be consecutively broadcast in their filming order.

By this point, the series' title had become blatantly ironic. Courted vainly by several beaux during the first three seasons, Lily Ruskin's romantic life had diminished more with each passing year. During the fourth season, she had no gentleman callers at all, unless one counts the cursory appearance of an old friend at the conclusion of "Aunt Emily" (April 7, 1958) or even the unrequited affection of Edward Everett Horton in "The Butler Show" (December 16, 1957). Parke Levy and his writers, evidently unconcerned about *December Bride*'s misnomer relative to its success as a series, chose for Lily to remain a merry widow.

All the while, Lou Derman continued to turn to his own experiences and interests for plotlines. When he splurged to buy a black-and-white Corvette, the experiences with the racer inspired him to write "Sports Car" (November 11, 1957) as a comic story for the character of Matt Henshaw. Derman's fear of flying was transferred to Pete Porter in "The Airplane Show" (January 6, 1958), while his successful attempts at bodybuilding were reversed for comic effect in "The Muscleman Show" (February 3, 1958) when Matt is inspired to improve his physique. Derman also borrowed ideas from cast members to create stories.

Lily helps Hilda win over her cranky landlord in "The Parrot Show."

When Spring Byington bought an electronic device to help her learn Portuguese as she slept, so did Lily in "Sleep Teaching" (March 24, 1958). Verna's love for pets provided the spark for "The Parrot Show" (January 13, 1958), in which Hilda's landlord threatens to evict her if she doesn't get rid of her parrot Wilma.

When Ruth suspects Matt of seeing another woman, Lily (RIGHT) and Hilda attempt to find her but get trapped into appearing with an African native in a theater lecture in "The Other Woman," 1957.

Most reviewers still could not understand the show's continued popularity. "It's a slight series for people who won't take their pleasure big," *Variety* noted after the season's premiere episode. "For others, it may be a filler, but whatever it is, it still has an audience potential." Most episodes that followed the premiere were merely mediocre, but several offered Verna a chance to shine. In "Mean Grandfather" (October 14, 1957), Lily and Hilda are determined to convince a teenage girl's grandfather that the popular music she loves is not that radically different from the rhythms of his youth. In the show's concluding moments, Verna holds her own with the bobbysoxers, joining in on the latest dance crazes. In the incorrectly titled "Aunt Emily" (April 7, 1958), Hilda must figure out a way to get rid of her visiting hypochondriac cousin Emily (Isabel Randolph). While Verna's physical stunts are not part of the action, her acting is topnotch. She's over the top in "The Butler Show" when Hilda is called in to distract Lily's undesirable suitor, but it's the type of performance audiences had come to expect of her. In "The Parrot Show," when Lily cooks up a scheme to get even with Hilda's hardnosed landlord, Hilda's apartment turns into a veritable zoo. As a baby elephant insistently gropes Verna's hip, searching for the peanuts she's using to keep it occupied during the dialogue, she never fails to break character. All the while, the audience roars with laughter. Critic Hal Humphrey noted of the episode, "You have to admire Spring Byington and Verna Felton, who play the leads, for having the stamina to get through these inane scripts."

As with the first three seasons of *December Bride*, Pete's wife Gladys continued to remain invisible, except for "Masquerade Party" (March 11, 1957), in which she appeared in a gorilla costume. When "The Airplane Show" aired on January 6, 1958, and viewers learned that Gladys was going to have a baby, they began to wonder if the baby would someday make an appearance on the show, or if Pete would simply talk about the infant as he did Gladys. According to Erskine Johnson's Hollywood gossip column, three weeks later, even Parke Levy was unsure. "The Airplane Show" had actually been filmed in early October, so the writers were evidently planning for the child to be born during the fourth season. But as the months moved along, Pete and Gladys remained parents-in-waiting, and viewers noticed that there were few subsequent mentions of baby Porter. Everyone was left hanging until the following season.

One wonders how much actual input the actors, especially Spring Byington, had in the show's plots. A United Press International item, released on May 8, 1958, quoted Parke Levy on the matter: "Spring Byington tells me what to do— and I like it. Whenever the angle is suggested for a show, it must be checked by Spring for plausibility. This way we can assure credibility. I've lived with my mother-in-law for many years, but a man just doesn't know all about women— especially mothers-in-law—as well as the woman herself." Of course, the item smacked more of public relations than anything else.

It's possible that there were times when Levy was annoyed by Spring's input, solicited or not. In early 1955, midway through the series' initial season, some papers reported that Spring was trying to convince Levy that characters Matt and Ruth ought to have a child. "Although mothers-in-law are often the butt of many jokes, our value as baby-sitters is undisputed," the actress asserted. "And I've got two sons-in-law, two daughters, and three grandchildren who will vouch for that." One month after this item was published, Levy responded in the March 18 issue of *TV-Radio Life*: "We are trying to keep *December Bride* entirely apart from the usual situation show, and for that reason we do not intend to let Frances

Lily and Hilda assist Pete in a run-through of getting Gladys to the hospital in time in "Baby Rehearsal," an episode filmed thirteen months before the Porters' baby arrived the following season.

Rafferty and Dean Miller, who play the young married couple, have a child in the story because then we'd just be another family show. Our program is about a charming mother-in-law—period."

Levy's son Robert, often a visitor on the *December Bride* set, recalled in a 2005 interview that a definite friction existed between the producer and his series star. However, Parke Levy's association with Verna Felton, according to the younger Levy, was a different story: "Verna was loved; Spring was not really well loved . . . I remember my dad calling Spring some names that weren't associated with 'lovingness.' But Verna was always wonderful." Parke Levy's daughter Linda Mickell, who also was present on evenings when the shows were filmed, remembered Spring as "distant" and Verna as more approachable. On the other hand, Spring's oldest granddaughter Lois Ann "San" Michel, who regarded her as "my mentor, advisor, and best friend," also remembered her as "a very private individual."

As the star of *December Bride*, Spring was expected to look more the part of glamorous widow than some of her more matronly film roles—and she enthusiastically responded. According to a 1959 *TV Guide* fashion profile, Spring believed older women could remain glamorous as long as they stayed focused on the charm, colors, and lines of their dresses. Her television wardrobe—about thirty new outfits per season—however, was composed of ready-made garments which she redesigned to suit her personal requirements, a skill she had picked up previously when costumed by the film industry's top designers. By the time of *December Bride*, Spring was considerably trimmer than she appeared in some of her film roles. At seventy-two, she sported a 26-inch waist, although possibly with some help—in some episodes, she appeared tightly corseted. To divert attention from her rather short neck, Spring invariably employed deep V-necklines, long beads, scarves, and collars. She often wore very high heels to add height to her five-foot-three frame. Because she knew the camera added weight, she was most often seen wearing black, forest green, navy blue, or deep red. All *December Bride* promotional photographs of the star appear heavily retouched, with virtually no signs of facial wrinkles or sagging flesh. She kept her hair colored a soft blonde— as she had for many years—and her bright blue eyes were enhanced by long false eyelashes.

On the other hand, Verna Felton cut quite a contrasting figure, and she would have been the first to admit it. She had long accepted the prematurely gray hair and extra pounds, both of which became more pronounced as she entered her forties. At five-foot-two, she also sought to augment her height with high heels, though by now she had surpassed the size-two's she wore in her slender youth. In press releases, Verna unashamedly admitted to 165 pounds, but at times that statistic might have been a little conservative. Still, she realized that her face and figure were her fortune. And she was not ashamed or embarrassed to wear unflattering outfits for comic effect—unlike the star of the series who was perhaps a little too self-conscious to wear a sleeveless flapper-style dress for the second season's "The Rudy Vallee Show." When Lily and Hilda dressed as bums in several episodes, Verna's attire was always more comical. If one of Verna's dresses accented her bulging middle, or if her horizontally-striped sweaters drew attention to an aged bosom, she thought it all the more like Hilda. She was not afraid to dress in wide stripes, loud floral prints, or large polka dots. Whenever

Hilda's matronly figure sharply contrasts with that of a buxom chorine in this behind-the-scenes gag shot of Verna and actress Joi Lansing during filming of "The Study Group," 1956.

Verna toned Hilda down a bit with a solid shade, her dress was still in contrast with the one Spring wore in the same scene, because Spring's was typically darker, and thus more slimming. Still, Hilda's outlandish choices and Lily's chic wardrobe helped the actresses to create characterizations that were very real to viewers. Rick Mitz, the author of *The Great TV Sitcom Book*, described the characters succinctly: "Lily was a flower—sweet and perfumed—and we could almost smell her in our living rooms. She was one of those TV people who never went to the bathroom. (Her friend Hilda definitely went.)"

Hilda's active appetite was often a source of jokes as in this scene from "Horse Phobia," 1958.

Like all supporting players of the period, Verna was bound by a contractual clause to supply her own wardrobe for any acting assignment, with the exception of period pieces. For the role of Hilda Crocker, she found this to be a pressing problem. "Buying clothes to fit Hilda's character is almost a full-time job," Verna confessed in 1956. "The clothing, as well as accessories, must be somewhat overdone to fit in with Hilda's ideas, and yet not to the point of clownishness." Since February 1956, when *December Bride's* filming day had been permanently moved from Saturday to Tuesday, Verna spent almost every Wednesday—her only free weekday in the series' stringent production schedule—shopping for Hilda's outfits. "I shop all over the San Fernando Valley, and sometimes my feet start killing me—just like Hilda's do, and she's at fault," Verna said with a laugh when interviewed in the summer of 1956. "By this time I have come to know many salespeople in a number of smaller shops in the Valley—I prefer them to the larger stores—and they are always on the lookout for something I might like." Two years later, when interviewed for *TV Radio Life*, she was still buying new costumes. Shop managers would call in to say, "We have a Hilda dress for you." Although she delighted in finding just the right thing to wear, Verna sometimes found it a chore to manage two wardrobes. "And my hats are a sizeable item. I also have many clothes I kept from my days on the stage and some I have used in *December Bride*. I keep most of my wardrobe in a guest house in the back and I also converted what was once the nursery for my son's baby into a storage room."

Since Verna had always loved hats, she decided that Hilda would become known for hers. Verna pulled some of her outdated chapeaux out of storage for Hilda to wear and then began looking for others suitable for the character's personality. When friends and fans began making hat donations, Verna's collection soon totaled over one hundred. Most were typically Hilda Crocker: fussy, showy, and *passe*. "Hilda chooses hats strictly with men in mind," Verna told *TV Guide*. "That's why so many birds and flowers. She thinks they're appealing to the opposite sex . . . Some have exclusive labels like Saks, Bullock's Wilshire, and Lilly Dache. Two trimmed with birds of paradise must have sold for at least $125 . . . I'll put a bee in your bonnet—I never pay more than $14.95 for a hat."

Verna appears to have never been inhibited about her generous figure, for she appeared onscreen before millions in quite a few unflattering outfits, whether gussied up in Hilda's street attire or the disguises she and Lily concocted for their schemes. For those former instances, the actress reasoned that man-crazy Hilda would see herself as more attractive by dressing in styles popular with 1950s youths. The results were always hilarious. In "The Shoplifter" (October 31, 1955), she wears a shell blouse and the equivalent of a "poodle skirt"—except Hilda's is covered in peacocks. In "The Golf Lesson" (October 21, 1957), she dons a cardigan with a huge "H" embroidered on the front, reminiscent of Penny Marshall's ever-present "L" in *Laverne and Shirley*. She dances the Black Bottom and the Shimmy wearing a test-pattern gypsy skirt in "Mean Grandfather" (October 14, 1957).

The live studio audience had come to expect to see Hilda in some wild get-up or elaborate hat, just as much as they anticipated her cheery entrances punctuated with her standard greeting "Yoo Hoo!" Sometimes—before Verna uttered a single line—she was greeted with gales of laughter because of her attire, such as one dress with a huge plaid pattern in "Sports Car" (November 11, 1957) or the *decollete* polka dot gown in "The Other Woman" (December 9, 1957). In "The Shoplifter," she was required to quickly enter the Henshaw's front door off-camera while the other four principals were conversing in the next room. The actors' dialogue was interrupted by spontaneous laughter at that point, because the studio audience was distracted by Hilda's peacock skirt. Similar responses greeted her when she dressed as a mini-skirted French maid in "The Microphone Show" (November 18, 1957) and as a Morticia Addams look-alike in "Matt-Pete Fight" (May 19, 1958), but Verna went to the greatest lengths for a costume for "The Butler Show" (December 16, 1957). When guest star Edward Everett Horton, playing a staid butler, becomes an unwelcome presence in the Henshaw household, Lily enlists Hilda to pose as her coarse "sister" with hopes that she'll run him off. For this scene, the original script called for Verna to wear "a silly hat with long feathers, red dress, ratty fur piece around her neck and lots of costume jewelry." This brief description was just enough for Verna's imagination to kick into high gear. She recalled the elaborate but out-of-style gowns she had saved from her stage career—a time when she had once weighed only ninety pounds—and realized she had just the thing to wear. Searching through her trunks, she removed a stunning evening gown she had worn during a 1921 engagement in Regina, Saskatchewan. Covered in thousands of iridescent lavender sequins with accents of dusty purple glass beads forming grape clusters accented by green seed-bead leaves, the dress featured a heavy train and a back flap decorated in the same style. While the gown had not been originally designed as formfitting, Verna knew that that it would now fit snugly on her matronly figure. In fact, when she tried it on, it was too tight to allow her to fasten the multitude of hooks and eyes in the back, but Verna was determined to squeeze into it. Realizing the back flap would hide the necessary bodice extensions and modern zipper, she requested Desilu's costume department to make the necessary bodice alterations. To accessorize, she chose a huge black picture hat covered in ostrich plumes and a pair of vintage Venus pumps she had also preserved from the gown's era. Despite Verna's efforts to have the dress let out, it still fit so tightly that she could barely exhale. She didn't care, though. The roars of laughter and thunderous applause greeting her that evening were well worth it.

While the season's succession of guest stars—like Horton—was impressive, Spring Byington hastened to explain to a Canadian journalist, "This is not a move to change the feel of the show, but to introduce a new face now and then." In fact, the five principals—Lily, Matt, Ruth, Pete, and Hilda—remained the show's only permanent cast members throughout the run of the series, unless one considers a few semi-regulars, like Dick Elliott as Hilda's longsuffering boyfriend Stanley Poole. This roly-poly actor, best known to television audiences as Mayor Pike on *The Andy Griffith Show*, was born as Richard Damon Elliott on April 30, 1886, in Salem, Massachusetts. Like Verna and Spring, he began his acting career as a stock player during the first decade of the 20th Century. He married actress Ora Esther Claud, who later gave birth to their only child, a son. With the advent of the Depression, Elliott found stage work too difficult to find, so he retreated to San Antonio where his wife's relatives lived. There he made a living selling aluminum-ware until making the big move to Hollywood in 1931. By the time he played Hilda's exterminator boyfriend, Eillott had filled over 300 minor roles in films and television programs. Widowed since 1949, Elliott was known for his high-pitched voice and distinctive speech pattern of whistling through his teeth. While he made eight *December Bride* episodes as Stanley, Dick Elliott had first appeared as two other incarnations of Hilda's boyfriends—Richard and Walter.

Other semi-regulars included a number of talented character actresses who played members of Lily and Hilda's social set: the Westwood Women's Cultural Club. Delightful Cheerio Meredith, best known to television fans as Mayberry's hypochondriac on *The Andy Griffith Show*, chalked up the most appearances as eye-rolling Hortense Miller. Eight days older than Verna Felton, Meredith (*nee* Edwina Lucile Hoffman) was born a grocer's daughter in St. Joseph, Missouri, on July 12, 1890. At nineteen, she gave up a nascent foray into vaudeville to marry Oklahoma City automobile salesman-racecar driver Conde Thompson Mosley. By 1927, when the youngest of her four children was born, Meredith's family was living in Hollywood, where she would divorce soon afterwards. It was not until her children were fully grown that Meredith picked up where she left off in 1910 and resumed her acting career. She once said she had been waiting years to become wrinkled so she could play daffy old ladies.

North Carolina native Elvia Allman, who had been a prolific radio performer for decades, put in a total of ten appearances on *December Bride*, with all but one as club member Sarah Selkirk. The inimitable Marjorie Bennett put in nine performances as jolly Edythea Walker during the last four seasons. Angular Almira Sessions was around for seven episodes, first as Madeline Schweitzer and then as Elsie Pringle for the remaining six. Although Gail Bonney appeared six times as gossipy Madeline Schweitzer, her character abruptly disappeared after the second season. However, Lily often referred to Madeline during the remainder of the run. Sweet little dumpling Madge Blake cheered up five episodes as another club member, variously identified as Anita Henderson or Margaret Wilcox.

A roll call of the rest of *December Bride*'s impressive array of character actors would require too much space, so only those appearing most frequently in nonrecurring roles make this list: Norman Leavitt, Rolfe Sedan, James Flavin, Lyle Talbot, Sid Melton, Harry Cheshire, Damian O'Flynn, Isabel Randolph, Peter Leeds, Pierre Watkin, Joseph Kearns, Sandra Gould, Byron Foulger, Raymond Greenleaf, Grandon Rhodes, William Forrest, Joi Lansing, Dick Wessel, and Frank Jenks. Closer to home, Verna's neighbor Howard McNear showed up five times in various parts, while her son Lee Millar and daughter-in-law Edith Simmons filled bit parts in eleven and nine episodes, respectively.

Despite the absence of *I Love Lucy*'s lead-in, *December Bride* ended its fourth season in ninth place on the ratings charts. This was even more remarkable, considering that season's feeble plots as well as the producer's episode-juggling strategy.

On March 12, 1958, about a week before Verna filmed the final episode of the season, she received a telegram from Ed Sullivan, the president of the National Academy of Television Arts and Sciences. She had been nominated for an Emmy Award in the category of Best Continuing Supporting Performance by an Actress in a Dramatic or Comedy Series during the year 1957. The other contenders, all of whom had been nominated in previous years, were Ann B. Davis for *The Bob*

Cummings Show, Pat Carroll for *Caesar's Hour*, Marion Lorne for *Sally*, and Vivian Vance for *I Love Lucy*. Two of them—Carroll and Vance—had previously won for performances on the same shows. Spring Byington also received her first Emmy nomination that same year for best leading actress in a comedy or drama. The awards ceremony was held at the Cocoanut Grove in Hollywood on Tuesday evening, April 15. Disappointingly, neither Verna nor Spring won. Instead the awards went to Ann B. Davis and Jane Wyatt of *Father Knows Best*.

A little more than a week before the ceremony, Verna had appeared in the Beverly Hills Easter Parade, which was televised live on Los Angeles station KTTV. Bill Welch hosted from the corner of Santa Monica and Wilshire Boulevards on that cool, damp Easter Sunday. The parade marked the end of the 1958 Easter Seals campaign, honoring many local crippled children by inviting them to ride in the automobiles with the celebrity participants. Among those waving to the crowd from their cars were a very polite Lauren Chapin of *Father Knows Best*, an upbeat Jerry Mathers of *Leave It to Beaver*, gushing gossip columnist Louella Parsons ("All my life I've wanted to be in a parade!"), plus Adolphe Menjou, Jane Withers, and Kathy Nolan and Tony Martinez of *The Real McCoys*. Just after Amanda Blake of *Gunsmoke* passed the camera, it began to rain. By the time Frances Rafferty, waving and grinning, followed along in her car, it was coming down too hard for the driver to stop for the camera. But shortly afterwards, as a white Ford convertible approached the intersection, Welch slowed it down long enough to speak to Verna, riding in the back seat with a boy and girl. Her Easter bonnet was very simple, nothing like some of Hilda's monstrosities.

"Happy Easter, Verna," Welch said. "I'm glad you got the top up!"

She laughed, "Yes, a happy *wet* Easter!"

As the car moved out of camera range, Verna waved to an eager fan. He asked in an upbraiding voice, "How come we don't see you on radio no more?"

Her reply began, "Oh, well, I'd love to—" then trailed off as undecipherable as the Ford moved away. Verna must have wondered where this fan had been for the past four years to not know that her television career consumed too much time to consider regular radio appearances—even though she still missed performing in that medium.

Yet, just two months later, Verna was delighted by a rare opportunity to perform with Lee in a local radio drama. The production, which was sponsored by the Episcopal Theatre Guild, also reunited her with old friends Robert Young and Gil Stratton. The guild had been founded in 1952 by a small group of entertainment professionals who wanted to serve their church through their talents. Their primary objective was to aid worthy parish and mission projects of the Diocese in southern California through radio and stage productions. Numbered among the members were Robert Young, Lyle Talbot, Art Gilmore, Stanley Farrar, Marvin Miller, Lurene Tuttle, and Sarah Selby.

Lee and Verna perform on radio for the Episcopal Theatre Guild, June 1958.

Lee had been briefly associated with the Episcopal Theatre Guild in 1955, when it produced *Once Upon a Saturday*, a one-act musical he had co-written with Wayne Hamilton, a fellow actor from Lee's days on KTTV's *Without Fear*. Hamilton (*nee* Wayne Hamilton Pilcher) had been born in Oak Park, Illinois, in 1922. With only a grammar school education, he joined the army in 1943. Following his military service, he turned toward Hollywood to pursue the career of his dreams. Despite Hamilton's musical talents, he found it quite difficult to make a mark for himself. Eventually, he found various jobs in the entertainment industry—including a stint as a promotion man for Capitol Records and a behind-the-scenes position with the *Queen for a Day* television show—all less than fulfilling. Although Lee had more industry connections than Hamilton, neither seemed able to reach stardom. In 1954, as a way to supplement their income, the men entered into a partnership they named Songs Unlimited, "a service offering everything in musical and lyrical composition for the entertainment and advertising world." They prided themselves on their unique songwriting team; both men were capable of writing lyrics and composing music. By 1957, Hamilton had moved into Verna's empty guest house, where he would reside for the next several years.

Unlike the previous three summers, Verna found herself without a movie role during the 1958 hiatus from *December Bride*. She also found herself without a housekeeper—Lillian Nishijama had left her employ. Usually when Verna's housekeepers took a vacation, she would enlist the help of either of her old friends, Zora Blazic or Ida Graves, who would come and stay for several weeks and do the cooking and cleaning. This summer, just as Verna was wondering what to do about the vacant position, Arden Allen Jr.—Pearl's nephew—phoned from his home in Sebastopol. Verna had remained close to all of her stepfather's family, so close that they felt comfortable enough to ask favors when necessary. Arden's request involved his eighteen-year-old daughter Daphne, who had just graduated from high school. "I was a disaffected teenager and didn't want to be home," Daphne remembered in 2006. Arden asked if his daughter could perhaps stay with Verna for the summer, feeling that a change of scenery would be beneficial and suggesting that she could help out around the house. Verna agreed that the girl could do the cooking in exchange for bed and board. Although Daphne possessed the skills to prepare a basic meal, she admits she to being "a typical self-centered teenager, not giving a hoot about anyone else." As a result, her culinary efforts were not very successful, and after a while Verna decided she really needed to find someone else. Asking Daphne to move back downstairs to free up the housekeeper's apartment, she allowed her young relative to stay for the remainder of the summer, doing other tasks, like gardening.

"I thought she was a great lady," Daphne recalled. "She just had a very wonderful mind, and of course, a wonderful sense of humor, but she lived very simply, without pretension. Her lady friends would come over and they'd play cards, and their conversations were of the most ordinary kind . . . She changed her sheets every day. She wasn't a fanatic about other cleanliness, but she did like clean sheets every night when she went to bed. I remember the unlimited amounts of ice cream in the freezer, and I gained a lot of weight that summer . . . She adored her grandchildren—they were her life . . . I had met [Verna] before that summer—once was when I was about eight or ten years old, visiting at my grandparents' house on Judah Street in San Francisco. And she said, 'I wish I could put you in my pocket and take you home!' And all I could think of was, 'Oh, god, I want to go, I want to go, I want to get out of here!'. . . It was kind of a transforming experience for me to grow up in a small town of 3,000 and then to be down in Hollywood and Los Angeles. Of course, my grandmother [Dorothy Allen] thought that I should go on the stage. She kept asking my mother, 'Well, does she want to go on the stage?' My grandmother was so enamored with a stage career—in her book, that was the only thing that one could do. But no, I didn't have the talent or the looks or anything that would have gotten me there." Before the summer ended, Daphne got to see professional actors behind the scenes when she accompanied Verna to the studio to watch the filming of an episode of *December Bride*. After returning home, she eventually decided to attend UC-Berkeley.

Besides maintaining contact with her Allen relations, Verna also kept in touch with the Canadian relatives of Margaret Thomas Felton, who had married Verna's brother Clayton more than forty years before. In the summer of 1957, Margaret's younger brother Bert Thomas and his wife, residents of Victoria, British Columbia, had visited Verna on the *December Bride* set. After she told them she was contemplating a visit to Canada the following summer, they happily spread the news to relatives in Ladysmith, where officials were already planning events for British Columbia's 1958 centennial celebration. William Hallinan, chairman of Ladysmith's celebration committee, wasted no time in inviting Verna—hailed in the local press as "the most illustrious person associated with the early theatrical life of Ladysmith"—to be the guest of honor at the upcoming ceremonies. Fourteen miles away, in the larger city of Nanaimo, similar events were scheduled for the day when Her Royal Highness Princess Margaret would make a brief stop during her two-week tour of the province. Officials in Nanaimo also wanted Verna as one of their city's honored guests, although many had not been around fifty years earlier when Verna had first made a name for herself in Canada. But everyone knew her as Hilda, and to have a Hollywood celebrity attend their event would put the proverbial icing on BC's birthday cake.

All centennial events were planned around Princess Margaret's historic visit, which would was set for Wednesday, July 16—one week before Verna was to report to the studio to begin rehearsals for the season's first *December Bride* rehearsals. In late May, she wrote to Hallinan, saying her plans hinged on obtaining a release from CBS to attend the events. When the network okayed her trip, Verna arranged to fly from Los Angeles to Victoria on July 15.

Victoria was suffering an oppressive heat wave when Verna arrived, inappropriately attired in a dark blue suit, red hat framed in clusters of cherries, and her prized set of six stone martin scarves. "It's hot, isn't it?" she gently exclaimed when Nanaimo's mayor and the city council greeted her at the airport.

The weather on the following day offered no relief. At noon, a cavalcade of six automobiles, headed by a Royal Canadian Mounted Police car and flanked by two scarlet-coated RCMP motorcycle outriders with a third covering the rear of the procession, drove up to the Nanaimo City Hall. More than one thousand people who lined the drive gave Princess Margaret a hearty cheer as she emerged from her car. She was dressed sensibly in a sleeveless floral chemise of pink roses on a beige background, accented by a beige cloche and "the familiar double string of matched pearls." Escorted by Lieutenant-Governor Frank Ross and members of the official royal party, the princess was greeted on the steps of the city hall by Mayor Pete Maffeo, in his brand new robes of royal purple and wearing his golden chain of office. Waiting in the council chamber were several mayors and dignitaries from neighboring towns as well as four Nanaimo alderman and their wives. The only American in the room was Verna Felton.

Previously, a card with information about Verna had been handed to the princess's official escort. The mayor then asked the princess if he would be permitted to present Nanaimo's famous visitor. "Of course, where is she?" rejoined the princess. Then she walked quickly across to Verna and shook hands. "It took my breath away," exclaimed Maffeo. "She was so quick to respond. She is a real lady." Princess Margaret chatted with Verna for several minutes, expressing keen interest in *December Bride*. The princess asked hopefully whether the show would be aired on British television in the near future, adding that she would look forward to seeing it if possible. This brief exchange caused a stir afterwards when the aldermen and their wives—standing by and waiting to be presented to Her Highness—were unintentionally forgotten. The princess and her hosts left immediately for a quick tour of the city, stopping at a large parking lot where an estimated 10,000 people had gathered to watch Princess Margaret cut the mammoth birthday cake, reportedly weighing 10,000 pounds. She was wildly cheered when she popped a piece of cake in her mouth and munched on it with obvious relish. After heartily congratulating the cake's designer, the princess departed amid cheering goodbyes.

That afternoon, Verna was the guest of honor at a centennial tea held at the Canadian Legion Hall and hosted by her old friend Mrs. C. H. Barker. According to the *Nanaimo Daily Free Press*, "Miss Felton met so many old friends that she was overwhelmed. There wasn't even elbow room so many came to pay her tribute."

Ladysmith resident Bill Hallinan was in charge of Verna's itinerary on the following day. He and his wife met her in Nanaimo that morning and took her to Ladysmith, where first they toured the city's new General Hospital. The entire hospital personnel gathered near the main entrance to greet her. As noted in the local newspaper, Verna wore "an ensemble which featured a light wool coat in soft mauve shade, with a flowered dress in tones matching her small feathered hat in a deep mauve. More than one staff nurse was heard to say in admiration, 'It just suits her.'. . . Miss Felton walked leisurely through the whole hospital, visited and talked with the patients, members of the staff and signed dozens of autographs, relaxed in the coolness of the administration office where she was invited to sign the visitors' book."

From there, Hallinan led Verna on a tour of other sites, including schools, the municipal building, the newspaper office, and the offices of the Comox Logging and Railway Company. After lunch at Manana Lodge, overlooking the magnificent view of Ladysmith's harbor, Hallinan's committee accompanied Verna on a harbor cruise to "The Green," where the Allen Players had once camped during summer rehearsals. As she surveyed this site—one she had not visited for over thirty years—the memories flooded back. She felt pangs of loss, not only for the summer home her family had been forced to forfeit, but also for her parents and husband who had camped with her in that verdant spot between the lovely Silver Strand and Shell Beaches. She turned to Hallinan and told him that the area was more beautiful than she remembered it. She then confessed that if she ever retired, she would like to return to Ladysmith. "I don't think you appreciate what

Verna has her morning coffee in Nanaimo, July 17, 1958. IMAGE I-68910
COURTESY OF ROYAL BC MUSEUM, BC ARCHIVES. JIM RYAN, PHOTOGRAPHER.

you have here," she said, speaking of the beauty she encountered on her trip
up-Island from Victoria.

That evening the Native Daughters, Post No. 7, hosted a reception for the
actress in the Native Sons Hall, decorated with a huge sign that read "Welcome
Home Verna." Hundreds had assembled beforehand, and they all rose to their feet
as Verna made her entrance, wearing a slate blue satin suit and matching hat.
"This is one of the most exciting days of my life," she said in a voice choking
with emotion. "It has brought so many pleasant memories. Thank you for
your wonderful reception." She then was asked to present Centennial scrolls to
a group of local pioneers who had resided in British Columbia for more than
seventy years. After the ceremony, she sat for more than one hour signing

Verna greets a longtime Ladysmith resident as she signs autographs at the Native Sons Hall.

autographs. The *Ladysmith Chronicle* reported, "The only flaw in the evening was the fact that it was oppressively hot and people in charge became concerned about the way Miss Felton was hemmed in by the crowd which pressed forward to speak to her. Later Mr. Hallinan managed to form them into a line to file past the table at which she was seated."

Verna was tireless during the rest of the weekend's schedule, which included a major stock car race in Nanaimo on Friday night. As the guest of honor, she kissed the winner and presented him with the cup. "So our friend Hilda finally got to kiss a man," she laughed. "He was a pretty attractive young fellow, too." While in Ladysmith, she stayed in the home of Margaret Felton's niece, Thelma Jones Paton. On Sunday, which was Verna's sixty-eighth birthday, they attended the morning service at St. Mary's Catholic Church and afterwards "went to the convent where [Verna] spent a pleasant half hour with the Sisters." That afternoon, Thelma invited some of her houseguest's old friends to a birthday tea. The cake's inscription read, "To Our December Bride."

Upon her arrival home, Verna told the *Long Beach Independent*: "The whole trip was a sheer delight for me, like something out of a dream. I'm happy to be back at work on the show, but it was great to recall the memories of those wonderful old days."

Meanwhile, others in Canada recalled those "old days." After reading columnist Mamie Maloney's profile of Verna's recent visit, several Vancouver residents felt the urge to respond. One reader, identified only as "Bessie," who was a waitress at the Castle Hotel in Vancouver, remembered the kindness of Pearl Allen who gave her weekly passes to the Allen Players and thus "helped her endure what could been a cold and lonely winter—her first in Canada." F. W. Hurley wrote that he was a "callow youth in the bald-headed row at the top price of four-bits every Monday" when Verna played at Calgary's Grand Theatre, circa 1912. "I used to nearly cry," he wrote, "when I'd look back to appraise the house because there would be less than a couple of hundred people while the new movie palaces would get full-houses for tripe like *The Perils of Pauline* and *The Iron Claw*." Maloney concluded, "The cycle has once again come full circle with films losing out to TV and resurgence of the live theatre. And Verna, who has been through it all, is still going strong."

During Verna's absence, daughter-in-law Edith had been rehearsing for the part of Mary Magdalene in the Hollywood Hills Theatre's production of *The Pilgrimage Play*. When the director needed children for a crowd scene, she took along Lisa. The family was hopeful that the four-year-old would become the family's fourth generation to join the acting profession. Verna loved to tell the story of an incident during the run of this show that foretold her eldest grand-daughter's inclination not to follow the family tradition. "Little Lisa came over to see me one afternoon and said, 'Oh, gosh, Gramma, the director gave me a real scolding yesterday.' I asked her why and she said, 'I picked my nose.'"

Meanwhile, Lee and his partner Wayne Hamilton had spent the summer rewriting a full-length musical called *Extra Special Day*, set in New Orleans and based on an original story by Robert Neil Porter. Earlier in the year, when theatrical producer Donald Lloyd Young showed interest in the work, Lee and Wayne had signed a contract for him to lease their musical, which boasted twenty scenes, a cast of thirty-five, and a fifteen-member orchestra. In the meantime, Young engaged the Civic Playhouse, an "intimate theatre" on La Cienega Boulevard, as the ideal venue for *Extra Special Day*'s opening in the fall. Young lined up a cast that featured a handful of film actors known for their secondary roles, including Shirley Mills, Robert Arthur, Clarence Muse, Barbara Pepper, and Alan Carney. The musical was set to open as a limited engagement on November 18. Rehearsals began on November 2, the playbills were printed, and all was set—or so it seemed. At the last minute, Young postponed the opening for one week, cit-ing financial difficulties. When it failed to open on November 25, Lee was crest-fallen; he had put all of his energies into the musical. With his acting career less than progressive and a family to support, he found himself more and more finan-cially dependent on his mother.

Despite her heavy involvement in the lives of her son's family, Verna didn't see herself as a meddling presence—at least, that's the impression she gave in Jack Holland's profile of her in the August 2 edition of *TV Radio Life*: "My son lives a few blocks from me so I spend some time with him, his wife Edith, and my two grandchildren. Not too much time, mind you. I don't believe in being the nosey [*sic*] mother-in-law. In fact, I have one rule I strictly observe as a mother-in-law—I keep my mouth shut. And if I find I can't shut up, I just leave."

Around this same time, Verna, as a patroness of the Film Welfare League, was busy selling tickets for its annual benefit luncheon and fashion show. It had been founded in 1929 "for the purpose of rendering aid to the needy in all branches of the theatrical profession." The league's policy was to give immediate aid, especially to those professionals who were not eligible for assistance from the Motion Picture Relief Fund. Its members included a considerable number of silent screen actresses, including May McAvoy, Laura LaPlante, Viola Dana, Corinne Griffith, and Gloria Swanson. Verna also remained active in the Radio Women's War Service, which by now had turned its attention to other charities, including donating supplies and clothing to Native Americans. They also financially supported a Korean orphan.

"My home life follows the line of general activity," Verna told Holland. "People are forever dropping in unexpectedly and the barbecue is going most of the time. We usually gather around the pool . . . there are two things I wouldn't give up—my garbage disposal and my pool." Verna, however, did part with one luxury when common sense prevailed. Her hectic schedule during the previous decade had not allowed her much chance to use the small boat she had purchased, so she eventually sold it.

In the midst of all this summertime activity, Verna returned to work on *December Bride*'s fifth season with a certain amount of apprehension, a feeling shared by the entire cast and crew. Their coveted Monday-night time slot had been given to another Desilu production, *The Ann Sothern Show*, while *Bride* had been moved to Thursday evenings at eight, following reruns of *I Love Lucy*. *Bride*'s new competition was Walt Disney's *Zorro* on ABC and a new NBC sitcom *The Ed Wynn Show*. The latter only lasted fifteen weeks, but the former proved to be quite popular in a season already dominated by westerns. In addition to the schedule change, the producers dispensed with filming *Bride* in front of a live audience, a switch that would give episodes a different look—and sound, considering the annoying laugh track now accompanying each episode.

Proving most detrimental to the series' success, though, were the feeble plots of the first ten or so episodes. On October 2, the season opener failed to win favor, even after employing the tactic of seasons past by featuring a celebrity guest star. Aptly titled "The Edgar Bergen Show," *Variety* noted that "Spring Byington took a back seat to her guest star . . . It was Bergen and not Miss Byington who got into the middle of floundering romance and straightened everything out by the half-hour finale . . . It's Miss Byington and her permanent party that have brought the viewing crowd to the series and the writers ought to spend more time with them." Six weeks later, when guest Zsa Zsa Gabor appeared in a "rambling" story, the situation—or the ratings—had not improved very much. *Variety* keenly observed: "Considering the fact that *December Bride* continues to hammer away at the same type of gag, week in and week out, the fact that it manages to remain a fairly engaging half-hour is a tribute to the enthusiasm of cast and the writers." Despite this bit of optimism, the show was continuously losing points in the ratings. It quickly fell from the top ten and then from the top twenty.

In an effort to salvage the season, CBS and the show's sponsor General Foods summoned Parke Levy to a brainstorming conference late that fall. Hollywood columnist Erskine Johnson later reported their lack of progress as Levy nixed every new gimmick handed to him.

"How about a marriage for Lily Ruskin?" they asked.

"No," Parke said. "Too many fans like her to be free."

"Then how about a marriage for Hilda?"

"But what would Hilda and her husband talk about?" Levy wondered.

"How about Matt and Ruth becoming parents?" someone suggested.

Levy emphatically rejected that idea. "Then Lily would be a grandmother, and we would have a grandmother show, which it isn't. It's a mother-in-law show."

Levy then reminded everyone that *December Bride* had one new gimmick going already—Pete and Gladys would soon become parents. The baby would be the first cast addition in five years, and future episodes would revolve around babysitting routines. He added that there were tentative plans for Lily and company to visit Europe or the Orient for a change of scenery. Then Levy broke up the meeting by thinking out loud: "We'll have Pete's baby grow up fast, buy her a pony, and then we'll have a western." The meeting adjourned then. Everything that could be done was being done for *December Bride*.

Never one to put all of her eggs in one basket, Verna utilized a free weekend that fall to rehearse and appear in a live appearance on *The Jack Benny Program*. The October 19 telecast, titled "The Millionaire," was a take-off on the currently popular CBS series by the same name. Marvin Miller guest-starred in his usual role of Michael Anthony, executive secretary to a multibillionaire whose hobby was giving away a million dollars to persons he had never met. This time the recipient will be Dennis Day. As the show opens, Verna, as Mrs. Day is at the ironing board, surrounded by piles of clothes and more hanging on the walls. Dennis enters and tells her he's leaving to make an appearance on Benny's television show. "You're going to do what?" she bellows. "How many times have I told you that I don't want you to working for that one-horned, blue-eyed, purple penny-pincher?" Just then Michael Anthony arrives at the door with a cashier's check for one million dollars, payable to Dennis Day. Mother and son dance a jig when they realize their newfound wealth.

Later, when Dennis fails to show up at the studio, Benny decides to visit his home to find out why. He finds the place totally redecorated and staffed with a maid and butler. Dennis enters wearing polo attire, but his mother's *nouveau riche* ensemble is even more absurd: an outlandish bouffant cocktail dress festooned with cabbage roses, not to mention gaudy diamond chokers, bracelets, and hair ornaments. She loftily carries herself across the room, a long cigarette holder poised in her jewel-encrusted hand. Thinking she is now in a position to put Benny in his place, she pushes him down on the sofa and lets loose with a fierce tirade—until the doorbell suddenly interrupts her. There stands an apologetic Michael Anthony, who announces that he has learned that "Dennis Day" is only the singer's stage name. He explains that the check was intended for the real Dennis Day—a butcher in Covina. Now the Days are right back where they started.

Due to the tight rehearsal schedule for this live episode, Verna had to resort to her old trick. In the opening scene, one can easily notice that she's reading her lines from notes pinned to the ironing board. There's a bumpy spot during her tirade when she speaks a line or two out of sequence, causing the sound technician to come in a little late with the doorbell, but it remains the best performance of those Verna did for Benny's television series. (Verna's first known appearance on the series was another live broadcast on February 20, 1955, which featured George Raft as the guest star in a sketch titled "Death Across the Lunch Counter." This episode had originally been planned for the previous fall with Alan Ladd in mind. In fact, he and Verna are in the Benny show's *TV Guide* listing for October 31, 1954, as guest stars. For some reason or another Ladd was unavailable, and a filmed episode "How Jack Found Mary" was substituted that evening.)

On December 30, during a two-week holiday break from *December Bride*, Verna suffered what physicians called a slight stroke. She was released from St. Joseph's Hospital several days later in good condition. By January 7, she was back at rehearsal for "The Hi-Fi Show" episode showing no visible effects of her recent ailment. However, just to play it safe, she didn't perform any more pratfalls or stunts for the remainder of the season.

There had been no apparent warning signs before the stroke. In an interview five months prior, Verna felt blessed "with great vitality." She took no vitamins or prescription medicines. She said she once took a Miltown tranquilizer because a doctor thought it might slow her down, but she ditched that idea when she almost went to sleep driving on the freeway. She stuck to no special diets. In fact, she continued to eat whatever she wanted. "She was a meat and potatoes kind of gal," her granddaughter Kate recalled. "She didn't like vegetables." Occasionally, she got some exercise swimming, but probably not often enough. And now she could empathize with friends Janie Morgan and Charlotte Treadway—both prior stroke victims. Charlotte's stroke had left her a cripple, but Janie had bounced back quickly and afterwards continued to appear on television's *Our Miss Brooks* until its cancellation. Like Janie, Verna prided herself on her positive outlook. At sixty-eight, not even a stroke would make her consider retirement.

Meanwhile, the *December Bride* episodes filmed in late fall and throughout the winter were noticeably superior to those produced during the first half of the

Elvia Allman, Spring Byington, and Verna in "The Beatnik Show," 1959.

season. One standout was the topical "Beatnik Show," in which Lily and Hilda try to persuade Hilda's college-dropout nephew to forsake the coffeehouse life in favor of academia. While only one episode ("Lily's Blind Date") dealt with Lily's romantic life, Hilda was luckier in that department. In fact, she almost became the series' namesake. She snagged a proposal from boyfriend Stanley in "Hilda's Engagement," prodded him to set a wedding date in "Lily's Advice Column," then had to reassure him when he got cold feet in "Stan Loses His Nerve." By season's end, Lily's best friend still had not corralled Stanley, and the storyline was left hanging.

Pete's friends congratulate him on the birth of his daughter in "Pete Has a Baby." From left to right, Dean Miller, Frances Rafferty, Harry Morgan, Spring Byington, and Verna Felton.

Conversely, another long-running storyline would finally see completion on January 15, 1959, when Pete's wife Gladys would give birth to baby daughter Linda. Gladys's maternal state had been announced on "The Airplane Show" on January 6, 1958, comprising what must be the longest pregnancy in television sitcom history. Playing the part of little Linda was infant Vikki Rubino, born on November 8, 1958. One day at the Desilu lunch counter, her grandfather-stuntman Albert Cavens overheard *December Bride*'s assistant director say that the program needed a baby for some forthcoming sequences, and he offered Vikki's services. Subsequent stories involved the baby's nurse—an old fussbudget named Miss Twilly—and Lily's involvement with the child. In general, these were the most outstanding episodes of the season, but they came too late.

Spring Byington and Verna Felton on the *December Bride* set during the filming on "Linda on TV," 1959.

By May 1, rumors were circulating in the press that *December Bride* would not return for a sixth season. By June 9, it was official—the show would cease production and be replaced in the fall by *The Betty Hutton Show*. Of course, this was a huge disappointment for the show's five principals who had grown so close, but they were quite proud of their indestructible record of remaining in the top ten for four seasons. Over the course of the show, Verna had won the respect of Frederick de Cordova, who had moved from the position of producer to series director beginning with the fourth season. Although not mentioning her by name, de Cordova alluded to Verna in his memoir *Johnny Came Lately* when he wrote that the show boasted "a remarkable group of underrated character actors and actresses who proved, week after week, that the geriatric picture need not be a gloomy one."

Perhaps the most enduring relationship Verna shared with any of the *December Bride* cast was her friendship with Harry Morgan, the only surviving cast member at this writing. In 2004, four days after his eighty-ninth birthday, the actor was interviewed for TV Legends, the video oral history program of the Archive of American Television. By this time, his career had spanned more than sixty years. The session started out well, with Morgan providing many details about his family background and early stage career in New York. Later when the discussion turned to Morgan's considerable television work, the pace slowed down as Morgan provided increasingly simple responses. Although the interviewer gave him many prompts to describe some of his fellow actors, Morgan was not able to offer much in the way of anecdotes, this due perhaps to his advanced age. (However, even back in 1967, a *TV Guide* profile described him as "the kind of guy who never says a lot when a little will do.") When discussing Morgan's experiences on *December Bride*, he attempted to jog the elderly actor's memory by listing some of the show's guest stars like Edgar Bergen, Zsa Zsa Gabor, and Joel Grey. Failing at this, he asked if Morgan had a favorite among the show's episodes. Perking up a little, he replied, "No, not really, but we had *Verna Felton*, and [she] and I had a lot of scenes together, and I *loved* Verna. She was really a wonderful person, a wonderful actress. We did a lot of shtick together, and she was a lovely person." Though not overly expressive, it is important to note that Morgan singles out Verna as his fondest memory of *December Bride*. Luckily for both of them, the show's cancellation did not mean that they would never work together again.

CHAPTER 14

THE LAST ACT

On the evening of May 6, 1959, the eleventh annual Emmy Awards were presented during a telecast originating from three locations—the Moulin Rouge in Hollywood, the Ziegfeld Theatre in New York, and the Mayflower Hotel in Washington, D.C. For the second consecutive year, Verna Felton and Spring Byington were nominated for their *December Bride* roles, in the respective categories of Best Supporting Actress in a Comedy Series and Best Actress in a Leading Role in a Comedy Series. But when the winners were announced, it was an exact rerun of the previous year. No one seemed more surprised than Ann B. Davis of *The Bob Cummings Show* when Dinah Shore handed her the statuette for the supporting category. In fact, Davis had not prepared a speech. Likewise, an ecstatic Lauren Chapin of *Father Knows Best*— accepting for absent leading-actress winner Jane Wyatt—found it hard to offer more than a simple thank-you.

However delighted they might have been to be twice nominated for an Emmy, neither Verna nor Spring was present for the awards ceremony. Since May 2, Spring had been spending a ten-day holiday in her native Colorado, returning there at the request of Governor Steve McNichols to help publicize "Rush to the Rockies," the state's centennial celebration. During her stay, she was honored at events in Pueblo, Central City, and Cascade, but the highlight of her vacation was a visit to the Lowry Air Force Base in Denver. Ever since she had first flown in a "Jenny," Spring had maintained a "lively interest in flying." In fact, she had learned to fly under the tutelage of Tom Ryan, brother of future First Lady Pat Nixon during *December Bride*'s 1955 hiatus, but her dream was to fly in a jet— especially to prove to friends younger than herself that the aircraft "is safer than riding in an automobile on the freeway."

The morning after the Emmy Awards ceremony, Spring joined a group of Strategic Air Command bomber crew members to tour the Air Force Physiological Testing Center at Lowry Field. She was instructed in the problems of high-altitude jet flight, oxygen masks, ejection seat techniques, while as a finale she was placed in a decompression chamber where altitudes of fifty thousand feet were simulated. She emerged asking, "Now where is our jet?" Weather at Denver forced them to drive to Colorado Springs for the flight. As disbelieving airmen gathered around, seventy-two-year-old Spring was fitted with parachute and hard hat. Safely strapped into her seat, she waved jauntily at the crowd before the T-33 jet took off for its flight above the Pikes Peak area. Thirty-five minutes later, she emerged from the jet, announcing, "It was absolutely wonderful."

One *Colorado Springs Gazette-Telegraph* writer described Spring as "a vivacious lady with as much bounce as her first name," but another who attempted to discover her age was disappointed. "An actress should be ageless," she coyly answered. "I play parts of persons in and around my age group." However, another *Gazette-Telegraph* columnist had already exposed her true date of birth to readers just seven months earlier. Eighty-three-year-old Dora Foster, a spinster school teacher-turned-journalist, remembered from childhood when Spring's educator-father bought eggs and milk at her family's ranch outside Colorado Springs during summers when the Byington family camped nearby. To learn Spring's exact age, this amateur sleuth turned to surviving nonagenarians who attended school under the "jolly plump professor" some seventy years earlier. They recalled not only when Spring was born, but also that several female students had presented a bouquet of flowers to Professor Byington and his wife upon the occasion. The year, Foster asserted positively, was 1886.

Just as Spring remained noncommittal on her birth date, she was not forthcoming about the future of *December Bride*. The final first-run episode of the show—airing on May 7—coincided with her visit to Colorado. Two days before, Spring was quoted in the *Gazette-Telegraph*: " 'If we don't do this show again, we have some other plans,' she said with a smile, but refused to divulge what her plans are." By this time, of course, the actress had already been informed of the show's cancellation, and she was exploring possible film and television assignments. In August, she would start work on what would become her final feature film: *Please Don't Eat the Daisies* with Doris Day and David Niven.

While Spring was visiting her home state, Verna was entrenched in a new film role, which coincided with her usual *December Bride* hiatus. *Guns of the Timberland* was the project of actor Alan Ladd, whose contract with Warner Brothers insured that the studio would finance two films a year for Ladd's own Jaguar Productions— a decision that Jack Warner later regretted because of the typically inferior quality of Jaguar's products. *Guns of the Timberland* was no exception. Originally planned as a 1958 summer production, the film was postponed until the next year when the chief writer abruptly defected. Ladd then engaged young actor-writer Aaron Spelling to salvage the project with an overnight rewrite, but the production continued to remain plagued. Ladd, haunted by a string of box-office flops, was increasingly dependent on sleeping pills and alcohol.

Yet plans for the film moved ahead with the selection of the film's location site. Plumas County, California, located in the northern section of the scenic Sierra Nevada, was chosen for most of the action. On April 27, Verna and other members of the cast, which included Jeanne Crain, Gilbert Roland, Lyle Bettger, Frankie Avalon, and Noah Beery Jr., settled into their hotel rooms in Quincy, the county seat where some of the filming would take place. Most scenes, however, would be shot some thirty miles east, between Clio and Portola, including two at Blairsden's train depot where old Engine Number Eight, pride of the Quincy Short Line Railroad, would play a stellar role in the production. Afterwards the company would relocate to Chilcoot, near the Nevada border, for the final location shoot. This mountainous area was certainly not foreign to Verna since Sierra County bordered Plumas County on the south. Forest City, the town where her parents had met over seventy years earlier, was less than seventy miles away. Even closer was Downieville where her Lawrence forebears had operated a successful hotel in the days when miners still hoped to strike it rich. In those days, Plumas County had its share of prospectors as well, but around 1910—with the advent of the Western Pacific Railroad—the timber industry began to emerge as the county's primary economic force, one that was still thriving in 1959.

This locale lent itself perfectly to *Guns of the Timberland*, which was based on Louis L'Amour's story of a feud between lumberjacks and ranchers. Ladd played the leader of a logging team in search of timber. When they come upon some fresh forestland, the local ranchers, led by Crain, implore the lumberjacks not to cut down their forest. Without it, their homes will be buried in mudslides after the first heavy rain. Of course, a romance between the leads is hinted at, but not before the townspeople and loggers take turns dynamiting each other. When Crain's ward Avalon is nearly killed, Ladd realizes the error of his ways. In the final shot, he leaves town with Crain as his bride.

Verna, as Crain's feisty Aunt Sarah, delivers a very natural performance, especially in scenes where she demonstrates a sincere affection for Crain and Avalon. She slips into caricature only once, and this occurs in an odd scene during the town dance when Avalon sings a 1950s teenybopper number blatantly incongruous with the 1890s costumes. Still, Verna makes the best of things in a film that could only be described as weak.

As Ladd biographer Beverly Linet noted, neither Spelling's rewrite nor Robert Webb's direction could "succeed in lifting the film from the damning category of 'minor Western'—so minor, in fact, it was the only Alan Ladd movie the *New York Times* failed to review." Columnist Dorothy Kilgallen was blunt in her review of the star's performance: "[Alan Ladd has] gained so much weight he looks quite different from the actor [whom audiences] remember as the star of other films." Indeed, Ladd's features appear bloated, and his performance is totally lackluster. Besides his addictions, the star suffered other physical problems during the shoot. On April 29, only two days into production, it was rumored in the *Feather River Bulletin* that Ladd had suffered a heart attack while filming near Clio. Later he fell off a horse, was bitten by a snake, and contracted the flu, prompting precautionary flu immunizations for the entire movie company on May 5.

"Give him more rein! Don't tighten, or he'll throw ya!" Aunt Sarah advises the character played by Jeanne Crain in the corral scene from *Guns of the Timberland.*

Verna's experience on the film was happier. She showed no signs of the stroke she had suffered four months earlier and even engaged in a pratfall during her character's opening scene. Hailed as "without question the darling of the set" by the *Nevada State Journal*, Verna renewed acquaintances with Jeanne Crain, with whom she had worked in *Belles on Their Toes*, and Regis Toomey, who had appeared as one of Lily's suitors on *December Bride*. And she reminded Noah Beery Jr. that she had appeared with his father in her very first film *The Chosen Prince* back in 1917. On Monday, May 11, when the company moved east to shoot scenes on the Guidici Ranch near Chilcoot, they made the Mapes Hotel in Reno, Nevada— some thirty-five miles south—their headquarters. While there, Verna was delighted to play tourist with the Blazics who motored up from Oakland the following weekend. During their visit, Verna's friends took her to nearby Virginia City, where her mother had endured an unhappy stay at the convent school run by the Daughters of Charity. In addition to touring the Mackay Mansion, Gold Hill,

Alana Ladd, Frankie Avalon, and Verna in *Guns of the Timberland*.

and the Silver Terrace Cemetery, they posed for a photograph outside the Bucket of Blood Saloon, a Virginia City fixture since 1876—and one which would have been in existence for several years before Clara Lawrence fled the fabled city. Back in Reno, Verna's visitors dined at the Mapes Hotel's Coach Room with her and fellow film stars Ladd, Crain, Roland, Bettger, Avalon, and visitor Carolyn Jones, then the wife of Aaron Spelling. Location filming ended early the next week.

Verna returned home that spring with the sad realization that for the first time in five years, she would not be a part of a steady television series. However, she was still grateful for *December Bride*'s popularity. Reruns would continue airing during primetime on CBS until September 24, and then four days later, the show would premiere on the network's weekday morning schedule. (Producer Parke Levy had recently sold his fifty-percent interest in the series to the network for more than half a million dollars.) Although the repeat broadcasts would provide lucrative residuals, Verna instructed her agent to scout for guest spots on shows preparing their fall production schedules.

In the meantime, Verna was content to enjoy the summer with her family. In March 1959, Lee and Edith had sold their house on Beck Avenue and moved to 11351 Dilling Street—just around the corner from Verna. Their rear yard now abutted the southern side of Verna's property so a gate was installed between the two houses. Verna could pass through whenever she liked to visit her granddaughters, and, likewise, Lisa and Kate could enter Verna's yard to enjoy her pool and play with her new dog. By then, all of Verna's cocker spaniels were gone, but she had acquired a black dachshund-Chihuahua mix, which she named Henry—in honor of Henry "Harry" Morgan. "He was long like a dachshund, with really short legs,

Verna with friends in Virginia City, 1959. From right to left are Zora Blazic, Kathy McClure, and Lois Blazic.

a curly tail, and one ear up and one ear down," Lisa happily recalled. "He was the best dog ever! That was her baby." Kate added, "He always looked like he was signaling for a left turn. She had a gray cat named Veronica, and she always had parakeets. She would try to teach them to say, 'Verna Felton's baby bird.' "

Living next door Lisa and Kate learned more about their "Gramma's" likes and dislikes. "Her favorite color must have been purple," surmised Lisa, "because her entire bedroom was wallpapered in a floral print of violets. She even used some of it to put under the glass tops of her dressers and the desk." Kate agreed, "She wore purple a lot and used violet perfume. Even her living room was a subtle shade of purple." According to Lisa, this room was adorned with two purple plush velvet armchairs, as well as Oriental prints, lamps, and small sculptures.

Verna at the wedding reception of Margaret and Tom Hier, Alhambra, California, August 15, 1959. The groom was the son of Verna's second cousin Virginia Lawrence Hier. Verna had added the lilies of the valley to her hat for a *December Bride* episode earlier in the year.

Verna in 1950 with her second cousin and namesake Verna
Lawrence, aunt of the groom.

The girls remembered that holidays were a special time for their grandmother.
She delighted in serving a huge Thanksgiving meal, inviting so many guests
that she often hired help to serve and wash the dishes. "I tell you, when my
grandmother had Christmas dinners, it was never just family," Lisa said. "There
was always somebody from *wherever*. She had a lot of friends that used to come.
We used to have to sit at the children's table because there was never enough
room. One of the traditions she started was really cool. She had a red tablecloth
at Christmas, and everybody that stayed for dinner had to sign it or write a little
comment on it. Then she'd embroider over their signatures in white thread.
When that original cloth was completely filled with autographs, we started a new
one—and we still follow her tradition." At Christmas and Easter, Verna was
generous with gifts to her granddaughters. "We pretty much got the same things,
but different colors," Lisa said. "At birthday time, we'd make a list, and she'd buy
everything on it," recalled Kate.

Verna with one of her many parakeets, 1955.

Around this time, Verna once overstepped the boundaries of grandparenthood. "I remember one time my parents got mad at her because she took me and had my hair all cut off," Lisa laughingly recalled. "I guess I had long hair at the time, and I came back with a 'Twiggy' cut—and it was before Twiggy made that style famous!"

By this time, Lee had probably come to expect such from his mother. "They had a very close relationship," observed Kate. "He would do anything for her. I think she kind of doted on him, and he was a mama's boy—the only child, you know . . . I do think that at times she was perhaps overbearing."

Kate and Lisa Millar.

At times, Edith Millar must have keenly felt the aura of Verna's matriarchal tendencies. Lisa commented on their relationship: "I think on the [surface] it was good. I remember my mother complaining about her being very domineering and very 'in charge.' You know, like it's her house, and 'it's going to be done my way, whether you like it or not.'" During Lisa's infancy, when Lee and Edith were still living in the guesthouse, a remark was made which offended the new mother. As Edith was attending to her crying baby, Verna said something like, "Oh, is that big old bad mommy doing things to you that shouldn't be done?" Lisa recalled, "I'm sure that she was jesting, but my mother being as sensitive as she was, probably took it to heart."

Debbie Leff remembered a similar incident from her own childhood. When Thelma Leff once punished her daughters by not allowing them to leave their yard, Verna leaned over the fence and asked, "How are my babies? Does your mother still have you in prison?" Debbie asserted, "DeeDee delighted in playing the two mothers against their girls."

Still, the neighboring families remained close. "When Lisa and Kate were born, DeeDee never turned us aside," Debbie affirmed. The Leff girls were in and out of DeeDee's house all the time. Every Friday night, they would go to Verna's after dinner to watch *Rawhide*. During the summer of 1960, while their house was being enlarged, the three girls slept at Verna's every night. Each year, as a holiday tradition, they even helped DeeDee decorate her Christmas tree. Debbie recalled, "On one family vacation, in the '50s, she came with us to San Diego and Tijuana. She was quite recognizable, even on the streets in Tijuana, and people stopped her everywhere for autographs. I think we got special treatment there because of her fame." At one point on the trip, little Sandy Leff climbed up on the hotel pool's high diving board when a lifeguard attempted to stop her. "Leave her alone. She can do it," assured Verna, who, as Sandy's swimming coach, had every faith in the girl.

Back home in North Hollywood—just as in Tijuana—Verna was often stopped on the street or in stores when passersby recognized her famous face or distinctive voice. The daily reruns of *December Bride* kept Verna in the public eye, and the residuals kept her in spending money. Lee and Edith also reaped residuals from their own appearances on the show. In fact, that seems to have been their only steady source of income during most of 1959, supplemented by a few television bit parts here and there. Edith filmed one episode of *Fibber McGee and Molly*, but Lee was a little more fortunate, finding work on *Dennis the Menace*, *The Twilight Zone*, and *Tightrope*. Once again, he turned his attention toward the stage. In the spring, Lee had enjoyed a ten-week run of the satirical musical comedy *The Boy Friend* at the Ivar Theater in Hollywood. Then, in November, he and famous dwarf actor Billy Barty garnered more praise than any of the other actors in the San Bernardino Civic Light Opera Association's production of *Li'l Abner*. But, neither theatrical production became the career springboard Lee needed.

Meanwhile on September 27, Verna was honored by the Radio and Television Women of Southern California for her sixty years in show business. The Sunday afternoon luncheon fete was held in the Crystal Room of the Beverly Hills Hotel. More than two hundred radio, television, and film actors, writers, and technicians were on hand to toast the veteran actress. Those unable to attend sent their regrets via telegrams, chief among them being Howard Keel, president of the Screen Actors Guild, and Harry Ackerman, president of the Academy of Television Arts and Sciences. Hollywood's most flamboyant gossip columnist also sent an apology: "Hi Pal. Sorry I can't be there to help celebrate. Just can't believe it is sixty years. Hope you go on another sixty. My love and devotion always, Hedda Hopper."

Verna accepted the award with typical humor by confiding, "I shouldn't say this, but it's killing me to be here." She explained that she had to tear herself away from her television set to arrive at the luncheon on time. "The Dodgers were ahead 5 to 1 when I left. Anybody bring a transistor?" While acknowledging her lengthy career, she declared unabashedly: "And don't everybody stand up at once now and ask me my age. I was born at Salinas in 1890. That makes me 69." However, there was one important little inaccuracy—Verna had only been in show business for fifty-nine years. After all these years, she still believed that her debut at San Jose's Victory Theatre had taken place the year her father died, when it had actually been the following year. By 1959, though, there were few left living to refute her claim. And her devoted friends would have probably agreed that fifty-nine years was close enough to give anyone an award for succeeding so long in such an industry.

That fall, Verna filmed three guest appearances on some of television's most popular situation comedies. The first—an episode of *The Many Loves of Dobie Gillis*—would turn out to be Verna's best post-*December Bride* television performance. Titled "Deck the Halls," the show revolved around the holiday disillusion suffered by Dobie's grocer-father, Herbert T. Gillis. As a succession of inconsiderate customers visits his store on Christmas Eve, Gillis (Frank Faylen) tries valiantly to hold his composure, but a call from irascible Mrs. Lapping (Verna) proves to be the last straw. Depositing an eighteen-pound frozen turkey she bought six months before on his counter, the old lady delivers a rambling excuse of why she can no longer use the bird for her holiday meal. Furthermore, she demands to be paid the current price of sixty-nine cents per pound instead of the forty-nine cents it cost her in June. When Gillis refuses to accept her return, she goes off: "Well, *now*'s when I'm returning it! I've been keeping it in my refrigerator all this time, and with all that electricity!—and *you'll* sell it for sixty-nine, wanting to give me *forty-nine* while you're selling it for sixty-nine, making two profits! And at Christmas time, too! This is when everyone should be their kindest—(singing) Deck the halls with boughs of holly! Fa-la-la-Give me my money!" With that, Gillis explodes, ranting about all the kooky notions of his clientele, and throws the turkey through his front window. Old Lady Lapping is so frightened she runs out screaming for the police. When Gillis is sent before the judge, he's still out of control and lands in jail. That night his family comes down to bail him out and take him home, just in time to receive a group of carolers, including a repentant Mrs. Lapping. Ray Allen's script is right on the mark, while the loud and fast-paced exchange between Verna and Faylen is absolutely brilliant, notwithstanding her increasing inability to memorize lines; only once is she obviously looking at the cue cards. It is one of her finest performances ever.

During the filming of "Devery's White Elephant," an episode of *The Ann Sothern Show*, Verna was reunited with the show's star twenty years after the two had performed together in the 1939 MGM film *Joe and Ethel Turp Call on the*

Mrs. Lapping (Verna) demands a refund for a turkey she bought from Mr. Gillis (Frank Faylen) six months earlier in *The Many Loves of Dobie Gillis.*

President. Sothern played Katy O'Connor, the assistant manager of the Bartley House, an upscale Manhattan hotel. In this episode, her boss James Devery (Don Porter) had gotten himself into a pickle by remodeling a luxury suite and then being unable to rent it—at $3,000 per month. When eccentric Alaskan millionaire Emma Kittridge (Verna) appears on the scene, Devery pressures Katy into entertaining the old girl so she will sign a lease. Katy then finds it difficult to keep up with Mrs. Kittridge who likes to stay out on the town until three in the morning. While Verna played the sizeable part with warmth and gusto, Sothern responded by generously sharing close-ups with her veteran guest star.

In "Cousin Naomi," a midwinter installment of *The Real McCoys,* Verna played Naomi Vesper, a sly moocher who descends on the McCoys while her cousins George and Flora McMichael—the McCoys' neighbors—are out of town. In no time at all, she gets under the skin of Grampa McCoy (Walter Brennan) as she takes over his bedroom, gobbles up all of their food, and has the entire family hopping to her beck and call. Every time he aims to ask her to leave, she fakes a hang-dog expression and pitiable cough. Only when the McMichaels return is Grampa free of the old sponger—and then he has to help them get rid of Cousin Naomi.

Flora (Madge Blake) and George McMichael (Andy Clyde) try to reason with their Cousin Naomi (Verna) on *The Real McCoys*.

Meanwhile, this lighter workload enabled Verna to focus more on community projects. During the post-war years, the Radio Women's Workshop, formerly the Radio Women's War Service, had remained her pet organization. The Workshop now donated volunteer hours to various charity groups, including the VIPs (Volunteers in Psychiatry) of the Los Angeles County General Hospital. In 1959, after Verna had helped raise funds for the Los Angeles Fire Department, she was made Honorary Fire Chief. In that capacity, she personally visited all fire stations, from Woodland Hills to San Pedro, often enlisting the aid of actor friends, including Spring Byington, Frances Rafferty, and Dennis Day, for fundraising events. Verna considered her new title as the "most fun" honor ever bestowed on her, especially since it allowed her the privilege of riding on any fire wagon or official car. Never one to meet a stranger, she made friends among firemen all over the county.

Verna and Spring have fun in a fire engine at Station 38 in Wilmington, California, April 14, 1959.

The following year, another appointment would keep Verna even busier. On February 9, 1960, she was inaugurated as the honorary mayor of North Hollywood during the forty-sixth annual installation banquet of the North Hollywood Chamber of Commerce. The gala event, held at the Sportsmen's Lodge in Studio City, also celebrated local accomplishments of the previous year. Nine past Chamber presidents were present, as was eighty-one-year-old Fred Weddington, an early-day community leader and Valley resident for over sixty years. Verna, herself with more than twenty-two years of North Hollywood residency, had been selected as a perfect choice to fill the position left vacant by outgoing honorary mayor John Raitt. And she did not disappoint.

In fact, in a very short time, Verna was regarded as "just about the greatest public relations factor North Hollywood has ever had." No matter how busy her schedule, she gave graciously of her time to events promoting the Girl Scouts, the North Hollywood Little League and the North Hollywood Business and Professional Women's Club. She also proved herself as a "ribbon cutter par excellence for the openings of new businesses in the city," everything from the Sizzler Steak House and the Golden Do-Nut Shop to the Studio Dodge dealership. On

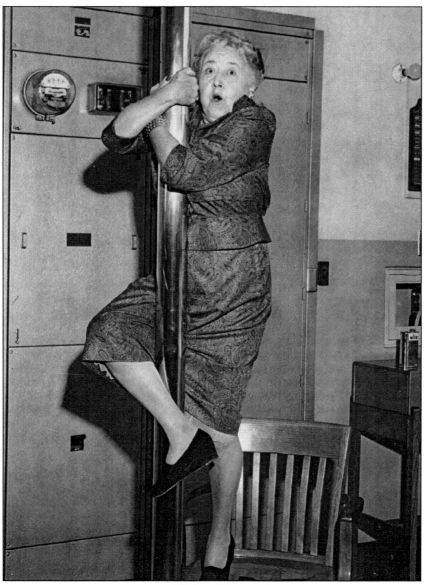

Verna, always fun and obliging for photographers, 1959.

April 5, 1960, when the Ventura Freeway opened, Verna and North Hollywood postmaster Everett Carpenter were among the first to try it out—in a vintage 1910s touring car.

Former Chamber of Commerce president Everett "Barney" Oldfield—not to be confused with the pioneer auto racer of the same name—acted as the public relations director for many of Verna's appearances for the Chamber. A mere two months younger than Verna, Oldfield was a tall and dapper gentleman who drove

Newly inaugurated "mayor" Verna Felton confers at the annual North Hollywood Chamber of Commerce banquet with Russell Quisenberry, seated at left, and B. S. Hand. Standing from left are councilmen Lemoine Blanchard and Everett Burkhalter, new chamber president Everett Carpenter, and William McCann, executive assistant to Los Angeles mayor Norris Poulson, February 9, 1960.

Verna helping break ground for the chapel at St. Joseph's Hospital, Burbank, circa 1962. Walt Disney looks on.

Riding in the 1959 North Hollywood Christmas parade with Lisa and Kate.

her to many of the openings, picnics, and parades, including the famous Santa Claus Lane Parade in downtown Hollywood. Lisa and Kate, as well as the Leff girls, accompanied their grandmother on some of these parades. In fact, during the Hollywood parade, Lisa first realized that a lot of people knew her grandmother: "That was probably the only time I realized that she was famous enough to be doing something like that. But I never felt like she was a celebrity. She didn't have airs, didn't act like she was one, at least around us. I was about six or seven [at the time]." Likewise, at the 1964 parade, Kate, then nine years old, was impressed with her grandmother's celebrity status when they were introduced to child actors Lisa Loring and Ken Weatherwax of *The Addams Family*, who were near them in the parade lineup.

Verna also used her honorary post to promote causes like the International Guiding Eyes, a North Hollywood philanthropic group which donated trained guide dogs to blind persons across the United States. She also participated in a campaign to educate the public about the importance of seat belts. But most enthusiastically, Verna the avid baseball fan, promoted the annual North Hollywood Night at Dodger Stadium. Each summer, the Chamber of Commerce sold game tickets, including round-trip bus transportation from North Hollywood to Chavez Ravine. Verna mugged for local newspaper photographers as she boarded the bus, gave a pep talk to Dodgers manager Walter Alston, and wound up her pitching arm while practicing to throw out the first ball.

Choosing an honorary mayor was a common custom among the local communities in the Los Angeles area. At one time or another, Walter Brennan, Donna Reed, Frank Wilcox, Tippi Hedren, and Amanda Blake, among others, served in similar capacities in locations such as Granada Hills, Panorama City, and Northridge. Some even circulated their positions, serving one year in one place and the following year in another. Actually, Verna had been the honorary mayor of Studio City in 1958, but her schedule of activities then was miniscule compared to the work she would do for the North Hollywood Chamber of Commerce.

As for her mayoral duties, Verna took it all in stride. "The only thing I can't stand are the long speeches women give at their clubs," she once told an interviewer. "I wish they'd come to the point and get it over with." However, she admitted the job had its benefits: "I get an air-conditioned car in the summer and a heated one in the winter to take me to a ground-breaking ceremony or ribbon-cutting. All I have to do is jump out of the car, break the ground or cut the ribbon and jump back in if it's too hot or cold. I'm pretty good with a shovel, but that's hard ground out there."

Near the time of her installation as North Hollywood's honorary mayor, Verna was chosen for another honor. She would be among the 1500 celebrities—past and present—to be initially included in the Hollywood Walk of Fame, a project sponsored by the Hollywood Chamber of Commerce, in cooperation with the Hollywood Property Owners Association and the Hollywood Improvement Association. The Chamber envisioned the new sidewalks as a way to bring back "the buzz of showbiz activity" to Hollywood Boulevard, while preserving the memory of entertainers responsible for putting Hollywood on the map. On February 8, 1960, ground was broken for the Walk of Fame—15,000 feet of charcoal-colored terrazzo sidewalks inset with coral stars, each having the celebrity's name and peripheral outline of the star set in bronze. With an estimated cost of $1.25 million, the Walk of Fame officially opened on November 23 to coincide with Hollywood's annual Santa Claus Lane Parade. Nearly 100,000 persons lined Hollywood Boulevard that night to see grand marshals Roy Rogers and Dale Evans lead the way for more than 200 entertainment personalities—Verna Felton included—riding in the parade. With all the excitement and commotion, it is

Harry Morgan and Verna appear ecstatic about their reunion for the pilot *For Pete's Sake*, 1960.

doubtful Verna even got near the star commemorating her work in television. It had been placed at 1717 Vine Street, between film icon James Dean and producer John Nesbitt. Spring Byington had rated two stars on Hollywood Boulevard: one for motion pictures and another for television.

That same year Spring and Verna each filmed a television pilot. Both had been terribly disappointed when *December Bride* ended and began looking into the possibilities of another regular series, especially Spring who now preferred television over motion pictures. Spring chose *Here Comes Melinda*, a half-hour comedy in which she starred as Melinda Gray, a baby sitter for the Westwood Baby Sitters Service. She described the character to Hedda Hopper as "an ordinary woman who always says, 'Let's see what we can do; let's not be downed by anything.'" Co-starring Charlie Ruggles, the pilot aired in May as "The Sitter's Baby" on an episode of *Goodyear Theater*. However, it failed to attract a sponsor.

The opposite was true of *For Pete's Sake*, the pilot Verna filmed on January 29, 1960. For several years, Parke Levy had believed that Harry Morgan could carry a show of his own; almost as soon as *December Bride* left the airwaves, he put this idea into action. Morgan could easily reprise his popular role of Pete Porter for the spin-off, Levy reasoned, but the series would benefit from an additional familiar face. Verna Felton was the logical choice. As gung ho Hilda, her audience appeal was assuredly bankable. Besides, the sarcastic banter Hilda traded back and forth with Pete on *December Bride* could be amplified on this new series, providing a reliable source of gags. Spin-offs at this time were television rarities, but even more groundbreaking was Levy's idea to utilize two former cast members of a previously cancelled show in a new offshoot. Lily, Matt, and Ruth would be missing this time around, but viewers would finally be introduced to Gladys.

Levy found casting the part a little tricky. "You have never seen Gladys [on *December Bride*]," he once explained, "because I don't know how to cast her. We had a contest to decide who to use in the part and the suggestions ran over such a wide variety that we gave up."

Harry Morgan admitted to the same problem. "I cannot quite visualize [Gladys]. She might be very attractive and probably bigger than I am but very sweet. She'd have to be to accept all the cracks in good faith and not leave me or beat my brains out. She may be a little like Judy Holliday, scatterbrained. But I'd think twice about stepping on her toes. Because she's probably a big girl."

Eventually, an attractive redhead named Cara Williams was selected to play Pete's wife. Ten years Morgan's junior, Brooklyn-born Williams (*nee* Bernice Kamiat) had been a performer for most of her life. A 1961 *TV Guide* profile revealed: "When her parents separated, her mother, believing that her child's liking for dancing and singing and mimicry was an indication of natural talent, hauled her off to California. For a while they lived in a tent, and it was some time before the child's earnings—she did small parts and acted as the voices for caricatures of film stars in Porky Pig cartoons—enabled them to eat normally." Williams began her film career in 1941 as Bernice Kay, but soon adopted the moniker Cara Williams, one she later insisted that she loathed. After twenty films, her main claim to fame was her best-supporting actress Oscar nomination for 1958's *The Defiant Ones* starring Tony Curtis and Sidney Poitier. When *For Pete's Sake* was filmed, Williams was contemplating a divorce from her husband John Drew Barrymore.

Levy hired Bill Manhoff as his co-writer for the pilot's script. Pete Porter's background would remain somewhat the same; he was still an insurance salesman, but he was no longer a father. Baby Linda, introduced in the final season of *December Bride*, would be written out. Gladys would not turn out to be the shrew Pete described during the run of *Bride*. Instead, she was pretty, although a bit daffy. The pilot opened with Pete and Gladys moving into a new house at 2633 Poplar Drive in Westwood. Their neighbor Hilda popped in to welcome them,

Dennis Day tests his mother's strength in "Murder Across the Lunch Counter."

but the next-door neighbor Phil Martin (Bill Heyer) was not so friendly. The remainder of the plot involved a struggle between Pete and Phil, which later affected Gladys's relationship with Phil's French wife Michele. The pilot was long on slapstick, a departure for Morgan whose brand of humor on *Bride* had been mainly verbal.

By April 7, CBS had agreed to add *For Pete's Sake* to its Sunday night line-up, tentatively placing it in the ten o'clock slot, while it courted Bristol-Myers, Inc., as the show's sponsor.

North Hollywood's honorary mayor surrounded by swimmers fresh from the pool, from left, Sandy Leff, Lisa Millar, Kate Millar, Billy Mannara, and Jerry Houser, 1960. Verna's dog Henry makes sure he is not left out of the action.

As Verna waited for production to begin on *For Pete's Sake*, she accepted another guest part as Mrs. Day on *The Jack Benny Program*, now directed by her old friend Frederick de Cordova. "Murder Across the Lunch Counter"—a rewrite of the 1955 telecast in which she had also appeared—was filmed in May by Desilu. Verna's brief scene included a confrontation with Benny after Mrs. Day ("Miss Bulldozer of 1960") throws guest star Dan Duryea out of his dressing room so her son Dennis can have the space. It would be the final time Verna bellowed the character's trademark line, "Aw, Shuddup!" Like many of Benny's shows, this episode was filmed far in advance—it would not air until the following December.

Meanwhile, the summer of 1960 was like most others at 4147 Bakman Avenue. The pool was a lively place, and one of the newest regulars was eight-year-old Jerry Houser, who lived around the corner on Aqua Vista Street. "Miss Felton had the only pool in the neighborhood," recalled Houser. "And you'd figure, here she is, a celebrity, but she was great about it . . . and she'd be there a lot of the times. I remember we knew she was an actress on TV, but I don't know that we knew her credits that well, but we knew she was sort of special. I remember her house perfectly. I remember that she had an electric gate at her driveway, which was always really cool. I thought she must be in the chips! I remember her being warm and very inviting. In those days, there was a lot more neighborhood togetherness." Ten years later, while a student at North Hollywood High, Houser would be discovered by a casting director and signed for a part in the film *Summer of '42*. Other film and television roles would follow, but today Houser is best known for his prolific career as a voice actor. In 1992, he joined the ranks of Verna Felton and other past Disney voice artists when he became a Disney voice talent in the animated feature *Aladdin*.

Since the pool was such a popular place, Verna found it necessary to lay some ground rules. Foremost, the children were to address her as "DeeDee" or "Mrs. Millar," but never as "Verna." Once when Sandy Leff misbehaved, Verna called her down, reminding her that if she wanted to continue swimming, she would have to follow the rules. Sandy sassily retorted, "I don't want to swim in your dumb, dirty pool, *Verna*!" For this serious infraction, the girl was banished from the pool for several days.

Though overly generous with her pool, Verna, naturally, could not allow the entire neighborhood to come into her house for necessities or refreshments. "Of the hundreds of times I went swimming there over many summers, I probably only went in her kitchen only ten times or less," recalled James Simons. "It was not what you were supposed to do. One could readily understand that with five to eight wet kids traipsing through your kitchen, you'd have puddles and puddles." To stop the children from asking Verna or her housekeeper for drinks of water, Lee and Edith installed an outdoor drinking fountain next to the pool.

Debbie Leff maintained that the actress was a "very generous person, but not when it came to food." Although the Leffs and Verna were quite close, Debbie never recalled being offered something to eat at Verna's. She remembered that sometimes Sandy would tell Lisa and Kate to ask their grandmother to fix them all an ice cream cone. "DeeDee would not think of offering us something to eat on her own—she had to be instigated." Debbie also recalled the actress's sparse refreshments when her canasta circle came to play cards. "Dee's housekeeper did not work on the weekends, so on Saturday nights, DeeDee always prepared the same snack—little pizzas made from English muffins, tomato sauce, and mozzarella cheese." On New Year's Eve, when this same group of ladies usually gathered at Verna's, they would end up going down to the Leff's house which they knew would have a bigger spread of food. The Leffs could not completely understand Verna's parsimony when it came to sharing food, but they reasoned it must have stemmed from the lean years of the Great Depression.

Daphne Allen, who as a teenager spent the summer of 1958 as Verna's guest, also recalled Verna's frugality. "When I was living upstairs in the housekeeper's apartment, I made a long distance call to a fellow student at Santa Rosa Junior College. The phone call came to more than sixty dollars. Verna was quite angry, as she was a penny-pincher. I worked off the phone bill by doing some garden maintenance for her."

Verna found other ways to save money. When James Simons was about eleven years old, she hired him to paint her latticed pergola, which was by then in sad disrepair. "I was paid ten or fifteen dollars—to me a princely sum," he said. "It wound up taking about ten hours, but I was a pretty careful worker, even though I did get some white paint on some of the ferns and such, which I felt bad about. She never said anything about it, though. I guess you could say this was a lady who probably didn't want to spend the fifty dollars that it would have taken to hire a professional to do it. She was not lavish, but I don't think she could afford to be. And her life experience taught her it wasn't smart to be that way."

Simons's rationale seems to be right on the mark. Verna had been a freelance artist most of her life; she never knew when the demand for her services might run out. Furthermore, she may have been watching her pennies for a less selfish reason. As one family insider put it, "one of Verna's biggest problems was the fact that Lee wasn't financially secure—without her help. She was pretty good at making sure that he and his family had enough money to live on. She was a very doting grandmother. She bought the girls things and provided for them in many ways. And they loved her and admired her."

For these reasons, Verna was hopeful for the success of her new television series, which began filming in July. Now renamed *Pete and Gladys*, the show's premise was the same, but with a few other crucial tweaks administered by network executives. They saw in Cara Williams the potential to become the "next Lucille Ball." (The more famous redhead had ended her long run on CBS that spring with plans to pursue a career on the stage.) Promoting Williams as such, CBS won over both Goodyear and Carnation Milk as sponsors. Williams, now viewed as more of an equal to Morgan, would take over the plots' zany slapstick routines, while Morgan would essentially assume the role of longsuffering husband. "In *December Bride* I couldn't help but look good," Morgan said. "All I had to do was walk in and shoot my mouth off for five minutes of the best lines, and that was it. But now, I'm on most of a half-hour, which is a lot different."

As for Hilda, the character's exact history with Pete and Gladys was never explained, not even in the pilot. While it was evident that they knew each other previously, no mention was made of Lily Ruskin or the Henshaws. The producers now saw Hilda as a "best friend" figure for Gladys, one who sometimes persuaded Gladys to pursue crazy schemes, without actually getting involved in them

The stars of *Pete and Gladys*: Harry Morgan, Cara Williams, and Verna Felton, summer 1960.

herself. This was a huge switch from the Hilda who aided Lily Ruskin time and again. Still, Hilda traded barbs with Pete, and in effect, became the butt of his jokes, in the same way as his much maligned (but never seen) mother-in-law had been on *December Bride*. Consequently, several columnists reviewed *Pete and Gladys* and referred to Verna as Gladys's mother. "Although I love her like my own mother," said Morgan, "I must, in the interests of accuracy on our show, deny that 'Hilda' is my mother-in-law in *Pete and Gladys*. I awake in fear and trembling when I dream of what kind of mother-in-law probably will be created for me by Parke Levy." Morgan's "fears" would go unrealized; no such character would ever be created. Besides, such comments were intended purely for laughs—unfortunately a rare commodity on the set of *Pete and Gladys*.

"There was a problem with *Pete and Gladys*," recalled Debbie Leff, who sometimes visited dress rehearsals as Verna's guest. "Cara Williams was the meanest person. She was not nice to Verna Felton at all." Nor was the series star compatible with Harry Morgan or Parke Levy. "She was terrible," said Robert Levy, the producer's son. "My dad was afraid to go down to the set half the time because she was just such a bitch. I worked on that show one year as a script supervisor, which all I did was rehearse their lines with them, and [Harry and Cara] wouldn't speak to each other for the whole season. And it's not that unusual, but it just makes it very awkward to work [together] every day. Cara was a great talent, but she was one of those who was her own worst enemy." Indeed, before *Pete and Gladys*, Williams had earned a reputation for her temper and volatility. Most recently, she had clashed with Lauren Bacall and walked out of the 1959 pre-Broadway production of *Goodbye Charlie*. She also walked out on the leading role in a road company of *Born Yesterday*. Even becoming Gladys Porter started with typical Cara Williams fireworks.

Auditioning actresses for the role, Parke Levy finally met Cara and said, "I never heard of you, young lady."

"I never heard of you, either," Cara snapped back.

Soon after the television series first aired, the actress admitted, "I've walked out on success every time. I even started writing a book, *My Climb to Nowhere*. I guess I really never wanted to be a star—until now." Evidently, Williams's newfound drive affected the production right from the beginning. On Levy's personal script for "The Bavarian Wedding Chest," the first episode filmed in July, he wrote, "Cara bitching again."

In this episode, Bill Heyer and Delphine Seyrig appear, as they had in the pilot, as the Porters' next-door neighbors. Inexplicably, they never show up in any subsequent episodes, only to be succeeded by a string of replacements. Whether this casting instability was a result of Williams's abrasive attitude is a matter for speculation, but at least one fellow performer quickly fell prey to the hot-tempered series lead.

Hazel Shermet, who, ironically, had played Gladys eight years earlier on the radio version of *December Bride*, was hired to play Gladys's buddy Pamela for "Gladys Rents the House," an episode co-written by Shermet's husband Larry Rhine. "It went well, and Cara was very pleased and thrilled," recalled Shermet, who was subsequently signed for a second episode—"Oo-La-La"—with the understanding that she would soon be offered a regular contract. "And the next show I did, it was about [Gladys and Pam]. We were going to do a charity thing, doing the French can-can and everything. And in the living room [scene], as part of the story, [my character] had a French song that [she] wanted to do in the show . . . so I sang this very funny French song, and it threw Cara so badly because I got a hand from the crew. And Cara . . . couldn't think of her next line. So they said, 'Do it again, Hazel.' And I did it again, and she couldn't think of her next line. And she said, 'She can't do that song because I can't think of my lines when

Despite the image portrayed in this promotional shot from the episode "Gladys Rents the House," Cara Williams and Verna did not make beautiful music together.

she's finished. It does not belong in the show.' She did *not* want *me* doing anything funny like that, you know. It was *her* show. You can't blame her in a way, you know, but there were going to be lots of [episodes]. This was just one. I was to sign to be on the entire series, you know, to be the neighbor and Cara said she was not going to have . . . competition on her own show . . . so I was devastated."

Verna was not unaccustomed to such temperament. In May, a few months before the strife with Williams began, she told an interviewer, "Youngsters who get a 'star complex' after one or two years in TV make me a little sad. If they only realized the way down is faster than the way up. Look at the actors who have never had star billing but who have worked steadily through the years."

Verna was equally philosophical when her role as Hilda was eventually whittled down to brief, cursory appearances—usually popping in to say hello on her way to the beauty parlor or someplace. Originally, Hilda had occupied more of the storylines, serving as a real buddy to Gladys in early episodes like "Bavarian Wedding Chest," "Movie Bug," and "Oo-La-La." This switch may have had more to do with her increasing problem of memorizing lines. Robert Levy recalled an uncomfortable set when Verna stumbled through "The Handyman," an early episode directed by Jack Arnold:

"Verna had a problem with her memory. Naturally, she was an older woman. And they used to write her lines on the set, underneath a cup of coffee, wherever . . . I remember this one episode, Verna was supposed to come in, and her line was 'Nurse Crocker, reporting for duty' and then she had a couple of lines after that. [According to a script dated June 14, 1960, the actual line was "Nurse Crocker reporting for duty. I hear disaster has struck your tiny house-hold."] She would come in and say, 'Hello, Nurse Crocker reporting for duty, and I'm here to—' and she'd flub the line. And they'd do another take, and they did more and more takes . . . She would remember less and less of the lines . . . It was a mental block. They were begging the director Jack Arnold to break it up, into close-ups or whatever. 'We can't do a master [shot],' they were saying, 'She's not going to get through it . . . and he would not break it up. He sat there . . . in his little chair. He just wanted for some reason—and I was young and I didn't appreciate directing—the coverage master . . . I don't know how many takes they did. I don't remember if they finally gave up or whatever, but I know it was in the twenties. And, you know, you started to feel terrible for her. You knew that she was going to come in, and you hoped that she got half of the stuff right."

Early in the season, Verna was given some physical shtick reminiscent of the *December Bride* days. In "Bavarian Wedding Chest," she valiantly tried to help Pete and Gladys move a monstrous piece of furniture, using her head—encased in a straw hat resembling a bee skep—as a battering ram. But her finest hour was "Oo-La-La," which was telecast on October 24. The script was written by Bob O'Brien, but one would have guessed Lou Derman was behind it—the plot was pure *December Bride*. (Interestingly, Derman and O'Brien would become writing partners on *Mr. Ed* the following year.) As members of the Westwood Women's Civic Club, Gladys and Hilda help put on a charity show which features a can-can as the finale. Gladys asks former professional dancer Collette (Joyce Vanderveen) to lead the number, but her new husband, ex-prizefighter Rocky Murdock (Karl Lukas), forbids it. When she agrees to help without telling her husband, he goes ballistic.

Halfway through the episode, Verna is given a chance to shine in a terrific bit of physical comedy. She also proves herself with a masterful delivery of the scene's lines. Hilda has been put in charge of wardrobe, and Pete meets her, pushing a rack of costumes:

> **PETE**
> Hilda, aren't you going to do anything in the show?

> **HILDA**
> No. I refuse.

> **PETE**
> Why?

> **HILDA**
> They didn't ask me. Thirty-one years in show business
> and they didn't ask me!

> **PETE**
> Thirty-one years?

> **HILDA**
> Yes, and I'll tell you something else.
> Plays were written for me—good plays.

> **PETE**
> Well, of course, that Shakespeare was a great writer.

> **HILDA**
> I'll tell you one thing—you stand right there while I climb
> up on the scaffolding and drop a sandbag on your head!

Meanwhile, Rocky arrives, expecting to find Collette at the dress rehearsal. Gladys asks him to stay and see their number. While Collette hides, another performer fills her dancing shoes: Hilda! Bouncing out in a short can-can costume, the old girl tries to kick her bowed legs as high as the young beauties. Not knowing the routine, she keeps watching their feet, and of course, is always a few steps behind. Rocky snarls, "Hey, what's going on here?" Thinking quickly, Pete covers for the women, "Well, when we couldn't get Collette, we decided to play the number for comedy!" Rocky roars with laughter as Hilda attempts to lower herself to her knees. Once settled, she unabashedly flashes a peek at her black panties. Then, lifting herself up, she twirls around and bends over to give her audience another look. Throughout the scene, it's obvious that Verna was having

Cast members of *December Bride* and *Pete and Gladys* help Parke Levy (RIGHT) celebrate at the wedding of his daughter Linda to Sherman Mickell (LEFT), October 9, 1960. At the bride's left are Cara Williams, Verna, Harry Morgan, and Spring Byington. Mickell wryly observed that the wedding guests paid more attention to the four actors than to the newlyweds.

a field day. Unlike the majority of *Pete and Gladys* episodes which award Cara Williams all the funny bits, "Oo-La-La" is truly an ensemble piece, allowing Morgan, Williams, and Verna to share the limelight more equally.

Even though Verna maintained her "co-starring" status in the opening and closing credits throughout the season, her weekly contributions soon dwindled away. Barbara Stuart as Alice Brown, the wife of Pete's co-worker Howie (Alvy Moore), was featured more prominently as Gladys's confidante. And by January, veteran stage and screen performer Ernest Truex had come aboard as "Pop" Hooper, Gladys's father. Verna and Truex—ten months older than she—shared a common career thread: as children, each had played the lead in *Little Lord Fauntleroy* in stock companies. Truex—appearing in six episodes which would air near the end of the season—was given more to do with his role than Verna ever had. Pop was a likable old fellow, but like his daughter, he tended to get himself into sticky situations, causing heartaches for Pete. On February 2, Parke Levy announced to the press that viewers might expect to see a December-December romance develop between Pop and Hilda, but no such plans ever made it to paper, much less celluloid. However, Lee Millar was featured in small roles on two *Pete and Gladys* episodes co-starring Truex: "The Garage Story" (filmed on January 4) and "Secretary for a Day" (filmed on February 9).

Verna in costume and makeup for the "No Man Is Japan" episode of *Pete and Gladys*.

On February 4, Verna was featured for the fourth time in *TV Guide*—this time as "The Mad Hatter of Television." Since hats were as much a part of Hilda as her hi-jinks, the editors thought it would be fun to feature part of Verna's vast collection. Dancing a little jig, Verna posed for the photographer in front of a white wall hung with seventy-five of Hilda's hats, most of which were either blue, purple, or fussily trimmed in flowers and feathers. The subject of the article had chosen a dress of lavender lace, but perched on her head was a tricornered hat of folded newspaper.

Meanwhile, as the season's end neared, Verna was inexplicably excluded from six of the final episodes filmed. Hilda had originally been included in the scripts for at least two of these—"Gladys Goes to College" and "The Mannequin Story"—but the character was deleted from them before filming began. Viewers may have wondered why Verna's name still appeared on the credits, yet the actress did not show up in the episodes. Later in the year, it became evident that Verna had been released from *Pete and Gladys*.

When the show's second season debuted on September 18, there was no mention of Hilda. The *Los Angeles Mirror*'s Hal Humphrey telephoned Verna for confirmation that "Hilda Crocker, that bumptious old neighbor gal" had been kicked off the block. "Yes, it's true," replied Verna. "After six years, they've decided Hilda didn't belong in the show. Isn't that something? I'd rather not go into detail about it. I'm too old to fight." Levy said Verna was dropped because there was no logical reason for Hilda to be a friend of Gladys Porter, and that viewers believed she was Gladys's mother. Humphrey could see through that flimsy explanation. "Apparently Verna is the victim of that old show biz adage about there being room for only one comic to get laughs in a show," he said. "Somebody else took precedence over Verna."

Unlike *December Bride*, *Pete and Gladys* never made it to the top ten. In fact, it was not among the top twenty-five shows for the 1960-61 season. That fall, eleven new situation comedies had debuted on network television. All would be cancelled at season's end, except three: *The Andy Griffith Show, My Three Sons,* and *Pete and Gladys*. The former two were long running, but *Pete and Gladys* only lasted one additional season. Harry Morgan was tight-lipped about the experience. "Let's say I wasn't sorry to see it end," he later told *TV Guide*. Cara Williams would attempt a comeback with another sitcom, *The Cara Williams Show*, in 1964, but it was a terrific flop. Her career fizzled fast.

For Verna, Hilda's premature demise was a huge disappointment. In November 1960, she had told the *Louisville Courier-Journal* that she hoped to play Hilda for five more years. "After that, I plan to do a series already titled *Miss Rachel*," she announced. "I play a 75-year-old screwball with an 85-year-old girl friend." Both aspirations turned out to be only that. (Most curious is the octogenarian character Verna mentioned. One wonders if she had been inspired by Verna's faithful friend Jane Morgan, who was indeed a decade older than she.)

Nevertheless, Verna scoped out new television guest spots soon after her release from *Pete and Gladys*. First, she reported to the RKO Studios to film an episode of the syndicated *Miami Undercover*, a half-hour crime drama starring Lee Bowman as private detective Jeff Thompson, a troubleshooter hired by the Miami Hotel Owners Association. Bowman's co-star in this low-budget series was former boxing champ Rocky Graziano. In "Cukie Dog," Verna played Aramintha, a wealthy dowager whose pet pug Pekingese is "dognapped" from a canine beauty salon. The old girl pays a $50,000 ransom, and the dog is returned; Jeff is hired to find the snatchers. The episode aired as early as May 27, depending on when local stations chose to air it.

By the time "Cukie Dog" was telecast, Verna was filming her final appearance on *The Jack Benny Program*. Rehearsals for "Dennis's Surprise Birthday Party" began on May 29, with filming being completed on Friday, June 2. Ironically, the script did not call for Verna to share a scene with Benny, nor did it allow Mrs. Day any of her typically bombastic moments. When Benny wants to throw a surprise birthday party for Dennis, he calls a "cease fire" with Mrs. Day in order to solicit her help. On the pretense of discussing a change in Dennis's song for an upcoming Benny show, the star asks Dennis to arrive that evening at Benny's home where all the costumed party guests will be assembled. Dennis, however, sees no need for the song change, and to prove it, he serenades his mother with his choice: "The Boys from the County Armagh." She enthusiastically joins him on the chorus the second time through, but firmly insists that he meet with Benny anyway to discuss the change. Later, after Dennis accidentally discovers the ruse, Mrs. Day—totally out of character—sympathizes with Benny and warns her son, "I'm not going to let you spoil his surprise." She instructs Dennis to attend, but is unaware that the dense young fellow has decided to show up costumed as a leprechaun, thus ruining Benny's evening. By this time, Verna's professional reputation not only afforded her top billing among the other non-regulars on this episode, but her pay also demonstrated her worth—$1,000 for the week. In comparison, supporting players Ann Doran and Bill Walker earned half as much, while Verna's old pal Shirley Mitchell, in the uncredited voiceover role of the telephone operator, received one hundred dollars for one day's work. To put these figures into even sharper perspective, Lee and Edith Millar—just one week earlier—had respectively earned $125 and $100 daily for two days' work on the Benny show when they filmed "Jack Goes to a Cafeteria."

By this time, Lee and Edith's film careers were disappointingly static. In fact, the Jack Benny episode was most likely Edith's final television credit. "She always said she wanted to be God's gift to the American theatre," recalled Kate, "but she didn't quite make it." Besides the *Pilgrimage Play*, Edith had only been associated with one other West Coast stage production—the 1958 ill-fated *Crazy October* starring Tallulah Bankhead. The stage manager had been Ed Strum, a friend of Lee and Edith's from their New York stage days. He recommended Edith as Joan Blondell's understudy. Edith's movie career was equally unimpressive. Her only known film was 1960's *The Apartment*, for which she supplied the off-screen voice of Fred MacMurray's wife. By late 1961, Edith finally redirected her focus. For the past year, her theatrical representative had been her old friend and former New York roommate Louise Winter LaCount, now known as Linda Brittin and employed by the Grady-Towers Agency. When LaCount opened her own business—The Brittin Agency on Cahuenga Boulevard—Edith signed on as a client, but simultaneously became LaCount's business partner. Among the artists they represented were Bill Bixby and Lee Millar, who left Jack Weiner, the agent he had long shared with Verna.

As for Lee, he continued to rely on the residuals from various television bits, mostly playing photographers or reporters—roles for which he'd laughingly warn his daughters, "Don't sneeze, or you'll miss me." In the summer of 1961, when new offers failed to come his way, Lee sought a role in *The Kansas Story*, a musical spectacular produced to commemorate the state's centennial. This huge outdoor extravaganza, performed in both Topeka and Wichita during June and July, depicted the history of Kansas beginning with Spanish exploration and continuing through the first one hundred years of statehood. The production brought together local and national talent under the guidance of director Vladimir Rosing and musical director Meredith Willson, author of *The Music Man*. Lee was part of the eleven-member vocal cast recruited from California, including his writing partner Wayne Hamilton and William A. Forester, the husband of actress Reta Shaw. Assembled in a trailer offstage and invisible to the audience, the sound cast spoke into microphones while the actors onstage lip-synched the lines. The resulting performance was quite impressive. As one spectator recalled, "There was a cast of one thousand. There were seven different stages. There were lights shining down on it all. It was almost like watching parades go across different stages. Here go the cowboys and here go the Conestoga wagons with their pioneers and here go the Conquistadors in their Spanish garb, and I remember thinking it was great." Lee would later equate his month-long stay in Kansas with Verna's experience when she filmed *Picnic*: the locals treated him like royalty.

Soon after Lee's return to California, Verna hosted one of Pearl Allen's great-nephews for a lengthy stay. Although all of Pearl's siblings were deceased, Verna kept in touch with the younger generations of the Allen family, some of whom still resided in Pearl's native Chico. Twenty-year-old Clyde Allen Bowman Jr., the grandson of Pearl's youngest sister Meda, was one of them. A hopeful actor, Bowman came south intent on breaking into the entertainment industry. Until he established himself in a regular job, there seemed no better place to stay than the home of a sixty-year veteran with whom he shared a family connection. Since her housekeeper occupied the upstairs apartment, Verna ensconced Clyde in the guesthouse by the pool. Meanwhile, he took acting lessons from her friend Lurene Tuttle in her apartment right off Sunset Boulevard in Hollywood.

For several months in the summer and fall of 1961, Clyde was privy to the dynamics of the Millar household on Bakman Avenue. He quickly developed a firm and fast admiration for his hostess, but this was only natural—Verna Felton enjoyed being around people. "I spent quite a bit of time with her for a short while. She was quite a lady," Clyde recalled. Even after he moved into an apartment in Burbank, Clyde regularly visited Verna. "We went to dinner several times a week, and I drove her a lot of places because she was getting older and she didn't like to drive too far. She would drive to the store and all that stuff, but when it came to driving [outside North Hollywood], I would drive. I'd take her out to visit friends at the actors' home in Woodland Hills, take her shopping, and we went over to the studios a few times . . . Verna had kind of a routinized lifestyle.

A lady came over and gave her a massage once or twice a month, in the afternoons. When Verna would have her dinner at night, sometimes I was there, and sometimes other people were there. A lot of times I guess she was alone, except for the housekeeper. I remember she spent a lot of time going next door to see the girls Lisa and Kate . . . Whenever Lee used to come into Verna's back door, he'd say, 'Hey, Ma, are you home?' They seemed to get along fine . . . Edith's mother would stop by quite often, once or twice a week. She'd stop by, and they'd have a cocktail. They got along famously . . . Not too many actors came to the house, outside of the McNears. The ones that were always going in and out of the house were the Leffs, her granddaughters, and the McNears. I don't remember anyone else coming in, except the women she played cards with."

For several years before Clyde's extended stay, Eva Liston Barwick had served as Verna's housekeeper and cook. Widowed since 1952, she had been a resident of southern California for almost twenty-five years. Eva was born a farmer's daughter on November 11, 1897, in that part of Indian Territory which later became Oklahoma. As a young lady, she moved to Kansas City, Missouri, where she obtained a job as clerk for the local telephone company. There, she met Maurice Barwick, a dairy sales manager, whom she married in Los Angeles in 1937. While Barwick established himself in a printing business, his wife settled into the life of a Burbank homemaker. The couple had no children, so when Eva became widowed, she looked for a position to support herself until reaching retirement age. As Verna's housekeeper and cook, she was given weekends off, but otherwise, she prepared all the meals at 4147 Bakman Avenue. "I recall her cooking meat, potatoes, and vegetables—generally wholesome food, but not really fancy fare," offered Clyde Bowman. "Eva became more of a companion than a housekeeper," remembered Debbie Leff. "She ate dinner with DeeDee, and she went shopping with her."

Clyde and Debbie each remembered some of Verna's dietary preferences. "I know that Verna liked barbecued food—grilled meats, steaks, and chicken," Clyde said. Debbie reminisced about her neighbor's ever-ready supply of chocolate-covered raisins, pickled watermelon rind, and Limburger cheese, kept in a refrigerator container labeled "Stinky Cheese" with a figural mouse on top. At Christmastime, she enjoyed making fondants using fresh dates she bought at the local farmers' market. While Debbie recalled Verna's fondness for Old Fashioneds, Clyde instead remembered her before-dinner gimlets. "She also bought a case of Budweiser twelve-ounce cans from the store about every other week," he said. "She quite often had a beer—only one—and watched some TV in the living room before retiring for the night."

There was no television in Verna's guesthouse, so Clyde often watched programs with Verna in the evenings. "She watched *Dr. Kildare* with Richard Chamberlain regularly. She also liked *Ben Casey*. Doctor shows were big with her. She watched several things on daytime TV, and she especially liked [fitness guru] Jack LaLanne. I don't think she was a real night owl. She watched TV until after the news—10:30 p.m. or so—and retired. Sometimes she would retire early if she was going to the studio."

As Verna and Clyde watched various television programs, he would ask her about certain actors and directors. "I know that she and Cara Williams didn't get along, but I don't know if that was the reason that Verna was not on the second season [of *Pete and Gladys*]. She said Cara Williams was not a very nice person. And I know that Verna and Harry Morgan were troupers from way back. And apparently Cara Williams had an ego trip and was pretty much an insecure person. I remember that [Verna] did not like Cara Williams very much. Verna did not talk a whole lot about Spring Byington, but she liked Spring Byington. I think that they had a professional relationship that was very cordial. They had a mutual respect for each other."

During Clyde's stay, *December Bride* reruns were being broadcast daily, while repeats of the first season of *Pete and Gladys* were aired each Monday evening that summer. Consequently, Verna was still very much a part of the television scene. "When I would take her places—whether it was to the doctor or running errands—everywhere we went, people would just stream over to talk to her. She'd always take time to stop and talk to people. And she had such a distinctive voice that sometimes she would go into places and start talking, and people would look up and then come flocking over—because even though they didn't see her, they knew who she was because her voice had such a different quality. So she would stop and talk with everybody. In fact, she loved it. Verna was very down-to-earth."

Even Verna's automobile was unostentatious: a brown-and-white 1957 Ford Fairlane coupe. Clyde explained, "At that time, most Hollywood personalities drove inconspicuous cars. There was a big thing about 'reverse status symbols' during this period. I remember Lurene Tuttle telling me that her business manager hit the roof when she bought a new red 1962 Chevrolet convertible."

Clyde often drove Verna's Fairlane when they went out to dinner. Verna enjoyed Italian food, especially pasta. "We also went several times to her favorite Mexican restaurant on Ventura Boulevard. It had no beer or wine license, but the owner had no problem with us bringing our own beer in. There was a liquor store a few doors down where we bought Budweiser and took it in. The owner doted on Verna as one of his best customers."

Clyde, however, was not around one afternoon that summer when several NBC-TV trucks pulled up in front of Verna's home and a crew of a dozen men began unloading lighting equipment, reflector boards, and cameras. The actress had been selected as one of the celebrity interviews on a popular daytime half-hour show called *Here's Hollywood*, which was hosted by her fellow *December Bride* alum Dean Miller. Debuting in September 1960, the show stuck close to home during its first season but began tracking stars across the globe the following spring. Previous to arriving at Verna's that summer, Miller had interviewed Paul Newman, JoAnn Woodward, and Louis Armstrong in Paris, as well as Yves Montand and Shirley MacLaine in Tokyo. The foreign assignments were not all work, though, because they also served as part of Miller's honeymoon itinerary. On June 9, he had wed his Ohio hometown honey, Ida Wagner.

Miller suggested Verna to producer Pier Oppenheimer as a possible subject for *Here's Hollywood*. But what would they discuss? The veteran actress had no film or television roles lined up. Miller, who had experienced firsthand Verna's joy for living, explained that the angle could be her plan for staying young. Since it was summertime, and Verna enjoyed her pool so much, Miller and Oppenheimer thought it best to interview her at poolside, and perhaps even show her swimming. Verna was game. To amplify her youthfulness, they told her to invite all the neighborhood kids to frolic around her in the water—just as it was on any other summer day. James Simons, then fifteen years old, remembered being impressed with the trucks crowding their normally quiet street: "There was a lot of excitement amongst the kids. We got to be extras in a television show." Naturally, Lisa and Kate were part of the action, too, as well as Henry, Verna's dog.

Clyde Bowman saw the show when it was telecast the week of September 6: "As the show opened, Dean Miller said, 'Here we are at the home of Verna Felton. Let's go in and see if she's here. And you didn't see her, but you heard her go 'Yoo Hoo!' And the camera followed the sound of her voice, and there she was, sitting on top of the slide at her pool. And then she goes down the slide and into the pool. And she had a bathing cap on, so then she swims to the edge and gets out of the pool. And by the time they come back [from the commercial break], she's dried off, and they're sitting out in the yard by the guesthouse for the interview. What they discussed, I don't remember, but I thought her stunt was so typical of who she was because, you know, Verna was just like her character on *December Bride* and *Pete and Gladys*—she wasn't a little old lady who just sat around being a little old lady. Remember the way she played off Spring Byington? She was kind of like Spring Byington's alter ego, doing all these stunts. And Verna was that way every day. Totally unpretentious—the same on or off camera. And her voice was the same, and her voice inflections were the same. I know that even when she was serious, she still sounded like Hilda. You know, like when she was talking about something serious—like when we would go out to the Motion Picture Country Home, and she would see some of her friends out there, which was at times a sobering thing. But it was still her! She was an unforgettable person, unforgettable."

With no acting assignments on the horizon, Verna enjoyed a leisurely summer with Lisa and Kate that year. Kate described a typical day in what was to be her grandmother's sunset years: "We kind of took off our shoes and put on our bathing suits at the beginning of summer and took them off at the end of the summer. [We] spent a lot of time in the pool. And she spent a lot of time in there with us, playing. It was relaxing. She would have a huge barbecue-type party for her birthday in July . . . She used to take us when she went shopping in downtown North Hollywood. There was a place called Rathbun's Department Store and

Verna (wearing orchid) surrounded by friends gathered at poolside for her
birthday in 1962. Seated in the foreground, left to right, are Howard McNear,
Katie Robinson, Eddie Strum, Helen Rourke, Lee Millar, and Wayne Hamilton.
Standing directly behind them, left to right, are Kate Millar, Mary Edith Stahl,
Gertie Virden, Verna, Jane Morgan, and two unidentified friends. In the rear,
left to right, are Violet MacKaye, Grace Simmons, Clyde Bowman Jr., Edith
Millar, Lisa Millar, and an unidentified friend.

the May Company, as well as little stores on Tujunga—that was where her jewelry
store was. We went there a lot." Lisa also remembered going with her grandmother
and her dog Henry to get ice cream. "I remember her as being lots of fun! To me,
she was a lot like 'Hilda.' "

Verna allowed the girls to play dress-up with her costumes. "There was a very small room in the guesthouse, which had originally been Lisa's nursery," recalled Kate. "And then they turned it into a storage room. We always called it 'the Hilda room.' On one wall were sliding doors with shelves behind them with all her hats on them. And on the other side were closets with all these wardrobe bags that you could get six dresses in. She also had one for her shoes. It was amazing. And we would get in there and try on all of her clothes and jewelry and hats." Lisa laughed, "Everything she wore and used for that role was in that room—it was just called 'the Hilda room.'"

Around this time, Edith had hired a strict Costa Rican housekeeper who watched after the girls in their parents' absence. The woman took it upon herself to discipline the girls severely. Once she hit Kate in the mouth with a hairbrush, but the girls were scared to tell anyone else because the housekeeper threatened to beat them more if they did. When Verna noticed Kate's swollen lip, she asked what caused it. "I had to lie," said Kate. "I had to tell her that I fell over this little step by the gate that went between the two houses. And we went out there with a shovel, and she fixed it. I felt so bad because I had lied to her." Later, Kate summoned the nerve to tell Verna, whispering the truth into her grandmother's ear. "Oh, she got mad!" Kate said. Needless to say, Verna's ire led to the termination of that housekeeper.

In the fall of 1961, Verna received an acting offer she could not refuse. In fact, she considered it a gravy train. She would not be required to memorize lines, hit her marks on the soundstage floor, or wear stage makeup. Only her unmistakable voice was needed. On November 6, Verna became Fred Flintstone's mother-in-law.

Produced by William Hanna and Joseph Barbera, *The Flintstones* was the first prime-time cartoon series made especially for television. During its first season (1960-61), the ABC series had landed a spot in the top twenty. Set in the Stone Age, *The Flintstones* was often referred to as an animated version of *The Honeymooners*, but years later, hardly anyone involved with the show agreed on its actual inception. As for the caveman angle, comic strips like "Alley Oop" had been around for years. Verna, especially, knew that the concept was nothing new. In 1933, she had been a leading player in *The Mud Caves*, a radio serial in which the caveman characters grappled with everyday problems.

The Flintstones would reunite Verna with four co-workers from her radio days. Alan Reed, with whom she had appeared on radio's *December Bride*, supplied the booming voice of quarry worker Fred Flintstone. Jean Vander Pyl, a *Lux Radio Theatre* alum, provided the voice of Fred's longsuffering wife Wilma. Mel Blanc, with whom Verna had worked most closely on *The Judy Canova Show*, was next-door neighbor Barney Rubble, while Bea Benaderet, Verna's friend and co-worker in a multitude of radio series—including *Tommy Riggs and Betty Lou*—gave voice to Barney's wife Betty.

Fred Flintstone was at times a chauvinistic blowhard, but he met his match in "Trouble-in-Law," the episode which introduced Mrs. Slaghoople, his domineering

Friends gather in Verna's lavender living room, Christmas 1961. Verna (REAR CENTER) is flanked by Grace Simmons (LEFT) and Violet MacKaye. Seated are Helen Rourke and Myme James. On the floor (LEFT) is Hazel Delphine. The others are unidentified friends.

mother-in-law, played by Verna. If the plot perhaps seemed a little familiar to Verna, then it was only natural. "Trouble-in-Law" could be described as a meld of two *December Bride* episodes: "Lily Ruskin Arrives" and "The Texas Show Part One." When Fred learns that Mrs. Slaghoople has sold her home to move in with Wilma and him, he desperately tries his hand at matchmaking. He introduces his mother-in-law to Melville J. Muchrocks, a wealthy Texas rancher, and it's love at first sight. Later, when Wilma overhears that a con man posing as a wealthy Texan is preying on women in town, Fred and Barney kidnap Muchrocks and throw him on an outbound train. Mrs. Slaghoople is heartbroken and begins making Fred's life miserable. Things change when she gets a check from the oil well her erstwhile suitor had her invest in. After quickly packing her bags, she sets off to locate and lasso her old beau. A jubilant Fred lifts her luggage too eagerly and hurts his back in the process, so Mrs. Slaghoople decides to remain there to help him recuperate.

Verna evidently had a field day with the battleaxe part of Mrs. Slaghoople. Dropping her voice into a lower register—even lower than that of Mrs. Day—Verna used volume and vitality to bring the old buffalo to life, but with a remarkable range. In the amusement park scene, she's delightfully giddy when riding the roller coaster with her sweetie, but she is equally effective later when squalling over his sudden disappearance. Even though her name was not included among the final credits, viewers would have had no trouble identifying the source of that famous voice. Even the animated character resembled Verna, except for the familiar red topknot she shared with daughter Wilma.

In December, Verna joined the ensemble cast of the one-hour television special *Henry Fonda and the Family*, a comedy review produced by Bud Yorkin and Norman Lear. Taped in front of a live audience, Fonda presented a series of sketches which one reviewer described as "a peeping-tom survey of the American family in its native habitat, the suburbs." Yorkin and Lear conceived the idea earlier in the year. "The whole project is unique for television these days," said Yorkin. "First came the idea, then the sale, then the script and, finally, casting." Since the production featured four actors starring in weekly television series, rehearsals and the taping were scheduled late in the month when most companies had shut down for the holidays. Dick Van Dyke, Dan Blocker, Cara Williams, Paul Lynde, Carol Lynley, Michael J. Pollard, and Verna were all chosen to fill comedy roles. Ironically, the experience brought together three members of the Broadway cast of *Bye Bye Birdie*—Van Dyke, Lynde, and Pollard, not to mention what might have been an uncomfortable reunion for Verna and Cara Williams. If there were any fireworks on the set, director Yorkin must have squelched them. "Everything has worked out fine," he told *TV Magazine*. "No cast feuds, no problems about roles, no troubles at all."

Verna appeared in three brief sketches. In "Father and Son," a mechanically challenged Lynde—in his typically prissy manner—tries to repair his little son's bicycle. When he accidentally cuts his finger, he cries for his unsympathetic mother, Verna. "Would you like to have me kiss it first and make it all well?" she coos sarcastically. To which he deadpans, "If there's anything I can't stand it's a smarty-pants old woman." Another sketch, focusing on America's senior citizens, featured Verna as the granddaughter of a 104-year-old man, played by Van Dyke. Later, Verna plays the frustrated mother of Lynde who is obsessed with his home movie camera. ("You better look out, or I'm going to *zoom in* on you!" she tells him.) While they are picnicking, he insists that she strike a candid pose after stumbling on a rattlesnake. The chemistry between Verna and Lynde were among highlights of this mildly comic spoof.

Henry Fonda and the Family aired on CBS on Tuesday, February 6, 1962. The following evening, Verna appeared in minor role on *Wagon Train*, the number-one rated show on television that season. In "The Lonnie Fallon Story," a young cowboy (Gary Clarke) is smitten with pretty Kathy Jennings (Lynn Loring), but her father (Frank Overton) disapproves of the match. Jennings is taking Kathy to

The cast of *Henry Fonda and the Family*. Front, left to right, are Carol Lynley, Henry Fonda, Marianne Finney, Verna Felton, Flip Mark, and Michael J. Pollard. Standing, left to right, are Dick Van Dyke, Cara Williams, Paul Lynde, and Dan Blocker.

California, and he warns Fallon that if he attempts to follow the wagon train, he will shoot him. Jennings does not know that Kathy is already married to Fallon and expecting his child. Verna played Kathy's taciturn grandmother who secretly gave the young couple consent to marry. Near the episode's conclusion, she speaks up to reveal the true story.

Meanwhile, Clyde Bowman had not only found work in radio production at KMPC in Los Angeles, but he had also decided to marry nursing student Ruth Okuda in a ceremony planned for February 10 in Chico. That weekend, Verna flew to San Francisco where Clyde's sister JoAnn and her husband were waiting in the airport to drive her the rest of the way to Chico. "She was quite a character," JoAnn Mondon recalled. "We knew which flight she was on. All the people got off the flight and came down the escalator, and we didn't see her. So we thought, 'Oh, dear.' It was pouring down rain, and we thought maybe she didn't make it or something. About that time, we heard a big racket and a lot of people. And this whole big gang of people was coming down the escalator, and Verna was in the middle of them. People had recognized her and started following her. So when she got down the escalator, she came over to us. She had on a really expensive fur

Henry Fonda interviews the granddaughter of a 104-year-old man on *Henry Fonda and the Family.*

coat, and over that she had a plastic raincoat with a big safety pin holding it shut. That's the way she was—totally unpretentious."

On the three-hour drive to Chico, Verna entertained JoAnn and her husband with tales of moviemaking, particularly about her latest film, *Guns of the Timberland.* She related the now fabled stories of Alan Ladd's lack of height and how he positioned himself on orange crates to appear taller than his leading ladies. "We were driving over near Orland, out in the rice fields," recalled JoAnn, "and a pheasant flew out in front of us. We smacked him a good one, and we were kind of half-sick about it—the feathers were flying. So the following Christmas, Verna sent me a Christmas card. And in it, she said, 'I almost had a pheasant, but it got away.' She had a good sense of humor about a lot of things."

Verna was particularly amused by the reception she received at JoAnn and Clyde's parents' home in Chico. "My parents' grandkids or somebody went out and told the neighborhood kids that 'Hilda' was there. So the next thing we know, here's all these kids with binoculars looking into our house from the back yard! It was quite the talk of the neighborhood that Verna had come up for the wedding. That was quite a weekend."

Once Verna returned to southern California, a few acting assignments dribbled in. She appeared on the April 26 telecast of another top-twenty television series: *My Three Sons.* Fred MacMurray starred as widower Steve Douglas who was raising sons Mike, Robbie, and Chip, but with the help of the boys' "all-bark-and-no-bite" grandfather Bub (William Frawley). In "Coincidence," Steve Douglas stumbles upon another household of five that closely mirrors his own in regards to names,

Verna (RIGHT) visiting with JoAnn Mondon (LEFT) at the home of Louella and Clyde Bowman Sr. (CENTER), Chico, California, 1962.

ages, and dispositions—except this family is all females. The grandmother Mub (Verna) barks orders to her granddaughters, just as her male counterpart Bub does in his household. The teenage girls have boy problems, just as the reverse is true for Mike and Robbie Douglas. And the girls' mother tries to keep her calm amid all the confusion, just as stalwart Steve Douglas does in his own home. Although the episode was not fraught with humor, its touch of surrealism made it a fan favorite in later years. Verna moves rather slowly and carefully as she comes down a staircase, but she packs appropriate force into her lines as the grouchy Mub. Surprisingly, she was billed as the episode's "special guest star," even though her time onscreen barely amounted to sixty seconds.

Ironically, on Verna's next project she was not given any screen credit for the first time in over twenty years. This oversight can only be explained by the overall inferiority of the production itself. *The Man from Button Willow* was the creation of actor Dale Robertson, best known for his roles in movie westerns and the NBC series *Tales of Wells Fargo*, now near the end of its six-season run. Robertson had recently formed his own production company to handle his film, television, and personal appearance activities, but his pet project was an animated feature about the legendary exploits of Justin Eagle, the first United States government agent. The title—not even remotely related to Eagle—was chosen by Robertson who was charmed by the picturesque name of Buttonwillow, a small settlement twenty-five miles outside of Bakersfield, California.

Envisioning a western tale suitable for the entire family, the naïve Robertson thought the production of an animated feature was "merely a matter of getting script writers, a director, animators, and actors to supply the voices." When production began in 1962, he had no idea it would take three years to get the film to the screen. Robertson hired David Detiege—an animation writer for Disney shorts who had graduated to Bugs Bunny and Mr. Magoo—to write and direct *The Man from Button Willow*. The producer was Detiege's wife, Phyllis Bounds, the niece of Walt Disney's wife Lillian. Several former Disney and Warner Brothers animators also worked on the film. Robertson, who provided the voice of the title character, was joined by a bevy of veteran voice actors, including Verna, Barbara Jean Wong, Clarence Nash, Herschel Bernardi, Shep Menken, and Pinto Colvig. Film actor Edgar Buchanan, frequently seen in westerns, played Eagle's rustic sidekick.

Verna voiced three *Button Willow* roles: the doctor's hawk-nosed wife, a San Francisco cable-car passenger, and Mrs. Pomeroy, a plump middle-aged widow with eyes for Justin Eagle. As the self-appointed leader of the town's Ladies Monday Afternoon Knitting, Social, and Discussion Club, Mrs. Pomeroy approaches Eagle with an ingratiating offer—she thinks she is the perfect candidate as surrogate mother to his juvenile Chinese ward (Barbara Jean Wong). This role gives Verna a choice opportunity to demonstrate the mastery of her craft, and she does not disappoint. Beginning with a voice gushing with insincere flattery and transparent pomposity, she deflates with indignant disgust when Eagle quietly refuses her proposal.

The main action of *The Man from Button Willow*, though, revolves around a much more serious problem. As railroads expanded to the west, unscrupulous land speculators took advantage of the situation by buying up the necessary land and selling it back at a profit. The United States government sent Senate investigators to put a stop to this, sometimes employing the use of an undercover man like Justin Eagle. Had filmmakers stuck to this story, *The Man from Button Willow* might have been more successful. Instead, they injected songs and tedious slapstick sequences involving a multitude of animals, all of which bogged down a solid plot.

In addition, Robertson had too many irons in the fire. During *Button Willow*'s production, he was filming three live-action features, including one on location in Africa. *Button Willow* had been originally slated for a June 1963 release, but was then postponed until Thanksgiving that year, finally reaching theaters in April 1965. By that time, Verna and the rest of the cast had given up wondering what had happened to it.

When interviewed by Marty Halperin in February 1964, Verna was still hopeful for the success of *The Man from Button Willow*. While the animation was far from Disney quality, she was impressed particularly by a sequence she had been shown depicting a horse fighting a mountain lion. Furthermore, she had been led to believe that Robertson was serious about producing an animated television series for children—a possibility that Verna would find increasingly appealing.

Composite scene of *The Man from Button Willow* characters created to serve as Dale Robertson's Christmas card to his friends, 1962.

Meanwhile, Verna's successful guest spot on *The Flintstones*, which had aired on March 16, 1962, brought her an offer to reprise the role of Mrs. Slaghoople. She returned to the studio on the evening of May 9 to record "The Little Stranger," an episode created by former *December Bride* writer Herb Finn. Though Verna was quite effective once again as Wilma's no-nonsense mother, her contribution was almost incidental, being brought in for the final five minutes of the episode. After Fred overhears Wilma mentioning "a little visitor," he thinks she is pregnant and begins treating her like a queen. When he learns that a baby nurse could cost eight dollars a day, skinflint Fred—hoping to save money—telephones his mother-in-law to invite her for a long visit. Not until after her arrival, Fred learns "the little stranger" is a neighborhood kid whom Wilma has agreed to keep while his parents go on vacation.

Much of the subsequent summer was involved with Verna's new investment: a house at Laguna Beach. For some time previous, she had owned a mobile home on a rise overlooking the ocean in this town some sixty miles from North Hollywood. In July, Verna decided to purchase a more permanent summer retreat, and the gray house at 261 San Joaquin Street suited her just fine. Even before Verna was born, Laguna Beach—detailed by one historian as "a small, flat basin surrounded by steep cliffs, water-etched coves, and rolling hills"—was a tourist town where vacationers sought relief from inland heat. At one time, film stars like Mary Pickford, Rudolph Valentino, Charlie Chaplin, and later Judy Garland, Bette Davis, and Mickey Rooney maintained homes there. By the 1960s, Laguna Beach boasted a thriving artist colony. Though Verna's family enjoyed the use of her pool, they delighted in the seashore retreat. Lee, especially, frequented his mother's beach house, located just off the Pacific Coast Highway.

Verna's carefree summer schedule was interrupted twice near season's end when Hanna-Barbera called her to record two additional episodes of *The Flintstones*.

On August 30, she voiced Mrs. Slaghoople for the third time in "Foxy Grandma." Similar to her previous appearance, Verna's input was not needed until the final moments of the program when Mrs. Slaghoople saves Fred and Wilma by tossing out two bank robbers who have been holding them hostage at home. On September 7, in "Mother-in-Law's Visit," Mrs. Slaghoople was more central to the story when expectant father Fred tries—unsuccessfully—to please the old grouch. He takes a job as a cab driver—disguised in a cap and bushy moustache—to earn money for a baby crib. His first passenger is his suspicious mother-in-law who thinks "that tub of lard" is out carousing. They end up spending the evening together, searching for Fred. Finally, he bets Mrs. Slaghoople that she will find her son-in-law in the library. She, of course, disagrees. Fred races into the reading room, pulls off his disguise, and allows her to find him perusing books on baby care. The old lady admits she has misjudged Fred and makes amends—until Barney Rubble blows Fred's cover about the cabbie's true identity. While Verna is more than competent in this, her final *Flintstones* offering, her performance somehow lacks the spark of the previous ones, especially the more enjoyable "Trouble-in-Law."

By this point, Verna's increased difficulty with memorizing lines made assignments like *The Flintstones* more appealing—voice work allowed her to rely on the script in her hand. Besides, these assignments reminded her of the golden days in radio, which she still missed. Nevertheless, in the fall of 1962, Verna accepted a guest part on the popular television sitcom *Dennis the Menace*. It would prove to be a most unhappy experience, one that would sour her on television work for the rest of her life.

Verna later discussed the episode—"Aunt Emma Visits the Wilsons"—with Marty Halperin: "It was supposed to be a Christmas show, and we rehearsed all day on Wednesday. And on Thursday while we were rehearsing—about six o'clock—they called up and said, 'Disregard the script. We're not going to do a Christmas show.' Friday, we got there, and they started [with] this other [script]. So we [rehearsed] it through, went home, studied it some more. [We] got there the next morning, and they said they didn't like this [new] script, so they said, 'Give me that.' And [it was replaced by a third one]. Later that day—on the last day of filming—we were sitting, reading the last few lines, and they came in and handed to me *nineteen* pages of manuscript. And I said, 'What's that for?' And they said, 'Well, don't pay any attention to what you've got—just throw it out.' And I said, 'I'm going to do this now in place of the others?' They said yes, so I said, 'Then pull up the idiot board because I *cannot* deal with it. Just put up the idiot board! If you think [that] I can think of dresses and changes and new lines at this point . . . it's *impossible* to [learn] this.' And it wasn't possible for *anybody* to do. So they had to put the idiot board up so that we could get out—they wanted to get out—we got off about at eight o'clock at night. But [writers] don't think [the] way [an actor does]. They've worked on [the script], and as they've worked, they memorized it, but *we haven't*!"

Verna's frustration with the *Dennis the Menace* script dilemma is clearly reflected in her performance as the wealthy aunt of John Wilson (Gale Gordon). For a role that should have been filled with bombastic vigor, Verna disappoints those viewers familiar with her past capability for such characters. A few times, her voice is almost strong enough to suit, but her facial expressions lack the necessary spark. And there are brief glimpses of Verna's customary delivery, but it's like Hilda in slow motion. Standing between the robust Gordon and statuesque Sara Seegar—playing his wife—Verna even appears to have physically shrunk since her vibrant days on *December Bride*. The script calls for her to hit it off with Dennis (Jay North), but even their scenes lack spunk. She is obviously reading cue cards in one as they discuss Dennis's prized bug collection. All in all, it is a sad sitcom swan song for Verna. The show's producers were evidently displeased with the final product: they chose to air it as the final first-run episode of the series, buried in the middle of July 1963 reruns.

After this fiasco, Verna resolved not to pursue any more live-action roles. Instead, she preferred to wait for more opportunities to record for *The Flintstones* or other cartoons. The wait lasted perhaps longer than she had imagined. On June 29, 1963, she wrote to Nancy Felton Koster, a distant relative living in Newcastle, California, who had just published an updated family history: "Forgive me for not writing sooner but was away on vacation . . . We have a home in Laguna now, so slip away when we can, right near the beach. Things in T.V. are very slow, nothing much in sight for next year. But the re-runs help a lot."

Around this time, Verna resorted to auditioning for television commercials, but she needed assistance getting back and forth to the studios. She had not driven since the fall of 1962 when she gave her car keys to Debbie Leff as a birthday present. Now sixteen, Debbie had earned her driver's license and happily became Verna's chauffeur. Debbie remembered taking her to one audition—for Parson's Ammonia—but, infortunately, Verna was not selected as the product's spokesperson.

In late July, Verna experienced more disappointment when it became evident that she would not reprise her role as Mrs. Slaghoople on upcoming episodes of *The Flintstones*. For whatever reason, the part had been taken over by voice actress Janet Waldo, who was then providing the voice of teenager Judy Jetson on Hanna-Barbera's *The Jetsons*. Thirty-nine-year-old Waldo had worked with Verna many times during their radio careers, but in 2005, when questioned by the author as to why Verna was replaced, the actress was clueless. In fact, not only was Waldo unaware that Verna had preceded her in the part of Wilma Flintstone's mother, but she also mistakenly believed that Verna had died prior to the advent of Waldo's cartoon career. (Waldo still held Verna in high regard: "Not only was she a brilliant actress but a remarkable person. I still have on my kitchen sink an adorable china rooster—combination coffee, cream, and sugar piece—that she gave me for my bridal shower.")

In late August, Verna conceded to appear in a bit part on a Bob Hope television special, which boasted Dean Martin, Barbra Streisand, James Garner, and

Bob Hope embraces Verna during a rehearsal of his comedy special, 1963.

Tuesday Weld as Hope's guests. Ever since Verna's appearances on Hope's radio show a decade earlier, the comedian had regarded her as one of his favorite character actresses. In fact, he had requested her once before for a television special—back in February 1954 when she played an old harridan of a landlady. For the 1963 special, Hope's opening sketch paired him with Weld as a couple of married actors whose shows air at the same time on competing networks. One evening as they watch television, the phone rings, and their maid—Verna— enters to answer it. When she tells them that a representative from the Neilsen Ratings is on the line, the stars grapple for the receiver, at which point Verna intercepts it and yells into the mouthpiece, "I don't know who they're looking at, but I'm watching *The Flintstones!*" Perhaps Hope's writers had chosen the cartoon show for this punchline without knowing Verna's connection to it, or perhaps not. After she delivers the jab, Verna gives Hope what could be interpreted as a knowing wink and exits. Whatever the case, when the special aired on September 27, it would mark the last time Verna would enact any role on television. Almost two weeks later, Fairfax Nisbet of the *Dallas Morning News* reported that Verna would soon make "a rare TV appearance on one of the Bob Hope drama series episodes." However, no available credits for *Bob Hope Presents the Chrysler Theatre* reveal that Verna fulfilled Nisbet's prophecy. It is quite likely that Hope extended the invitation, however.

During the dry spell that had begun with Verna's departure from *Pete and Gladys*, Verna proved she was not averse to appearing on television game shows. At least they would not require the memorization of lines. In 1961, she had appeared on *About Faces*, which featured pairs of contestants whose paths had crossed previously—the first contestant to recall their association won a prize. In the fall of 1963, Verna was asked to appear on NBC's *Your First Impression*, a daytime show with a panel of three celebrities who tried to guess the identity of mystery guests. For Verna's segment, she would pose with three young girls, only one of whom would be her real granddaughter. By asking questions of the girls, the panel would have to decide which child actually belonged to Verna. Lisa remembered that the family "really wanted to send Kate, but she looked too much like Gramma, and I didn't look anything like her." Lisa proved to be a wise choice. When one panelist asked her the funniest thing she had ever seen her grandmother do, Lisa recalled seeing her grandmother come down the slide into the family swimming pool. Trying to imagine Verna in a swimsuit, the panelists thought the occurrence very unlikely. They chose an impostor as Verna's granddaughter.

"Lisa was so tickled," Verna later told Marty Halperin. "She was so proud of herself because we had said, 'If you do anything, you do the slightest little thing, they'll catch you right away, and they'll know who it is and you'll give away the secret.' 'Oh, no,' she said, 'I wouldn't do that.' 'Well,' we said, 'then you do it right.' And she did. She just did it beautifully. So then she got prizes from Spiegel. She sent for two bicycles, one for her sister and one for herself, and she got roller skates. Oh, she had the best time. She said, 'Please, Gramma, find me another job!'"

As for talk shows, it is not known if Verna ever appeared on any besides *Art Linkletter's House Party*, on which she guested in the fall of 1959. However, in early 1964, she was asked to participate on *Social Security in Action*, a public-service program with a talk-show format. Since 1958, the Social Security Administration had been conducting interviews with public personalities and celebrities for their weekly show, which was produced in Hollywood. Verna happily joined the ranks of such entertainment legends as Cecil B. DeMille, George Cukor, Edward G. Robinson, as well as the lesser-known character players like Marjorie Bennett, Barbara Pepper, and Hope Summers—all of whom were among more than three hundred individuals interviewed for *Social Security in Action*. The program's production schedule dictated that several interviews be taped consecutively on the same day. When Verna reported to the studio in January 1964, whom did she find waiting but Basil Rathbone. They shared a good laugh while reminiscing about Rathbone's slip of the tongue during a radio broadcast of *The Adventures of Sherlock Holmes* some twenty years earlier.

Arlyn Carr, the district manager of the Hollywood Social Security Office, conducted the interview, which progressed quite pleasantly. Of course, having been asked the same questions many times before, Verna had her replies down pat. Plus, with no script, she was more relaxed and animated in her responses. Chatting about the various stages of her career, Verna perpetuated several myths, chief among them that she became a professional at eight years old. When Carr asked how many other children had been in her family, she replied, "Just the one. I'm the one and only one." She discussed her radio career more at length than her other forms of entertainment: "I can tell you, I love radio best!"

Verna's true personality shone during the interview. When asked how she decided if a hat donation were worthy of her extensive collection, Verna answered, "Well, you just look at it, and if it isn't funny enough, why, you put it back in sackcloth and ashes!" Broaching the problems of aging, Carr asked what she thought about people working past the retirement age of sixty-five. "Well," she replied, "I used to think, when they're fifty, take 'em out and shoot 'em! Because that's the best thing for them—there's no aches and pains here and there, and then Social Security came out, and it's pretty good! In fact, it is wonderful." Carr persisted, asking Verna how long she thought a person should work. Half laughing, she replied, "Well, as long as they can stand up! If you can stand up, you're all right. If you fall down, go home and go to bed, that's all."

Then Verna told a funny tale about her old friend Charlotte Treadway, who had passed away the previous year. Treadway had always closely guarded her true age—even to her own detriment. "One of the girls in our radio club hadn't worked for years—she was crippled—and we were all supporting her. So I said to the girls, 'Hey listen, something's wrong. This gal is our age, she should be getting her Social Security.' So they said, 'Well, you go and tell her, not us.' I said, 'All right, I will.' So I went over and was talking to her, and she said, 'Why I'm not *that* old!' And I said, 'Now, listen, you're as old as the rest of us. We've

Marty Halperin interviews Verna Felton, February 1, 1964.

all grown up together, now listen.' But she wouldn't. So I went to Social Security, and I said, 'Now, we've got a gal on our hands, we're all supporting her. And I know she's eligible for Social Security—what are we going to do?' And the man said, 'Give me her name and address, and I'll pursue her.' So he went down, knocked on her door, and she wouldn't let him to see her. He had an awful time getting in. Well, do you know that silly thing had $500 waiting for her? And she had it every month. And she came to me, and I said, 'Well, what do you think [about your monthly check]?' And she said, 'If you tell the girls how old I am, I'll never forgive you!' "

A few days later when Marty Halperin came to call, Verna related some of the same anecdotes and opinions from her fifteen-minute *Social Security in Action* interview. Thirty-six-year-old Halperin, a radio fan since childhood, was so discouraged by the industry's negligence in preserving its past that he had begun gathering scripts, transcriptions, and other mementos of radio's colorful shows that had long since fallen victim to television. In addition, he had recently initiated an oral history project to preserve the memories of the medium's veteran players. Halperin's ultimate intention was to donate his taped interviews to a proposed Hollywood museum.

Born in Michigan, Halperin had moved to California in 1944. The following year, working as a page at NBC, he sometimes passed Verna Felton in the hallways, never dreaming he would visit her home twenty years later. In the interim, Halperin was employed for ten years as a recording engineer for the Armed Forces Radio Service. At the time he interviewed Verna, Halperin was an audio engineer in the film department of North American Aviation while moonlighting as a broadcasting instructor at Los Angeles City College.

That afternoon, Halperin set up the reel-to-reel tape recorder on a table in Verna's lavender living room while she seated herself on the sofa. Her dog Henry settled near her feet. From the next room, the machine picked up sounds of Verna's parakeets chirping noisily in their cage, which was suspended from the ceiling of the solarium nook. Halperin directed the conversation from Verna's earliest days on the stage right up to the present.

When the talk rolled around to her Disney features, Verna admitted that she had not done any work for that studio in several years. Indeed, there had not been many opportunities for any voice actors in recent Disney features. Since the 1959 financial failure of *Sleeping Beauty*, Walt Disney had produced twenty-nine features, but only two were animated films: *101 Dalmatians* and *The Sword in the Stone*. Instead, the studio had concentrated on live-action comedies, dramas, and nature films.

Verna's take on the situation was candid and emphatic: "I don't think [Walt Disney] should *do* the things he's doing! I think he should stick to his cartoons—because no one can do them as well as he does." Then she related how impressed she was with the recent animation she had been shown for *The Man from Button Willow*, expounding on the project for a few minutes until Halperin—seeking clarification—directed her back to her comment about Disney.

"Now, you mentioned you wish he'd stay with this instead of the other things he's doing. By that do you mean the live-action things?"

"Oh, I hate live-action!" she exclaimed, but then added with a laugh, "I like a piece of paper I can hide behind!"

Although at that point, Halperin did not realize the reason for Verna's distaste, he would soon learn that it was directly linked to her recent experiences in television.

"Are you doing any television now?" asked Halperin.

"No, not a thing now, not a thing now . . . I have no future plans, to tell you the truth. I am waiting for these cartoons that they say are going to start. That's what I want to do: cartoons where you are not seen, and you can *read* your lines."

"In comparing the days of your acting with the way it's being done today, do you have anything to say on that?"

"I don't like television at all," she said. "Don't like television."

"What primarily do you have against it?" asked Halperin.

Verna sighed. "There's not the *warm* atmosphere in their people, if I could say that. They think they are all potential stars, or they feel they are—no matter who they are. In radio, everybody got the same amount of money—except the high scale players. But there was a sweetness and a warmth [during the radio days]."

Later during the interview, when Halperin expressed his envy of Verna's voluminous career, she credited her stage training: "Well, I'll tell you, I was very lucky in having all this work that we did with the repertoire companies that our children can't have now. They're taught, and who are they taught [by]? They're taught by amateurs. But you see [my mother and I] were with professionals from the time that we left [San Jose] and we watched what they did. And they'd say [to me], 'No Babe, don't do that, do this . . . don't turn that way, turn this way.' Nowadays, they turn any way. I just look at them, and I think, 'Ooooohhh!' Some of the directors would die that we had worked with. And it's not pretty. Some of them, you know, they cross up and then turn back. We used to have long dresses, you see, with trains, and if we were going to make a cross upstage and turn back to say something, why, you'd get an angle where you could go right up with that train straight, you see, and then as you'd say something to them, you'd turn and turn very slowly and as you did, why, that dress would go right around your figure and you'd just leave it out. And then when you left it, you just kicked it to the side. Those things, you were all taught. Here, they wear long dresses and you see them going way over this way to get their feet out of them. I said to little Shirley Mitchell one day, 'Why don't you *learn* how to walk in a long dress?' [She said,] 'How *do* you walk? *Is* there a different way?' I said, 'Of course, there's a different way.' So I showed what we were taught. She said, 'Why don't they teach us that?' There's no training ground at all now . . . I said to my son [once], 'It just makes me sick that you kids have all lost all that.'

During the course of the interview, Verna kept coming back to the subject of her flagging career, at one point even admitting that she had considered opening an acting school for children in her guesthouse "because I like children—I love children. I worked with children a lot." The whole idea, however, was perhaps nothing but a pipe dream, considering her age and physical condition.

Another curious mention was Verna's invitation to appear on a Toronto television show. Although she told Halperin she was going to be a mystery guest on *What's My Line?*, records indicate that there was no show by that title being produced in Canada in 1964. (There had once been a French Canadian version of the popular game show, but it evidently ceased production in 1959.) Earlier in the interview, Verna—showing early signs of forgetfulness—had misidentified several individuals and productions, so it is not surprising that she should bungle the name of an unfamiliar Canadian television series. Most likely, Verna was referring to the immensely popular CBC television show *Front Page Challenge*, which ran from 1957 until 1995. As explained by the program's moderator Alex Barris, "the game itself was quite simple. There was a challenger representing a front-page headline from the past. Ideally, the challenger would have a fairly direct connection with the headlined story. Members of the panel would take turns asking questions in an attempt to track down the headline, or, at any rate, the story . . . Once the game portion was completed, the guest challenger moved to another chair to face the panel and was then interviewed by the panel. The interview might be directly related to the story, or, if the challenger was a celebrity, might wander to other areas of interest to the public." Over the years, American challengers included Zsa Zsa Gabor, Walter Cronkite, and Agnes Moorehead. According to Verna, plans had been made for her to fly to Toronto on March 6, 1964. However, a thorough search of Toronto newspapers does not reveal any items about her being in the city around that time. Attempts to request a search of CBC records for documentation also failed. If Verna was a guest on the show, it was most probably her final television appearance. If she was not, then it is quite likely that the 1963 *Bob Hope Comedy Special* was her final network television bow. Neither could be considered her final professional engagement, however. That was to come two years later.

In the meantime, Verna was satisfied to devote most of her time to the family. Lee continued to rely on his mother's financial support, since—in Kate's words—"he didn't work steadily at anything." By now, Lee had all but forsaken his acting career, aside from a remarkable appearance in "Operation Fly Trap," a 1964 episode of *Combat*. He played an army radio operator—speaking his part entirely in flawless German. Like his mother, Lee wished for radio to make a comeback, believing he would have a better shot at success in that medium.

When Halperin asked if her son was currently acting, Verna replied, fumbling slightly, "Yes, well, he's writing now, and selling." What she meant was that Lee and his partner Wayne Hamilton were attempting to sell their scripts and short stories. Linda Brittin and Edith had given them a small office in the Brittin Agency, now located at 649 North Bronson in Hollywood. Although Verna told Halperin that Lee was "doing very well," he and Hamilton had not sold much at all, except a 1963 film script—a science fiction piece called *Kroma* which evidently was cast but never produced—and several stories for *Alfred Hitchcock's Mystery Magazine*.

For years, Lee had tried to cultivate interest in a family legend that stemmed back to his maternal grandfather—one that would have made an ideal episode on *Thriller* or *Alfred Hitchcock Presents*. According to the tale passed down from Clara to Verna, Dr. Felton learned that a woman he attended in San Jose had died of phosphorous poisoning—administered by her physician husband. The tip-off came from the doctor's maid, who claimed she saw the body glowing in its coffin. Lee had written a short story based on the tale, but it had gone unpublished. In 1963, he shared the mysterious legend with Hollywood scriptwriter Andy Wasowski who took a quick trip to San Jose to comb old newspapers, death records, and coroner's inquests—all to no avail. Wasowski told the *San Jose Mercury-News*, "It made interesting reading, but unfortunately, the end result was a blind alley. So I can only assume that the story was far different and only expanded and got bigger and better with the retelling."

Verna participates in the ceremonial ribbon-cutting for completion of the first phase of Laurel Canyon-Sherman Way underpass in North Hollywood, December 1962. From left to right are: Jack Elliott, president of the North Hollywood Chamber of Commerce, Ronald Ellensohn, field secretary to Los Angeles Mayor Sam Yorty, Supervisor Warren Dorn, and Donald Tillman, president of the Los Angeles Board of Public Works.

Meanwhile, Verna's duties as honorary mayor of North Hollywood kept her busy, and the job was full of perks. She and thirteen other honorary mayors once dined with Los Angeles mayor Sam Yorty at City Hall. On July 15, 1963, she was the only female among the dignitaries assembled as Yorty cut the ribbon for the opening of the four million dollar Laurel Canyon-Sherman Way underpass. The following February she joined fellow honorary mayor Buster Keaton in another ribbon-cutting ceremony for the May Company department store in Canoga Park. The attentive "Barney" Oldfield continued to serve as Verna's escort for these appearances, and the pair was often seen dining at Sitton's Restaurant on Magnolia Boulevard in North Hollywood.

Verna liked to remain active and "in the know," which she certainly was, according to newspaper blurbs. In October 1964, she supported Republican senatorial candidate George Murphy by attending a huge fundraising dinner at the Encino home of John Wayne.

Meanwhile, it seemed that Verna might have a nibble of a guest part on a new television series. On January 7, 1965, entertainment gossip columns included a tidbit stating that producer Parke Levy planned to use Spring Byington, Harry Morgan, and Verna in cameo roles in his current series *Many Happy Returns*, a

Lisa (LEFT) and Kate help Verna model birthday gifts, 1965. Others, left to right, are Helen Rourke, Wendy Swartz, and Myme James.

situation comedy starring John McGiver as the head of a returns department in a large department store. Levy thought it would be fun to see the former *December Bride* crew returning various items of merchandise, but the producer's idea never had a chance to get off the ground. CBS cancelled the program not long after this news blurb was published.

On February 5, the *Van Nuys Valley News* reported that Verna had recently been reinstalled for her sixth term as honorary mayor of North Hollywood during a dinner for 400 persons at the Sportsmen's Lodge. That evening, North Hollywood—known as "the gateway to the San Fernando Valley"—and its civic leaders were lauded by main speaker Ben Reddick, publisher of the *Valley Times*, for "accomplishing so much since 1914 when there were only a few bee farms, a few dairies, and a population of 1,000." With actor Ernest Borgnine serving as emcee, Eddie Holohan—a public relations executive for Flying Tiger Airlines—was installed that evening as chamber president. Also on hand was actress Tippi Hedren, honorary mayor of Universal City.

Winter and spring passed off rather quietly, but in July, Verna celebrated her seventy-fifth birthday surrounded by neighbors and friends in a poolside party at home. Her canasta club was well represented, including Violet MacKaye, Myme James, Hazel Delphine, and Helen Rourke. Helen and Howard McNear—the latter still weakened from his 1962 stroke—joined Verna in cutting the large birthday cake, spread out on a table under the pergola. Its frosting featured appropriate adornments: violets surrounding a mound of white daisies—the former being guest of honor's favorite flower and the latter representing the youthful blossoms now used for the opening credits of the syndicated version of *December Bride*. Afterwards, she opened her presents, including one gag gift befitting Hilda Crocker—a yellow-and-white checked hat bedecked with plastic grapes.

Two months later, Verna—perhaps by now thinking the entertainment industry had forgotten her—was surprised to receive a call from the Disney Studio to voice a character in their latest animated feature, *The Jungle Book*. Disney's treatment of the Rudyard Kipling classic was loose, to say the least. The names of characters were basically the same—the Indian boy Mowgli, the panther Bagheera, the tiger Shere Khan—but Kipling enthusiasts would be hard-pressed to find many more similarities. After being abandoned at birth, Mowgli is raised by a mother wolf. Ten years later, Bagheera advises the boy to leave the jungle because Shere Khan is rumored to be returning to his home territory. Their trip through the jungle in interrupted by a variety of encounters, including a squadron of elephants, led by Colonel Hathi and including his wife Winifred and their baby son. Walt Disney's fondness for Verna's portrayal of the matriarch elephant in *Dumbo* twenty-five years earlier made her a logical choice for Winifred, but it may have been Bill Peet who first thought of engaging Verna for the role. As the story man for *The Jungle Book*, Peet's job description included finding the voices to be recorded. Since he had also worked on *Dumbo*, it's likely that Verna immediately came to mind. On September 22, she recorded a portion of her two brief but humorous scenes, only to be called back the following year after more changes were made in the casting.

Meanwhile, the honorary mayor of North Hollywood continued to promote various civic and business affairs. On October 8, her photograph appeared in the *San Fernando Valley Times*, posing beside a vintage stagecoach to publicize a bus tour of six Valley landmarks, sponsored by the Valley Historical Society. Less than a week later—and wearing the same hat—she helped break ground for the Gelson's Market in North Hollywood. Verna was also scheduled to attend an annual dinner of the North Hollywood Business and Professional Women's Club on October 18, but a medical emergency precluded that.

Shortly after the Gelson's groundbreaking, Verna fell in her home and broke her right arm. Debbie Leff recalled that she tripped over her dog Henry, but physicians later said that her fall might have been caused by a mild stroke. Whatever the case, on October 22, the *Pasadena Independent* reported that Verna

Winifred and son Junior (voiced by Clint Howard) are members of the pachyderm parade in *The Jungle Book.* © WALT DISNEY PRODUCTIONS

was "seriously ill" in Burbank's St. Joseph's Hospital. Family and old friends rallied around her. Spring Byington visited Verna's hospital room daily to cheer her. Bob Hope, in true wisecracking form, sent a wire: "I have a star spot in a new series for you as soon as you finish your stock stint in St. Joseph's." Verna was hospitalized for almost three weeks, which perhaps indicates there were other medical issues besides a broken bone. An upbeat blurb in Mike Connolly's newspaper column on October 29 substantiates this: "Old-timer Verna Felton flipped out of St. Joseph's Hospital, fit as a fiddle and flip as a fuchsia following surgery—and bouncing like a buttercup to get back on TV's work rack."

However, nothing was further from the truth than this hype. With her arm set in a heavy cast, Verna was in no shape to return to work. She was not physically strong enough to resume her duties as honorary mayor, much less meet the mental demands of acting. As her sixth term as North Hollywood's honorary mayor neared its end, Verna informed the chamber that she could not continue in the position and made it official on February 8, 1966, relinquishing her gavel at the fifty-second annual installation of Chamber of Commerce officers.

That evening, at the Sportsmen's Lodge in Studio City, with four hundred persons in attendance, Eddie Holohan was installed for a second term as president. During the ceremony, the audience was surprised but delighted when

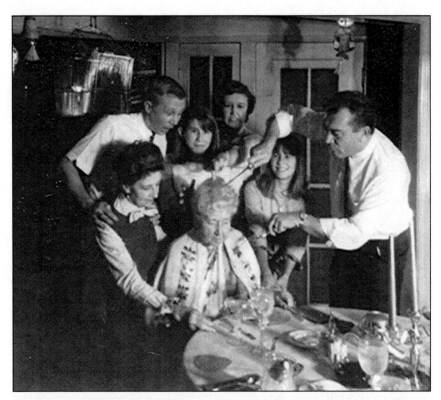

A gag snapshot of Verna posing as the family's Thanksgiving turkey while Wayne Hamilton pretends to "carve" her. Looking on, clockwise from left, are Grace Simmons, Lee, Lisa, Edith, and Kate, 1965.

local Boy Scouts, amid the sounds of tom-toms and Indian bells, appeared and began dancing around as they presented Holohan with an Indian headdress and an honorary title. The event, however, took on a "solemn and sentimental tone" as Verna was recognized for her six years of service. When Holohan announced that she would remain the community's "Ambassador of Good Will" for life, the audience rose to its feet with a lengthy ovation. In responseVerna said, "These have been six wonderful years serving you." Then, turning to actress Yvonne DeCarlo, who had agreed to become Verna's successor, she said, "I'm so glad to know that I've left my boys in good hands." She could not leave the podium without a touch of characteristic humor. "I'll say good night, but not goodbye because I'll be around the corner seeing what's going on." In the coming decade, Andy Griffith and Beverly Garland, among others, would serve as North Hollywood's honorary mayors, but, according to a retrospective published during the nation's bicentennial year, Verna reigned supreme: "Nobody anywhere has ever served a community anywhere with the generosity of spirit and unfailing cooperation of Verna Felton, stage and screen star, who was the beloved Honorary Mayor of North Hollywood for six years."

Eddie Holohan, elected to a second term as president of the North Hollywood Chamber of Commerce at the annual banquet informs retiring honorary mayor Verna Felton that she will be the community's Ambassador of Good Will for life and welcomes the new honorary mayor Yvonne DeCarlo of the popular TV series *The Munsters*, February 8, 1966.

By this time, Verna's agent had withdrawn her listing from *The Academy Players Directory*—a definite signal to those in the industry that the aging actress was no longer actively seeking employment. She would, of course, fulfill her pre-existing *Jungle Book* contract. On March 25, Verna returned to the Disney Studio to record additional dialogue for the film. Although she appeared healthy enough, her steps were slower and more deliberate, and her most prized physical asset—her voice—had changed drastically. As the dutiful but influential wife of blustery Colonel Hathi (expertly played by J. Pat O'Malley), she gave it her best. Yet, it is not the vigorous Verna Felton that Disney fans would recognize from *Alice in Wonderland*, for instance. Instead, her speech is definitely slurred—confirming the possibility of the 1965 stroke—and some lines leave her sounding quite old and tired.

Interestingly, the filmmakers must have been satisfied enough not to recast the part. In fact, even Winifred's animated features exhibit the disinterest and fatigue, evinced in Verna's dialogue. Likewise, the other characters were quite obviously shaped around the voices of Phil Harris, George Sanders, Sebastian Cabot, and Louis Prima, making it a remarkable showcase for character animation. That and the film's upbeat music helped to make the bright and breezy film a huge financial success. *The Jungle Book* would be the final animated feature bearing the personal stamp of Walt Disney, and ironically, it capped Verna Felton's professional career as well. She had come full circle, finally returning to the medium she loved. More importantly, her sixty-five years in the industry would end with a prestigious production—one bearing the name of one of the most important figures in twentieth-century American entertainment and culture.

Verna was still receiving fan mail as late as May 19, when one Eva Gutierrez wrote to her via Jack Weiner. Gutierrez informed Verna that she had watched *December Bride* in its heyday—until she returned to live in her native Norway. She requested an autographed photo from Verna, but most likely she never received one. Dr. Alfred E. Twomey, a history professor at Central Missouri State College, also wrote to Verna around this time, requesting a photo and biographical information for *The Versatiles*, his upcoming book on character actors. His request went unanswered, a fact he would regret enough to mention in his book's preface. Vera Jedlick Morgan, who had performed as a child actress with the Allen Players some forty years before, was also disappointed that Verna was unable to respond to her letter that summer. On July 19, Lee replied on his mother's behalf, explaining to Morgan that Verna was still recovering from a broken right arm and "is doing very little work these days." Normally, a broken bone would have healed enough after nine months for anyone to write so this does not seem to be the real reason for Verna's incapacitation. It was even more likely that the handicap preventing Verna from replying to any of these individuals was her deteriorating mental condition.

In the spring of 1966, Daphne Allen, by this time employed as a librarian, stopped in Los Angeles on the return trip from a convention in St. Louis. When she visited Verna that evening, she immediately noticed that Verna "just wasn't quite herself." Allen thought that her host appeared to be suffering from some sort of dementia. As the year wore on, Verna's condition grew tragically worse, saddening or confusing her friends and family. Debbie Leff recalled that at one time Verna insisted on hiding liquor in her shoe drawer. Kate, not yet eleven years old, did not understand when her grandmother did or said peculiar things. "She was seeing things that weren't there, and I didn't understand that she was ill. I can remember one in particular. She thought she saw the Cartwrights [from the *Bonanza* television show] coming up out of the ground by the water fountain near the pool. It was just bizarre. And we would be sitting at the table, and she would say things like, 'What have you done with your hair?' And we hadn't done anything at all." Dr. Carl Lund, Verna's personal physician since 1940, estimated that she had been suffering from arteriosclerosis for the past ten years. The condition had advanced gradually following her 1958 stroke but had intensified since the one she possibly experienced in 1965. For the past several years, Verna would lose her train of thought when conversing. Her problems with memorizing lines—quite well known now for a decade—were now obviously a direct result of the circulatory condition the doctor diagnosed.

This snapshot, taken at Verna's birthday party in 1966, is quite likely the last photograph of the actress. Her longtime friend Jane Morgan is seated at left.

Still, Verna was physically able to remain in her own home, as long as someone was around. "I remember [workers] going through the house and adding bars to the stairs going up and down," said Lisa, "and bars in her bedroom so she could get in and out of bed easier." By now, Eva Barwick had left Verna's employ, and in her place Pat Sheehan served as both housekeeper and caregiver. Edith Millar's mother Grace Simmons moved in, taking Barwick's apartment so she could look in on Verna as well.

Another significant dynamic had taken place by this time: Lee and Edith separated—although amicably—and he moved into Verna's beach house. Edith and the girls took up residency in Verna's guesthouse, and the Dilling Street house next door was put up for rent—a necessary move financially since the Brittin Agency had recently failed. Edith was now supporting herself with a job at the May Company.

Further tragedy struck that summer while Edith and the girls were vacationing in Virginia. Pat Sheehan's grandson accidentally set fire to the pergola out back, which quickly spread to an adjacent room where many family trunks were stored. Before firemen arrived, both structures were an entire loss. More than one lifetime's accumulation was reduced to ashes, for the trunks had contained theatrical mementos and scripts which had been gathered over the course of three generations, including a set of antique newspapers collected by Lee Millar Sr. Even more recent documents, including stories and scripts written by Verna's son, were lost in the blaze.

The only other landmark event of the summer was Verna's seventy-sixth birthday, celebrated in the customary style around the pool on July 20. For the occasion, the guest of honor chose an aqua print and had her hair coiffed in its usual upswept style, although—in keeping with the current fashion—perhaps a little more teased. She spent a most pleasant evening, chatting over drinks with old friends, including Janie Morgan, now eighty-five.

Summer passed into fall. The holiday season, which Verna had once relished so much, finally arrived. Happy trick-or-treaters streamed up and down Bakman Avenue on October 31. Three weeks later, the Millar family gathered for their annual Thanksgiving feast. But on December 12, with Christmas plans already underway, Verna suddenly became quite ill. Dr. Lund was summoned, but found there was nothing he could do. Verna had suffered another stroke—one that Lund quickly knew would prove fatal. It was decided to keep her as comfortable as possible at home, in her own bed. Even as two private-duty nurses were called in to take shifts around the clock, Verna's heart grew weaker. On the morning of December 14, one of the nurses, sensing that her patient would not make it through the day, telephoned Bernard and Thelma Leff, asking them to come say their final goodbyes. Lee and the rest of the family remained nearby all day, waiting for the inevitable. That afternoon at twenty minutes past five, Verna Felton quietly passed away.

Soon afterwards, as the Millar family began making funeral plans, they noticed that Verna's dog Henry was nowhere in sight. They discovered that faithful pet under the bed of his mistress, refusing to leave her. Lisa, who had formed a special bond with Henry, was sent in to retrieve him.

Meanwhile, four miles away, at St. Joseph's Hospital in Burbank, Verna's most recent employer lay dying. Walt Disney, suffering from lung cancer, had been a patient there for two weeks. On the evening of Verna's death, he discussed plans for EPCOT for several hours with his brother Roy, but on the following morning the world-famous visionary took a turn for the worse. Disney died at nine thirty-five, sixteen hours after "his favorite elephant" had gone on before him.

As news of both deaths spread, Lynn MacKaye Morgan—now a busy young mother—was caught unaware, barely catching the announcement on her television. "I thought they said that Verna had died, but I didn't catch all of it. I called the television station to verify it."

Morgan was among those who attended Verna's funeral on Saturday, December 17, at the Steen-Lorentzen Mortuary chapel on Magnolia Boulevard in North Hollywood. Frederick de Cordova delivered the eulogy, and Morgan recalled the service as "quite upbeat" with lots of humorous stories of Verna and her Hollywood career. Dennis Day attended, but there were few other celebrities present, recalled Debbie Leff, whose family rode to the funeral in a limousine with de Cordova. Lisa and Kate—although by now thirteen and eleven years old, respectively—were deemed by their parents as "too young" to attend.

Also absent was Al Blazic, for whom Verna Felton had been a second mother. Regretfully, he could not leave the family business he managed in Oakland. Clyde Bowman, by now a young father of two, was also unable to leave his home in northern California. Dolores "Dolly" Stelter, who had christened Verna as "DeeDee," had long lost touch with the Millars by this point and was not even aware of Verna's passing. When Verna had suffered her first stroke in 1958, Trudy Stelter told her daughter about it. "I was in high school at the time, and for some reason, I just automatically thought that Verna must have died then," recalled Dolores Stelter Neese in 2008. "And then years later, I went online to the Internet Movie Database and read that Verna had died in 1966, and I thought, 'Oh, my gosh, all that time she was alive, and I didn't know it!' And I just burst into tears because I thought, 'All that precious time I could have gone over there and talked to her.' Right now, it still catches me because I just didn't inquire further when my mom told me she had a stroke."

Cremation followed the funeral, and burial took place in The Garden of Prayer, an urn garden shaded by magnolias and evergreens at Grand View Memorial Park in Glendale. A small simple piece of granite reading "Verna Felton Millar 1890-1966"—outlined in an image of an open book—would mark the spot.

Floral tributes, cards, and letters poured in. On December 15, both the Los Angeles City Council and the Los Angeles County Board of Supervisors adjourned their sessions by standing in silent remembrance of Verna Felton.

Tributes also appeared in all the major newspapers. Verna's obituary in the *New York Times* concentrated on her most famous role: "In *December Bride*, she was known for risking life, limb, and sacroiliac in acrobatic feats that have been called worthy of a stunt man. The show's producer, Parke Levy, would have her roughhousing with wrestlers, trading half-nelsons, and getting involved in barroom-type free-for-alls. In one episode, she skipped rope with the boxer Art Aragon and later sparred with him. There was even a time when Mr. Levy told her to roll out of a window. She did—head first."

At the time of her death, Verna Felton's assets—including her North Hollywood home, a half-interest shared with Lee in the Laguna Beach house, her part-interest in the Carson family ranch near Stockton, plus bank accounts, residuals, furs, and jewelry—were roughly estimated at just under $575,000. Her last will and testament, signed on September 14, 1965, bequeathed the Bakman Avenue house in equal shares to Lee, Edith, Lisa, and Kate. She left her part of the

Laguna Beach house to Lee, while her interest in the Stockton property went to Lee and the girls. The residue and remainder of the estate was left to all four individuals.

To the rest of the world, Verna Felton left a greater legacy. Although few people—if any—recall today her prolific stage career, an ample supply of documents survive, attesting to her star stature on the Canadian stage. Many of her radio characterizations endure on MP3 files so that listeners can access these whenever they want to hear Blossom Blimp warble or Mrs. Day bellow, "Ahhh, Shudddup!" Employing DVD and Blu-Ray discs, film fans are delighted to find her performances as fresh and funny as they did over fifty years ago. A legion of Disney devotees still marvels at the talent behind Cinderella's beloved Fairy Godmother and Wonderland's roaring menace The Queen of Hearts. Diehard sitcom fans continue to seek treasured episodes of Verna Felton's signature series *December Bride,* while younger generations discover her bombastic voice on *The Flintstones.*

"It's been a happy life," Verna told Marty Halperin, "but I don't say I'd do it all over again." Then, in her best Hilda Crocker voice, she winked, "I think I might stay home and wash the dishes."

EPILOGUE

The Jungle Book was released on October 18, 1967, ten months after the death of Verna Felton. Its lively music numbers helped to make it a solid financial success, earning $13 million just from its domestic release.

Most of the people who knew Verna Felton intimately are gone now. Bernard and Thelma Leff died in 1991 and 1997, respectively. Their daughter Debbie died in 2006.

Zora Blazic, Verna's faithful friend for almost thirty-five years, died in Oakland at age ninety-two on January 6, 1997.

Ida Allan Graves, Verna's Canadian friend since girlhood, lived to see her ninety-seventh year. As the darling of the annual Calgary Stampede Parade, she rode for fifteen years in the lead carriage, including the year preceding her death which occurred on January 21, 1986.

Verna Arline Lawrence, Verna's cousin and namesake, remained unmarried and lived near relatives in Arcadia, California. She was retired from the Veterans Administration when she passed away on February 16, 1985, at age eighty-five.

Violet Harvey Allen, the widow of Verna's stepfather, married twice after Pearl Allen's death. She was approaching her ninetieth birthday when she died on December 28, 1993.

Pearl's younger brother Arden W. Allen died on October 19, 1960, just five days before his eighty-second birthday. His wife Dorothy survived him by seven years.

Margaret Felton, Verna's sister-in-law, died in North Vancouver, BC, on June 3, 1971, at age ninety-two. She had never remarried following the abandonment and subsequent death of her husband, Clayton Felton (*nee* Van Alstine). Ernest Richard Felton, Verna's only nephew, died in Nanaimo, BC, on December 28, 1982. He was sixty-seven.

Eva Barwick, Verna's housekeeper, retired and returned to live in Kansas where she died at age ninety-five in 1992.

As for Verna's *December Bride* crony, Spring Byington continued to act into her eighties. Following a two-year-stint as a regular in the television western *Laramie*, she made guest appearances on *Kentucky Jones* (with series regular Harry Morgan), *Batman, I Dream of Jeannie*, and *Blondie*. Her final guest-starring role was the Mother General on *The Flying Nun* in 1968. On September 7, 1971, at age eighty-four, she died of cancer in her Hollywood home. The veteran actress had held on to her secret: none of her obituaries reported her true age.

December Bride producer Parke Levy, weary of sponsor intervention during production of his 1964-65 sitcom *Many Happy Returns*, abandoned his career soon after the show's cancellation. He lived in retirement in Beverly Hills until his 1993 death from an aortic aneurysm at age eighty-four.

December Bride head writer Lou Derman went on to write for *Mr. Ed* and *All in the Family*. A sudden heart attack claimed his life as he drove to work one Sunday in February 1976.

Dean Miller,who played Matt on *December Bride*, returned to Ohio in 1965 and bought a small radio station which he owned until his death from cancer on January 13, 2004. He was seventy-nine.

Frances Rafferty acted only sporadically following *December Bride*, but made a few appearances during the second season of *Pete and Gladys* as Gladys's friend Nancy. She much preferred raising quarter horses on her California ranch. She died of heart disease on April 18, 2004.

Harry Morgan followed *Pete and Gladys* with nine other television series, including *The Richard Boone Show, Dragnet 1967,* and of course, *M*A*S*H*, playing Col. Sherman T. Potter, a role that finally won him an Emmy. As of this writing, Morgan survives at ninety-four.

Verna survived only two of her canasta cronies. Mamie Bush died of cancer in 1959, and Charlotte Treadway, who had continued to decline following her 1948 stroke, died in the Motion Picture Country Hospital in 1963.

All of the cronies who survived Verna surpassed her age at death. Gertie Virden, eighty-five, willed her body to scientific study before her 1967 death from heart disease.

Jane Morgan, suffering from dementia, took to her bed soon after Verna's death, but she lingered until January 1, 1972, when she died of heart failure at age ninety-one. By that time, Helen Rourke had moved out of Jane's home and acquired an apartment of her own. On March 21, 1976, at age eighty-two, she died of pneumonia at the Motion Picture and Television Hospital in Woodland Hills.

Prior to Verna's passing, Violet MacKaye had moved to Newport Beach, where she died of pancreatic cancer on June 13, 1973. "Vi" was seventy-nine. Myme James died at eighty-four on November 17, 1978.

Helen Delphine, who had worked in a theatrical agency for years, graduated to the real estate industry before her death on January 18, 1985. She was eighty-one.

Eighty-four-year-old Katie Robinson died in a LaCrescenta convalescent hospital on December 29, 1979. Her lifetime companion Mary Edith Stahl survived her by fifteen years and earned the distinction of living longer than any of the canasta cronies. Confined to a Glendale nursing facility for a number of years, Mary Edith died at ninety-three on February 1, 1995.

Verna's neighbor Helen McNear, also a card playing buddy, passed away on January 20, 1984, fifteen years after losing her husband Howard.

For a short time after his mother's passing, Lee Millar continued to pursue acting. After filling a few bit parts on television shows like *The Invaders* and *The Mothers-in-Law*, he temporarily abandoned this career to concentrate more on writing. In 1969, he became a senior editor for the *Newporter*, a small newspaper published in Newport Beach. Two years later, he switched to the *Laguna News-Post*, where he served for a brief time as a feature writer. From time to time, Lee also appeared in Laguna Playhouse productions. By 1974, he decided to sell the beach house to move back to North Hollywood, where he rented an apartment on Moorpark Street. Around this time, Lee resurrected his acting career, landing small roles in television series such as *Kojak, Baretta,* and *Police Woman*. He was also active in several theatre productions at the "Show" Place on Ventura Boulevard in Studio City. In 1978, Lee made a last-ditch effort to break into New York theatre, but it was all in vain. By this time, heavy drinking and smoking had wracked his health. In August 1980, a neck biopsy revealed that a malignant tumor had metastasized. On September 21—less than six weeks later—Lee died of cardio-respiratory failure at UCLA Medical Center. Like his father and both grandfathers, Lee did not live to see age sixty. His ashes were scattered at sea.

Edith, Lisa, and Kate moved into Verna's house, and the three continued to live there through the girls' teenage years. Edith left the May Company to become personnel manager at a local savings and loan association. She worked her way up to branch manager, a position she held until retirement. She never remarried or resumed her acting career. On March 30, 2004, after a bout with pneumonia, Edith passed away in Providence St. Joseph Medical Center in Burbank. She was eighty. Edith's mother Grace "Blossom" Simmons lived out her final days at the Bakman Avenue house as well, dying in 1979.

Lisa Millar married Reuben Kofman in 1973. As of this writing, they and their children—son Ryan Millar Kofman, daughter Abra Lee Kofman and her husband James Barrett—live at 4147 Bakman Avenue. Kate Millar married Shand Cunningham in 1979. They reside today in Burns, Oregon.

ACKNOWLEDGMENTS

First, I am greatly indebted to my friend Charles Stumpf, a fellow character actor enthusiast, who knew my particular passion for Verna Felton's work. It was he who, in 2004, suggested to BearManor Media publisher Ben Ohmart that I author this biography. I greatly regret his passing on August 28, 2009.

Sincere thanks go to Ben for having faith—and unending patience—in this project. He perhaps did not realize when he commissioned me that, as an amateur genealogist, I tend to get immersed in the details of people's lives. Even I had no idea that it would take five years to complete the job.

At first, I did not really know where to begin. When Ben suggested that I try to locate Miss Felton's surviving family, I turned to another character actor expert, John Nelson—a real Internet sleuth. With just a few keystrokes, John provided me with the necessary contact information.

Miss Felton's granddaughters Lisa Kofman and Kate Cunningham generously loaned their grandmother's personal papers and photographs, which had been sealed up in a wardrobe trunk since the actress's death. These musty and yellowed documents became the springboard for my research. Without them, this book would have never become a reality. In addition, Lisa and Kate graciously fielded my many questions, no matter how insignificant they may have seemed, and they opened doors which led to new sources of information. I have written this book, in part, as a means to thank them for their generosity.

I am extraordinarily grateful to Al Blazic, who knew Verna Felton for a longer number of years than any other person I interviewed. Al maintained a close relationship with the actress until the end of her life, and his memories greatly amplified my work. Ironically, just before I began my study, Al had begun to look into Miss Felton's family background, just to satisfy a personal interest. He happily aided my own search and unselfishly copied and shared rare photographs and home movies.

I will be forever thankful to Marty Halperin who kindly offered to provide a tape recording of his 1964 interview with Miss Felton. Without this source, readers would not know many of her views or opinions, not to mention the inside information she provided on individuals such as Jack Benny and Red Skelton. When I first listened to the recording on March 7, 2005, portions of it gave me the eeriest of feelings. Several times, Mr. Halperin asked Miss Felton questions I would have asked her, given the chance—and she supplied the answers I craved. At other points in the recording, she addressed issues that either I yearned to know or those which I would have never known otherwise. It was almost like Miss Felton was speaking to me. Most touching was Mr. Halperin's concluding remark that Saturday in February 1964: "I know that people in the future who listen to this are going to learn a lot about what you've done and the experiences you've had." Mr. Halperin, thank you for having the foresight to preserve Miss Felton's recollections.

No worthwhile biography can exclude genealogical information, so I set out to explore Miss Felton's lineage. My quest for her paternal ancestry was quite short lived. Fortunately, the Felton family history has been well documented over the past one hundred years, due in part to the ongoing efforts of the Felton Family Association, a group of descendants headed by the zealous Cora Felton Anderson. Thanks to Cora for providing relevant material from the scrapbook of the late Nancy Felton Koster. I am also grateful for this organization's continued interest in Miss Felton's life story and their willingness to share the Felton genealogy. In particular, one FFA member, the authoritative and skillful Richard Tivey, generously supplied the author with information linking Miss Felton—via her great-great-grandmother Felton—to King Edward III of England.

Miss Felton's maternal line was another matter entirely, but several individuals helped me put the pieces together. The biggest mystery revolved around the assertion of a young man I met through the miracle of the Internet. Although he possessed no documentation, Brad Felton insisted that his grandfather was Miss Felton's brother—a claim lost on her granddaughters who believed the actress was an only child. Furthermore, Brad informed, there was a second brother. When Al Blazic corroborated his story, a real search began. One year later, primary documents unearthed in the courthouse of Sierra County, California, revealed Clara Lawrence's first marriage, which produced sons Howard and Clayton—two individuals Verna Felton never mentioned in interviews. Brad Felton wanted to know the final fate of his grandfather, and so did I. That's where Emmitt McClendon came in.

As far as California historical and genealogical research, no one has been more helpful than Emmitt. Although he himself is not related to the Lawrence family, he is very interested their ancestors since his wife is a descendant. Emmitt introduced me to many beneficial online archives, often just when I was at my wit's end. I would have never located death record for Miss Felton's half-brothers had it not been for a suggestion from Emmitt. On this score alone, I'll always be grateful to him.

Others climbing the Lawrence family tree included Marge Hier, who shared vital information to solve another Lawrence family mystery—the connection of the Chicago branch of the family to the California lines. When I found a Verna Arline Lawrence on census records, the similarities were too glaring to ignore. Marge was the one source who could explain the relationship of "Big Verna" and "Little Verna."

Any career profile concerning Verna Felton would be incomplete without giving credit to the man behind her career—her stepfather Pearl Allen. Delving into his family background provided me with a whole new set of friends, including Clyde Bowman and Daphne Allen, who each lived in Miss Felton's North Hollywood home for a short time. Clyde and Daphne were able to provide inside information available nowhere else, and this work would have been quite incomplete without their contributions. John Bowman, the Allen family historian, as well as an entertaining raconteur, unselfishly shared his voluminous files with me, enabling me to connect the various members of the Allen clan. JoAnn Mondon put me in touch with these individuals and others when she hosted an Allen family reunion in her home in 2006. I cannot thank her and her husband Richard enough for their kind hospitality. I know now why Verna Felton embraced the Allens as her own kin.

I also salute Miss Felton's neighbors: Dolores Stelter Neese, Steven Stelter, Dr. James Simons, Debbie Leff, Sandy Leff Raab, Christopher "Kit" McNear, and Jerry Houser who shared their personal recollections of life on Bakman Avenue in the 1940s, 1950s, and 1960s. To each, I am indebted for their happy memories of "DeeDee."

Few people I contacted were more enthusiastic than Lynn MacKaye Morgan, the daughter of Miss Felton's friend Violet MacKaye. Lynn good-naturedly fielded question after question and supplied a rare insight into the lives of Miss Felton's canasta cronies.

Unfortunately, most of Miss Felton's co-workers and friends were deceased by the time this project began. *December Bride* co-stars Dean Miller and Frances Rafferty died within three months of each other in early 2004. I had written to both as early as 1987, long before this biography was ever considered. Rafferty never responded, but Miller immediately replied, apologizing that he needed to postpone sharing memories of the series and its stars until a less hectic time. Sadly, that day never arrived, and I regret not pursuing him. Out of the blue, however, he left a message on my answering machine in 1994, but included no telephone number where I could reach him. Alas, those were the days before the Internet placed so much personal information at our fingertips. In 2003, I again wrote to him, but by that time it was too late. All attempts to contact Harry Morgan ended in failure, as did my vain efforts to reach Cara Williams. I even flew to California expressly to meet Williams at a fan convention in 2007, but she failed to appear. Spring Byington's granddaughter Lois Ann "San" Baxley Michel politely refused to be interviewed. This only made me dig deeper for true information concerning her famous grandmother, whom she called "the greatest lady I ever knew." Still, I relished candid interviews with Parke Levy's surviving children, Robert Levy and Linda Levy Mickell. Linda Derman Kelemer, the daughter of *December Bride* writer Lou Derman, cheerfully took time from her busy schedule to read my episode guide and add behind-the-scenes comments regarding her father's inspirations for plots and characters.

Five of Miss Felton's fellow actors were particularly helpful in summoning memories of working with her. Sharon Douglas wrote copious details about their experiences in New York when performing on radio's *Sealtest Village Store*. Peter "Dix" Davis conversed at length about their escapades during rehearsals for *Lux Radio Theatre*. Mary Costa bubbled with delight when recalling the time they spent together in the recording studio for *Sleeping Beauty*. Regarding the pioneer television broadcast of *Oh, Miss Tubbs!*, Selma Stern freely shared her personal notes, while Peggy Webber reminisced at length about the production, even conducting a little research of her own to help answer my queries. All were unanimous in their high regard for Verna Felton's steadfast professionalism and winning personality. All have my sincerest gratitude.

For sharing their memories with me, I am grateful to other individuals who either knew and/or worked with Verna Felton: Mary Andrews, Lois Blazic, Hattie Gunton Brendel, Dann Cahn, Shirley Mitchell, Ferris Murdy, Dale Robertson, Jean Kirkpatrick Shively, Doris Singleton, Irene Sommerfeld, the late Gale Storm, the late Gil Stratton, Eleanor Kirkpatrick Weltmer, and Elizabeth Wilson.

I am indebted to the following personnel who assisted me in the research of the text: Freda Edwards of the Altamont Public Library; Phil Gries of Archival Television Audio, Inc.; Carol Bowers, Leslie Shores, and John Waggener of the American Heritage Center, University of Wyoming; Kayla McAlister of the Humanities Department, Calgary Public Library; the staff of the California Department of Health Services, Sacramento, California; John A. Gonzales of the California History Room, California State Library; Mary Jo Reitsema of the Carnegie Branch Library for Local History, Boulder, Colorado; Leni Panopio of the Cypress Lawn Cemetery Association, Colma, California; Paul E. Trejo, genealogist for the Diocese of Monterey, California; Lynn Eaton of the Hartman Center for Sales, Advertising and Marketing History, Rare Book, Manuscript and Special Collections Library, Duke University; the reference staff of the Fond du Lac Public Library; Sylvia Duffus of the Edmonton Public Library; Jim Bowman of the Glenbow Museum; Lindsay Moir of the Glenbow Museum Library; Elizabeth Cain of the Halstead Public Library; Ana Martinez-Holler of the Hollywood Chamber of Commerce; the office staff of the Ladysmith Chamber of Commerce; Josie Walters-Johnson of the Motion Pictures Division, Library of Congress; Lovelle Gant of the Registrar-Recorder/County Clerk's Office of Los Angeles County; Mona Gudgel and James Perry of the Monterey County Historical Society; Charles Dearman and Larry Hughes of the Motion Picture, Sound, and Video Branch of the National Archives; Claudia Koch of the Montrose Regional Library; the staff of the Museum of Television and Radio, New York City; Julio Gonzalez of the Otto Rothschild Collection, Music Center

Archives; Jeremy Megraw of the Billy Rose Theatre Collection, New York Public Library for the Performing Arts; the staff of the Oakland History Room, Oakland Public Library; Bruce Tabb of Special Collections, Portland Public Library; the reference staff of the Riverside Public Library; Kelly-Ann Turkington and Marion Tustanoff of the Royal British Columbia Museum; Maria Ruiz of the St. Charles Borromeo Church, North Hollywood, California; Brian Darr of the San Francisco Performing Arts Library and Museum; Tom Carey of the San Francisco History Center, San Francisco Public Library; Bob Johnson of the California Room, San Jose Library; Jan Parrish of the Superior Court of Sierra County, California; Jody Gripp of Special Collections, Tacoma Public Library; the reference staff of the Thunder Bay Public Library; Lauren Buisson, Arts Library Special Collections, Young Research Library, UCLA; Nancy Mason of the Special Collections Department of the University Library, University of New Hampshire; the staff of the Special Collections Division of the University of Washington Libraries; and Dave Smith of the Walt Disney Company Archives.

Heartfelt thanks are extended to Betsy Tolley, head of the Interlibrary Loan Department of the Spartanburg County Public Library. Over the course of four years, Betsy has diligently—and with great cheer—searched for and retrieved microfilm holdings of innumerable newspapers to aid my research. She would say it's all part of the job, but Betsy went the extra mile.

I would also like to recognize with particular appreciation the support I have received from individuals who served as volunteers for their organizations: Nancy Peterson of the California Genealogical Society; Carolyn Swift, director of the Capitola Historical Museum; Nancy Pratt-Melton of the Golden Nugget Library; Bill Dahlquist and Don Dodd of the Los Angeles Fire Department Historical Society; Deborah Ogden of the Grand Lodge of California, Independent Order of the Odd Fellows; Margaret Castle of the Grass Valley Museum; Wallace Ginn, archivist for North High School, Denver, Colorado; Gary Carlsen of the Monterey County Genealogical Society; Barbara Doucette of the Peabody Historical Society and Museum; and Gretchen Collins of the Tacoma-Pierce County Genealogical Society. Special thanks go to the persevering Janene Crawford of the Santa Clara County Historical Society, who located a death record for Verna Felton's maternal grandfather.

Three paid researchers proved their worth by uncovering material not readily available to me. I applaud the discriminating efforts of Melinda Herzog-Landrith, Auburn, California; Maria E. Brower, Grass Valley, California; and Maryanne McGrath, Victoria, British Columbia.

I also extend warm thank-you's to a number of individuals who provided me with information, photographs, or audio/video recordings: Berwin Berlin, Sidney Bloomberg, Kent Bowman, Bud Buczkowske, James Bush, Dr. Virginia Cooke, Carolyn Dowd, Joe Doyle, Ron Evans, Katie Green, Tim Hollis, Debbie Hurt, David Inman, Tom Kiefer, Christy King, Joan Kirkaldie, Tom Kleinschmidt, Chuck Knuthson, Laura Leff, Robert Leszczak, Alan Levy, Joel Lobenthal, Mary

Marchetti, Hank Moore, Mary O'Donnell, Gary Myer, John Ottinger, Matt Ottinger, Diane Peacock, Elizabeth Peters, Bruce Reitherman, John Rotella, Eldon Russell, Chuck Schaden, Bob Schuster, Ivan Shreve, Gregg Simon, Michael C. Smith, Robert Stiles, Tyler St. Mark, Glenn Sundstrom, Candace Taylor, Molly Webster, Neil Wilburn, Chad Woodruff, and John Wulf. Special thanks go to Dale Sheldon who offered leads in my search for biographical information related to Spring Byington.

Ben Ohmart knew what he was doing when he chose Valerie Thompson as this book's designer. Just like Cinderella's fairy godmother, Valerie has worked magic to create a visually stunning tribute to the life and career of Verna Felton. And is it any wonder? Not when you realize that she and Verna share the same birthday! Valerie, your sincere enthusiasm and meticulous attention to details are deeply appreciated.

I am most grateful for the support I have received, in friendship, interest, and encouragement, from Harry Bayne, Ben Branscom, Mary Ann Brockman, Tracey Bruce, Sara Cannon, Teresa Coan, Rex Crews, Sheila Dobbins, Kathy Edge, Andy Hall, John Harrington, Cathy Humphries, Cecelia James, Everett Johnston, Sammy Keith, Jeff Lerner, Graig Luscombe, Charles MacArthur, Rodney Mangum, Danny McGarr, Nancy McMakin, Cheryl McNeace, Ken Mitchell, Jackie Moore, Brian Poole, Shawn Poore, Jeff Smith, Nancy Smith, Sam Staggs, Maris Steinberg, Lois Stokes, and Cheri Wofford. They have all allowed "Verna" to share their time with me these past five years.

This book would not have come together without the input of my friend Tony Waters who suggested appropriate revisions and provided constant feedback all along the way. His steadfast friendship and enthusiasm for this project have been invaluable.

Finally, I humbly thank my mother, Ruth Ann Tucker, who urged me to use every spare moment to complete this biography. I must have neglected her numerous times in the process of "getting that book finished," but being a fellow Verna Felton fan, she always understood. Thankfully, Mamma was once an English teacher: she assisted with the proofreading, too. Her unwavering support and devotion are priceless.

APPENDICES

AUTHOR'S NOTE: While it is virtually impossible to present a comprehensive list of Miss Felton's stage and radio appearances, readers may consult the main text of this work for the majority of those credits. To locate other possible radio appearances, readers may browse the website RadioGoldIndex (www.radiogoldindex.com), which offers a partial listing of Miss Felton's prolific radio credits.

APPENDIX A: VERNA FELTON FILMOGRAPHY

1917:	*The Chosen Prince*
1939:	*Joe and Ethel Turp Call on the President*
1940:	*Northwest Passage*
	If I Had My Way
1941:	*Dumbo*
1945:	*Girls of the Big House*
1946:	*She Wrote the Book*
1948:	*The Fuller Brush Man*
1950:	*Cinderella*
	Buccaneer's Girl
	The Gunfighter
1951:	*New Mexico*
	Alice in Wonderland
	Little Egypt
1952:	*Belles on Their Toes*
	Don't Bother to Knock
1955:	*Lady and the Tramp*
1956:	*Picnic*
1957:	*The Oklahoman*
	Taming Sutton's Gal
1959:	*Sleeping Beauty*
1960:	*Guns of the Timberland*
1965:	*The Man from Button Willow*
1967:	*The Jungle Book*

APPENDIX B: VERNA FELTON TELEVISION APPEARANCES

NOTE: This list—most likely incomplete—excludes Verna Felton's appearances as a regular on *December Bride* and *Pete and Gladys*, which are documented in subsequent appendices.

28 October 1951	*The Colgate Comedy Hour*
8 February 1952	*The Dennis Day Show*
22 February 1952	*The Dennis Day Show*
7 March 1952	*The Dennis Day Show*
21 March 1952	*The Dennis Day Show*
4 April 1952	*The Dennis Day Show*
18 April 1952	*The Dennis Day Show*
2 May 1952	*The Dennis Day Show*
16 May 1952	*The Dennis Day Show*
6 June 1952	*The Dennis Day Show*
27 November 1952	*The George Burns and Gracie Allen Show*
26 January 1953	*I Love Lucy:* "Sales Resistance"
19 February 1953	*The George Burns and Gracie Allen Show*
17 April 1953	*The Adventures of Ozzie and Harriet:* "Whistler's Daughter"
27 April 1953	*The George Burns and Gracie Allen Show*
27 April 1953	*I Love Lucy:* "Lucy Hires a Maid"
11 June 1953	*Amos & Andy:* "Kingfish Has a Baby"
30 November 1953	*The George Burns and Gracie Allen Show*
16 February 1954	*The Bob Hope Special*
18 February 1954	*Place the Face*
8 July 1954	*Where's Raymond?*
26 October 1954	*The Halls of Ivy:* "Professor Warren's Novel"
20 February 1955	*The Jack Benny Program:* "Death Across the Lunch Counter"
25 September 1955	*The Jack Benny Program:* "Jack Goes to Dennis's House"
26 September 1956	*The Vic Damone Show*
30 April 1957	*Climax!:* "The Disappearance of Amanda Hale"
23 June 1957	*Flamingo Theater:* "The Old Lady" (KTTV-Los Angeles production)
19 October 1958	*The Jack Benny Program:* "Millionaire"
3 November 1959	*Art Linkletter's Houseparty*
22 December 1959	*The Many Loves of Dobie Gillis:* "Deck the Halls"
18 January 1960	*The Ann Sothern Show:* "Devery's White Elephant"

25 February 1960	*The Real McCoys:* "Cousin Naomi"
4 December 1960	*The Jack Benny Program:* "The Lunch Counter Murder"
17 January 1961	*About Faces*
1 June 1961	*Miami Undercover:* "Cukie Dog"
6 September 1961	*Here's Hollywood*
14 January 1962	*The Jack Benny Program:* "Dennis's Surprise Party"
6 February 1962	*Henry Fonda and the Family*
7 February 1962	*Wagon Train:* "The Lonnie Fallon Story"
16 March 1962	*The Flintstones:* "Trouble-in-Law"
26 April 1962	*My Three Sons:* "Coincidence"
2 November 1962	*The Flintstones:* "The Little Stranger"
1 February 1963	*The Flintstones:* "Mother-in-Law's Visit"
8 February 1963	*The Flintstones:* "Foxy Grandma"
7 July 1963	*Dennis the Menace:* "Aunt Emma Visits the Wilsons"
27 September 1963	*The Bob Hope Comedy Special*
Fall 1963	*Your First Impression*
28 January 1964	*Social Security in Action*

APPENDIX C: *December Bride* Episode Guide

NOTE: Episodes denoted by an asterisk (*) are ones not personally viewed by the author. Synopses for these episodes were derived from Parke Levy's copies of the original scripts, housed at the American Heritage Center, University of Wyoming. [Parke Levy Papers, Accession Number 3148: Boxes 2, 3, 4, and 5.]

December Bride
The First Season: 1954-55

Cast:	Spring Byington as Lily Ruskin
	Dean Miller as Matt Henshaw
	Frances Rafferty as Ruth Henshaw
	Harry Morgan as Pete Porter
	Verna Felton as Hilda Crocker
Creator:	Parke Levy
Producer:	Frederick DeCordova
Director:	Jerry Thorpe
Writers:	Parke Levy, Phil Sharp, Bill Freedman, Milton Rosenblum, Marvin Kline, Al Schwartz, Ellis Marcus, Lou Derman, Herb Finn, Joel Kane, Ben Starr
Composer:	Eliot Daniel
Conductor:	Wilbur Hatch
Director of Photography:	Karl Freund
Production Manager:	W. Argyle Nelson
Editorial Supervisor:	Dann Cahn, A. C. E.
Film Editor:	Bud Molin, A. C. E.
Art Director:	Claudio Guzman
Set Dresser:	Theodore Offenbecker
Assistant Director:	Marvin Stuart
Re-recording:	Editor: Robert Reeve
Sound:	Glen Glenn Sound Co.
Announcer:	Dick Joy
Sponsor:	General Foods Corporation

"LILY RUSKIN ARRIVES" Oct. 4, 1954
EPISODE #1 FILMED ON THURSDAY, FEBRUARY 25, 1954
WRITERS: PARKE LEVY, PHIL SHARP
GUEST CAST: HARRY CHESHIRE AS GUS WARNER,
MORONI OLSEN AS LIEUTENANT MORGAN, SAM MCDANIEL AS THE PORTER

Architect Matt Henshaw and his wife Ruth have been married for five years when Ruth's widowed mother Lily Ruskin comes to Los Angeles for a visit. On the train from Philadelphia, Lily becomes infatuated with fellow passenger Gus Warner, who claims to be a wealthy investor. Gus promptly proposes marriage, but Matt suspects he has made his money illegally. Lily decides to take the $3200 engagement ring to the police to see if it's been reported as stolen; meanwhile Gus discovers it's missing and phones the same police department. When Lily arrives there, Lieutenant Morgan suspects her as the thief. Matt, Ruth, and Gus arrive soon and set the record straight, but an argument ensues and Gus breaks his engagement to Lily. In the closing vignette, Lily greets Lt. Morgan, her new suitor, at the door. Ruth asks where she's going, and Lily responds: "How do *I* know? I'm in the arms of the law."

NOTES: This is the pilot for the series. Verna Felton does not appear in this episode. Sam McDaniel (1886-1962) was a brother of beloved character actress Hattie McDaniel, best known for her Academy Award winning role of Mammy in *Gone With the Wind*.

"CHICKEN SALAD" Oct. 11, 1954
EPISODE # 3 FILMED ON SATURDAY, AUGUST 14, 1954
WRITERS: PARKE LEVY, PHIL SHARP, AND BILL FREEDMAN
GUEST CAST: JOHN QUALEN AS BOB THOMPSON

Matt is concerned because Lily is spending all of her free time with her new friend, Hilda Crocker, who has Lily's calendar filled with lectures, art shows, ballet performances, and meetings of the Westwood Women's Cultural Club. That evening, over a dinner of Lily's chicken salad, Matt tells Lily and Hilda they should be saving some time for dating. Hilda's response: "Who needs men?" This infuriates Matt, so he invites meek Mr. Thompson, the hardware store owner, to dinner, hoping he'll hit it off with Lily. Soon after Mr. Thompson arrives, Hilda phones to remind Lily of her speaking engagement at their club meeting. Lily leaves in a rush, and Mr. Thompson feels rejected. A few days later, Hilda drops by to ask Lily to make a large tray of chicken salad every other day to be sold at the Helping Hand Auxiliary's ongoing bazaar. Later Pete tells Matt and Ruth that he saw Hilda at the movies with Mr. Thompson, even though "she led us all to believe men were poison." Everyone is speechless when Hilda soon comes to the door with Mr. Thompson and announces their engagement. He beams as he brags on Hilda, "Nobody makes chicken salad like my Hilda." Lily casts a suspicious eye toward Hilda as the scene fades. In the vignette, Lily burns her recipe for chicken salad.

"THE CHINESE DINNER" Oct. 18, 1954
EPISODE # 4 FILMED ON SATURDAY, AUGUST 21, 1954
WRITERS: PARKE LEVY, MILTON ROSENBLUM, AND MARVIN KLINE
GUEST CAST: RICHARD LOO AS LEE FONG, KEYE LUKE AS SOO YUNG,
WEAVER LEVY AS THE AMERICAN CHINESE MAN, GRADY SUTTON AS MR. DAVIS
THE EMPLOYMENT AGENT, CHEERIO MEREDITH AS MRS. LACEY, CAROL
LEONARD AS THE DANCER

When Matt is asked to entertain Lee Fong, a Chinese business associate, Lily thinks it would make the man feel more at home if she serves a Chinese dinner. She invites a Chinese dancer to perform and selects pressed duck as the *entrée*, stacking piles of books on the bird. (Pete: "What a way to go—crushed by an encyclopedia!") Meanwhile Matt engages a Chinese waiter, Soo Yung, to serve the meal. When Yung arrives, Lily and Ruth mistake him for the businessman and because he speaks no English, they amuse him by continuously serving him cocktails. When Fong finally arrives, Lily assumes he's the waiter Matt hired so she sends him to the kitchen. He good-naturedly plays along, serving the dinner until Yung realizes their mistake and rushes out to the kitchen. Lily is terribly embarrassed and Matt apologizes profusely, but Fong is so impressed at Lily's thorough planning that he agrees to negotiate with Matt at the office the next day. Lily vows to never meddle in Matt's affairs again.

NOTES: Verna Felton does not appear in this episode. The screen credits list Parke Levy and Lou Derman as the writers for this episode, but the original script cites those writers listed above.

"THE ACCIDENT" Oct. 25, 1954
EPISODE # 2 FILMED ON SATURDAY, AUGUST 7, 1954
WRITERS: PARKE LEVY, PHIL SHARP, AND BILL FREEDMAN
GUEST CAST: PAUL HARVEY AS ELLIOTT J. GORDON, JAMES PARNELL AS THE
DEFENSE ATTORNEY, DOUGLAS EVANS AS THE CITY ATTORNEY, ROBERT BURTON
AS THE JUDGE, NORMAN LEAVITT AS THE CLERK

Inexperienced driver Lily comes home after an accident (Pete to Matt: "There's an accordion coming up your drive!"), but she insists it was not her fault. Matt agrees to testify on her behalf at a hearing, not knowing the other driver was his boss, Mr. Gordon. When Lily learns that Gordon has also asked Matt to be his character witness, she feels responsible for creating a strain between the two men. To ease these tensions, she tells the judge that she caused the accident by driving 70 mph while in a drunken condition and with drops in her eyes, further aggravated by her attempts to comb her hair while looking in the rear-view mirror. The judge sternly orders Lily to his chambers where he tells her he's never heard such a pack of lies. He is so charmed by her efforts to throw the case that he asks her to lunch with him at Romanoff's.

NOTES: Verna Felton does not appear in this episode.

"THE VETERINARIAN" Nov. 1, 1954
EPISODE # 5 FILMED ON SATURDAY, AUGUST 28, 1954
WRITERS: PARKE LEVY, AL SCHWARTZ, BILL FREEDMAN
GUEST CAST: RALPH DUMKE AS DR. CHARLES J. NELSON, ROLFE SEDAN AS
MR. WILSON, RAYMOND GREENLEAF AS MR. HARPER, RALPH MONTGOMERY
AS JIM

When Lily wants to return to Philadelphia, Matt thinks it's because she is lonely for the opposite sex. He invites an acquaintance, Dr. Nelson, to dinner, relying on the man's profession to make him an impressive suitor. But when the doctor arrives, he's an obnoxious clod. Lily is more charmed by Mr. Harper, a department store manager, who has dropped in to woo her. Matt mistakenly believes Harper is a lowly sales clerk unfit for Lily's attentions, so Pete tries to keep Nelson from leaving by pretending to have an injured arm. Then they discover the doctor is actually a veterinarian.

NOTES: Verna Felton does not appear in this episode.

"MY SOLDIER" Nov. 8, 1954
EPISODE # 6 FILMED ON SATURDAY, SEPTEMBER 4, 1954
WRITERS: PARKE LEVY, ELLIS MARCUS
GUEST CAST: RUTH BRADY AS BLANCHE ROBERTS, SALLY FRASER AS BETTY
SHOEMAKER, HERB VIGRAN AS EUSTACE BUDLONG, DICK BENNETT AS BUNNY

As a participant in a Red Cross program, Lily has been pen pals for quite a while with a soldier named Eustace Budlong. When she receives Eustace's telegram, saying he will drop by that evening, she is frantic with worry. Lily has lied about her age to keep his interest ("What soldier would write to Whistler's Mother?"), making him believe she is 21 years old. Hilda volunteers her niece Blanche to pose as Lily, but the girl turns out to be too cerebral, spouting quotes from Kierkegaard and Proust. So they substitute bobby-soxer neighbor Sally, but her jealous boyfriend intervenes. Finally a middle-aged soldier arrives, saying that his buddy Eustace could not make it. Lily is relieved, but pretends that she is her own mother, informing the soldier that Lily is not at home. As the soldier turns to go, he cannot keep from admitting the truth: *he's* Eustace and he lied about *his* age. Lily bursts into laughter with her own admission: "*I'm* Lily!"

"GRUNION HUNTING" Nov. 15, 1954
EPISODE # 8 FILMED ON SATURDAY, SEPTEMBER 18, 1954
WRITERS: PARKE LEVY, LOU DERMAN
GUEST CAST: BYRON KANE AS JOE THE STOREKEEPER, JAMES FLAVIN AS MIKE
THE COP

Pete is upset that Matt always has plans with Lily whenever Pete invites him to do something with him. However, the boys are unaware that this entire conversation has been recorded on Matt's new tape recorder. After Lily and Hilda accidentally hear the recording, they decide that Lily should become very busy every night so the boys can spend some time together. Instead of joining a card game with Matt, Ruth, and Pete, Lily tells them she and Hilda are going down to the beach "to see the *bunions* run." They are amused by her new interest but are a little doubtful. Then Hilda arrives in rain hat, raincoat, denim pedal-pushers, and sneakers, carrying a bucket and a baseball bat. She and Lily leave on the pretense to hunt grunion, but wind up in a fish market where they learn that the grunion aren't running. Meanwhile the others realize that Lily and Hilda must have heard the recording. When the ladies return home without grunion, Pete apologizes to Lily, and all is well.

"LILY'S MOTHER-IN-LAW" NOV. 22, 1954
EPISODE # 9 FILMED ON SATURDAY, SEPTEMBER 25, 1954
WRITERS: LOU DERMAN, PARKE LEVY, ELLIS MARCUS
GUEST CAST: GRANDON RHODES AS HARVEY ADAMS, ESTHER DALE AS MRS. ADAMS, MARIO SILETTI AS THE WAITER

When Pete observes Lily giving Matt and Ruth advice on cooking and clothing styles, he quips, "One day Lily will be one-fifth mother and four-fifths law!" Then he learns that Lily's new *fiancé* Harvey is taking Lily home to meet his mother. (Pete: "Matt, you are about to witness the sweetest revenge: a mother-in-law getting a mother-in-law!") That evening at the Adamses' residence, Harvey's overbearing mother dictates what Lily should cook for Harvey, makes comments about Lily's choice in earrings, etc. The old lady insists that Lily and Harvey live with her after their marriage. Lily is polite until she can take it no more, proceeding to tell Mrs. Adams that she never tells her daughter how to cook or what to wear. Then she catches herself and realizes she's just gotten a dose of her own medicine from Mrs. Adams. Seeing that Harvey will always believe his mother is right, Lily breaks their engagement.
NOTES: **Esther Dale was less than a year older than Spring Byington, and Grandon Rhodes was almost eighteen years Byington's junior.**

"LILY HIRES A MAID" NOV. 29, 1954
EPISODE # 10 FILMED ON SATURDAY, OCTOBER 2, 1954
WRITERS: PARKE LEVY, LOU DERMAN, ELLIS MARCUS
GUEST CAST: NANCY KULP AS LOUELLA SIMPSON, LYLE TALBOT AS OSCAR BUTTERFIELD, FRANCES MERCER AS DOROTHY BUTTERFIELD, FRANK JENKS AS HAPPY LARSON

Lily surprises Matt and Ruth by hiring live-in maid Louella Simpson for a month to "give the kids a vacation in their own home." But when the dowdy, gum-chewing Louella arrives (driving a 1936 Plymouth with Cadillac hubcaps), Lily has second thoughts. (Lily: "We're very fastidious." Louella: "That's all right, m'am, I've worked for nervous people before.") Louella dons a pinafore with gigantic ruffles and begins to dust while simultaneously chewing gum and singing "Flat Foot Floogie." Lily learns that Matt has invited an important client and his wife to spend the weekend in the Henshaw home so she informs Louella she'll have extra chores to perform. (Louella: "I'm going to need a month to *recruperate*!") The last straw comes when Lily catches Louella sweeping cigarette ashes under the rug. When reprimanded, Louella quits just minutes before the guests arrive. To save Matt embarrassment, Lily poses as the Henshaws' maid. As she waits on the guests, she overhears the client's wife make disparaging remarks about her own mother-in-law. Then out in the kitchen Lily is surprised by the arrival of a frisky sailor who had arranged a blind date with Louella. He assumes that Lily is Louella and practically chases her back out to the living room. Hilda unexpectedly arrives and immediately blows Lily's cover. The client's haughty wife, indignant that the maid is actually Matt's mother-in-law, bursts out of the house. Lily explains it all to the client who finds the whole situation very amusing. Lily promises Matt no more surprises for the evening, but she wonders what to do with the sailor in the kitchen. Hilda takes off her hat and grabs Lily's maid's cap, declaring "Just give me that uniform, and call me Louella!"

"THE GIGOLO" DEC. 6, 1954
EPISODE # 11 FILMED ON SATURDAY, OCTOBER 23, 1954
WRITERS: PARKE LEVY, LOU DERMAN, HERB FINN
GUEST CAST: FORTUNIO BONANOVA AS RINALDO MONTEZ, TRISTRAM COFFIN AS MR. WAGNER, RAY WALKER AS DAN WINTERS

Hilda is taking mambo lessons from 41-year-old Rinaldo Montez ("Ten dollars an hour — he's worth every wiggle!"), but Lily thinks he's taking advantage of Hilda since she's the one who pays for all of their nightly dates. Pete tells Lily he's heard of opportunists like Montez who persuade women like Hilda to invest in nonexistent ventures. Lily is then afraid Hilda will invest $2000 in Montez's chain of dance studios. She tries to convince Hilda that Montez is a fortune hunter, but Hilda (in a ponytail tied up with streamers) brushes her off, exclaiming, "This is the first time in years I've gone out with a man with hair!" Lily is determined to expose Montez as a gigolo so she asks Hilda to hide behind a screen and eavesdrop when Lily invites Montez over to teach her to mambo. Hilda refuses, but Lily threatens to reveal her true age ("You voted for McKinley!") so Hilda agrees. When Montez arrives, Lily tells him she's a millionaire. He turns on the charm, kissing her hand and vowing to become her slave. When Lily mentions Hilda, Montez calls Hilda a hippopotamus. Hilda bursts from behind the screen, chasing Montez with the fireplace bellows. She screams, "You double-crossing Don Juan! I'll break every bone in your body!" She knocks him down behind the sofa, beating him with the bellows. He escapes, but Hilda sends a vase hurling after him before she falls into Lily's arms sobbing.

"THE RICH MAN" Dec. 13, 1954 *
Episode # 13 Filmed on Saturday, November 6, 1954
Writers: Parke Levy, Lou Derman, Herb Finn
Guest Cast: Paul Cavanaugh as Gerald Hawkins, Walter Woolf King as Mr. Firestone, Olaf Hytten as Hudson

Lily has a bump-up with a tall handsome man driving a powder blue Cadillac. While exchanging information, they mistakenly swap driver's licenses. Later the man phones her to arrange a meeting to swap them back. He's so charmed by Lily that he also invites her to go on a drive. By reading his address on the license, Lily assumes he's a millionaire because he lives in an exclusive neighborhood. Actually Hawkins works for a millionaire and was driving his boss's car the day of the accident. His boss, Mr. Firestone, leaves town and tells Hawkins to have some fun while he's away. Before Hawkins arrives at the Henshaw home, Hilda tells Lily,"You have all the luck. You bump into Cadillacs and get boyfriends — I bump into trucks and get sued." She then coaches Lily on how to snag Hawkins, telling her to pretend she's rich so Hawkins won't think she's a gold digger. Lily pooh-poohs all the suggestions and goes upstairs to change shoes. Hawkins arrives, and Hilda takes matters into her own hands. She tells him that Lily is very rich but unpretentious. Later Hawkins confesses to Hudson, Firestone's butler, that Lily and the Henshaws jumped to the conclusion that the Firestone estate was his. He is quite charmed by Lily and doesn't want to jeopardize their budding romance, so he asks Hudson to play along. Hawkins invites Lily, Matt, Ruth, Pete, and Hilda all for dinner at the mansion. During the evening, Firestone phones to inform Hawkins that he's on his way home. Hawkins admits his deceit to Lily. She doesn't know what to say, but Hilda does: "Is this employer of yours single?"

"THE CHRISTMAS SHOW" Dec. 20, 1954
Episode # 12 Filmed on Saturday, October 30, 1954
Writers: Parke Levy, Lou Derman, Herb Finn
Guest Cast: Chris Olsen as Dannie, Will Wright as Mr. Jordan, James Flavin as the policeman

Lily is at a loss for what to buy Matt and Ruth for Christmas when Dannie, the young grandson of her grumpy neighbor, enters. He tells Lily he wants snow for Christmas because he's never seen it. This jogs Lily's memory of Matt's earlier remark about missing the snow back east so she decides to order a refrigerator truck full of snow from Arrowhead. After it arrives, Pete and Matt get into a snowball fight which is interrupted by Mr. Jordan, Dannie's grandfather. Jordan complains that the melting snow is making the sidewalks slippery. A policeman enters the scene and informs Jordan that the Henshaws have broken no laws. Jordan huffs off but returns later when everyone is singing carols. He threatens to sue the Henshaws because he slipped on the snow, but his heart is soon melted at the sight of Dannie building a snow man. Jordan then joins in the caroling.

NOTES: Will Wright, who also played with Verna Felton on radio's *My Little Margie*, appears here in a Scrooge-like role similar to the one he played six years later on The Andy Griffith Show as town merchant Ben Weaver. Actors Rolfe Sedan (as the professor) and Anne O'Neal (as Martha) appear in the original script of this episode; if their scenes were filmed, they were deleted before the broadcast date. In the vignette, Spring Byington appears as herself: "Friends, this is the holiday season, and we of *December Bride* wish you the happiest of times with this one reminder for yourself and for those you love—please drive carefully. When those wonderful parties are over, make sure that 'one for the road' is coffee." She then sips from a cup, a subtle reminder of the show's sponsor, Maxwell House Coffee.

"THE LUAU" Dec. 27, 1954
EPISODE # 14 FILMED SATURDAY, NOVEMBER 13, 1954
WRITERS: PARKE LEVY, LOU DERMAN, HERB FINN
GUEST CAST: PAUL HARVEY AS MR. GORDON, DAMIAN O'FLYNN AS MR. TREMAINE, GEORGE MEADER AS MR. HIGBY, MEL MANA AS JOE

Ruth is overjoyed when Matt plans a Hawaiian vacation, but the plans quickly go astray when his boss Mr. Gordon asks him to entertain an important client, Mr. Higby, a misogynistic, vegetarian teetotaler. To perk Ruth up, Hilda suggests to Lily that she host a surprise luau in the back yard. Lily goes the whole hog with the decorations, music, and menu by asking Joe, a native Hawaiian, to supervise the event, including roasting a pig in a pit. When Ruth arrives, she's moved to tears at her mother's thoughfulness. Mr. Gordon and another client, Mr. Tremaine, drop in and join in on the celebration. When Matt arrives with his uptight client, Higby is appalled at the drinking, music, and the pig in the pit. Then Hilda, wearing a long Hawaiian print dress and flowers in her hair, begins singing and dancing the hula. She attempts to get Higby in the mood by bumping hips with him, but he flees, thoroughly insulted. Matt regrets losing the Higby account until Tremaine, a restaurateur, asks him to design his new establishment. Lily beams when Tremaine cites her carefully planned Hawaiian atmosphere as his inspiration.

"LILY WANTS TO PAY HER WAY" Jan. 3, 1955
EPISODE # 15 FILMED SATURDAY, NOVEMBER 20, 1954
WRITERS: PARKE LEVY, LOU DERMAN, HERB FINN
GUEST CAST: KATHRYN CARD AS MRS. DENNIS THE SCRUBWOMAN, EDDIE GARR AS THE DRUNK, IRENE TEDROW AS THE HOTEL MAID

When Matt's boss refuses his request for a raise, Lily thinks it's time she paid room and board, but Matt adamantly disagrees. After two failed attempts to help out with expenses, Lily sees no alternative but to move out. Without telling Matt and Ruth, she checks into a hotel where she is miserably unhappy. When Hilda drops in, Matt and Ruth convince her to tell them Lily's whereabouts.

Meanwhile Lily has taken pity on the hotel scrubwoman who is working on her 25th wedding anniversary. She sends the woman to her husband and gets down on her knees to finish scrubbing the floor. Matt and Ruth enter, and, thinking Lily's now "paying her way," they urge her to quit her job. She won't be convinced until they tell her that Matt got his raise after all. Then the three of them happily finish scrubbing the floor.

NOTES: Kathryn Card (1892-1964) had been a member of the Allen Players with Verna Felton in Edmonton, Alberta, in 1921-22.

"LILY THE ARTIST" JAN. 10, 1955
EPISODE # 16 FILMED ON SATURDAY, NOVEMBER 27, 1954
WRITERS: PARKE LEVY, LOU DERMAN, HERB FINN
GUEST CAST: SIG ARNO AS PROFESSOR SPINELLI, PETER BROCCO AS ARTHUR POMEROY, WILLIAM FORREST AS MR. DOBSON

Lily's art teacher, Professor Spinelli, pretends she has talent so that she will continue to buy brushes, paint, canvases, and lessons from him. Her family and friends think her paintings are wretched. She creates one for Pete called "Chicken on a Bicycle," prompting Pete to quip that he's seen oil used better in a sardine can. Matt recognizes that Spinelli is taking advantage of Lily so he hatches a plot to get her to quit painting. He brings home a genuine Dulac, valued at $900, from an art gallery on approval, pretending he painted it years ago. He criticizes it, telling Lily that any amateur who can't do better than "his" painting should just give up. He hopes Lily will realize that she has no talent for painting. After he leaves, Lily tells Hilda that Matt's painting has no definition; she paints over it to "give it new meaning" and in the process ruins the Dulac. When Matt finds out, he admits his ruse and confesses that he must now buy the Dulac. To reimburse Matt, Lily decides to hawk her paintings on La Cienega Boulevard, where Hilda assists by yelling to passersby that their goods are right off the boat from France and that Lily is "Grandma Moselle." Mr. Pomeroy of the Pomeroy Art Institute happens by and, after talking with Lily, he denounces Spinelli as a charlatan. He also critiques her paintings, calling them frightful. Hilda admits to Lily that Matt and Ruth don't like them either. When Pomeroy offers $25 to buy the canvases for his students to reuse, Lily realizes that she can undo her work on the Dulac using turpentine. However, she discovers a portrait under the Dulac. Mr. Dobson of the art gallery recognizes the original work as that of Jorgensen, saying it's worth $1500. Matt sells it to him at a profit of $600, and with a sigh of relief, Lily vows to give up painting.

NOTES: Series writer Lou Derman was an art collector who bought many paintings from artists on La Cienega Boulevard.

"THE GRANDFATHER CLOCK" JAN. 17, 1955
EPISODE # 17 FILMED ON SATURDAY, DECEMBER 4, 1954
WRITERS: PARKE LEVY, LOU DERMAN, HERB FINN
GUEST CAST: ALMIRA SESSIONS AS MADELINE SCHWEITZER, GAIL BONNEY AS
VIRGINIA APPLETON, LOUISE LORIMER AS KITTY MAXWELL

Lily's three-generation family heirloom, a grandfather clock, is shipped from Philadelphia, but its charm soon wears off when it chimes incessantly, keeping the household awake. Lily learns it will be too costly to repair so she decides to donate it to her club's white elephant auction. Matt is delighted at its removal, but then he stumbles on a letter from Lily's sister Mary to Ruth: "Oh, my child, the memories that clock must have for your mother! I can just see us now standing around it on that fateful day in November, 1918, when it chimed the hour of the armistice of World War One. And we knew then that the man who was to become your father would be coming home safely. In 1929, when the world seemed to crash and take everything with it, this clock was the only thing your parents could salvage. Somehow through the years, your mother never thought of it as a clock, but rather as a tall sincere friend standing quietly in the hallway. In fact as a child she could never say 'grandfather clock.' She used to address it as Mr. Tick Tock. And, oh, the secrets they must have shared!" Just as the clock is about to be moved, Matt flatly states, "The clock stays." He tells Lily they'll get it fixed because that's the least they can do for Mr. Tick Tock.

NOTES: This is the first appearance of members from Lily and Hilda's Westwood Women's Cultural Club. In the original script, Almira Sessions was to play Virginia Appleton, and Gail Bonney was to play Madeline Schweitzer, however, the roles were reversed onscreen. In all subsequent episodes, Bonney plays Madeline's part, and Sessions plays a similar character named Elsie Pringle. The script credits Gail Bonney with the voiceover role of Aunt Mary. The popular song "Grandfather's Clock," written by Henry Clay Work around 1876, is heard as background music throughout this episode.

"THE SENTIMENTALIST" JAN. 24, 1955
EPISODE # 18 FILMED ON SATURDAY, DECEMBER 11, 1954
WRITERS: PARKE LEVY, LOU DERMAN, HERB FINN
GUESTCAST: HARRY ANTRIM AS CHARLES WOODRUFF, LUDWIG STOSSEL AS
TASHA ZIMMERMAN THE WAITER, ALADDIN AS THE VIOLINIST

After receiving a letter from an old beau she has not seen in 35 years, Lily becomes wistful as she plans a reunion date with him. She recalls Charles Woodruff as a handsome, muscular quarterback who spontaneously created poems while wooing her. She remembers the place where he gave her his fraternity pin: a little Hungarian restaurant complete with gypsy violinist and fortune teller. Lily then decides she'll recreate that scene when Charles comes to town. Matt tells Ruth that Lily is foolish for being so sentimental, but Ruth defends her mother and her gender by saying that such things are important to women. She reminds

Matt of the night he proposed, but he has no desire to look back at the past. In the meantime, Lily fusses with every little detail of her plans for date with Charles, even finding the perfume ("Gardenia") she wore when they dated. When Charles arrives he is not as Lily has envisioned. He's put on considerable weight, so much that he can't fit in the restaurant booth. He is more interested in the menu than in Lily's reminiscences, and he mistakes her perfume for "what they spray to kill the kitchen odor." When Lily mentions the poetry Charles once wrote, he reveals that the only writing he does now is advertising jingles for Finkel's Flea Powder. When he denies proposing to her many years ago, Lily realizes that their reunion is a mistake. She requests that the violinist play "The Old Grey Mare — She Ain't What She Used to Be." Meanwhile Matt and Ruth return to the courtyard of the Gourlet Restaurant where she insists he re-enact his proposal at the wishing well. He clumsily drops her ring into the well and falls in trying to retrieve it. Back at home, Lily confesses to Ruth that "if you try to relive a beautiful memory, you destroy it." Ruth sadly agrees.

"THE URANIUM SHOW" JAN. 31, 1955
EPISODE # 19 FILMED ON SATURDAY, DECEMBER 18, 1954
WRITERS: PARKE LEVY, LOU DERMAN, HERB FINN
GUEST CAST: FRED SHERMAN AS FREDDIE SHERMAN, TYLER MCVEY AS MR. CLINTON

Lily and Hilda want to go on a vacation trip but cannot decide where, until Matt tells them about a man who found uranium in the desert. Lily then convinces Hilda to spend a week near Bakersfield hunting for uranium. When Matt bets Ruth that they won't last a week, Ruth bargains with him for a Persian lamb coat if he loses. Hilda later arrives wearing Bermuda shorts, knee socks, boots, and a pith helmet with a veil. She's carrying a pick ax, canteen, and a Geiger counter. Lily bounces downstairs looking equally ridiculous, dressed in overalls and miner's cap and carrying a sifting pan. Off they go to seek their fortune. Two days later they burst through the door, proclaiming they found uranium. When planning ways to spend their new money, Hilda says she's going to buy a YMCA. Lily buys new furniture, a color television set, and a Persian lamb coat for Ruth. Later Mr. Clinton, the representative sent by the investment company to buy Lily's claim, informs her that the vein of uranium weakened when it crossed her boundary line. The cost to mine it would outweigh the benefits. Lily is crestfallen, telling Ruth she'll have to return all she bought. Matt offers to pay for the coat so Ruth can keep it. Then Hilda strolls in, wearing diamonds, a hat bedecked with bird-of-paradise feathers, and a full-length mink coat. Her solo rendition of "A Pretty Girl Is Like a Melody" is interrupted when she's informed of the worthless claim. She takes one look at her newly bought finery and quips, "In the morning I'll be a nudist!"

"THE INSURANCE SHOW" FEB. 7, 1955
EPISODE # 20 FILMED ON THURSDAY, DECEMBER 23, 1954
WRITERS: PARKE LEVY, LOU DERMAN, HERB FINN
GUEST CAST: FRANK WILCOX AS BILL EMERSON, JAMES TODD AS MR. JENKINS

After Lily accidentally bumps her head on a store awning, the store's insurer, The Delta Insurance Company, wants her to either sign a release of liability or accept a monetary settlement. But she refuses, saying she was unhurt. ("People should sign less and trust each other more.") The company also happens to be Pete's employer, so he tries his hand at convincing Lily to either sign or accept compensation. When she politely refuses once more, Pete gets into an argument with Matt regarding Lily's inability to see reason. Lily feels responsible when they refuse to speak to each other. When Mr. Emerson, Pete's boss, phones her for an appointment, Lily assumes it's because Pete failed at persuading her to sign the release. She doesn't want to endanger his job so she has Hilda, who's been taking a civil defense course, bandage her head and arm before Emerson arrives. She convinces him she's seriously hurt but soon confesses the truth when Matt and Pete arrive arm-in-arm. Pete is so overcome by Lily's efforts to help him that he loses control and, to everyone's amazement, kisses Lily. He protests, "All right, so I kissed a mother-in-law!"

"SURPRISE PARTY" FEB. 14, 1955
EPISODE # 22 FILMED ON SATURDAY, JANUARY 8, 1955
WRITERS: PARKE LEVY, LOU DERMAN, JOEL KANE
GUEST CAST: ROLFE SEDAN AS JOE, JERRY HAUSNER AS THE FIRST CUSTOMER, MIKE ROSS AS THE SECOND CUSTOMER

Lily finds a present hidden in the kitchen cabinet and assumes it's a surprise birthday gift from Matt and Ruth. Hilda rushes to open it, but she drops the package and breaks the contents, which they think is a ceramic Chinese warrior with a clock in his stomach. Lily wants to replace it before Matt and Ruth find out. She locates the gift shop where it was purchased, but they no longer have any in stock. They recommend that she get in touch with another customer who bought one. When Lily finds the man, she offers him $20 for his clock. He has to leave his diner to get the clock, so in his absence, Lily mans the counter. She makes a mess of the orders, but finally Joe arrives with the clock and she makes the switch, only to drop it again! Before she can admit her deception, Matt and Ruth give her a wristwatch for her birthday present. Matt notices the package containing the broken clock and tells Ruth that a client gave it to him over a year ago and he meant to get rid of it by now. In the vignette, Matt, Ruth, Pete, and Hilda toast Lily on her birthday.

"JEALOUSY" FEB. 21, 1955
EPISODE # 21 FILMED ON THURSDAY, DECEMBER 30, 1954
WRITERS: PARKE LEVY, LOU DERMAN, JOEL KANE
GUEST CAST: REGIS TOOMEY AS TOM ANDERSON, RUTH BRADY AS THE SECRETARY, JOI LANSING AS DIANE SULLIVAN, MAURICE MARSAC AS MR. LABROSSE

Lily is being courted by Tom Anderson, a wealthy widower, who showers her with poetry and flowers. But she becomes jealous when he hires buxom blonde Diane Sullivan as his new secretary. Lily attempts to change Tom's mind about his selection, but he tells her that an attractive secretary is good for morale, makes a man feel young and keeps the men in the office on their toes. (Lily: "One look at Miss Sullivan, and this place will look like a ballet school!") Lily decides to find out if Tom is the jealous type. She hires a young French tutor to become amorous with her while Tom is present. Her ploy works, and she throws Tom's philosophy right back at him: "Look, Tom, I'm on my toes!" Tom offers to fire Miss Sullivan, but Lily maintains that they should trust each other. Suddenly Tom proposes marriage to Lily. She accepts, and they plan to be married in two weeks.
NOTES: Verna Felton does not appear in this episode.

"WEDDING PREPARATIONS" FEB. 28, 1955
EPISODE # 23 FILMED ON SATURDAY, JANUARY 15, 1955
WRITERS: PARKE LEVY, LOU DERMAN, JOEL KANE
GUEST CAST: REGIS TOOMEY AS TOM ANDERSON, GLADYS HURLBUT AS MISS SELBY

Matt generously offers to pay for Lily's wedding reception, but he's dismayed when the guest list climbs from 16 close friends to over 150 friends and relatives from all over the country. Miss Selby, the wedding consultant, recommends that it be a formal affair since a large number of guests will attend. Matt becomes increasingly concerned about the cost until Tom advises that he will help with all the expenses. Tom informs Lily that he won't be able to attend the wedding rehearsal because he must leave on a business trip in the morning. Hilda directs an impromptu rehearsal in the Henshaw living room, during which Lily and Tom receive several phone calls, necessitating Pete to fill in as a the bride and, at one point, Lily as the groom. By the end of the rehearsal everyone is so confused by Hilda's direction (including Hilda) that she begs Lily to elope. In the vignette, Pete kids Lily that when people hear about the free meal she's serving at the reception they'll come from as far away as Africa. She laughs it off until she reads the latest letter of acceptance: "Dear Cousin Lily, Expect me at the wedding. Am bringing a hundred spear carriers. Do not bother buying a wedding ring as your Aunt Nairobi will be glad to give you the one she wears in her nose. Love, Cousin Pete-chee from Tanganyika, Africa." They all look accusingly at Pete who hurries out, "I leave now. Africa speaks!"
NOTES: *Africa Speaks!* (1930) was an early documentary of a safari into the Belgian Congo.

"THE BREAKUP" MAR. 7, 1955
EPISODE # 24 FILMED ON SATURDAY, JANUARY 22, 1955
WRITERS: PARKE LEVY, LOU DERMAN, JOEL KANE
GUEST CAST: REGIS TOOMEY AS TOM ANDERSON, JESS BAKER AS WILFRED
KETTNER, PEGGY KNUDSEN AS AUDREY KETTNER, BUTCH BERNARD AS STEVIE
KETTNER

Lily happily opens wedding gifts from her family and friends (Matt and Ruth: crystal vase, Pete: coffee service, Hilda: carving set). She is excited about Tom's daughter, son-in-law, and grandson coming from New York to attend the wedding. Meanwhile at the airport, these three are waiting for Tom and Lily to pick them up. Audrey Kettner, Tom's daughter, reveals her shrewish temperament and resentment towards Lily by telling her husband that Lily will ruin Tom's life. Furthermore, she forbids her son Stevie to kiss Lily when she arrives. When she does meet Lily, Audrey informs her that they will not be staying with the Henshaws as planned. They'll rent a hotel room instead. Then she gives her father and Lily the brush-off, refusing their offer to drive them to the hotel. Later at the Henshaw home, the Kettners are very cool toward their hosts. Audrey makes snide remarks about the size of their home and the wedding gifts. Lily is alone in the kitchen when Stevie comes in from surveying the back yard. He lists all the things he saw: the orange tree, the lemon tree, the barbecue, and the fish pond. Then he asks to see Lily's hooks, "the ones Mother says you're trying to get into Grandpa." He says his mother said Lily was a gold digger. Lily asks Stevie if he thinks she should marry his grandfather, and he flatly tells her no, saying that his mother has said she'll break up Lily and Tom before long. Lily tries to hide her tears but knows it's futile to go ahead with the wedding plans. In the vignette, Hilda asks Lily why she doesn't fight for Tom, and she replies that she loves her children too much to subject them to Audrey's scorn.

"MEXICO" MAR. 14, 1955
EPISODE # 25 FILMED ON SATURDAY, JANUARY 29, 1955
WRITERS: PARKE LEVY, LOU DERMAN, JOEL KANE
GUEST CAST: NESTOR PAIVA AS MIGUEL, JULIAN RIVERO AS SENOR PRADO,
VICTOR MILLAN AS TINO THE ATTORNEY, FLORITA ROMERO AS THE YOUNG
MEXICAN GIRL, AND JOSE GONZALES-GONZALES AS PEPE

Lily decides to go to Mexico to forget her sadness over the broken engagement to Tom. Hilda asks to accompany her. (Pete: "America's loss will be Mexico's catastrophe.") In a small Mexican town, Lily and Hilda are arrested for shoplifting. A storekeeper thinks Lily stole the Mexican handbag she brought with her from Los Angeles (a birthday gift from Madeline Schweitzer). The police chief, whom they learn is a son of the storekeeper, locks them in a cell (Hilda: "We're prisoners behind the enchilada curtain!"). An attorney, another son of the shopkeeper, advises them to plead guilty, but Lily refuses. Miguel finally realizes they're innocent and invites them to stay for a fiesta. Hilda hikes up her skirt and does her best to keep up with a senorita doing the Mexican hat dance. **NOTES: Series writer Lou Derman had vacationed in Mexico just prior to writing this episode.**

"LILY'S NIECE" MAR. 21, 1955
EPISODE # 26 FILMED ON SATURDAY, FEBRUARY 5, 1955
WRITERS: PARKE LEVY, LOU DERMAN, JOEL KANE
GUEST CAST: SALLY FRASER AS HELEN WILSON, JOSEPH KEARNS AS CECIL
RUFUS, HAVIS DAVENPORT AS AGNES CARLISLE

Lily's 18-year-old niece Helen breaks up with her boyfriend and runs away from Philadelphia to Hollywood to become an actress. Her mother phones Lily to convince the headstrong Helen to come back home. Helen has hired bogus acting coach Cecil Rufus who has promised to make her a star. Lily confronts him: "Helen couldn't act frightened if the ceiling fell down." She concocts a scheme to send Helen packing. She pretends that Rufus thinks Lily also has great acting potential. Lily invites Helen to observe her rehearse with two of Rufus's "pupils," Cynthia Caldwell and Rock Farley, who are actually Hilda and Pete in disguise. Hilda has chosen a scene from a dreadful play which the Westwood Women's Cultural Club once produced. She sweeps through the front door wearing a flowery formal, a black boa, and huge picture hat. Pete enters in an Inverness cape and top hat. With a dramatic flourish, Hilda sets the scene: "I'm a lady of *30*. I'm sitting in my drawing room on Gramercy Square waiting for my *fiancé*." Pete, of course, plays her suitor, and Lily plays Hilda's mother. Even naïve Helen realizes their acting is terribly amateurish. She can't believe that "Cynthia" and "Rock" have been studying for eight years. Helen quickly realizes that in another eight years, she'll be 26, and her beau Bill will be married to someone else. Right on cue, the phone rings (Lily has timed it perfectly). It's Bill, and once Helen hears his voice, she starts packing her bag to rush home to him.

"MATT COOKS" MAR. 28, 1955
EPISODE # 27 FILMED ON SATURDAY, FEBRUARY 19, 1955
WRITERS: PARKE LEVY, LOU DERMAN, BEN STARR

Ruth spends three hours at the beauty parlor but gets upset when Matt doesn't even notice. An argument ensues, and Ruth decides she will ask Gladys to go with her to Palm Springs for the weekend. Ruth tries in vain to get Matt to ask her not to go, but he tells her that things will fine at home without her. He and Pete plan to clean house, cook, etc. Ruth reluctantly goes ahead with her plans, departing for the desert with Gladys. The next day Pete and Matt busy themselves with dusting and cleaning. Their nonchalant attitude about their absent wives has Lily very fretful. She and Hilda decide to sabotage the big dinner the boys have planned in order to make them admit they need the girls. They put bubble bath in the soup, plaster of Paris in the cake mix, and add red pepper, black pepper, and horseradish to the barbecue sauce. The desired results occur, perfectly timed to coincide with Ruth's return. Matt confesses he's glad she's back, and Ruth admits she had no choice—Lily didn't put her suitcase in the car.

NOTES: Only the five principals appear in this episode.

"THEATER TICKETS" APR. 4, 1955
EPISODE # 28 FILMED ON SATURDAY, FEBRUARY 26, 1955
WRITERS: PARKE LEVY, LOU DERMAN, BEN STARR
GUEST CAST: PITT HERBERT AS MR. STEVENS THE BOX OFFICE MANAGER, PERCY HELTON AS WHITEY, EMORY PARNELL AS MR. MCGRUDER THE POOL HALL MANAGER, PHIL TEAD AS BOOMY

Lily tells Matt and Ruth that her anniversary gift to them is tickets to a hit play ("Hail the King!"). Then she discovers that Hilda, who was supposed to pick them up, let her down. Now Lily must buy two more tickets without the children knowing it. When she goes to the box office she learns it's a sellout. A scalper called Whitey offers her a pair of tickets for $24. Considering the original price was $4.80 each, Lily loudly protests, frightening him away. When she later regrets not buying them from Whitey, Lily gets a tip that he can be located at 442 Aspen Street. Before they head there, Lily and Hilda leave a NOTES with their whereabouts for Madeline Schweitzer, who's expected to drop by. In the meantime Matt and Pete decide to go bowling, but they realize Matt's ball is in the car that Lily took. They follow the girls to 442 Aspen Street, which, unknown to either party, is McGruder's Pool Hall. Once there, Lily and Hilda decide to play pool ($1.00 an hour) while they wait for Whitey. Never having played before, they make up the rules as they fumble along. When Matt and Pete arrive, they're shocked to find Lily and Hilda (in hats and gloves) playing pool with some rather shady characters. Soon Whitey arrives, and while Matt's distracted, Lily buys the tickets.

"THE PSYCHIATRIST" APR. 11, 1955
EPISODE # 29 FILMED ON SATURDAY, MARCH 12, 1955
WRITERS: PARKE LEVY, LOU DERMAN, BEN STARR
GUEST CAST: GRANDON RHODES AS DR. MILTON CARLTON, EDITH SIMMONS AS MISS HODGES THE NURSE, HOWARD MCNEAR AS MR. MAYO, BENNETT GREEN AS THE DELIVERY BOY

Lily is excited about taking cello lessons from Mr. Mayo, but Ruth thinks it's her mother's way of dealing with the recent breakup with Tom Anderson. Vowing to get Lily interested in dating again, Ruth seeks help from Hilda who suggests, as a possible date, an analyst who's a cousin of her current boyfriend. Knowing that Lily is wary of matchmaking, Hilda pretends to need psychiatric help and asks Lily to meet her at Dr. Carlton's office. She tricks the doctor, too, telling him that Lily needs therapy. When Lily waits alone in the doctor's private office, she sees notes he left behind describing her symptoms (*per* Hilda). Lily realizes she's been set up and becomes furious with Hilda's scheme. To make herself unappealing to the doctor, she puts on a real show for him, swatting at imaginary flies and ducking from bats and flying saucers. She also tells him that she lives on Mars because the taxes are lower. Dr. Carlton soon catches on to her ploy and confides that he, too, has been the victim of matchmaking recently. When he asks her out to dinner, Lily tells him she'll cancel her trip—the flying saucer will have to leave without her.

NOTES: Grandon Rhodes played Lily's beau earlier in the season in Episode #9 "Lily's Mother-in-Law." Edith Simmons, Verna Felton's daughter-in-law, made the first of her nine *December Bride* appearances in this episode. Howard McNear, fondly remembered by television fans as Floyd the barber on *The Andy Griffith Show*, was Verna Felton's neighbor and friend.

"GOSSIP" APR. 18. 1955
EPISODE # 30 FILMED ON SATURDAY, MARCH 19, 1955
WRITERS: PARKE LEVY, LOU DERMAN, BEN STARR
GUEST CAST: GAIL BONNEY AS MADELINE SCHWEITZER

Matt announces that he and Pete are taking Ruth and Gladys to Big Bear for the weekend, but Ruth refuses to leave Lily alone with a bad cold. Lily doesn't want to ruin their getaway so she asks Hilda to stay with her. Later Madeline Schweitzer arrives to confront Lily about a rumor circulating among their club members. It's traced back to Hilda who claimed Madeline got a facelift. Lily explains that Hilda must have gotten mixed up when she overheard Lily say, "Madeline's having a facial, and I'm giving her a lift." Madeline leaves in a huff, putting all the blame on Hilda. Lily broaches the subject tactfully with Hilda, suggesting she apologize to Madeline, but Hilda becomes indignant and blames Madeline for being a tattletale. An argument follows between the best friends, and Hilda stomps out, "If you like Madeline Schweitzer so much, *she* can stay with you!" The children cancel their trip, and Lily feels responsible. When Hilda comes over to return everything she's ever borrowed, Lily apologizes sweetly and begins to reminisce over all the items, including the handbag that landed them in the Mexican jail. She puts a grass skirt (from "The Luau" episode) around Hilda who begins to hula. Now all is well, and the children rush off to pack for the trip.

"MATT'S MUSTACHE" APR. 25, 1955
EPISODE # 31 FILMED ON SATURDAY, MARCH 26, 1955
WRITERS: PARKE LEVY, LOU DERMAN, BEN STARR
GUEST CAST: JOHN QUALEN AS SVEN JORGENSON

Ruth hates Matt's new mustache so much she refuses to kiss him until he shaves it off. Lily believes if she's out of the house for a while, they'll have to end their feud and make up. She tells them she's going to Philadelphia to visit her sister Mary, but in reality she's decided to check into the Belfair Hotel downtown. She asks Mr. Jorgenson, a friend she's met at night school, to take her to the hotel. Later while Lily's out, Ruth takes a phone message confirming Lily's hotel reservation and then another one from Mr. Jorgenson who simply says, "I got the license." Ruth and Matt assume it's a marriage license and that the happy couple plan to stay at the Belfair after their elopement. (When they tell Hilda, she rushes out to enroll in night school!) Later Lily is confused when she's showered with gifts from the children, Pete, and Hilda. When Mr. Jorgenson arrives, he's stunned by the gifts for him as well. After Matt tells them they know they're planning to elope, Lily explains that Mr. Jorgenson got a license to barber. She also tells them that she thought they'd settle the issue about the mustache if she weren't around. Embarrassed by Lily's thoughtfulness, Ruth tells Matt to keep the mustache, but he says no. They kiss, and Ruth whines, "Oh, Matt, shave it off!" In the vignette, Matt comes downstairs with his face bandaged. A nervous Mr. Jorgenson follows him, "I've been a barber for 33 years, but I've never been so close to being a bridegroom!"

"THE LINE-UP" MAY 2, 1955
EPISODE # 32 FILMED ON SATURDAY, APRIL 2, 1955
WRITERS: PARKE LEVY, LOU DERMAN, BEN STARR
GUEST CAST: JOHN GALLAUDET AS CAPT. MULLAHAN, NORMAN LEAVITT AS JOE THE MOVER, JACK LOMAS AS OFFICER PHILLIPS, LESTER DORR AS SPERBER THE PLAINTIFF

Lily wants to surprise the children by having their living room furniture re-upholstered. Hilda recommends a man for the job (Mr. Millar), but since he won't pick up the furniture Lily decides to rent a trailer. Now she must convince the children to go to Coronado for the weekend so the furniture will be ready when they return. Ruth doesn't want to leave Lily alone, but Lily fibs and says Hilda's sister has invited them to San Francisco. Not keen on the idea of going away, Ruth tells Matt they'll just go for a long drive and come back after Lily and Hilda have left. But when they arrive home and find their living room furniture missing, they call the police to report the robbery. The police then pick up Lily driving the trailer and arrest her, thinking she stole the furniture. She tells them to call Hilda, "She planned all of this." The police captain orders a car to 1123 Edgemont, Hilda's address. Lily is then put in a lineup with two other women, both taller and larger, and is identified by Mr. Sperber as the woman who robbed his poultry market the night before. Hilda enters, with disheveled hair, and is shoved into the line-up. Sperber yells, "That little fat one was with her. She's the one who chased me with a meat cleaver!" Hilda retorts, "Well, for your information, last night I was in a steam bath with Madeline Schweitzer!" Just then Matt and Ruth rush in and identify Lily and Hilda. In the vignette, Captain Mullahan tells Lily that while she was in the line-up, someone stole her furniture off the trailer outside.

"THE OTHER COUPLE" MAY 9, 1955
EPISODE # 33 FILMED ON SATURDAY, APRIL 9, 1955
WRITERS: PARKE LEVY, LOU DERMAN, BEN STARR
GUEST CAST: ROBERT HUTTON AS BILL NOVAK, JEAN HOWELL AS ANN NOVAK

Newlywed Ann Novak is upset because her husband doesn't want her mother to move in with them. Lily suggests that Ann bring him to her house to see how well Matt, Ruth, and she get along. But in the meantime, Matt and Ruth have had an argument over Matt's separate bank account. Lily begs them to be cordial while the Novaks are visiting. They practically kill each other with kindness, but it fools the young couple so well that Ann's husband agrees for her mother to live with them. Matt and Ruth make up after Matt gives Ruth a fountain pen and this NOTES: "Use this pen. Write any amount. From now on, you share my account."

"LILY'S SONG" MAY 16, 1955
EPISODE # 34 FILMED ON SATURDAY, APRIL 16, 1955
WRITERS: PARKE LEVY, LOU DERMAN, BEN STARR
GUEST CAST: FRANK FERGUSON AS MR. SCHUYLER, HY AVERBACK AS MARK HARMON

Lily and Hilda must write a sentimental song to close their club's show. They select a poem, "The Wonder of Your Smile," and set it to music. After it's performed (to mixed reviews by Matt and Ruth), Hilda manages to get a spot on a TV show called "Bring It and Sing It," designed for one amateur to introduce a new song and another to sing it on the air. The winning song will be published, and the winners collect $2500 as prize money. Elsie Pringle's son Roland is chosen to sing it, but at the last minute he gets laryngitis. Lily pinch hits for him, and Hilda accompanies her on the piano. But once Lily is in front of an audience, she freezes. Matt, who has called the lyrics "trite" and the tune "nothing," steps in and sings the song for Lily. He realizes the words express his true feelings for his mother-in-law. They embrace when he concludes. Later at home, Mr. Harmon, the show's emcee, phones with the news that Lily and Hilda's song won by a close margin. Matt apologizes to Lily for thinking the song was corny.
NOTES: **In the concluding scene, Hilda is jumping for joy upon hearing the good news. She bumps into Pete, knocking him flat on the coffee table. She bounces off of him, falling backward onto the sofa. Harry Morgan tries to hide his smile after this stunt; it's very obvious he's about to break up.**

"LILY IS BORED" MAY 23, 1955
EPISODE # 7 FILMED ON SATURDAY, SEPTEMBER 11, 1954
WRITERS: PARKE LEVY, LOU DERMAN
GUEST CAST: HERBERT HEYES AS DR. PRITCHARD, JOHN MEEK AS STEVIE, SHIRLEY MITCHELL AS MARGIE, RUSSELL TRENT AS TOM THE POLICEMAN, MELINDA PLOWMAN AS KATHY, WALTER KINGSFORD AS ERIC RODNEY,

ELVIA ALLMAN AS NORA HIGBY, LU LEONARD AS MILDRED MORRISON, KIRK KIRKHAM AS SANDORO

Matt and Ruth call a doctor for Lily because she's been "tired and listless." The doctor can find nothing physically wrong with her, but he tells Matt and Ruth that her fatigue is perhaps psychosomatic. He recommends that they keep Lily stimulated so her boredom will pass and she'll return to health. So Matt and Ruth invite an assortment of folks over to help fill Lily's time. What they don't know is that Lily is tired and listless because she already has an assortment of visitors each day. Stevie comes over to practice his violin for Lily. Newlywed Margie needs cooking lessons (her husband said her eggs weren't fried—"they were electrocuted!"). Tom the cop likes to stop by for coffee and a chat. Kathy shows off her pirouettes. By the time they leave, Lily is exhausted. Hilda, recently returned from Las Vegas, bustles in and finds Lily frazzled. She reassures Lily, "We all crack up at times." Then she jumps in to an imitation of Sophie Tucker's trademark song, "Some of These Days." Lily is amused but she wonders why Hilda is trying to entertain her. Hilda explains that Ruth sent her over to keep Lily occupied. She then sings and dances to an old number, "The Bobolinks Fancy Ball," which she performed with her brother George when they first broke into show business. (They called their act "Songs, Dances, and Unpaid Hotel Bills.") It's a rather silly song, and even Hilda says, "You know, I think it killed vaudeville!" She rushes off but first warns Lily that Matt and Ruth are sending others to amuse her. Soon Eric Rodney enters. He proceeds to tell Lily all about his African adventures living among the natives. When Nora Higby arrives she picks up the pace by swinging Lily around in a doesy-doe. Rotund Mildred Morrison ("You can call me 'Slim'") interrupts the square-dance to invite Lily on trip through Mexico by jeep. When magician Sandoro releases doves from his hat, Lily flees the scene.

NOTES: This episode is incorrectly reported on internet websites as being the second episode of the series, however, it aired much later in the season, probably due to its obvious overhaul. The original script does not include the characters of Hilda, Eric, Nora, Mildred, and Sandoro. Verna Felton sang "The Bobolinks Fancy Ball" (written in 1901 by Louis W. Jones) early in her stage career. Shirley Mitchell (born 1919) was a regular on the radio show *Sealtest Village Store* which also featured Verna. Elvia Allman (1904-1992) performed with Verna on radio and was a member of the Radio Women's War Service, which Verna helped to found. Lu Leonard (1927-2004) went on to perform in Broadway musicals, but her fifteen minutes of fame came when she appeared in the movie *Micki and Maude*.

DECEMBER BRIDE
THE SECOND SEASON: 1955-56

CAST:	Spring Byington as Lily Ruskin
	Dean Miller as Matt Henshaw
	Frances Rafferty as Ruth Henshaw
	Harry Morgan as Pete Porter
	Verna Felton as Hilda Crocker
DIRECTOR:	Jerry Thorpe
CREATOR:	Parke Levy
PRODUCER:	Samuel Marx
WRITERS:	Parke Levy, Lou Derman, Ben Gershman, Samuel Marx, Kay Lenard, Bill Freedman, Peggy Chantler, Bill Davenport
COMPOSER:	Eliot Daniel
CONDUCTOR:	Wilbur Hatch
DIRECTOR OF PHOTOGRAPHY:	Karl Freund, A.S.C.
PRODUCTION MANAGER:	Argyle Nelson
ART DIRECTOR:	Claudio Guzman
SET DRESSER:	Theodore Offenbecker
ASSISTANT DIRECTOR:	Marvin Stuart
RE-RECORDING EDITOR:	Robert Reeve
FILM EDITOR:	Doug Hines
EDITORIAL SUPERVISOR:	Dann Cahn, A.C.E.
SOUND:	Glen Glenn Sound Co.
ANNOUNCER:	Dick Joy
SPONSOR:	Instant Maxwell House Coffee

"THE BOXING SHOW" OCT. 3, 1955
EPISODE # 36 FILMED ON TUESDAY, AUGUST 30, 1955
WRITERS: PARKE LEVY, LOU DERMAN, BEN GERSHMAN
GUEST CAST: ART ARAGON AS HIMSELF, JOHN GALLAUDET AS JIMMY FORBES, DOUGLAS EVANS AS MR. HARRIS, JOHN INDRISANO AS BILLY, SAM MCDANIEL AS SAM THE TRAINER

While brainstorming for fundraising projects for the Children's Sunshine Camp, Lily reads a newspaper item about a charity fight in Chicago. When she searches for boxers in the local telephone book, Pete suggests that Art Aragon would draw a crowd. Lily and Hilda seek out Aragon at his gym, but he quickly declines to help them. He's given up boxing for acting. ("Monroe gave 'em curves, the golden boy's gonna give 'em muscles.") He refuses to discuss the matter with the ladies and begins jumping rope. Hilda, in an effort to get his attention, jumps into the rope and lasts five or six turns, but he still won't listen. Then Lily proposes a bargain he can't refuse. If she secures Aragon a role in the Westwood Playhouse's production of *Golden Boy*, he will consent to box for the club fundraiser. However, when she talks to Mr. Harris at the playhouse, she is crestfallen to discover that he has decided to produce *The Women* instead. Meanwhile, Matt and Pete feel badly about not helping Lily find a boxer, so they decide to be Lily's fighters and begin practicing in the living room. When Aragon comes to see Lily, he mistakes the boys as his competitors for the stage role. A little bout ensues but is thankfully interrupted by the arrival of Lily and Hilda who inform Aragon that the play is off. After confiding that he was first coached in boxing at a charity camp when he was a kid, he shrugs off the news and volunteers to fight in the fundraiser. In the vignette, Ruth suggests that Lily and Hilda pose for publicity photos wearing boxing gloves and pretend to fight the boys. Hilda socks Pete to the floor, and Lily knocks Matt down. Then Pete declares them the new champions, holding their arms over their heads while they put their feet on top of Matt as Ruth snaps the picture.
NOTES: Art Aragon (1927-2008), a colorful and popular contender in both the lightweight and welterweight divisions, was boxing's "Golden Boy" in the 1950's in Los Angeles. Sam McDaniel had the distinction of being the only African American who ever appeared on *December Bride*. He supported on both of the opening episodes for the first and second seasons.

"THE PIZZA SHOW" OCT. 10, 1955
EPISODE # 35 FILMED ON TUESDAY, AUGUST 23, 1955
WRITERS: PARKE LEVY, LOU DERMAN, BEN GERSHMAN
SUPPORTING CAST: ROBERT CLARK AS JOHNNY STONE, DAMIAN O'FLYNN AS MR. LLOYD, JERRY MATHERS AS THE CUB SCOUT

After Lily is escorted home by a Cub Scout, she wonders if it's because of her age. She doesn't want to grow old, so she decides to look for a job. Hilda wants one, too. After striking out with every employment agency in town, they run a large ad in the newspaper, seeking work. Humiliated by this stunt, Matt says it makes him look like he's penniless. Later Lily and Hilda have lunch in a small café whose struggling owner, Johnny Stone, wants to sell it. They convince him to convert it into an Italian restaurant in order to attract a buyer, and they volunteer to work as waitress and cook. To keep peace at home, Lily pretends she's working as an interior decorator. Several weeks later a prospective buyer is expected to visit the restaurant. Matt and Pete decide to have lunch there the same day, not knowing that Lily and Hilda work there. Hilda tries to hide behind the spaghetti she's tossing, and Lily covers her face with a menu and assumes a phony Italian accent. (Pete: "How is the pizza?" Lily: "She is-a like-a home." Pete: "Like-a home, eh? Well, that kills that!") Lily soon blows her cover, but Johnny comes out from the kitchen to announce that the restaurant sold. The new owner asks Lily and Hilda to stay on, but Lily says no. She says now that they've proven that women their age can be useful, they're ready to move on to new things. In the vignette, Lily and Hilda sit at the kitchen table as Lily reads a postcard from Johnny who has moved back to Kansas to be with his convalescent wife. He writes: "If you and Hilda need a job, come and see me. I have opened an Italian restaurant in Hutchinson."

NOTES: This vignette was not part of the original script, but it was added as a way for Verna Felton to recognize her fans in Hutchinson, Kansas, where she had filmed *Picnic* earlier in the summer.

"LILY AND THE WOLF" Oct. 17, 1955
Episode # 38 Filmed Saturday, September 17, 1955
Writers: Parke Levy, Samuel Marx, Kay Lenard
Guest Cast: Charles Coburn as Jonathan Applegate, Lilian Hamilton as Mrs. Pemberton, Eric Wilson as James the Butler

While Lily is depressed that she can't find a job, Matt is discouraged because a wealthy client continues to reject his sketches. Lily turned down her last job offer, private secretary to a 70-year-old man who's had a succession of twelve secretaries in a short amount of time. It's soon realized that this man and Matt's fussy client are one and the same. Lily reconsiders taking the job to persuade the client to approve Matt's sketches, but Matt prefers that Lily not interfere. She ignores his wishes and is promptly hired by the client's sister who shows Lily a photo gallery of her brother's former secretaries, all young and beautiful. Mr. Applegate calls the display "my playground." Lily informs him, "I have news for you—school is out." Applegate is not dismayed and chases Lily around the room. When he kisses her hand, she says his flirtatious ways are "corny." She refutes his claim to be a man of the world, feigning that she has known many such men in exotic locales like the Isle of Capri. Applegate says he won't fire her until he proves to her that he's not a cornball. Meanwhile Hilda spills the beans to Matt and Ruth that Lily is Applegate's new secretary (for $150 per week). Horrified that rumors of Applegate's wolfish behavior might be true, Matt and Pete rush to bring Lily home. Before they arrive, Lily convinces Applegate to choose Matt's sketches. When the boys burst in, they find Applegate with his arms around Lily. The old fellow is merely trying to help her with a stuck window, but Matt demands "the old goat" release Lily. When Applegate realizes Lily is Matt's mother-in-law, he finds her even more charming because of her shrewd deceit. Furthermore, he promises to retain Matt as his architect and relinquish Lily from his employ.

NOTES: Charles Coburn (1877-1961) played with Spring Byington in several films such as _Heaven Can Wait_ and _Louisa_. He and she were so popular in the latter that they were once considered as co-stars in a television series. Coburn was seventy-eight years old when he filmed this episode. Byington was one month shy of being sixty-nine. It was one of the few times when the actor playing Byington's love interest was actually older than she.

"RUTH NEGLECTS MATT" OCT. 24, 1955
EPISODE # 39 FILMED ON SATURDAY, SEPTEMBER 24, 1955
WRITERS: PARKE LEVY, LOU DERMAN, BILL FREEDMAN
GUEST CAST: JOI LANSING AS LINDA

Ever since Ruth became chairman of her charity club, she spends all her time away from home. Lily sees trouble brewing so she feigns a broken wrist so Ruth will have to stay home to clean and cook for Matt. But her tactic backfires when Ruth tells her to hire a maid with the allowance Matt gives her. Lily reacts by hiring a buxom blonde to make Ruth jealous. Later when Matt and Pete meet Linda, who's actually a professional model, they go gaga. Pete: "She could cook arsenic, and I'd eat it." Matt confesses he'd rather have Ruth at home so he decides to play along with Lily's scheme. Ruth comes home after 8 p.m. and finds Linda wiggling her hips as she waits on Matt. After Matt declines Pete's invitation to go bowling and Lily accepts Hilda's suggestion to go to a Rudolph Valentino movie, Ruth's hesitant about leaving Matt alone with Linda. When a club member phones Ruth to remind her about a late meeting, Ruth asks if she can have a position not requiring her to leave the house. Matt smiles, "Welcome home, honey." They kiss.

NOTES: Joi Lansing (1929-1972) made a career out of playing models. At the time this episode was filmed, she appeared as a semi-regular on _The Bob Cummings Show_ as model Shirley Swanson.

"THE SHOPLIFTER" OCT. 31, 1955
EPISODE # 37 FILMED ON TUESDAY, SEPTEMBER 6, 1955
WRITERS: PARKE LEVY, LOU DERMAN, BEN GERSHMAN
GUEST CAST: GAIL BONNEY AS MADELINE SCHWEITZER, ALMIRA SESSIONS AS ELSIE PRINGLE, ROY ROBERTS AS JAMES BLACK, FRITZ FELD AS MR. DECORDOVA, RUSSELL TRENT AS MR. FLYNN, BENNETT GREEN AS THE MESSENGER

When Lily arrives home after a Friday of shopping, Matt gives her some exciting news—he has arranged for her to interview for a job as the social director of the

Parkside Country Club. She's delighted, but she has some exciting news, too. While she was trying on a "darling little red hat with white feathers" in Bentley's Department Store, she witnessed a woman shoplifting. ("I wouldn't be seen in the things she stole.") When the evening paper arrives, she discovers that her name has been mistakenly switched with the name of the shoplifter (Maude Hackett). Because a correction cannot be printed until Monday, Lily is concerned about her reputation in the interim. Matt assures her that none of her friends will read it. But the next day, as Lily is preparing for a luncheon interview with Mr. DeCordova, the manager of the country club, she receives a surprise visit from Madeline Schweitzer and Elsie Pringle, officers in Lily's women's club. They cast suspicious glances at Lily's stunning new outfit before getting down to business. They have heard (from Hilda) about Lily's job interview so they suggest that she resign as club treasurer, on the pretense that they're doubtful she'll have time to handle both positions. Quickly realizing their true motivation, Hilda comes to Lily's defense, "Why don't you two old buzzards stop circling? Swoop down and get it over with!" And then she explains to Lily, "Can't you see what's happened? They read it in the paper, and they think you're going to fly away to South America with the club's crummy twelve dollars and twelve cents!" When Madeline and Elsie don't deny this, Lily angrily turns over the club treasury and ushers them out. Then Mr. DeCordova's secretary phones to cancel the job interview, citing the newspaper item as the reason. Lily immediately phones James Black, the editor of the Westwood Gazette, who, fearful of a lawsuit, agrees to publish her dictated retraction, including the statement that she never stole anything in her life. When Ruth finds an unfamiliar hat in the hall closet, Lily is horrified to discover that she walked out of the department store without paying for it. Now her conscience won't allow the retraction to be printed, but neither does she know how to return the hat without casting doubt on her reputation. So, Hilda, without Lily's knowledge, slips out of the house with the hat. Mr. DeCordova arrives to tell Lily that she can report to work the next day without waiting for a retraction to be printed. When she replies that none will appear in the paper, he asks if she shoplifted or not. Unable to answer him, Lily forfeits her job as social director. Then Mr. Black arrives, saying he did not clearly understand Lily's reason to stop the retraction. As she begins to explain about the hat, Hilda rushes in, "Lily, all of your problems are solved. I took your hat back, and no one will ever know you stole it." Mr. Black is baffled, so Lily explains the entire story, admitting, "I became a shoplifter." Luckily, Mr. Black's amused by it all, and furthermore, he's very impressed with Lily's writing ability, citing her retraction as a classic. He then asks her to write a human interest column for his paper, which she suggests calling "Laughing at Life with Lily."

"LET YOURSELF GO" Nov. 7, 1955
EPISODE # 40 FILMED ON SATURDAY, OCTOBER 1, 1955
WRITERS: PARKE LEVY, LOU DERMAN, BILL FREEDMAN
GUEST CAST: ROLFE SEDAN AS MR. O'BRIEN

When Ruth breaks the grocer's rule at Harry's Market and squeezes tomatoes when he's not looking, Lily is inspired to write a column to urge readers to "throw off their imaginary shackles and inhibitions." She says people should do what they want to do, things that make them happy. She titles her column, "Let Yourself Go," to which Hilda replies, "Lily, look at my shape—I've went!" After the column runs, Elsie Pringle dies her hair champagne pink, Matt starts smoking cigars (against Ruth's wishes), and Pete takes up the saxophone ("For years I've wanted to play it, but Gladys says it's too noisy—her mother *whispers* louder than this thing can play!"). Hilda bursts through the front door wearing a leather jacket, gloves, and goggles and announces she's bought a motorcycle, something she's wanted since she was a little girl. Lily is amazed at the changes her column has wrought, but then her editor, Mr. O'Brien, arrives at her door, sporting a black eye. A reporter he discharged three years earlier came back to the office and socked him in the eye. The henpecked Mr. O'Brien is now scared to go home to his wife. Pete has marital worries also: Gladys locked him out of the house for three hours one night, demanding he get rid of the saxophone. Hilda is arrested for driving her motorcycle on the street after being frightened by a horse, while Ruth is having no luck convincing Matt to give up the cigars. Ruth decides to teach Matt a lesson by substituting his cigars with exploding ones that she orders from the Globe Novelty Company. Mr. O'Brien returns to inform Lily that he took her advice and locked his overbearing wife in her room. When he let her out, she respected him so much for standing up to her that she kissed him. Matt invites Mr. O'Brien to celebrate by smoking one of his cigars, and it explodes in his face. They all have a good laugh over that. Then Pete goes home to try Mr. O'Brien's tactic on Gladys. Soon he phones to say that Gladys locked *him* in *his* room instead.

NOTES: This is the first of six appearances for character actor Rolfe Sedan (1896-1982), a veteran of over 200 movies, including *The Wizard of Oz*. The original script credits Ben Gershman as the third writer instead of Bill Freedman. Since series writer Lou Derman played the saxophone, he chose to assign the same instrument to Pete Porter.

"THE LAUNDROMAT SHOW" Nov. 14, 1955
EPISODE # 41 FILMED ON SATURDAY, OCTOBER 8, 1955
WRITERS: PARKE LEVY, LOU DERMAN, BILL FREEDMAN
GUEST CAST: HERBERT MARSHALL AS HIMSELF, MAXINE SEMON AS LULU THE LAUNDROMAT CUSTOMER, BILL FORREST AS THE DIRECTOR, KAM TONG AS CHOU LAI

Lily forgets to tell the dry cleaners not to put starch in Matt's "lucky" shirt. Ruth: "Starch irritates his skin." Hilda: "He's lucky—it stretches mine." Matt will not conduct an important business deal without his lucky shirt so Lily takes it to a laundromat to wash it for him. When she and Hilda get there, there are no available washers, except for one being loaded by film actor Herbert Marshall. He's leaving soon for a location shoot in Hong Kong for his new picture *Terror in the Orient*. He needs some clothes laundered right away. Lily asks if he would allow her to put Matt's shirts in with his load. When he agrees, Hilda throws in her handkerchief just to say it was washed with Herbert Marshall's clothes. But instead of going home with Matt's shirt, Lily and Hilda take one of Marshall's. When they cannot find his home in Beverly Hills to make the switch, they go to his studio where they get parts as extras in Marshall's movie. During a scene in which they play Chinese peasants on a boat, Lily passes a NOTES to Marshall explaining the mix-up. He stops filming to inform them that Matt's shirt is packed in a trunk bound for Hong Kong. Lily then buys Matt a new shirt to pass off as the lucky one, but he is not fooled. Marshall then arrives at the Henshaw home with Matt's shirt. He went all the way to the pier to retrieve it because he understands Matt's feelings completely. As it turns out, Marshall never makes a motion picture without his own "lucky shirt."

NOTES: This episode is also known as "The Herbert Marshall Show," but the actual script in the Parke Levy Papers is titled "The Guest Star Show." Bill Freedman is credited onscreen as the third writer, but the script lists Ben Gershman instead. Maxine Semon (1909-1985) has a funny bit as a rude customer in the Laundromat.

"SKIDROW" Nov. 21, 1955
EPISODE # 42 FILMED ON SATURDAY, OCTOBER 15, 1955
WRITERS: PARKE LEVY, LOU DERMAN, BEN GERSHMAN
GUEST CAST: IRENE TEDROW AS PHYLLIS BAXTER, PERCY HELTON AS HARRY, JOE BESSER AS JOE, MICHAEL GARTH AS THE TV HOST, LOUIS NICOLLETI AS THE COUNTER MAN

When Lily hears that the city's soup kitchens are facing closures due to a lack of funds, she plans to research them for a series of articles. She doesn't want Matt and Ruth to worry about her safety in these neighborhoods, so she keeps her whereabouts a mystery. She and Hilda disguise themselves as the homeless, dressed in battered hats, moth-eaten sweaters, and old skirts, in an attempt to blend in with the other derelicts at the soup kitchen. Suddenly a television camera crew enters to film a live broadcast of *This Is Your City*. Matt, Ruth, and Pete are watching at home when they spot Lily and Hilda among those who are interviewed regarding the plight of the soup kitchen regulars. Lily makes a plea for viewers to help the homeless. Shortly thereafter, Phyllis Baxter, Lily's friend from Philadelphia who's visiting Los Angeles, arrives. She's seen the broadcast also, and she begins to berate Matt for allowing his mother-in-law to go around in such rags. Lily and Hilda soon arrive, but Phyllis doesn't believe Lily's explanation. She overreacts with tears, and before rushing out, presses a ten-dollar bill in Lily's hand, which Lily decides she'll use as her first contribution toward saving the soup kitchen. In the vignette, Lily receives a phone call from the television station with the news that they've received over $400 in donations. Hilda drags in, saying she's been locked out of her apartment because the new janitor didn't recognize her wearing rags.

NOTES: Pete calls Hilda "Tugboat Annie" when he sees her disguise. At one time Verna Felton was hopeful she'd be cast in a television series based on that MGM movie which starred Marie Dressler, but the title role was given to Minerva Urecal (1894-1966). Ben Gershman received screen credit as the third writer for this episode, but Bill Freedman's name appears on the script.

"BIG GAME HUNTER" Nov. 28, 1955
EPISODE # 43 FILMED ON SATURDAY, OCTOBER 29, 1955
WRITERS: PARKE LEVY, LOU DERMAN, BEN GERSHMAN
GUEST CAST: HARRY CHESHIRE AS STANLEY POOLE, PIERRE WATKIN AS MR. LEGRANDE

Lily makes Matt and Ruth believe she has a boyfriend so they'll stop needling her about dating. (They think she's spending too much time on her column.) When they press her for details, Lily makes up the name Roger Crofton, claiming he likes to hunt big game in Africa. Matt insists she invite Roger to dinner that evening because he's entertaining a special client, Mr. LeGrande, who's very interested in Africa. Lily asks Hilda if her new boyfriend, Stanley Poole, would pose as Crofton. Stanley's an exterminator, and Hilda and Lily track him down under a house where he's trying to catch a mole. Hilda tries "sweet talk" first, then threatens, "Are you gonna have to go up to Mulholland Drive alone tomorrow night?" Stanley agrees to help, but later phones to say he can't make it. Eventually he does show up at the Henshaw home, but he's drunk and looking for Hilda ("Where's my Butterball?"). Having forgotten he's posing as a big game hunter, Stanley confuses LeGrande and Matt when they ask him about his methods. ("I use traps, spray . . . if that doesn't work, I step on 'em!") Pete, not realizing Stanley came through after all, arrives in safari attire, posing as Crofton. This really confuses everyone until Lily explains the whole situation. LeGrande wonders why Lily must resort to making up a boyfriend. When he announces that he's an available bachelor, everyone eases out of the room. In the vignette, Lily reads the card accompanying the large bouquet LeGrande has sent her: "Lions, tigers, buffalo await our rendezvous—would you care to join me this Sunday at the zoo?"

NOTES: Harry Cheshire (1891-1968), who appeared in the *December Bride* pilot episode as Lily's love interest, is perfectly delightful in this episode as a tipsy Stanley. Bill Freedman is credited as a writer in the original script, but Ben Gershman is not. At the time of this episode, Mulholland Drive, which looks down on the nighttime lights of Hollywood, was a fabled location for lovers to park.

"FAMILY QUARREL" DEC. 5, 1955
EPISODE # 44 FILMED ON SATURDAY, NOVEMBER 5, 1955
WRITERS: PARKE LEVY, SAMUEL MARX, PEGGY CHANTLER
GUEST CAST: GAIL BONNEY AS MADELINE SCHWEITZER, MADGE BLAKE AS
ANITA HENDERSON, JOE FORTE AS HECTOR FLAGG

Matt writes a letter in praise of Lily for a contest ("What I Think of My Mother-in-Law"). However, as usual, Pete doesn't spare the criticism of his own mother-in-law in his contest entry. Matt convinces him to rewrite his letter and stuffs Pete's first draft in the living room desk where Lily finds it later and assumes the writer is Matt. Believing that Matt thinks she's meddlesome, Lily attempts to make Matt and Ruth displeased enough to ask her to move. She devises what she thinks is a perfect plan. She invites her fellow club members to bring the animals they've collected for a wildlife exhibit to the Henshaw home. Madeline brings a squawking parrot, Anita arrives with a raccoon named Wilbur ("Don't sing 'Davy Crockett'—he goes into convulsions!"), and Hilda enters with Marlon, a chimp dressed in overalls, sunglasses, and Tyrolean hat. When Matt and Ruth come home, Lily tells them the animals will have to stay in their living room for two days while Madeline's garage is painted. Expecting Matt to hit the ceiling, Lily is confounded when he beams, saying he'll have his own private zoo. Then Mr. Flagg, the contest representative, arrives to announce Lily as the winner. When he shows Lily the letter Matt wrote, she's very touched and begs Matt's forgiveness. She tells him to put her with the animals because she made a monkey of herself.
NOTES: **Madge Blake (1899-1969) was one of television's busiest character actresses, playing sweet old ladies in everything from *I Love Lucy* to *Batman*.**

"HIGH SIERRAS" DEC. 12, 1955
EPISODE # 45 FILMED ON SATURDAY, NOVEMBER 12, 1955
WRITERS: PARKE LEVY, LOU DERMAN, BILL FREEDMAN
GUEST CAST: DAN DURYEA AS HIMSELF, DOUGLAS FOWLEY AS CHARLIE, JOEY
RAY AS THE POLICE OFFICER

Actor Dan Duryea and his pal Charlie, a film director, have chosen a cabin in the High Sierras as a retreat from Hollywood's paparazzi. Their solitude is disturbed when Lily and Hilda, also vacationing in the mountains, stumble upon them. The ladies don't recognize Duryea, but when Lily tells him she's a newspaper columnist, he decides the only way to get rid of them is to scare them away. Duryea and Charlie enact a scene from a movie, making Lily and Hilda think they are convicts on the lam. They leave their cabin but tell Lily and Hilda to be gone by the time they return. However, Lily and Hilda discover their vehicle has two flat tires so Lily gets on the ham radio to plead for help. Then she discovers a cigarette lighter engraved with Duryea's name. She and Hilda realize they've been tricked so they decide to turn the tables on the men when they return. They cook up some soup, and once the men have eaten it, the ladies tell them it was laced with rat poison. Before any more confusion transpires, a police officer arrives at the door. He's heard Lily's S.O.S. on the radio. At this point, Duryea admits his true identity, and Lily gets an interview with him for her paper. In the vignette, Duryea drops by the Henshaw home to admit to Lily that he had the final laugh. The biographical details he shared with her at the cabin were actually those of actor Richard Widmark.

"RATE YOUR MATE" DEC. 26, 1955
EPISODE # 46 FILMED ON SATURDAY, NOVEMBER 19, 1955
WRITERS: PARKE LEVY, LOU DERMAN, BILL FREEDMAN
GUEST CAST: HOWARD WENDELL AS LAWRENCE WESTON, JOEY FAYE AS JIM,
DICK ELLIOTT AS RICHARD

Lily wonders if she and her new beau Lawrence Weston would make a good team. Hilda: "Lily, do you want to get married or pull an ice wagon?" As it turns out, Lily has good reason to question Lawrence's character. It is revealed during a locker-room conversation between him and his buddy Jim that Lawrence hasn't worked in ten years and that he has a terrible temper. Later that evening, Hilda introduces a game to Lily and the Henshaws and their guests. The object of "Rate Your Mate" (invented by Dr. Thornhill, a psychologist) is to determine if two people are compatible. Hilda is the moderator, asking the participants questions like, "Do you cry when you see movies? Do you lose your temper easily? Do think marriages are made in heaven?" When she tallies the results, Hilda announces that Lily and Lawrence averaged 98% whereas Ruth and Matt averaged 22% compatibility. This leaves Ruth so disturbed she wakes Matt to find out why he married her if they have nothing in common. He confesses he married her simply because he loves her, but an argument ensues and he spends the rest of the night on the living room sofa. The next evening, over a bridge game with Lawrence, Hilda and her boyfriend Richard, Lily learns Lawrence's true character when he criticizes her card-playing ability. She tells him she won't see him anymore. Meanwhile, Matt convinces Ruth that "Rate Your Mate" is not an accurate picture of their true feelings for one another. They kiss and make up.
NOTES: The original script for this episode identifies Hilda's boyfriend as "Stanley Poole," the same name used in Episode #43 when Harry Cheshire played that part. Cheshire was unavailable when this episode was filmed, and since Dick Elliott served as his replacement, the writers changed the character's name to avoid confusion.

"OPERATION COLESLAW" JAN. 2, 1956
EPISODE # 47 FILMED ON SATURDAY, NOVEMBER 26, 1955
WRITERS: PARKE LEVY, LOU DERMAN, BILL DAVENPORT
GUEST CAST: ROBERT EMMETT KEANE AS MR. PRITCHARD, GAIL BONNEY AS
MADELINE SCHWEITZER, MADGE BLAKE AS ANITA HENDERSON, PAULA
WINSLOWE AS EDYTHEA WALKER, TITO VUOLO AS MR. CARUSO

Mr. Pritchard, an old fussbudget who's a prospective buyer for the house next door, interviews the Henshaws about the neighborhood. He lists his many dislikes: dogs in his yard, loud noise, trash-burning violations, etc. Pete and the Henshaws realize quickly that Pritchard's an undesirable neighbor. Meanwhile, Lily and Hilda are consumed with their quest for donated cabbages, needed to make coleslaw for The Youth Center jamboree. Without their knowledge, Pete and Matt order 200 heads of cabbage so that Lily and Hilda will be available to help them concoct a scheme to rid the neighborhood of Pritchard. Meanwhile, both Hilda and Ruth order cabbages without telling anyone. As a result the Henshaws' front lawn is littered with surplus cabbages, which inspires Pete's plan: they'll use a cement mixer (originally rented to construct a patio) to grind the cabbages up. When the noise attracts an angry Pritchard, Lily tells him they're making coleslaw. He becomes furious, vowing not to buy the house next door. Mission accomplished!

"THE TRAILER SHOW" JAN. 9, 1956
EPISODE #48 FILMED ON SATURDAY, DECEMBER 3, 1955
WRITERS: PARKE LEVY, LOU DERMAN, BILL DAVENPORT
GUEST CAST: FRED SHERMAN AS MELVIN COOPER, JEAN HOWELL AS MARCIA COOPER, JAMES FLAVIN AS THE POLICEMAN, ROBERT BURTON AS MR. BICKFORD, ROBERT FOULK AS JOE, NORMAN LEAVITT AS BILL, RONNIE AND GARY STAFFORD & RAY AND TODD FARRELL AS THE COOPER BOYS

Lily befriends the Coopers, a couple with four young sons, when their car and travel trailer break down in front of the house. She invites them to wait inside while the mechanics make the necessary repairs. When Matt arrives and finds the Cooper boys running around and causing havoc, he's upset that the house is too noisy to entertain an important client he's invited over. In the meantime it's discovered that the youngest Cooper boy, Bucko, has the mumps. Since Matt and Ruth have never had the disease, they and Lily wait for Matt's client, Mr. Bickford, in the Coopers' trailer. Bickford soon arrives, but a cop interrupts, demanding an explanation for why the trailer is blocking the street. When Matt takes the officer in the house to meet Mr. Cooper, Lily and Bickford get locked inside the trailer. Lily tries to calm the very testy Bickford, who's afraid he's going to miss his flight. After serving him coffee and aspirins, Lily calmly shows him Matt's plans. When Bickford expresses his enthusiastic approval, Matt fulfills his promise to take Ruth on a second honeymoon trip to Tacoma—after he buys a new travel trailer.

NOTES: Verna Felton does not appear in this episode. The Cooper boys were played by two sets of brothers. James Flavin (1906-1976) makes the second of his six appearances as a cop.

"MATT'S MOVIE CAREER" JAN. 16, 1956
EPISODE #49 FILMED ON SATURDAY, DECEMBER 10, 1955
WRITERS: PARKE LEVY, LOU DERMAN, BILL DAVENPORT
GUEST CAST: KATHLEEN HUGHES AS AMBER WINSLOW, FRANK JENKS AS JIM
THE MILKMAN, MADGE BLAKE AS ANITA HENDERSON, GAIL BONNEY AS
MADELINE SCHWEITZER, ALMIRA SESSIONS AS NANCY, PAULA WINSLOWE AS
EDYTHEA WALKER

Lily directs the Westwood Players' production of *Women of Sparta*, featuring her club members as Spartan warriors and Matt and Pete as the opposing Roman soldiers. The next morning Hilda is disgruntled when she's not mentioned in the newspaper review: "I lead an army into battle, kill five Romans, capture a general, and bring in four prisoners—why, I was practically a Greek Audie Murphy!" The drama critic gives Matt a passing nod for his performance, but things really go to Matt's head when he receives a phone call from Maurice Flexner, the director of the Hollywood Playhouse, who asks him to audition for the lead role in *Cyrano de Bergerac*. Night after night he rehearses with another of Flexner's students, Amber Winslow, a buxom blonde. Ruth becomes very jealous but is unsuccessful in convincing Matt to give up acting. Pete exposes Flexner as a charlatan who takes advantage of amateur actors, promising them starring roles in plays that never open in exchange for his expensive coaching. When Matt discovers that Amber is actually Flexner's wife, he realizes he's been duped, and he promptly trades in his script for a make-up kiss from Ruth.
NOTES: **Madge Blake, Gail Bonney, Almira Sessions, and Paula Winslowe have no lines in their brief scene as actresses in Lily's play. Miss Sessions had played Elsie Pringle in previous episodes, but the original script identifies her character as "Nancy." This episode is sometimes identified on websites as "Stage Struck."**

"THE RUDY VALLEE SHOW" JAN. 23, 1956
EPISODE # 50 FILMED ON SATURDAY, DECEMBER 17, 1955
WRITERS: PARKE LEVY, LOU DERMAN, BILL DAVENPORT
GUEST CAST: RUDY VALLEE AS HIMSELF, BENNY RUBIN AS MARTY, CHEERIO
MEREDITH AS HORTENSE MILLER, ALMIRA SESSIONS AS ELSIE PRINGLE, HAVIS
DAVENPORT AS THE CIGARETTE GIRL, LEE MILLAR AS JOE THE PHOTOGRAPHER
CHOREOGRAPHY BY JACK BAKER

Lily and Hilda buy some of Rudy Vallee's personal memorabilia at an auction gallery, including a record of one of his trademark songs, "My Time Is Your Time." When Matt imitates Vallee's nasal rendition, they carry on like schoolgirls. Meanwhile, Vallee is distressed to learn that the record was sold my mistake. After his manager tracks down the buyer, the notoriously thrifty Vallee phones Lily with an offer to buy it back "for any reasonable sum up to $4." Instead Lily bargains with him to pose for photographs promoting her club's charity drive in exchange for the record. When Vallee offers to come to Lily's house the following day, Hilda is so excited she exclaims, "Lily, get the oxygen! I'm blacking out!" She collapses onto the sofa and accidentally lands on the prized record, smashing it to bits. The next day Lily and Hilda walk all over town to find a copy of the record, but to no avail. Matt and Pete volunteer to make a counterfeit copy, with Matt supplying an imitation of Vallee's voice. When Vallee arrives that evening, Lily explains that she and her fellow club members are dressed in the styles of Vallee's heyday, the 1920s, to make the publicity photos more colorful. Vallee says those days are long gone, but Hilda disagrees by enthusiastically dancing the Charleston. When the photographer asks the ladies to "look a litte more coquettish," Hilda hikes her squirt, puts one foot forward, and fawns over Vallee. (Pete: "This is sheer juvenile delinquency.") Lily gives Vallee the phony record but is shocked when he breaks it over his knee. He admits that it was the last existing copy of a recording where he went flat in the third measure. The vain Vallee wanted to insure that no one would ever hear his embarrassing sour NOTES. Lily and the gang don't let on that Hilda broke the original, and the girls all smile adoringly at Vallee as he sings "Tavern in the Town."

"THE TEXAS SHOW" (Part One) Jan. 30, 1956
Episode # 51 Filmed on Thursday, December 22, 1955
Writers: Parke Levy, Lou Derman, Bill Davenport
Guest Cast: Lyle Talbot as Bill Jeffreys, Howard McNear as Hal Norton, Louise Lorimer as Kitty Maxwell

Kitty Maxwell visits Lily with exciting news about a fascinating Texan she sat beside on the plane. He became very interested in meeting Lily after seeing a snapshot Kitty happened to show him. Lily agrees to meet him, and when Bill Jeffreys arrives that evening, Hilda's prediction ("Lily, you've struck oil!") is correct. Tall, beefy Bill, complete with huge Stetson and cigar, wastes no time in offering Lily a chance to invest in a gusher that's about to come in. Later Matt doubts Bill's true intentions, saying that he talks too big for a wealthy person. Lily refuses to believe Bill's a "confidence man," and informs Matt and Pete that she's invested $1000 in Bill's new oil well. (Pete: "That's the worst investment since I paid $2 for a marriage license!") Without Lily's knowledge, Matt and Pete visit Bill in his hotel room and demand the return of her check. The next morning, Hilda runs in, with high heels clipping across the floor, to show Lily a newspaper item announcing that Bill's new well came in, and that he named it "The Lily Ruskin." Matt slumps when he realizes what he's done, and sorrowfully shows Lily the check. She appeases him, "I could have never figured out the income tax." When Bill arrives, Lily congratulates him. He informs her that he's going to accept her check despite Matt's intervention. She confounds Bill by refusing his magnanimous offer, and furthermore explains that he doesn't know her very well. He admits he'd like to get to know her and invites Lily, the Henshaws, the Porters, and Hilda to fly out to Texas as his houseguests for a couple of weeks.

"THE TEXAS SHOW" (PART TWO) FEB. 6, 1956
EPISODE # 52 FILMED ON THURSDAY, DECEMBER 29, 1955
WRITERS: PARKE LEVY, LOU DERMAN, BILL DAVENPORT
GUEST CAST: LYLE TALBOT AS BILL JEFFREYS, GAIL BONNEY AS MADELINE SCHWEITZER

Pete and Hilda show their enthusiasm for their upcoming Texas trip by showing off their new western wear, but Lily suggests that Hilda needs to alter her leather jacket because it's a little snug. Pete is less subtle—when Hilda exits, he accompanies her: "There might be some Indians out there—I'll need a covered wagon to hide behind." Bill soon arrives, and when the conversation turns to Hilda, he remarks that his ranch foreman Steve Farrell might take a liking to her even though Steve normally prefers women a little slimmer than Hilda. After Bill leaves, Lily tells Ruth that she's worried that Hilda will be lonely if Bill and she decide to marry. To insure that Steve is impressed with Hilda, Lily concocts a scheme to get Hilda to lose weight. She pretends that her doctor has ordered her to diet, so she asks Hilda to spend the week with her and diet along with her. At one point they wind up at Hilda's apartment where Lily puts Hilda through some hilarious moves on a stationary bike. Later Lily is disappointed to find food hidden all over Hilda's apartment, so when she must leave she arranges for Madeline Schweitzer to supervise Hilda's calisthenics. Hilda discovers hidden food in a purse Lily leaves behind, and Madeline confesses Lily's scheme to help Hilda lose weight. Hilda thinks Lily is ashamed of her, and she reacts by telling Lily she isn't going to Texas and that furthermore she never wants to speak to her again. Bill intercedes by showing Hilda a telegram from Steve who's anxious to meet her. He reminds her that Lily's motives were based on her love for Hilda, but Hilda remains firm. Later at the airport, just before everyone is ready to board, Lily spots Hilda hiding behind a post. She explains her presence by saying she's flying to Canada to visit her daughter, but when her suitcase accidentally falls open, her western garb is revealed. "Aw, Lily, I just wanted you to ask me once more!" The two friends embrace, and all is well.

"THE TEXAS SHOW" (PART THREE) FEB. 13, 1956
EPISODE # 53 FILMED ON SATURDAY, JANUARY 7, 1956
WRITERS: PARKE LEVY, LOU DERMAN, BILL DAVENPORT
GUEST CAST: LYLE TALBOT AS BILL JEFFREYS, DICK WESSEL AS STEVE FARRELL, LOU KRUGMAN AS BART ROGERS, LOUIS NICOLETTI AS BOB HAGGARTY, JACK LOMAS AS JIM BUCKNER, THE FRONTIERSMAN AS THE BAND

On Bill's ranch outside Houston, the Henshaws, Porters, Lily, and Hilda are having a grand time riding horseback. Hilda especially enjoys flirting with Steve Farrell who calls her his "little tumbleweed." Bill is showing Lily lots of attention as well, and he's planned a big party to introduce her to all of his friends. When his fellow millionaires, Bart, Bob, and Jim arrive for the party, each is amazed at the resemblance Lily bears to Bill's late wife, Kathleen. They explain that Bill hasn't allowed any furnishings to be moved or replaced since her death three years ago. Lily is a little surprised when Bill insists she wear the party outfit he's chosen for her. That evening around the swimming pool where 1,000 orchids float, it's very evident that for Bill there is no other place on earth. As he and Lily dance, the band plays "I'll Take You Home Again, Kathleen." The coincidence is too great for Lily, and she begs to go inside for a wrap. Hilda discovers her inside staring at a portrait of the late Mrs. Jeffreys wearing the very same western outfit Bill has chosen for Lily. She whispers to Hilda, "He doesn't love me. He loves a memory. He'd never be mine." She asks Hilda to ask the band to play a special song for her: "California Here I Come."

"SUNKEN DEN" FEB. 20, 1956
EPISODE # 54 FILMED ON SATURDAY, JANUARY 14, 1956
WRITERS: PARKE LEVY, LOU DERMAN, BILL DAVENPORT
GUEST CAST: DESI ARNAZ AS HIMSELF, JOSEPH KEARNS AS MURRAY, RICHARD DEACON AS JENKS THE BUTLER, HARRY HARVEY, JR. AS JIMMY THE FAN CLUB PRESIDENT
CHOREOGRAPHY BY JACK BAKER

Lily feels responsible when Desi Arnaz sues Matt's firm, Gordon & Co., for $50,000. She neglected to deliver Matt's revised plans for a house adjacent to Mr. Arnaz, and without them, a construction company didn't put in a retaining wall before beginning their work. As a result, the hillside on which the Arnaz house was built caved in, causing his den to sink two feet. The insurer for Gordon & Co. is Delta Insurance Company, which, coincidentally, is Pete's firm. When Pete woefully informs everyone that Delta won't cover the cost of the damage to the Arnaz house, Matt is fearful of losing his job. Mr. Arnaz's attorney will not allow Matt to speak with Arnaz, so Lily takes matters into her own hands. Accompanied by Hilda, Lily tries to get an appointment with Mr. Arnaz, but his butler, Jenks, prevents their entry. Undaunted, the pair finds an unlocked exterior door and enters the "sunken den." When they hear Jenks coming Lily hides in the fireplace, and Hilda conceals herself in a storage nook in a revolving wet bar. Jenks doesn't notice either of them as he tidies the room and locks the door through which they entered. After he leaves, the girls set off the burglar alarm when they try to leave via the locked door. Frantically they search for another exit until Lily suggests they go out a window. She carefully climbs on the sofa and eases herself out the window. Hilda gets a running start and jumps onto the sofa before diving headfirst out the window (and into a fish pond)! Back at the Henshaw house, Hilda suggests to Lily that they go see a movie to forget about their disastrous attempt at meeting Mr. Arnaz. While checking movie ads, she notices an item about Desi Arnaz's teenage fans being invited to his home that evening so the two decide to join the club. To blend in with the gang, Lily and Hilda don saddle oxfords, bobby socks, and Desi sweatshirts. Hilda even sports bangs and a ponytail. While they attempt to mix with the crowd someone puts on a jazzy record, and

Hilda holds her own, dancing with a bespectacled teen. Desi soon enters and quickly notices the "new members." (Lily: "We're *charter* members!" Hilda: "Since 1925!") Jenks then recognizes them, and Lily quickly explains the real reason for attending, apologizing for the damage done to the den. Desi's agent, Murray, arrives to inform him that a leak in the Arnaz swimming pool actually caused the hillside to collapse. Lily and Hilda are relieved and then overjoyed, especially when Desi asks them to join his fan club. ("That gives me 38 against Lucy's 21,005,075.") He asks the girls if they'd like to stay for the dancing, but they don't intend to be wallflowers. Lily beams, "Sure, I rock." Hilda, hand on waist, bounces her hip up and down, "And I roll!"

NOTES: Desi Arnaz (1917-1986) was celebrating his 15th year in motion pictures when this episode was filmed. He plugs his current feature *Forever, Darling* (co-starring Lucille Ball) in his first scene. Joseph Kearns (1907-1962) makes his first of five appearances on *December Bride*, while Richard Deacon (1922-1984) makes his first of three. Deacon's character was named for actor Frank Jenks, who himself appeared on *December Bride* a total of four times.

"THE WRESTLER" FEB. 27, 1956
EPISODE # 55 FILMED ON SATURDAY, JANUARY 21, 1956
WRITERS: PARKE LEVY, LOU DERMAN, BILL DAVENPORT
GUEST CAST: SANDOR SZABO AS KARL MANHEIM, SANDRA GOULD AS FRIEDA MANHEIM, FRANK JENKS AS JIM THE MILKMAN, FRANK KREIG AS CORKY, JULES STRONGBOW AS JULES THE ANNOUNCER, TOM RICE AS HIMSELF, BENNY GOLDBERG AS THE REFEREE

When Lily loses Matt's car bumper by towing both Elsie Pringle and Madeline Schweitzer's cars, she promises him that she will stop helping so many people. Soon after, Hilda persuades Lily to counsel her niece Frieda, who's threatening to leave her husband, a pro wrestler named Karl Manheim. Later that evening, when the Manheims arrive, Lily greets tall, brawny baritone Karl who's quite a contrast to his wife, the small, birdlike, and shrill Frieda. Frieda orders Karl to sit down, explaining to Lily, "I think he's too talented to spend the rest of his life wrestling with those big musclebound baboons." Hilda, with a dreamy glint in her eye, exclaims, "It should only happen to me." Frieda insists Karl's best talent is his singing voice. (Hilda: "Well, it's a rather unusual combination—a singer and a wrestler! A sort of a half-Nelson Eddy!") At Frieda's insistence, henpecked Karl sings "Hold Me Close." Lily loves Karl's voice, volunteering to get him an interview with Mr. Mozier, a movie producer. To show his gratitude, Karl gives Lily tickets to the Friday night wrestling match. The next day, Lily and Hilda go down to the gym to tell Karl that a screen test for Mozier's new motion picture, *Passion Under the Palms*, is too expensive. But Lily's convinced the producer to watch Karl wrestle on television. She persuades Karl that it will be the perfect time to audition for the part of the shiek. When the milkman returns the wrestling tickets that Lily gave him, Matt figures out that Lily's up to her old stunts again. He, Ruth, and Pete go down to see the match where they're startled to see Lily and Hilda wearing balloon pants and veils. They accompany Karl the Singing Shiek into the ring as his trainers, complete with carpet and hookah. His opponent is Tom Rice the Hillbilly Heathen, whom Hilda attempts to distract with hilarious results. Karl sings "Hold Me Close" into the camera whenever he pins the Heathen, but he's so distracted with trying to audition that he's defeated. (Karl: "What happened?" Hilda: "He held ya close!") In the vignette, backstage Lily phones Mozier who's unimpressed with Karl's singing. Outside the fans are heard chanting, "Shiek!" Frieda rushes in to tell Lily that Karl's been offered a three-year contract for $1,000 a week. Frieda is so happy she's willing to give up the idea of Karl's singing career.

NOTES: Olympic and former world heavyweight champion Sandor Szabo (1906-1966) was a huge draw in California matches in the 1930s, 40s, and 50s. He makes the first of his three appearances in this episode. Professional wrestler and former USF football star Tom Rice (1914-1996) and former wrestler and Los Angeles area promoter Jules Strongbow (1906-1975) were also recruited to lend authenticity to this episode. According to the script, actor John Indrisano was slated to appear as the referee, but he was replaced by former featherweight boxer Benny Goldberg (1919-2001). Sandra Gould (1916-1999) is best known as Gladys Kravitz #2 in the *Bewitched* television series. Writer Lou Derman borrowed the character names Karl and Frieda from his best friend and C.P.A., Karl Schultz and his wife Frieda.

"RUTH GETS A JOB" MAR. 12, 1956
EPISODE # 56 FILMED ON TUESDAY, FEBRUARY 7, 1956
WRITERS: PARKE LEVY, LOU DERMAN, BILL DAVENPORT
GUEST CAST: SARA BERNER AS THE HOTEL GUEST IN THE SHOWER, EMORY PARNELL AND GEORGE MEADER AS THE HUNG-OVER GUESTS, PETER LEEDS AS BRUCE THE GROOM, CHARLOTTE LAWRENCE AS BERNICE HARPER, DOUGLAS EVANS AS MR. HOLMAN THE HOTEL MANAGER, JOI LANSING AS MILDRED THE BRIDE, RUSSELL TRENT AS THE HOUSE DETECTIVE, PITT HERBERT AS THE BELLBOY

Ruth complains about the Henshaw's worn-out refrigerator, but Matt refuses to buy a new one. So Ruth gets a job ($40 a week) as a switchboard operator in a hotel. She embarrasses Matt when she tells him that his boss's wife came to the hotel for lunch and saw Ruth working. He's ashamed for others to know that he can't support his wife on his salary alone. The next morning when Ruth's co-worker Bernice arrives to take her to work, Matt appears in a frilly pinafore and dust cap. He begins cleaning house, hoping to embarrass Ruth enough to quit her job. But she leaves, furious. Later Lily visits Ruth at work and takes over during her break, playing havoc with the guests' phones, plugging the wrong holes with the wrong plugs. When the customers storm the front office, the manager asks Lily to leave and fires Ruth. This is just what Lily had intended. When they get home, a brand new refrigerator, wrapped in a big bow, is waiting in the kitchen.

"HANDCUFFS" MAR. 19, 1956
EPISODE # 57 FILMED ON TUESDAY, FEBRUARY 14, 1956
WRITERS: PARKE LEVY, LOU DERMAN, BILL DAVENPORT
GUEST CAST: DICK ELLIOTT AS WALTER HIGBY, IRVING BACON AS MR.
BOLTON, JUNE KIRBY AS BETSY BAER

Hilda's in a pickle. After her breakup with boyfriend Walter, she answered a lonely hearts ad. Now she has a blind date with a man from Pomona, a Mr. Bolton. She doesn't want to meet him at her apartment because it's being painted. Lily agrees for them to meet at her house that evening, laughing when Hilda admits she told Bolton she was about forty years old. Just then Walter rushes in, begging Hilda's forgiveness. ("I can't eat, I can't sleep, I can't work! All I do is stand around and stare at those old used cars and think of you!") Hilda relents, but makes him promise he'll never be jealous again. Walter insists that Hilda join him on a date that evening. She finally agrees to meet him at her apartment at 8 p.m. After Walter leaves, Hilda wrangles, successfully, to persuade Lily to take her place with Bolton. Pete arrives, asking the girls to help him practice a new magic trick for the church benefit. He handcuffs them together, but is mystified when the handcuffs stay locked. He rushes out to find a key. Matt and Ruth hold Lily and Hilda a captive audience while they rehearse their song-and-dance ("You're the One I Love") opener for Pete's act. After they exit, Walter phones, saying he's coming right over. Hilda panics, thinking he'll walk in while Bolton is there. To prevent Walter from knowing they're handcuffed, Hilda sits with her arm extended behind the sofa while Lily crouches behind. Hilda tells Walter she can't go on their date because Lily is upstairs sick. In fact, he'd better leave immediately because "this place is just crawling with *streplococci* germs!" He refuses to go until she sends him to the drug store for aspirin. In the meantime, kindly Mr. Bolton knocks at the door. Hilda and Lily switch places. Lily beckons him to come in, apologizing that her sprained ankle prevented her from answering the door. When she tells Bolton that Hilda's "tied up" and cannot keep her date, he's obviously charmed by Lily and sweetly offers his box of candy. Just then, Walter's car is heard approaching. Lily sends Bolton to the kitchen to get her a glass of water. The girls rush to change places again but are caught by both Walter and Bolton. When Walter demands an explanation for the handcuffs, Hilda deadpans, "We escaped from a chain gang." Finally Pete arrives with the key. Once the girls are "free," they go out on a double date with Walter and Bolton.

NOTES: In all subsequent episodes, Dick Elliott appears as Stanley Poole, Hilda's exterminator boyfriend, a role originated by Harry Cheshire. Series writer Lou Derman was himself an accomplished amateur magician, performing each Friday night at the Hollywood Magic Castle.

"PETE'S BROTHER-IN-LAW" MAR. 26, 1956
EPISODE # 58 FILMED ON TUESDAY, FEBRUARY 21, 1956
WRITERS: PARKE LEVY, LOU DERMAN, BILL DAVENPORT
GUEST CAST: ARNOLD STANG AS MARVIN FISHER, PIERRE WATKIN AS COL.
FRANK BRADBURY, EDNA HOLLAND AS MRS. BRADBURY, DICK WESSEL AS THE
TOP SERGEANT, SHARON LEE AS THE GIRL

Pete's tired of Gladys's nerdy brother Marvin hanging around the house. After Lily and Hilda visit their friend, Colonel Frank Bradbury, Pete and Matt get the idea to convince Marvin to enlist in the Marines. But poor Marvin is rejected because of his weak vision. Lily offers to invite the Bradburys to dinner to see if he can help. Marvin thinks his thick glasses will discourage the colonel from assisting him so he attempts to memorize the room so he can maneuver around without them. Things go afowl when the colonel sits in the chair designated for Marvin, and the very blind Marvin sits on top of him. Later he offers to mix martinis but walks into the hall closet, thinking it's the kitchen. With a sigh, Pete tells him to put on his glasses. The colonel thinks there's a possibility he can recommend Marvin for an office job. Pete is elated until he learns that Marvin's been assigned to the recruiting offices at 8th and Figueroa Streets for at least one year. Marvin beams, "You can expect me home for dinner every night!"

NOTES: According to Robert Levy, son of *December Bride* writer-creator Parke Levy, Arnold Stang (1918-2009) was a family friend who often dined in their Beverly Hills home.

"LILY IN A GAS STATION" APR. 2, 1956
EPISODE # 59 FILMED ON SATURDAY, JANUARY 28, 1956
WRITERS: PARKE LEVY, LOU DERMAN, BILL DAVENPORT
GUEST CAST: FRANK CADY AS CHARLIE FINN, OLIVER BLAKE AS JOE WATSON,
PAUL MAXEY AS THE CUSTOMER

Matt is offered a junior partnership in his firm's New York office, but he's concerned that he and Ruth might not be able to find a two-bedroom apartment there. Lily overhears their discussion, and, not wanting to stand in their way, encourages Matt to take the position. Later when she tells Hilda of the situation, she invites Lily to move in with her. Lily knows the children will try to persuade her to relocate with them, so she tells them that she and Hilda have bought a gas station. Actually, Lily's friend Joe Watson has just bought one, and Lily plans to work there to convince Matt and Ruth that it's her operation. Ruth is fearful to leave Lily behind, but Hilda tells her, "I'll take as good of care of Lily as if she were my own mother!" Charlie Finn, the man Matt will be replacing in New York, comes over to brief Matt on the new position. Matt and Ruth barely recognize him—he's lost over 100 pounds. He's popping pills right and left, saying his doctor told him he's headed for a nervous breakdown. He tells Matt that he won't spend much time drafting; instead he'll be busy entertaining clients. Matt and Ruth begin to have second thoughts about the move. Meanwhile at the station, a uniformed Lily and Hilda wait on a huge man driving a Volkswagen. While he's using the pay phone, Lily lets the gas tank overflow and Hilda tries to put water in the tires. As he climbs back in the car, Lily calls out, "Next time, get some of our pink gas—it's so pretty!" When he starts the engine, it explodes! Lily has put gasoline in the radiator. Matt and Ruth arrive during the cleanup to tell Lily that they've decided against the New York job. Matt jokes that if he did move to New York, Lily would have to go, too, and then Hilda would tag along: "Manhattan would never be the same—the Indians wouldn't take it back!"

"RUTH'S HAIRCUT" APR. 9, 1956
EPISODE # 60 FILMED ON TUESDAY, FEBRUARY 28, 1956
WRITERS: PARKE LEVY, LOU DERMAN, BILL DAVENPORT
GUEST CAST: MABEL ALBERTSON AS BEATRICE HENSHAW

Matt's mother is coming for a weeklong visit, and Ruth wants to get a shorter, Italian haircut, but Matt doesn't agree. Ruth says that long hair is old-fashioned, and Matt counters that his mother is sort of old-fashioned. While he's golfing, Lily and Hilda, although they have no experience, give Ruth a haircut. Standing on each side of her, they hack at her hair until it's a lopsided mess. Ruth goes to Victor's Salon to get it repaired, coming home sporting a much shorter and smarter hairstyle. However, Matt is not convinced that it's more attractive or economical. He continues to make cracks about Ruth's mannish appearance, calling her "Friar Tuck" and "Gorgeous George." His annoying jokes end when his mother arrives sporting a new haircut—hers is identical to Ruth's.

NOTES: "Gorgeous George" was the professional name of George Wagner (1915-1963) who, as one of television's first wrestling superstars, grew his hair long and bleached it blonde.

"JAYWALKER" APR. 16, 1956
EPISODE # 61 FILMED ON TUESDAY, MARCH 6, 1956
WRITERS: PARKE LEVY, LOU DERMAN, BILL DAVENPORT
GUEST CAST: KING DONOVAN AS OFFICER GABRIEL WADSLOWSKI, HOWARD MCNEAR AS MR. PAISLEY, ARTE JOHNSON AS EUGENE GALVIN

Matt and Ruth are surprised by a visit from prissy Mr. Paisley, membership chairman of the Architect's League, whose duty it is to screen applicants. He invites them, as prospective members, to attend a dance the following Saturday. The next day Lily is fined for jaywalking when she entered the street to search for a lost earring. She gets testy with the arresting officer, telling him she's going to write about her unjust treatment in her newspaper column. She refuses to pay the fine, and engages Hilda's nephew Eugene, recently admitted to the bar, as her legal counsel. After Matt reads Lily's column, he worries that Paisley will also see it and consequently blackball Matt from the league because of his "crackpot" mother-in-law. Lily spends a sleepless night, consumed with worry about the consequences of her editorial. She confesses her second thoughts about Eugene's inexperience to Hilda, who invites her to go to the ballet (*Swan Lake*) to get her mind off her troubles. Instead of accepting the invitation, Lily decides to take a nap. Soon she begins to dream . . . she's in a courtroom as a prisoner on trial. She wears stripes and carries a ball and chain. Sitting on the bench and wielding an oversized gavel is Mr. Paisley. She pleads her innocence of the jaywalking charge, demanding a trial by jury. Police Officer "Gabriel" Wadslowski descends on angel wings, attesting to her guilt. Matt and Ruth are called as character witnesses, and they enter, zombie-like, in their dance clothes with black balls floating over their heads. The judge quickly dismisses their credibility. Eugene, in a kid's sailor suit, roller skates in to defend Lily, but he's tempted by a judicial bribe (an oversized ice cream cone) and with his baby talk, denounces Lily, "Ha, Ha, Ha! You guilty!" As a last resort, Lily begs for Hilda to be called to tell what happened on the street that day. Hilda flutters out in a feathered headdress and tutu, refusing Lily's plea, "Not tonight, Lily—I'm dancing in *Swan Lake!*" The judge pronounces Lily guilty, sentencing her to hang by the earrings for 30 days. She then confesses and throws herself on the mercy of the court, promising to pay the fine. Lily wakes abruptly from her dream, now motivated to drop the case. She searches in the desk for Eugene's phone number and stumbles across the earring she thought she'd lost. In the vignette, Matt and Ruth come home from the dance with the happy news that he was accepted into the league. Lily tells them that now Hilda is being defended by Eugene; she drove through a stop sign at Wilshire Boulevard and North Palm Drive.

"BEAUTY PAGEANT" APR. 23, 1956
EPISODE # 62 FILMED ON TUESDAY, MARCH 20, 1956
WRITERS: PARKE LEVY, LOU DERMAN, BILL DAVENPORT
GUEST CAST: ALMIRA SESSIONS AS ELSIE PRINGLE, CHEERIO MEREDITH AS HORTENSE MILLER, MARJORIE BENNETT AS EDYTHEA WALKER, SANDRA SPENCE AS JAN DARLING, LEE MILLAR AND PETER GRAY AS THE PHOTOGRAPHERS, ELAINE BRUCE, SUSAN BROWN, AND CAROLE COLE AS THE MODELS
CHOREOGRAPHY BY JACK BAKER

The Westwood Women's Cultural Club meets at Hilda's apartment to discuss their annual charity show. Lily asks the girls to sing the opening number they've been rehearsing. With Hilda at the piano, Elsie, Hortense, and Edythea sing a maudlin yet sappy tale of a fawn falling to its death over a cliff. Lily is not pleased at all, and Hilda admits, "It sounded like four cats on the back fence." While brainstorming for a central theme for their show, Hilda suggests a be-bop concert and Elsie offers to engage her nephew's jazz band. Lily rejects both ideas as unenlightening. When she finally settles on "The March of Science," the other club members protest her choice, citing its lackluster content and the meager advance ticket sales. They ask for Lily's resignation as entertainment chairman, but she begs for one day to devise a way to attract an audience. Later that evening, Lily is inspired when observing the fawning members of Matt's camera club photographing a young model in a swimsuit. She changes the name of her show to "Scientific Follies" and advertises it with the teaser: "Girls! Girls! Girls!" Lily dresses her club members in vintage swimsuits, complete with ruffled hats and stockings, but wisely uses young swimsuit models to assist them down a short flight of stairs as they sing about four major inventions. Edythea wears a model of Robert Fulton's steamboat around her waist. Hortense portrays "The Spirit of Flight," her arms suspended by airplane wings and wearing a propeller on her cap. Elsie stands siffly as Miss Penicillin, encased in a giant hypodermic needle. And Hilda sports antenna on her head and a television screen around her middle, hamming it up in the chorus-line finish when the television set bumps her chin as she does the high kicks.

"LILY AND THE SAILOR" APR. 30, 1956
EPISODE # 63 FILMED ON TUESDAY, MARCH 27, 1956
WRITERS: PARKE LEVY, LOU DERMAN, BILL DAVENPORT
GUEST CAST: NESTOR PAIVA AS JAKE, GIL PERKINS AS MIKE THE BARTENDER, HUBIE KERNS, RAY SANDERS, RED MORGAN, AND RICHARD ELMORE AS SAILORS (STUNTS)

When Matt forgets his wedding anniversary, Ruth feels like she's taken for granted, telling him that he can celebrate alone. The next day she announces that she and Gladys are going to Palm Springs without their husbands. Pete counters with the suggestion to Matt that they go to Las Vegas while the girls are out of town. Lily tries to think of a way to keep both couples at home. When Hilda mentions their friend Sally's romance with a sea captain, Lily drags Hilda down to a seaside bar in hopes to meet a sailor to participate in her scheme to patch up things between Matt and Ruth. They meet a roughhousing sailor named Jake to whom Lily offers $25 if he will be her escort that evening. Meanwhile a barroom brawl ensues, and Hilda's purse makes a handy weapon for one sailor. Hilda joins the fracas to retrieve it, climbing up on the bar and batting every man within reach. That evening Jake arrives at the Henshaw home, calling for "Lil." Matt and Ruth can't understand the appeal Jake holds for Lily, especially after they see his former girlfriend's image tattooed on his arm. Lily explains, "I've been high and dry too long. It's time I got my feet wet." She and Jake go out to the kitchen to make drinks (hot buttered rum). Matt and Ruth decide not to leave town for fear of what Lily and her sailor might do. Hilda bustles in, and, as usual, spills the beans about Lily's ploy. Matt and Ruth decide to get even, telling Lily they've cancelled their vacations to help with her wedding plans. Jake jumps ship ("I'll see you in Singapore!"), and Lily is relieved to have reunited the children. Ruth: "Mother, isn't $25 a lot to spend for a date?" Lily: "Yes, but not for an anniversary present."

"LILY THE MATCHMAKER" MAY 7, 1956
EPISODE # 64 FILMED ON TUESDAY, APRIL 3, 1956
WRITERS: PARKE LEVY, LOU DERMAN, BILL DAVENPORT
GUEST CAST: NANCY KULP AS FLORENCE EDDINGTON, ROBERT FOULK AS JACK SCHUYLER, STANLEY ADAMS AS HENRY CLARK, RICHARD DEACON AS BUD HODGES THE TELEVISION REPAIRMAN

Lily tries to help Florence Eddington, the quiet and colorless daughter of an old friend, snag a husband. She enlists the aid of Hilda to find Florence an escort to a masquerade party that the Henshaws are attending. Lily asks Henry Clark, a traveling salesman who works for Edythea Walker's husband, to come by and meet Florence. Hilda tempts Jack Schuyler, a friend of Walter's, to meet Florence by describing her as a charming and glamorous blonde. Lily is distressed to know that both men are set to arrive at the same time. When Henry arrives, he struggles to make conversation with the taciturn Florence. Meanwhile a television repairman arrives to work on Matt's set. Soon Jack rings the bell, and Lily takes him to the kitchen on the pretense to unjam an ice tray. Jack takes one look at Florence and exits quickly to the kitchen, bumping into Henry. When he realizes that the two men have been set up, Jack warns Henry, "This is a trap—they got a preacher in there disguised as a TV repairman!" They both run out the back door, despite the desperate pleas of Lily and Hilda. Lily frets over how to tell Florence that her dates flew the coop, but is amazed when she reenters the living room to find Florence having a friendly conversation with the repairman whose gentle personality is much compatible with that of Florence. Things end happily when he asks her to attend a dance. Lily and Hilda beam with approval.
NOTES: Character actor Stanley Adams (1915-1977), intimate friend of Lou Derman, made his first of three appearances in this episode.

"SWIMMING POOL" MAY 14, 1956
EPISODE # 65 FILMED ON TUESDAY, APRIL 10, 1956
WRITERS: PARKE LEVY, LOU DERMAN, BILL DAVENPORT
GUEST CAST: FRANK JENKS AS GEORGE BIGELOW, JOAN BANKS AS MARY LOU BIGELOW, DAMIAN O'FLYNN AS ED, KATHRYN CARD AS MRS. BIGELOW, EDITH SIMMONS AS JANET, JACK ALBERTSON AS MR. CROFT, KEVIN CORCORAN AS ED AND JANET'S SON

Lily is honored when she's asked for an interview by a writer from *The Ladies Home Digest* after she delivers a speech on mothers-in-law. Meanwhile Matt and Ruth argue over Matt's plan to install a swimming pool in the back yard. When Ruth asks Matt to consider the expensive consequences, Lily suggests they visit the home of Kitty Maxwell's son-in-law George Bigelow who has recently built a pool. Good-natured George welcomes them at the door wearing his robe, which conceals his swim trunks. The pool is visible through an open glass door, and the rowdy laughter of the swimmers is heard. Mary Lou, George's wife, enters wearily from the kitchen where she's been preparing food for all of their guests. She disparagingly mentions George's mother whose brief visit has been lengthened indefinitely because she's enjoying the pool so much. The senior Mrs. Bigelow then enters in her swimsuit, chattering about the shortage of clean towels and sandwiches, all the while dripping water on the living room rug. A family of five then arrives, and George escorts them out to the pool. Mary Lou complains about the noise, the extra work, and the increasingly expensive grocery bill since adding the pool. Then Ed runs in from the pool, covered in blue paint—some kid dumped a whole bucket in the water. An argument ensues between the Bigelows, and one soon erupts between Matt and Ruth when he blames Lily for suggesting they visit the Bigelows. He thinks he was set up by Ruth and her mother so he leaves in a huff, saying he'll walk home. Hours later, Ruth looks out her living room window, hoping to see Matt return. Pete drops in just before the arrival of the writer who's going to interview Lily, who's fretting that Matt's absence won't be understood by the interviewer. Pete takes it upon himself to pose as Matt to save face for Lily. He spreads it on thick for Mr. Croft, the interviewer: "Marriage has made me realize that the three most beautiful words in the English language are *mother-in-law*." When Croft insists they all pose for a photo to appear in the magazine, Pete tries to hide his face. Croft persuades Pete to kiss Ruth in the next pose, and just then a confused Matt walks through the door. Pete immediately calls Matt "Pete," and Ruth and Lily play along. Matt, who has obviously reconsidered a lot of things on his walk, then extols Lily's virtues as a mother-in-law. He then apologizes to Ruth for their argument and instinctively embraces her. They enjoy a lengthy kiss while a shocked Mr. Croft looks on. Lily sets Mr. Croft straight on the men's true identities and subsequently vows to never get involved in another of her children's arguments.

December Bride
The Third Season: 1956-57

CAST:	Spring Byington as Lily Ruskin
	Dean Miller as Matt Henshaw
	Frances Rafferty as Ruth Henshaw
	Harry Morgan as Pete Porter
	Verna Felton as Hilda Crocker
DIRECTOR:	Jerry Thorpe
CREATO AND PRODUCER:	Parke Levy
ASSOCIATE PRODUCER:	Mary Morriss
WRITERS:	Lou Derman, Parke Levy, Bill Davenport, Al Schwartz, Bill Derman, William Cowley, Budd Grossman, Nate Monaster, Ben Starr
COMPOSER:	Eliot Daniel
CONDUCTOR:	Wilbur Hatch
DIRECTOR OF PHOTOGRAPHY:	Sid Hickox, A.S.C.
PRODUCTION MANAGER:	W. Argyle Nelson
ASSISTANT DIRECTOR:	Marvin Stuart
ART DIRECTOR:	Claudio Guzman
SET DRESSER:	Theodore Offenbecker
CAMERA CO-ORDINATOR:	Maury Thompson
MAKEUP:	Otis Malcolm
HAIR STYLIST:	Lorraine Roberson
RE-RECORDING EDITOR:	Robert Reeve
SOUND RECORDER:	Cameron McCulloch
EDITORIAL SUPERVISOR:	Dann Cahn, A.C.E.
FILM EDITOR:	Douglas Hines
SOUND:	Glen Glenn Sound Co.
ANNOUNCER:	Dick Joy
SPONSOR:	General Foods Corporation

"THE RORY CALHOUN SHOW" Oct. 8, 1956
Episode # 66 Filmed on Saturday, July 21, 1956
Writers: Lou Derman, Parke Levy, Bill Davenport
Guest Cast: Rory Calhoun as Himself, Leo Fuchs as the grocer, Ruth Marea Brewer as Evelyn

In the third season opener, Matt wants to move when he discovers a reasonably priced lot in the Pacific Palisades. He suggests that Pete and Gladys buy an adjoining lot so they will still be the Henshaws' neighbors when they sell the Westwood house. A week later, no one has shown an interest in the house. Then comes the news that the airport has changed its flight pattern, and for the next six weeks, lots of planes will be flying directly over the neighborhood. This distresses Matt, but Hilda tries to cheer him up with a lead on a potential buyer, Rory Calhoun the movie star. She says that Elsie Pringle and Calhoun's cook take cha-cha lessons together, and the cook said that Calhoun wants to buy a smaller house. Hilda and Lily decide to go down to the Royal Market where Calhoun shops on weekends. After a three-hour wait, he appears. The girls have to compete for his attention with a zealous grocer who wants to break into pictures. Finally, Calhoun agrees to see the Henshaw home. Matt and Ruth fret that planes going over every three minutes will deter Calhoun from considering it so Lily locks heads with Hilda on another plan. That evening, Calhoun stops by on his way to a film preview (*Flight to Hong Kong*). Matt tries to give him a rushed tour to outrace the noise of the planes. Then Pete, Lily, and Hilda (all three wearing fake beards) arrive at the door, disguised as a mission band that bangs drums and crashes symbols each time a plane soars overhead. Calhoun recognizes the women, and laughs at their efforts. As it turns out, the Henshaw house is a little too small for him. He wants a house with four bedrooms.
NOTES: Leo Fuchs (1911-1994), star of New York's Yiddish Theatre on Second Avenue, was one of Lou Derman's best friends.

"THE MARJORIE MAIN SHOW" Oct. 15, 1956
Episode # 67 Filmed on Tuesday, July 31, 1956
Writers: Lou Derman, Parke Levy, Bill Davenport
Guest Cast: Marjorie Main as Herself, Franco Corsaro as Carlos Montalvo

When a man named Carlos Montalvo phones Lily with an interest to see the Henshaw house, she is sure he'll buy it if it's decorated in a Spanish theme. Before his arrival, she and Hilda decorate it elaborately with sombreros, bulls, serapes, etc. He's greeted at the door by Lily, then Hilda, wearing flamenco dress and mantilla, makes her entrance, snapping her castanets and batting her eyelashes at the distinguished Mr. Montalvo. He's quite amused, but explains he's not Mexican (he's from Jersey City), and furthermore, it's his client, a movie star, who's interested in seeing the house. He will reveal nothing but her initials, *M.M.* Pete immediately assumes it's Marilyn Monroe, and now he has no intention of

selling his own house. That evening at eight when the doorbell rings, the movie star is revealed to be Miss Marjorie Main. There she stands in a huge black tricorne hat. She acts very much like her screen persona, laughing heartily at her own jokes and slapping Lily on the back a few times. From a thermos she takes a swallow of goat's milk, explaining it's doctor's orders. She's not interested in seeing every room of the house, and features like the garbage disposal don't impress her. She says she has her own garbage disposal: her pet goat, Debbie, who gives three quarts of milk daily. When she promptly gives Matt a check ($35,000) for the house, he compliments her as fast worker, but she replies, "Not fast enough, sonny, or the name wouldn't be *Miss* Main!" After she exits, Pete explodes, "How am I going to sell my house with a goat next door?" The Henshaws are not certain they want to sell to Miss Main, but have little time to decide how they'll get out of it because she arrives early the next morning with Debbie. She remarks that Debbie is sensitive to noise, and puts her in the back yard. Then she informs them that she's moving in three hours later. Matt explains that the house has to go through escrow and that they have nowhere else to go. She says they can "bunk with her" until they find a new place. Miss Main's also unfazed by the planes passing overhead. They try everything to discourage her from moving in but aren't successful until Lily arrives from outside with a glass of Debbie's milk. Miss Main takes a sip and is shocked to find the milk sour. Lily offers the passing planes as an explanation. Miss Main grumps, "What ain't good for Debbie ain't good fer me. Gimme my check back." After she leaves, Lily casually mentions how handy the Henshaws' lemon trees are.
NOTES: **Film actress Marjorie Main makes a rare television appearance in this episode, perhaps at the invitation of her friend Spring Byington.**

"HOUSE ON BLOCKS" Oct. 29, 1956
EPISODE # 68 FILMED ON TUESDAY, JULY 24, 1956
WRITERS: LOU DERMAN, PARKE LEVY, BILL DAVENPORT
GUEST CAST: GEORGE MEADER AS MR. WESLEY, SANDRA GOULD AS MRS. WESLEY, LENNIE BREMEN AS MIKE THE HOUSE MOVER, JAMES FLAVIN AS THE FIRST COP, BARNEY PHILLIPS AS THE SECOND COP, EDWARD BROPHY AS THE POLICE SERGEANT, JACK RICE AS A POTENTIAL HOUSE BUYER

During an open house at the Henshaws', Mr. and Mrs. Wesley, who've been displaced by freeway construction, show a strong interest in making a deal, but they can't come up with the down payment until they sell their house, currently sitting on blocks and awaiting a move. Hilda impulsively offers to buy the Wesley house, but Lily thinks she's doing it mainly to help Matt and Ruth. Then Hilda tells her she's been intending to buy a beach lot from Sally Benson, and the Wesley house will be perfect for it. Hilda can't reach Sally by phone to make arrangements to leave the house on her lot, but she hires Mike, a mover, to take the house there. When he arrives at the Benson property, he finds it's been converted into a parking lot. Hilda and Lily meet Mike there in order to think of another place to park it. Finally at 1 a.m., Lily remembers an empty lot that Anita Henderson's been planning to build a restaurant on. She sends Mike there before she and Hilda head home. Meanwhile, Matt and Ruth are attending a party and have no awareness of these helpful efforts. When they arrive home before Lily, they're surprised to find her bed empty. The phone rings, and Mike leaves a cryptic message for Lily: "The gang's coming over to knock your blocks off." What he means is that the house is sitting too high to go through an underpass, and Mike's hired some help to lower it before the police notice the traffic backed up behind it. Matt mistakenly believes Lily's in some kind of trouble with a gang of crooks so he, Ruth, and Pete rush to the police station to report the threat. Meanwhile a weary Lily and Hilda arrive home and decide to call Anita to make sure she still owns the vacant lot. They learn that her lot's only 6 feet by 15 feet (she only wanted to open a hot dog stand), so they rush out to search for Mike. At the police station, Matt tries to explain the situation to the sergeant when an officer brings in Lily and Hilda on a speeding charge. Their attempts to enlighten the sergeant fail, and he orders all five of them to take a sobriety test. The next day, Mr. Wesley backs out on the deal to buy the Henshaw house, and phones Hilda with an offer to buy back his little house. She jumps at the chance.

"THE PRIZE FIGHTER" Nov. 5, 1956
Episode # 69 Filmed on Tuesday, September 11, 1956
Writers: Lou Derman, Parke Levy, Bill Davenport
Guest Cast: Arnold Stang as Marvin Fisher, Art Aragon as Himself, Beverly Long as Susie Martin, Stanley Clements as Steve Dundee, Roy Glenn as Ben

Pete's nerdy brother-in-law Marvin is visiting again. He's seeking a medical discharge from the Marines and intends to move into Pete and Gladys's new house in the Palisades when it's completed. The Henshaws doubt that Marvin would live with the Porters if he were married, but naturally Marvin doesn't know any girls to date. Lily suggests Susie Martin, who's recently broken up with her boyfriend, professional boxer Steve Dundee. When brutish Steve discovers Susie trying to teach Marvin to dance, he challenges Marvin to a boxing match. Everyone advises Marvin not to fight, but when Susie kisses him and declares he's the bravest man in the whole world, he's determined to keep the match. Hilda suggests boxer Art Aragon as a coach for Marvin. When Art meets scrawny Marvin, he doubts there's any way Marvin can win. But because Art dislikes Steve, he agrees to help. The next day, he sets Steve up by telling him that Marvin's a killer. With Steve looking on, Art takes a fall when Marvin swings at him during their short bout in the ring. Steve sees Marvin in a new light and frantically wishes Marvin and Susie lots of luck as he exits the gym.

"RITZY NEIGHBORHOOD" Nov. 12, 1956
EPISODE # 70 FILMED ON TUESDAY, AUGUST 7, 1956
WRITERS: LOU DERMAN, PARKE LEVY, AL SCHWARTZ
GUEST CAST: SHIRLEY MITCHELL AS VIKKI YOUNG, CHEERIO MEREDITH AS
HORTENSE MILLER, MARJORIE BENNETT AS EDYTHEA WALKER, ALMIRA
SESSIONS AS ELSIE PRINGLE, HARRY ANTRIM AS MR. CRANDALL, KING
DONOVAN AS HAL BOSWORTH, DORIS PACKER AS MRS. CRANDALL, PETER
LEEDS AS JIM YOUNG

Matt sells the house to a Mr. Crandall, who uses a one-year-old turquoise Cadillac as a down payment. Considering the upcoming move for the Henshaws, Lily regretfully informs the Westwood Womens Cultural Club that she must resign as its president. The Henshaws and the Porters are invited to attend a formal cocktail party given by Jim and Vikki Young, who will become their neighbors once they build their new homes in the Palisades. Matt and Pete immediately feel out of place among the Youngs and their materialistic friends, who talk about nothing but swimming pools, mink coats, sailboats, and the country club. Pete says their new homes would be "twin poor houses in the middle of Fort Knox." The next day, Matt tells Ruth and Lily that he should back out of the deal with Crandall. Matt's mechanic phones, suggesting that the Cadillac has been in an accident, considering all the problems he's found with it. Matt sees this as his "out," but Crandall refuses to budge on the deal, saying his wife really likes the neighborhood and hopes to make lots of friends in Westwood. With a twinkle in her eye, Lily invites Crandall's wife over to meet some of her neighbors-to-be. The next morning as Mrs. Crandall and Lily get to know each other, Hortense bounces in. Right away she warns Mrs. Crandall about Hilda Crocker, the biggest man-chaser in the neighborhood. "She broke up my home . . . Bruce used to follow me around like a dog." To Mrs. Crandall's consternation, Hortense then begins pocketing little items like vases and bric-a-brac. Lily says nothing, merely smiles knowingly at Mrs. Crandall. Hortense leaves abruptly, saying she has to go to a board meeting downtown. Lily elaborates: "It's her parole board. She has to report twice a month." Then Edythea saunters in with her Great Dane, Jupiter. She seats him on the sofa beside an uneasy Mrs. Crandall. Her visit is cut short when Elsie pops in to remind Edythea that they're late for a cha-cha lesson. After they leave, Lily explains that Elsie lives next door, and her wild parties last until 4 a.m. Mr. Crandall enters with Matt, but before Mrs. Crandall can comment on her visitors, Hilda saunters in, dressed in a low-cut, clinging knit gown. She's also wearing a black wig and dangerously long eyelashes. She immediately begins flirting with Mr. Crandall, cuddling close to him, "Where did you get those dimples?" Mrs. Crandall bristles with anger, "Harry, you buy this house, and you'll live in it yourself!" She marches out. Her dutiful husband agrees to take back the Cadillac and call off the deal. Matt is so overjoyed he offers to kiss Hilda, who warns, "Look out, Matt, you'll knock off my eyelashes!"

"LILY AND THE PROWLER" Nov. 19, 1956
EPISODE # 71 FILMED ON TUESDAY, AUGUST 14, 1956
WRITERS: LOU DERMAN, PARKE LEVY, WILLIAM COWLEY

When Matt refuses to help Ruth do the dishes, so does Pete. They say that's woman's work. More words fly, and before they know it, Matt and Pete are kicked out of their bedrooms. They sleep in the Henshaw living room with Matt on the sofa and Pete on an army cot. Matt tells Pete that they must remain aloof toward Ruth and Gladys until their wives break down and apologize. Two days later, their differences have not been resolved. Lily tells Hilda she's worried about the standoff. She tries to persuade her friend to rattle the garbage cans after everyone's asleep so Ruth will run in fear to Matt's side. Hilda: "Yes, and Matt will come out with a baseball bat and rattle a few of my teeth!" But she agrees to do it. At 1 a.m., Ruth hears the racket and rushes into Matt's arms. Lily comes downstairs, too, saying she saw four burglars outside. Suddenly Hilda bursts through the side door, chased by a dog. She feebly explains that she was passing by on her way home from a late show and seeing the men in the yard, decided to investigate. Ruth: "I would have run." Hilda: "Running from men is completely against my nature." The five friends end the evening with a cup of coffee, and Matt helps Ruth wash the dishes.

NOTES: Only the five principals appear in this episode.

"THE JOCKEY" Nov. 26, 1956
EPISODE # 72 FILMED ON TUESDAY, SEPTEMBER 18, 1956
WRITERS: LOU DERMAN, PARKE LEVY, BILL DERMAN
GUEST CAST: ARNOLD STANG AS MARVIN FISHER, NESTOR PAIVA AS CHARLIE DYKES, CHEERIO MEREDITH AS HORTENSE MILLER

Lily's club has invested in El Peppo, a racehorse. They choose Pete's slightly built brother-in-law Marvin to be their jockey, but he's not too keen on the idea. He's afraid of heights and is very nearsighted. Once they cajole him to mount the horse, Hilda snaps a photo, and the horse takes off running at lightning speed. Everyone immediately assumes that Marvin and El Peppo have an electric chemistry, but when Marvin tries to get the horse to repeat his performance, he fails. Pete tells Marvin he's not cut out to be a jockey, and Marvin gets so upset he locks himself in his room for a week. Meanwhile, El Peppo is getting slower and slower in his test runs, only a mile in six minutes. They think the animal misses Marvin, so they ask Pete to persuade Marvin to come out of his room. Marvin only agrees to if Pete will paint his bedroom ceiling. Just as Pete climbs the ladder with his brush, Mr. Dykes, the stable owner, comes by to inform him that a camera flash scared the horse into running a mile in 1.36 minutes. When Pete realizes that it was not Marvin who motivated El Peppo, he hands Marvin the paintbrush. In the end, the club raffles off El Peppo to Frances Ferguson, whom Lily says is worthy, "Her husband just left her, and this will help her forget."

"THE DECORATING SHOW" DEC. 3, 1956
EPISODE # 73 FILMED ON TUESDAY, AUGUST 28, 1956
WRITERS: LOU DERMAN, PARKE LEVY, WILLIAM COWLEY
GUEST CAST: HOWARD MCNEAR AS THE PAINTER, GRANDON RHODES AS ROY KENDALL, HAROLD FONG AS THE WAITER

After the Henshaw house doesn't sell, Matt and Ruth finally decide to redecorate their house instead of moving. Ruth has a hard time pleasing herself with the choices she makes. The lamp she selects doesn't look the same when she gets it home. The painter can't seem to capture the right shade of gray (the same as in Matt's pajamas) for the living room. So Lily suggests they try a decorator. Ruth hires Roy Kendall for the job. He flirts openly with Lily and invites her out for dinner. At a Chinese restaurant, Kendall recommends the same atmosphere for the Henshaw home. Lily is unsure the children will appreciate that style so Kendall offers to send over one Chinese piece at a time until they grow accustomed to it. When the first piece, a chair, arrives, the Henshaws aren't pleased with it at all, but they're reluctant to admit that to Lily. They don't want to hinder the budding relationship she seems to have with Kendall. Things change quickly when Hilda shares the latest gossip. She says that four acquaintances have all used Kendall as a decorator, and he's suggested a Chinese motif for each one. And he wooed the women on Chinese food. But the worst part is that Kendall is a married man. Matt smells a rat and decides to look at the manufacturer's label on the underside of the chair. He finds the furniture store's telephone number listed there also, and when they investigate further, it turns out that Kendall owns the store. Lily's outdone, "At my age I ought to know chop suey from baloney!" After this fiasco Matt and Ruth decide to postpone redecorating for several weeks.

"THE INDIAN SHOW" DEC. 10, 1956
EPISODE # 74 FILMED ON TUESDAY, OCTOBER 30, 1956
WRITERS: LOU DERMAN, PARKE LEVY, BILL DERMAN
GUEST CAST: RALPH DUMKE AS HENRY, JOSEPH KEARNS AS THE GUIDE, RODD REDWING AS THE INDIAN SHOPKEEPER, NORMAN LEAVITT AS THE CARPENTER, JEAN G. HARVEY AS MARY

Matt's boss wants him to call on several clients in the Midwest so Matt decides to go by car and take the Ruth and Lily. The timing's perfect because the house renovations can be completed while they're away. When Hilda hears about the trip, she mentions that her uncle in Muncy, Indiana, wants her to invest in a chicken farm, and wonders if she can hitch a ride to check on her investment. When questioned about her experience with such a farm, she quips, "What's to know? Every time a chicken sits down—Bingo!" Pete is interested in making an investment in the farm also. Since Gladys has gone to New York to await the arrival of her sister's baby, he's free to join the gang on their road trip. The next morning as Matt's station wagon is loaded, he admonishes everyone about the lack of space for souvenirs. Lily and Hilda don't heed his warning, and on the first stop in New Mexico they buy a total of $145 worth of Indian souvenirs, including a skin dress for Hilda ("Do you have my size? Heap Big 44 Stout!") They plan to ship them back to California but find that the nearest post office is 38 miles away. The shopkeeper refuses to accept returns, so they hide their purchases in their hotel room closets, and even in the electric Murphy bed. Later Lily and Hilda decide they must sell their loot without Matt finding out. They open their own Indian trading post but don't have much luck, especially after Hilda's Indian dance turns into a Charleston. When Matt, Ruth, and Pete stroll by, they hide behind ceremonial masks. When the fellows grow suspicious, they unmask a disappointed Hilda and Lily. Then Matt gives his approval for them to take along all of their souvenirs because he's bought some of his own.

"MAN TOWN" DEC. 17, 1956
EPISODE # 75 FILMED ON TUESDAY, NOVEMBER 6, 1956
WRITERS: LOU DERMAN, PARKE LEVY, BILL DERMAN
GUEST CAST: JAMES BURKE AS HARRY HENSHAW, HARRY O. TYLER AS THE
HOTEL CLERK, CHARLES WATTS AS TOM THE SHERIFF, WILLIAM "BILL" PHILLIPS
AS THE DEPUTY, HANK PATTERSON AS HIRAM HIGGLEBY, FRANK RICHARDS AS
THE CROOK, PHIL ARNOLD AS THE BALD MAN

The gang makes a side trip to Pinewood, Oklahoma, where Matt's bachelor uncle is the local newspaper editor. Pinewood is a booming oil town where the men outnumber the women eight to one. In the hotel lobby filled with men, Hilda attracts wizened old Hiram Higgleby who invites her to the town dance that evening. Ruth gets noticed, too. Matt accuses her of wiggling ("You walked across that hotel lobby like you were churning butter."). Soon the sheriff arrives, announcing he's there to search the premises for a bank robber who's hiding in the area. Pete is arrested when the hold-up weapon is found under his pillow. Professing that he's been set up, Pete is carried off to jail. When Lily and Hilda visit him, Hilda offers him a salami. "It's good for you—it's full of iron." (She's hidden a file in it.) Matt's uncle enters with the news that the real crook should have a bump on his head from a scuffle with the bank guard. Lily and Hilda promise Pete they'll exonerate him. That evening at the dance, Lily and Hilda rub the heads of every man they're partnered with. Finally the criminal is found during the apple-bobbing contest: Hilda holds the men's heads in the tub while she feels for bumps.

"FOOTBALL HERO" DEC. 24, 1956
EPISODE # 76 FILMED ON TUESDAY, OCTOBER 2, 1956
WRITERS: LOU DERMAN, PARKE LEVY, BILL DERMAN
GUEST CAST: HARRY CHESHIRE AS MR. NORRIS, PARLEY BAER AS COACH
ANDERSON, JOE CONLEY AS BUTCH FARRELL, GARY GRAY AS TOMMY HART,
YVONNE LIME AS SANDY CUMMINGS, RALPH SANFORD AS THE SECURITY GUARD,

BURT MUSTIN AS POP, LENNIE BREMEN AS A FAN, JOE BROWN AND FREDERICK FORD AS FOOTBALL PLAYERS

In Missouri, the travelers stop in Matt's college town for lunch. Some cheerleaders come in the malt shop, talking about tomorrow's football game. Ruth introduces them to Matt because she's proud he made the scoring touchdown for the championship game ten years ago. The kids insist he attend the game, but Matt says they need to make it to Kansas City by nightfall. Ruth and the rest pressure on him to change his mind, and as soon as he does, he regrets that he must tell Ruth the truth. His team was already ahead by sixty-two points when he scored the final touchdown. Dreading he'll be exposed the next day, Matt breathes a sigh of relief when he learns the game is a sellout. In the meantime, Lily bumps into the coach when she's at the box office. She explains who her son-in-law is, and Coach Anderson arranges not only to get them seats but to meet Matt on the field after the game. The next day at half-time, Lily and Hilda strike up a conversation with the father of the star quarterback from the team ten years ago. Lily beams when she tells Mr. Norris that her son won the championship game. Being a diehard fan of the team, he removes from his wallet an old newspaper clipping which reveals that Matt was actually on the third string that year, brought in for the final moments of the game because he hadn't played in a game all season. Lily and Hilda are crushed by this news, and because she feels responsible for setting up the meeting between Matt and his old coach, she tells Hilda that she must explain things to Coach Anderson before the end of the game. She and Hilda don helmets and cover themselves with blankets, sneaking past a guard onto the field where the home team is huddled on the sidelines. To blend in, they even do warm-up exercises, during which Hilda is knocked to the ground and exposed. Before they can speak to the coach, the guard escorts them away. When the game is over, Ruth approaches the coach to ask about that touchdown ten years ago. He doesn't disappoint Lily (who's passed him a NOTES via the guard) and boasts that Matt went over the goal line with three 200-pound opponents hanging onto him.

"NEW YEAR'S PARTY" DEC. 31, 1956 *
EPISODE # 77 FILMED ON TUESDAY, OCTOBER 9, 1956
WRITERS: LOU DERMAN, PARKE LEVY, BILL DERMAN
GUEST CAST: JESSLYN FAX AS AUNT CORA HUNTER, VERA MARSHE AS RENEE,
BYRON FOULGER AS CHARLIE BROWN THE WESTERN UNION MAN, EDITH
SIMMONS AS FAY BOWER THE NURSE

On the day before New Year's Eve in Hilda's hometown of Chicago, all of the nightclubs are booked for the following evening, except for one with three available seats. When Matt, Ruth, and Pete refuse to go without Lily and Hilda, Lily pretends that Hilda's old friend Sophie Lawrence has invited them to a swanky party at her apartment in the Carlton Arms. Meanwhile, Pete's been tracked down by Gladys's Aunt Cora who insists that he spend New Year's Eve with his in-laws, watching their home movies. The next morning, while Lily and Hilda have their hair done in the hotel beauty parlor, Pete enters to tell them he's going to ditch Gladys's family for a fun night with Matt and Ruth. When Aunt Cora suddenly enters, looking for Lily, Pete sits at a dryer, hiding under a sheet and towel. Aunt Cora soon notices a lit cigar nearby, which Hilda hastily begins to smoke, but then she sees Pete's shoes poking from under the sheet. She gently chides him for hiding and then rushes a sickened Pete off to tour the art institute, aquarium, planetarium, etc. before their family dinner. That evening, as Matt and Ruth prepare to leave, Hilda and Lily emerge from the bedroom in elegant evening attire. They tell the children that they want to make a good impression on Sophie's high society friends. When Matt promises to phone them at Sophie's at midnight, Lily and Hilda panic. They don't want them to know that they have nowhere to spend the evening. Knowing that Sophie has planned to go out, Hilda suggests they hang at her apartment until the children call. At 11:30 p.m., Ruth, Matt, and Pete (who's escaped his in-laws) phone the girls at Sophie's to say they're having a miserable time at the nightclub so they want to drop by Sophie's to wish them all a happy new year. Lily tells Hilda that they've got to fill Sophie's apartment with guests so it will appear as if they're having a party. She sends Hilda out on the street and throughout the building to find "friendly strangers" while she rounds up some food. A short time later, the strangers begin to arrive, including a Western Union man, a nurse, a cop, a homeless woman, three merchant seamen, some frowsy women, and a butler, none of whom appear to resemble Sophie's high society friends. They've all been enticed by different tales told to them by Hilda. Lily's worried that they won't fool the children, so she asks the friendly strangers to play along with her scheme. When the Henshaws and Pete are taken aback by the appearance of the guests, Hilda quickly explains it's a costume party. The guests do their best to use proper English and converse about things such as foreign travel, the yacht club, etc., but Lily cannot greet the new year with a lie. When she confesses her ruse, the children forgive her, and the real party begins.

"ROYALTY" JAN. 7, 1957
EPISODE # 78 FILMED ON TUESDAY, OCTOBER 16, 1956
WRITERS: LOU DERMAN, PARKE LEVY, BILL DERMAN
GUEST CAST: JOHN QUALEN AS COUNT GUSTAV ROMANI, IPHIGENIE CASTIGLIONI AS THE DUCHESS, GORDON RICHARDS AS THE BUTLER

Hilda is dreamy-eyed when she comes to breakfast in the hotel suite. She danced the night away with Count Gustav Romani, whom she met at Sophie Lawrence's party. She says he wasn't really tall or handsome, but she made him laugh, and his age was perfect: "When I said I was thirty, he told me he was forty." The count, whom Hilda calls Gus, phones later, asking her to accompany him to the ballet that evening. When he meets Matt, Ruth, Lily, and Pete, it's obvious to them that Gus is charmed by Hilda's wit and vitality. The next morning, his aunt, the Duchess, requests to meet Hilda on the following day. Gus explains that she wants to know more about Hilda's family background, but Hilda confesses she doesn't know much about her family tree. Gus promises to help her find a genealogist to chart her lineage. After he leaves, Hilda cries to Lily: "The duchess wants my pedigree. They're looking for a poodle, and I'm just a mutt." The next afternoon, Hilda meets Gus's Aunt Patricia, the duchess, who has a dignified and slightly condescending air about her. Hilda sees right away that the old lady is very domineering. She tells Hilda that there are times when Gustav forgets his obligation and duty as a nobleman. After she and Gus exit the room to discuss a few things, Lily arrives with Prof. Schultz (Pete wearing a pince-nez), who has researched Hilda's family lines. Hilda asks him not to share the fake family chart he's prepared (it includes Cleopatra and Sir Francis Drake) because she knows that any relationship she has with Gus will be overshadowed by his devotion to his aunt. When the Romanis re-enter the room, he affects a German accent and creates a long tale about all the black sheep in Hilda's line, such as Sam Crocker who helped Benedict Arnold escape and Senor Pepe Sanchez Alvarado Figueroa Crocker who led the effort to blow up the battleship Maine in Havana Harbor. The duchess can bear no more and excuses herself with a terrible headache. Gus realizes it's futile to think he and Hilda have a future together. So does Hilda. They part as friends.

"CHICKEN FARM" JAN. 14, 1957
EPISODE # 79 FILMED ON TUESDAY, NOVEMBER 13, 1956
WRITERS: LOU DERMAN, PARKE LEVY, BUDD GROSSMAN
GUEST CAST: IRVING BACON AS ANDY, WILL WRIGHT AS THE DOCTOR

The happy quintet finds themselves lost when searching for Hilda's uncle's Indiana farm. A gas station attendant gives them directions to Ned Washburn's place, but when they arrive they find that Uncle Ned is not home. He left a note informing them that he's gone to Chicago to pick up his new bride. (Hilda: "He's almost seventy!") Uncle Ned, however, has left a list of chores for Hilda and her friends, but warns them all to be very careful of his three prize Plymouth Rock hens. They attempt to do their best, but farm life is really roughing it for these Los Angelinos. Pete falls in the pig sty, then has to take a bath in tin tub near the wood stove. Meanwhile Matt gives Lily a ring for safekeeping. Since he and Ruth eloped, she never had an engagement ring. For their anniversary, he wants to surprise her with this diamond ring. Out in the hen house, Hilda and Lily gather eggs. Lily shows Hilda the ring, but when Hilda suddenly sneezes she drops it. They search but cannot find it anywhere. Then they look suspiciously at the Plymouth Rock hens. Late that night, they take the hens to the home of a doctor and beg him to determine if one of the chickens swallowed Ruth's ring. He asks them to hold the chickens behind his fluoroscope for the tests, but nothing shows up. Meanwhile back at the hen house, Pete finds the ring on the floor and shows it to Matt. Matt's a little disappointed that Lily was so irresponsible, but then

Ruth runs in saying she saw shadows moving toward the barn. Soon Hilda and Lily enter the hen house to resume their search. Lily apologetically explains where they've been but is quickly overjoyed when Matt reveals the ring and puts it on Ruth's finger.

"THE HOMECOMING SHOW" JAN. 21, 1957
EPISODE # 80 FILMED ON TUESDAY, NOVEMBER 20, 1956
WRITERS: LOU DERMAN, PARKE LEVY, BUDD GROSSMAN
GUEST CAST: ELVIA ALLMAN AS SARAH SELKIRK, MARJORIE BENNETT AS EDYTHEA WALKER, MADGE BLAKE AS MARGARET WILCOX, ALMIRA SESSIONS AS ELSIE PRINGLE, CONNIE VAN AS SELMA

Six weeks after being on the road, the gang arrives back in Los Angeles to find the Henshaw home totally redesigned, inside and out. Gone is the Early American look, and in its place a more modern décor. They are all awestruck by its sleek beauty, but Ruth is especially taken with the new furniture and carpet. She politely asks Pete to not put his feet on the window seat nor his head on the chair cushion. Then she asks him to be careful with his cigar. She's instantly protective of the new furnishings, suggesting to Matt that they buy plastic slipcovers that evening. Pete takes it all in stride until the next day when Ruth follows him around with a silent butler to catch every little ash. (Pete: "I've got the feeling I'm being followed by an alligator.") When one ash accidentally hits the floor, Ruth brusquely remarks that she must sweep the rug. Matt tries to smooth things over, but Pete, feeling unwelcome, says, "This house has always been a refuge for me. When things got a little rough for me at home, I could scoot over here and relax until the storm blew over. Maybe it's time I found myself a new storm shelter." The next day, Matt goes over to Pete's and finds him in the garage, watching television on a seven-inch screen, amid all the clutter of garden tools, wheelbarrow, old furniture, etc. When Ruth comes over to invite Pete to lunch at her house, he declines, "I wouldn't be comfortable without a tie." She doesn't understand his jab, but Matt does, and when Ruth leaves, he chastises Pete for acting like a spoiled child. Pete quietly asks him to go. That evening, as Lily and Hilda are preparing for a surprise engagement party their club is giving Elsie Pringle, Pete enters with a silver tray Gladys sent over. When Pete hears the party is to take place in the Henshaws' new living room, he wonders how Ruth ever gave Lily permission to host it. When Lily considers that the girls may spill food on Ruth's rug, Pete volunteers his garage as a last-minute substitution. That evening, as the rain falls, Pete is kept busy emptying buckets in his leaky garage while Lily's club members decorate with balloons and prepare to surprise Elsie. Soon Margaret gives the signal that the bride has arrived. When Elsie enters, the ladies yell "Surprise!" Elsie's overcome with emotion as she unwraps her presents (including a blue negligee, three sets of steak knives, and an electric heating pad). Then Ruth and Matt enter, looking for Lily. When Ruth can't understand why Lily is hosting the party in Pete's garage, Matt explains, "Do you know what we've done?

We've let our new furniture come between old friends." Ruth is remorseful, but suddenly she takes Matt back to their living room to get a present for Elsie. They return with the plastic slipcovers, inviting the party guests to cover the food and gifts, and themselves, and move the party to the Henshaws' living room. When Lily protests, Ruth tells her, "We won't be needing them anymore." Then, as the laughing party guests exit, Ruth gives Pete a cigar. In the vignette, Hilda tells Lily she bought a waffle iron to replace the set of steak knives she bought for Elsie. Then Margaret drops by to find out on which train Elsie's departing. She wants to give her the waffle iron she exchanged for the set of steak knives she bought. Lily takes them both by the arm to accompany them to the department store because, she explains, Ruth is out buying a waffle iron for Elsie.

"THE BUDGET SHOW" JAN. 28, 1957
EPISODE # 81 FILMED ON TUESDAY, NOVEMBER 27, 1956
WRITERS: LOU DERMAN, PARKE LEVY, BUDD GROSSMAN
GUEST CAST: ANN DORAN AS MISS MOORE, GENEVIEVE AUMONT AS MISS LAROUCHE, MILLIE BRUCE AS THE MAID, DEE SHARON AS MODEL #1, IRENE KING AS MODEL #2, MARJORIE MAY AS MODEL #3

When Matt accuses Ruth of spending too much money, she cites his extravagances as well. They challenge each other to stick with a budget, but the very first day Ruth goes off her budget, spending $89 on a green dress at an exclusive shop, Yvonne's. She plans to hide it in the back of her closet so Matt won't notice it. Moments later, he suddenly walks in, and seeing Lily holding the dress, assumes it's hers. Hilda bustles in to invite Lily to a movie premiere the next evening, but Lily moans that she has nothing to wear. Matt suggests the new green dress. To get out of the predicament, Lily says she'll just buy a less expensive green dress to wear, doubting Matt will ever notice the difference. Ruth hides her dress back in the closet, but Matt accidentally finds it. He demands she take it back. When the shop owner refuses to accept the return, Matt and Pete go down to demand satisfaction. Instead, they're so charmed by the store models and Miss LaRouche, the buyer for Yvonne's, that Pete buys a dress for Gladys and Matt allows Ruth to keep her green dress.

"STUDY GROUP" FEB. 4, 1957
EPISODE # 82 FILMED ON TUESDAY, DECEMBER 4, 1956
WRITERS: LOU DERMAN, PARKE LEVY, BUDD GROSSMAN
GUEST CAST: JOSEPH KEARNS AS PROF. THORNHILL, KING DONOVAN AS HERB THE DIRECTOR, JOI LANSING AS CANDY RUSSELL, BARBARA STUART AS BARBARA COLEMAN, JAN KAYNE AS JEAN BOWERS, GLORIA PALL AS HELEN WILLES, LEE MILLAR AS JOE THE PHOTOGRAPHER

Lily interviews Prof. Thornhill who's written a book on marital problems. He's of the opinion that the number of divorces would decline if wives kept up mentally with their husbands by joining a study group. This gets Ruth to wondering if she and Matt are mentally incompatible. She joins a study group in order to "save her marriage," but she ends up spending so much time at the library studying Socrates and Sophocles that it leaves Matt very discouraged. With a mischievous look in her eye, Lily suggests he start his own study group. And she knows just the perfect students to join it: four chorus girls she's been interviewing for an assignment. They arrive the next evening just before Ruth is to leave for the library. Of course, they all have knockout figures and dazzling smiles, leaving Ruth a little daunted by their beauty and doubtful of what they plan to study. She hangs around to find out. Meanwhile Pete arrives to check out the group, and when he meets the members, he immediately joins. Ruth hears loud laughter coming from the den. When she goes in to investigate, she finds the girls gathered around Matt's chair, planning future meetings on the terrace of one girl's apartment, the perfect location to enable them to "get close to nature." When Ruth storms out of the room, Matt follows her, asking what she'd do if he left home every night of the week. She realizes she's neglected him and decides to quit her study group. Soon thereafter, Lily reads an item in the newspaper—Prof. Thornhill's wife is leaving him. He spent so much time trying to save other marriages that he never came home.

"MOTHER-IN-LAW GROUP" FEB. 11, 1957
EPISODE # 83 FILMED ON TUESDAY, DECEMBER 11, 1956
WRITERS: LOU DERMAN, PARKE LEVY, BUDD GROSSMAN
GUEST CAST: SARA HADEN AS MRS. HAWKS, SUSAN MORROW AS JANET
SINCLAIR, PAUL PICERNI AS GEORGE SINCLAIR, RUTH WARREN AS MRS.
HOKINSON, DORIS KEMPER AS MRS. KANE, NETTA PACKER AS MRS. PREBBLES,
LILLIAN CULVER AS MARY PALMER

Lily writes a column about the virtues of mothers-in-law, and receives such positive feedback that she decides to form a mother-in-law group to further promote her opinions. Television talk show host Mary Palmer phones Lily to ask for a preliminary interview to determine if the club would make a good topic for one of her future broadcasts. Another mother-in-law who notices Lily's column is the mother of one of Matt's old girlfriends, Janet Sinclair, who, coincidentally, is visiting Los Angeles and wants to visit Matt. Mrs. Hawks explains to Lily that Janet is still infatuated with Matt, although she loves her husband George very much. She confides that whenever there is a slight disagreement, Janet tells George that she could have married a perfect man: Matt. So when Mrs. Hawks read Lily's column, she instinctively felt that Lily could help strengthen her daughter's marriage. When George comes by to pick up Mrs. Hawks, Lily is very impressed with him so she decides to help Mrs. Hawks. She shares with Matt and Ruth her plan to shatter Janet's illusions of Matt. When Janet arrives, Ruth, looking quite haggard, is working like a slave. A slovenly, shirtless Matt comes downstairs, barking orders to Ruth and spitting tobacco juice on the floor. He tells a bewildered Janet that he's not very happily married, then screams at a black-eyed Lily to bring in the coffee. As she goes to fetch it, he snarls to Janet, "How I've put up with that old bag all these years, I'll never know!" Janet asks about Lily's eye, Matt suspiciously explains that she bumped into a door. Then Hilda enters from outside, hair askew and dressed in grimy overalls. She looks meekly at Matt, "I waxed your car, son." Matt is not impressed and demands to know if she polished the chrome. Hilda's lip trembles when she tells him it was getting dark so she quit. She sobs, "Can I have my dinner now?" He refuses to feed her until she's finished with his car. Pete, posing as the grocery boy collecting on the large bill Matt's run up, is literally kicked out of the house by Matt. By the time Mary Palmer arrives for her appointment with Lily, Janet has had enough. Before she exits, she angrily confesses to Mary that she had to drive 2,000 miles to have her eyes opened. Matt has fallen from his pedestal. An embarrassed Lily finally explains the whole situation to Mary when Hilda re-enters, "I've finished your car, son. Can I please have my dinner now?"

"THE PIANO SHOW" FEB. 18, 1957
EPISODE # 84 FILMED ON TUESDAY, DECEMBER 18, 1956
WRITERS: LOU DERMAN, PARKE LEVY, BUDD GROSSMAN
GUEST CAST: ARLENE HARRIS AS MILLICENT, CHICK CHANDLER AS JOHNNY LAFFERTY

Ruth wants a piano for the living room, but Matt doesn't think they can afford it. Pete enters, jubilant that he's been accepted into the Hypnotists League of America. A doubtful Hilda, who's just dropped in to show them a tricycle she bought for her landlady's son, is persuaded to let Pete try out his new skill on her. Everyone is amazed when Hilda is hypnotized into thinking she's three years old, but Pete is unable to stop her from riding around the room on the tricycle until Lily whispers in her ear, "Crawford's Department Store is having a sale." Later Ruth is still sulking about not having a piano so Lily decides to secretly appear on a quiz show called *Pay the Piper* to win one. In order to claim her prize, Lily must allow a stranger named Millicent, posing as Lily's old friend, to stay in the Henshaw guest room for one week, no matter what happens. In order to get Matt and Ruth to kick her out, Millicent wreaks havoc on the kitchen, dumping cake batter on Pete and soaking Matt with the sink hose. She makes insulting comments, fills the bathtub with goldfish, and plays bongo drums at midnight. To help the Henshaws, Pete hypnotizes Millicent into thinking she must go home, and for a frantic last hour before the week Lily must do her best to keep Millicent in the house. Soon Mr. Lafferty arrives and awards the piano prize to Lily. In the vignette, Lily is plunking out "Chopsticks" when Hilda scoots beside her on the piano bench. She begins playing "She's Only a Bird in a Gilded Cage" while warbling terribly off-key.

"DUCK HUNTING" FEB. 25, 1957
EPISODE # 85 FILMED ON TUESDAY JANUARY 8, 1957
WRITERS: LOU DERMAN, PARKE LEVY, NATE MONASTER
GUEST CAST: RAYMOND GREENLEAF AS PAUL FARNUM, BYRON FOULGER AS MR. BURNS, EDITH SIMMONS AS THE RECEPTIONIST (VOICE ONLY)

Lily is hopeful that Farnum and Sons, a publishing company, will be interested in her novel, *The Lady Said Yes*. However, Paul Farnum tells Mr. Burns, an editor, that it's the worst piece of drivel he's read in years, assuming its author is a gushy, moonstruck adolescent. Timid Mr. Burns is hesitant to tell Lily their company has rejected her manuscript so Farnum offers to do so. He is immediately charmed by Lily and promptly asks her to lunch. He continues to court Lily, taking her dancing and to dinner, all the while feigning an interest in revising her novel. When he returns her manuscript, he accidentally encloses an interoffice memo to Burns which criticizes Lily's weak plot and flat characters, etc. Lily, feeling she's been led on by Paul, cancels their date for the evening and refuses to take his calls. Ruth suggests that Matt and Pete take Lily along on their planned duck-hunting trip to help cheer her up. But she also tells Paul where he can find Lily. He surprises a resistant Lily at the duck blind, then wins her back when he quotes one of her characters: "Happiness is such an elusive thing that two people should leave no stone unturned to seek it." He reminds her of her two characters who decide to marry and suggests they do the same.

"THE ENGAGEMENT SHOW" MAR. 4, 1957 *
EPISODE # 86 FILMED ON TUESDAY, JANUARY 15, 1957
WRITERS: LOU DERMAN, NATE MONASTER
GUEST CAST: RAYMOND GREENLEAF AS PAUL FARNUM, DICK ELLIOTT AS STANLEY POOLE, ELVIA ALLMAN AS SARAH SELKIRK, MADGE BLAKE AS MARGARET WILCOX, CHEERIO MEREDITH AS HORTENSE MILLER, FRANK ORTH AS HAL CARTER, PIERRE WATKIN AS HERB DAVIS, BYRON FOULGER AS JOHN BURNS

Lily excitedly shows Matt, Ruth, and Pete her engagement ring from her beau, book publisher, Paul Farnum. She describes how it happened, "Well, after lunch we took a drive through Nichols Canyon, and Paul parked the car at tip top of the cliff." Pete interjects, "Naturally. Any man thinking of marriage *must* have suicidal tendencies." When Hilda sees the ring, she exclaims, "Oh, Lily, look at it sparkle. You can stand on the beach and signal battleships. I'm so happy for you." It's the first time the two best friends have seen each in over two weeks because Lily has been so involved with Paul. She fears Hilda has been spending a lot of time alone since her last quarrel with Stanley, her boyfriend. Lily decides to help rekindle their romance. When she visits Stanley at his office, she finds he's still interested in seeing Hilda but he won't make the first move. Lily encourages him to take Hilda out to dinner at Armando's. When Hilda learns later that Lily had a hand in their date, she retorts, "I don't need people arranging dates just because they feel sorry for me. I've been finding my own men for forty, uh, thirty years." After Hilda leaves, Lily tells Ruth she must find a way to boost Hilda's ego. She decides to invite several single gentlemen to her buffet supper that week, in hopes that one will be attracted to Hilda. But when the men mingle with the ladies, none seems interested in Hilda. Matt's co-worker, Herb Davis, is instead interested in Sarah Selkirk's Mayan silver bracelet while Pete's friend Hal Carter prefers to compare aches and pains with fellow hypochondriac Margaret Wilcox. And John Burns, Paul's editor, renews an acquaintance with former dance-school partner, Hortense Miller. When they all exit to the patio, Hilda is left sitting alone. Then Stanley arrives. Hilda greets him like a long-lost friend, touched that he came over after finding out her whereabouts from her landlady. He gazes at Hilda, "You look beautiful tonight, Poopsie." Hilda responds, "And you look beautiful, cupcake," as they proudly exit hand-in-hand toward the patio.

"MASQUERADE PARTY" MAR. 11, 1957
EPISODE # 87 FILMED ON TUESDAY, JANUARY 22, 1957
WRITERS: LOU DERMAN, NATE MONASTER
GUEST CAST: RAYMOND GREENLEAF AS PAUL FARNUM, FRIEDA INESCORT AS
MISS PRUDHOMME, EDITH SIMMONS AS EDNA THE MAID, ROBERT BURTON AS
BOB CARRADAY, LEE MILLAR AS GEORGE THE PARTY GUEST

Lily and her fiancé Paul Farnum plan to wed on the first day of the following month. Paul plans to announce their engagement at a party he's giving for Bob Carraday, one of his authors. When he mentions he's searching for a party theme, Lily suggests that he ask his guests to dress as their favorite fictional characters. He likes that idea, but he instructs Lily to let his housekeeper, Miss Prudhomme, take care of all the party plans. He invites Lily to visit his home the following day to see if there's anything she would like to change before she moves in. The next day, Lily and Hilda are greeted by the tall and austere Miss Prudhomme, who carries herself with an almost regal bearing. As Lily makes suggestions about changes in decorating, particularly a pair of gaudy lamps, Miss Prudhomme reacts coldly. When Paul arrives, it's obvious that "Prudie" is quite devoted to him. Hilda's reaction: "Lily, I don't trust that woman. She's been top sergeant of this outfit for twenty-two years, and you're coming in as a buck private." Later that week Paul drops in to tell Lily that they must postpone the wedding for a couple of weeks. Bob Carraday wants Paul to accompany him to New York to get a jump on publicizing his forthcoming book. As he's leaving, Hilda arrives to give Lily a little preview of the costume she selected to wear as Scarlett O'Hara. When she sits on the sofa, the hoop skirt flips up, exposing her pantaloons. Then the caterer phones with confusing news for Lily—the formal dinner she planned was changed by Paul to a buffet. On the evening of the party, as the guests depart, they're bid farewell by Lily (as Madame Butterfly) and Paul (as a naval officer). Matt and Ruth (as Hansel and Gretel) call for Pete, who enters from the patio dressed as Trader Horn. He's happy that he and Gladys won first prize for their costumes. When he beckons her, Gladys enters the room carrying a trophy. She's wearing a huge gorilla costume, waving to Lily as she exits. In passing conversation, Lily learns from Bob Carraday that it was not his idea to fly to New York on the first; Prudie phoned him, saying it was important that Paul be there then. When all the guests have gone, Lily addresses Miss Prudhomme: "This is your hour of triumph. You managed to see that the lamps were kept. The sit-down dinner became the buffet you wanted, and I find that even my wedding date is at your mercy. I congratulate you, Miss Prudhomme, you're batting a thousand." When she sees Paul approaching, the housekeeper reacts for his benefit, running upstairs in tears, threatening to move back east. Paul frantically chases after her, ignoring Lily's calls. She sadly realizes she can't compete with a woman who has a twenty-two year headstart on her.

NOTES: Series writer Lou Derman borrowed the character name Prudhomme from his daughter Linda's piano teacher, whom Linda recalled also had a regal bearing.

"KISSING BOOTH" MAR. 18, 1957
EPISODE # 88 FILMED ON TUESDAY, FEBRUARY 5, 1957
WRITERS: LOU DERMAN, BEN STARR
GUEST CAST: ELVIA ALLMAN AS SARAH SELKIRK, ROBERT FORTIER AS BILL CHAMBERS, FRANK JENKS AS THE MAN AT THE KISSING BOOTH, EDNA HOLLAND AS THE BRENTWOOD CLUB MEMBER

Matt becomes jealous when Ruth's old friend Bill Chambers gives her a peck on the cheek at a party. Meanwhile Lily is having trouble finding a girl for her club's kissing booth at a charity bazaar. Hilda's neighbor, who's a model, cancelled out, and even Madeline Schweitzer's niece can't fill the space (Lily: "She's a dumpy girl with wild hair and big ears.") Hilda coyly poses with both hands under her chin, but Lily is not moved, "No, Hilda, not even for charity." Pete offers Gladys, "With her mouth, she could kiss 'em two at a time!" They're trying to come up with the perfect girl when Bill Chambers (tall, handsome, and energetic) comes to ask for Ruth's help in planning a party for a mutual friend. When he exits with another kiss for Ruth, Matt is steaming with jealousy, and Ruth is angrily embarrassed that Matt was rude to Bill. Suddenly Matt suggests Ruth ("Miss Pucker Puss") to fill in at Lily's booth. She accepts! The next day, the men are lined up to kiss Ruth when Matt enters the bazaar. Pete advises Ruth to step out of the booth before Matt finds here there. Hilda is a poor substitute; all the men drop out of the line and go over to the competing booth where the Brentwood club members are selling pies. Matt speaks to Sarah Selkirk, a member of Lily's club, who informs him that if they don't make their quota, some underprivileged child will go without toys. Matt approaches Ruth and tells her that they were both wrong. Then he instructs her, "Get in that booth!" In the vignette, Lily and Hilda are happily counting the $149 they took in. Pete gives them one more and kisses both ladies. Lily winks, "See, Hilda, we haven't lost our sex appeal!"

"THE HOBO SHOW" Mar. 25, 1957
Episode # 89 Filmed on Tuesday, January 29, 1957
Writers: Lou Derman, Nate Monaster
Guest Cast: Parley Baer as Morgan, Dick Wessel as Big Sam, Sid Melton as Weehawken, Donald Randolph as Commissioner McDermott, Lillian Culver as Harriet Adams

Matt's first assignment as the advisory architect on the city planning commission is to find a site for the new city dump. He's stuck between two choices: the community of Saugus and a railroad yard. He's reluctant to suggest the latter due to the necessary displacement of the hoboes who live there. Later Lily stumbles upon Matt's city map on which he's marked the hobo jungle. She then decides that hoboes would make an interesting topic for her next column. She convinces Hilda to accompany her to the jungle to get a real feel for hobo life. Disguised in ragged clothes, Lily and Hilda introduce themselves as Sadie and Philadelphia Fanny to three hoboes they find living under a railroad trestle. Morgan is the most erudite of the three, and it's he who suspects the girls' sincerity, having noticed their manicured fingernails. He sends Big Sam to follow them when they leave the hobo camp. Back at the Henshaws' house, Lily discovers she's forgotten her key. To enter the house without the knowledge of Matt and Ruth (who would have disapproved of their jungle visit), they attempt to climb a ladder to Lily's bedroom. Big Sam thwarts their efforts and forces them back to camp where Morgan informs them that their criminal behavior will draw attention to all the hoboes and thus put an end to their Shangri-La. The next morning, Big Sam reads in the paper that the city planning commissioner and assemblywoman Adams are coming to camp to investigate rumors of it being an eyesore. Lily is determined to help the hoboes because she respects their great integrity and honesty. She cleans up and decorates the camp while Hilda shampoos the men and makes them dress in fresh clothes. When the commissioner and Mrs. Adams arrive, he's amazed at their civility, but she sees the situation as an impressive charade. Matt arrives and is speechless to find Lily there. She explains that hobos don't add much to society, but they don't take away from it either. Lily wins over the commissioner who winks and confesses that he's partial to Saugus.
NOTES: Harriet Adams was the real-life wife of actor Stanley Adams, good friend of Lou Derman.

"THE ENGLISHMAN" Apr. 1, 1957
Episode # 90 Filmed on Tuesday, February 12, 1957
Writers: Lou Derman, Ben Starr
Guest Cast: Paul Cavanaugh as Mr. Hawthorne, Lewis Martin as Henry Henshaw

Lily introduces Matt to Mr. Hawthorne, a charming elderly Englishman whom Lily has engaged as a guest lecturer for her club. Hawthorne impresses Matt when he informs him that Englishmen are the masters of their own homes. The next day, Ruth and Matt argue when he refuses to run her errands. Ruth, in turn, balks when he demands that she retrieve the evening paper and have it waiting for him when he comes home. She tells him to buy a dog to do that job. Several days later, Matt grows a goatee like Mr. Hawthorne's, telling Pete that the American husband is a sucker and he's not going to stand for it anymore. So that Matt will have to wait on himself, Ruth decides she'll spend a few days in Las Vegas. But she changes her plan when she learns that Matt's dad is flying in for a visit. That eveing, Matt and Lily are having a nice visit with Mr. Henshaw when Ruth enters with a cumbersome load of firewood. She refuses help from her father-in-law, and then fussily fluffs his cushion, lights his cigar, and then drags his suitcase clumsily up the stairs. Mr. Henshaw questions her strange behavior, and Matt admits that Ruth's trying to embarrass him. He explains about his admiration for Mr. Hawthorne's customs. His father asks how long Hawthorne's been married, and Lily interjects that he's a bachelor. They both look at Matt as he realizes his foolish behavior.

"DO IT YOURSELF" APR. 8, 1957
EPISODE # 91 FLIMED ON TUESDAY, FEBRUARY 19, 1957
WRITERS: LOU DERMAN, NATE MONASTER
GUEST CAST: HARRY CHESHIRE AS MR. HORNSBY, NORMAN LEAVITT AS THE
SECOND TV REPAIRMAN, LEE MILLAR AS THE FIRST TV REPAIRMAN, DICK JOY
AS THE TV ANNOUNCER (VOICE ONLY)

Matt is upset over a stack of bills so Lily tries to save him some money by fixing the blender, cuckoo clock, toaster, etc. When she demonstrates how she repaired the vacuum cleaner, it blows Hilda's wide-brimmed straw hat off her head. Her sink repair job ends up spraying Matt right in the face. Matt instructs Ruth to call a repairman to have the TV set repaired before an important client, Mr. Hornsby, comes over to discuss business and watch the fights. Lily and Hilda are not aware of this, and after the repairman leaves, they attempt to fix the set themselves. They take out every tube, dust them off, and replace them. Now the picture jumps all over the screen. When Ruth tells Lily it must be in perfect working condition for tonight, Lily rents a television for the evening. Ruth rents one as well, but neither of them work very well. Mr. Hornsby, a sports enthusiast, does not want to miss a minute of the fights so he runs between the three sets, trying to see the video on one and listen to the audio on another. When all three sets fizzle out, Hornsby runs out to his car to listen on the radio. Lily is frantic with worry that she's ruined Matt's business deal, but soon Hornsby comes inside and informs them that his man won the fight. He's so happy he tells Ruth she should be proud of Matt because he's chosen him to design Hornsby's stadium.

"THE OLD MAN" APR. 15, 1957 *
EPISODE # 92 FILMED ON TUESDAY, FEBRUARY 26, 1957
WRITERS: LOU DERMAN, BEN STARR
GUEST CAST: DICK ELLIOTT AS STANLEY POOLE, CHARLES CANTOR AS WILBUR POOLE

Hilda is hopeful that Stanley will propose marriage to her, provided that his father gives his permission. To insure that this happens, she asks Lily to spend some time with "Dad" Poole in order to promote Hilda's finest qualities. Lily agrees, so when Mr. Poole arrives in Los Angeles, Lily invites him to come over with Stanley and Hilda. The senior Mr. Poole turns out to be a spry health fanatic and a spendthrift, insisting that he and Stanley walk the four miles to Lily's house. The exercise exhausts Stanley, but his father is obviously invigorated. And he's instantly charmed by Lily, who plays right up to him, giving the impression that she's just as frugal. When he promptly asks Lily to go boating in the park, she accepts the invitation. Several days (and dates) later, Mr. Poole asks Lily to marry him. Hilda's responds, "Oh, Lily, if you marry him and I marry Stanley, then . . ." She throws her arms around Lily, "MOTHER !" Lily says she has no intention of marrying Mr. Poole, but she's afraid her refusal will antagonize Hilda's chances of becoming Stanley's wife. Hilda adds, "If I lose Stanley, that's it, sister. I've already gone through the entire phone book." Then Lily remembers the doctor sketch that Pete's been rehearsing for his insurance convention so she decides to enlist his help for the evening. When Mr. Poole arrives (carrying a bouquet of dandelions), Lily pretends to be having trouble with her sacroiliac. Matt and Ruth play nurse, massaging her neck, administering her pills, etc. Matt also phones her doctor, despite Lily's protests regarding the financial costs. Mr. Poole becomes more and more uncomfortable, realizing that the woman he thought would be a good wife is actually a sickly (and costly) burden. "Dr. Pete Porter" arrives, promptly reminding Lily that the best place for her recovery is Switzerland. He prescribes caviar and "Welsh Rabbidia" as miracle cures, but he adds that they're very expensive. After he helps Matt and Ruth escort Lily to her bedroom, Mr. Poole takes Hilda aside, saying he goofed when he proposed to that "walking pill box." Then he wishes Hilda well with Stanley before informing her that he's skipping out on Lily. Hilda cautions, "She'll turn California upside down till she finds you." Mr. Poole replies, "Well, she ain't going to, because I'll be in Florida." After he makes a hasty exit, Hilda beckons the rest downstairs with the news that Mr. Poole has left for his home state. Lily laughs, "I hope he enjoys the walk."

"SONG PLUGGING" APR. 22, 1957
EPISODE # 93 FILMED ON TUESDAY, MARCH 5, 1957
WRITERS: LOU DERMAN, BEN STARR
GUEST CAST: SANDOR SZABO AS KARL MANHEIM, SANDRA GOULD AS FRIEDA MANHEIM, SID MELTON AS JOE COOPER, FUZZY KNIGHT AS LENNY SPERBER, DICK CROCKETT AS FINGERS, ROBERT HOY AS BOOMY, DAVE SHARPE AS ZIGGY

Hilda's niece Frieda has thrown her henpecked husband Karl, the pro wrestler, out of the house again because he won't give up his career in favor of something less dangerous. Hilda asks Lily to intervene, but she's reluctant to help the Manheims because Matt and Ruth will think she's meddling again. Frieda is confident that Karl could become a professional nightclub entertainer if only he could find a hit song. Lily and Hilda decide to help by visiting a pair of down-on-their-luck songwriters, Joe and Lenny. When they're offered $50 to compose a song for Karl, they come up with "I Called My Mother 'Father' Because I Never Had a Dad." Hilda: "What else have ya got?" Lily explains they want something romantic, so Joe and Lenny sing another creation, "Some Wonderful Day." The girls love it, and they're delighted to know that Joe and Lenny can arrange for three musicians to record Karl's rendition right in the Ruskin home. Lily insists that they do it while Matt and Ruth are out. That evening, Karl and Frieda arrive to make the recording, but their attempts are ruined several times by things like Hilda's applause, the phone ringing, and Frieda's tears. During a break, they all go out to the kitchen. When one musician, Fingers, re-enters the living room to search for a cigarette lighter, Ruth enters and sees him opening drawers. She thinks he's the neighborhood prowler and uses the jujitsu moves Karl has taught her. Soon Boomy and Ziggy enter the room, and she brings them to the floor alongside Fingers, kicking them until Lily and the rest rush in to explain their presence. The musicians are insulted and leave in a huff. Lily frets that it's all her fault, but Karl insists it's his own fault for attempting to change his career. When Frieda begins to protest, Karl sets her straight: "I was a wrestler when you married me, and a wrestler I'm gonna be! Now go sit in the car and wait for me!"

"MOUNTAIN CLIMBING" APR. 29, 1957
EPISODE # 94 FILMED ON TUESDAY, MARCH 12, 1957
WRITERS: LOU DERMAN, BEN STARR
GUEST CAST: MOREY AMSTERDAM AS HIMSELF, SANDRA SPENCE AS NANCY, EDDIE RYDER AS HARRY

Matt and Pete plan to go mountain climbing despite Ruth's protests that it's too risky. Then her concern grows into jealousy when she meets their buxom young guide, Nancy. In the meantime, Lily and Hilda prevent a runaway car on La Cienega Boulevard from striking a pedestrian by driving their automobile into the path of the runaway, whose driver turns out to be comedian Morey Amsterdam. When he drops by with an offer to repay Lily and Hilda for their bravery, Lily asks him to help Ruth. Later that evening, Morey returns and follows a scheme hatched by Lily. Upon meeting Ruth, Morey flirts shamelessly with her, declaring that she should be in the movies. He rushes to phone a producer, "Forget Lana! Forget Ava! Dump Marilyn!" Then he practices a romantic scene with Ruth, after which he instructs Matt to have her at the studio the next morning at 10 a.m. After Morey exits, Matt cancels his mountain climbing trip with Nancy, citing the unfavorable weather forecast. Ruth happily makes up with Matt.

"LILY-HILDA FIGHT" MAY 6, 1957
EPISODE # 95 FILMED ON TUESDAY, MARCH 19, 1957
DIRECTOR: NORMAN TOKAR
WRITERS: LOU DERMAN, BEN STARR
GUEST CAST: DORIS PACKER AS HELEN KINGSLEY, MARJORIE BENNETT AS EDYTHEA WALKER, RODNEY BELL AS JACK THE DRUNK TRAIN PASSENGER

Helen Kingsley, Lily's new neighbor, calls on Lily after noticing her excellent taste in clothes. When she learns that Lily has designed and created many of her own dresses, Helen, who owns a chain of dress shops, offers her a job as a designer. When Lily spends an increasing amount of time with Helen, her friendship with Hilda suffers. Hilda, fighting back tears, confides to Ruth that she intends to leave that evening to visit her daughter in Canada. In fact, she may stay there indefinitely. Knowing that Hilda doesn't get along well with her daughter's husband, Ruth now realizes how hurt Hilda is about the rift between her and Lily. Ruth races to the Oyster Shack where Lily and Helen are dining to tell her mother about Hilda's plans. In the meantime, Lily and Helen have left there and have returned to the Henshaw home where Edythea Walker is modeling Lily's latest creations for full-figure women. Edythea jokes: "I used to be a *perfect* 14. Oh, those kindergarten days!" As Lily and Helen discuss Edythea's dress, they disagree over its design. An argument is about to reach the boiling point when Ruth, Matt, and Pete rush in to hurry Lily off the train station to catch Hilda in time. They find Hilda in an upper birth, but she's unmoved by Lily's sincere pleas for forgiveness. Even Pete cannot convince her to stay. When she learns that Lily and Helen have severed their business ties, Hilda makes up with Lily. In the vignette, Hilda invites Lily to accompany her to Canada after all, especially since she's discovered that her son-in-law is in Mexico.

DECEMBER BRIDE
THE FOURTH SEASON: 1957-58

CAST:	Spring Byington as Lily Ruskin
	Dean Miller as Matt Henshaw
	Frances Rafferty as Ruth Henshaw
	Harry Morgan as Pete Porter
	Verna Felton as Hilda Crocker
CREATOR AND PRODUCER:	Parke Levy
DIRECTOR:	Frederick DeCordova
WRITERS:	Lou Derman, Arthur Julian, Bill Davenport
MUSIC COMPOSER AND CONDUCTOR:	Wilbur Hatch
THEME MUSIC COMPOSER:	Eilot Daniel
PRODUCTION MANAGERS:	Edward Hillie, James Paisley
PRODUCTION SUPERVISOR:	W. Argyle Nelson
DIRECTORS OF PHOTOGRAPHY:	Henry Cronjager, Sid Hickox, A.S.C.
CAMERA COORDINATOR:	Maury Thompson
ASSISTANT DIRECTOR:	Ted Schilz
EDITORIAL SUPERVISOR:	Dann Cahn, A.C.E.
FILM EDITOR:	Douglas Hines
RE-RECORDING EDITOR:	Robert Reeve
SOUND RECORDER:	Eldon Ruberg
SOUND:	Glen Glenn
ART DIRECTOR:	Claudio Guzman
SET DECORATOR:	Theodore Offenbecker
PROPERTY MASTER:	Sandy Grace
MAKEUP:	Otis Malcolm, S.M.A.
HAIR STYLIST:	Eve Kryger
WARDROBE:	Helen Scovil Roup

"VALLEE'S PROTÉGÉ" Oct. 7, 1957 *
EPISODE # 96 FILMED ON TUESDAY, AUGUST 6, 1957
WRITERS: LOU DERMAN, ARTHUR JULIAN
GUEST CAST: RUDY VALLEE AS HIMSELF, JOEL GREY AS JIMMY GRANT, MILTON PARSONS AS THE BUTLER, FRANK WILCOX AS JULES BRENNAN, DOLORES DEMARTIN AS HELEN THORPE, CINDY ROBBINS AS BETTY ZANE, DONNA JO BOYCE AS LITA JONES

Lily's nephew Jimmy Grant, who's won several amateur singing contests, arrives from Philadelphia to seek his fortune in Hollywood. Lily asks Matt to get his friend, the talent agent Jules Brennan, to represent Jimmy, but Matt seriously doubts Jimmy's ability to break into the competitive world of show business. Lily decides to ask Rudy Vallee, whom she and Hilda met earlier in the year, for his opinion of Jimmy's vocal talent. After Jimmy's solo, Vallee tells him that his voice has possibilities, but that the rock and roll style is too disagreeable to his own tastes. He predicts that rock music is a passing fad. Comparing it to his own musical style of the 1920s, Vallee opines, "Mine was the age of inspiration. This is the age of perspiration." He tells Jimmy that the world is waiting for another Vallee and offers to coach Jimmy in emulating him. Hilda volunteers to accompany on the piano while Jimmy sings through a megaphone "I'm Just a Vagabond Lover." (Hilda, breathlessly: "For years I thought that was the national anthem.") Vallee encourages Jimmy that the correct way to sing is not through the diaphragm, but through the nostrils. When he finally gets it right, Vallee declares, "Sound the clarion, the new Vallee is born." Several nights later, Mr. Brennan comes to the Henshaw home to hear Jimmy audition. Lily has also invited three teenage girls to serve as charter members of Jimmy's fan club. When Jimmy arrives and begins his Vallee-esque rendition of "Vagabond Lover," complete with megaphone, Brennan is aghast, and the girls, completely disgusted with the music, walk out. Jimmy dejectedly leaves the room. Brennan explains to Lily that Jimmy must switch to a swing style if he hopes to be a financial success. When Vallee arrives, Brennan tells him that no one is buying the megaphone and vagabond lover routine today. He tells Vallee that if he added rock and roll to his Las Vegas act, Brennan could get him ten thousand dollars more a week. In no time at all, Jimmy is coaching Vallee in the elements of rock and roll.

"MEAN GRANDFATHER" Oct. 14, 1957
EPISODE # 97 FILMED ON TUESDAY, AUGUST 13, 1957
WRITERS: LOU DERMAN, ARTHUR JULIAN
GUEST CAST: JOEL GREY AS JIMMY GRANT, GAIL GANLEY AS MARGIE CROFT, FRANK TWEDDELL AS MR. CROFT, RAY KELLOGG AS THE POLICEMAN, JACK DIMOND AS HAL, PAUL KENT AS LARRY, DOLORES DEMARTIN AS LINDA, CINDY ROBBINS AS SANDY

Jimmy really likes Margie Croft, but her strict grandfather interrupts their dates by enforcing a 9 p.m. curfew for Margie. Mr. Croft believes that rock and roll music has corrupted the country's youth. Lily decides to convince the old grouch that today's teenagers are respectful and polite so she invites him to meet some of Margie's friends. That evening she coaches Jimmy, Margie, and their friends on how to behave around Mr. Croft., insisting that they not use any slang expressions. Hilda enters wearing a wild outfit (sequined top and gypsy skirt) and carrying waltz records, a checkerboard, and a stereopticon. The kids all agree to "play it square." When Mr. Croft enters, he's delighted to find Hilda accompanying Jimmy's solo of "Jeannie with the Light Brown Hair." Croft is further impressed as he watches the teenagers waltz. Before leaving, he agrees that Margie may stay out that evening until 10 p.m. As soon as he's out the door, Hilda shouts, "Roll up the carpet, and have a ball!" The kids began dancing to rock and roll music, but are soon interrupted by Croft's unexpected return. When he realizes he's been deceived, he blames Margie. Lily and Hilda come to her defense. Lily asks Croft,

"What's so terrible about these children? How did you dress when you were a boy? Bell bottom trousers! Were they any better?" Hilda questions Croft, "And why do you insist that their dances are all crazy? When *you* were young, what were you dancing? I'll tell you—you were doing the Charleston!" She then shocks him by giving a lively demonstration of the Charleston, the Black Bottom, and the Shimmy. Lily asks Croft, "Did any of the things you did keep you from growing up into a fine citizen?" He thinks it over and then asks if there's room at the party for ex-fuddy duddy. Hilda runs to the turntable, "This joint is going to jump tonight!" As the kids dance, Hilda cuts in on Jimmy and Margie. She wows them all at her ability to keep up with the kids, and for one evening at least, the generation gap is closed.

"THE GOLF LESSON" OCT. 21, 1957
EPISODE #98 FILMED ON TUESDAY, AUGUST 20, 1957
WRITERS: LOU DERMAN, ARTHUR JULIAN
GUEST CAST: JOEL GREY AS JIMMY GRANT, LESTER MATTHEWS AS MR. EVANS, DAMIAN O'FLYNN AS BILL, HAL K. DAWSON AS HARRY, ROSS FORD AS ROSS, LEE MILLAR AS LEE

Jimmy is discouraged because he can't get an interview with the producer of a new musical. When Lily and Hilda learn that the man is going to be on the golf course at a certain time, they plan to make his acquaintance and introduce Jimmy. That afternoon, they attempt to play the game, using incorrect terminology and improper tactics, while stalling at the same hole until they spot a man who looks like a producer type. He and his golf partner grow increasingly frustrated as the ladies take forever to putt. Finally, Jimmy arrives with a radio. He asks Hilda to switch the radio stations often during his "audition" for the two men looking on. As the music changes, Jimmy entertains them with different dances, such as a polka and a waltz. He also performs some amazing acrobatics and impresses them with a bit of improvisation as a French chef. Unfortunately, after all of their efforts, Jimmy and the ladies are embarrassed to learn that neither of the men watching is Mr. Hampton, the producer. Hilda: "Lily, I'll flip you to see which one of us jumps in the little hole first." Pete rushes onto the scene to tell Jimmy that Mr. Hampton's office called to say he's been given an interview. In the vignette, Lily is pleased to discover that Jimmy got the part after all and is headed to New York for rehearsals.

"THE PHOTOGRAPHY SHOW" Nov. 4, 1957 *
EPISODE # 99 FILMED ON TUESDAY, JULY 30, 1957
WRITERS: LOU DERMAN, ARTHUR JULIAN
GUEST CAST: PETER LEEDS AS THE SHORE PATROL, DICK WINSLOW AND PAUL SMITH AS SAILORS, BOB DUGGAN AS THE MAN

Matt is so pleased with a candid photo he took of a sailor kissing his girlfriend that he decides to enter it in a photography contest. While he's at a football game with Pete, Lily accidentally scoops up the photo and its negative with some gift-wrapping paper Hilda left behind. Lily doesn't discover her blunder until it's too late—the photo and negative were incinerated along with the other paper. She doesn't want Matt to know that his photo was destroyed. She decides to make things right by having Pete and Ruth pose as the sailor and his girl at the exact same location in the park while Lily snaps the picture. After they leave, Hilda drops in and, as usual, spills the beans to Matt about his lost photo. He rushes off to the park. Meanwhile, just as Lily is about to release the shutter for a perfect shot, a member of the shore patrol ambles in. When he sees Pete kissing Ruth, he arrests him for misconduct, despite everyone's protests. Then Matt arrives just in time to capture another candid shot of a different sailor and his girl.

"SPORTS CAR" Nov. 11, 1957
EPISODE #100 FILMED ON TUESDAY, AUGUST 27, 1957
WRITERS: LOU DERMAN, ARTHUR JULIAN
GUEST CAST: NINA BARA AS NATASHA, RAY MONTGOMERY AS GEORGE

Matt buys a Ferralini, a new sports car, which only accommodates two riders. (Pete to Ruth: "We'll miss you, kid!") When Ruth hears that the car's maximum speed is 140 miles per hour, she doubts its safety. Her concern grows when she learns Matt's entered a race. Lily asks a gypsy fortuneteller named Natasha to read Matt's palm and "predict" that the race will end in tragedy. He shrugs it off, claiming he's not superstitious. That night, Lily and Hilda sneak into the garage to sabotage his car and thus prevent him from competing in the race. When they hear someone coming, they hide. Ruth enters and she quietly removes a part from under the hood. Pete slips in later and does the same thing. In the meantime, Matt has reconsidered Ruth's opinions about the car and has decided to sell it to his friend George. When they can't get the car to start, they're perplexed. Pete and the girls don't remember where the removed parts fit, but in the end Natasha buys the car.

"THE MICROPHONE SHOW" Nov. 18, 1957
EPISODE # 101 FILMED ON TUESDAY, SEPTEMBER 17, 1957
WRITERS: LOU DERMAN, ARTHUR JULIAN
GUEST CAST: HOWARD MCNEAR AS WILBUR SEDGELY, MARJORIE BENNETT AS
EDYTHEA WALKER, ELVIA ALLMAN AS SARAH SELKIRK, WILLIAM FORREST AS
HENRY THOMPSON, CHEERIO MEREDITH AS HORTENSE MILLER

The executive council of the Westwood Women's Cultural Club meets at Lily's house to organize the next American Women's Convention. Lily assigns duties to the various chairs, including Hilda who's in charge of renting an auditorium. After Hilda pays a deposit on Regents Hall on Cahuenga Boulevard, Matt looks over the contract and finds that it says nothing about the necessary amenities, such as microphones, amplifiers, scenery, usher service, etc. Hilda insists that those were included in a verbal agreement she had with Mr. Thompson, the auditorium's owner. Lily phones him, asking for a refund of the $100 deposit. When he flatly refuses her request, Lily invites Wilbur Sedgely of the Better Business Association to attend the club's next meeting. Sedgely is already familiar with Thompson, whom he describes as a slippery character. When he advises Lily to secretly tape record Thompson's false promises she decides to pose as the president of another club who's interested in renting the auditorium. Pete and Matt rig a hidden microphone in a lamp base in the living room while they covertly operate the tape recorder in the den. That evening, when Thompson arrives, Lily attempts to make him stand near the lamp as he promises to include all of the amenities in the rental fee. When the tape accidentally breaks, Pete sends Hilda out in a French maid's outfit to relay a coded message to Lily: "Madame! Ze goose—he is not cooking! The pressure cooker is not *spinning* around." Thompson is anxious to leave, but Hilda entertains him with a spry can-can while humming "Madamoiselle from Armentiers" until she spins and falls into his arms. Pete emerges from the den, posing as a German plumber, to inform Lily that everything is fixed. Lily gets Thompson to repeat himself regarding the contract's details, but suddenly he discovers the microphone. Before he can leave, Lily and Hilda demand not only a refund of their club's deposit, but an additional $2500 on behalf of the other clubs he has rooked by using the same tactic. Hilda instructs him, "Add an extra dollar for the can-can. I'll need it for liniment."

"MATT'S GRAY HAIR" DEC. 2, 1957
EPISODE # 102 FILMED ON TUESDAY, SEPTEMBER 24, 1957
WRITERS: LOU DERMAN, ARTHUR JULIAN
GUEST CAST: LARRY THOR AS RALPH BENNETT, FRANCES ROBINSON AS PHYLLIS
HARVEY, AMZIE STRICKLAND AS MARILYN ENRIGHT

Hilda tells Lily about Marilyn Enright whose boyfriend won't pop the question, "He won't even walk down the middle aisle of a movie." The trouble is that his friends have convinced Ralph that marriage ages a man. Lily decides she'll introduce Ralph to Matt and Ruth to convince him that his pals are wrong. Meanwhile,

Pete brings over a can of gray hair dye that his mother-in-law bought by mistake. He thinks perhaps Lily or Hilda can use it. (Lily: "Madeline Schweitzer's daughter puts a silver streak in her hair." Hilda: "Oh, you should see her head—it looks like a divided highway.") When Matt and Ruth come home from a cocktail party, Ruth's upset because a party guest told Matt he looks younger every time she sees him and that Ruth looks as if she needs more rest. Matt boasts that he can't help it that women age more quickly than men. This only infuriates Ruth more. When Matt's asleep, she sprays his temples with the hair dye. The next morning, Matt's distraught to find he's gone gray overnight. Ruth innocently suggests that he's been worrying too much. When Pete detects that Matt's hair has been sprayed, Matt plans to embarrass Ruth in front of her visiting friend Phyllis. Soon after Phyllis arrives, Lily enters with Marilyn and Ralph. They're all shocked when a white-haired Matt creeps downstairs in a cardigan, hobbling over to be introduced to the guests. He hams it up, saying that marriage had an aging effect on him. Ruth is so disgusted she snatches Matt's wig off to reveal his bald head underneath. Lily explains to Marilyn and Ralph that her children's pranks actually keep them young.

"THE OTHER WOMAN" DEC. 9, 1957
EPISODE # 103 FILMED ON TUESDAY, SEPTEMBER 10, 1957
WRITERS: LOU DERMAN, ARTHUR JULIAN
GUEST CAST: BARBARA EDEN AS MISS WILSON, HILLARY BROOKE AS DIANE BENNETT, TYLER MCVEY AS MR. INGRAHAM, JACK BOYLE AS JOE THE STAGE MANAGER, MAURICE KELLY, CASSE JAEGER, JAMES ELSEGOOD, ILA MCAVOY AS THE NATIVES

Ruth grows suspicious when Matt comes home late three nights in a row. He tells her he's been playing ping-pong with Pete, but actually he doesn't want Ruth to know they've been playing poker. Pete's out $88 and doesn't want to quit playing until he wins it back. Matt agrees to phone Pete during that evening's game at Jim's, pretending to be Gladys asking him to come home and thus allowing Pete to quit while he's ahead. That evening, Ruth is quizzical when Matt arrives bearing flowers, then distrusting when she overhears part of the telephone conversation in which Matt tells Pete he "can't make it tonight." Ruth immediately concludes that Matt is having an affair. Her fears are substantiated when she finds the NOTES on which Matt has scribbled the phone number. When Lily informs Hilda of Ruth's suspicions, Hilda boldly calls the number and reaches a maid who informs her that she's reached the residence of Diane Bennett, who's delivering a lecture that evening. Lily and Hilda are determined to end the "affair" by talking to Miss Bennett. They march down to the auditorium but are refused admission to Miss Bennett's dressing room. Miss Bennett, recently returned from Africa, has brought back the tallest of all Africans. In order to speak with her, Lily and Hilda disguise themselves as African natives and join the others onstage. Lily identifies herself as "Bonga Bonga" and Hilda introduces herself as "Toura Loura." They make spectacles of themselves by trying to keep up with the native dancers who tower above them. Meanwhile back at home, a remorseful Ruth learns the true reasons for Matt's behavior the past few days.

"THE BUTLER SHOW" DEC. 16, 1957
EPISODE # 104 FILMED ON FRIDAY, NOVEMBER 1, 1957
WRITERS: LOU DERMAN, ARTHUR JULIAN
GUEST CAST: EDWARD EVERETT HORTON AS CLAYTON

Mr. Gordon, Matt's boss, goes to Europe for six weeks, leaving his butler, Clayton, to serve the Henshaws. Soon the very fastidious Clayton becomes a little annoying, requiring Matt to dress for dinner and ordering cases of champagne, caviar, smoked sturgeon, etc. He's smitten with Lily's gentility and grace and consequently becomes overly attentive, making fresh lemonade for her, assisting in her garden, and reciting Lord Byron's "She Walks in Beauty." He invites her to join him for a ride along the beach on his day off, "Six days a week I'm a butler but on Tuesday, I'm a man!" Lily politely declines his invitation then realizes how serious Clayton's attraction is when he refuses to join the Gordons in Switzerland. She knows she must convince him to leave, but only with Hilda's help. That evening, Lily tells Clayton that her sister has recently returned from Alaska where she operated a saloon, complete with dancing girls. His apprehension turns to complete consternation when Hilda bursts through the door, wearing a huge picture hat with ostrich plumes, a sequined evening gown that's much too tight, and ratty fur piece. She spreads it on thick, flirting outrageously with Clayton ("I been up in that cold country so long—defrost me!") and using crude talk ("I better bring my grips in. Where do you want me to shack up?"). Lily tries to defend Hilda's behavior, saying she's just earthy. Clayton counters, "If she were earthier, she'd have gophers!" When Hilda downs a triple-decker sandwich and announces she's going to move in, it's the last straw for Clayton. He immediately phones the airline for a plane ticket to Switzerland.

"RUTH GOES HOME TO MOTHER" DEC. 23, 1957
EPISODE # 105 FILMED ON TUESDAY, JULY 23, 1957
WRITERS: LOU DERMAN, ARTHUR JULIAN
GUEST CAST: MARY LAWRENCE AS DOROTHY RICH, LEWIS MARTIN AS HENRY HENSHAW

Lily's been offered a job writing an article for American Travel magazine. In order to complete it without being interrupted, she decides to move into the spare room over the garage. Meanwhile, Pete's house is being fumigated so Lily offers her old bedroom to him. Matt berates Ruth for disorganizing his newspaper, not knowing that her friend Dorothy actually did it when she was visiting. Ruth gets mad and tearfully moves in with Lily over the garage. Lily's troubled that the children are not speaking to each other, so attempts to induce Ruth to move back in with Matt by inviting Hilda to share the cramped space in the garage room while her apartment is being painted. Even when Hilda brings in her parrot Wilma, Ruth still won't budge. When Matt's father phones with the news that he's flying in for a visit, Lily finds a solution. She asks Mr. Henshaw to take the garage room, sends Hilda home, puts Pete on the living room sofa (Pete: "It's like I never left home!"), and reclaims her own bedroom. Now Ruth must bunk with Matt in their bedroom. A reconciliation is accomplished when Ruth suggests that they order a double subscription for the newspaper. As they kiss and make up, they crumple the newspaper Matt holds between them, prompting Matt: "Well, if we're going to mess up the paper, this is the way to do it."

"HOT MEAL" Dec. 30, 1957
Episode # 106 Filmed on Tuesday, Oct. 15, 1957
Writers: Lou Derman, Arthur Julian
Guest Cast: Dick Elliott as Stanley Poole, Mary Jane Croft as JoAnn, Allen Jenkins as Mr. Schnellbocker the plumber, Pierre Watkin as Col. Donovan

Matt comes home after a rough day only to learn that once again Ruth did not cook dinner because she spent all day volunteering at the USO. Ruth promises to have a home-cooked meal waiting for him the next evening, but when she comes home late that afternoon she learns that Lily has been out all day and that Gladys forgot to come over and put out Ruth's frozen turkey to thaw. Ruth's frantically upset because Matt will be home soon and dinner will not be ready. Hilda suggests, "Can't you wrap it in a heating pad?" When Matt discovers that dinner will be late, he hits the ceiling, demanding that tomorrow's meal must be on the table at 6 p.m. He even dictates the menu: filet mignon, potatoes au gratin, Caesar salad, Baked Alaska, etc. The next day Ruth decides to hire a caterer so she can go with JoAnn to a party at the USO, but she's left in the lurch when the caterer's kitchen catches fire. With eighteen minutes to prepare Matt's dinner, Ruth and Lily employ Pete, Hilda, Stanley, and even the plumber to assist in the kitchen. Disastrous results occur as they scurry about. Hilda knocks the salad onto the floor. JoAnn bumps Stanley, sending egg whites all over his shirtfront. The steaks burn. Ruth cries. Then Matt phones to say he's having dinner with his boss.

"THE AIRPLANE SHOW" Jan. 6, 1958
Episode # 107 Filmed on Tuesday, October 8, 1957
Writers: Lou Derman, Arthur Julian
Guest Cast: Larry J. Blake as the man in the airport, Margie Liszt as his wife, Stephen Wootton as their son Herman, Edith Simmons as the woman with a baby, Barbara Pepper as the fat lady

While the gang watches home movies of their trip to Palm Springs, Gladys phones Pete to tell him she's expecting a baby. For the first time, he's speechless. Then he regains his composure, "I just had a horrible thought. What if the baby looks like my mother-in-law?" The next day Matt shows Pete some designs for the new nursery, which is expected to cost $2500. Pete realizes he will need more income with the baby on the way. He's been offered a promotion but has been reluctant to accept the new job because it involves a lot of travel and he's afraid to fly. Then his boss gives him an ultimatum: if he doesn't fly to San Francisco on a business trip tonight, then he will be denied the promotion. Lily decides to help Pete overcome his fear by showing him a film taken from an airplane ride so he can imagine what flying is like. Pete's so scared of flying he doesn't even want to watch the film, but Hilda and Matt force him to sit through it. Even afterwards he still refuses to fly to San Francisco. Then Gladys phones to tell him that her mother is expected for a weekend visit. This changes his mind, and soon he's at the airport awaiting his flight. He's a nervous wreck until a fellow passenger asks him to hold her baby for a minute while she searches for her ticket. Once he looks down at the adorable little child, he realizes how ridiculous his behavior is. Just before he boards, he hands Matt a large box he's been carrying. He tells him to return it to the army surplus store. When Matt looks inside, he finds a parachute.

"THE PARROT SHOW" JAN. 13, 1958
EPISODE # 108 FILMED ON WEDNESDAY, OCTOBER 2, 1957
WRITERS: LOU DERMAN, ARTHUR JULIAN, BILL DAVENPORT
GUEST CAST: WILLARD WATERMAN AS SAM WINSLOW, WILL WRIGHT AS MR. SCHUYLER, MEL BLANC AS THE VOICE OF WILMA THE PARROT

Hilda's new landlord, Mr. Schuyler, is evicting any tenants who own pets. Hilda has a parrot but doesn't want to move because she likes all her neighbors, plus she's invested a lot in decorating her apartment. She tries to hide Wilma's cage under a lampshade, but grouchy Mr. Schuyler discovers the bird after it quotes lines from TV westerns. He gives Hilda until the next morning to get rid of Wilma. Hilda takes her parrot over to Lily's to spend the night but both the bird and its owner can't sleep without the other. Lily mentions Hilda's plight to Sam Winslow, an attorney, who recalls a court case involving an animal trainer who claimed his animals weren't pets because he used them in his vocation. This gives Lily an idea. The next day, when Schuyler knocks at Hilda's door, Lily answers it wearing a clown costume. She explains her appearance by informing him that she and Hilda are going back to the circus act they performed years ago. Hilda enters dressed in a pith helmet and safari outfit. She's carrying a whip and leading a chimpanzee (dressed in hula skirt and lei). She tells Schuyler that she wants to make some changes in her apartment, such as a stronger chandelier for Irving to swing from. Schuyler is not amused, nor is he impressed when a trained seal emerges from the bedroom and does tricks for Hilda. When he threatens to evict Hilda, she insists that the animals are her business partners and that she'll take him to court. Schuyler is not convinced to reconsider until Dolly, a baby elephant, appears at Hilda's side. This is the last straw. Schuyler allows

Hilda to keep her parrot on the condition that she must get rid of the other animals. She happily agrees.

"THE ANTIQUE SHOW" JAN. 20, 1958
EPISODE # 109 FILMED ON TUESDAY, NOVEMBER 5, 1957
WRITERS: LOU DERMAN, ARTHUR JULIAN
GUEST CAST: FRANCES ROBINSON AS PHYLLIS HARVEY, FRANK JENKS AS THE SINGING TELEGRAM MAN

Ruth is expecting to receive a wristwatch as an anniversary present from Matt, but the day before their anniversary, Matt gives her a toaster. She is so angered over this impersonal gift that she decides that two can play at this game. Instead of giving him gold cuff links, she gives him a new window screen for his bathroom. An argument ensues, and when Phyllis asks her out for dinner, Ruth accepts the invitation even though it's her anniversary night. Later Matt accidentally finds the cuff links in his coat pocket when he retrieves it from the hall closet. In the meantime, Lily and Hilda plot to keep Ruth at home that evening. They ask her to pose in a pair of stocks (donated for their club's antique sale) while they snap a picture for the brochure promoting their sale. They pretend to have lost the key to the lock so they head out to the garage to search for a hack saw. Meanwhile, Matt enters with the wristwatch Ruth was expecting. While she's still captive, they kiss and make up.

"HOUSEMOTHER" JAN. 27, 1958
EPISODE # 110 FILMED ON TUESDAY, NOVEMBER 11, 1957
WRITERS: LOU DERMAN, ARTHUR JULIAN, BILL DAVENPORT
GUEST CAST: IRENE TEDROW AS DEAN FILLMORE, OLIVE STURGESS AS MARGIE, CAROL LEIGH AS MARCIA, EILENE JANSSEN AS SUE, SUE ENGLAND AS ESTHER, LUANA ANDERS AS BEE, VAL BENEDICT AS TURK, NEIL GRANT AS MOOSE

Lily is asked to take over the duties of housemother at the Sigma Sigma Phi sorority house to enable her to gather background information for her new article on college students. The girls cry on Lily's shoulder after the dean lays down the law: no more dances, dates, or fellows until the sorority sisters' grades improve. Lily promises the dean she won't allow one single male to set foot in the house. Later when test scores come in, the girls and Lily are thrilled that every sorority member has passed. Lily agrees to speak with the dean to allow the girls go to the prom that night. Meanwhile Matt and Pete go to the sorority house to deliver beanies. When the girls see the dean and Lily approaching, they hide the men in the closet. After a few close calls, they're still concealed when Dean Fillmore rescinds her order and permits the girls to attend the prom.

"THE MUSCLEMAN SHOW" FEB. 3, 1958
EPISODE # 111 FILMED ON TUESDAY, NOVEMBER 19, 1957
WRITERS: LOU DERMAN, ARTHUR JULIAN, BILL DAVENPORT
GUEST CAST: MIKE MASTERS AS DICK CONWAY, JEANNE TATUM AS RITA CONWAY, RAY KELLOGG AS THE DELIVERY MAN, JETT ROBERTS AS GEORGE, JIM STOCKTON AS STAN

Lily's new assignment is to interview Dick Conway, the winner of the Mr. Muscles contest. Consequently, she must decline Hilda's invitation to a double-feature horror movie in order to photograph and interview Dick. Hilda's response: "You mean one of those big beautiful men, the ones with the glorious physique? Oh, the heck with Frankenstein! I can do my screaming right here!" When the body-builder arrives and begins flexing his chest muscles for the camera, Hilda quips, "He can do the cha-cha standing still!" Matt's pretty impressed with Dick's talents, too. When Dick tells him that he used to have the same build as Matt prior to weightlifting, Matt decides to invest in some equipment from McClary's Gym. Ruth is skeptical and tells Matt that he's not cut out to be a muscleman. Determined to prove his masculinity, Matt attempts to lift a barbell over his head. When it gets stuck across his shoulders, Pete takes it from him but crashes onto the coffee table. The next day, Matt is so sore he can't stand up straight. His pride won't allow him to quit weightlifting, especially since Ruth has predicted he won't stick with it longer than three days. When Lily learns about the strict regimen that Dick's wife must follow to support her husband's hobby, such as squeezing 500 oranges a week, milking a goat, entertaining his bodybuilder buddies, and giving him nightly rubdowns, she thinks Ruth needs to observe Mrs. Conway's lifestyle. That evening after Lily and the Henshaws arrive at the Conways' home, Dick comes home and hands his wife a huge box of alfalfa for her to carry to the kitchen. Then he demonstrates for Matt an exercise for building the deltoids by lifting Ruth over his head. Soon his training partners arrive. One promptly does pull-ups on the door casing until it pulls loose. The other lifts Ruth some more. Then Matt tries to lift her, with disastrous results. Ruth's had enough—she refuses to be a human barbell and commands Matt to return his weightlifting equipment the next morning. He's not one bit angry. As they embrace he tells Ruth that one beautiful body at their house is enough.
NOTES: Mike Masters (1929-2003) was a stuntman for television shows like "Combat!" and "The Wild, Wild West."

"CONTOUR CHAIR" FEB. 10, 1958
EPISODE # 112 FILMED ON TUESDAY, NOVEMBER 26, 1957
WRITERS: LOU DERMAN, ARTHUR JULIAN, BILL DAVENPORT
GUEST CAST: LEE MILLAR AS BURT THE NEPHEW, RUSSELL TRENT AS THE OTHER NEPHEW, NORMAN LEAVITT AS THE PANHANDLER, MURRAY ALPER AS THE NEWSPAPER VENDOR

Matt buys what he calls a "health chair," which resembles a vibrating recliner.

Ruth deems it unsightly and asks him to get rid of it. He refuses, saying a man's home is his castle. When Phyllis phones Ruth to ask if their club can meet at the Henshaw house, Ruth gets Pete to move the chair out to the garage so she won't be embarrassed by its presence in the living room. In the meantime, Lily and Hilda have asked Madeline Schweitzer's nephews to come over and load the donated items they've been collecting for a sale sponsored by the Los Angeles Youth Foundation. The men pick up Matt's contour chair, too, thinking it's a donated item. Lily and Hilda then haul the trailer downtown, but soon they run out of gas in a run-down section of the city. When they get out of the car to phone Ruth for help, they discover they've locked the car keys and their purses inside. First Hilda hikes her skirt to hitch a lift. A bicyclist passes by and wisecracks, "Are you kidding?" Then Hilda attempts to earn the dime needed for a phone call by becoming a street performer. She rummages through the donated goods on the trailer until she wraps herself in a shawl and clutches a rose between her teeth. Lily cranks a Victrola, playing "La Cucaracha" as an accompaniment to Hilda's dance, but they get no donations. Just when they think the situation is hopeless, Pete (who's been sent by Ruth when she discovered that Matt's chair was missing) arrives to save the day. When the three finally arrive home with the heavy chair, a weary Hilda moans, "This health chair is making me sick." And even Matt finally admits that the chair's vibrating action is too erratic. When Matt tells Pete it's strong enough to throw someone out the window, Pete buys it for Gladys's mother.

"THE FRED MacMURRAY SHOW" FEB. 17, 1958
EPISODE # 113 FILMED ON TUESDAY, JANUARY 21, 1958
WRITERS: LOU DERMAN, ARTHUR JULIAN, BILL DAVENPORT
GUEST CAST: FRED MacMURRAY AS HIMSELF, KATHLEEN FREEMAN AS MARIE, JACK ALBERTSON AS TOM DESMOND, RALPH DUMKE AS MR. BRODERICK, BENNETT GREEN AND HENRY EAST AS THE DOG TRAINERS, BLAZE AS TRUE HEART THE DOG

Lily's newspaper, the *Westwood Gazette*, enters a contest with its competitor, the *Westwood Star*, to name an honorary mayor of Westwood. Readers of each will vote for their favorite candidate. When Lily asks Hilda for suggestions for the *Gazette's* candidate, she suggests actor Fred MacMurray, a Westwood resident (at 428 N. Glenview Drive). Lily loves that idea and invites Hilda to accompany her to MacMurray's house to ask him in person. Before they arrived, MacMurray's involved in rehearsing a scene for an upcoming western film. His cook Marie, wearing a two-gun holster, beats him to the draw every time they practice the scene, explaining, "I worked for Gary Cooper for eight years." MacMurray is charmed by Lily and agrees to run for the honorary position. The next day, he's dismayed to learn that his opponent will be True Heart the Wonder Dog, a German Shepherd who's the star of his own television series. Later, when MacMurray's agent informs him that the dog's ahead by 71 votes, Lily suggests that MacMurray "do some tricks" to win more votes the next day at a public gathering. He considers playing his saxophone, but Lily tells him that Pete can teach him some easy magic tricks to perform instead. However, on the following day, the crowd is more entertained by True Heart. MacMurray attempts a *piece de resistance* stunt by untying himself from a chair at the count of five. When he's unsuccessful, True Heart comes to his rescue and unties the rope, to the audience's delight. A dejected MacMurray leaves the contest before he hears the final tally: 1242 votes for True Heart and 1243 for Fred MacMurray.

NOTES: Kathleen Freeman (1919-2001), most famous as Jerry Lewis's frequent foil, makes the best use of her screen time as Marie. Her scene is the highlight of this entire episode.

"BABY REHEARSAL," FEB. 24, 1958
EPISODE # 114 FILMED ON TUESDAY, DECEMBER 3, 1957
WRITERS: LOU DERMAN, ARTHUR JULIAN, BILL DAVENPORT
GUEST CAST: EDITH SIMMONS AS THE NURSE, OLAN SOULE AS MR. KENT, WILLIAM TRACY AS MR. FERGUSON

Matt, claiming he's coming down with the sniffles, wants sympathy from not only Ruth, but from everyone. He describes his fluctuating temperature to Hilda, asking if she's ever experienced that. Hilda answers, "Once—when I got stuck between my stove and refrigerator." When Pete finds Matt moaning on the sofa, he offers no sympathy either, "What's the Camille routine?" When Matt acts hurt by Pete's callousness, Pete admits he hurt Gladys's feelings that morning, too, by asking, "If the baby looks like your mother, can we keep it in the hospital until it can have plastic surgery?" Lily and Ruth chide Pete for being so insensitive toward Gladys, and he confesses his jokes about the baby mask his fear of becoming a father. He's afraid he'll panic once it's time for the baby to be born. Lily suggests they rehearse, practicing the necessary steps to leave the house with Gladys, etc. Pete panics even in the rehearsal, so Lily then suggests he visit the fathers' waiting room at the hospital. Once there, Pete sits with two expectant fathers, Ferguson and Kent, who appear calm and collected. Pete nervously smokes and then begins asking Ferguson about his baby's doctor. When he learns the doctor is very young, Pete expresses doubts about his experience and expertise. He makes Ferguson, a nonsmoker, so nervous that he starts puffing on two cigarettes. When Pete learns that the doctor of Kent's baby is over 70 years old, he wonders about his capability also. Kent becomes so agitated with worry that he paces back and forth. Finally the fathers ask Pete about his wife and her doctor. When Pete replies that his baby's not due for six months and he's there to get over his nervousness, Kent and Ferguson are ready to oust him from the room. The nurse enters and informs the two fathers of their babies' arrivals. Ferguson excitedly passes out cigars, "My boy had a wife!" And when Kent hears he has a daughter, "Wonderful! Wait till I tell my wife!" Pete sighs to Lily, "I'm glad those two fellows aren't going to be here six months from now. They could

make a fellow awfully nervous."
NOTES: Pete's comment regarding the "Camille routine" is a reference to the classic stage and screen production, from which the heroine's lengthy death scene is often parodied.

"ARMY BUDDY" Mar. 3, 1958 *
EPISODE # 115 FILMED ON TUESDAY, DECEMBER 10, 1957
WRITERS: LOU DERMAN, ARTHUR JULIAN, BILL DAVENPORT
GUEST CAST: RICHARD ERDMAN AS MAJ. JERRY HIGGINS, LYLE TALBOT AS TOM WINTERS, ROSS FORD AS CAPT. ERNIE ROSS, JEAN HOWELL AS LIZ ROBERTS

Matt panics when he receives a letter from the Air Force saying he owes the government $250,000 for an airplane he lost when he was stationed in Italy in 1945. He explains to Ruth and Lily that he and a buddy, Jerry Higgins, used the plane to fly to Naples for a double date, but when they got back to the airfield the plane was gone. Little does Matt know that Jerry, now an Air Force major stationed at March Field in Riverside, is playing a prank on him by sending this phony letter. He's actually seeking revenge because on the night in question, Matt ditched Jerry for a date with both girls, leaving him home with their mother. Tom Winters, an attorney friend, helps Matt track down Jerry whom Matt needs as a defense witness. Meanwhile everyone thinks of ways to help Matt pay back the government. Ruth wants to get a job while Lily offers to cash in her savings bonds. And Hilda gives Matt a check, insisting she doesn't need the money, "In twenty-five years I start collecting Social Security . . . It would be a lot sooner if I weren't such a liar." Jerry phones Matt, posing as a general in Washington, but when the operator calls later informing Matt that he'll have to pay overtime for the call from March Field, Matt realizes he's been duped. Lily hatches a plot to get even with Jerry who's expected at the Henshaw house that evening. When he arrives with his *fiancée* Liz, he finds the living room bare of any furniture except two orange crates. Matt explains that they've had to sell the house and all its furnishings to pay for the missing plane. Ruth enters in overalls, explaining she cannot stay because she must report for work at the aircraft factory. Jerry offers to straighten out the whole thing with Washington, but the doorbell rings, and there stands Lily, pretending to be from The Traveler's Aid. She tells Jerry, "We've been trying to find you for months. I have a big surprise for you, Major. Your mother-in-law is here, all the way from Italy." An angry Liz turns to Jerry for an explanation, but suddenly Hilda, dressed as an Italian, bursts through the door, followed by Pete, who's costumed much like Chico Marx. They both rush to embrace and kiss Jerry on both cheeks. Jerry denies knowing them, although Lily insists he married Hilda's daughter in Italy in 1944. Jerry hotly refutes this claim, but Matt calmly states that he was the best man at the wedding. Hilda adds, "You should-a see your two beautiful bambinos, they look just-a like you," prompting Liz to give her engagement ring back to Jerry. Finally Lily and Matt set the record straight, and Jerry promises no more practical jokes.

"THE ED WYNN SHOW" MAR. 10, 1958
EPISODE # 116 FILMED ON TUESDAY, JANUARY 28, 1958
WRITERS: LOU DERMAN, ARTHUR JULIAN, BILL DAVENPORT
GUEST CAST: ED WYNN AS HIMSELF, ROBERT CARSON AS TED SIMMONS,
FRANKIE DARRO AS SONNY WILLIAMS, NORMAN LEAVITT AS LESTER, JOHN
ELDREDGE AS MR. McGUIRE, DICK BARON AND MICKEY MARTIN AS THE JOCKEYS

Matt invites Ed Wynn, a new member of his camera club, to come to the house to take some pictures. When Lily expresses her delight with Ed's comedic performances, he informs her that he wants to audition for a dramatic role: Abe Lincoln on an upcoming *Playhouse 90* production. She asks Ed to counsel her friend Sonny Williams, a horse jockey who wants to break into acting. When Ed plays host to Lily and Sonny the next evening, he learns from his agent that the *Playhouse 90* producer, Mr. McGuire, will not consider Ed for the Lincoln role because he's too short. Lily suggests that Ed audition with actors shorter than he, and she knows just the right fellows: Sonny's jockey friends. The following night, Lily plays Mary Lincoln to Ed's Abe (in a towering stovepipe hat) while the jockeys stumble over their lines. The only serious element of their audition is when Ed recites Lincoln's farewell address he made when leaving Springfield, Illinois, for Washington, D.C. It's effective enough to win him the role.

"THE BOUNCER SHOW" MAR. 17, 1958 *
EPISODE # 117 FILMED ON TUESDAY, JANUARY 7, 1958
WRITERS: LOU DERMAN, ARTHUR JULIAN, BILL DAVENPORT
GUEST CAST: SANDOR SZABO AS KARL MANHEIM, SANDRA GOULD AS
FRIEDA MANHEIM, FRANK SCANNELL AS MR. HOWARD, AND JUNE TOLLY AS
THE CIGARETTE GIRL

Lily agrees to act as a marriage counselor (again) for Hilda's niece Frieda and her husband Karl. Frieda has taken a job as a car hop so that Karl can quit his wrestling job while he builds his singing career, but Karl doesn't approve of her new line of work. Lily suggests that Karl combine his two talents by forming a quartet of singing wrestlers. After the men rehearse at Lily's, she suggests that they audition for Mr. Howard, a nightclub owner who's looking for novelty acts. However, Mr. Howard is unimpressed with their talent, but he does hire Karl as a bouncer. Meanwhile, when Matt scolds Ruth for opening his mail, she bets him that he'd open her mail out of curiosity also. When he vehemently disagrees, she sets him up by sending herself a phony letter with the cryptic message "Meet me tonight, same place, same time." Matt falls for the bait, reading Ruth's letter and assuming that she's secretly meeting a man that night. Later Ruth tells Matt that she's spending the evening with her knitting club, hoping he'll follow her to Karl's nightclub where she's agreed to meet Lily and Hilda. Then Karl phones Lily to say that Frieda got the night off to hear him sing at the club. He's afraid of what will happen when she learns he's merely a bouncer there. Lily arranges with Howard for Karl to sing one number that evening. At the club, while Ruth expectantly waits for Matt, she sets the scene by positioning a burning cigar in her table's ashtray. When he arrives and demands to know where her date is, she breaks into laughter as she explains her ruse. Then as Karl begins his solo, several hecklers get into an argument with Matt and Pete, resulting in a fistfight. Karl never misses a note as he performs his duties as a bouncer by knocking the heads of the hecklers together.

"SLEEP TEACHING" MAR. 24, 1958 *
EPISODE # 118 FILMED ON TUESDAY, JANUARY 14, 1958
WRITERS: LOU DERMAN, ARTHUR JULIAN, BILL DAVENPORT
GUEST CAST: TOM BROWNE HENRY AS MR. GORDON, HELEN KLEEB AS FLORENCE

Lily buys "Sleep Teaching" equipment so that she and Hilda can learn Spanish as they sleep. She demonstrates for Hilda how it works by putting a small speaker under Hilda's pillow. It's connected to an automatic timer that starts the recorded Spanish lesson one hour after falling asleep. (Hilda: "Lily, if you want me to hear that thing, you better put it in my refrigerator.") Ruth wants to take a trip to Europe but Matt thinks it's too expensive. When she's unsuccessful in convincing Matt to ask his boss for a raise, she uses Lily's equipment that night to play a recording of her own voice, urging Matt to ask Mr. Gordon for the raise. Matt wakes during the middle of the recording, but, realizing Ruth's ploy, he decides to play along with it and pretends to sleep as the message drones on. The next morning, Matt arranges for Pete to phone, pretending he's Mr. Gordon. During the phone conversation, Matt intends to demand a $100-a-week raise or he'll quit his job. When Ruth answers and hands the phone, he launches into his ultimatum, calls Gordon a "miserable old weasel" and hangs up. Then he is sickened to realize that, by coincidence, Mr. Gordon actually phoned him before Pete could. When Matt goes to Gordon's home to apologize, he's refused admittance by the housekeeper. Knowing that Stanley plans to exterminate the Gordon home the following week, Lily hatches a plan to gain entrance immediately. She and Hilda pose as Stanley's assistants, explaining to the housekeeper that Mr. Poole is unavailable next week. The housekeeper, Florence, warns them not to disturb Mr. Gordon, who's asleep on a chaise lounge on the patio. To prevent the gardener from noticing them, Lily and Hilda push the lounge into the living room. Hilda occupies Florence in the kitchen while Lily attempts to speak to Gordon's subconscious, whispering, "Matt Henshaw is a brilliant young architect. You need him. You're going to hire him back." When Gordon suddenly wakens amused, he asks Lily, "How can you fire a brilliant young architect with a beautiful wife to support? And, may I add, an extremely attractive mother-in-law?" Then Hilda comes tearing in, afraid that the approaching Florence will see that Gordon's lounge chair is inside the house. Not realizing he is awake, she pushes the lounge out the door, flying out of sight. A crash is heard. Then Hilda, shamefaced, enters the house, "Lily, they're building the pools too close to the houses these days."

"THE GILBERT ROLAND SHOW" Mar. 31, 1958
Episode # 119 Filmed on Tuesday, February 25, 1958
Writers: Lou Derman, Arthur Julian, Bill Davenport
Guest Cast: Gilbert Roland as Himself, Edward Colmans as Don Pablo, Marya Stevens as Lucia, Benny Baker as Pete, Mary Beth Hughes as Shirley, Thayer Roberts as Eddie, and the Guadalajara Trio

When Hilda wants to prove to a friend in Chicago that she knows some famous people, Lily suggests they go down to the Farmers' Market to see if any movie stars are hanging out there. They discover Gilbert Roland having lunch, and he graciously agrees to pose for a photo with Hilda. During a quick interview conducted by Lily for her newspaper column, Roland reveals that he's infatuated with a beautiful Spanish lady he met briefly in a hotel lobby. However, her father will not allow Roland to court her. Lily suggests that Roland serenade Lucia under her window. That evening, as a hired trio is playing quietly in the background, Roland calls up to Lucia, proposing marriage. Her father appears beside her at the window and permits his daughter to give her answer. When Roland finally hears this calm, dark beauty speak, he's taken aback by her rapid and brash tone. He later describes her to Lily and Hilda as a Spanish Donald Duck. So now Roland's in a worse predicament; he doesn't want to marry the abrasive Lucia. But Spanish custom dictates that the only way he can get out of the pending marriage is for Lucia's father to call off the engagement. Lily offers to help. The next day, when Don Pablo and Lucia arrive at the Henshaw home (for the purpose of meeting Roland's family), Ruth poses as Roland's maid whom he kisses passionately right in front of his future bride and father-in-law. Then Lily enters, pretending to be his mother whom he scornfully commands to go outside and stomp grapes with "Aunt Maria." Matt and Pete pose as Roland's browbeaten brothers, Antonio and Pedro, whom he belittles and abuses. Then "Aunt Maria" (Hilda) enters in peasant blouse and kerchief (*a' la Lucy Ricardo*), complaining of being exhausted from stomping the grapes ("With my left foot I was pressing burgundy, with my right foot, muscatel."). When Roland tells Aunt Maria that Lucia can help her stomp grapes tomorrow right after the wedding, it's the last straw for an insulted Ron Pablo. He denounces Roland as a barbarian and calls off the wedding. After he leaves, Roland kisses Lily and Hilda (on the lips) in appreciation for their help. Lily playfully informs him that they have a custom, too: any man who kisses them must marry them.

"AUNT EMILY" Apr. 7, 1958
Episode # 120 Filmed on Tuesday, February 11, 1958
Writers: Lou Derman, Arthur Julian, Bill Davenport
Guest Cast: Isabel Randolph as Emily Randolph, Byron Foulger as Henry Bixby, Rolfe Sedan as Mr. Gibbons, Gavin Gordon as Lucian Davis

When Lily learns that her old beau, Lucian Davis, is coming to town, she invites Hilda and Stanley to go on a double date, but Hilda wearily declines, citing her visiting cousin Emily as the reason. Health-conscious Emily doesn't want to go out anywhere, preferring to stay at with her iron pills and blood tonic she regularly purchases from the pharmacist. Lily advises Hilda that all Emily needs is a man in her life, "someone with zing and pep and vigor, someone that will show her it's fun to be alive." When Lily sees Pete disguised as an old man for a costume party, she asks for his help. The next day Hilda and Emily present a striking contrast when they arrive at Lily's. Emily removes her dowdy overcoat to reveal a drab cardigan (buttoned to the throat) over a plain dress. Hilda sports a spring bonnet, floral dress, six-inch heels, and a see-through plastic handbag. When Pete arrives in a gray wig and beard, he invites Emily to dance. Ruth puts on a zippy record, and Pete charms Emily as he shakes her all over the rug. Much to Lily and Hilda's delight, Emily ecstatically leaves on a date with Pete. For the next three nights, Pete and Emily paint the town, but then Emily asks him to come to Hilda's to discuss something personal. Fearing that Emily is really serious about a relationship with Pete, Lily and Hilda conspire to turn Emily's attentions to Mr. Bixby the druggist. However they don't know that Emily has been seeing Bixby on the sly. When Pete meets Emily, she refuses to date him any longer, saying he's too old for her. Then Lily enters on cue, disguised in a gray wig and eyeglasses as Pete's "girlfriend," wielding an umbrella and chasing a two-timing Pete out the door. Emily explains to Hilda and Lily that she's engaged to Bixby. Then Lucian arrives looking for Lily, but when he sees her in the old lady getup, he makes a hasty retreat, with Lily trailing after him.

"THE MICKEY ROONEY SHOW" APR. 14, 1958
EPISODE # 121 FILMED ON TUESDAY, MARCH 18, 1958
WRITERS: LOU DERMAN, ARTHUR JULIAN, BILL DAVENPORT
GUEST CAST: MICKEY ROONEY AS HIMSELF, BENNY RUBIN AS HENRY, MARY TREEN AS MRS. SCHULTZ, JAN ARVAN AS HAL, JAMES FLAVIN AS THE FIRST POLICEMAN, JOHN P. MONAGHAN AS THE SECOND POLICEMAN, MIKE SMITH AS DASH HARDWICKE, PETER VOTRIAN AS LEFTY, BART BRADLEY AS SPUD, TOM MASTERS AS MIKE, MARK "BUTCH" CAVELL AS ITCHY

Hilda encourages Lily to ask Mickey Rooney to chair her committee on juvenile issues since he's currently casting a movie about juvenile delinquents. When he admits that he's having a difficult time finding young actors, Lily wonders if he could use a boy right off the street. The next day he hosts a small party for four delinquents that Lily and Hilda have found. While Lily and Hilda prepare the refreshments, Rooney initiates a game of Blind Man's Bluff, but while he's blindfolded, the streetwise kids rob him blind, taking silver candlesticks, punch bowl, etc. That afternoon, Lily, Hilda, and Rooney go downtown to find the boys. To blend in with the other toughs, they're wearing what they consider to be the proper attire. Lily's in a ratty cardigan and dowdy dress while Hilda fills out a moth eaten sweater with horizontal stripes. With Rooney they shoot craps for hubcaps, making the right kind of noise to attract the boys they intend to help.

In a bit, the boys come along with sacks of Rooney's possessions, asking to join the game. A policeman threatens to run them all in until Rooney convinces him of his true identity. Then Rooney, instead of pressing charges against the little thieves, counsels them. He tells them he's known a lot of people who had nothing but didn't resort to stealing. He convinces them that working for a living is the best way to go. They return all of Rooney's stuff, and he takes them back to his house to finish the party.

NOTES: Mary Treen (1907-1989) shines as the pushy stage mother of Dash Hardwicke, a no-talent kid auditioning for Rooney's movie.

"LILY'S BIRTHDAY DRESS" APR. 21, 1958 *
EPISODE # 122 FILMED ON TUESDAY, DECEMBER 17, 1957
WRITERS: LOU DERMAN, ARTHUR JULIAN, BILL DAVENPORT

When Lily admires a red velvet dress for sale at Mayfair's, Ruth suggests to Matt that they buy it as a surprise birthday present for her. They hide the wrapped package in Ruth's trunk in the garage, but Lily and Hilda accidentally find it when they're searching for a belt for Lily to wear on a double date with Hilda and Stanley. Hilda tempts Lily to open the package, and she's delighted to find the dress of her dreams. Suddenly Matt and Pete surprise Lily and Hilda, and there is no time to put the dress back in the trunk. Lily throws it in the front seat of the car. When Matt questions their presence in the garage, Lily tells him that Hilda needs to borrow some paint, which Matt accidentally spills on his head as he takes it off the shelf. Matt reaches for the dress Lily intended to wear on the date, and thinking it is a rag, wipes his face with it. Crestfallen, Lily realizes that she doesn't have anything dressy enough for the date until Hilda suggests that she wear the red dress. Thinking the children will be away from home when she leaves on the date, Lily agrees that it's the only way out. Later, Ruth suggests to Matt that they give Lily her birthday present early. When they exit on the pretense of going to the movies, Lily comes downstairs wearing the new dress. When she hears the children approaching, she covers the dress with her coat. Ruth and Matt present her with the package, but Lily stalls them by saying she heard a noise upstairs. When they go up to inspect, Hilda tries to help Lily get out of the dress, but the zipper's stuck. The children come back downstairs and insist that Lily open the box. She lifts the lid only about an inch, exclaiming, "Oh, the dress from Mayfair's! Thank you, Matt. Thank you, Ruth. I'll go try it on right away." As she runs up the stairs, Ruth decides to follow her to help her get dressed. Hilda screams a warning to Lily, who immediately comes down the stairs in her new dress. The children are astonished that she changed so quickly. (Lily: "I loved the dress so much, I practically jumped into it.") She and Hilda make a hasty exit, as Matt says to Ruth, "And it takes you all night to get dressed."

"WEDDING FLOAT" Apr. 28, 1958
Episode # 123 Filmed on Tuesday, February 4, 1958
Writers: Lou Derman, Arthur Julian, Bill Davenport
Guest Cast: Elvia Allman as Sarah Selkirk, Marjorie Bennett as
Edythea Walker, Cheerio Meredith as Hortense Miller, Leon Belasco
as Prof. LaStratza, Steven Peck as Mr. Murcott

The theme for the Westwood Chamber of Commerce Parade is "The American Family," so Lily suggests that her club decorate their float with a wedding tableau. She volunteers Ruth and Matt to be the bride and groom. Edythea, Hortense, and Sarah all want to sing "O Promise Me" as the accompanying background music on the float, but Hilda cracks, "There's enough gravel in those three voices to pave a road to Mexico City!" So Lily asks Prof. LaStratza to judge their vocal talents. None of the ladies make a favorable impression upon the professor, who diplomatically suggests that they all three sing together. After looking at their wedding photos, Matt criticizes Ruth for not always looking as feminine as she did on their wedding day. She responds in an equally immature way by preparing his breakfast the next morning while wearing a black sequined evening gown and matching elbow-length gloves. An argument ensues, and Matt sorely tells Lily to get another guy to be the groom on the float. As his replacement, Hilda offers Mr. Murcott, her dance instructor, a tall handsome man with a very seductive voice. This fails to make Matt jealous until the last minute when he sees Ruth dressed in her bridal gown. Then they kiss and make up. Ruth and Lily rush Matt to change into the cutaway suit they've rented, only to learn that he rented one for himself to wear on the float.

"THE CAPISTRANO SHOW" May 5, 1958
Episode # 124 Flimed on Tuesday, February 18, 1958
Writers: Lou Derman, Arthur Julian, Bill Davenport
Guest Cast: Shirley Mitchell as Nancy Gordon, Jack Rice as the
professor, Lester Dorr as Henry Simpson, Jesslyn Fax as Margaret
Simpson, Richard Monahan as the delivery boy

Nancy Gordon, the niece of Matt's boss, arrives from Philadelphia for a weeklong visit with the Henshaws. She quickly wears out her welcome by making snide remarks about the size of their home, dictating a menu to Lily, and dispatching Ruth to the airport to retrieve her 17 bags of luggage. A camera bug, Nancy insists that the Henshaws take her sightseeing. She goads Ruth into sticking her head between the bars of Jack Benny's gates in order to get a closer picture of his house, only to end up with Ruth getting stuck. Then she directs Hilda to stand so closely to the La Brea Tar Pits that she falls in. (Hilda: "The guide said I was the youngest thing ever pulled out of the La Brea Tar Pits!") Nancy plans to extend her visit for one week in order to witness the swallows' return to Capistrano, but Lily and the rest are so sick of her, they plot to trick Nancy into thinking the swallows have arrived a week early. They choose squabs as a replacement, hoping

Nancy will be fooled, but when Pete releases the birds from their crate, they discover they've been given chickens instead. When Nancy arrives at the mission, Hilda and Lily try to convince her that the birds are actually "swallchicks," a cross between the two species. Finally Nancy packs her bags and heads home, only to write Lily later that she intends to return for a Christmas visit. Lily proposes that she and the Henshaws go to Philadelphia for the holidays and wave at Nancy as their trains pass in Chicago.

"LILY ON THE BOAT" MAY 12, 1958
EPISODE # 125 FILMED ON TUESDAY, MARCH 11, 1958
WRITERS: LOU DERMAN, ARTHUR JULIAN, BILL DAVENPORT

Lily is having a run of bad luck. In the past week, she's broken Matt's golf club, backed his car into the garage door, exposed his film, and turned the sprinkler on him. She decides to get out of his hair for a while and books a 21-day cruise to San Francisco, Seattle, Vancouver, and Anchorage. When everyone says their goodbyes in Lily's cabin, she apologizes to Hilda departing on her birthday. Hilda, fighting tears, responds, "That's all right—there'll be another one in 3 years." Later that day, Lily arrives at Hilda's door, admitting that she didn't really want to go on the cruise. She asks Hilda to let her stay there for a while and tearfully exits to the guest room. When Matt, Ruth, and Pete arrive with a cake as a surprise for Hilda's birthday, Lily comes out of hiding and apologizes for being such a pest. She tells them all to sit down while she prepares Hilda's party, pushing Matt into a chair holding the cake. When he rises with white frosting smeared all over his dark suit pants, he greets Lily with "Welcome home!"

"MATT-PETE FIGHT" MAY 19, 1958
EPISODE # 126 FILMED ON TUESDAY, MARCH 4, 1958
WRITERS: LOU DERMAN, ARTHUR JULIAN, BILL DAVENPORT
GUEST CAST: JOSEPH KEARNS AS MR. BARNABY, DICK ELLIOTT AS
STANLEY POOLE

Matt becomes insulted when Pete reminds him of a ten-dollar debt. An argument develops, and three days pass without the boys speaking to each other. When Ruth hears that Pete is planning to sell his house, she begs Matt to apologize, but he refuses. When Mr. Barnaby, a prospective buyer for Pete's house, phones Lily to interview her about the neighborhood, she invites him to visit the next day. Meanwhile she conspires with Hilda and Stanley to pose as some characters they saw in the double-feature matinee ("The Fantastic Puppet People" and "The Amazing She-Monster"). The next day, Barnaby is greeted by Lily in a long Victorian gown. Her hair is astray, and with a wild look in her eye, she repeats, "Did I tell you *they're* among us?" Barnaby is somewhat uncomfortable with her behavior, but even more so when Stanley enters wearing a miniscule derby and Bermuda shorts and carrying a shovel. He's been burying people in the sand at the beach. Barnaby is taken aback when Hilda descends the stairs looking like Morticia Addams, offering Barnaby a steaming goblet with a deep and eerie tone, "Would you care for a cordial?" When Stanley invites Barnaby to go to the beach with him, he rushes out saying he won't be buying the Porters' house. Later Lily asks Matt to help prepare dinner by peeling onions, knowing it will make him teary. Then she phones Pete to say that Matt needs his consolation because Ruth is leaving Matt. When Pete comes over, Lily's scheme is obvious, but Matt apologizes and Pete reciprocates.

DECEMBER BRIDE
THE FIFTH SEASON: 1958-59

CAST:	Spring Byington as Lily Ruskin
	Dean Miller as Matt Henshaw
	Frances Rafferty as Ruth Henshaw
	Harry Morgan as Pete Porter
	Verna Felton as Hilda Crocker
PRODUCER AND DIRECTOR:	Frederick DeCordova
CREATOR AND EXECUTIVE PRODUCER:	Parke Levy
ASSOCIATE PRODUCER:	Mary Feldman
WRITERS:	Lou Derman, Arthur Julian, Bill Davenport
MUSIC COMPOSER AND CONDUCTOR:	Wilbur Hatch
THEME MUSIC COMPOSER:	Eilot Daniel
PRODUCTION MANAGER:	James Paisley
PRODUCTION SUPERVISOR:	W. Argyle Nelson
DIRECTOR OF PHOTOGRAPHY:	Sid Hickox, A.S.C.
CAMERA COORDINATOR:	Maury Thompson
ASSISTANT DIRECTOR:	Ted Schilz
EDITORIAL SUPERVISOR:	Bill Heath
FILM EDITOR:	Douglas Hines
RE-RECORDING EDITOR:	Robert Reeve
SOUND RECORDER:	Dave Forrest
SOUND:	Glen Glenn
ART DIRECTORS:	Ralph Berger, Kenneth A. Reid
SET DECORATOR:	Theodore Offenbecker
PROPERTY MASTER:	William Black
MAKEUP:	Otis Malcolm, S.M.A.
HAIR STYLIST:	Eve Kryger
COSTUMER:	Marjorie Henderson

"THE EDGAR BERGEN SHOW" Oct. 2, 1958
Episode # 127 Filmed on Tuesday, August 19, 1958
Guest Cast: Edgar Bergen as Himself, Frances Bergen as Herself, Robert Easton as Bob Bigelow, Kathy Case as Alice, Rolfe Sedan as the man at the airport, Edith Simmons as the lady with a baby

On her return train trip from a summer vacation in Philadelphia, Lily becomes acquainted with entertainer Edgar Bergen who sits beside her. When she discovers that they've accidentally switched valises, she and Hilda go to his home to exchange them. Bergen agrees to give Lily an interview for her paper, but first he introduces them to his ventriloquist dummies Charlie McCarthy and Effie Klinker. When his shy brother-in-law Bob arrives and suddenly excuses himself to another room, Bergen follows him to find out what's wrong. Bob's downcast because his girlfriend Alice, whom he's been dating for a year, has called it quits because she's tired of waiting for a proposal. Bergen explains to Lily that Bob's too shy to pop the question. When they learn that Alice is flying back to New York to live, Bob decides to rush there to stop her. Lily suggests that Bergen accompany him to the airport in case Bob gets too nervous to speak. They coach Bob on being Bergen's new dummy; if he can't get the words out, Bergen, seated nearby and wearing a disguise, will mimic Bob's voice. Eventually, Bob manages to propose on his own, and the young couple plan an elopement.

"THE ALASKA SHOW" Oct. 9, 1958
Episode # 128 Filmed on Tuesday, August 5, 1958
Guest Cast: Pierre Watkin as Col. Kenneth Donovan, Peter Leeds as Maj. Andy Walker, Maria Tsien as Tanana, Bob Duggan as the quartermaster sergeant

Since Lily knows Matt has always hoped the Air Force would call him back for training, she asks her friend Col. Donovan to pull some strings. The colonel asks Maj. Andy Walker to arrange Matt's two weeks' active duty, but the major switches assignments. Instead of sending Matt to Palm Springs, Walker gives him the duty intended for himself: Glacier Island, Alaska. When Matt protests, the repugnant major promises Matt that he'll love the "balmy tropical climate" in Alaska. Lily hatches a plan to persuade Walker to switch the duties back so that Matt can avoid the frozen north. That evening, after Walker arrives at the Henshaw home, Pete, posing as Capt. Nielsen, drops in to give Matt a briefing on Glacier Island. He spouts a lot of nonsense about how the island is a "tropical Shangri-La of the Arctic, sheltered by a mountain range and warmed by a Japanese current." He claims the women, who outnumber the men fifty-to-one, are descendants of Tahitians. In fact, he says, he married one such young native, Tanana, whom he invites inside, along with her mother, Oona (Hilda in disguise). When the beautiful Tanana greets Walker with a kiss on the lips, he quickly offers to let Matt go to Palm Springs. Lily's plan worked like a charm; the major packs his bags for the flight to Alaska.

"FENWICK ARMS" OCT. 16, 1958
EPISODE # 129 FILMED ON TUESDAY, AUGUST 26, 1958
GUEST CAST: ELVIA ALLMAN AS SARAH SELKIRK, MARJORIE BENNETT AS
EDYTHEA WALKER, CHEERIO MEREDITH AS HORTENSE MILLER, LILLIAN
BRONSON AS MARY PERKINS, RALPH MOODY AS MR. GATES, ROSS ELLIOTT AS
CHARLIE HAMILTON, GEORGE R. SANDERS AS MR. SCOTT, JEAN CARSON AS
MRS. HAMILTON, LINDA DANSON AS MRS. SCOTT

Lily's friend, the meek and mild Mary Perkins, is afraid she'll lose her job as
manager of an apartment house, the Fenwick Arms, if she can't keep the apartments
rented. When next-door neighbors the Hamiltons and Scotts feud constantly,
Lily makes attempts at a reconciliation so the two couples won't move out. She
employs Matt, Ruth, and the gang to help. They stage an annual reunion for
former residents of the Fenwick Arms to impress the Hamiltons and Scotts that
it's a great place to live. Matt and Ruth pretend that they fell in love as tenants at
the apartment complex while Pete is proud that he was a member of the Fenwick
Arms baseball team. As they sing the "alma mater," Hilda and the girls in her club
bustle in, wearing their Fenwick Arms cheerleading uniforms. Mr. Gates, the
overbearing owner of the complex interrupts their little pep rally, demanding an
explanation. When he tries to fire Mary, the Scotts and Hamiltons patch up their
differences and agree to continue to lease their respective apartments.

"BRIDE'S FATHER-IN-LAW" OCT. 23, 1958
EPISODE # 130 FILMED ON TUESDAY, JULY 29, 1958
GUEST CAST: ROSCOE KARNS AS DAD HODGES, RUTA LEE AS CAROL HODGES,
ROSS FORD AS TOM HODGES

When Ruth decides to go to Balboa to help friends Phyllis and Fred patch up
a quarrel, Matt forbids her to meddle in their affairs, adding tactlessly that in her
absence, Lily will have to "do your job," cooking and cleaning. To his chagrin,
Ruth goes anyway. Meanwhile, Carol, a newlywed across the street, is having her
own problems. Her widowed father-in-law has taken over all of the household
chores, including cooking, washing, ironing, etc. Lily has a solution that will kill
two birds with one stone. She calls Ruth at Balboa and tells her not to worry because
"that cute little blonde in the shorts" is running the Henshaw house now. Ruth
arrives home almost immediately to find Matt eating Carol's elegant dinner. She
tries to resume her wifely duties, but to no avail. Carol's husband Tom comes
over and finds Carol sewing a button on Matt's shirt (while he's still in it). When
Tom questions Carol, she tells him that his father does all those things for him
so she decided to help Matt out while Ruth was away. Lily offers Tom a taste of
Carol's pot roast, and he loves it. Then his dad comes in to tell them to come home
to Tom's favorite: leg of lamb. But Tom says he's going to eat Carol's dinner instead.
A reconciled Matt and Ruth join them. Lily eases Dad's hurt feelings by reminding
him that he can never replace Tom's mother, but he'll always be a father to him.
Then they sit down to eat Dad's leg of lamb.

"THE CHIMP SHOW" OCT. 30, 1958
EPISODE # 131 FILMED ON TUESDAY, AUGUST 12, 1958
GUEST CAST: RETA SHAW AS ELEANOR BASCOMB, WALLY BROWN AS HENRY BASCOMB, SID MELTON AS THE DELIVERYMAN

Hilda tells Lily that her friend Henry Bascomb got married, but his new wife doesn't like living with Suzie, his pet chimp. The domineering Eleanor resents having to feed her and take her for walks. The next day, Lily and Hilda decide to visit Henry and offer their support. When they arrive, they learn that Eleanor gave Henry an ultimatum before she left to visit her mother: get rid of Suzie by 6 p.m. Henry sadly concludes that he will have to sell Suzie to a zoo. When Suzie comes in on a scooter and then affectionately climbs in Hilda's lap, Hilda volunteers to keep her for a few days. But without Henry, Suzie refuses to eat. Lily has an idea. She calls Henry and tells him to bring Eleanor to Suzie's veterinarian's office. When the Bascombs arrive, Matt, posing as an army colonel, informs them that Suzie's been chosen to be sent to the moon. Pete, looking very professional as "Dr. Porter," begins to examine Suzie while Eleanor hesitantly asks about the mission, "Is Suzie going to come back?" Matt asks Henry to sign the permission forms to use Suzie in the moon, but Eleanor obviously has second thoughts. When Dr. Porter brings Suzie out wearing an astronaut suit, Suzie jumps into Eleanor's arms, and that's all it takes. Eleanor breaks down and refuses to allow her to participate in the moon flight. To everyone's surprise, she begins using baby talk with Suzie, and referring to herself as "Mama," as she carries her out of the vet's office. Lily and Henry exchange victorious glances at each other.

"HILDA'S ENGAGEMENT" NOV. 6, 1958
EPISODE # 132 FILMED ON TUESDAY, SEPTEMBER 9, 1958
GUEST CAST: DICK ELLIOTT AS STANLEY POOLE, MARJORIE BENNETT AS EDYTHEA WALKER, ELVIA ALLMAN AS SARAH SELKIRK, CHEERIO MEREDITH AS HORTENSE MILLER, FRITZ FELD AS MR. BAGBY THE LANDLORD

When Hilda hears that fellow club member Edythea Walker is engaged to be married, she's suddenly consumed with envy. Lily tries to cheer up by suggesting that the news may give Hilda's boyfriend, Stanley, the motivation to finally propose. When Edythea smugly shows off her engagement ring and offers to give Hilda tips on how to land Stanley, Hilda impulsively blurts, "I don't need any tips. We're already engaged." Knowing that Edythea will spread the word to everyone in town, Hilda's worried that Stanley will find out about her blunder when he returns from his exterminators' convention. After Hortense Miller plans a double engagement party for Edythea, Hilda, and their boyfriends, Hilda is loath to admit to her friends that she is not engaged. Lily insists there must be a graceful way out. She instructs Hilda to go home and take a nap while she works on Stanley. Inviting him over on the pretense of spraying for bugs, Lily casually mentions that Hilda went to a dance the night before with a fellow named Maurice. When he says that he thought that he and Hilda had an understanding,

Ruth interjects, "It don't mean a thing if you ain't got that ring." Stanley considers the matter for a minute, then exits suddenly, telling Lily that he will head to Hilda's as soon as he buys an engagement ring. When Lily phones Hilda to alert her, she discovers that Hilda's taken an extra sleeping tablet. She rushes over to make sure Hilda is awake by the time Stanley arrives. When her landlord calls to collect the rent, Hilda is so groggy she thinks he's Stanley and gives him a big kiss. As he exits, wiping his face with his handkerchief, Stanley enters, "Poopsie, you can forget him. I'm here to propose to you." He holds Hilda in a long embrace as he pops the question. With her head resting over Stanley's shoulder, Hilda quickly falls asleep until Lily passes smelling salts under her nose. She immediately wakes and accepts the proposal. Stanley is ebullient, "I feel like celebrating. Why don't we arrange an engagement party?" Lily agrees, "That's a wonderful idea, Stanley, but we'd better hurry. We're due there in about half an hour."

"THE ZSA ZSA GABOR SHOW" Nov. 13, 1958
EPISODE # 133 FILMED ON TUESDAY, SEPTEMBER 16, 1958
GUEST CAST: ZSA ZSA GABOR AS HERSELF, LYLE TALBOT AS BILL MONAHAN, EDITH SIMMONS AS THE MAID

Ruth dreads to tell Matt that someone backed into their car when she was downtown. He's furious until the other driver shows up at the front door: film star Zsa Zsa Gabor. He welcomes her into the living room, fawning over her, as does Pete when he drops in. She so charms the men that Matt claims the accident was Ruth's fault, and Pete, as Matt's insurance agent, tears up the claim form. After she leaves, Lily learns that Senator Crandall can't speak at the campaign dinner for accident prevention. She wonders if Zsa Zsa would consider being the guest speaker, so she and Hilda go to the movie set to ask her. They're thrilled when Zsa Zsa agrees, but on the night of the dinner, Zsa Zsa is a no-show. Hilda volunteers to go on stage, "I'll do a couple of cartwheels if someone will help me push my cart." Finally, Zsa Zsa arrives, still in her dance hall costume because she had no time to change. She's wearing a formal length coat over the skimpy outfit, but Hilda steps on its hem as Zsa Zsa climbs the steps to the stage. Now she must speak to the audience wearing her movie costume. The men in the audience are so taken with her voluptuous figure that they carelessly cause all kinds of accidents. The waiters crash into each other, spilling food and dishes. The cameraman falls from his perch. (Hilda: "She's shootin' em outa the trees now!") And through it all, Miss Gabor continues to speak on the importance of accident prevention.

"HORSE PHOBIA" Nov. 20, 1958
EPISODE # 134 FILMED ON TUESDAY, SEPTEMBER 30, 1958
GUEST CAST: GLENN TURNBULL AS LARRY GILBERT, NORMAN LEAVITT AS MR. FOSTER, ROBERT CARSON AS PAUL REYNOLDS

Pete is eager to sell a big insurance policy to Paul Reynolds, who owns the biggest horse ranch in the valley. Since Pete knows nothing about horses, Lily offers to help him learn some horse facts so he will have something in common with Mr. Reynolds. Later Pete reports to Lily that he did his best to clinch the deal by discussing horses with Mr. Reynolds, but he failed to get his signature on a contract. Reynolds invites Pete to the ranch to ride an overnight trail, but Pete's deathly fear of horses prevents him from accepting. Lily arranges a riding lesson for Pete, but he chickens out and doesn't even climb up on the animal. Then she recalls a Shetland pony that a neighbor rented for her son's birthday party. When Mr. Foster arrives with Dynamite, Lily hoists Pete into the saddle while Hilda holds the reins. At first Lily and Hilda walk Dynamite slowly around the back yard. When they let Pete fly solo, the pony bolts and runs amok with Pete holding on for dear life. Mr. Reynolds arrives just in time to see Lily and Hilda chasing Dynamite (and Pete) across the yard. In the vignette, Lily tells phone-mate Madeline that she and Hilda will go along with Pete on Mr. Reynolds's trail—to hold the pony.

"TOUGH MOTHER-IN-LAW" NOV. 27, 1958
EPISODE # 135 FILMED ON TUESDAY, OCTOBER 7, 1958
GUEST CAST: LESTER MATTHEWS AS SIDNEY HARLOW

When Pete's mother-in-law Hazel starts dating Sidney Harlow, an Australian sheep rancher who's visiting Los Angeles, Pete has high hopes that Harlow will propose. ("I've finally achieved the dream of every son-in-law. We'll be separated by six thousand miles of shark-infested waters.") Meanwhile Sarah Selkirk phones to invite Lily to lunch the next day. Sarah wants her to meet her visiting cousin, a nice man with a sheep ranch in Australia. The next day when Harlow arrives at the Porters' house, Pete desperately does a hard sell on his mother-in-law, but Harlow regretfully informs him that he must break his date with Hazel to attend his cousin's luncheon. Pete bids him farewell, "Please drive carefully. The life you save may be mine." Later that afternoon, Pete is crestfallen to learn that Harlow is taking Lily out to dinner that evening. Harlow continues to date both ladies over the next few days, but Pete moans, "Of all the people in town, he would have to meet an attractive woman like Lily. The first day he came here, I should have locked him in the guest room and broken both his legs." When a rumor circulates that Lily is engaged to marry Harlow, Pete congratulates her. She sets the record straight by saying she's not at all interested in marrying him. (Matt: "If you want to get rid of a man, all you have to do is say no." Hilda: "I used to get rid of men by saying yes.") When Lily recalls that Harlow's twenty-year-old son is the apple of his eye, she realizes that Harlow wouldn't want to marry a woman who wouldn't make a good mother for his son. When Harlow calls on Lily that evening, he finds a much different woman than the one he's been persistently wooing. As she and Harlow exchange pleasantries, Lily rings a little bell for Matt to bring coffee. When he attempts to converse with Harlow about Australia, Lily cuts him off by ringing the little bell again. She admits to Harlow that if she didn't rule Matt with an iron hand, he wouldn't have a penny to his name. She beckons him again with the bell, "Matt, didn't you get paid today?" He produces his pay envelope, and Lily expertly flips through the bills for a quick count. Hilda arrives at the door, dressed in a woolen shawl and wrinkled dress, posing as Matt's mother, "Mrs. Ruskin, I just wanted to give Matt his cake. Today is his birthday." Lily replies brusquely, "Why don't you leave the cake and go? You know how I feel about two mothers-in-law under the same roof." Harlow watches the scene with growing amazement. Hilda: "May I come again next year?" Lily: "Yes, but please call first." Just then, Ruth, who's been in Palm Springs for a few days and is unaware of the situation at home, comes in. Before she can ruin the scheme, Lily orders her to her room. When she protests, Lily commands Matt to take Ruth upstairs. After she goes kicking and screaming, Lily calmly asks Harlow to tell her more about his son. Instead, he bids a hasty farewell. Suddenly Pete enters: "He just went into my house. Mrs. Ruskin, you are a doll!" Then Hilda enters again, "Lily, now can I watch him blow out the candles?" Ruth shakes her head in bewilderment as the rest break into laughter. In the vignette, Lily tells her phone-mate Edythea that Pete is trying to break up his mother-in-law's romance with Harlow, who wants to sell his ranch, marry Hazel, and move in with Pete and Gladys.

"POWER SAW" DEC. 4, 1958
EPISODE # 136 FILMED ON TUESDAY, OCT. 21, 1958

When Lily gives Matt a power saw for his birthday, he ends up spending every waking minute in the garage with his new toy. Ruth grows frustrated that Matt is ignoring her, so Lily suggests she find a real interest. Ruth chooses skin diving, hoping that her absence from home will provoke Matt into spending less time with his saw. (When Hilda sees Ruth in her wetsuit, she's startled, "I had frog's legs last night, and I thought he'd sent a friend to get me!") But Ruth's plan doesn't work; Matt continues to spend all his spare time crafting objects with the saw. Ruth and Lily are weary of the unending drone of the saw, so they plot with Hilda to overload the electrical circuit while Matt's using it. They operate every lamp, fan, vacuum, stereo, and kitchen appliance at the same time. When the power is kicked off, they scramble to disconnect everything before Matt enters from the garage. He can't figure out what happened, and when he resumes operating the saw, the ladies do their dirty work once more. Pete sees what's happening and reports it to Matt, who enters the kitchen, feigning amnesia. He says the only thing he remembers is that a board hit him in the head when the power went off. Ruth smells a rat, and when she threatens to knock him back into reality with another blow to the head, he snaps out of it. Later Lily tells Hilda that Ruth's taken up carpentry—she nailed the garage door shut because Matt refuses to give up his power saw.

NOTES: Only the five principals appear in this episode.

"THE POST OFFICE SHOW" DEC. 11, 1958 *
EPISODE # 137 FILMED ON TUESDAY, OCTOBER 28, 1958
GUEST CAST: DAMIAN O'FLYNN AS PAUL MARTIN, ROLFE SEDAN AS THE FIRST POSTMAN, FRED SHERMAN AS THE SECOND POSTMAN, STANLEY ADAMS AS MR. CLAYTON THE SUPERVISOR, LEE MILLAR AS CLERK JENSEN, ADDISON RICHARDS AS ELIOT GORDON

Lily writes a column about procrastination called "Do It Now," which causes problems when her friends and family take the advice too quickly to heart. Paul Martin, a friend of Matt's, offers to set him up in his own business if he will resign from Gordon and Company. Matt doesn't seriously consider it until he learns he's not getting a Christmas bonus check from Mr. Gordon. In a fit of anger, he writes a letter of resignation and has Lily mail it to Gordon's residence while she's running errands. In the meantime, Mr. Martin drops in to thank Lily for her column. After consideration of his many years of hard work, he's decided to retire to South America. This leaves a despondent Matt in the lurch. When Lily hears the news, she feels responsible so she determines that she must get that letter back. Early the next morning, she, Ruth, and Hilda wait at the drop box where Lily deposited the letter. When the mailman arrives to empty the box, Lily asks him for the letter, but, by law, he is not allowed to give it back to her. He sends her to the Westwood post office to file a claim to get the letter back, but since they arrive before business hours, Lily and Hilda use the employees' entrance. Inside it's a bedlam of activity, and no one sees them enter. Soon a postman enters, and they recognize him as the one who picked up the mail from the drop box. As Lily and Hilda approach the table where he's unloaded his bag, they are finally spotted by the supervisor, who mistakes them for temporary workers sent to help with the Christmas overflow. He instructs them to sort letters, but they make such a mess of things that he redirects them to close and lock the bags of outgoing mail. Hilda's charm bracelet gets locked onto one bag, and when a clerk comes by to collect the bags, he drags Hilda along with them. She bumps into a pile of carefully stacked packages, knocking them over. Lily tries to help her up and reassemble the packages, as the supervisor glares down at them. Later, Lily explains to Matt that she and Hilda did not find his letter. ("After all the confusion we created in the post office, a lot of Christmas mail won't be delivered until Easter.") Then Mr. Gordon drops in to explain why Matt didn't get a bonus check; he's decided to make him a junior partner in the business instead. Matt tries to find the words to tell Mr. Gordon about his resignation letter when Hilda enters with the morning mail. Lily discovers that the desperately sought letter has been returned for insufficient postage; she affixed a three-cent stamp instead of a four-cent. Matt happily breathes a sigh of relief as Lily tears up the letter.

"CAR FOR CHRISTMAS" DEC. 18, 1958 *
EPISODE # 138 FILMED ON TUESDAY, NOVEMBER 11, 1958
GUEST CAST: ELVIA ALLMAN AS SARAH SELKIRK, CHEERIO MEREDITH AS
HORTENSE MILLER, MARJORIE BENNETT AS EDYTHEA WALKER, JAMES FLAVIN
AS THE COP, SANDRA WRIGHT AS DOROTHY

Ruth wants a yellow convertible for Christmas, but Matt is unwilling to spend the money. Ruth shops the want ads for a used car and surprises everyone when she drives home in a twenty-seven-year-old jalopy she bought for $25. It's her way of shaming Matt into buying her the car she wants, but he doesn't immediately fall for it and encourages Ruth to keep on driving the wreck. Finally, after Ruth's fixed five flat tires, Matt commands her to get rid of the embarrassing car, which she conspicuously parks on the curb in front of the house. When he leaves to play golf, he tells Ruth to make sure the car is gone when he gets back. When she stubbornly refuses, Lily determines that she and Hilda must do something about the car. (Hilda: "Why don't we stick a tail on it and push it into the La Brea Tar Pits?") Lily decides there's no alternative except to make it look like the junker was stolen. Later when Ruth discovers it's missing, she suspects Matt is the culprit so she phones the police. Meanwhile, the car has broken down on the road with Hilda and Lily. A policeman on a motorcycle pulls up and begins emptying items from the small trunk attached to his bike. He says, "I believe you dropped a few things, ladies," as he hands them a tail light, muffler, license plate, hubcap, etc. He's about to write them a ticket for littering when a bulletin comes over his police radio, describing their car as a stolen vehicle. (Hilda: "Go easy on us, officer. It's our first job.") Lily tries to explain, but the officer takes them into custody. By this time, Matt thinks Ruth got rid of the old car and has offered to buy Ruth the yellow convertible, leaving her confused as to who stole the jalopy. Then the policeman arrives with Lily and Hilda in tow. Ruth drops the charges, but she's afraid that if Matt sees the old car outside now, he'll change his mind about the new car. When Lily's club members drop in to rehearse Christmas carols, Lily herds them outside to push the car away. Meanwhile, Ruth tries to stall Matt from leaving to go to the dealership to buy her new convertible. When they go outside, Lily, Hilda, and the club members conceal the junker from view by standing in front of it. They sing "Deck the Halls" as Ruth whisks Matt past them. In the vignette, Lily tells Ruth she sold the old car to Ruth's friend Dorothy, who wants a new car for Christmas, too.

"CHILD OF NATURE" DEC. 25, 1958
EPISODE # 139 FILMED ON TUESDAY, OCTOBER 14, 1958
GUEST CAST: TOM BROWN AS RALPH TURNER, FRANK WILCOX AS DR. CRAIG,
ROSS FORD AS HARRY GIBSON, FREDERICK DECORDOVA AS MR. TAYLOR

Lily makes the acquaintance of Mr. Taylor, a producer of television commercials, who gives her free tickets to a movie preview. When Lily offers them to the children, Ruth declines, insisting that she and Matt are going to the ballet that evening. When Matt and Pete learn the movie is *Child of Nature*, the latest film featuring French film star Suzette Garneau ("The Bikini Bombshell"), they grab the tickets, leaving Ruth and Gladys to go to the ballet without them. The next morning, Matt raves about the film, describing it as a dramatic story of a runaway orphan who must face the cruel realities of life. Ruth denounces it as a peep show when Matt shows off a life-size cutout of Suzette he was given by the theater manager. In it, Garneau is coyly depicted as a curvaceous, barefoot blonde in a short cotton dress. Matt plans to use the cutout in some gag shots when his camera club meets that evening. Ruth, seething with jealousy, draws a moustache on Garneau. ("I wanted you to see how the 'Child of Nature' looks when she grows up.") When Ruth begins to doubt her own attractiveness, Lily decides that her wholesome, all-American look could be used in one of Mr. Taylor's commercials, thereby boosting her self-esteem. However, that evening, Ruth has a different plan in mind. Before Matt's staid camera club members arrive, she comes downstairs costumed as Suzette Garneau, wearing a sexy, provocative smile on her face. She affects a French accent and a childish tone as she plays with Matt's hair, untucks his shirt, and runs away with his exposure meter. When he trips and lands on his knees, Ruth impishly sits on his back and holds his neck like a horse. Just then Pete and the camera club members enter, but Ruth continues with her act as the uninhibited "child," throwing herself stomach-down on the sofa, chin resting on the arm of the sofa, and kicking her legs up behind her. All the men are instantly charmed, and Matt has a difficult time getting their attention away from Ruth and to a bowl a fruit he's chosen as their photographic subject. Instead they want to take pictures of Ruth so a very nervous Matt tries to hide as much of her legs as possible. Just as Ruth is laughing childishly and affecting a cute pose on top of the desk, Lily arrives with Mr. Taylor, who is shocked to learn that this is the wholesome daughter Lily recommended for his commercials. When he leaves abruptly, Ruth, still in her French accent, asks Lily, "Is something wrong, Ma-ma?" Lily shrugs, "I'm afraid Ma-ma made la goof." By the following evening, all is well, and the gang is preparing to go to the ballet. When Lily realizes that she forgot to pick up the tickets, she turns to the rest, "I hope this is a good night for television." Ruth and Hilda look at her balefully while Matt and Pete kiss Lily appreciatively.

"THE BEATNIK SHOW" JAN. 1, 1959
EPISODE # 140 FILMED ON TUESDAY, NOVEMBER 18, 1958
GUEST CAST: ELVIA ALLMAN AS SARAH SELKIRK, ROSEMARY ELLIOTT AS CONSUELO, KIP KING AS HAROLD, ANDRE PHILLIPPE AS ANDRE, DON R. RIZZUTI AS IGOR

Hilda's concerned when her nephew Harold decides to drop out of college. He's been influenced by the beatniks who hang out at the Snake Pit, an underground coffeehouse. When Matt and Pete offer to visit the Pit to talk Harold out of spending so much time there, Lily and Hilda decide to go along. Harold tries to assure them that he knows what he's doing. He doesn't want to be "one of the herd," but instead he wants to discover himself as an individual. When it's time for the beatniks to share their latest creations, a heavily made-up girl named Consuelo shares her abstract expressionistic painting of her mother, done in oil, watercolor, and pancake batter. Another beatnik who's written a poem ("Sweet Taste of Defeat") on his shirt is accompanied by a bongo player, Igor. Matt reminisces about a poem he wrote in college. After he's encouraged to share it, the beatniks go crazy for it. The next day when both Hilda and Sarah wear identical new hats, both guaranteed to be "original" creations by milliner Mr. Schultz, they are both completely outdone that neither is wearing a unique *chapeau*. Sarah complains, "It's no fun to be different unless you *are* different," prompting Lily to compare this to Harold and the beatnik situation. She tells Hilda she has a solution. That night, Lily and Hilda go back to the Snake Pit, but this time they're dressed as beatniks. Lily's almost unrecognizable in thick mascara and eye shadow. Like Lily, Hilda sports a ponytail, and her ample figure fills out a pair of Capri pants. Harold can hardly believe his eyes. Hilda: "Did you ever see a generation more beat?" Then Lily shares her painting ("Despair in a Delicatessen") which awes Consuelo, especially when she learns Lily used chopped liver, sour cream, mayonnaise, and mozzarella cheese as her media. She announces that she and Hilda are dedicated to spreading the movement, starting with their club, the Westwood Women's Cultural Club-niks. Hilda adds, "Next we're going to form the PTA-niks, the DAR-niks, and the YWCA-niks. As Hilda beats the bongo drum, Lily recites her latest poem, "Bless-ed Are the Depress-ed." It's so miserably meaningless that Harold decides to abandon the beat generation. As he exits, he tells the beats that he's going back to the UCLA-niks. Lily: "Hilda, we've done it! Now we can go home." Hilda: "What are you, a square? I dig this beat the most, *man!*" She beats the bongo as the beatniks smile their approval.

NOTES: Andre Phillippe (1928-2007), born in New York as Everett Cooper, was a personal friend of writer Lou Derman and had previously made a name for himself as a "French" chanteur in Paris.

"NURSE SHOW" JAN. 8, 1959 *
EPISODE # 141 FILMED ON TUESDAY, NOVEMBER 25, 1958
GUEST CAST: ISABEL RANDOLPH AS KATHLEEN TWILLY, RICHARD ERDMAN AS ROY MILLER

With Pete and Gladys's baby due any time, Lily helps them find a nurse when theirs suddenly elopes. She gets Pete an interview with sixty-year-old Miss Twilly, but warns, "She's a little on the straight-laced side and very fussy. She told me she only works for conservative, quiet couples." Pete reacts, "Well, you can't find a quieter couple than Gladys and me . . . most of the time we barely speak to each other." Then he begins a new magic trick, involving breaking eggs into a lady's purse. When he's interrupted, he puts the purse down on the desk near the door and goes home to dress for the interview. Meanwhile, Lily arranges a elaborate tray of cookies, coffee, etc., to impress Miss Twilly. ("If I could, I'd have put gloves on all the ladyfingers.") When the conservative Miss Twilly arrives, she puts her handbag near the one Pete left behind. Soon he comes in, wearing a double-breasted suit, gloves, Homburg, and carrying a rolled umbrella. He assures Miss Twilly that his household is very quiet and, in fact, dull. Miss Twilly seems pleased and promises to confirm things later with a phone call. After she leaves, Pete takes a purse off the desk and resumes his trick. Then Miss Twilly returns with Pete's purse she picked up accidentally. When she recognizes her own bag in Pete's hand, she takes it, saying she meant to write down his phone number. As she reaches into her bad, she's indignant to find raw eggs in it. She leaves in a huff. Pete then decides he'll become the nurse for his baby. Since Matt has a friend who's a new father, he invites Roy Miller over to give Pete some tips on caring for a baby. But Lily soon ushers him out when his tips make Pete less secure about being a nurse. Lily thinks he can win Miss Twilly back if she thinks his baby will be put in the hands of a "stupid bumbling woman." That evening, Miss Twilly arrives to pick up a new purse Pete bought to replace the one he ruined. When Hilda appears at the door in a World War I nurse's uniform, she's introduced as Miss O'Toole, the baby's new nurse who agreed to come out of retirement to take the job. Miss Twilly regards her with suspicion and distaste, especially when Hilda drinks "cough syrup" from her thermos, wheezes, pounds her chest, and shouts, "Kill the Kaiser!" Lily and Miss Twilly observe as Miss O'Toole uses a rubber doll to teach Pete about infant care. When she tosses the doll to Pete, he misses, and it drops to the floor. Hilda warns, "Butterfingers . . . you're going to have to do better than that." When Miss Twilly questions her practices, Hilda snorts, "Butt out . . . this is my case." Then she absentmindedly puts the doll in the refrigerator while she's teaching Pete how to prepare the formula. The last straw comes when she roughly bathes the doll in the kitchen sink using the spray attachment. Miss Twilly shuts off the water and informs Hilda that she's off the case. Miss Twilly assures a very happy Pete that she will be available for duty as soon as his baby arrives.

"PETE HAS A BABY" JAN. 15, 1959
EPISODE # 142 FILMED ON TUESDAY, DECEMBER 2, 1958
GUEST CAST: LOUISE GLENN AS ANN NICHOLS, TERRY BECKER AS LT. JOE CARTER, BARNEY PHILLIPS AS CHAPLAIN RANDOLPH, SID MELTON AS MR. JACKSON, HELEN JAY AS THE NURSE, STAFFORD REPP AS THE COP

Lily asks Pete to do a magic act for her club's new show, and Hilda asks her friend Ann Nichols to design the advertising poster for it. When Hilda learns that Ann's boyfriend, a Marine named Joe Carter, has dumped her, she invites Ann over to Lily's to console her. Pete arrives, and asks Ann to help him practice a new magic trick, but he and she wind up getting locked together in handcuffs. Then Ann's boyfriend Joe arrives with his chaplain in tow. Joe's changed his mind; he wants to marry Ann before he ships out to Japan later in the day. As Pete tries to explain about the handcuffs, he gets a call from Phyllis who excitedly informs him that Gladys went into labor during their luncheon date and that she's driving her to the hospital now. He explains that he can't miss the birth of his baby, so he suggests that Joe and the rest join Ann and him at the hospital where the young couple can be married as they wait for someone to unlock the handcuffs. A little while later, everyone's assembled in the delivery waiting room, except Pete and Ann. Since Joe's plane leaves in ninety minutes, he's anxious that Ann won't arrive in time. No one realizes that Pete and Ann had a flat tire on the way to the hospital. To make matters worse, a policeman gives Pete a ticket for parking next to a fire plug and then threatens to arrest them when he sees them handcuffed together. Finally Pete convinces him to take them to the hospital where Joe and Ann are finally married despite constant interruptions. Pete and Ann are still handcuffed when the nurse comes out to congratulate Pete on the birth of his daughter. He takes off running down the hall with Ann in tow. In the vignette, Pete's finally free of the handcuffs when he toasts Matt as godfather, Ruth as godmother and Lily as god-grandmother. Lily raises her glass, "To the health of Little Miss Porter."

"NURSE IS FIRED" JAN. 22, 1959
EPISODE # 143 FILMED ON TUESDAY, DECEMBER 9, 1958
GUEST CAST: ISABEL RANDOLPH AS KATHLEEN TWILLY

Miss Twilly, the live-in nurse for Pete and Gladys's baby daughter Linda, is so strictly regimented that she won't even let Pete hold the baby. When Lily and Hilda visit, she orders them to wear surgical masks and not to advance more than two steps into the baby's room. Disgusted with the treatment they receive, Lily and Hilda leave. (Hilda: "Was there a baby in there? I didn't see a baby in there—'could be a puppy!" Lily: "Next time we'll bring our binoculars.") Later Pete considers replacing Miss Twilly, who allows Linda to cry so "she won't be spoiled, and it's good for her lungs." As Linda continues to wail, Miss Twilly forbids anyone to enter her room. While Miss Twilly is in another room, Matt and Pete climb through Linda's window. As soon as Pete holds her, she stops crying. When they hear footsteps approach, they hide in the closet. Lily steals in to hold Linda, but she, too, takes cover in the closet when she hears someone coming. It's Ruth, but just as she holds the baby, an angry Miss Twilly enters, commanding all of the visitors to leave. Pete faces a showdown with Miss Twilly, who threatens to quit if he doesn't put Linda down. He refuses, and she leaves immediately. For the next three nights, Pete stays up with a squalling Linda. He's miserable and exhausted because neither of them can sleep. Lily, Ruth, Matt, and Hilda all drop in to offer their help. (Hilda to Linda: "Auntie Hilda's going to bring you a pizza, and we'll have a midnight snack!") Just then Miss Twilly comes to the door, saying she was passing by and saw the lights on so she decided to stop and get a uniform she left behind. After she goes into the baby's room, where Pete has put Linda down, they notice that Linda's crying subsides. Then over the intercom, they hear Miss Twilly softly talking to Linda, calling herself "Nana," and explaining that she only wanted Linda to have separate times for sleeping, eating, and love. The others all realize that Miss Twilly's intentions were in Linda's best interest. Seeing that she's an old softie underneath, Pete asks Miss Twilly to come back to work, which she happily agrees to do.

NOTES: The name for Pete's baby was chosen by Lou Derman in honor of his own daughter, Linda Derman.

"LILY'S BLIND DATE" Jan. 29, 1959 *
Episode # 144 Filmed on Tuesday, December 16, 1958
Guest Cast: Roscoe Karns as Charley Allen, William Forrest as Harry Howard, Paul Bryar as the detective, Henry Hunter as Daniel Turner, Margie Liszt as Mrs. Turner

Matt and Ruth try their hand at matchmaking by secretly setting Lily up to meet Matt's business associate in Caruso's Market, but Hilda lets the cat out of the bag first. She persuades Lily to go the market anyway to get a peek at the man. When a handsome man strikes up a conversation with Lily, she and Hilda assume he's the one the children intended for her to meet. As it turns out, the man is a counterfeiter, and Lily and Hilda are almost arrested when a detective finds a roll of phony bills planted in Lily's grocery cart. Later Lily takes a phone message for Matt from Mr. Scott who explains that he was prevented from keeping the appointment Matt made for him. Lily realizes she just spoke with the man whom she was to meet, but she's determined that the children won't arrange any more chance meetings. Hilda opines, "If you'd have gone out with that counterfeiter, that would have taught them a lesson." A gleam shows in Lily's eyes, and Hilda moans wearily, "Oh, I can see now, it's going to be one of those nights." That evening, Lily tells the children that she met a charming man at the market and that she invited him over to meet them later in the evening. Then she nonchalantly mentions the phone message from Mr. Scott. Little do they know that Lily has asked her friend Charley Allen the auctioneer to pose as her new romantic interest. When Charley arrives with candy for Lily, she leaves the room to put it in a dish. This gives Matt a chance to find out more about Charley, who says he deals in diamonds, furs, and jewelry. He pulls back his coat sleeves to display six watches on each wrist and even offers to sell some to Ruth and Matt at a good price. From a large box he brought in, he takes out a $2000 mink coat, drapes it over Ruth, and offers to sell it for $50. The Henshaws and Pete begin to suspect Charley's a crook, especially after he ducks behind the sofa when he hears a fire engine's siren. He knows the kids are on to him, so he makes a quick exit, promising to meet Lily the next day at City Hall. They beg her not to marry him, admitting their guilt of setting her up and their sorrow that Lily is now mixed up with a thief. When they confess that they've learned their lesson, Lily agrees to give up her new boyfriend. Then she rolls up her sleeves to reveal six watches strapped about her arm. She feigns regret as she takes them off, saying, "He wanted me to wear these to see which one I liked."

"LILY'S ADVICE COLUMN" FEB. 5, 1959
EPISODE # 145 FILMED ON TUESDAY, DECEMBER 23, 1958
GUEST CAST: DICK ELLIOTT AS STANLEY POOLE, LEE MILLAR AS DENNIS, BILLY STREET AS JOHNNY

Lily temporarily takes over her newspaper's advice column while columnist Harriet Adams is away. When Hilda hears this, she sees it as a perfect opportunity to prod her *fiancé* Stanley into setting a wedding date. She phones Stanley to suggest that he write Harriet Adams for her opinion on the matter. Hilda wants to get married in June, but exterminator Stanley protests, "That's when the bugs come out." When he finally agrees to write Harriet, Lily plans to advise him that June is the best month for a wedding. Meanwhile, Matt decides to secretly write Harriet Adams after he has an argument with Ruth who insists that he attend art exhibits, ballets, and concerts with her. The next day at the newspaper office, Lily opens Matt's letter (signed "Weary Husband"), not knowing it's from her son-in-law. She responds, "This problem is bound to arise when a sensitive intelligent girl married a cultural oaf." Furthermore she advises him that he's fortunate to have a wife who attempts to raise his cultural level. When Lily gets home, Ruth tells Lily about her disagreement with Matt, leaving Lily horrified that she's interfered in her children's issues. She's further distressed to learn that the paper has gone to press, meaning Matt will be expecting the answer in that evening. Lily writes a more supportive response to "Weary Husband," then gets the printer to print just one page with the new reply for her to insert in Matt's paper. Later Matt smugly reads Harriet's response to Ruth, "You should be able to choose your own form of relaxation because you're the breadwinner." Stanley is angered when he learns from Matt that Lily actually responded to his letter also, but Lily assures Stanley that she would have advised him in the same way had she not known his real identity. Hilda hustles Stanley out while Matt goes upstairs to change clothes so he can take Ruth to an art exhibit. Lily decides to write a letter to Harriet Adams, begging her to come back from vacation and signing it "Weary Mother-in-Law."

"THE HI-FI SHOW" FEB. 12, 1959
EPISODE # 146 FILMED ON TUESDAY, JANUARY 13, 1959
GUEST CAST: NANCY KULP AS THE LIBRARIAN, ROBERT HOY AS THE FIRST LIBRARY PATRON, PERRY IVINS AS THE SECOND LIBRARY PATRON

Matt refuses to allow Ruth to keep a $275 hi-fi set she brought home on approval. He wants to spend his bonus income check for something else. Ruth appeals to Matt's pride by playing a song ("Some Wonderful Day") he recorded on their second date, hoping it will persuade him to allow her to keep the hi-fi. [Pete's response to Matt's solo: "May I have a lock of your hair?"] Matt reconsiders the hi-fi set and endorses his check, secretly hiding it inside Ruth's library book. Later when Lily and Hilda inform Ruth they're going downtown to return a yellow slacks suit Hilda bought at Mayfair's (Hilda: "When I spread out my arms

I look like a taxi with the doors open."), she asks them to return her library book, not knowing the check is inside. Later Matt tells Lily about the hidden check so she and Hilda go to the library to retrieve it. In their search, they disturb every library patron there, particularly one poor man standing on a rolling ladder whom Hilda pushes right out the window into a fish pond. All ends well, though, when the twosome arrives home with the check, just in time for Ruth to re-hide it in the book and feign surprise when she finds it, with Matt looking on.

NOTES: This was the first episode Verna Felton filmed following the mild stroke she suffered in late December 1958. Producer Parke Levy appears as an extra in the library scene.

"THE SCOTCH SHOW" FEB. 19, 1959
EPISODE # 147 FILMED ON TUESDAY, JANUARY 20, 1959
GUEST CAST: RUSSELL ARMS AS RONNIE MACDOUGALL, BETHEL LESLIE AS NANCY LEE FAIRBURN, DAVID THURSBY AS ANGUS MACDOUGALL, TED DE CORSIA AS MR. FAIRBURN

Lily offers to help Nancy Lee Fairburn, a young exchange student from Scotland, who feels she cannot marry the man she loves because of a longstanding feud between their families. Lily invites Ronnie MacDougall, Nancy's boyfriend, over to learn more about the dispute, which began 300 years ago when a MacDougall stole a sheep from a Fairburn. Ronnie's in favor of marrying Nancy without their fathers' consent, but Lily suggests inviting both men to Los Angeles. When crusty Mr. MacDougall arrives from San Francisco, he's charmed by Nancy, until he learns she's a Fairburn. In fact, he storms out, refusing to wait for her father's arrival from Scotland. Lily entices him to return by promising to have Pete, posing as the elder MacDougall, end the feud with Nancy's father. MacDougall scoffs at Pete's ability to pull off a true Scottish appearance, and once again leaves. Soon Nancy arrives with Mr. Fairburn, who, thinking Pete is Angus MacDougall, gives his blessing for the marriage. When Nancy blows the whistle on Pete's ruse, Lily explains everything to her father. Just then MacDougall returns and quickly begins an argument with Fairburn. To settle matters once and for all, Ronnie offers to pay Fairburn for the sheep stolen long ago. Fairburn accepts his offers but stipulates that Ronnie should pay interest as well, which he calculates to be $2000. Nancy reasons that the $2000 would be due to the entire Fairburn clan, and since there are approximately 2000 living descendants, Ronnie's share would only be $1. Lily persuades the fathers to see how much the young couple loves each other, and they give their approval for the union of their children.

NOTES: Scotland native David Thursby (1889-1977) gives one of his final television appearances in this episode. Acclaimed stage actress Bethel Leslie (1929-1999) does a fine job affecting a Scottish accent in her role as Nancy.

"THE MARTIAN SHOW" FEB. 26, 1959 *
EPISODE # 148 FILMED ON TUESDAY, JANUARY 27, 1959
GUEST CAST: ROGER PERRY AS JIMMY MAYFAIR, DICK ELLIOTT AS STANLEY POOLE, GRANDON RHODES AS MR. GRAVES, DAYTON LUMMIS AS MR. MAYFAIR, ANTHONY WARDE AS THE COP

When Lily advises Jimmy Mayfair, a young reader of her column, to pursue his dream to become a singer, she incites the wrath of his father who intends for the lad to assume the leadership in the family business, Mayfair's Department Store. The elder Mayfair, as the newspaper's biggest advertiser, threatens to take his business elsewhere if the editor doesn't fire Lily for giving such advice. Regretfully, Mr. Graves, the editor, agrees. He explains the situation to Lily, who tells him that Jimmy is coming over that day to thank Lily for her advice. Graves suggests that she talk him out of becoming a singer, but Lily hesitates to do so until she talks to Jimmy. Later, when Lily discovers that Jimmy is on his way to audition for a television talent show, she invites him to sing the number for her. She is very impressed with his talent and doesn't regret the advice she gave him at all. After the audition, Jimmy drops by to tell Lily that he was chosen to sing on the show that evening, but he's not sure he should do it because he knows it costs Lily her job. Meanwhile, Hilda and Stanley drop in on their way to the Exterminators' Association Dance, or as Hilda calls it, the "Bug Ball." Jimmy is confused by their grasshopper costumes, saying that for just a minute he thought they were Martian invaders. This gives Lily an idea for a way to convince Mr. Mayfair to watch Jimmy perform on television. Later that evening, she arrives at the Mayfair home, frantically informing him that a flying saucer carrying two little green people just landed on his roof. (Mayfair: "Did they appear to be armed?" Lily: "One of them had a spray gun . . . uh, ray gun.") He thinks she's daffy until he sees Hilda and Stanley in their green costumes peering and waving into his window. Lily tells him to turn on the television to catch any related bulletins about the Martian invasion. Just then a cop's voice is heard outside, and Lily knows the gig is up. Mayfair opens the door and finds the cop clutching Hilda and Stanley's shoulders. ("I found these two loonies dancing around on your lawn.") Lily admits their deceitful trick, but she insists that Mayfair listen to Jimmy sing. As Stanley and Hilda argue with the cop, Mayfair sits down quietly and is charmed by his son's talented voice.

"LILY BABYSITS" MAR. 5, 1959
EPISODE # 149 FILMED ON TUESDAY, FEBRUARY 3, 1959
GUEST CAST: DICK WESSEL AS MOM, EDDIE RYDER AS THE BELLBOY, LENNIE BREMEN AS THE THIRSTY CUSTOMER, LEE WARREN AS THE NAVAL OFFICER, GEORGE BARROWS AS THE HOT CUSTOMER, LEE MILLAR AS THE TELEGRAM DELIVERYMAN, AND STUNTS BY HARVEY PARRY, DALE VAN SICKEL, FRED GABOURIE

When Pete and Gladys go to Balboa for a second honeymoon, Lily substitutes for Miss Twilly, Linda's nurse. Hilda volunteers to help, "It'll do me good to have a change of refrigerators." A nervous Pete leaves a long list of instructions for the two "nannies," but Lily and Hilda assure him all will be fine while he's gone. That evening, Lily and Hilda walk Linda for almost two hours to get her to fall asleep before deciding to take her for a ride in the car. When they get lost in a thick fog, they realize they've run out of milk for Linda. Through the mist they see a café called Mom's Bar and Grill. Thinking it's a reputable establishment since the owner is a mother, they go inside but are surprised to find out that Mom is actually a burly mustachioed bartender and the father of six. When he holds Linda she stops fretting, but when he tries to hand her over to Lily again, she starts crying. So Lily tends bar. Meanwhile at Pete's hotel, a well-meaning bell-boy is incredulous that Pete went on vacation without Linda. This upsets Pete, and he rushes back to Los Angeles to check on Linda. Back at the bar, Mom fees Linda and even offers to lead Lily and Hilda through the fog back to Pete's. They arrive just in time to greet Pete, whose fears are calmed after he sees that Linda is all right. Much later that night, a singing telegram ("Rockabye Baby") from Pete arrives for Linda, to which an exhausted Lily sends a reply: "Dear Daddy, I am asleep. Why aren't you? Love, Linda"

"RUTH THE BRAIN" MAR. 12, 1959
EPISODE # 150 FILMED ON TUESDAY, FEBRUARY 10, 1959
GUEST CAST: FRANK CADY AS PROF. MCCULLOUGH, FRANCES ROBINSON AS PHYLLIS HARVEY

After being tricked by Matt into an argument, Ruth claims she's smarter than him, insisting that they participate in an IQ test designed by Prof. McCullough whom Lily has recently interviewed. (Lily to Hilda: "If my daughter is smart, she'll try very hard to be stupid.") When the scores are returned, Ruth is disappointed to learn that they each scored 120 so she secretly changes hers to 220. Later when Lily reads the results, Matt is incredulous, but Lily admits that Ruth was a very bright baby. Pete quips, "With that IQ, she could've delivered herself!" Matt begins to feel insecure about his lower score. Then Hilda cheerfully delivers the news the Westwood Women's Cultural Club is going to nominate Lily as Mother of the Year since she's the mother of a genius. Later when Ruth's absent, Prof. McCullough drops in to pick up some photos Lily took of him. When Ruth's high score is mentioned, he disputes it, saying it was 120. Matt and Pete closely examine the notification letter and see Ruth's alteration. Hilda has reservations, "Lily, about that Mother of the Year . . ." Lily, aggravated and embarrassed, suggests, "Just run me for the Jackass of the Month!" They all hatch a revenge plot against Ruth. Later, Lily enters with McCullough posing as Prof. Nickel, head of the federal government's research department. He tells Ruth that the White House has sent him to ask her to join "Operation Brainstorm." She's honored until she learns she won't be able to return home for five years. Lily: "We'll keep a star in the window for you." When McCullough tells her she'll be the property of the U.S. Government, Ruth admits her fraudulent deed, "I'm not really a genius, Matt. I'm just as stupid as you are."

"STAN LOSES HIS NERVE" MAR. 19, 1959
EPISODE # 151 FILMED ON TUESDAY, FEBRUARY 17, 1959
GUEST CAST: DICK ELLIOTT AS STANLEY POOLE, JIM DAVIS AS DON MARTIN, LINDA GAYE AS LISA MARTIN

Hilda's down in the dumps because Stanley has called off their wedding due to his dissatisfaction with the exterminating business. He feels he's too old to handle the job after several recent mishaps. Stanley wants to begin a new career, necessitating the postponement of his marriage to Hilda until he's more confidently settled into a new occupation. Lily consoles Hilda, "Don't worry, dear. We'll have him squirting before you can say DDT." They visit Stanley at his office, but their persuasive tactics fail. Stanley confesses he's lost the "killer instinct," so he intends to accept Pulaski Exterminating's offer to him buy out. Lily cooks up a scheme with neighbor Don Martin, a rugged television star, to help Stanley conquer his fears. That evening while Stanley and Hilda are her dinner guests, Lily invites Martin, posing as a novice exterminator, to treat her house. When Lily tells him her closet has moths, he merely sprays in that general direction. Stanley intervenes, "Get a little closer, son. With what you're doing, they won't even look up from their lunch." Stanley gives Martin some other advice, and Martin agrees with him that exterminating is a young man's game. But when Martin feigns fright of a spider, the rotund Stanley takes over, bravely climbing under the fireplace hood and spraying up the chimney, telling Hilda, "This one's for you, Poopsie." His confidence regained, Stanley decides to return to exterminating, thus making Hilda very hopeful for a wedding later in the year.

"THE TEXAN, RORY CALHOUN" MAR. 26, 1959
EPISODE # 152 FLIMED ON TUESDAY, FEBRUARY 24, 1959
GUEST CAST: RORY CALHOUN AS HIMSELF, RALPH REED AS BOBBY HAMILTON, SID MELTON AS BILL, STANLEY ADAMS AS CHARLIE, FUZZY KNIGHT AS ANDY, GLENN TURNBULL AS MR. GILLIAM

Bobby Hamilton, the 17-year-old son of Lily's friend in Philadelphia, is visiting the Henshaws while he prepares for an entrance exam to Cal Tech. Matt invites Bobby to go with him to the ranch of television star Rory Calhoun, who's asked Matt to design his new guesthouse. Right away Bobby is keenly interested in the rugged life of a rancher, and soon he abandons his plans to study science at Cal Tech. Lily convinces Calhoun that he must make Bobby believe that life on his ranch is softer than it really is. When Lily and Bobby arrive at Calhoun's the next day, they find a fancy trailer there. Calhoun explains that tonight, they'll dine on Cornish game hen cooked inside the trailer. One of the ranch hands, Bill, informs Calhoun that the string quartet can't play tonight so he's setting up a croquet game. Andy, another hand, enters bearing a bouquet of Black-Eyed Susans, which he's grown for the table centerpiece. Bobby's confused and asks who's watching the herds. Andy says they've been tranquilized so they won't stampede. Charlie, a third hand, arrives, reporting that he got carsick during the cattle roundup today. Bobby sees through their ploy and is insulted. Calhoun explains that research and discovery can be just as exciting as ranching. He reminds Bobby that they're lots of cowboys around, but there's only been one Edison, Marconi, or Salk. Bobby realizes the truth in this statement, and enrolls in Cal Tech after he passes the entrance exam.

"LINDA ON TV" APR. 2, 1959
EPISODE # 153 FILMED ON TUESDAY, MARCH 3, 1959
GUEST CAST: PETER LEEDS AS LENNIE HELLER, HAYDEN RORKE AS FRED MASON, PAMELA MASON AS THE WAITRESS, VIKKI RUBINO AS LINDA PORTER

Obnoxious Lennie Heller brags that his infant daughter Susie is prettier than Pete's daughter Linda. In fact, he says she's been used in a color magazine ad for Dr. Schultz's Non-Chafing Talcum Powder. When he boasts that Susie has been offered an audition for the *Playhouse 90* television show, Lily and Hilda are determined to get Linda a chance to audition for the same show. Remembering that Lennie said the show's producer, Fred Mason, lunches every day at the Café Sunset, Lily and Hilda decide to accidentally meet him there. Lily finds Mason at a quiet table on the sidewalk so she casually strolls Linda's baby carriage back and forth under his eye. He ignores her attention-getting methods until Hilda arrives on the scene acting as a passerby enthralled with Linda's beauty. Mason realizes the ladies' intent, and when he finally looks at Linda, he agrees she should have an audition. Pete is so thrilled when Linda subsequently wins the role that he invites Lennie over the night of the broadcast to rub it in. Just before the show airs, Gladys calls saying the production office called to apologize that Linda's scene was cut from the final version due to time limits. When Lily takes Pete out in the kitchen to give him the news, he wants to retreat through the back door, but Lily convinces him to face Lennie despite his disappointment. When they return to the living room, they find that Lennie has left in shame because he couldn't accept the fact that Linda beat his daughter out of the role. When Mason phones Pete to offer Linda another role, he declines, saying she's retiring from show biz.
NOTES: The waitress was played by Pamela Mason, then the wife of film actor James Mason, who visited the set during the filming of this episode.

"LILY GOES FISHING" APR. 9, 1959
EPISODE # 154 FILMED ON TUESDAY, MARCH 10, 1959
GUEST CAST: ROBERT FOULK AS THE FIRST FISHERMAN, HARRY CHESHIRE AS THE SECOND FISHERMAN, HERB VIGRAN AS HARRY SIDNEY, LEE MILLAR AS THE BAIT SALESMAN

Matt and Pete are to perform magic tricks for Lily's club's show, but the only time she can reserve the auditorium is the same weekend that the boys plan to go on a fishing trip to Ensenada. (The Westwood Bird Lovers have booked their annual chicken dinner at the auditorium the weekend that Lily wanted it.) Matt and Pete volunteer to cancel their trip, opting instead to fish at Malibu for the day. When Matt catches a prize corbina (3.5 feet long), Lily decides to surprise him by cooking it for dinner as repayment for giving up the weekend trip. She takes it to the market to be filleted, only to learn later that Matt intends to be photographed with the fish. She and Hilda hurry to the pier to catch another corbina, but after getting their lines tangled with the other fishermen, Lily decides to buy a mounted corbina she spies in a bait shop. Back at the Henshaw home, Harry from the fish market arrives with Matt's corbina, which he could not bring himself to fillet. Later Lily arrives with the mounted fish and tries to pass it off as Matt's catch. Hilda offers an explanation of their speedy preservation, "It's a drive-in taxidermist—he stuffs while ya wait." When Lily and Hilda see the fresh corbina, Matt advises them to read a plaque carefully before buying one the next time. Lily reads hers, "Caught by Irving Green, July 12, 1941."

NOTES: Lee Millar, Verna Felton's son, makes the last of his eleven DB appearances in this episode.

"LILY HELPS TWILLY" APR. 16, 1959
EPISODE # 155 FILMED ON TUESDAY, MARCH 17, 1959
GUEST CAST: ISABEL RANDOLPH AS KATHLEEN TWILLY, LEO FUCHS AS FELIX KOSLO, STEVEN GERAY AS THE MAITRE'D, SUE BAKKENSON AS THE WAITRESS

When Miss Kathleen Twilly, the nurse for Pete's baby, seems distracted, Lily and Hilda drop by to see if anything is troubling her. Miss Twilly confesses that she has recently learned that an old boyfriend, Felix Koslo, is back in town. He's playing the violin each evening at the Café Budapest. Miss Twilly has not seen him for thirty years, ever since they had a quarrel. Normally after a disagreement, Felix would appear under her window and serenade Miss Twilly with "I'll Take You Home Again, Kathleen," but on that final occasion, he didn't show up. Without Miss Twilly's knowledge, Lily and Hilda go to the café to learn if Felix is a married man. (Hilda: "Let's flirt with him. If he flirts back, he's married.") After some casual conversation about his music, Hilda lets the cat out of the bag by asking Felix, "Do you know 'I'll Take You Home Again, Miss Twilly'?" Felix is anxious to find out more about Miss Twilly but admits his shameful failure to become a concert violinist in Europe. He sadly declines Lily's offer to arrange a meeting with Miss Twilly. The next evening, Lily decides to hire Felix to play for

Ruth's elegant supper she's prepared for Matt. Next door at Pete's house, Lily, Hilda, and Miss Twilly are playing cards when they hear loud, frantic violin music coming from the Henshaw home. Miss Twilly goes over to tell them the music will disturb the baby. Pete and Ruth are dancing energetically when Miss Twilly enters, and then Felix turns around. He stops playing; Miss Twilly clutches her heart with her hand and flees. She enters the Porter house in tears, "Oh, Mrs. Ruskin, I wish you hadn't done that." Lily tells her that she and Felix belong together. Softly, from outside, come the tender strains of "I'll Take You Home Again, Kathleen." Then Felix enters. As Lily and Hilda quietly steal out, Felix and his Kathleen embrace. In the vignette, Lily informs her phone-mate Madeline that Miss Twilly is now Mrs. Felix Koslo.

"LILY, THE EXAMPLE" APR. 30, 1959
EPISODE # 156 FILMED ON TUESDAY, MARCH 24, 1959
GUEST CAST: JESSE WHITE AS HARRY, ALLEN JENKINS AS JOE, CLINTON SUNDBERG AS MR. SCOFFIELD, HAL K. DAWSON AS THE IMPATIENT CUSTOMER, GAIL BONNEY AS THE CASHIER

When Ruth forgets to pick up Matt at the airport, he holds up Lily as an example, saying she would never do such a thing. He cites further evidence of his mother-in-law's abilities by reminding Ruth that Lily remembers to pick up Matt's laundry and shops around for better prices on clothes Ruth admires. An argument ensues, and when Lily feels caught in the middle, she quickly accepts Hilda's invitation to a "nice little cafeteria down at the beach." Once there, Lily muses over how she can stop Matt from holding her up as an example to Ruth. Meanwhile, two gentlemen, Harry and Joe, ask to share the table with Lily and Hilda. When she explains her problem to them, Harry responds with this advice: "Vacate de premises." Hilda tells Lily not to listen to him, but Lily decides to accept a job offer from the cafeteria manager and to move out of Matt and Ruth's house. She finds a small apartment near the beach, telling the children she needs to get out of Los Angeles on her doctor's advice. She lies that the smog causes her severe headaches. Three days later when Hilda drops by the Henshaw home, she, as usual, spills the beans and tells them Lily is working as hostess in a cafeteria. When Matt and Ruth visit Lily there, they insist that she come back home. Her new friends, Harry and Joe, argue that the situation there is uncomfortable. Matt is remorseful about making Lily an example. When Harry sees that Matt is an "okay guy," he reverses his decision and urges Lily to go back home. In the vignette, Hilda cautions Lily to not set too good of an example for Ruth. Then an alarm clock goes off, and Lily explains, "That's to remind me to forget to pick up Matt's shirts."

NOTES: Gail Bonney, who played Lily and Hilda's friend Madeline Schweitzer in six episodes, appears here as the cafeteria cashier. Although she has no lines, her incredulous expression when noticing the quantity of food on Hilda's tray is priceless.

"BALD BABY" MAY 7, 1959
EPISODE # 157 FILMED ON TUESDAY, MARCH 31, 1959
GUEST CAST: PORTLAND MASON AS GLORIA, BEN LESSY AS UNCLE LOU ELLIOTT, JEROME COWAN AS DR. HEATLEY, RICHARD ERDMAN AS MR. KESSLER, EDITH SIMMONS AS THE RECEPTIONIST

Pete frets that his four-month-old baby has no hair yet. Everyone tries to convince him that she's all right, but he says, "I'm just thinking ahead. Some day my poor baby will come home in tears. Some wise guy opened the window on the school bus, and her wig blew off!" Pete then asks Lily to go with him to the doctor's office to see what he can do to help Linda. The doctor explains that only six women out of one hundred become bald, with heredity playing a part. After telling Pete that a baby's mother carries traits for baldness, Pete begins to worry that Linda has inherited that trait from Gladys. He's anxious to meet Gladys's Uncle Lou who's expected to arrive from Chicago that evening. That afternoon while Pete and Gladys are away, Uncle Lou wanders over to the Henshaw home where he finds Lily and Hilda on the patio. When they learn that he is Gladys's uncle, they attempt to look under his hat to check for baldness. Finally when he removes it, their fears are confirmed. Hilda mutters, "Poor Linda." Lily explains Pete's phobia to Uncle Lou, who agrees to wear a toupee when he meets Pete. When the toupee falls off, Pete is grief stricken. Then Uncle Lou introduces his daughter Gloria, whose long tresses Pete tests by pulling on them. Pete's fears are calmed when Uncle Lou tells him that Gloria had no hair until she was six months old. In the vignette, Pete shows Lily a new photo of Linda, on which he has painted some hair.

NOTES: Edith Simmons, daughter-in-law of Verna Felton, makes the final of her nine DB appearances in this episode.

APPENDIX D: *PETE AND GLADYS* SEASON ONE EPISODE GUIDE

NOTE: Episodes denoted by an asterisk (*) are ones not personally viewed by the author. An incomplete collection of *Pete and Gladys* scripts are among the Parke Levy Papers [Accession Number 3148: Box 11] at the American Heritage Center, University of Wyoming. These scripts, as well as available film versions of episodes, were consulted to construct this guide.

PETE AND GLADYS
THE FIRST SEASON: 1960-61

CAST:	Harry Morgan as Pete Porter
	Cara Williams as Gladys Porter
	Verna Felton as Hilda Crocker
CREATOR/PRODUCER:	Parke Levy
ASSOCIATE PRODUCER:	Bill Manhoff
DIRECTORS:	William D. Russell, Jack Arnold, Gene Reynolds, Earl Bellamy, Norman Abbott, James V. Kern, Seymour Berns
WRITERS:	Parke Levy, Bill Manhoff, Fred S. Fox, Iz Ellenson, Jim Fritzell, Everett Greenbaum, Samuel Locke, Nathaniel Curtis, Bobby O'Brien, Alan Campbell, Bill Berney, Norman Paul, Hal Goodman, Larry Klein, Danny Simon, Joel Rapp, Milton Pascal, Larry Rhine, Stan Dreben, Jack Roche, Charles Fleming, Louis M. Heyward, Bill Freedman, Henry Sharp, Joe Quillan, Harry Crane, George Beck, Larry Markes
COMPOSER/CONDUCTOR:	Wilbur Hatch
DIRECTOR OF PHOTOGRAPHY:	Lester Schorr, A.S.C.
ASSISTANT DIRECTOR AND UNIT MANAGER:	Frank Mayer
PRODUCTION MANAGER:	W. Argyle Nelson
FILM EDITOR:	Fred Maguire
ART DIRECTORS:	Hal Pereira, Albert Heschong
SET DECORATORS:	Sam Cooper, Robert R. Benton
SOUND EFFECTS EDITOR:	Gene Eliot

MUSIC EDITOR:	Gene Feldman
MAKEUP:	Harry Ray
HAIR STYLIST:	Lillian Shore
CASTING:	Kerwin Coughlin
RE-RECORDING EDITOR:	Joel Moss
SOUND:	Glen Glenn Sound Co.
SPONSORS:	Goodyear Tires & Carnation Milk
	Filmed at Paramount Studios

"FOR PETE'S SAKE" SEPTEMBER 19, 1960
EPISODE # 1 FILMED ON FRIDAY, JANUARY 29, 1960
GUEST CAST: BILL HEYER AS PHIL MARTIN, DELPHINE SEYRIG AS MICHELE MARTIN, ELVIA ALLMAN AS GLORIA THE BEAUTICIAN, BARBARA MORRISON AS THE COUNTY TAX APPRAISER

The Porters move into a new house and meet their new neighbors, Phil and Michele Martin.

"CRIME OF PASSION" SEPTEMBER 26, 1960*
EPISODE # 2
GUEST CAST: CESAR ROMERO AS RICKY VALENTI, PEGGY KNUDSEN AS MRS. VALENTI, TED KNIGHT AS THE NEIGHBOR, PETER HELM AS THE DELIVERY BOY

Gladys wants Pete to join her in taking dancing lessons.

"BAVARIAN WEDDING CHEST" OCTOBER 3, 1960
EPISODE # 3
GUEST CAST: BILL HEYER AS PHIL MARTIN, DELPHINE SEYRIG AS MICHELE MARTIN, JAMES FLAVIN AS THE POLICEMAN, BUDDY LEWIS AS THE MOVER

Pete brings home a huge Bavarian wedding chest. Gladys thinks it's a monstrosity, so Pete tries to sell her on the idea that it's supposed to bring good luck.

"THE HANDYMAN" OCTOBER 10, 1960*
EPISODE # 4
GUEST CAST: PETER LEEDS AS GEORGE COLTON, SHIRLEY MITCHELL AS JANET COLTON, CHEERIO MEREDITH AS THE RED CROSS WORKER

Tired of the taunts of George Colton, his needling next-door neighbor, Pete decides to prove that he's a match for anyone as handyman around the house.

"MOVIE BUG" OCTOBER 17, 1960
EPISODE # 5
GUEST CAST: JACK ALBERTSON AS COLES, JOEY FAYE AS THE ASSISTANT DIRECTOR, WILLIS BOUCHEY AS MR. SPRINGER, NETTA PACKER AS MARIE, KEN LOWRY AS MENLO RAND, BAMBI HAMILTON AS SUZY

Unknown to Pete, Gladys lets a movie company use the Porter residence for some exterior shots. Then she proceeds to badger the producer for a part in the picture.

"OO-LA-LA" OCTOBER 24, 1960
EPISODE # 6
GUEST CAST: KARL LUKAS AS ROCKY MURDOCK, JOYCE VANDERVEEN AS COLLETTE DuPRES, HAZEL SHERMET AS PAMELA

Pete persuades a French girl named Collette to do a can-can number at a charity show. But he hasn't bothered to check with Collette's husband—a burly customer named Rocky.

"THE GOAT STORY" OCTOBER 31, 1960*
EPISODE # 7
GUEST CAST: RONNY HOWARD AS TOMMY, HENRY NORELL AS TORRANCE

That nasty man from the animal pound is after little Tommy's pet goat. So Gladys and Hilda come to the rescue. They hide the goat in Gladys's house.

"PETE'S PERSONALITY CHANGE" NOVEMBER 7, 1960
EPISODE # 8
GUEST CAST: WHITNEY BLAKE AS AGATHA HENDERSON, BARBARA STUART AS ALICE BROWN, WILLIS BOUCHEY AS MR. SPRINGER, ROLFE SEDAN AS THE WAITER, WILLIAM BOYETT AS THE HUSBAND, JAN BROOKS AS THE WIFE, DON LOSBY AS THE NEWSBOY

Pete loses a big sale, so his boss calls in a psychologist to put some oomph back into his salesmanship.

"CAMPING OUT" NOVEMBER 14, 1960*
EPISODE # 9
GUEST CAST: ALVY MOORE AS HOWIE BROWN, BARBARA STUART AS ALICE BROWN, MICKEY SIMPSON AS MAN MOUNTAIN

Pete and his pal Howie want to go on a camping trip, but to get their wives' approval, they have to prove that they're tough. They decided on a trial in Pete's back yard.

"BOWLING BRAWL" NOVEMBER 21, 1960
EPISODE # 10
GUEST CAST: GALE GORDON AS UNCLE PAUL, SHIRLEY MITCHELL AS JANET COLTON, WILSON WOOD AS THE WAITER

Pete thinks it's time Gladys and his uncle Paul ended their long-standing feud. But Gladys isn't satisfied just to "make up." She decides she's got to prove she's a good sport.

"PETE TAKES UP GOLF" NOVEMBER 28, 1960*
EPISODE # 11
GUEST CAST: WILLIS BOUCHEY AS MR. SPRINGER, HOWARD CAINE AS BURKE, MILTON FROME AS JOHNSON

Pete wants to join the country club for its golf links, and Gladys wants him to join it for social links.

"GLADYS AND THE PIGGY BANK" DECEMBER 5, 1960
EPISODE # 12
GUEST CAST: PETER LEEDS AS GEORGE COLTON, SHIRLEY MITCHELL AS JANET COLTON, MURIEL LANDERS AS CLAIRE, SHIRLEY MELLINE, GAINES KINCAID, AND HARRIETT ARGENBRIGHT AS EXTRAS

It's the Coltons' anniversary and Pete and Gladys are trying to think of an appropriate gift. Gladys can't remember just what kind of gift they got from the Coltons but figures it must have been a cheap one—so she and Pete reciprocate with a worthless doodad.

"NO MAN IS JAPAN" DECEMBER 12, 1960
EPISODE # 13
GUEST CAST: BARBARA STUART AS ALICE BROWN, PHILIP AHN AS HORACE SUKI, BEULAH QUO AS MRS. SUKI, JUDY DAN AS FUMIKO MITZU

There's a possibility that Pete may become the manager of his firm's Tokyo branch, and he's all excited about becoming "oriented." He arranges for a Japanese exchange student to move in and help him learn the customs.

"MISPLACED WEEKEND" DECEMBER 19, 1960
EPISODE # 14
GUEST CAST: DAVID LEWIS AS CHARLES FLEMING, ANN LEE AS MRS. FLEMING, DONALD FOSTER AS MR. STEPHENS, CHARLES WATTS AS THE FAT MAN

Gladys and Pete want to get away from it all and spend a few days in Palm Springs. So Gladys uses the sick-grandmother bit on Pete's boss, Mr. Fleming.

"GLADYS RENTS THE HOUSE" JANUARY 2, 1961
EPISODE # 15
GUEST CAST: MOREY AMSTERDAM AS WALLY, STANLEY ADAMS AS FRED, HAZEL SHERMET AS PAMELA, WILLIS BOUCHEY AS MR. SPRINGER, JANE DULO AS DORA, SANDRA GOULD AS SYLVIA, SID TOMACK AS MANNY, FRANK KREIG AS JACK, DICK BERNIE AS CONVENTIONEER

Gladys wants a vacation in Hawaii. She starts raising funds for this jaunt by renting a room to a couple of lodge members, in town for the big Antlers' convention.

"GLADYS' POLITICAL CAMPAIGN" JANUARY 9, 1961*
EPISODE # 16
GUEST CAST: SHIRLEY MITCHELL AS JANET COLTON, JAMES FLAVIN AS OFFICER HARRITY, NANCY KULP AS MISS HOTCHKISS, JOYCE COMPTON AS MRS. WILSON, DORIS PACKER AS MRS. MCGILLICUDDY, DON BEDDOE AS MR. SCHUYLER, ALVY MOORE AS HOWIE BROWN, PAT ROSSON AS THE BOY

Pete's fast becoming the "forgotten husband," as Gladys campaigns for the presidency of the Women's Civic League.

"COUSIN VIOLET" JANUARY 16, 1961
EPISODE # 17   FILMED ON DECEMBER 6, 7, AND 8, 1960
GUEST CAST: MURIEL LANDERS AS VIOLET, TOMMY FARRELL AS STEVE MAGRUDER, ALVY MOORE AS HOWIE BROWN

Cousin Violet, a plump lass, has sent Gladys's photo to her Navy pen pal, Steve Magruder, implying it's a picture of herself. Steve gets leave from duty and decides to pay Violet a visit.

"THE HOUSE NEXT DOOR" JANUARY 23, 1961*
EPISODE # 18
GUEST CAST: ALVY MOORE AS HOWIE BROWN, CHRISTINE NELSON AS EDITH HALSEY, WILLIAM NEWELL AS MR. HIGGINS, CHARLES LANE AS MR. VINCENT, IRENE TEDROW AS MRS. VINCENT, JOHN CLOSE AS OFFICE HANNITY

Gladys rents the house next door for a friend, but there's been a mix-up somewhere—moving day comes and complete strangers take possession of the place. She and Pete masquerade as owners of a theatrical school in hopes of driving the new tenants out.

"INSURANCE FAKER" JANUARY 30, 1961*
EPISODE # 19
GUEST CAST: ALVY MOORE AS HOWIE BROWN, BARBARA STUART AS ALICE BROWN, MYRNA DELL AS MRS. WINGFIELD, DON O'KELLY AS BIG TONY, GEORGE BARROWS AS SWIFTY, BARRY BERNARD AS HEWETT

Gladys finds herself fleeing from a cutlass-swinging villain when she attempts to unravel an apparent insurance fraud and is mistaken for a confederate by two hoodlums.

"SKIN DEEP" FEBRUARY 6, 1961*
EPISODE # 20
GUEST CAST: ALVY MOORE AS HOWIE BROWN, BARBARA STUART AS ALICE BROWN, FRED EASLER AS OTTO INGLEHOFFER, ANN LEE AS MRS. FLEMING

Pete gets a raise—and a reduction in his work load. He just tells Gladys about the reduction, and she, thinking less work means less money, decides to get a job. **NOTE: This episode is sometimes known as "The Great Stone Face."**

"SIX MUSKETEERS" FEBRUARY 20, 1961
EPISODE # 21
GUEST CAST: ALVY MOORE AS HOWIE BROWN, BARBARA STUART AS ALICE
BROWN, SHIRLEY MITCHELL AS JANET COLTON, PETER LEEDS AS GEORGE
COLTON

Pete and Gladys have planned a weekend in the mountains, but they have to share the one cabin with two other couples.

"THE PANHANDLER" FEBRUARY 27, 1961
EPISODE # 22
GUEST CAST: ADDISON RICHARDS AS BENNINGTON CARSTAIRS, LILLIAN
BRONSON AS MARTHA CARSTAIRS, HERB ELLIS AS THE CABBIE, JACK ALBERTSON
AS MR. MURPHY, LILLIAN CULVER AS THE LADY IN THE PARK, HOWARD DAYTON
AS THE BEATNIK, JOSEPH MELL AS THE DELICATESSEN OWNER, GAIL BONNEY AS
THE TELEPHONE OPERATOR (VOICE ONLY), ALEX DUNAND AND WILLIS ROBARDS
AS EXTRAS

Gladys attends the dress rehearsal of community play. After the rehearsal, still dressed in tramp clothes for her part in the play, she starts homeward—without any money.

"GLADYS OPENS PETE'S MAIL" MARCH 6, 1961*
EPISODE # 23
GUEST CAST: ALVY MOORE AS HOWIE BROWN, BARBARA STUART AS ALICE
BROWN, ROY ROWAN AS TOM WILSON, ALLAN RAY AS THE MAILMAN

Pete can't seem to break Gladys from opening his mail. Howie gives him a great idea—write himself a letter implying that he's in serious trouble.

"THE GARAGE STORY" MARCH 13, 1961*
EPISODE # 24 FILMED ON JANUARY 4, 1961
GUEST CAST: ERNEST TRUEX AS POP, JACK ALBERTSON AS MR. SIMPSON, LEE
MILLAR AND RICHARD BULL AS THE DRIVERS

Gladys's father has been staying with her since he retired. Gladys forces Pete to take Pop to work with him (a less-than-brilliant idea, it develops), and then suggests he get Pop a job at a service station.

"THE ORCHID STORY" MARCH 20, 1961
EPISODE # 25
GUEST CAST: ERNEST TRUEX AS POP, ALVY MOORE AS HOWIE BROWN, SID
KANE AND DON AMES AS THE DELIVERY MEN

Pop's many and varied interests all have one thing in common—they all mean trouble for Pete.

NOTE: Verna Felton does not appear in this episode.

"SECRETARY FOR A DAY" MARCH 27, 1961
EPISODE # 26 FILMED FEBRUARY 9, 1961
GUEST CAST: ERNEST TRUEX AS POP, WILLARD WATERMAN AS HIGGINS, BARRY KELLEY AS SLOCUM, BARRY BERNARD AS SPRINGER, KAREN MORRIS AS THE AIRPORT GIRL, DOROTHY KONRAD AS THE DELICATESSEN WOMAN, LEE MILLAR AS KREBS, JOEL WESLEY AS THE POLLSTER

Gladys wants to run off a batch of resumes for her job-hunting father, but Pete won't allow her to use his office duplicating machine. Then Pete is asked to work on Saturday—and Gladys eagerly volunteers to substitute for him at the office.

"THE FUR COAT STORY" APRIL 3, 1961*
EPISODE # 27
GUEST CAST: JOHN FIEDLER AS CHARLEY BROWN, PETER LEEDS AS GEORGE COLTON, BERNICE MCLAUGHLIN AS HELEN BROWN, JOHN HART AS MERVIN

On the eve of their anniversary, Pete hedges again on his six-year-old promise of a fur coat for Gladys. He doesn't want to "squander" money on a luxury like that—he's saving for a motorboat.

"PEACEFUL IN THE COUNTRY" APRIL 10, 1961
EPISODE # 28
GUEST CAST: WILLARD WATERMAN AS HIGGINS, JOHN DAY AS JOE WALKER, DICK CROCKETT AS LOU ABLE

Pete and Gladys are to weekend at his boss's cabin in the mountains, so that Pete can show the place to a couple of prospective buyers. But Hilda has put Gladys in charge of a monstrous great Dane named Strongboy—and there's nothing to do but take him along.

"JUNIOR" APRIL 17, 1961
EPISODE # 29
GUEST CAST: ALVY MOORE AS HOWIE BROWN, JONATHAN HOLE AS INSPECTOR PERKINS, DON AMES AS MARKET CHECKER, FRANK JENKS AS DETECTIVE SGT. CARY, ALLEN JENKINS AS DETECTIVE SGT. KRAUSE

Gladys convinces Pete that they should care for her friend's seven-year-old for a couple of days. Junior turns out to be a chimpanzee.

"GLADYS COOKS PETE'S GOOSE" APRIL 24, 1961*
EPISODE # 30
GUEST CAST: CHRISTINE NELSON AS EDITH HALSEY, TOM BROWN AS RAYMOND CHARLES, PETER BROCCO AS MR. SOHAN

Gladys always garbles Pete's business messages, and she is determined to make up for it. Having found a telegram in his pocket about a Mr. Sohan from India, she decides to help Pete impress his prospective client by preparing an exotic Asiatic feast.

"STUDY IN GRAY" MAY 1, 1961*
EPISODE # 31
GUEST CAST: ERNEST TRUEX AS POP, BARRY KELLEY AS MR. SLOCUM

Pete's in a dilemma because the painter can't come to re-decorate his boss's den—so Gladys cheerfully proposes Pop for the job.

"POP'S GIRLFRIEND" MAY 8, 1961*
EPISODE # 32
GUEST CAST: ERNEST TRUEX AS POP, FIFI D'ORSAY AS CHARMAINE DUMONDE, OLAN SOULE AS MR. OLDFIELD, HARRY CHESHIRE AS JOHN, HELENE HEIGH AS MARTHA, VICTOR MASI AS THE MESSENGER

Pop inherits Uncle Harry's estate, and decides to move into an apartment of his own. Gladys doesn't want the old boy to get lonely—so she decides to shop for a roommate for him.

NOTE: Verna Felton does not appear in this episode.

"RING-A-DING-DING" MAY 15, 1961*
EPISODE # 33
GUEST CAST: BARRY KELLEY AS MR. SLOCUM, LURENE TUTTLE AS MRS. SLOCUM, RICHARD DEACON AS FOSTER, MOLLIE GLESSING AS WINNIE, ARTHUR GOULD-PORTER AS THE BUTLER

The pastries and dips at Mrs. Slocum's party are extra-rich this evening—it seems Gladys has managed to lose a valuable ring belonging to her hostess somewhere among the goodies.

NOTE: Verna Felton does not appear in this episode.

"THE MANNEQUIN STORY" MAY 22, 1961
EPISODE # 34
GUEST CAST: ERNEST TRUEX AS POP, ALAN HEWITT AS CLAUDE FENTON, DONNA DOUGLAS AS THE MODEL, SANDRA GOULD AS THE MOTHER, MICHAEL FLATLEY AS THE LITTLE BOY

Invited to a plush party, Gladys has her eye on a dress she just can't afford. Pop, who has just taken a job at a swank department store, thinks he can help his daughter get her heart's desire.

NOTE: Verna Felton does not appear in this episode.

"THE PROJECTIONIST" MAY 29, 1961*
EPISODE # 35
GUEST CAST: MURIEL LANDERS AS VIOLET, STERLING HOLLOWAY AS LESTER SMITH, ROLFE SEDAN AS ENGSTROM, JOE WALL AS THE BURLY MAN, KEN DRAKE AS GARY MILHOUSE, PAT ROSSON AS THE YOUNG MAN

Gladys's cousin Violet is back—still trying to trap a man. So Gladys begins a program designed to reduce her plump relative and smooth the road to romance.

NOTE: Verna Felton does not appear in this episode.

"GLADYS GOES TO COLLEGE" JUNE 19, 1961
EPISODE # 36
GUEST CAST: FRANK WILCOX AS FRANK BRENNER, ELEANOR AUDLEY AS MRS. BRENNER, NAN LESLIE AS JOSIE, WILLIAM TANNEN AS MR. BROWN, JOSE GONZALES-GONZALES AS THE DRIVER, TINA MENARD AS THE PASSERBY, RODOLFO HOYOS AS DIEGO, NACHO GALINDO AS THE ENGLISH-SPEAKING WAITER, MANUEL LOPEZ AS THE POLICEMAN

Gladys goes to college for a night course in Spanish. Pete, taking her at her word when she brags that she has learned to order a full meal in Spanish, invites his district manager and wife to a Mexican restaurant—so Gladys can impress them.

NOTE: Verna Felton does not appear in this episode.

BIBLIOGRAPHY

NOTE: This bibliography does not include the many magazine and newspaper articles, films, television and radio shows, and DVD commentaries that were also used for research, but information pertaining to them can be found in the text itself.

BOOKS AND MANUSCRIPTS

Adams, T. R. *The Flintstones: A Modern Stone Age Phenomenon.* Atlanta: Turner Publishing, Inc., 1994.

Alexander, Philip W. *The History of San Mateo County.* Burlingame, California: Press of Burlingame Publishing Company, 1916.

Andrews, Bart. *The "I Love Lucy" Book.* Garden City, New York: Doubleday & Company, Inc., 1985.

Arden, Eve. *Three Phases of Eve: An Autobiography.* New York: St. Martin's Press, 1985.

Arnaz, Desi. *A Book.* Cutchogue, New York: Buccaneer Books, 1976.

Barrier, Michael. *The Animated Man: A Life of Walt Disney.* Berkeley: University of California Press, 2007.

Barris, Alex. *Front Page Challenge: History of a Television Legend.* Toronto: Macmillan Canada, 1999.

Benny, Mary Livingstone, Hilliard Marks, and Marcia Borie. *Jack Benny.* New York: Doubleday & Company, Inc., 1978.

Billips, Connie, and Arthur Pierce. *Lux Presents Hollywood: A Show-by-Show History of the Lux Radio Theatre and the Lux Video Theatre, 1934-1957.* Jefferson, North Carolina: McFarland & Company, Inc., Publishers, 1995.

Blanc, Mel, and Philip Bashe. *That's Not All Folks!: My Life in the Golden Age of Cartoons and Radio.* New York: Warner Books, 1988.

Bordman, Gerald. *American Theatre: A Chronicle of Comedy and Drama, 1869-1914.* New York: Oxford University Press, 1994.

_____. *American Theatre: A Chronicle of Comedy and Drama, 1914-1930.* New York: Oxford University Press, 1995.

Breschini, Gary S., Mona Gudgel, and Trude Haversat. *10,000 Years on the Salinas Plain.* Carlsbad,California: Heritage Media Corp., 2003.

_____. *Early Salinas.* Charleston, South Carolina: Arcadia Publishing, 2005.

Buxton, Frank, and Bill Owen. *The Big Broadcast, 1920-1950: A New, Revised, and Greatly Expanded Edition of Radio's Golden Age.* New York: Viking Press,1972.

Campbell, Robert A. *Sit Down and Drink Your Beer: Regulating Vancouver's Beer Parlours.* Toronto: University of Toronto Press, 2001.

Canemaker, John. *Paper Dreams: The Art and Artists of Disney Storyboards.* New York: Hyperion Press. 1999.

Clark, Barrett H. *A Study of the Modern Drama: A Handbook for the Study and Appreciation of the Best Plays, European, English, and American, of the Last Half Century.* New York: D. Appleton and Company, 1925.

Clements, Cynthia, and Sandra Weber. *George Burns and Gracie Allen: A Bio-Bibliography.* Westport, Connecticut: Greenwood Press, 1996.

Cohan, Steven. *Masked Men: Masculinity and the Movies in the Fifties.* Bloomington: Indiana University Press, 1997.

Coyne, Steven Sanders, and Tom Gilbert. *Desilu: The Story of Lucille Ball and Desi Arnaz.* New York: William Morrow and Company, Inc., 1993.

De Cordova, Fred. *Johnny Came Lately: An Autobiography.* New York: Simon and Schuster, 1988.

DeLong, Thomas A. *Radio Stars: An Illustrated Biographical Dictionary of 953 Performers, 1920-1960.* Jefferson, North Carolina: McFarland & Company, Inc., Publishers, 1996.

Dier, Caroline Lawrence. *The Lady of the Gardens: Mary Elitch Long.* Hollywood, California: Hollycrafters, 1932.

Doucette, Barbara A. *Peabody: The First 150 Years.* Peabody, Massachusetts: The Peabody Historical Society and Museum, 2000.

Dunning, John. *On the Air: The Encyclopedia of Old-Time Radio.* New York: Oxford University Press, 1998.

Durham, Weldon B., ed. *American Theatre Companies, 1888-1930.* New York: Greenwood Press, 1987.

Eisner, Joel, and David Krinsky. *Television Comedy Series: An Episode Guide to 153 TV Sitcoms in Syndication.* Jefferson, North Carolina: McFarland & Company, Inc., 1984.

Fein, Irving A. *Jack Benny: An Intimate Biography.* New York: G. P. Putnam's Sons, 1976.

Felton, William Reid. *A Genealogical History of the Felton Family: Ancestors and Descendants of Lieutenant Nathaniel Felton.* Rutland, Vermont: The Tuttle Company, 1935.

Fradkin, Philip L. *The Great Earthquake and Firestorms of 1906: How San Francisco Nearly Destroyed Itself.* Berkeley: University of California Press, 2006.

Gabler, Neal. *Walt Disney: The Triumph of the American Imagination.* New York: Alfred A. Knopf,2006.

Gargiulo, Suzanne. *Hans Conried: A Biography; With a Filmography and a Listing of Radio, Television, Stage and Voice Work.* Jefferson, North Carolina: McFarland & Company, Inc., Publishers, 2002.

Garvis, Jann E. *Roar of the Monitors: Quest for Gold in the Northern Sierra.* Nevada City, CA: Graphic Publishers, 2004.

Gehring, Wes D. *Seeing Red: The Skelton in Hollywood's Closet.* Davenport, Iowa: Robin Vincent Publishing LLC, 2001.

Ghez, Didier, ed. *Walt's People, Volume 2.* Xlibris, 2006.

Gilbert, Lauren Miranda, and Bob Johnson. *San Jose's Historic Downtown.* Charleston, South Carolina: Arcadia Publishing, 2004.

Goldberg, Isaac, and Hubert Heffner, eds. *Davy Crockett and Other Plays.* Princeton: Princeton University Press, 1940.

Goldrup, Tom, and Jim Goldrup. *Feature Players: The Stories Behind the Faces, Volume One.* Selfpublished, 1986.

Grams, Jr., Martin. *Radio Drama: American Programs, 1932-1962.* Jefferson, North Carolina: McFarland & Company, Inc., Publishers, 2000.

Grant, John. *Encyclopedia of Walt Disney's Animated Characters.* Boston: Hyperion Books, 1998.

Green, Katie Willmarth. *Like a Leaf Upon the Current Cast.* Nevada City, California: Lectramedia, 2004.

Guin, J. M. *History and Biographical Record of Monterey and San Benito Counties.* Los Angeles: Historic Record Co., 1910.

Holtzman, Will. *William Holden.* New York: Pyramid Publications, Inc., 1976.

Hull, Betty Lynne. *Denver's Elitch Gardens: Spinning a Century of Dreams.* Boulder, Colorado: Johnson Books, 2003.

Hyatt, Wesley. *A Critical History of Television's "The Red Skelton Show," 1951-1971.* Jefferson, North Carolina: McFarland & Company, Inc., Publishers, 2004.

Inge, William. *Picnic: A Summer Romance in Three Acts.* New York: Random House, 1953.

Inman, David. *The TV Encyclopedia: The Most Comprehensive Guide to Everybody Who's Anybody in Television.* New York: The Putnam Publishing Group, Inc., 1991.

Johnson-Cull, Viola, ed. *Chronicle of Ladysmith and District.* Victoria, British Columbia: Morriss Printing Company, Ltd., 1980.

Johnston, Ollie, and Frank Thomas. *The Disney Villain.* New York: Hyperion Books, 1993.

Johnston, Robert B. *Old Monterey County: A Pictorial History.* Monterey, California: Monterey Savings and Loan Association, 1970.

Josefsberg, Milt. *The Jack Benny Show: The Life and Times of America's Best-Loved Entertainer.* New Rochelle, New York: Arlington House Publishers, 1977.

Kleno, Larry. *Kim Novak: On Camera.* San Diego: A. S. Barnes & Company, Inc., 1980.

Koster, Nancy Felton. *The Felton Family: Descendants of Nathaniel Felton Who Came to Salem, Massachusetts in 1633.* Self-published, 1963.

Krantz, Lynn Blocker, Nick Krantz, and Mary Thiele Fobian. *To Honolulu in Five Days: Cruising Aboard Matson's S. S. Lurline, 1933-1963.* Berkeley: Ten Speed Press, 2001.

Kubey, Robert. *Creating Television: Conversations with the People Behind 50 Years of American TV.* Mahwah, New Jersey: Lawrence Erlbaum Associates, 2004.

Kurtti, Jeff. *Disney Dossiers: Files of Characters from the Walt Disney Studios.* Bellevue, Washington: Becker & Mayer, 2006.

Lackmann, Ron. *Same Time, Same Station: An A-Z Guide to Radio from Jack Benny to Howard Stern.* New York: Facts on File, Inc., 1996.

Lamparski, Richard. *Whatever Became of —?: Tenth Series.* New York: Crown Publishers, 1986.

Leff, Laura. *39 Forever: Second Edition, Volume 1 (Radio) May 1932-May 1942.* North Charleston, SC: Book Surge LLC, 2004.

_____. *39 Forever: Second Edition, Volume 2 (Radio) October 1942-May 1955.* North Charleston, SC: Book Surge LLC, 2006.

Leff, Leonard, and Jerold L. Simmons. *The Dame in the Kimono: Hollywood Censorship and the Production Code.* Lexington, Kentucky: The University Press of Kentucky, 2001.

Linet, Beverly. *Ladd: The Life, The Legend, The Legacy of Alan Ladd.* New York: Arbor House, 1979.

Logan, Joshua. *Movie Stars, Real People, and Me.* New York: Dell Publishing Company, Inc., 1978.

Mackenzie, Harry. *Command Performance, USA!* Westport, Connecticut: Greenwood Press, 1996.

Maltin, Leonard. *The Disney Films.* New York: Crown Publishers, Inc., 1973.

Mars, Amaury. *Reminiscences of Santa Clara Valley and San Jose.* San Francisco: The Mysell-Rollins Company, 1901.

Martin, Harry, and Caroline Kellogg. *Tacoma: A Pictorial History.* Virginia Beach, Virginia: The Donning Company/Publishers, 1981.

Marx, Arthur. *Red Skelton: An Unauthorized Biography.* New York: E. P. Dutton, 1979.

Matson, Cecil. *Seven Nights—Three Matinees: Seventy Years of Dramatic Stock in Portland, Oregon 1863-1933.* Self-published, c. 1981.

McNeil, Alex. *Total Television: A Comprehensive Guide to Programming from 1948 to the Present.* New York: Viking Penguin, Inc., 1984.

Mitz, Rick. *The Great TV Sitcom Book.* New York: Richard Marek Publishers, 1980.

Morino, Marianne. *The Hollywood Walk of Fame.* Berkeley: Ten Speed Press, 1987.

Muller, Kathleen. *San Jose: City with a Past.* San Jose: The Rosicrucian Press, 1988.

Nathan, George Jean. *The World in Falseface.* New York: A. A. Knopf, 1923.

O'Neil, Thomas. *The Emmys: Star Wars, Showdowns, and the Supreme Test of TV's Best.* New York: Penguin Books, 1992.

Parish, James Robert, and Vincent Terrace. *The Complete Actors' Television Credits, 1948-1988, Second Edition, Volume 2: Actresses.* Metuchen, New Jersey: The Scarecrow Press, Inc., 1990.

Quirk, Lawrence J. *The Films of William Holden.* Secaucus, New Jersey: The Citadel Press, 1973.

Schaden, Chuck. *Speaking of Radio: Chuck Schaden's Conversations with the Stars of the Golden Age of Radio.* Morton Grove, Illinois: Nostalgia Digest Press, 2003.

Schickel, Richard. *The Disney Version: The Life, Times, Art and Commerce of Walt Disney.* New York: Simon and Schuster, 1968.

Schilling, Jr., Lester Lorenzo. *The History of the Theatre in Portland, Oregon, 1846-1959: A Thesis Submitted in Partial Fulfillment of the Requirement for the Degree of Doctor of Philosophy at the University of Wisconsin,* 1961.

Shapiro, Mitchell E. *Radio Network Prime Time Programming, 1926-1967.* Jefferson, North Carolina: McFarland & Company, Inc., Publishers, 2002.

Sies, Leora M., and Luther F. Sies. *The Encyclopedia of Women in Radio, 1920-1960.* Jefferson, North Carolina: McFarland and Company, Inc., Publishers, 2003.

Sinnott, James J. *Alleghany and Forest City: Treasure Towns.* Volcano, California: California Traveler, Inc., 1975.

_____. *Downieville: Gold Town on the Yuba.* Volcano, California: California Traveler, Inc., c. 1972.

Storm, Gale. *I Ain't Down Yet: The Autobiography of My Little Margie.* Indianapolis: The Bobbs-Merrill Company, Inc., 1981.

Stumpf, Charles, and Ben Ohmart. *The Great Gildersleeve.* Boalsburg, Pennsylvania: BearManor Media, 2002.

Terrace, Vincent. *Fifty Years of Television: A Guide to Series and Pilots, 1937-1988.* New York: Cornwall Books, 1991.

_____. *Television Specials.* Jefferson, North Carolina: McFarland & Company, Inc., Publishers, 1995.

Thomas, Frank, and Ollie Johnston. *Disney Animation: The Illusion of Life.* New York: Abbeville Press, 1984.

Thompson, Robert J., and Gary Burns, eds. *Making Television: Authorship and the Production Process.* New York: Praeger Publishers, 1990.

Tucker, David C. *The Women Who Made Television Funny: Ten Stars of 1950s Sitcoms.* Jefferson, North Carolina: McFarland & Company, Inc., Publishers, 2007.

Voss, Ralph F. *A Life of William Inge: The Strains of Triumph.* Lawrence, Kansas: University of Kansas Press, 1989.

Waters, Jr., Walter Kenneth. *George L. Baker and the Baker Stock Company: A Dissertation Submitted to the Department of Speech and Drama and the Committee on the Graduate Division of Stanford University,* 1964.

Webb, Graham. *The Animated Film Encyclopedia: A Complete Guide to American Shorts, Features, and Sequences, 1900-1979.* Jefferson, North Carolina: McFarland & Company, Inc., Publishers, 2000.

Wiberg, Ruth Eloise. *Rediscovering Northwest Denver: Its History, Its People, Its Landmarks.* Niwot, Colorado: University Press of Colorado, 1995.

Williams, Gregory Paul. *The Story of Hollywood: An Illustrated History.* Los Angeles: BL Press LLC, 2005.

Wilson, Gerald, and Martin Grams, Jr. *The Railroad Hour: A History of the Radio Series!* Albany, Georgia: BearManor Media, 2007.

Wood, Carlyle, ed. *TV Personalities Biographical Sketchbook, Volume 2.* St. Louis: TV Personalities, 1956.

_____. *TV Personalities Biographical Sketchbook, Volume 3.* St Louis: TV Personalities, 1957.

Wood, Ruth Kedzie. *The Tourist's Northwest.* New York: Dodd, Mead & Company, Inc., 1916.

Young, Jordan R. *The Laugh Crafters: Comedy Writing in Radio and TV's Golden Age.* Beverly Hills: Past Times Publishing Co., 1999.

SELECTED NEWSPAPER AND PERIODICAL ARTICLES

"A Case of Identity." *Press* (Pittsburgh), November 13, 1960, TV section, p. 2.

"Attention, Mothers-in-Law." *TV Guide* Vol. 2, no. 49 (December 4, 1954): 13-15.

Bahn, Chester B. "Two Continents Know Spring Byington of Temple Stock Troupe." *Syracuse Herald* (Syracuse, New York), June 5, 1927, p. 8.

Baumann, Ursula. "Verna Stars in Movies—But You Rarely See Her." *Citizen-News* (Hollywood), April 5, 1955.

Belgum, Deborah. "'50s Star a Springs Native." *Gazette-Telegraph* (Colorado Springs), November 29, 1987, p. D2.

Bigsby, Evelyn. "Spring Byington's Fashions for Older Women." *TV Guide* Vol. 7, no. 11 (March 14, 1959): 12-14.

Brooks, Maggie. "Valley Que Presents Verna Felton." *The Valley Que* Vol. 1, no. 9 (May 1960), p. 3, 19.

Byington, Spring, and Wambly Bald. "Act My Age? Not Me!" *Family Circle* Vol. 50, no. 5 (May 1957):37, 70-73.

Carter, Peggy. "Clever Is the Word for Verna." *Radio Life* (December 17, 1944): 6, 26.

Cerf, Bennett. "Trade Winds." *Saturday Review* Vol. 39, no. 9 (March 3, 1956): 5.

Cini, Zelda, ed. *El Valle de Toluca: "The Fertile Valley" of North Hollywood, 1847-1975.* Sherman Oaks, California: San Fernando Valley Magazine, 1975.

"December Bride." *TV Guide* Vol. 2, no. 50 (December 11, 1954): 14.

DeLong, Jack. "Nanaimo Throngs Cheer Princess." *The Sun* (Vancouver), July 17, 1958, p. 6.

Dempsey, Lotta. "The Idols of Yesteryear." *The Daily Star* (Toronto), undated clipping.

Derman, Lou. "Plotting the Situation Comedy." *Variety* (January 8, 1958), p. 100.

Eiten, Myles. "The Voice is Familiar." *The American Weekly*, February 16, 1958, p. 1.

Felton, Verna. "Love That Red-Head!" *Radio Mirror* Vol. 29, no. 2 (January 1948): 46-47, 81-82.

Fessier, Jr., Mike. "You Ought to See What They've Got Harry Doing Now." *TV Guide*, Vol. 15, no. 18 (May 6, 1967): 29-32.

Foster, Dora. "Park Region Yesterdays." *Gazette-Telegraph* (Colorado Springs), October 12, 1958, p. B3.

Freeman, Frank. "The Glow Has Died Down." *Mercury-News* (San Jose), August 18, 1963, p. 10L.

Garcia, Joel. "Indian Ceremonies Install North Hollywood CC Slate." *News* (Van Nuys, California), February 10, 1966, p. 13-A.

Gehman, Richard. "The Wild, Wild World of Cara Williams." *TV Guide* Vol. 9, no. 27 (July 8, 1961), p. 12-16.

Goode, Betty. "My Secret of Happiness." *Radio-TV Mirror* Vol. 40, no. 4 (September 1953): 68-69, 84-85.

Gordon, Shirley. "Kilocycle Queen of Caricature." *Radio Life* Vol. 13, no. 19 (July 14, 1946): 4-5, 8.

_____. "Vaguely Vera." *Radio Life* Vol. 14, no. 10 (November 10, 1946): 4-5, 39.

Graham, Sheilah. "Spring is Perennial." *Rocky Mountain Empire Magazine* (June 25, 1950): 8.

Hall, Joy. "What's New With Verna?" *Radio-Television Life* Vol. 22, no. 1 (September 1, 1950): 3, 34.

Handman, Stanley. "Spring is Eternal." *Weekend Magazine* Vol. 8, no. 21 (May 24,1958): 6-9.

"Harry Morgan Has In-Law Troubles." *TV Guide* Vol. 5, no. 11 (March 16, 1957): 14-16.

"Harry Morgan's Wife Doesn't Scare Him — On TV!" *TV Guide* Vol. 4, no. 40 (Oct. 6, 1956): 17-19.

"Hilda Causes Stir." *Daily Colonist* (Victoria, British Columbia), July 18, 1958, p. 15.

Holland, Jack. "God Bless the Mothers-in-Law." *TV-Radio Life* (March 18, 1955): 4.

_____. "She Puts the Life in Living." *TV-Radio Life* Vol. 37, no. 35 (August 2, 1958): 48.

"Honorary Buff." *TV Channels* Vol. 2, no. 6 (February 5, 1961): 7.

"How to Get Away from It All." *Complete TV* Vol. 3, no. 5 (January 1958): 44-47.

Humphrey, Hal. "Verna Felton Tossed Off Block Where 'Pete and Gladys' Live." *Mirror* (Los Angeles), October 4, 1961, section 4, p. 10.

"Inside Secrets of the Three Face Contest." *TV-Radio Life* (April 30, 1954): 4.

"Is Television Going to Be Like This?" *Radio Life*, 1945.

"Jane Morgan." *Radio and Television Mirror* Vol. 31, no. 6 (May 1949): 18.

Johnson, Erskine. "Hollywood Today." *The Evening Standard* (Uniontown, Pennsylvania), December 1, 1960.

Judge, Frank. "Gleam of an Idea Sold a Unique TV Project." *TV Magazine*, February 4, 1962.

Keatley, Patrick C. "Remember the Old Empress?" *Daily Province* (Vancouver, BC), February 26, 1949, magazine section, p. 8.

Ladd, Bill. "Her Honor Verna Felton Has a Well-Feathered Wardrobe." *Courier-Journal* (Louisville, Kentucky), November 6, 1960, section 6, p. 6.

Law, Aline. "Honorary Mayor Verna Felton Takes Time for Cooking." *Valley Times Today* (North Hollywood), October 6, 1960, p. 19.

Lieber, Leslie. "Grandma Cuts Capers." *The Herald* (Boston), September 9, 1956.

McClelland, Doug. "Vera Vague: Of Mirth and Men." *Films of the Golden Age Issue* 34 (Fall 2003): 48-65.

McMurphy, Jean. "Lily, Hilda Are Young at Heart." *The Times* (Los Angeles), August 24, 1958, part VII, p. 2.

McNeil, Jean. "Spring Byington's Serious Side." *Portland Press Herald* (Portland, Maine), February 26, 1956.

Molina, Elsa. "Happiness Knows No Season." *TV Radio Mirror* Vol. 44, no. 6 (November 1955): 40-41, 93-94.

Morath, Glad. "Spring Byington Delighted with Flight in T-33 Jet." *Gazette-Telegraph* (Colorado Springs), May 8, 1959, p. 4.

Morgan, Vera E. J. "It Was Fun Being in Show Business Here." *News-Tribune and Sunday Ledger* (Tacoma, Washington), September 11, 1966, p. 4-5.

"Mrs. Dr. Byington Is Dead." *The Enterprise* (Montrose, Colorado), April 16, 1907, p. 1.

Murphy, Paul. "Verna Felton Finds Her Face a Passport." *News-Herald* (Hutchinson, Kansas), May 26, 1955.

"NBC Personalities—Verna Felton." *NBC Advance Program Service* (San Francisco), Vol. 2, no. 40 October 29, 1933, p. 1.

Nisbet, Fairfax. "Robertson Completes Feature." *Morning News* (Dallas), April 29, 1965, p. 26.

_____. "Robertson Here for Convention." *Morning News* (Dallas), February 7, 1963, section 3, p. 7.

"Pioneer in Theatrical Life Plans 1958 Visit." *Free Press* (Nanaimo, British Columbia), October 29, 1957, p. 7.

"Radio's Golden Age Has Special Significance for Marty Halperin." *Los Angeles Skywriter*, July 10, 1964, p. 3.

Rasky, Frank. "Verna Felton Recalls 'Old Empress' Days." *Sun* (Vancouver, British Columbia), July 8, 1946, p. 5.

Rathbun, Joe. "Joe's Radio Parade." *Sunday Times-Signal* (Zanesville, Ohio), April 4, 1943, p. 7.

"Reflections of Passing Events in the Screen World." *The New York Times*, October 19, 1941, p. X5.

Ross, Jerry. "When Road Shows Folded, She Built New Career in Radio." *Globe-Democrat* (St. Louis), May18, 1947, p. 4F.

Ross, Mildred. "TV Is Duck Soup: It's Like 'Doin' What Comes Naturally' for Verna Felton." *TV-Radio Life* Vol. 25, no. 19 (July 4, 1952): 5, 34.

"Sealtest Village Store." *Tune In* Vol. 2, no. 3 (July 1944): 10-13.

"Second Stroke Kills TV Actress." *The Province* (Vancouver, British Columbia), December 15, 1966, p. 2.

Shaffer, Bill. "The Summer of Picnic." *Kansas Heritage* Vol. 13, no. 1 (Spring 2005): 6-12.

"Spring Byington: Flying Grandmother." *TV Guide* Vol. 4, no. 10 (March 10, 1956): 13-15.

"Spring Gives a Party." *TV Stage* Vol. 4, no. 5 (September 1957): 32.

The Gazette (Colorado Springs, Colorado), December 29, 1891, p. 4.

"The Mother-in-Law Joke." *Time* (March 12, 1956): 62.

"Time Hasn't Lowered the Curtain." *TV Guide* Vol. 6, no. 24 (June 14, 1958): 5-7.

"TV's Happiest Outlaws." *Look* Vol. 19, no. 25 (December 13, 1955): 178-181.

Tyrell, Tom. "Radio News." *The Shopping News* (San Francisco), May 26, 1947, p. 1.

Urban, Glenn. "Ageless Spring Byington Pays Visit to Native City." *Gazette-Telegraph* (Colorado Springs), May 5, 1959, p. 1,6.

Vera, Dorothy. "T.V.'s Verna Felton—Born in Salinas—Papa Was One of Town's Early Doctors." *Californian* (Salinas), October 29, 1960, p. 8A.

"Verna Felton, 76, Dies of Stroke." *Herald-Examiner* (Los Angeles), December 15, 1966, p. F-7.

"Verna Felton, 76, TV Actress, Dead." *Times* (New York), December 16, 1966, p. 47.

"Verna Felton Comes to Dinner." *The News-Herald* (Hutchinson, Kansas), June 9, 1955, p. 24.

"Verna Felton: $500-A-Word Star." *TV Guide* Vol. 3, no. 23 (June 4, 1955): 12.

"Verna Felton Honored for Career as Actress." *The Times* (Los Angeles), September 28, 1959.

"Verna Felton Is Unofficial Queen of the Roughhouse." *TV Guide* Vol. 5, no. 38 (September 21, 1957): 17-19.

"Verna Felton: Mad Hatter of TV." *TV Guide* Vol. 9, no. 5 (February 4, 1961): 12-13.

"Verna Felton Moved by Warmth of Local Welcome." *Chronicle* (Ladysmith, British Columbia), July 24, 1958, p. 1.

"Verna Felton, Radio and TV Actress, Dies." *Times* (Los Angeles), December 15, 1966, Section 3, p. 16.

Wiberg, Ruth Eloise. "Rediscovering Northwest Denver." *North Denver Tribune*, September 24, 1987, p. 2.

Wilkinson, Harry. "Looking Hollywood Way." *Good Old Days* Vol. 7, no. 11 (May 1971), p. 34.

Willett, Bob. "Verna Felton Is Still Tops." *Sun* (Vancouver, British Columbia), August 2, 1952, magazine section, p. 1.

"William Gardner: Founder, Gardner School and District." *The Trailblazer* Vol. 25, no. 1 (February 1984): 3-5.

Williams, Mollie. "Spring Byington: The Secret She Won't Tell." *TV Star Parade* Vol. 4, no. 11 (February 1957): 38-39.

INTERVIEWS

Allen, Daphne. Telephone interview. 4 March 2006.

Andrews, Mary. Telephone interview. 4 March 2006.

Blazic, Albert. Telephone interviews. 12 April 2005, 27 April 2005, 22 May 2005, 9 June 2005, 5 August 2005, 26 February 2006. Personal interview. 5 June 2006.

Bowman, Clyde. Telephone interviews. 15 February 2006, 4 May 2008.

Bowman, John. Telephone interview. 19 February 2006.

Brendel, Hattie Gunton. Telephone interview. 12 March 2006.

Cahn, Dann. Telephone interview. 8 January 2007.

Costa, Mary. Telephone interview. 15 February 2005.

Cunningham, Kate Millar. Telephone interviews. 23 May 2004, 16 January 2005, 15 April 2008.

Dahlquist, Bill. Telephone interview. 13 March 2005.

Davis, Peter "Dix." Telephone interview. 15 March 2008.

Dodd, Don. Telephone interview. 26 February 2005.

Halperin, Marty. Telephone interviews. 5 January 2005, 13 March 2005.

Houser, Jerry. Telephone interview. 8 January 2005.

Kelemer, Linda Derman. Telephone interview. 23 October 2006.

Kofman, Lisa Millar. Telephone interviews. 30 May 2004, 16 January 2005, 24 May 2005.

Leff, Debbie. Personal interview. 30 September 2007.

Levy, Robert. Telephone interview. 30 March 2005.

McNear, Christopher "Kit." Telephone interview. 14 March 2005.

Mickell, Linda Levy. Telephone interview. 30 March 2005.

Mondon, JoAnn Bowman. Telephone interview. 13 February 2006.

Morgan, Lynn MacKaye. Telephone interview. 12 April 2008.

Murdy, Ferris. Telephone interview. 4 April 2007.

Neese, Dolores Stelter. Telephone interview. 14 April 2008.

Shively, Jean Kirkpatrick. Telephone interview. 13 April 2009.

Simons, James. Telephone interview. 21 October 2008.

Sommerfeld, Irene. Telephone interview. 1 May 2009.

Stern, Selma. Telephone interview. 8 July 2008.
Storm, Gale. Telephone interview. 22 January 2005.
Stratton, Gil. Telephone interview. 24 January 2005.
Webber, Peggy. Telephone interview. 16 March 2005.
Weltmer, Eleanor Kirkpatrick. Telephone interview. 13 April 2009.
Wilson, Elizabeth. Telephone interview. 7 May 2005.

LETTERS

Fox, Sharon Douglas, to Fredrick Tucker, 16 April 2005, 18 April 2005, 14 May 2005.
Kelemer, Linda Derman, to Fredrick Tucker, 18 December 2006.
Lee, Janet Waldo, to Fredrick Tucker, 21 April 2005.
Leff, Debbie, to Fredrick Tucker, 1 June 2005, 9 July 2005.
Michel, Lois Ann Baxley, to Fredrick Tucker, 19 April 2008.
Mitchell, Shirley, to Fredrick Tucker, 21 March 2005.
Morgan, Lynn MacKaye, to Fredrick Tucker, 5 April 2008, 6 April 2008, 30 May 2008, 9 June 2008, 12 June 2008.
Raab, Sandy Leff, to Fredrick Tucker, 21 November 2007.
Robertson, Dale, to Fredrick Tucker, 21 March 2005.
Singleton, Doris, to Fredrick Tucker, 16 April 2005.
Smith, Dave, to Fredrick Tucker, 22 April 2005.
Webber, Peggy, to Fredrick Tucker, 26 March 2005, 15 April 2005.
Weltmer, Eleanor Kirkpatrick, to Fredrick Tucker, 27 April 2009.

INDEX

MacNeil, Jack, 123-125
Maher, Wally, 289, 300-303, 342
Main, Marjorie, 333, 481, 497, 652-653
Maltin, Leonard, 381, 383, 418, 420, 423, 425
Malyon, Eily, 230
Mana, Mel, 614
March, Hal, 441, 447
Margaret, Princess, 516-517
Marsac, Maurice, 619
Marsh, Myra, 162, 299
Marshe, Vera, 659
Marshall, Herbert, 490, 632
Marsky, Meta, 32, 38, 48, 51, 90
Martin, Lewis, 669, 680
Martin, Mickey, 688
Marx, Groucho, 300, 326
Masi, Victor, 726
Mason, Pamela, 715
Mason, Portland, 718
Masters, Mike, 684
Masters, Tom, 691
Mathers, Jerry, 513, 628
Matthews, Lester, 676, 701
Maxey, Paul, 645
Maxwell, Marilyn, 397, 398
May, Marjorie, 663
McAvoy, Ila, 679
McCrea, Joel, 262, 495
McDaniel, Sam, 608, 628
McDevitt, Ruth, 469
McKinley, William, 46-47, 49-50
McLaughlin, Bernice, 725
McNaughton, Anna, 163, 166, 167, 171, 174, 175, 180-183, 185, 246, 251
McNaughton, Mary, 13
McNear, Christopher "Kit," 389, 482, 487, 600
McNear, Howard, 263, 296, 302, 388-389, 392, 482, 512, 566, 586, 597, 622, 623, 639, 646, 657, 678

McNear, Helen, 296, 297, 302, 388-389, 390, 392, 482, 597
McQuarrie, George, 38, 51-52
McVey, Tyler, 617, 679
Meader, George, 614, 643, 653
Meek, Donald, 150, 237, 306
Meek, John, 625
Mell, Joseph, 724
Melton, Sid, 512, 669, 672, 699, 707, 714
Melville, Rose, 166
Menard, Tina, 727
Mercer, Frances, 611
Meredith, Cheerio, 491, 512, 609, 638, 647, 655, 656, 666, 678,693, 698, 699, 704, 720
Merrill, Lou, 263, 287
Methot, Mayo, 171-172
Michel, San Baxley, 455, 482, 600
Mickell, Linda Levy, 507, 558, 601
Millan, Victor, 620
Millar, Edith Simmons (daughter-in-law), 394-396, 412, 430-431, 484-485, 487-488, 512, 520,-521, 532, 537, 538, 551, 561, 566, 567, 583, 588, 591-593, 597, 622, 623, 649, 659, 666, 667, 681, 686, 697, 700, 718
Millar, John Edgar (father-in-law), 176-178, 254
Millar, John "Jack" Walter (brother-in-law), 176, 177, 178, 293
Millar, Kate Carson (mother-in-law), 177-178, 213, 243, 244, 246, 488
Millar, Kate Walker (granddaughter), 488, 497, 523, 532, 533, 535, 536-538, 545, 550, 551, 561, 563, 565-567, 578, 583, 588, 590, 593, 597, 598
Millar, Lee Carson, Jr. (son)
 acting career, 430-431, 538, 561-562, 597
 birth, 212

Breinigsville, PA USA
20 May 2010
238365BV00002B/3/P